PHONETICS
Theory and Application

McGRAW-HILL SERIES IN SPEECH

John J. O'Neill, *Consulting Editor in Speech Pathology*

Aly and Aly: *A Rhetoric of Public Speaking*
Armstrong and Brandes: *The Oral Interpretation of Literature*
Baird: *American Public Addresses*
Baird, Knower, and Becker: *Essentials of General Speech Communication*
Baird, Knower, and Becker: *General Speech Communication*
Fisher: *Small Group Decision Making: Communication and the Group Process*
Gibson: *A Reader in Speech Communication*
Hahn, Lomas, Hargis, and Vandraegen: *Basic Voice Training for Speech*
Hasling: *The Audience, the Message, the Speaker*
Henning: *Improving Oral Communication*
Kaplan: *Anatomy and Physiology of Speech*
Kruger: *Modern Debate*
Mortensen: *Communication: The Study of Human Interaction*
Myers and Myers: *The Dynamics of Human Communication: A Laboratory Approach*
Ogilvie and Rees: *Communication Skills: Voice and Pronunciation*
Reid: *Speaking Well*
Reid: *Teaching Speech*
Robinson and Becker: *Effective Speech for the Teacher*
Tiffany and Carrell: *Phonetics: Theory and Application*
Wells: *Cleft Palate and Its Associated Speech Disorders*

WILLIAM R. TIFFANY, PH.D.
Professor of Speech and Hearing Sciences
University of Washington

JAMES CARRELL, PH.D.
Professor Emeritus of Speech and Hearing Sciences
University of Washington

Phonetics
THEORY AND APPLICATION

SECOND EDITION

McGraw-Hill Book Company

New York   St. Louis   San Francisco   Auckland   Bogotá   Düsseldorf
Johannesburg   London   Madrid   Mexico   Montreal   New Delhi
Panama   Paris   São Paulo   Singapore   Sydney   Tokyo   Toronto

Library of Congress Cataloging in Publication Data

Tiffany, William R
    Phonetics, theory and application.

    (McGraw-Hill series in speech)
    In the 1960 ed. J. A. Carrell's name appeared first
on the t.p.
    Includes bibliographies and indexes.
    1. English language in the United States—Phonetics.
2. Speech. I. Carrell, James A., joint author,
II. Title.
PE2815.T5 1977   421'.5   76–4970
ISBN 0–07–064575–2

PHONETICS
Theory and Application

1234567890 DODO 783210987

This book was set in Times New Roman. The editors were
Ellen B. Fuchs and Phyllis T. Dulan; the cover was designed
by Anne Canevari Green; the production supervisor was
Angela Kardovich. The drawings were done by J & R Services, Inc.
R. R. Donnelley & Sons Company was printer and binder.

Contents

v

Preface to the Second Edition

Since the manuscript of the first edition of this book was completed in 1958, there has been what can only be called a deluge of publication in the speech sciences, much of it having implications for phonetics. Scholars working in such major centers as the Haskins Laboratories in New Haven, the Speech Transmission Laboratory of the Royal Institute of Technology in Stockholm, the speech and hearing science laboratories at a number of universities in the United States and other countries, and elsewhere have been reporting their findings at a continuously accelerating rate.

In 1970, for example, *LLBA: Language and Language Behavior Abstracts* summarized more than 10,000 books and journal articles appearing in a single year. The number of journals carrying articles in this area had so increased that *LLBA* felt obliged to examine the contents of nearly 800. The literature of speech acoustics and speech physiology, cognitive psychology, and linguistics has been particularly valuable in understanding better the nature of speech sound systems and the behavior of speakers.

For this and other reasons a revision of the first edition of this book after more than a decade is clearly in order; accordingly the text has been almost completely rewritten. Although we cannot lay claim to a complete synthesis of all that has gone on in phonetics during this interval, one major objective has been to present in this second edition an account of systematic phonetics in general, and the American English sound system in particular, in terms which are compatible with the new insights provided by recent research.

Our central purpose remains the same, however: to offer beginning students a sound and scholarly treatment of phonetic theory, explained in the clearest possible terms, in order to help them become aware of speech as a significant form of behavior. If we succeed, they will be prepared with the information and techniques needed to change their own speech or that of others, or to pursue other theoretical or applied interests in the study of speech and language.

Things we have tried to do which make the second edition somewhat different from the first include these: (1) even greater care has been taken not to be "prescriptive" in commenting on pronunciation, and to give more emphasis to understanding the kinds and sources of *diversity* in American speech; (2) discussions of the bases of speech and language analysis have been updated, including attention to *distinctive feature theory*; (3) for those with no previous preparation for the study of phonetics there is given a more detailed review of the perceptual, articulatory, and acoustic backgrounds for speech behavior; (4) the *dynamic* nature of speech production is emphasized more strongly, and the description of its *prosodic* or *nonsegmental* elements is greatly expanded. Finally, we have not only retained all the original exercises, but have added an exercise section to each chapter on phonetic theory in Part One as a way of encouraging students to begin developing insights and skills in speech analysis from the start of their studies.

A note about the modified title: We have dropped the last three words of the original title, *Phonetics: Theory and Application to Speech Improvement*, not because of any lessened concern for speech improvement; nothing from the first edition which contributed to this goal has knowingly been omitted from the second edition. However, the deleted phrase is thought possibly to imply a kind of "schoolmastering" which is not present, and it may also lead to misunderstandings about the nature of the treatment we have tried to give our subject matter. We hope the new title will reflect more accurately our intention to provide a scholarly presentation of phonetics, with guidance in the development of technical skills, which will not only meet the needs of those concerned with speech improvement, but also be useful to anyone with alternative reasons for studying speech.

With regard to the change of order in naming the authors, the shift from "Carrell and Tiffany" to "Tiffany and Carrell" was made mainly to emphasize that the two editions, taken together, are truly coauthored (and because we were taught early that "turnabout's fair play"). The author now named first did have somewhat greater responsibility for selecting the material which is new to the second edition, but each chapter has been a full collaboration. Whatever merits or demerits the book may earn must be shared equally.

Finally, we must acknowledge a great debt to Professors John O'Neill and John W. Black, who reviewed the manuscript of this edition. We are particularly obligated to Professor Black, who called upon his wide knowledge of theoretical and applied phonetics for many valuable suggestions.

William R. Tiffany
James Carrell

Preface to the First Edition

Although it might prove difficult to find his counterpart in real life Prof. Henry Higgins, the phonetician in Shaw's *Pygmalion*, at least illustrates in dramatic form the simple truth that better speech is beyond no one. We profess no particular desire to emulate the professor by transforming the Eliza Doolittles of the world, and we certainly deny belonging to the "How now brown cow?" school of speech improvement.

We have attempted, however, to offer some assistance to a considerable and varied group of persons who are concerned in one way or another with what may be called the *form* of speech. These include the English-speaking student—in or out of school—who wishes to speak his native language acceptably, and thus effectively. Next are those who are learning English as a new language and need to become familiar with its patterns. We have had in mind also the speech therapist or teacher, for whom a thorough knowledge of the speech sounds and their dynamics is absolutely essential, and any others who may have reason to inquire into the details of English speech.

Finally, it would be gratifying to think that there may be some who would like to know about this aspect of their language as a matter of general culture.

The whole premise of this book is that the acquisition of accurate and effective speech—or the teaching thereof—depends first upon understanding certain principles of speech form and next upon applying them intelligently in learning or teaching the oral use of language. The surest road to effective speech lies in this direction, since the acquisition of good speech involves a good deal more than vocal drill and exercise.

A word of caution: throughout the process of speech improvement one must keep a sense of proportion; there is no single standard of correctness that can be applied, as we shall presently explain. Furthermore, good speech is never to be thought of as a kind of superficial gloss, applied to make the surface shine. It cannot make one a different kind of person. Skill in the mechanics of speech can, however, help one avoid mannerisms and inadequacies of pronunciation or articulation which might stand between the true personality and its full expression. Good speech form naturally can never substitute for *content;* it is an elementary principle that form complements content and makes it effective.

More specifically, the application of phonetics to speech improvement involves a careful study of the sounds of English—their production and the ways in which they change in connected speech—and an understanding of the characteristics of speaking—stress, intonation, and other aspects which will be discussed in due course. As a method, phonetics leads the student to a more nearly accurate perception of speech patterns—the speech sounds individually and in context. As he becomes sophisticated phonetically, he will find himself better able to recognize acceptable speech patterns as he hears them. He is then in a better position to become perceptive about his own speech—a basic requirement in the development of expressive skills.

Although the potential value of such an approach to speech improvement seems to be generally accepted, there has not been an entirely satisfactory text or manual to apply phonetic theory and method, at an appropriate level, to speech improvement. Consequently the gap between the academic and the practical has appeared wide. This is not to find fault with the academic phonetician; he may legitimately and profitably be occupied entirely with the scholarly study of spoken language. However, even those who might wish to bridge theory and practice have found no way to do so. In this text we have at least made an earnest attempt to achieve this goal, believing that the effort is thoroughly worthwhile.

Among those persons who have managed only a bowing acquaintance with phonetics there is some complaint that the whole subject has been made much too complicated and needlessly detailed for anyone whose interests lie more in speaking well than in academic matters. The accusation that a study of phonetic theory is an unnecessarily long and difficult route to speech improvement is quite unfounded, as we hope to demonstrate; it is, instead, the most direct and efficient approach. The charge that phonetic theory has been made unduly obscure may have some evidence for its support. In studying what purport to be elementary discussions of phonetics, one often gets the feeling that they have been written with the assumption that the reader already knows a great deal about the subject. This error also we try earnestly to avoid. At the same time, it is our purpose to present what seems to be sound theory and adequate basic information, including even some reference to research findings. Along with this is an introduction to terminology and principles which should prepare the student for further excursions into phonetic literature, if he finds the subject interesting.

It seems obvious that such a book as this will be of greatest use to the student if he also enjoys the guidance of a skilled teacher. No one can describe the sound of speech accurately by writing about it; speech is something that must be heard, so that written descriptions are not fully meaningful unless they can be supplemented by spoken examples provided by an informed and resourceful instructor.

Nevertheless, we have tried, in so far as possible, to make this text a "do it yourself" book. We have hoped to accomplish this by presenting understanding theory along with liberal exercise materials. No apology is made for this attempt, nor does it seem to us that any supposed demands of scholarship make such an apology necessary. We frankly should like to feel that a student who reads this book and follows its counsel can, with no other help, become a better and more effective speaker. Of course we recognize the practical impossibility of completely achieving such a goal, but it seems to us that this is the manner in which any textbook should be written.

The authors wish to express their thanks for help in arranging the use of broadcast speech samples to John King, secretary, Queen City Broadcasting Company, Seattle; Milo Ryan, professor, School of Communications, University of Washington, and the Columbia Broadcasting System. They are grateful also to Mrs. Frances Howard and Miss Ann Cannon for typing the original manuscript of this book.

James Carrell
William R. Tiffany

PHONETICS
Theory and Application

Part One

Theory

Chapter 1

Approaches to Phonetics

In this chapter we shall attempt to lay the groundwork for an appreciation of the scope and significance of phonetics, the science of speech sounds. First, the authors present their major premise: that speech deserves to be better understood because it is among our most significant forms of behavior, and because such study can facilitate the processes of communication upon which human beings so greatly depend. A word will be said about the principal fields of interest among phoneticians. Introduced next is the important principle that speech is a dynamic process, comprehensible only if one takes into account the phenomena of its *production* by a speaker in relation to its *perception* by a listener. To be discussed also are the many and significant sources of *variation* in speech among those who speak a common language—variations which must be understood and appreciated, as sometimes they are not, if social, emotional, and language problems are to be avoided. Because of the light it may shed on present speaking practices, a brief historical review of the evolution of modern English as a spoken language is given. Finally, for those who may have an interest in changing their own speech or the speech of others, some options on speech form are considered.

A POINT OF VIEW

It is a paradox that something as familiar and useful as human speech should be so little understood by those who use it. Through teaching we have been made quite aware of the details of writing and reading—the derivatives of speech—but most speakers know little about the nature and form of spoken language itself; regrettably, much of what they believe they know often proves to be incorrect. A common misconception, and one which interferes seriously with efforts to become adept in the analysis of speech, is to suppose that the form of speech is like that of writing. As we shall presently make clear, the relatively static letters of the alphabet, singly or arranged into words, are a most inadequate representation of the dynamic sound patterns of speech.

An even more significant difference between writing and speaking is the way in which they are acquired. From the time children begin to talk they are largely on their own. They find it unnecessary to attend consciously in order to talk, so there seems to be little reason to make them aware of the details of the process. Not so with learning to write and to spell. During much of our early school life, attention is directed by teachers and other critics to our written communication—the way we form our letters, arrange them into words, and punctuate. Great effort is devoted to making us conscious of the *form* of writing, and of our departures from what is considered an acceptable form.

Contrast with this the relatively light emphasis placed on the form of speech. Only the most grievous lapses from an acceptable pronunciation are likely to receive attention, and then only unsystematically. Certainly the average pupil is far more poorly informed about speech than about writing, and is given far less encouragement in achieving skill in its use—this despite the fact that language is spoken much more often than it is written, by a factor which we would suppose is greater than 10 to 1. It can be argued that since speech seems to be learned successfully by most through a kind of cultural osmosis there is little need for concern about the details of speaking. The rejoinder, of course, is that neither *language competence* nor *speech performance* reach their highest degree of efficiency if they are neglected.[1] Human communication ought never be taken for granted.

It is fashionable in some quarters to assert that one way of talking is as good as another and that it is best, as one writer puts it, to "leave your language alone" (Hall, 1950). Up to a point there is some logic to this admonition, for neither written nor spoken language need conform to any parochial set of rules governing what is "correct"; one's speech, without

---

[1] Those familiar with linguistics will recognize here the distinction made between *competence*—mastery of the shared system of rules which relate symbols to meaning—and *performance*, through which one puts abstract rules into operation. Phonetics deals primarily with the latter. (See also page 33.)

apology, reveals one's cultural, ethnic, and geographic origins—and one's personal idiosyncracies as well. It is a simple fact, however, that one way of talking is *not* as good as another if it fails in some respect to communicate effectively, or if it attracts unfavorable attention in the social group with which the speaker wishes to be identified.

Our view, then, is that there are differences in modes of speech which need to be subjected to the same kind of scientific scrutiny that might be given other facets of behavior in which there is reason to be interested. It is not our intention to approve some of these differences while condemning others as "substandard," "bad," or "incorrect." Instead, they are to be examined within the context of phonetic theory to the end that teachers, and speakers themselves, can appreciate the nature and significance of these differences, and so become better prepared to deal with them in the pursuit of whatever speech goals are chosen.

THE SCOPE OF PHONETICS

The lines of inquiry which will help us understand speech are several. First, there are certain generalities about the sound structure of all spoken languages, and English in particular, which are basic to the study of speech form. Next is the related question: What is a "speech sound," and what are those sounds of English, or American English, which we should be able to distinguish? It also seems necessary to know the way in which the speech system operates to produce these sounds. These facts will, we hope, lead to an understanding of the important *distinctive* properties of speech sounds. It will then become possible to classify the speech sounds meaningfully from each of several points of view on the basis of their common properties.

But since speech is a dynamic process, we must also examine with care the way in which individual sound segments are blended in the complex patterns of connected speech, and the changes they undergo when placed *in context*. We must also become aware that there are *nonsegmental features* —the prosodic melodies of speaking—which may do quite as much as the words themselves to make meanings clear. There are many interesting collateral matters to be touched on: questions of speech styles and usages, and choices among them; kinds and sources of variations that may arise among speakers of a common language; and numerous others. Finally, it is of the greatest importance that these inquiries be complemented by measures to develop a high level of skill in *speech analysis*,[1] for this is an indispensable tool for both theoretical studies and practical applications.

---

[1] The term *speech analysis* can be used to designate any of several methods of describing the components of spoken language, but here and at numerous other points in our discussions it is used in the special sense of *analytical listening*. This is the method which allows the auditor to recognize details of the sound structure of speech samples by means of his or her own perceptual processes. Chapter 3 discusses this basic phonetic technique, and the acquisition of skill in its use is a major purpose of exercise materials throughout the text.

Our approach to phonetics will be by way of these topics, and we shall deal with them in the approximate order of their mention. Phonetics can, of course, be treated simplistically. One might, for instance, limit oneself to the discovery that spoken language does indeed consist of sounds; one may learn their names, observe superficially their manner of production when spoken alone, and even develop some skill in identifying broadly those sounds which make up the words one hears. Perhaps this is as far as children need go when they are introduced to "sound families" as a step in learning to read by the *phonic* method. This level of understanding will not suffice for their teacher, however; nor will it serve in any measure the purposes of a student who has a serious interest in the phenomena of spoken language as an end in itself, or one who wishes to deal with problems in speaking. We venture the comment that the details of phonetics will not, after all, prove too difficult to master.

There are numerous fields of language study, many of them with shared subject matter. *Phonetics* is broadly the science of speech sounds as elements of language, and the application of this science to the understanding and speaking of languages. Special fields of interest are *physiological* or *articulatory phonetics*, which is concerned particularly with formation of speech sounds and the dynamics of speaking; *acoustic phonetics*, which studies the physical nature of speech; and *auditory* or *perceptual phonetics*, which deals with speech analysis and speech recognition. Classification of speech sounds is the subject matter of *taxonomic phonetics*. *Experimental phonetics* employs objective laboratory techniques in the analysis of spoken language. For our present purposes the term *phonology* may be taken as synonymous with *phonetics*. *Linguistics*, which has many branches, embraces the study of language in the most inclusive sense. One area, *structural linguistics*, is in part devoted to speech sound structures, with particular emphasis on their linguistic function.

SOME PERSPECTIVES ON PHONETICS

Anyone who embarks on the study of phonetics should appreciate the place of speech sound production in the total process of communication. Consider a simplified model of what happens when meanings are carried verbally from speaker to listener. Reacting to a stimulus from without (perhaps a question) or to some inner state (aching feet!), the speaker *encodes* a message, a most extraordinary process mediated by neural circuits in the brain which still are incompletely understood. The *verbal formulation*—what the speaker means to say—is translated into complex motor responses of the speech system to produce an audible signal, "My feet are killing me!" It still remains for the listener to *decode* the message, a step accomplished by means of the *cognitive* or "knowing" operations of the brain.

It would be fascinating to explore all phases of communication, but we must limit ourselves to some important generalities about the last two steps: *speech production* and *speech perception*. First, in no way can speech sounds be considered analogous to typewriter letters, which are essentially always the same when a given key is struck. A spoken word is not a series of invariant sounds like the discrete symbols of a printed word. The speech system functions *dynamically*, producing flexible *sound patterns* which vary in response to many influences; sounds are not fixed in form. What these influences are and the changes they produce in the nature of speech await later explanation, but this basic premise must be kept in mind as an important principle of phonetics.

The second generality relates to speech perception. If we are interested in sounds as carriers of meaning, which is their *linguistic function*, it follows that the way they are *perceived* by a listener has a great deal to do with what they *are* as units of spoken language. The answer to the schoolboy puzzler, "If a tree falls in the forest when no one is around, did it make a sound?" depends, of course, on what is meant by "sound." If the word is used in a psychological sense, there is no sound without a listener. In the sense of being meaningful units of spoken language, the audible energies generated by the speech system are not "speech sounds" until they have been processed by the auditor's decoding system. By the same logic that says that beauty is in the eye of the beholder, speech sounds are in the ear of the listener. If the point seems abstract, it nevertheless has significant implications for anyone who wishes to understand the relationship between *sound* and *meaning*.

Because of their importance to phonetic theory and its applications, some ramifications of these ideas call for further discussion.

Dynamic Sound Production

The unique characteristics of speech sound production can be made somewhat clearer if we expand on the warning that the mechanism for articulation is not analogous to such language-signal generators as typewriters or teletypes. Although complexity of design is not the most important difference, it is nevertheless a fact that the speech mechanism has a great many more "moving parts" than the most sophisticated mechanical printer. Speech is produced by a system (described more fully in Chapter 4) which requires both simultaneous adjustment and serial movement of three physiological systems: respiratory, laryngeal, and articulatory, each of which has other life-serving functions for the organism. Each of the three is composed of both slow- and fast-moving structures which are moved so rapidly that we easily speak at a rate which matches a typing speech of 15 or more characters per second. Only a system with some such degree of complexity could originate a signal as multidimensional as human speech.

A difference which is of the greatest possible theoretical and practical significance is that the articulatory system, unlike a mechanical printer, produces speech sounds which are never exact replicas of one another; instead, they show variations which are the result of its dynamic flexibility of operation. In contrast, when a given key on a mechanical printer is struck, the result is almost invariably the same. This distinction is basic to the study of phonetics. Speech sounds can be examined individually, and this is a necessary step. However, for a full understanding of spoken language such an analysis of the *common properties* of each sound must be complemented by a study of the *variations* it may show when placed in *context*.

Physiologically, the explanation for the amazingly flexible operation of the speech mechanism lies in two directions. First, it is set in motion by exceedingly complex and diverse instructions from the brain, not simply by pressing a key. Next, its moving parts are a matrix of finely coordinated muscles capable of highly versatile neuromuscular responses, not a system of levers and relays. Whereas a machine has only one way to produce a symbol, human beings have the ability to generate a given sound in different ways. For example, the *oo* in "boot" is usually spoken with rounded lips, but the "same" sound can be produced by changing tongue position with the lips left unrounded. This enables the speech system to "correct" itself by using alternative conditions for production of sounds.

It would take us too far afield to explore what is known and what is not known about the way the brain is programmed for these exceedingly variable speech responses, nor can we look into the physiological processes of sound production beyond what is to come in Chapter 4. As a perspective from which to begin our phonetic studies we must content ourselves with a summary of some of the major reasons for the differing patterns of speech sounds. Some kinds of changes occur because of their context, which introduces such later topics as *coarticulation*, *assimilation*, and *ellipsis*. Others are simply a result of a speaker's idiosyncracies, for no matter how consistently people share the basic language rules of a community, they still differ from one another—both in their interpretation of the rules and in the way in which they apply them. This and other factors relate to *free variation*, which is treated in Chapter 2. Later in the present chapter still other sources of variation are discussed.

Speech Perception

The reason for the phonetician's interest in perception has already been stated: because the phenomena of speech can be understood only if its *production* and *perception* are viewed as interrelated and interacting elements of a *single* process. This generalization has both theoretical implications and some of a more concrete nature. For beginning students, perhaps the most immediate value in knowing something about the way in which speech is perceived is that this information may help them to acquire skill in *perceptual analysis*, a phonetic technique which calls for sophisticated listening skills. They must realize from the outset that to comprehend the *meaning* of a word or sentence does not mean that the structural details of its *sound pattern* have been perceived. Yet this they must be able to do if they are to analyze normal or abnormal speech.

The topic of speech perception can be approached by reviewing some of the problems involved in comprehending and describing spoken language. Human speech is an extraordinarily complex auditory stimulus. Even a single speech sound combines a large number of *distinctive features* which provide the information on which an auditor bases recognition of the sound. Sometimes the distinctions between speech sounds are obvious, but often they are quite subtle, a fact which makes discriminating between them not unlike differentiating two intricate visual designs which may differ by a single small detail.

One of the remarkable facts about human perceptual capacities is that we can quickly and usually with little effort make sense out of speech patterns of enormous complexity. A point which is important for students to realize, however, is that in speech *analysis* they will be called on not only to recognize the sounds under study, but also to *describe* their characteristics—a feat which is considerably more demanding than simply grasping what was said.

The remarks just made apply to difficulties in perceiving the complex dimensions of a single speech sound. Running speech multiplies these. The composition of the speech signal fluctuates in time, how much and how often depending on the nature and length of the speech sample. If the simile is not too contrived, speech is like a flowing stream with currents, eddies, and waves which change the appearance of its surface from instant to instant. On the basis of research studies, time relations may introduce the most difficult of all perceptual elements, especially when the stimuli occur at ordinary speech rates or faster (about four to six syllables per second).

For example, speech scientists (see Ladefoged, 1967) have tested the ability of listeners to identify the time location of clicks which were superimposed on samples of tape-recorded speech, comparing the positions where subjects reported hearing the clicks with their actual position. The margin of error in judgment was surprisingly great under some conditions, and, in fact, at times listeners tended to locate the click a full word distant from its actual position. There have been other impressive demonstrations of our relatively poor ability to analyze accurately the temporal relations of rapidly occurring auditory stimuli. One investigator (Warren, 1969) spliced together a number of short nonspeech sounds on a recorded tape loop which allowed continuous repetition of the sequence. Sounds were a high-pitched tone, a low-pitched tone, a hiss, and a buzz, repeatedly presented without pauses. At speeds comparable to the rate of speech, errors in judging the order of stimuli were gross, and a learning period was needed before the subjects could even identify the sounds.

The apparent discrepancy between these findings and the ease with which we can, in fact, understand spoken language is not hard to account for. Our perceptual set is usually to listen for *meanings*, and it proves that meaning can be apprehended without necessarily utilizing every potentially available acoustic cue. This is only to say that a word can be understood even if it is only partly heard, just as we can recognize an elephant merely by glimpsing its trunk. Communication engineers refer to the *redundancy* of speech, and they have succeeded in filtering, condensing, clipping, and otherwise modifying its form without serious loss of understandability. When interested in speech as a unique kind of sound, however, the phonetician is required to adopt a special listening set in order to note its salient features.

The Motor Theory of Speech Perception   This hypothesis about the way spoken language is perceived is related to, and may have been suggested by, certain psychological theories about the nature of thought processes. Psychologists agree generally that *thinking*, except possibly in the case of some nonverbal forms, is mediated by verbal symbols. In the formulation of some psychologists, thinking is carried out by means of *covert* or *subvocal* speech; we think, they theorize, by "talking" silently to ourselves by means of inner speech movements.

Explained simplistically, the motor theory of speech perception holds similarly that spoken language is perceived on the basis of *covert* (or, on occasion, *overt*) articulatory movements. That is, the listener "repeats" the message and apprehends its meaning from cues provided by inner speech responses. The most persuasive proponents of an advanced form of this hypothesis are Liberman et al. (1967), who have developed in some detail the thesis that "the speech decoder works by referring the incoming speech signal to commands that would be appropriate to its production." A review of the research evidence for and against the motor theory would require more space than seems justified. There are, however, a number of generally accepted explanatory principles about perceptual processing which have been brought together under an *analysis-by-synthesis* model, and these will be discussed in the next section.

Analysis-by-Synthesis   This formulation of what takes place in the process of speech perception runs as follows: At the initial stage, the incoming speech signal is received by the sensory end organ of hearing in the ear and transmitted to the brain via the auditory pathways. It is assumed that under ordinary listening conditions the sensory data which reach the brain are to some degree incomplete by reason of limitations in both the producing systems of speakers and the receiving systems of listeners. It may also be that not all the incoming information gets fed into the perceptual processing circuits of the brain because of the filtering effect of attention, perceptual set, and for other reasons.

Up to this point, only physical energy in the form of sensory nerve impulses will have reached the brain, although it is theorized that some sorting and interpretation of the physical input may have taken place in the inner ear. Under the analysis-by-synthesis formulation, brain circuitry next organizes the data it has received into the *percepts* on which recognition is based. However this takes place, *structuring* is an essential feature. Neisser (1967, p. 196) suggests the possibility that "hearing an utterance, the listener constructs one of his own in an attempt to match it." As an aside, some of the difficulties in language recognition suffered by brain-injured patients (*agnosia*) are thought to be due to a breakdown of this structuring capacity, not a loss of memory traces for language itself.

There are at least partial answers to some of the questions about speech perception. Recognition based on fragmentary information—a word incompletely heard—involves a principle the psychologist calls *closure*, this being the tendency of the mind to supply missing details. An auditor's perceptions are conditioned by certain presumptions made on the basis of past experience. In the case of speech, these presumptions are the product of learning, and take the form of some kind of "known" or "standard" speech sound, or on a phonological "rule." The *constancy* principle inclines us to perceive a given figure as always the same, regardless of variation in details of the stimulus. Percepts are thus made to fit one's a priori presumptions, and cues not consistent with the presumptions are rejected.

Many of these observations can be illustrated in the visual realm by the way in which incomplete or ambiguous figures are reconstructed. For instance. in deciphering the incomplete figures of Leeper (1935) shown in Fig. 1, we have only greatly fragmented visual stimuli upon which to base our perceptions. How well we are able to "make sense" out of such figures depends upon how well closure can supply the missing details from our prior experience and on the basis of unconscious expectations about what we *ought* to see. Knowing that the upper right-hand figure is an office machine makes the fragments of the figure easier to reconstruct. Knowing in advance that one figure is a typewriter enables us to spot this particular picture quite easily.

One's ability to understand spoken language is made highly efficient through analysis-by-synthesis, of course. Its principles are also significant for general communication theory. Our immediate interest, however, lies in the implications analysis-by-synthesis may have for the problems of perceiving phonetic characteristics of speech. A basic premise would seem to be that our habitual perceptual set, which is to listen to speech for its meaning, must be replaced by one which allows us to perceive details of its *form*. It should help to realize that our descriptions of speech form are likely to be biased,

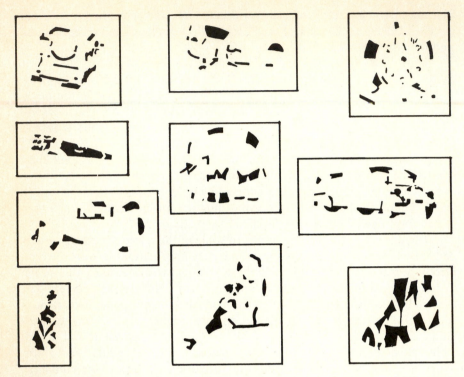

Figure 1-1 Incomplete figures of Leeper (1935). A visual analogy of the problem of human perception of meaningful forms from incomplete data. (Permission for reproduction of this figure by The Journal Press, Prentice-Hall, Inc., and Professor Robert W. Leeper. Figure from Ulric Neisser, *Cognitive Psychology,* © 1967, reprinted by permission of Prentice-Hall, Inc., Englewood Cliffs, N.J.).

not necessarily because we are bad listeners, but by reason of the very factors which enable us to grasp meaning efficiently; they work *against* the recognition of structural details.

A second premise which is also basic is that a full knowledge of possible speech forms provides a memory bank from which to draw in matching features that have been detected in a sample under study with known *articulatory possiblities*. It is not through practice alone, or because they necessarily have unique abilities, that trained linguists can describe accurately the form of a spoken language they never before have heard and which they understand poorly or not at all. For this reason one who has only a "practical" interest in speech should not be reluctant to study phonetic theory, since this is the route by which practical goals can be reached most effectively. The point is of the utmost importance to the speech improvement teacher and to the speech pathologist who must diagnose and correct deviant speech, as well as to the descriptive linguist engaged in the study of spoken language forms.

KINDS AND SOURCES OF VARIATION
IN SPEECH

As words are spoken by persons who share a common tongue, they must necessarily be pronounced in a way that will make them understandable to all members of the language community. So it is that for its spoken words each language has configurations of sound which are agreed-upon and known to all members of the language group. These pronunciations we record in the dictionary as best we can, and pass on to each following generation by formal and informal education. In the broadest sense, these usages make up the *standard speech* of the language community.

Obviously those who speak the same language must, within limits at least, obey the rules for its pronunciation, else there would be no communication. What these rules are and how they operate is, in one way or another, the business of a variety of scholars including, of course the phonetician. These same scholars, and particularly the phonetician, are also keenly interested in speech differences, which we shall call *variations*, that can be observed among members of a broad language community. Such variations are numerous and their sources many.

The reasons for this interest are several. From the standpoint of phonetic theory alone, the question of what is *correct* is not uppermost; the term *standard* in this context means only that the speech usages fall within accepted rules of the spoken language well enough to fulfill their communicative function. There are many observable variations within these broad limits. The descriptive phonetician seeks only to understand the phonological rules which apply, and to note the way in which the rules operate. On the other hand, the question of what is desirable, in the sense of what serves the individual's communicative needs well, is not unimportant. The recommendation that you should "leave your speech alone" is not a good one.

Most variant forms of speech are referred to in phonetic literature as dialects. McDavid (1966, p. 211) has defined the term simply as "a habitual variety of language, regional or social. It is set off from all other such habitual varieties by a unique combination of language features; words and meanings, grammatical forms, phrase structures, pronunciations, patterns of stress and intonation."

The broadest generalization that can be drawn is that geographic, social class, and cultural *isolation* are principally responsible for the emergence of dialect forms. To the extent that members of a language community are not separated by barriers such as these, they will tend to have a common currency of speech. To the degree that they are isolated, their speech patterns will diverge, just as a species of animal may in time evolve differences when cut off from the parent stock. Note, for instance, the dialect differences that have grown up among the English-speaking peoples of the United States, Australia, and the British Isles.

Interesting as they are, the whole subject of dialects is much too involved to be covered here. Because of their particular interest for students of speech we shall, however, touch on some of the major kinds of variations among speakers of American English, confining ourselves mainly to their sources.

Regional Dialect

One of the most obvious kinds of isolation which produces speech and language change is geographic, and more attention has been paid to regional influences on American English than to any other source of variation, at least until recent times. The early difficulties in North-South travel in the New World, combined with some degree of difference in the dialect characteristics of the original settlers themselves, operated to produce three major regional speech forms in the Eastern part of what is now the United States: *Northern*, *Midland*, and *Southern*. It is on the basis of these divisions and their branches that most dialect experts describe the multitude of minor dialect groupings which can be heard in American speech.

However, the dialect map of American English can no longer be drawn in terms of colonial categories. Social and dialect centers of gravity have moved away from the East toward the West; North-South distinctions are no longer as marked as was once the case. The ease with which Americans can and do migrate from one region to another, and their constant exposure to the speech forms of television, radio, and the motion pictures could have no other result. Historically, there has been not only a westward flow of early dialects, but also a fanning out of settlers which brought about extensive dialect intermixing. There has emerged as a consequence, in the view of some dialectologists, a new General American (GA) dialect, now heard most commonly outside the Eastern seaboard and the South, but destined perhaps to infiltrate these regions quite thoroughly in the course of time.

Regional American dialects continue to be described primarily in terms of the original three major areas, each with a number of subdialect regions. Their designation as Eastern American (EA), Southern American (SA), and General American (GA), although still used by some writers, tends to be supplanted by other terms which many dialectologists feel better identify the major dialect regions. While dialect geographers differ in this and other respects, the breakdown of Nist (1966) provides a good basis for discussion.

He lists 10 major dialect regions which have grown out of the parent Northern, Midland, and Southern divisions of colonial times. Generally, the Northern dialect area has generated subregional forms which include the dialects of *eastern New England*, the *North Central* region (Chicago, Cleveland, Minneapolis area), and the *Southwest* (Arizona, Nevada, and California generally).

The Midland area has evolved the dialects of *New York City*, the *Middle Atlantic* area, *western Pennsylvania*, the *Central Midlands* (the "vast heart-

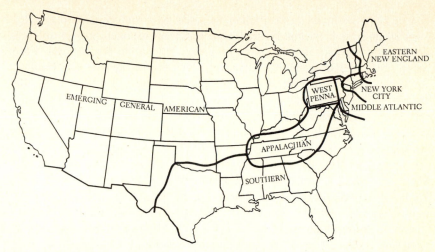

Figure 1-2   Dialect map of Nist showing the approximate boundaries of major American dialects as spoken in 1965. (From J. Nist, *A Structural History of English*, St. Martin's Press, Inc., 1966, by permission.)

land" of America), the *Northwest*, and *Appalachia*. The *Southern* area is distinguished by numerous subregional dialects heard generally in or close to the old Southern Confederacy.[1]

The dialect map prepared by Nist (see Figure 1-2) identifies the boundaries of what he considers to be the seven most prominent varieties of American English being spoken today. It is his view that there is presently going on "a gradual wearing away of pronunciation differences among the four regionalisms that cover most of the land mass of the continental United States: North Central, Southwest, Central Midland, and Northwest." He feels that there is emerging a General American dialect which in time may become the accepted American standard.

Whatever the trend may be for the future of American speech, it is evident that even today the residents of the vast Central and Western regions of the United States constitute the largest relatively homogeneous dialect population, and conceivably the one which may prove the most influential in the future. Their speech, incidentally, is closest of all the major dialect regions to the "network standard" of television and radio. Differences within the GA are less marked, and hence less obtrusive to those who speak this form, than the variations between their usages and those of eastern New Englanders, residents of Appalachia, and Southeasterners.

None of these observations is meant to imply that any one dialect is somehow better than another. As Wise (1957) sensibly points out, one cannot

---

[1] In addition to Nist, McDavid (1958) and Wise (1957) would be suitable references for anyone wishing to supplement our brief description of dialect regions.

charge that the mode of pronunciation used by some 90 million people, or even 30 million, is wrong. Actually, the really noticeable regional differences among educated speakers from each of the major areas are few; most of the more obvious distinguishing features center around the way the "*r*-family" of sounds are handled and upon the sound given certain vowels and diphthongs. There are a number of fine points of pronunciation, intonation, and stress, but these are not apparent to the average listener. Genuine subregional dialects which might be sufficiently conspicuous to attract much attention outside their own milieu are spoken by relatively few persons.

One critical point must be appreciated. It would be ideal if the study of phonetics could be carried on independently of any particular dialectical form, but this is not possible. Examples must be used, and the instructor must speak in *some* dialect. Much of the discussion in this text is couched in terms of General American, particularly the illustrations and exercise materials. This dialect framework has been selected not only because it is the speech of the authors, but also because it is the one most widely used by American English speakers. Although this might seem to constitute a tacit recommendation of GA as somehow better than other forms of American speech. such is not our intent. Any views the authors may have on the choices, if any, on a standard of speech are reserved for the final paragraphs of this chapter.

Social Class Dialect

America has no genuine social class dialect in the sense of a socially approved standard such as the Received Pronunciation (RP) of the British upper class. This "King's English," based on the grammar and pronunciation of educated persons from the South of England, became the distinguishing mark of social class in that country—a state of affairs which was the subject of the delightful ironies of George Bernard Shaw in his play *Pygmalion*, but perhaps better known to some through the musical comedy *My Fair Lady*. In the early days of the United States there were serious attempts by some of its better-known figures to prevent the "deterioration" of speaking and writing by establishing a standard—by law if necessary—but their efforts came to nothing. These doings are entertainingly recounted by H. L. Mencken in his book *The American Language* (1963). That there ever could be such a standard seems incompatible with the American temperament, and even in England Received Pronunciation no longer enjoys the prestige it once had.

Nevertheless, there are American social class dialects whose significance has only lately begun to be appreciated by students of *sociolinguistics*. Judgments about people's cultural and educational level *are* made on the basis of the way they talk. As research studies have demonstrated, there are certain traits of speech which listeners tend to associate with status; and while there may be no invariable set of characteristics which would, for all speakers in all places, mark them as members of a particular social class, there is a general tendency for certain speech patterns to be downgraded by biased or naïve observers.

Linguists and phoneticians have made a great many studies of Black, "ghetto," "inner-city," and other minority dialects which are, by some, taken as an indication of social class. Many of the so-called status markers prove to be variations in grammar and word usage, but there are also distinctive phonological characteristics. An example is the substitution of *d* or *t* for *th* as in "I tink dey are" for "I think they are," or the neutralization of *th* and *f* in a final position, so that "both of us" becomes "bof of us" or "bof us." There is also a simplification of consonant clusters, leading to "Muss you do dat?" for "Must you do that?" Grammatical ellipsis results in omission of sounds in such forms as "He here," "It mine," "She come," and so on. An excellent analysis of Black English will be found in Labov (1970).

Beyond pointing out that such usages may be interpreted by some as unfavorable indications of social class, there is not much more to be said on the subject in a discussion such as ours. As a student of language, and particularly when reflecting on nonstandard dialect, the phonetician only observes that these are speech forms which have developed from their own logic. In the milieu in which they are standard, they seem to facilitate transmission of the kind of information needed for successful survival in that culture. Such speech forms are legitimate in the phonetic sense, and phoneticians pass no judgment that they are "substandard," "bad," or "disadvantaged" speech. They prefer to form any opinions they may have about a social group on extralinguistic grounds.

Not everyone agrees, of course. Consequently, an extraordinary amount of heat has been generated, especially by friction between that faction among educators who believe that black dialect should be vigorously attacked in the schools and all children taught to talk alike, and their equally vocal opponents. The latter offer a number of arguments. Some say such linguistic traits are the rightful mark of a culture in which they take pride, and that in any event these speech differences are of no significance and should be ignored. Others contend that linguistic differences in this case are only by-products of the exploitation of one social group by another and that solution of this deeper problem would be followed by disappearance of this particular symptom. The phonetician cannot be the arbiter of this controversy.

Foreign Dialect

Among the commonest variations one is likely to hear, notably in certain urban areas, are those in the speech of persons who have taken on English as a second language. These variations consist of deviations in word usage and grammar, in the pronunciation of sounds and words, and in patterns of intonation and stress. Typical foreign dialects are so familiar that it seems unnecessary to give illustrations. As a general point of theory, the forms are variant because the speakers apply the phonological rules of their native language to English, which is only to say that they have learned English imperfectly.

More specifically, some sounds may deviate because they are missing from the native language and have not been mastered; this accounts for the difficulties some speakers have with *th* as in "think." Probably more often the native languages have sounds which somewhat resemble English sounds, but which differ in some important respects. This may account for subtle dialect differences in the shading of vowels and in the way such sounds as *r*, *l*, *s*, *t*, and others are pronounced. In fact, nonnative speakers are likely to have more difficulty with English sounds having "relatives" in their own language than with those for which they have no preexisting habits. In some cases they are misled by spelling, causing the Norwegian to say "yump" for "jump" because of the way the letter *j* is pronounced in that language. Variations in stress and intonation probably do most to give foreign dialect speech its flavor, although they are much more difficult to describe.

To some persons, and in some subcultures, foreign dialect speech is taken as an indication of social class, but probably much less often than in the case of minority dialects. Most of the comments about the latter would apply equally well to foreign speech. The principal problems it presents are peda-gogical, not social, and relate to the teaching of English as a second language —a matter which may be of great importance to nonnatives attempting to develop speech forms in English which are adequate to their needs. Those of us who have struggled to achieve reasonable proficiency in speaking other languages can appreciate the difficulties.

Dialects of Age and Sex

Although the term *dialect* may not seem quite the right term to describe them, there are interesting variations due to age and sex. Voice and speech would seem to be obvious indicators of sex, and this proves to be the case. It is less a matter of common knowledge that there are reliable indicators of age in voice. In one unpublished study (Tiffany and Hollien) observers were asked to estimate the age of 30 female speakers in their thirties and 60 who were in their forties. Of the older women, only seven were judged to be as young as thirty years of age or younger. The ages of none of the younger group were guessed to be as much as forty years, and only three were estimated to be older than thirty. Shipp and Hollien (1969) report comparable results for male speakers. In their study the correlation coefficient between actual and estimated age was .88, which means that the chances of guessing correctly was nearly 8 in 10.

Speech Style

A kind of variation in speech which differs from any mentioned thus far arises from the nature of the speech situation itself. This is more than a casual observation, for it appears that a basic characteristic of speech behavior is that it is conditioned by the nature of the communicative situation, and by the relationship between speaker and listener. For want of a better term we shall speak of *style* to describe this situationally conditioned variation. Quite unconsciously, style is adjusted to maximize the transmission of information, both verbal and nonverbal, with least effort. At a deeper psychological level, this change of manner reflects the operation of subtle processes whereby one member of a social group relates to another.

Surface differences in speech style are easily noted. Joos (1967) distinguishes five: *intimate, casual, consultative, formal,* and *frozen.* There is no need to describe each in detail, but they represent points on an informality-formality continuum from the elliptical intimate form to such rigid language as might be met in legal discourse or ritualistic utterances. On occasion one may, and perhaps should, exercise some conscious judgment in selecting a manner of speaking, but for the most part the choice is unconscious. Nor is the listener particularly aware of style, as such; nevertheless, a great deal of information is transmitted by it. A child reads clearly the difference in meaning between the formal address, "Charles Addington Jones, this intolerable behavior must cease at once!" and "Hey, Chuck, what're y' doing?" When style seem inappropriate, it may not be so much that the speakers are failing to obey the rules of language, but more that they are insensitive to the situation, have a rigid personality, or that conscious or unconscious attitudes are coming through.

Most of the time we speak what has been called "easy English." This familiar *elliptical* style is not only sparing in vocabulary, but also in phonetic structure—which is consistent with the definition of "elliptic" in *Webster's New Collegiate Dictionary* (1974) as "marked by extreme economy of speech." Rate tends to be more rapid than in formal styles, and the speech is rich in fragmented forms such as "I'm" not "I am," "it's" instead of "it is," "shouldn't" rather than "should not," and so on. Among educated speakers who would be thought of as using language properly one hears—and is not disturbed by—such elliptical forms as "frinstance" for "for instance," "'spose" for "suppose," "lesko" for "let's go," and similar comfortable forms. At the other end of the continuum, in a full formal style grammatical constructions are complete, the subject and predicate of each sentence is explicit, rate is usually slowed, and each word contains all its expected sounds.

If one were to make a value judgment, one could only say that style should fit the occasion—which seems to call for informality in speech most of the time. It would be wrong, however, to suppose that informal styles are in any way careless; articulation is not imprecise, and pronunciations are always within the limits of an acceptable usage. Despite its informality the speech form is, so to speak, well groomed. Actually, we hear very few examples these days of classical formal styles, although speakers naturally talk more formally on some occasions than they might in an intimate face-to-face situation. A study of the public utterances of contemporary figures we consider effective shows their style to be quite informal for the most part.

Defects of Speech and Voice

Communicative disorders are variants which have great social and educational significance. While dialects of the kind we have discussed thus far are natural and legitimate variants, speech and voice defects are not; dialect forms are shared by a whole community, but deviant communication *isolates* an individual from the community. Viewed theoretically, dialect represents a normal conversion of language competence into speech performance. Defective speech springs in some cases from language *incompetence*, or it may arise from an inability to convert competence into performance. The attributes of defective communication are well described by Van Riper (1972, pp. 1–50), as is their significance for the individual. Communication is defective, he says, when it is adversely conspicuous, interferes with communication, or is a source of stress for the individual—or any combination of these.

We can do no more than touch briefly on these conditions. Developmental disorders of language and articulation perhaps receive the most attention. Children who suffer from a developmental *language* disorder are slow to talk and in extreme cases may never talk at all. Those who do learn to talk, with or without trained help, are likely to have problems in vocabulary and language usage in speaking, and possibly also in reading and writing. Misarticulation of speech sounds is common among them. These are children whose *competence*, and hence their *performance*, is impaired. They have not learned the rules of language for one or a combination of reasons such as defective intellect, sensory deprivation, unfavorable environment, or brain dysfunction. Other children appear to have language competence, but continue to be "baby talkers" long after they should have mastered the sounds of speech. In severe cases their speech may be a virtual jargon.

Structural defects in and about the mouth (*orofacial defects*) can also cause speech abnormalities in children and adults, although these possibly account for a smaller proportion of cases than is generally supposed. A child with congenital cleft of the palate, for instance, is born with a split in the roof of the mouth. Even when given the best possible care by a plastic surgeon and other specialists early in life, it may be impossible for such a child to close the opening into the nose as the physically normal child does when speaking or swallowing. The speech of such children will then sound as if they are "talking through the nose," which indeed they are. Voice may be unpleasantly nasal, and the speech sounds may be distorted to a point where they are unintelligible, or nearly so. Other abnormalities in structure due to birth defect, growth failure, or injury, including the common dental malocclusions, can make normal speech production difficult or even impossible.

Injury to or disease of the nervous system can also cause defects of language, speech, and voice, since the brain and peripheral nerves mediate these functions. Among children the commonest of such conditions is *cerebral palsy*, in which the brain has been damaged—most often before or during birth—with the result that its victims may have a range of possible motor, sensory, and learning disabilities, including language problems and imperfect control of speaking movements. Accidental injury to the nervous system and neuromuscular disease, which are commoner among adults than in children, may cause a form of faulty articulation called *dysarthria*. These injuries and diseases, if they damage the language circuits of the brain, can cause difficulties in language comprehension or language expression—or both—in what is called *dysphasia*. Those of us with a relative or acquaintance who has suffered a stroke may have observed some of these latter peculiarities.

Disorders of voice are possibly of less interest to phoneticians than they are to speech pathologists or to the person who has one. They nevertheless can obscure the voiced-voiceless distinction between certain pairs of speech sounds, pervert natural intonation patterns, and otherwise contribute to variant speech forms. Abnormalities of voice (*dysphonia*) are usually divided into three types: disorders of *pitch*, *loudness*, and *quality*. Any of these can be the result of poor use of the vocal instrument, or they may have physical causes.

Vocal pitch can be higher or lower than is appropriate to the age and sex of the speaker, and the pitch patterns may deviate from the usual inflectional melodies of English speech. The voice can be too weak or too loud, and the patterns of stress may be unlike those to which we are accustomed. There are sundry vocal qualities which may attract adverse attention, but *hoarseness* is the most noteworthy since it suggests the possibility of laryngeal disease or aggravated abuse of the vocal mechanism. Complete loss of voice (*aphonia*) from either organic or nonorganic causes is not rare and has an obvious effect on the form of speech.

Finally, the variant forms associated with hearing loss must be mentioned. Speech cannot be learned naturally without the sense of hearing, except for whatever unconscious use is made of visual cues. Hence children born deaf acquire little or no speech unless they are given special educational training. Language problems of the deaf have been studied extensively because of the marked difficulties these individuals experience in achieving language competence by reason of their severe sensory deprivation.

Losses less severe than deafness, especially if they are present during a child's developmental years, can be expected to have an effect on speech and language commensurate with their severity. If the loss is mild, its principal effect may be to blur the recognition and discrimination of speech sounds, particularly certain consonants, with resultant misarticulations attributable to faulty learning. Moderate hearing loss brings more aggravated problems in speech sound learning, and may begin to interfere with language development. A child with severe hearing loss faces essentially the same problems as one who is deaf, but they are less acute.

THE EVOLUTION OF SPEECH FORM

Language and speech have their own evolutionary history. Just as human beings, as members of the animal kingdom, have undergone—and continue to undergo—many changes in form and feature over the span of time, speech continues to evolve, although at a much faster rate. Study of the history of language is a field in itself, but a brief review of some of the broad trends may help the student of phonetics to realize that speech form is not static, but continues to change.[1]

English is classified as one of the languages derived from the Germanic branch of Indo-European. Originally there were three such Germanic branches: (1) East Germanic, represented by the now-extinct Gothic; (2) North Germanic, from which Scandinavian arose; and (3) West Germanic, which was the parent of English, High and Low German, and Frisian (spoken by the inhabitants of Friesland, a province of the Netherlands). The ancient origins of English are traced to three tribes who settled in the British Isles in the fifth century: the Jutes, Angles, and Saxons. Three general periods or "kinds" of English are recognized:

> Old English (OE): prior to 1100
> Middle English (ME): from 1100 to 1500
> Modern English (MnE): from 1500
>   Early Modern: from 1500 to 1700
>   Late Modern: from 1700

Because of numerous circumstances, complicated and interrelated processes of growth took place in each of these periods. Old English, sometimes called Anglo-Saxon, was made up predominantly of native words brought by these migrants from northwestern Europe. After the arrival of the new dwellers the tongue they brought was subjected to numerous influences. From the eighth to the eleventh century the Scandinavian conquests introduced many hundreds of new words into English, including many place names. As early as the tenth century, when what was called West Saxon

---

[1] An excellent reference for those who wish to inquire further into the history of language is Baugh (1957).

became predominant, there developed a strong tendency for the language to become homogeneous throughout the English-speaking area.

A large number of French words came into the language during a period of some 350 years after the beginning of the Norman Conquest in 1066. The language of the Normans, which was a northern French dialect, was in general use by the higher classes for some time, although it presently was spoken in a modified fashion, French ceased to be the language of court and church after about 1350, but the influx of French words continued. By this time, however, Parisian French, rather than the northern dialects, exerted the greater influence, complicating the situation still further.

Large numbers of words were borrowed from Latin by scholars of the Middle English period, and many of these imports became a part of the common language. It is said that there is no language from which English has not borrowed words at some time or another. One analysis of contemporary dictionary words classifies their origins as follows: native, 18.4 percent; French, 32.4 percent; Latin, 14.4 percent; Greek, 12.5 percent; and other, 23.3 percent. It is easy to appreciate that the pronunciation of these words must have been altered, both when they first found a foothold in English and later when they were subjected to modification by generations of English speakers.

Historical phoneticians agree generally that there was no spoken standard until the sixteenth century, when the speech of upper classes in London and Oxford became the pattern which educated persons throughout the country followed. By 1800, however, usages had undergone great changes in London, although the older standard persisted in the north of England. These events are regarded as having laid the groundwork for the present differences between northern and southern (London) British dialects. Early American settlers brought with them a variety of dialects, but one of the most important was the earlier London and Oxford standard.

Spelling—Pronunciation

Spelling-pronunciation relationships are involved in considering speech form. During the period when loan words were coming into the language in great numbers, English speakers tended to retain some semblance of their original pronunciation, particularly in the case of French derivatives. In due course these pronunciations were altered—by a shift in accent and otherwise —but often original spellings were retained. When French was the fashionable language, even some native English words took on a French flavor in their pronunciation. There remain many words whose pronunciation in English is still close to that of the original language. Others, however, have been more or less completely anglicized, with the net result that one cannot safely infer pronunciation of loan words from their spelling.

Throughout the history of the language, spelling practices have been much more stable than pronunciations. Spelling conventions were first fixed by scribal tradition and later, after the invention of printing, by published books and manuscripts. Today, of course, dictionaries are the major factor in maintaining relatively inflexible spelling practices. They do not, however, fix pronunciations in quite the same way. In theory, editors of a dictionary only report what they believe to be the usages of "educated" or "authoritative" speakers (such as experts in a technical field); if these usages change, appropriate alterations are made in later editions of the dictionary. This being the case, the pronunciation a dictionary gives for some words may well lag behind the usages one hears most commonly in speech.

A most noteworthy characteristic of spoken English is the change that has taken place in its sound structure since Old English. These evolutionary developments are altogether too complex to be included in our discussion;[1] suffice it to say, however, that they are extensive. One of the most prominent was the *great vowel shift* which occurred during the fifteenth century (see Potter, 1950). For instance, the modern word "life," which Chaucer would have rhymed with our "leaf," came to be pronounced with the vowel we use in "safe;" Chaucer might have rhymed "house" with the modern "moose," but by Shakespeare's day it had the vowel sound we use in "dose." There was also the loss of some consonants and the appearance of new ones, such as the *ng* in "sing" and *zh* as in "measure." While facts such as these may be mainly of historical interest, they should nevertheless help one appreciate the living and growing nature of spoken language.

SPEECH FORM OPTIONS

It has been stressed in this introductory chapter that in the phonetician's view as an academician there is no prescribed standard or norm for speech which *must* be adhered to by members of a language community. Nevertheless, the question "What is best?" continues to be asked, and legitimately so; and although speech improvement is not a branch of phonetic science, the body of phonetic information we shall study does contain the facts needed by anyone who wishes to exercise options on speech form. In addition to the student perhaps, this will include for certain the speech pathologist, those who teach English as a second language, the instructor of the deaf and hard of hearing, the speech teacher, and numerous others with like applied interests.

Questions about speech form have many motivations. Except for the mavericks among us, the need to *conform* is strong; and those who feel this need must realize that judgments—right or wrong—are made on the basis of

[1] Baugh (1957) covers this subject in detail.

speech traits. It seems undeniable that manner of speaking is among the personal characteristics which can be of importance in reaching social and vocational goals. Given this premise, it would appear to follow that each of us should exercise options on speech form. If it is true, as Emerson suggests, that every man might well be occupied in writing his own bible, it is equally true that we should be formulating, in an intelligent way, our own standard of speech.

We are venturing a few specific comments and recommendations, based frankly on the authors' own biases. The most elementary requisite of good speech form—and there should be little disagreement about this—is *intelligibility*. To be clearly understood, the speaker's articulation of the speech sounds must be sufficiently accurate to make the words easily distinguishable; if they are not spoken in this way, the speaker simply will not communicate, and may likewise give an undesirable impression.

Barring some physical handicap, articulation which is adequate for effective communication is not difficult to achieve. The only requirements are that movements of the articulators be sufficiently vigorous and precise to give the speech sounds the characteristics they should have and that the individual speech sounds be blended properly into the patterns of connected speech. An understanding of the nature of the individual speech sounds and the dynamics of sounds in context will aid in meeting these requirements.

Unfortunately many persons fail at the elementary level of intelligibility. The reasons may be numerous, but they should never prove insurmountable for physically normal speakers with sufficient motivation. They must become aware of the need for distinct articulation, develop the capacity for perceptive listening so that they can recognize correctly articulated speech in themselves and others, and be willing to monitor their own articulation by conscious attention to their manner of speaking. Practice will naturally be needed, and for this purpose a generous amount of exercise material is included in later sections.

A second requisite of good speech form is pronunciation which conforms to some chosen acceptable practice. At this point the question arises as to what attitude one should take toward culturally inherited dialect characteristics in speech. If one is from the South and talks as do the educated individuals in that area, need one feel any obligation to eradicate the traces of one's speech origins? This question is naïve, of course, and the answer has already been given: standard, clearly articulated speech from any of the major dialect areas is good anywhere. There may be legitimate reasons for changing one's speech practices, although, strictly speaking, no reason need be offered if this is the option of choice. Those who find themselves in a situation where most persons speak a standard different from their own may wish to conform for business or social reasons. Movement toward General American has been noted.

An earlier comment about limitations of the dictionary as a guide to pronunciation needs amplification. Despite certain reservations to be noted, one can and should turn to any recent standard dictionary for an authoritative statement about the pronunciation or alternative pronunciations of any English word. Bear in mind, however, that except for certain *prououncing dictionaries*, of which the most widely used for American English is Kenyon and Knott (1953), most list only the formal, literary pronunciation, or more properly, the *lexical* pronunciation. Since this is how the word is pronounced when spoken carefully by itself, allowance must be made for the changes that may occur in connected speech.

The possibility that a dictionary one might be likely to consult could be out of date was mentioned previously. Pronunciations do not change from day to day, of course, but shifts do take place quite rapidly as the historian measures time. Most of the changes can be accounted for in retrospect by the lawful operation of known phonetic principles, but social changes and quite unexplained fashions in speech may also be factors. When the editors of a dictionary record current usages, they have no wish to "freeze" pronunciations, even if they were so unrealistic as to believe that they could if they tried. Altered pronunciations in the habitual speech of educated persons are listed as soon as they are judged by the dictionary editors to meet the criterion of use. Since dictionaries can be revised only at fairly long intervals, a usage may become common before it receives dictionary sanction. Furthermore, the average person does not buy each new edition fresh from the press. Editors of lexical dictionaries also have a natural and understandable tendency to be conservative about adopting changes in recognized pronunciations.

As a matter of common sense, accepted usages do not change so rapidly that the current edition of an authoritative dictionary is likely to be seriously out of date. On the other hand, it does not need to be followed slavishly, provided an "unauthorized" pronunciation is in common use among those who set standards. These latter are the "educated" persons we know as a group, but whose individual members are sometimes a bit difficult to identify. Nevertheless, everyone has an opportunity to hear good speakers in business and social contacts, in the pulpit, on radio and television, and elsewhere. No one person will suffice as a model of speech form, but from a wealth of observations it will be possible to draw useful conclusions. Herein lies a unique value of a phonetic method; one develops a heightened perception of speech form, supported by an understanding of theory.

It seems fitting to end this introductory chapter by observing that the ultimate purpose of our exploration of phonetics will be to gain a better appreciation of an important facet of human communication. We must be mindful that the way one talks is the result of many factors, some of which we have noted. What seems to us "normal," because of the way we perceive speech and because of our own particular language experiences, may appear deceptively simple. We must not overlook the complex and fascinating diversity in the *ways* of talking. The study of phonetics at its best is not simply an analysis of what is average, "correct," or even most intelligible, but rather is an effort to understand the nature of the revealing and human differences in modes of speech.

EXERCISES

1 Following are a number of sample terms for a glossary of Chapter 1. Add other terms you think should be included, and furnish a short definition of each:

analysis-by-synthesis	Old English
Black English	perception
borrowed words	percepts
class dialect	perceptual analysis
competence/performance	phonetic context
constancy	phonetics
dialect	phonology
elliptic speech	physiological phonetics
General American	Received Pronunciation
great vowel shift	regional dialect
lexical	sociolinguistics
Midland dialect	speech style
Modern English	standard speech
motor theory of speech perception	structural linguistics
nonstandard speech	substandard speech

2 One purpose of this chapter has been to encourage you to become more aware of the sound structure of your language—to make you more *sound-minded*. The *Slurvian Translation Test* given below is a kind of test of your ability to distinguish between sound patterns and "word" patterns. These slurvianisms (see Tiffany, 1963) are sentences which, when spoken in a normal conversational manner, are *ambiguous* sound structures in the sense that they can convey more than one meaning. For example, "most a fuss stew" also sounds like "most of us do." The sentences below will test your ability to identify alternative sound patterns (perhaps one of the ingredients of *sound-mindedness*). Spend no more than 30 seconds per item looking for the translation, then compare your results with the answers in Appendix E. We found that most students can solve about half of these sentences in the time limit specified. When you have finished, invent some slurvianisms of your own. At least you might "trite 'n sea few ken."

    1 Rocker buy bay bee inner treat hop.
    2 Padder keg padder keg peggers mend.
    3 Turnips outs fir ply.
    4 Roland's tone gadders Nome ahs.
    5 Sinkers honkers sick spent.

    6 Lawn tent britches full in town.
    7 Diamond died weights fur Nome Ann.
    8 But tune toot a gather.
    9 My tea hoax farm ladle egg horns crow.
   10 Home other rubber winter thick upper.
   11 High pled jelly gents two thief lag.
   12 A fit furs chewed own suck seed dry egg hen.
   13 Want a drain sit bores.
   14 Win rum douche a romance stew.
   15 Thoroughly Burt gashes swarm.

3 From the everyday unstudied speech of persons around you begin to collect instances of what you believe may be nonstandard speech. Include examples based on differences in pronunciation, articulation, stress, rhythm, and voice quality, but not word usage or grammar. Classify these into two groups: (*a*) those you think sufficiently different to be conspicuous, and (*b*) those probably not conspicuous, but which nevertheless seem to you not fully standard and acceptable. Listen for forms such as "cancha" for "can't you." and other examples of truncated, slurred, or unexpectedly informal usages. Submit 10 examples of each group to your instructor for comment. On the basis of your experience, frame a definition of standard speech; decide if your ideas have changed.

4 If your instructor can supply them, or you can find them elsewhere, listen to recordings of foreign, regional, and other dialect variations of spoken English and analyze them in the following ways: (*a*) on the basis of speech alone, decide what kind of person you think the speaker is; (*b*) list the specific sounds which seem to be pronounced in a way different from yours; (*c*) describe also differences from your speech in rhythm, stress, or melody pattern and try to identify their nature; (*d*) rank the speech samples in an order which reflects your own preferences from "most like to hear" to "least like to hear" and compare your rankings with those of other students; decide the basis on which you believe you ranked the speakers; and (*e*) rank the samples in order of intelligibility, or ease of understanding; are the *preference* and *intelligibility* ranks the same? Why or why not?

5 Test your own pronunciation standards against those of the dictionary in the following way:

    In the list below, two pronunciations are given for each word, depending on which syllable receives the primary stress. Which pronunciation do you think should be listed first in the dictionary? Which sounds better to you, and which do you use? Compare your choices with the keys in Appendix E. The D key gives the consensus of six popular American abridged dictionaries. The P key indicates the usages preferred by a normative group of more than 100 university students from the state of Washington, as reported in a study by Tiffany and Bennett (1966). Any surprises?

  1 ab*domen*/*ab*domen   **3** adver*tise*ment/ad*vert*isement
  2 a*dult*/*a*dult   **4** al*lies*/*all*ies

5 as*pir*ant/*a*spirant
6 *com*batant/com*bat*ant
7 com*par*able/*comp*arable
8 comp*trol*ler/*comp*troller
9 con*trac*tor/*con*tractor
10 con*ver*sant/*con*versant
11 de*cad*ent/*dec*adent
12 de*fect*/*def*ect (noun)
13 ex*quis*ite/*ex*quisite
14 fi*nance*/*fi*nance
15 for*mid*able/*for*midable
16 *fre*quents/fre*quents*
17 *grim*aced/grim*aced*
18 har*ass*/*har*ass

19 *hos*pitable/hos*pit*able
20 *im*potent/im*pot*ent
21 in*cog*nito/ in*cog*nito
22 in*dis*putable/indis*put*able
23 *in*quiry/in*quiry*
24 irre*fut*able/irre*f*utable
25 *lam*entable/la*ment*able
26 *mis*chievous/mis*chiev*ous
27 *pi*anist/pi*an*ist
28 *pre*cedence/pre*ced*ence
29 re*search*/*re*search
30 *re*source/re*source*
31 ro*bust*/*ro*bust
32 *ro*mance/rom*ance*

Chapter 2

The Nature of Spoken Language

As a point of departure for our study of phonetic theory we shall now examine certain facts which will help us to grasp the basic nature of speech sounds and the *sound structure* of spoken language. Specific topics to be covered in this chapter include (1) the concept that a language can be described in terms of its *phonemes,* or classes of distinctive sounds; (2) the *nondistinctive* differences among speech sounds which may arise because of *allophonic variation* and *free variation;* and (3) the nature of *speech segments* and *syllables,* which are functional units of speaking. This information will prepare for an introduction to some of the tools and techniques for *speech analysis,* which is to follow in Chapter 3.

Out of the virtually limitless number of sounds human beings can make with their organs of speech, a relative few are used in the languages of the world. Each, however, has its own unique set of sounds which is exactly like that of no other language. Because the speech producing system is physically the same in all human beings, certain *articulatory possibilities* are more likely to be adopted than others,[1] with the result that languages may have sounds in common—especially if they have a common ancestry, as do members of the Indo-European family. Yet the differences among languages often seem more significant when sound structures are examined closely. Some of the variations in shared sounds are slight; others are marked, as are the dissimilar forms of *r* in English, French, and German.

Speech sounds have a fundamental *linguistic function*. When combined in various sequences into syllables, words, phrases, and even longer configurations, they make up much of the audible code through which *meaning* is communicated from one person to another. When language is written or printed, the letter symbols represent speech sounds, except for the few languages which use *ideographs*, or stylized "pictures" to stand for spoken words. One who studies only isolated speech sounds will, of course, have an incomplete understanding of spoken language, since speech is a good deal more than individual sounds joined together. Nevertheless, an analysis of the speech sound elements is necessary and is important to both phonetic theory and its applications.

PHONEMES AND DISTINCTIVE SOUNDS

When the sound structure of a language is to be described, one first step is to determine what are called its *phonemes* or *distinctive sound classes*. Broadly defined, a phoneme consists of a *family* of phonetically similar sounds which, in serving linguistic function, *contrast* with one another in such a way as to differentiate the meaning of spoken words. Such contrasting sound *classes* are said to be the *phonemes* of the language under study.

Note that a phoneme is not defined as a sound, but as a class or family of sounds. As we shall learn, individual sounds from a given family differ in a number of ways, just as may members of a human family despite the strong family resemblances among them. Differences of this kind are termed *nondistinctive* in the sense that one member of the sound family could be substituted for another in a given word without changing its meaning—although its pronunciation would be affected.

As an illustration of what is meant by distinctive sounds, consider the word "kitten." This can easily be converted into the word "cotton" merely by substituting an *ah* vowel (spelled in this case by the letter *o*) for the sound represented by the letter *i* in "kitten." The same kind of meaning change

---

[1] The term *articulation* is used in this text to refer primarily to the actions of the speech structures (tongue, lips, and so on) in the formation of the sounds of speech in verbal communication. There obviously are also many nonspeech or "nonarticulate" sounds made with vocal organs: sneezing, coughing, grunting, sighing, and other basic human noises—polite and impolite. We are not counting these as "articulate," although many of them play a very important role in our communicative code.

would occur if these vowels were to be transposed in the words "lit" and "lot." Clearly, then, these two sounds are *contrastive*, and each must be included as members of distinctive sound classes of English; they belong to different phonemes. Excluding the diphthongs, which present some special problems, we customarily say that there are 36 or 37 such distinctive classes of sounds, or phonemes, in English. The exact number depends upon the dialect from which the count is made, and on some matters of interpretation as to what constitutes a phoneme—but these are details which need not concern us here.

It is important to remember that sounds belonging to a single phoneme are not physically identical, largely because of the influence of the surrounding phonetic context. For example, the vowels in "lit" and "kick" are *phonetically* different, although this fact may go entirely unnoticed by the casual listener. A decision as to whether or not two sounds are variants within a single phoneme is usually made by applying the *minimal-pair* test. In the case just cited, interchange of the vowels in "lit" and "kick" as they are customarily spoken would not suffice to cause a change in the meaning of the words; hence the two vowels are *phonemically* the same. Pairs of words such as "lit" and "lot" which do contrast in meaning by reason of a change in one sound only are called *minimal pairs*.

Additional examples of minimal pairs might help to clarify the important principle of phonemic differences. In addition to the "lit-lot" comparison, other illustrations of contrasting sounds which occur in the same phonetic context (pay no attention to spelling) are the vowels in "pet-pat" and "sin-sun," the initial consonants in "pad-bad" and "book-look," the medial consonants in "minor-miser" and "penny-petty," and the final sounds in "pat-pad" and "base-bait." By searching out the minimal pairs in a newly encountered language, one could determine its distinctive or contrasting *sound patterns*—provided one had access to a sufficiently large speech sample and, when needed, the services of a native informant.

In addition to having the same linguistic role, sounds belonging to any particular phoneme do tend to have certain phonetic traits in common. In general, they will be produced with largely similar articulatory movements, although occasional exceptions to this rule can be found. Most important, they will be *perceived* as the same by the native speaker of a language even though they do not always have identical acoustic characteristics. We usually judge the *t* in "team" and the *t* in "water" to be the same sound even though they may differ markedly in some dialects of American English, as the reader may be able to discover. The two forms of the sound are made with broadly the same articulatory movements, however, and some phoneticians have suggested that in this and similar cases listeners perceive the sounds as the same because they unconsciously sense this similarity in their formation.

A Network of Differences

From the standpoint of linguistic theory the most noteworthy fact about the phoneme system of a language is that it functions as *a network of differences*. Its sole function in language, as Hockett (1958) points out, is to keep utterances *apart*. He comments further: "In this frame of reference, the elements of a phonological system cannot be defined in terms of what they 'are,' but only negatively in terms of what they are *not*, what they contrast with" (p. 24). In some views of language theory it is a person's knowledge of this system of phonemic contrasts which constitutes in part what we have referred to earlier as language *competence* (see page 4).

In Table 2-1 will be found an example of such a contrast network as Hockett describes, in this case for vowels only. The nature of such a contrast matrix can best be grasped by speaking each set of contrasts aloud. Among the exercises at the end of this chapter is one suggesting that the reader construct a similar network with consonants.

Distinctive Feature Theory

The characteristics of sounds which cause them to be perceived as contrastive are commonly enumerated in terms of *distinctive feature theory*. A fuller treatment of this subject is reserved for Chapter 5, but the theory runs generally as follows: Each sound consists of a matrix of physical properties or *features* which make of it a *feature bundle*. Taken together, these distinctive features

Table 2-1   Vowel Contrast Network Showing the Manner in Which the Vowel Phoneme System May Be Defined as a Network of Meaningful Contrasts

Contrasting vowels	h——d	b——d	p——l	k——d	f——l
[ē]	heed	bead	peel	keyed	feel
[ĭ]	hid	bid	pill	kid	fill
[ā]	hayed	bade	pail	cade	fail
[ĕ]	head	bed	pell	ked	fell
[ă]	had	bad	pall	cad	
[ä]	hod	baaed	poll	cod	
[ô]	hawed	bawd	Paul	cawed	fall
[ō]	hoed	bowed	pole	code	foal
[ŏŏ]	hood		pull	could	full
[ōō]	who'd	booed	pool	cooed	fool
[ŭ]	hud	bud		cud	
[ĕr]	heard	bird	pearl	curd	furl

provide the information on which recognition of the sound is based. Sounds may differ from one another by a single feature or several.

Phoneticians disagree somewhat in their lists of distinctive features. Most agree on the *voiced-voiceless* contrast, which can be used for illustration. This is the distinctive feature distinguishing the following *minimal distinctive feature pairs*: "*p*ad-*b*ad," "ba*t*-ba*d*," "*f*erry-*v*ery," and "*t*o-*d*o." The *nasal-nonnasal* contrast, on which there is also general agreement, is important in differentiating such pairs as "*m*any-*B*enny," "*n*ew-*d*ew," and "wi*ng*-wi*g*." The distinctive feature concept is not only important theoretically, but also has been applied to a variety of matters such as theories of speech sound acquisition in children, techniques of teaching language, and methods of diagnosing and correcting speech disorders.

Summarizing, the basic elements of spoken language consist of sounds which are grouped into classes called *phonemes*. Sounds in each phoneme *contrast* with those of all other phonemes so that utterances can be "kept apart" in the way which is necessary if ambiguity in *meaning* is to be avoided. Distinctions among phonemes can be said to depend upon *distinctive feature* differences. With this background, we are now ready to discuss, in the following section, *nondistinctive* differences and sources of variation among sounds within a phoneme.

PHONETIC VARIATION

The nature of nondistinctive differences among sounds belonging to any particular phoneme—that they are *not contrastive* in the linguistic sense—should be clear from previous explanations. They can be referred to as *phonetic differences* to distinguish them from the *phonemic differences* among the *contrasting* distinctive sounds. In the kind of speech analysis necessary for many applications of phonological theory, phonetic variations are of great importance. This is true of dialect studies, for instance, or the kind of analysis-in-depth which is essential in the diagnosis and treatment of deviant or non-standard speech. The two principal types to be discussed in this section are (1) *allophonic variation* and (2) *free variation*.

Allophonic Variations

Variations are said to be allophonic when they occur systematically as a result of the influence of sounds on one another when they are embedded in a phonetic context. Theoretically the number of *allophones* which may exist in any phoneme is extremely large; the number identified in a given discussion will depend upon how fine a distinction the investigator wishes to make, and upon the refinement of his or her techniques for detecting differences among sounds. In contrast to allophonic variations, *free variations* are idiosyncratic in the sense that they arise from factors other than phonetic context under circumstances to be discussed presently.

The manner in which phonetic context produces changes in connected speech will be explained more fully in the chapters to follow. At this point we do not need a full understanding of these causes, since our present purpose is only to become aware of the importance of allophonic variations in the sound structure of spoken language. For this, some illustrations should suffice. One was given in the preceding section when the differences between the *i* vowel in "lit" and "kick" were pointed out, but additional examples may help to clarify the concept.

Compare the initial *k* in "key" and "caw," pronouncing the words in a natural conversational manner. It should be possible to hear and "feel" small differences between them: The *k* in "key" may well seem to be made at a more forward point in the mouth than the "hard *c*" in "caw," even though one would generally say that the two are the same sound. This variation is due, at least in part, to the fact that the *ee* in "key" is a vowel customarily produced with the front of the tongue raised in the forward part of the mouth. This favors a relatively forward point of articulation for *k* in this context, since we unconsciously adopt articulation movements which enable us to blend sounds with a minimum of effort. Because the *aw* vowel in "caw" is usually made with the posterior part of the tongue back and in a low position, the tongue is influenced toward a more retracted position for the sound which precedes it. Both forms of *k* are *allophones* of the *phoneme* /k/.[1]

As a further illustration, note the allophonic variations in sounds of the /l/ phoneme in "lee" and "law" and of /s/ in "see" and "saw." In both of these word pairs the initial consonant is influenced by the following vowel as were the forms of /k/ in the previous example. In a similar way, a given sound may be affected by the one which comes just before. This would be the case with variants of the final /l/ in "awl" and "eel." In this case "aw" is a *back* vowel, leading to a more retracted final sound than in "eel," which contains a *front* vowel. Consonants can influence adjacent vowels, as can be sensed in the varying quality of "ee" in the words "tea" and "key."

Repeating an earlier remark, the sound configurations of spoken language are so diverse that the number of allophones that might be found for any phoneme is large. Nevertheless, allophones of a given phoneme are generally made with broadly similar articulation movements and are perceived as the "same" sound. In linguistic nomenclature, the allophones of any phoneme are said to be in *complementary distribution* because no two allophonic variants will occur in the same phonetic context. Since they do not contrast in such a way as to effect a change in meaning, the differences between allophones of a phoneme are *non-distinctive*.

---

[1] When needed for clarity, phonetic or allophonic symbols will be enclosed in brackets ([k]) and phonemic class labels in virgules, or "slants" (/k/).

Free Variation

It regularly happens that a speaker's pronunciation of a particular allophone varies from one utterance to another, even though the phonetic context remains the same. Unlike allophonic variation, this is a kind of instability or fluctuation in sounds which stems from an idiosyncracy of the speaker or from the speaking conditions. Differences due to free variation are small in most instances, yet they are important to anyone interested in analyzing speech samples in the finest possible detail.

There are many possible reasons for free variation, and it would be exceedingly difficult, if not impossible, to enumerate them all. To begin with, there is the general philosophical observation that in nature no two events ever happen twice in exactly the same way. The quality of the vowel in " pen " is no more likely to be spoken in precisely the same way twice by a given speaker, or identically by two speakers, than are two clouds ever likely to be exactly the same.

Doubtless some free variations are no more than random fluctuations due to the inability of the human motor system to duplicate exactly, in successive trials, any complex response, whether it be speaking a word or signing one's name. Among persons with speech defects, structural abnormalities or neuromuscular impairment may contribute to unstable articulatory responses. It also seems possible that lags in neuromuscular maturation may be responsible for free variations which take the form of speech sound difficulties among certain types of speech-delayed children.

One broad rule that can be formulated is that much free variation depends on the speaker's manner from one time to another: on speech rhythms, patterns of stress, rate factors, and so on. These *prosodic* or *nonsegmental* features of speech help make meanings clear and reflect the way the speaker feels about what he or she is saying. These subjective states lead to free variation in the elements of utterances. Vowel length is greatly affected, to give only one example: The vowel in "say" varies considerably between a noncommittal "You don't say" and an astonished "You don't say!" There are other free variations which depend on subtle factors which are difficult to identify. The final consonant of "but" can be pronounced with an audible release of breath (*aspirated*); alternatively, the breath release may be inaudible (*unaspirated*). The word may even be spoken with no breath release on the final sound (*unreleased*). In American speech all three forms occur in the same phonetic context, and many other comparable examples can be found.

Points made about the differences among phonemes, allophones, and free variants might be clarified further by an analogy with printed language. In Figure 2-1 are four different *graphemes*, or letters of the alphabet. For each grapheme we have given three different *allographs* or variants of the letter— Roman capital, Roman lower case, and Gothic—out of the larger number

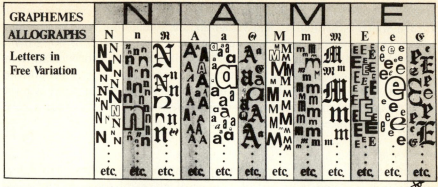

Figure 2-1 Graphemes—allographs—free variants analogy illustrating the differences among phonemes, allophones, and sounds in free variation in speech. Illustration by Jeff Wright.

that could be found. Each of these "means" the same thing, but the printer does not ordinarily mix them at random; one could say they are in *complementary distribution*. There are a number of variants in the Roman and Gothic which can be likened to free variations in speech.

SPEECH SEGMENTS AND SYLLABLES

Up to this point our discussion of the nature of speech has centered primarily on the manner in which the sound structure of language serves for the communication of meaning. This linguistic function, as we have seen, is carried out by a speech sound system whose basic elements are contrasting phonemes with their allophonic and free variants. From a somewhat different point of view, spoken language can be analyzed into what are called *segments* and *syllables*. This kind of description is useful to the linguist, and is of particular value when studying the physical and physiological phenomena of spoken language.

Speech Segments

The term *segment* is frequently encountered in phonetic and linguistic literature. In the broadest possible sense, a segment is any kind of physically or psychologically separable unit into which, for immediate purposes, one may choose to divide samples of spoken language. One such unit is the individual speech sound, of course, and through usage the term *segment* has tended to replace *speech sound* in a good deal of the phonetic literature. When linguists use the term *phonemic segment*, as they do on occasion, they are referring to a distinctive sound class of language, rather than to an individual sound.

To the acoustic phonetician a segment may be any kind of a speech event which has some clearly defined acoustic boundary, such as that between a resonant vowel and a following consonant, or some other separable unit of speech which is of interest. Individual speech sounds are sometimes called *phones*, a term which is especially appropriate when reference is being made to their audible characteristics—to the "sound of the sound." The term *malphone* has found its way into some of the speech pathology literature to designate misarticulated sounds. Incidentally, it is incorrect to use the term *phoneme* when one means *sound* or *phone*; thus, it is poor usage to say, "He mispronounced one of his phonemes."

Syllables

When speech is analyzed simply as a kind of sound, and without reference to meaning, it is found to consist of a series of pulses of sound energy called *syllables*. That speech is divisible in this way is, of course, perfectly familiar. Words of one syllable are *monosyllables*; those with two or more, *polysyllables*. One can easily recognize that words such as "me," "bomb," and "chair" have a single energy pulse. Examples of two-syllable words might be "baseball" and "midway"; three pulses can be sensed in "precedent" (prece-dent) and "catacomb" (ca-ta-comb). There are four syllabic pulses in "automobile" (au-to-mo-bile) and five in "refrigerator" (re-fri-ge-ra-tor). Note that some of these words have been divided into syllables at places different from those indicated in dictionaries; this is deliberate, for reasons that will be made clear in the discussion of *juncture* in Chapter 6.

Syllabification can be discussed in simple or complex terms, depending upon how deeply one cares to go into technical considerations. Simplistically, the existence of syllabic pulses seems easy to confirm merely by listening with reasonable care to the speech around us and to speech samples such as the illustrations given above. Syllable boundaries are more marked in some cases than in others, however. In "midway" the division is relatively prominent, except at fast rates; it is less so in "any," yet there are two peaks that can be distinguished. In words such as "fire" there is sometimes one peak, sometimes two, depending on stress and individual pronunciation. In all cases, however, the syllable consists of a breath pulse preceded and followed by a more or less brief interval of reduced energy flow.

A few phoneticians, it must be noted, question the concept that speech can be segmented in this way. They argue in part that when it is examined in the laboratory, no physical or acoustic phenomenon can be found to mark the exact point where one syllable ends and the next begins. This observation has some merit since, in connected speech, there are "transition zones" or *nodes*, rather than complete "breaks" between successive speech segments of any kind, as will be explained more fully when the dynamics of sounds in context are discussed. Nevertheless, it seems quite clear that speech can be segmented into syllabic pulses with definable boundaries. In our subsequent discussions this working hypothesis will be the basis for certain points of theory, and also for some suggestions about methods of speech improvement.

Properties of Syllables Syllables vary widely in their configurations, but all have certain acoustic and physiological properties in common. Acoustically, each has a *nucleus* consisting of some vowel or vowellike resonance. Physiologically, this *vowel target* marks the point within the syllable where the vocal tract is most open. At the syllable boundaries, as noted earlier, there occurs a node marked by either a significant reduction in energy flow or a brief interval of relative arrest of the breath pulse. The exact acoustic and physiological characteristics of syllable boundary areas are determined not only by the place and degree of the articulatory constriction, but also by the nature of the transition, or juncture, with the next syllable.

Phoneticians have been interested in the physiological conditions which cause syllabic breath pulsing, but disagree on their precise nature. Articulation movements certainly play a major role. In some cases there may be a complete, although momentary, cessation of breath flow. This occurs, for instance, when the breath is completely stopped in the usual production of *t* in such a word as "catkin." In other cases, articulation movements at the syllable junction cause a marked decrease in breath flow without stopping it completely. This can readily be noted in the sentence "You may win!" Stetson (1961) interprets experimental findings as supporting the idea that syllable divisions result from arresting movements of the breathing musculature, but this explanation is not universally accepted. Those who object say in part that the apparent arresting action of these muscles is the result of syllabic division, not their cause.

Syllable Types Syllables may consist of only the vowel or vowellike resonance mentioned previously or be composed of a number of different vowel-consonant combinations. Sounds which by themselves can form syllables (mainly vowels and diphthongs) are said to be *syllabic*. Those sounds we customarily call consonants do not, as we shall learn, function as syllables except in certain special cases, and are therefore termed *nonsyllabic*. In terms of phonetic function, the division of individual sounds into syllabics and nonsyllabics is more satisfactory in some ways than the vowel-consonant dichotomy.

Syllables containing only a vowel or vowellike resonance are readily recognized. In the words "acorn" and "egress," for instance, one usually hears the initial syllable as a relatively "pure" stressed vowel. Often vowel (V) syllables receive no more than minimal stress, as in the first segments of the words "ago," "along," and "enough." Sounds which are usually nonsyllabic may function as syllabics. This is illustrated by the way we are likely to pronounce the sound represented by '*n* in the phrase "cat 'n mouse." If we say "Keep them out" in this conversational manner: "Keep 'm out," all that remains of the word "them" is a syllabic *m*. Similarly, one hears a syllabic *l* in the phrase "It'll do." When speech is transcribed phonetically, a procedure to be introduced in Chapter 3, a special mark is used to indicate that a sound which is usually nonsyllabic has become syllabic in the speech sample being recorded.

More often than not the syllable nucleus, if closely observed, is heard to have a shifting rather than a completely stable quality. For example, if one speaks this sentence in a conversational manner: "The last sound in the word 'boy' is *oy*," the segment represented by the letters *oy* clearly shows such a change in resonance. Classically, the sound in this case would be considered a diphthong or, loosely, a segment consisting of two closely blended resonances. Whether or not such *complex nuclei* as these can be classified as distinctive diphthongs raises some theoretical questions which will be discussed elsewhere (pages 187). At the moment, the point being made is simply that shifting resonance may be a prominent feature of syllables.

Turning next to syllables made up of consonants combined with vowels, the simplest possible configurations are the following: (1) consonant-vowel (CV), as in "to," "go," and "see"; (2) vowel-consonant (VC), as in "up," "ail," and "on"; and (3) consonant-vowel-consonant (CVC), as in "pot," "look," and "take." Much more complex combinations occur in speech, but these simpler types can be used to explain certain important facts about the function of nonsyllabic sounds in speech.

Note that in the case of all the illustrative monosyllabic words given above, consonants are found only at the *boundary* of syllables; that is, they function to *initiate* or *terminate* syllables or to do both. It is not quite correct to say that nonsyllabic segments cannot be spoken in isolation since some of their features can be prolonged in the case of *s*, *f*, and a few others. It is correct, however, to say that in the syllabic pulses of connected speech, consonants are always inseparably bound to a vowel nucleus—save for the kind of special case mentioned earlier where a consonant becomes syllabic.

In a CV syllable the consonant represents a position from which, or through which, the articulatory organs move to the posture for the vowel nucleus. This releasing action can be referred to as an *on-glide*. If the syllable is of the VC type, the consonant is produced by a movement from the articulatory position for the vowel nucleus to, or through, whatever point is characteristic of the consonant in question. Such a terminating action for the syllable is commonly referred to as an *off-glide*. The phrase "or through" was included in the description of consonant formation simply because the dynamics of connected speech are such that the articulators remain in a fixed position only briefly, if at all.

Earlier the most *open* part of the syllable was called the *vowel target*. Similarly, a syllable consisting of some vowel-consonant combination has one or more *consonant targets* at the most *closed* point or points at syllable boundaries. This statement relates to the vocal tract being markedly constricted at some point during consonant production, but relatively open for vowel production. Articulation could thus be viewed as the movements required to "hit"—or at least aim at—a rapidly sequenced series of syllabic and nonsyllabic targets.

Transitional Information   There are additional salient facts about syllables comprising vowel and consonant targets. Because any consonant is a *boundary phenomenon*, a result is that the acoustic cues for recognizing the consonant become encoded in the vowel-consonant *transitions* and even in the vowel nucleus itself. In other words, the listener may perceive a sound as *t* not only because it has certain distinctive features of its own, but also because of the way its characteristics affect the vowel which precedes or follows it. Similarly, the vowel influences the acoustic patterns of adjoining consonants. Such a monosyllabic word as "peak" is recognized on the basis of its unique total acoustic configuration, rather than as a *p* plus *ea* plus *k*. (See Chapter 6, pages 128–129.)

A further illustration may help us to understand the interaction between vowel and consonant elements in syllabic configurations. Pronounce the word "up," taking care not to open the lips at the end of the word, thus making certain there is no audible release of breath. Under this common articulatory condition, listeners do not usually experience any difficulty in recognizing the word or in identifying its final sound, even without watching the speaker's lips. There were no audible plosive release cues carried by the segment *p* alone, however. Correct judgments were based on the unique way in which the vowel nucleus was terminated; that is, on *transitional information*. The same phenomenon can be illustrated with words such as "at" and "back." Although this transitional information is *subliminal*, or below the conscious level, experiments with synthetic speech have shown that it suffices for accurate perception. (See, for example, Liberman et al., 1956.)

Consonant Clusters

Up to this point only simpler syllabic forms—V, CV, VC, and CVC—have been used as the basis for an explanation of some of the phenomena of syllables. Much more complex syllabic patterns are regularly heard in American English, and there have been numerous attempts to classify such syllables in terms of their consonant configurations. The findings of one such study (Moser, 1957) are presented in Table 2-2.[1] He found syllables containing

---

[1] Moser's *One Syllable Words* is recommended as a great storehouse of information relating to the sound structure of American English. It analyzes nearly all single-syllable words used in American speech, with rank orderings of the frequency of occurrence of sounds and sound combinations. One can, for example, identify words which begin with [*f*] and end with the consonant combination *nd*, or discover that there are 28 words which begin with [b] followed by the vowel of "he," but only 8 words which start with the syllable *ge-* (as in "get"). His painstaking and exhaustive compendium can be extraordinarily useful in preparing a variety of language materials, such as speech tests and exercises (and is even good for finding rhymes).

Table 2-2 Classification of Syllabic Types in One-Syllable Words*

Syllable type	Number of instances	Example
V	11	E
CV	178	to
VC	111	at
CVC	1,978	tot
VCC	160	eats
CCV	98	stir
CVCC	2,845	socks
CCVC	1,069	stack
VCCC	34	arks
CCCV	12	straw
CCVCC	1,423	steaks
CVCCC	622	barks
CCCVC	135	sprig
CCVCCC	252	spanks
CCCVCC	161	sprigs
CVCCCC	8	sixths
CCCVCCC	15	sprints
CCVCCCC	4	sphinxed

* Taken from Moser (1957). C is a consonant; V is a vowel

as many as seven sounds (CCCVCCC as in "sprints," for example). The fact that the boundaries of syllables may consist of *consonant clusters* rather than individual consonants does not, however, alter the basic principles governing the way in which they function as syllable boundary phenomena. From the foregoing it is evident that syllable boundary events are in an important sense a way of getting from one vowel to the next—a method of joining vowels, so to speak. Here we encounter the dynamics of "joining" or *juncture*, which will be elaborated in Chapter 6. A thorough understanding of the syllable will do much to clarify the complexities of juncture.

In actuality, when words are uttered in connected speech, the articulatory targets may be considerably more intricate than when even the most complex syllable is spoken as an isolated monosyllabic word. Since words are not ordinarily isolated from one another under the conditions of ongoing speech, some extraordinarily complicated forms develop. For instance, the phrase "sixth squared" becomes a bisyllabic CVCCCCCVCC! How can combinations like these be produced at the rates known to be typical of human speech? Either articulation must be slowed down to accommodate the articulatory shifts needed to hit all the targets, or else exact canonical pronunciation must be sacrificed—as it is in ways to be discussed presently. In any event, these facts about syllable form give some appreciation of the remarkable ability required of the neuromuscular system if it is to generate normal speech.

All this information about syllabification is basic to a theoretical understanding of the way in which language is spoken. It also has important applications to techniques of speech improvement. Later these will be developed in some detail, but one of the principles is that for most purposes, the syllable rather than the individual speech sound is the segment which should be used in training a child or adult with a disorder of articulation, or in working with anyone in need of speech improvement.

EXERCISES

1 Here are several terms to include in a glossary for Chapter 2. Add to them and frame a concise definition for each term:

allophone	noncontrastive
complex nucleus	nonsyllabic
complimentary distribution	off-glide
consonant target	on-glide
consonant cluster	phone
contrast network	phoneme
contrastive analysis	prosodic feature
distinctive feature	segment
distinctive sound	syllable
free variant	syllabic
grapheme	syllabic nucleus
juncture	transition
minimal pair	vowel target

2 Prepare a contrast network for consonants patterned after that for vowels in Table 2-1. This should be designed to prove or disprove the theory that English contains the following contrastive sound classes (phonemes): /p/, /b/, /t/, /d/, /k/, /g/, /f/, /v/, /s/, /z/, /sh/, /h/, /m/, /n/, /l/, /w/, /wh/, and /r/. (A number of possible phonemes in English have been omitted from this list.)

3 Read the passage below as a carfully *spoken* message. Analyze what you have read into segments and syllables rather than letters and words. Count the number of each in each line and then turn to Appendix E for the results of the author's analysis. If they differ, repeat the exercise. If they still differ, consult a dictionary (although the dictionary is by no means an infallible guide). If you continue to differ, consult your instructor. Some variation is to be expected, but your counts should be within the indicated ranges. The passage:

He participated in an exceptionally interesting telephone conversation with several old friends who were acquaintances from his mathematician years at the University of Mississippi—years crowned with many athletic successes, schemes, and laughter.

4 As explained earlier in this chapter, words always contain a vowel (V) and usually a consonant or two, but many have an extremely complex syllabic

structure. "Sprints," you recall, is a CCCVCCC word. In this exercise try to find at least one word in addition to those listed in Table 2-2 with the following structures: V, CV, VC, CVC, VCC, CCV, CVCC, CCVC, VCCC, CCCV, CCVCC, CVCCC, CCVCCC, CCCVCC, CCCVC. All can be found among one-syllable words. Try next to find examples of the following two-syllable word forms: VCV, CVCV, VCVC, CVCVC, CCVCV, CCVCCV, CCVCVC, CVCCVC CCVCCVC, VCCCVC, CVCVCC, VCCCCVC. An example of each will be found in the answer key in Appendix E. After looking at the key (if necessary), can you find another word of each type? What other common structures can you think of? How about CCCVCCCVCC? It's a fairly common word!

Chapter 3

Phonetic Transcription

In this chapter we shall undertake a somewhat detailed discussion of the *phonetic alphabet* as a tool for the study of speech sounds. This will lead to a consideration of (1) some perspectives on the uses of a phonetic alphabet, (2) a presentation of the alphabet of the International Phonetic Association (IPA), and (3) a specific examination of some of the symbols most commonly used in the transcription of American English. A major objective will be to bring students to a point where they can recognize the principal American speech sounds, identify the classes into which they fall, and associate these sounds with the symbols of the International Phonetic Alphabet upon which we shall base much of our discussion of phonetic theory and its application. A start will be made on mastery of the techniques of phonetic transcription.

PHONETIC METHODS

A primary goal of phonetics is to study, in all its ramifications, spoken language as a unique and distinctively functioning form of *sound*. Sometimes the phonetician's purposes may be served best by laboratory examination of the acoustic and physiological phenomena of speech, but the most basic and indispensable technique for studying speech is what may be called *perceptual analysis*. This one accomplishes simply by listening analytically to spoken language, usually recording one's observations in written form by means of some system of *phonetic transcription*.

To make accurate observations of speech in this special way, phoneticians need to be armed with fundamental information about the behavior of speakers and the sound structure of languages in order that they can be alert to the *articulatory possibilities* they may encounter. Thus prepared, they must also acquire the ability to listen analytically, to direct their attention to the fine detail of speech. Because our usual set is to listen for *meaning*, this phonetic technique may seem difficult at first, but competence in its use can be acquired through practice by most persons with reasonably normal capacities. Without the ability to analyze speech in this way, neither academic phoneticians, language instructors, speech pathologists, nor any others who have reason for concern with the form of speech can be successful in their endeavors.

The study of speech presents a problem, for it is *momentary*. Spoken words leave no physical trace and thus are lost unless some way is found to record their passage. To be sure, they can be preserved by modern electronic instruments such as the tape recorder, but these devices only give the phonetician an opportunity to hear the samples as often as wished. Experimental phoneticians can report their findings by sound spectrograms, charts, and figures, but if the results of perceptual analysis are to be discussed and written about, there must be devised a symbol system—a kind of *phonetic vocabulary* —through which spoken language can be presented in *visible* form simply, conveniently, and with reasonable fidelity and consistency. In the following section we turn to some of the ways in which this has been attempted, and to some of the problems involved.

LANGUAGE—SPOKEN AND WRITTEN

Human beings early felt a need to communicate with their fellows in a way more enduring than speech, and from this need grew the invention of writing —perhaps the most important single event in our cultural history. There is no need to trace in detail the way in which modern alphabets developed, although the story is a fascinating one (see, for instance, Bolinger, 1968, or Brown, 1958). The point to be made is that the Roman alphabet, as we use it, has serious inconsistencies in the manner in which it indicates English pronunciations and is therefore an imperfect tool for the phonetician who wishes to record the sounds of spoken language.

Examples of this inconsistency are readily found. A particular English letter may stand for as many as three or four *phones*, as does the *a* in "law," "hat," "pay," and "father." On the other hand, a given sound is frequently represented by several different letters or combinations of letters. A case in point is the word "circle" which, by analogy, could just as well be written "sirkle," "sirchle," "psircle," or "circhle," to mention only a few of the numerous possibilities. Two letters, *x* and *q*, when taken by themselves, have no necessary phonetic function at all, and we have no real need for the letter *c*. Many sounds have no single symbol of their own—those in "*th*ink," "*th*at," "*sh*oe," and "*ch*oose," for instance—and are mainly handled with double letters.

Such lack of regularity in the relation between sound and symbol in English is found in the representation of both vowels and consonants, but vowel pronunciations are perhaps especially difficult to infer from spelling since we manage with the five vowel symbols *a*, *e*, *i*, *o*, and *u*, sometimes with awkward doubling of letters, to indicate a minimum of 11 vowel sounds in General American speech. The frequency of spelling errors even among educated adults is perhaps not surprising. Incidentally, even though movements for the reform of spelling have made little progress, a current tendency toward simpler phonetic spellings is quite marked; note, for instance, the relative respectability of "thru" and the universal American practice of writing "honor" and "labor" without the *u* found in British English.

An account of the historical origins of present spelling practices would lead us afield, but many discussions of the subject are available, including those in Potter (1950) and Baugh (1957). As we have indicated (see Chapter 1), English underwent rather dramatic alteration during the interval between Old and Modern English, but spelling conventions, although by no means fixed, did not always reflect changes in pronunciations. There are good historical reasons for the vagaries of modern American spelling, but none of them ameliorates the fact that the conventional alphabet has serious limitations if one proposes to analyze the sound patterns of spoken language.

SPECIAL SYMBOL SYSTEMS

Limitations of the conventional alphabet were obvious, of course, to early phoneticians and to others with an interest in spoken language, and proposals for revised, shorthand, and universal alphabets circulated in England as early as the sixteenth century. According to Abercrombie (1965) it was Francis Lodwick who was perhaps the most important of what he termed the "forgotten phoneticians." In 1686, in his "An Essay Towards an Universal Alphabet," Lodwick proposed an alphabet in which he says (to quote Abercrombie, p. 50): " 'All single sounds ought to have single and distinct characters,' and no one character shall 'have more than one Sound, nor any Sound be expressed by more than one Character.' "

Table 3-1 Comparative Chart of Phonetic Alphabets

IPA	Webster's 2d ed.*	Webster's New World†	American College‡	Webster's 3d ed.§	Linguist's alphabet
i	ē	ē	ē	ē	iy
ɪ	ĭ	i	ĭ	i	i
e	ā	ā	ā	ā	ey
ɛ	ĕ	e	ĕ	e	e
æ	ă	a	ă	a	æ
ɑ	ŏ	ä o	ä	ä	a
ɔ	ô	ô	ô	o	ɔ
o	ō	ō	ō	ō	o
ʊ	o͝o	oo	o͝o	u	u
u	o͞o	oo	o͞o	ü	uw
ʌ	ŭ	u	ŭ	ə	ə
ɝ	ûr	ûr	ûr	ər	ər
ə	(italics)	ə	ə	ə	ə
ɚ	ĕr	ĕr	ər	ər	ər
aɪ	ī	ī	ī	ī	ay
ɔɪ	oi	oi	oi	oi	ɔy
ju	ū	ū	ū	yü	yuw
aʊ	ou	ou	ou	au	aw
p	p	p	p	p	p
t	t	t	t	t	t
b	b	b	b	b	b
d	d	d	d	d	d
k	k	k	k	k	k
g	g	g	g	g	g
tʃ	ch	ch	ch	ch	č
dʒ	j	j	j	j	ǰ
f	f	f	f	f	f
v	v	v	v	v	v
θ	th	th	th	th	θ
ð	t̶h̶	t̲h̲	t̶h̶	t̲h̲	ð
s	s	s	s	s	s
z	z	z	z	z	z
ʃ	sh	sh	sh	sh	š
ʒ	zh	zh	zh	zh	ž
h	h	h	h	h	h
m	m	m	m	m	m
n	n	n	n	n	n
ŋ	ng	ŋ	ng	ŋ	ŋ
l	l	l	l	l	l
w	w	w	w	w	w
hw	hw	hw	hw	hw	ʍ
j	y	y	y	y	y
r	r	r	r	r	r

Note: Because of the different concepts of linguistic structure, dictionary pronunciation systems are not strictly comparable on a phoneme-to-phoneme basis. For this reason not all vowel symbols used by the dictionaries represented here are given—only those which most closely compare with the IPA symbols for the vowels of stressed syllables. For example, even when they are used by the dictionary in question, symbols for "half-long" or "r-diphthong" vowels are not included.

Over the years spelling reform has had the support of many well-known figures, including both Benjamin Franklin and lexicographer Noah Webster. Samuel Pepys and, later, George Bernard Shaw did their composition with phonetic systems. In fact, so great was Shaw's interest that he left his estate to a fund for development of a phonetic alphabet, but the will was subsequently broken by relatives whose concerns evidently lay elsewhere. Although spelling reform still has advocates (largely unsuccessful), the movement does not necessarily relate closely to the use of phonetic symbols for scientific purposes.

Two individuals who worked during the latter half of the nineteenth century gave great impetus to the concept of speech analysis and transcription by specially selected symbols. One was Sir Isaac Pitman (1813–1897), who invented the widely used shorthand system which bears his name. It is, incidentally, his grandson, Sir James Pitman, who devised the Initial Teaching Alphabet (ITA), now used extensively in England and elsewhere for teaching children to read and write. Another influential figure, Alexander Melville Bell, an instructor of the deaf, presented his *Visible Speech* symbols in 1867. Although the symbols were designed as a means of teaching the elements of spoken language to the deaf, the concepts on which they were based represented a significant contribution to phonetic science. Bell's system was developed further by Henry Sweet and others, and greatly influenced the work which led to the alphabet of the International Phonetic Association.

Current Systems   While our discussion is to be couched mainly in terms of the International Phonetic Alphabet, several other methods of indicating the sounds of speech are in current use. A comparison of some of the commonest of these will be found in Table 3-1. The various systems are not, however, precisely equivalent, being used for different purposes. Most dictionaries indicate pronunciation by *diacritical marks*, and these have become entrenched as the commonest method for everyday use. An especially common alternative to the IPA is the phonemically based alphabet found in much of the literature on linguistics. This "linguist's alphabet" is based upon some attractive concepts derived from language analysis. If regarded strictly as *phonetic* symbols, these two alphabets are approximately equivalent, as illustrated in Table 3-1, but the IPA in one form or another is used more commonly in the fields of speech, psychology, acoustic and physiological phonetics, and speech pathology.

---

* *Webster's New International Dictionary*, 2d ed. Springfield, Mass.: G. & C. Merriam Company, 1956.

† *Webster's New World Dictionary of the American Language*, college ed., Cleveland: World Publishing Company, 1954.

‡ *The American College Dictionary*, C. L. Barnhart (ed.), text ed., New York: Harper & Brothers, 1948.

§ *Webster's Third New International Dictionary*, Springfield, Mass.: G. & C. Merriam Company, 1961.

¶ Various texts in linguistics.

THE INTERNATIONAL PHONETIC ALPHABET

The central principle of a phonetic alphabet best suited for speech analysis is that it should consist of symbols which represent sounds with the greatest consistency and the least ambiguity, within the limits of what is possible. In theory this has been taken to mean that each phoneme class is represented by a single symbol and that, insofar as possible, provision is made for noting allophonic and other variations by means of diacritic marks. The first really successful alphabet of this kind was designed by scholars who were prompted by the needs of foreign language teachers, particularly the group who formed the International Phonetic Association.

The speech sound symbols used by the IPA were chosen with the premise that a common group of symbols could be used to represent a wide range of speech sounds which would have known and agreed-upon articulatory characteristics understood by scholars of all languages. There were symbols which could be used to describe both native and foreign speech patterns to other scholars and to students. They constituted essentially a *phonetic* (rather than a phonemic) alphabet. The idea of such a phonetic alphabet and its underlying principles were formulated in 1888 in the *Principles of the International Phonetic Association* and subsequently refined in 1949:

> When two sounds occurring in a given language are employed for distinguishing one word from another, they should whenever possible be represented by two distinct letters. . . .
>
> When two sounds are so near together acoustically that there is no likelihood of their being employed in any language for distinguishing words, they should as a rule, be represented by the same letter. Separate letters or diacritical marks may, however, be used to distinguish them in "narrow" transcriptions, or in scientific investigation . . . [p. 1].

The *Principles* are not altogether clear as to the difference between a phonemic and a phonetic alphabet. The symbols of the IPA have been used in both functions: to stand for *contrastive classes* of speech sounds, without regard to pronunciation, and also to stand for some particular pronunciation or range of pronunciations, without regard to contrast. This distinction may seem trivial, but it can be a very important one. The /t/ can stand only for an abstract class of events which contrast with other classes in a certain language, or it can stand, as [t], for a consonant produced in a certain specified manner, or having certain acoustic or physiological characteristics. The importance of this will be better understood as we discover that some variants within a phoneme class can have the same or nearly the same pronunciation as variants of some other class. As an example, one General American pronunciation of the /t/ in "butter" is essentially the same as the frequent English pronunciation of the /r/ in "very."

Table 3-2 Sounds of American Speech

Syllabics

Vowels

Front vowels		Back vowels	
symbol	key word	symbol	key word
i	heed [hid]	u	who'd [hud]
ɪ	hid [hɪd]	ʊ	hood [hʊd]
e	hayed [hed]	o	hoed [hod]
ɛ	head [hɛd]	ɔ	hawed [hɔd]
æ	had [hæd]	ɑ	hod [hɑd]

Central vowels		Diphthongs*	
ɝ-ɜ†	hurt [hɝt]	aɪ	file [faɪl]
ʌ	hut [hʌt]	aʊ	fowl [faʊl]
ɚ-ə†	under [ʌndɚ]	ɔɪ	foil [fɔɪl]
ə	about [əbaʊt]	ju	fuel [fjul]

Syllabic consonants

ṃ [kipṃ]	ṇ [hɪtṇ rʌn]	ḷ [pɛdḷ]

Nonsyllabics

Obstruent consonants

Stops		Fricatives	
p	pen [pɛn]	f	few [fju]
b	Ben [bɛn]	v	view [vju]
t	ten [tɛn]	θ	thigh [θaɪ]
d	den [dɛn]	ð	thy [ðaɪ]
tʃ (č)	chew [tʃu]	s	say [se]
dʒ (j)	Jew [dʒu]	z	zoo [zu]
k	kay [ke]	ʃ (š)	shay [ʃe]
g	gay [ge]	ʒ (ž)	beige [beʒ]
ʔ	"hu uh" [hʌʔʌ]	h	who [hu]

Sonorant consonants

Nasals and laterals		Glides	
m	some [sʌm]	w	way [we]
n	sun [sʌn]	hw (w̥)	whey [hwe]
ŋ	sung [sʌŋ]	j (y)	yea [je]
l	lay [le]	r	ray [re]

* Does not include the "nondistinctive" and centering diphthongs.
† [ɝ] and [ɚ] are the r-colored vowels. [ɜ] and [ə] are the pronunciations typical of r vowels in Eastern, Southern, and English speech.

But such complications need not sidetrack us from the basic fact that phonetic symbols can be used not only as class labels, but also as symbols for certain "standard" articulations, against which any actual utterances may be evaluated.

As a foundation for competence in speech analysis, one must acquire a set of *referents*, or articulatory and auditory images, for *standard* speech sounds, and learn the phonetic symbol used to designate each of them. Only by extensive listening to properly chosen speech samples can these percepts be developed. The words given to illustrate each sound listed in Table 3-2 were carefully selected as words likely to be spoken uniformly by General American speakers. From the outset, however, it is essential that the student listen attentively to as wide a variety of speech samples as possible to note similarities and differences among the phones in each phoneme class. It will be helpful to concentrate on the sound being listened for, without reference to either word meaning or spelling. The guidance of an instructor who can illustrate pronunciations is almost indispensable.[1]

The famous English phonetician Daniel Jones provided vowel models for his students termed *cardinal vowels*. These were defined in his *An Outline of English Phonetics* (1940) in terms of a standard range of tongue positions, from the extreme position of the sound [i] "in which the raising of the tongue is as far forward as possible and as high as possible . . ." to the opposite extreme of [ɑ] "in which the back of the tongue is lowered as far as possible and retracted as far as possible . . . [p. 31]" Other vowels were described as having equal degrees of acoustic separation between these extremes.[2]

Jones's students were highly skilled at phonetic transcription and, as Ladefoged (1967) suggests, this may have been a result of their firm grasp of model sounds to which others could be compared.

In addition to their scholarly concerns, Professor Jones and his students had a primary interest in teaching Received Pronunciation, which was then considered the proper diction of the educated English person. There is no comparable standard for American English, and, indeed, RP no longer occupies the place it once did in British culture. The procedure of matching to a model, however, illustrates one very important way in which listening skills may be achieved.

Some further general remarks should be made about the use of a phonetic alphabet. Written symbols do not "describe" the spoken sound. This may be

---

[1] A tape recording has been prepared to illustrate use of the phonetic alphabet, and to provide a set of referents for the IPA symbols as used by the authors. Copies of the tape can be obtained from the authors. They are not copyrighted, and may be duplicated without permission.

[2] The notion of equal acoustic separation would be thought suspect by most modern phoneticians, and it is difficult to imagine that Jones's models were not influenced to some degree by standard British pronunciations.

done only by means of a *feature analysis*, either acoustic or articulatory. It should also be remembered that each "key" word represents only one out of many possible allophones of the sound class represented. Thus, it is important to tune one's ear to the range of sound values that may be heard within a class as well as to the "cardinal" or standard sound.

The IPA alphabet is "international," but only within limits. For instance, the vowel [o] is a distinctive sound in both American and English speech, but it certainly is not pronounced exactly the same by native speakers of the two countries. This kind of variation is comparable to shades of difference between the pronunciation of sounds in the [æ] phoneme in Northern and Southern American speech.

Finally, one should remember that any phonetic alphabet represents its inventor's concept of the sound structure of the languages to which it is applied; if the inventor's theoretical formulations are faulty, so will be the symbol system. Scholars are still very much in the process of unraveling the mysteries of phonology, and not all phoneticians agree on the sound structure of language nor, therefore, on the best set of symbols.

We are ready now to begin a specific study of the sounds of speech by becoming familiar with the alphabet of the IPA as it may be applied to one American dialect, and to take some initial steps in speech analysis. The IPA symbols for the common American English speech sounds presented in Table 3-2 will be discussed below. From this point forward IPA symbols will generally be used in identifying sounds under discussion.

The Consonants

Note first that the IPA symbols for 16 of the consonant sounds are the same as familiar letters of the conventional alphabet, and indicate pronunciations usually associated with these letters by English speakers. The symbols which retain their usual associations are:

[p] as in "pen" [pɛn]	[s] as in "say" [se]
[b] as in "Ben" [bɛn]	[z] as in "bays" [bez]
[t] as in "ten" [tɛn]	[h] as in "hay" [he]
[d] as in "den" [dɛn]	[m] as in "some" [sʌm]
[k] as in "Kay" [ke]	[n] as in "sun" [sʌn]
[g] as in "gay" [ge]	[l] as in "lay" [le]
[f] as in "few" [fju]	[w] as in "way" [we]
[v] as in "view" [vju]	[r] as in "run" [rʌn]

There remain to be learned at this time only nine IPA consonant symbols. These are:

[θ] as in "think" [θɪŋk] and "thick" [θɪk]. This is a *voiceless* sound usually spelled with the letters *th* in English. The IPA symbol is the letter *theta* of the Greek alphabet.

[ð] as in "that" [ðæt] and "those" [ðoz]. This sound is similar to [θ] but is *voiced*. Both [θ] and [ð] are usually spelled *th*. The symbol [ð] is an Old English letter called *eth* or *edh*, It is still used in modern Icelandic.

[ʃ] as in "she" [ʃi] and "sugar" [ʃugɚ]. The IPA symbol employed for this "hishing" sound is similar to the mathematical integral sign and takes the form of a "stretched" letter *s*. Note that in writing this symbol, the tail should stretch below the line. The sound is sometimes called an *esh*.

[ʒ] as in "beige" [beʒ] and "vision" [vɪʒən]. This sound is a voiced counterpart of [ʃ]. In written form the tail of the symbol should also stretch below the line.

[tʃ] as in "chew" [tʃu] and "cheese" [tʃiz]. This symbol is composed of two characters, and when feasible may be written as a *ligature* (the two symbols touching or tied together). As an alternative so [tʃ], some systems of notation employ the character [č] ("*c*-wedge"), a usage which is becoming more common.

[dʒ] as in "Jew" [dʒu] and "age" [edʒ]. This may also be written where feasible as a ligature combining [d] and [ʒ]. The sound is a voiced counterpart of [tʃ]. Use of the single character [ǰ] ("*j*-wedge") for this sound is common.

[ŋ] as in "sing" [sɪŋ) and "sung" [sʌŋ]. This is a common English nasal sound often represented in conventional spelling by the letters *ng*. In form, the character resembles the letter *n* with the second down-stroke curled under below the line. The sound is often called an *eng*.

[hw] as in "when" [hwɛn] and "why" [hwaɪ]. This may also be written as a ligature if feasible. The sound is a voiceless counterpart of [w] and has been represented in various ways—with [w̥], [ʍ], and [ɥ], for example. We use the non-IPA form [hw] because of its use in many phonetics texts and dictionaries.

[j] as in "yes" [jɛs and "you" [ju]. This is the ordinary lower case *j*. In the IPA it stands for the sound we usually associate with the letter *y*.

One additional noncontrastive consonant sound should be introduced at this point. This is [ʔ], which symbolizes what is called a *glottal stop*. This is not usually listed among the "standard" sounds of American English, but it is frequently heard among all English speakers and is an especially common allophone in certain dialects. A verbal description of the sound is difficult, but it occurs most often as a variant of certain *stops* and is heard commonly in the words "hu uh" and "uh huh" [hʌ ʔʌ] and [ʔʌhʌ]. This stop is a momentary interruption of the breath flow at the *glottis*.

The Vowels

The symbols for the vowels require a number of new associations, but there should be no great difficulty in forming these if your dialect is standard GA. Some characters correspond to letters of the English alphabet, but others had to be borrowed from various sources. From 11 to 14 vowels are usually considered necessary for the broad analysis of most dialects of American English; hence the five vowel letters do not suffice. In forming new symbol-pronunciation associations for vowels, it will be best to ignore as much as possible the usual spelling.

It will help you to develop the necessary associations between vowel symbol and vowel sound if we draw your attention here to a fact which we shall enlarge upon later, that vowels are made by constricting the vocal tract in the *front* or *back* areas, constricting it to a greater or lesser degree (a *high* or a *low* tongue position), and producing the vowel with greater or lesser force or tension. It is primarily in terms of these categories of *fronting, height,* and *tension,* plus *lip rounding,* that we now describe each of the major vowel sounds of American English. As you look at the phonetic symbol and listen to the key words, also try to feel, and, where possible, to see, the tongue and lip positions—in yourself and in others. It may also help you to place your finger in your mouth as you utter each of the vowels. You will be able to feel the change of pressure of the tongue against your finger as you produce front, back, high, and low vowels.

Below are the standard vowel categories which we shall use as the basis for our discussions in succeeding sections, and as a beginning alphabet for use in phonetic transcription:

[i] as in "east" [ist] and "seen" [sin]. The symbol is a lower-case (small) printed dotted *i*. The tongue constriction should be felt as *tense*, in the front of the oral cavity, and higher (closer to the roof of the mouth) than in any other English vowel. The sound tends to be slightly dipthongal in some contexts.

[ɪ] as in "sit" [sɪt] and "build" [bɪld]. The symbol is a small capital ɪ. The sound is shorter than [i] as a rule, and the tongue, while still high and forward, is less so than for [i]. The tongue should also feel lax by comparison.

[e] as in "steak" [stek] and "rain" [ren]. The symbol is the lower-case *e,* but the sound to be associated with this letter is that which Americans often term "long *a.*" The tongue is fronted and its height is about midway between the positions for [i] and [æ]. It is a tense vowel and in stressed syllables is likely to be noticeably diphthongal.

[ɛ] as in "bed" [bɛd] and "head" [hɛd]. The symbol is the Greek letter epsilon. The sound is shorter than [e] and simpler (nondiphthongal). The tongue position is lower than for [e]. It is described as—and should feel—more lax.

[æ] as in "hat" [hæt] and "mass" [mæs]. The symbol is a ligature of the letters a and e. The tongue position is also front, but not so far as for the other front vowels, and it is markedly lower. The jaw too is usually markedly lower.

[u] as in "too" [tu] and "boom" [bum]. The symbol is the lower-case letter *u.* This is the highest of the back vowels. It is classed as tense and tends

to be longer and more dipthongal than the other high-back vowel, the [ʊ]. It is produced with strongly rounded lips.

[ʊ] as in "look" and "put" [pʊt]. The symbol is a small capital ʊ. This back-vowel sound is shorter and simpler than [u], the tongue is less high and less strongly retracted than for [u], and the lips are less closely rounded.

[o] as in "coat" [kot] and "note" [not]. The symbol is a lower-case *o*. In terms of tongue height it is *mid-back*—not high, not low. The sound is tense, often long and diphthongal, and the lips are strongly rounded.

[ɔ] as in some pronunciations of "law" [lɔ] and "caught" [kɔt]. The symbol is called the open *o*. The tongue position is slightly lower than for [o], and the lips are less tightly rounded. The sound is described as lax. This sound may present special problems for you if you have only one *ah* sound in your dialect (see below).

[ɑ] as in some pronunciations of "lah" [lɑ] and "cot" [kɑt]. The symbol resembles the script form of the letter *a*. The tongue position is far back, markedly low, but the lips are not rounded. Both [ɑ] and [ɔ] will provide difficulties for those whose dialect includes only one single low-back vowel— who do not distinguish between "cot" and "caught," and similar pairs. For them [ɑ] and [ɔ] are simply different allophones of a single phoneme. For other Americans the distinctions can be meaningful, however.

[ɝ] as in most American pronunciations of "term" (tɝm] and "stir" [stɝ]. The symbol is the reversed hooked epsilon. This vowel is usually described as *central*, but has a more complex tongue posture than other vowels, giving it a highly distinctive resonance called "*r*-colored." (See Chapter 10, page 216.)

[ɜ] as in some American (Eastern New England for example) pronunciations of "term" [tɜm] and "stir" [stɜ]. The symbol is the reversed epsilon. This is the non-*r*-colored mid-central vowel used by Americans who "drop their *r*'s." The tongue is lax and is *neutral* in its position. To Americans who do not use the [ɜ] it may sound something like a rough approximation of [ʌ]. For many of you a standard recorded reference or an *informant* will be necessary.

[ʌ] as in "cup" [kʌp] and "done" [dʌn]. The symbol is the caret or upside-down *v*. The tongue is a bit back of central but, it is not "back" as in British [ʌ]. The sound is simple, short, and lax.

[ə] as in "alone" [əlon] and "today" [təde]. The symbol is an upside-down backward *e*. This is the *reduced* vowel, or *vowel murmur*. It is all that is left of any vowel which becomes so weak or short that definite resonance is lost. It may sound a bit like a very short [ʌ], but we will find later that this is not actually a correct characterization of [ə]. This vowel is called the *schwa* and is the most common of all vowels.

[ɚ] as in "motor" [motɚ] and "later" [letɚ]. This *schwar* symbol is often called the *hooked schwa*, and is used to represent a weak, schwalike syllable with some *r* coloring retained. It, like the schwa, is not contrastive in the sense previously discussed. However, schwar and schwa are important allophones of other vowels.

The Diphthongs

We have chosen to include four *diphthongs* in the beginning list of common sounds of American English. In general, a diphthong can be described as a complex syllabic characterized by a prominent shift in vowel quality—or, loosely, a syllabic consisting of two perceptually distinct vowel resonances blended in a single syllable. Some phoneticians treat such complexes as vowels with various kinds of on- and off-glides, rather than as diphthongs. This involves some phonetic theory which we need not go into at this point, however, since our present objective is simply to recognize these somewhat unique syllabics in speech. The four diphthongs are these:

[aɪ] as in "high" [haɪ] and "spite" [spaɪt]. Notice that the beginning resonance is symbolized by [a]. This represents a vowel resonance midway between [ɑ] and [æ], approximating the British vowel in "path." Notice also that in the "standard" GA [aɪ] pronunciation glides only to a position approximating [ɪ], rather than to [i]. Notice finally that the major emphasis is on the [a], with a rapid *off-glide* to [ɪ]. Treated as a vowel-plus-off-glide, the same pronunciation might be transcribed as [aj].

[aʊ] as in "house" [haʊs], and "plow" [plaʊ]. Notice the nuclear and off-glide parts to this diphthong—from a stressed [a] to off-glide [ʊ], as usually pronounced by GA speakers. A rough verbal description of the [a] resonance was given above. If considered a vowel with off-glide, [aʊ] would be transcribed [aw].

[ɔɪ] as in "boy" [bɔɪ] and "noise" [nɔɪz]. This diphthong represents an off-glide from the nuclear [ɔ] (sometimes quite close to [o]) to the [ɪ]. It can also be written [ɔj].

[ju] as in "use" [juz] and "few" [fju]. This diphthong may also be transcribed as [ɪʊ], a choice which would be distinctly preferred in some pronunciations of certain British English words, and in a few American dialects as well. In our examples the more common American usage appears to be [ju]. It consists of an *on*-glide from [j] to [u], and is transcribed only as [ju]. Listen carefully and you may hear that in the [ju] of "you" the nuclear vowel [u] is glided *to*, rather than away from.

A further note should be made about the syllabic consonants, or the sounds which can function either as syllabics or nonsyllabics, depending upon circumstances. A dot below the consonant symbol, as in the phrase [hɪtn̩rʌn] "hit 'n run," signifies that a syllabic [n̩] has been uttered instead of a vowel plus [n]. There are a number of frequently used syllabic consonants, the most common being [m̩] as in "keep 'm" [kipm̩], [n̩] as in "button" [bʌtn̩], and [l̩] as in "puddle" [pʌdl̩].

The Nonsegmentals

Attention is called to the more common of the non- or suprasegmental symbols presented in Table 3-3. These enable one to record not only the speech sounds but also *stress, length, pauses,* and other nonsegmental features of speech. More elaborate ways of analyzing nonsegmental features will be discussed later, but even in broad speech analysis there may be a reason to use these common symbols. Absence of these marks in a transcription may mean simply that the transcriber was not interested in noting these features. If they appear at some points in a transcription but not at others, this usually indicates that there was nothing about the unmarked segments to which the transcriber believed attention should be called.

Primary stress is noted by the symbol [ˈ], as in the words "above" [əˈbʌv] and "absent" [ˈæbsənt]. The stress mark is placed before the stressed syllable, not after, as dictionaries usually do. If one chooses to mark a *secondary stress,* the symbol [ˌ] is used, again before the syllable. Examples might be [ˈtɛləˌfon] and [ˌlɛməˈned] for "telephone" and "lemonade." It will be helpful if you begin immediately to note that all words of more than one syllable have more stress on certain syllables than on others.

The duration of a sound is quite often a phonetically important feature. If so, a *long* segment can be indicated by [:] and a *half-long* segment by [·]. One might reprimand an untrained puppy who was guilty of an impropriety thus: [bæːd dɔgi]; or one might console the penitent animal by saying [tu·bæd], giving somewhat more than usual length to "too." In the speech of one who does not pronounce *r*'s, [bɜːd] might well be more accurate than [bɜd] as an indication of the greater-than-average length of the vowel in "bird."

Table 3-3   Common Nonsegmental Symbols

Symbol	Description	Example
[ˈ]	Primary stress	[ˈtɛləˌfon]
[ˌ]	Secondary stress	[ˈtɛləˌfon]
[ˌ]	Syllabic consonant	Especially [l̩] [m̩] [n̩]
[¹]	Low pitch level	
[²]	Medium pitch level	[¹ɪts ən ə⁴staˈ³nɪʃɪŋ²θɪŋ]
[³]	High pitch level	
[⁴]	Very high pitch level	
[↗]	Upward inflection	[wɛl↗]
[→]	Level inflection	[wɛl nau→]
[↘]	Downward inflection	[go hom↘]
[·]	Half-long	[nɑt bæ·d]
[:]	Long	[oː hi wɑz]
[|]	Short pause	[wɛl | aɪ dont no]
[‖]	Long pause	[dont ‖ nɑt hɪr]
[⁺]	Open juncture	[dʒæk⁺kəld]

Phonetic transcription can be punctuated by conventional means, but while periods, colons, semicolons, and commas often are correlated with pauses in speech, they are essentially linguistic rather than phonetic symbols. Where actual pausing is, for some reason, a matter of particular phonetic interest, a long pause can be indicated by [‖] and a short pause by [|]. Using these latter symbols, a long pause in uttering the phrase "No. It's not" could be transcribed as [no‖ɪts nɑt].

The Complete Alphabet of the IPA

Thus far we have introduced only those symbols which we find especially useful in "broad" transcription of American English. However, the official alphabet of the IPA contains a great many more symbols plus a large number of diacritic or modifying symbols to enable us not only to transcribe the sounds of other dialects and languages, but also to be more exact in transcribing our own speech. This, as you will recall from your reading of Chapter 2, is not always pronounced in the "standard" manner. Figure 5-3 is a reproduction of this official version. At this time the more complete IPA chart will raise some questions which we shall have to postpone answering until later, but

Table 3-4   Articulatory Modifiers

Symbol	Description	Example
[~]	Nasal resonance	[sĩŋ θrũ ðə̃ nõz]
[ᵥ]	Voiced, or weak and unaspirated	[bʌtɚ ɪz bɛtɚ]
[₀]	Voiceless (breathed)	[zæd̥] is about like [sæt]
[ᵤ]	Labialization (lip rounding)	[ræbɪt] is like [wæbɪt]
[ₙ]	Dentalization (linguadental rather than lingua-alveolar)	[t̪ɪm]
[ᵥ]	Retroflexed (palatized)	[ḑ] [ṇ] [ḷ] [ṭ] [ẓ] [ṣ]
[⊥]	Raised tongue	[ɪ⊥] is like [i]
[⊤]	Lowered tongue	[i⊤] is like [ɪ]
[⊣]	Fronted tongue (also [+])	[a⊣] is like [æ]
[⊢]	Retracted tongue	[æ⊢] is like [a]
[¨]	Centralized vowel	[ï] is like [ɨ]
[iᴵ]	Example of vowel modifier	[sɪtiᴵ]
[fᵛ]	Example of consonant modifier	[fᵛæn] is like [vⁱæn]
[‿]	Tie mark to indicate diphthong or affricate	[d͡ʒɔɪn]
[‾]	Unreleased	[hɑt‾taɪm]
[ᴺ]	Nasal release	[katᴺn]
[ᴸ]	Lateral release	[batᴸl]
[ʰ]	Aspirate release	[ha pʰ]
[']	Affricate release (sometimes used for aspirate release	[hɑt']

those of you who would like to forge ahead at a more rapid pace in your acquisition of phonetic transcription skills should consult it at this time.

To round out our introduction to phonetic symbolization, Table 3-4 presents a list of those modifying symbols and diacritics to which we will most often refer. They will be discussed at appropriate places later in the text.

PHONETIC TRANSCRIPTION

Because most of us already know how to spell, it is often assumed that we therefore are all equally aware of the sound shapes, or form, of our own language. However, as we have already learned, hearing sound shapes is not necessarily a simple task. It is, rather, one which requires careful, often repeated and sophisticated listening, especially in view of the twin facts that (1) spelling may seriously mislead us as to the sound structure of a syllable or word and (2) our perceptions may, as a result of incomplete reception or faulty analysis, be false to the facts. Nevertheless, it is possible to perform a perceptual analysis of speech, and to record our perceptions in the form of a phonetic transcription.

Phonetic transcription skill is ordinarily acquired in a series of relatively graded steps, which we suggest might proceed approximately as follows:

1 First learn the appropriate form of the symbols and make certain that you understand the distinction between phonemic and phonetic transcription.

2 Learn to associate each symbol with a model utterance which is a clear canonically pronounced example in a single stressed syllable.

3 Begin to identify the important variant forms, or allophones, typically found for each sound class studied.

4 Learn to identify the common complex consonant combinations in single syllable contexts.

5 Learn to transcribe both sound segments and stress patterns in short multisyllabic utterances, assigning the appropriate symbols to the *reduced* syllables.

6 Learn to transcribe the sounds which appear in unexpected, non-English sequences.

7 Learn to identify non-English phones and assign to them the appropriate symbols. These are the major sound classes not contrastive in English (bilabial fricative, flap, etc.).

8 Learn to transcribe "slurred" or reduced and elliptic speech as well as the sound patterns typical of speech defects.

Recall that phonetic transcription is a record of the listener's *impression* of what he or she hears. Your first task is to make sure that this impression is one which is based upon speech cues, not alphabet cues. In other words you should hear "ink" not as the letters *i, n,* and *k,* but as a speech sound series [ɪ], [ŋ], and [k]. You will need to forget how to spell for the moment—to know that "women" starts with [wɪ], that "phone" begins with [f], and that "ough" can stand for [o], [u], [ʌf], [aʊ], [əf], or [ʌp]. You need to *listen.*

If transcription is an auditory perceptual task, as we have stated, it follows that phonetic transcriptions are made of speech, not of writing. In turn this means that you can transcribe only real utterances. It is not possible to transcribe the word "through"—only some particular pronunciation of it. That pronunciation may be an imaginary one, made by a hypothetical model speaker who always pronounces the word in a clear and exact manner, in precise accordance with the known rules of the language, but as we have seen in Chapter 1, speech is never exact and the "rules" vary more widely than we usually assume. In any case, phoneticians, as distinct from linguists, are usually more interested in how speakers depart from expectation. Your expectation, if you are concerned with applications to speech improvement, learning, and abnormality, is that what you hear will *not* be a model utterance.

In practice, when phonetic transcriptions are made, they are usually of the speech of an "informant"—some speaker other than yourself, speaking at a normal rate. You should realize that at normal speech rates we are able to listen analytically to no more than one or two segments at a time. For that reason *repetition* is required. This can be accomplished in one of three ways: (1) through repetition of the utterance by the speaker (dangerous because repetition may bring about self-conscious changes), (2) by repeated listening to recordings of an utterance, or (3) by analyzing your own repeated imitations of the informant's speech. This last is obviously practicable only if you are in fact a good imitator.

Here are some additional details of procedure which are sometimes helpful in phonetic transcription:

1 In attacking a sample of speech, try to determine the number of syllables; remember that they will be heard as rhythmical pulses of sound energy. Since the syllable is a kind of basic element of speech, it should be located as the first step in transcription.

2 After the syllable divisions are determined, ask yourself what is the basic, distinguishing sound quality of each pulse—usually a vowel or diphthong resonance. These may then be recorded, allowing a suitable amount of space between them for the recording of the nonsyllabic symbols. The phrase "now let me sleep" might look like this: [aʊ ε i i].

3 Next decide how each syllable was started and stopped, and insert the appropriate consonant symbols or symbol combinations from your model set.

4 Next identify the manner in which each segment departs from "standard" and revise as necessary, by employing segmental symbols from a larger set, or by the use of modifying symbols.

5 Finally, add to the transcription the nonsegmental symbols necessary to your purpose (symbols for stress, length, pitch, quality, etc.).

The above strategy will not be the best for everyone. You may wish to adopt the strategy of setting down your own imitation of the utterance as a broad phonemic transcription, then checking it against the actual utterance item by item. "Now let me sleep" might be found, with either strategy, to be more appropriately and meaningfully recorded, for your purposes, as [nʌʊ ˌlɛmɪˈslijp↘], [nɑ̃ːlɛʔmɪj slip⁻] or in any number of other ways, depending upon the details of the sound pattern, your perceptual skills, and the purposes served by the phonetic transcription.

EXERCISES

1 Here is a list of terms for you to use in constructing a glossary for Chapter 3:

articulatory modifiers	International Phonetic	phonetic
c-wedge	Association	transcription
caret	*j*-wedge	primary stress
back vowels	ligature	reduced vowel
diacritical marks	long pause	*s*-wedge
diphthong	low vowel	schwa
epsilon	nonsegmentals	schwar
eth	open-*o*	secondary stress
feature analysis	perceptual analysis	short pause
front vowels	phone	syllabic consonant
half-long	phonetic alphabet	theta
high vowels	phonetic symbol	vowel murmur
IPA alphabet		*z*-wedge

2 Learn the proper form of each of the symbols of Table 3-2. Print carefully. Be sure to distinguish between capital and lower-case forms. Take note of the sizes of the symbols and their position on the line. These must be committed to memory just as you would learn a vocabulary for a foreign language.

3 Learn to associate each symbol of Table 3-2 with a target, or standard, pronunciation of the sound used in a stressed and carefully pronounced syllable (except for the allophones [ə] and [ɚ]). For this you will need an expert "informant" in the form of a teacher or a tape recording, or both. If a recorded model is available, listen carefully and then make your own recording for comparison with the model. Have the teacher or laboratory instructor criticize your pronunciations. It is important that you develop an appropriate auditory image for each sound. Listen to and produce the vowels in isolation and in different contexts. Do the same with the consonants in several vowel contexts. Strictly speaking, consonants cannot be produced in the absence of a vowel. It will, however, help to practice the *continuant* consonants ([f], [θ], [s], [m], etc.) as sustained sounds as well as in CV and VC syllables.

4 For each of the sounds of Table 3-2 construct a "loaded sentence." For example, "The fair-haired French fellow buried the bread" is loaded with the sound [ɛ]. It may prove a further challenge if you include a variety of spellings and phonetic contexts in your sentence. Underline the letter or letters which spell the sound in each instance. Have the sentence checked for accuracy.

5 Practice reading the following simple phonetic transcription. You should not have any difficulty, but if you do, try to analyze its source and nature.

1 [ju ɔt tu si ðə sɪks bɔɪz]
2 [dʒɪm traɪd tu lɜn hɪz e bi siz]
3 [fənɛtɪk trænskrɪpʃən ɪz izi sʌmtaɪmz]
4 [kaʊnt frəm wʌn hʌndrəd tə θri θaʊzənd baɪ tɛnz]
5 [ɪts fʌni ðət lɛtɚz ɑr nɑt prənaʊnst æz ðe ɑr spɛld]
6 [hwaɪ du wi juz ən i saʊnd ɪn bi si di i ænd pi]
7 [hwaɪ juz ən ɛ saʊnd ɪn ɛf ɛl ɛm ænd ɛn]
8 [onli wʌn lɛtɚ, ði o, ɪz prənaʊnst æz nemd]
9 [pliz rɪmɛmbɚ ðət wi du nɑt kæpətəlaɪz ɪn fənɛtɪks]
10 [dɪdʒu hæv ɛni trʌbl̩ ridɪŋ ðiz sɛntənsəz]

6 If we take away the orthographic conventions of spacing and punctuation, you may find the transcriptions more difficult to read. Try these:

1 [əfənɛtɪksɪstəmɪzəsʌmhwʌtsəmɛtrɪkl̩strʌkʃɚ]
2 [wikənfaɪndaʊtələtəbautitʃʌðɚθrudaɪəlɛktənæləsəs]
3 [hɪkəridɪkəridɑkɪzðəstɑrtəvənɜsriraɪm]
4 [nɑnsɛnsɪzəlɑthɑrdɚtuɛtəwɪnʃɚdlu]
5 [naʊmekʌpjɚonsɛntənsəzæntraɪðəmɑnjurfənɛtɪkfrɛndz]

7 The following transcriptions are full of obvious errors—five or more in each line. List the errors and note their type. An informal pronunciation is not an error. Check your results with your fellow students.

1 [Rɑdʒɚ Braun ɪz ə lɪŋgwst ofkənsɪdrəbl rɪnown]
2 [prose, laɪk poətri haz rɪθəm ɑn mitɚ ænə lɪtl̩ raɪm]
3 [θɛrs ɔlwez room æt ðə Bɑtəm so bring ə frɛnd]
4 [tu θre fʌr faɪv sɪzs ɑr ɑll wrɑng numbɜz]

8 Organize a "round-robin" group of two to four students and begin to practice dictating from phonetic transcriptions and phonetically transcribing the dictation of others. Numerous examples may be found in Part Two of this text. Compare the transcription with the original, discuss the errors with one another, and get help from the teacher or lab instructor when you cannot solve the problem within the group. Work from the simple to the complex, as suggested in this chapter (page 60).

9 Learn to read and to transcribe the *consonant combinations*. For each of the following find at least two words and transcribe them phonetically.

Initial consonant combinations followed by a vowel:

[pl pj br bl tr tw dr dw kr kl kw gr gl fl fr θr sp spr spl st str sk skr skw sw sl sm sn].

Final consonant combinations following a vowel:

[ps pt bz bd ts dz tʃt dʒd ks kt gd gz ft fs vz vd θs ðz ðd st sk sts sks sp zd ʃt mz md mp mps mpt nt nz ndz nts nst ntʃ ntʃt nd ndʒ ndʒd lz ld lts lt lp ldz lk lm ŋz ŋk ŋkt ŋks ŋd rz rdz rm rk rt rd rts]

10 As we have seen in one of the above exercises, there may be no "open spaces" in phonetic transcription. One word usually follows another just as one syllable follows another within a word. This exercise is a test of your ability both to read phonetic transcription and to identify an otherwise meaningless sound pattern as a logical part of a phrase which simply occurs across word boundaries. For each of the following phrase fragments identify some context in which the pattern would be logically found. There are many possible answers for most items. Try all 20 fragments before looking up the answers in Appendix E. If you had difficulty, can you identify its nature and source?

Examples: -bautɔl- That's *about all*.
-skwɪz- It's *quiz* time.

1	-vɪnd-	**11**	-məto-
2	-aundən-	**12**	-tʃətau-
3	-bɑlp-	**13**	-kwɛls-
4	-zɪŋt-	**14**	-ŋɔf-
5	-iṃo-	**15**	-stʃ-
6	-zidrɔ-	**16**	-rɔɪv-
7	-ʃælf-	**17**	-tʃəpɑl-
8	-odədæ-	**18**	uʃaɪ-
9	-ræpsi-	**19**	-zdino-
10	-snaɪt-	**20**	-rəlʌn-

11 Multisyllabic words are quite likely to have entire syllables omitted in informal rapid speech, and some words in English have more than one acceptable syllabic form, even in formal speech. The following is a list of words which often vary in syllable structure according to their rate of utterance and formality. Can you identify at least two syllabic forms for each? Phonetically transcribe a reduced (elliptic) form commonly heard in American English. When you have completed the exercise, check against some common reduced forms given in the key in Appendix E. Which forms do you think are substandard?

about	collect	didn't	our	regular
above	collision	especially	poetry	shouldn't
capacity	company	firing	president	similar
cafeteria	cooperate	flowering	probably	toward
chocolate	definite	naturally	realize	wouldn't

12 At this point you may wish to turn ahead to the phonetic transcription exercises in Part Two of this text. Here, for each of the major classes of speech sounds, you will find four aids to your perceptual training: (1) a practice paragraph which is loaded with the particular sound discussed in that section, (2) a list of illustrative words which are pronounced with that sound or some variant of it, (3) a list of "minimal pairs" which contrast two meaningful words which differ only by one phone each, and (4) a phonetic transcription of the careful "semiformal" pronunciation of the loaded paragraph by one of the authors. Compare your pronunciations with those of the authors.

Chapter 4

Articulatory and Acoustic Backgrounds

In this chapter we shall examine in some detail the physiology of speech production, which classically has been the principal subject matter of *physiological* or *articulatory phonetics*, along with certain anatomical and acoustic information which will enhance our understanding of the manner in which language is spoken. We shall approach these matters by a fairly wide-ranging review of what might be called the "articulatory possibilities" of human beings, starting with a consideration of a general physiological model of the speech system. We shall then describe the structure and function of the three subsystems which constitute the speech "mechanism": (1) the *respiratory system*, which provides the motive power for speech and voice; (2) the *phonatory system* of the larynx, which generates voice; and (3) the *articulatory-resonance system*, which shapes the outflowing breath stream into the sounds of speech. The chapter must be studied with care, since it contains the vocabulary and concepts constantly employed in the analysis of speech.

Strictly speaking, human beings have no unique or distinctive organs of speech which do not also have some other basic biological function. We "talk" with our entire body, in fact, since a good deal of what we think and feel is conveyed in the form of *nonverbal communication*, mediated by a tone of voice, the play of facial expression, gross and fine body movements and postures, and other cues which supplement, enrich, modify—or even deny— what is being said in words. But when human beings developed *verbal communication*, they utilized in a special way organs which are part of the respiratory and digestive systems. For this reason, some consider speech an *overlaid function*, since it employs organ systems which were already serving other biological needs.

Speech is not entirely an overlaid function, however, for in the course of evolutionary development certain structures have undergone changes which make them more efficient for speech production, but do not otherwise en-enhance their biological functions. Evolutionary changes in the larynx which facilitate phonation have been traced by Negus (1929, 1949); and an interesting sidelight is provided by Lieberman and Crelin (1971) and Lieberman (1972), who concluded, after vocal-tract measurements of reconstructed Neanderthal people, that these early humanoids did not have the anatomical prerequisites for producing the full range of human speech as we now know it. In addition to structure-function changes in what is sometimes called the *peripheral speech mechanism*, there have also evolved neural networks in the brain which serve both the symbolic processes of language and the neuro-muscular responses for its expression. It has been theorized that the neural circuitry for speech and language is inborn (see, for example, Lenneberg, 1967).

The fact that speech is produced with organ systems which originally had only a vegetative function is interesting to both the phonetician and the student of speech disorders. For instance, there are good reasons to suppose that the motor patterns human beings use to make speech sounds had their genesis, at least in part, as modifications of suckling, chewing, and swallowing movements. In the case of abnormal speech, it is evident that any physical or functional factor which disturbs vegetative function of the "organs of speech" is a potential cause for some kind of communication disorder. There may well be subtle connections between an infant's early feeding movements and both normal and abnormal development of the speech sounds.

The speech system functions as a whole, so that even the simplest speech act is a total integrated response. For purposes of description, however, a division into three subsystems is convenient: (1) the *respiratory system*, which is the source of the airflow needed to generate speech and voice; (2) the *phonatory system* of the larynx, which provides the constriction in the vocal tract needed to produce voice; and (3) the *articulation resonance-system*, which modifies the outgoing breath stream in various ways to produce and differentiate the sounds of speech. The throat, mouth, and nasal cavities which are part of this latter system also influence vocal quality and loudness.

VOCAL-TRACT ANALOGS

Before going on to further anatomical and physiological details, it might be instructive to examine some models of the speech system which scientists have constructed. In some cases their efforts were motivated by a desire to build an artificial "talking machine"; in others the theoretical models and *vocal-tract analogs* were devised as an aid to the scientific study and description of the phenomena of speech.

Best known of the early attempts to produce a mechanical talking device is probably that of Wolfgang von Kempelen in the latter part of the eighteenth century. Having first observed his own vocal mechanism, this ingenious German scientist designed a simple wooden box to serve as a mouth, with hinged shutters for lips, and a wooden flap for a tongue. To this apparatus he affixed a tube containing a reed vibrator which could be actuated by a set of bellows in such a way as to provide a sound source analogous to voice.

His experiments led him finally to a model similar to that shown in Figure 4-1. The reed vibrator lies inside the chamber marked *A*. Various combinations of resonators were added, the main one being that marked *C* in the diagram. "Speech" sounds were formed by manipulating the hands

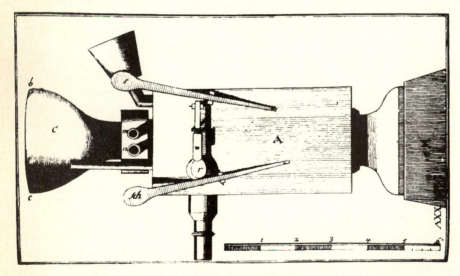

Figure 4-1 Artificial speaking machine of Wolfgang von Kempelen. The bellows arrangement *X*, when pressed, caused air to flow through chamber *A* in which is located a reed vibrator. The resulting tone is directed into the bell-shaped resonator *C*, whose resonances can be altered by manipulating one's hands over the mouth of the bell. Nasals and fricative sounds are produced by manipulating the appropriate levers. (By permission from an article by E. E. David, "Voice-Actuated Machines: Problems and Possibilities," *Bell Laboratories Record,* 1957).

over the bell-shaped resonator, with some of the consonant sounds being produced with the aid of accessory sound and resonance sources. His device is said to have "talked" surprising well, and though crude by modern standards, von Kempelen's machine was entirely analogous to the human speech system, containing a source of air pressure, a tone generator, and a resonance-articulation analog.

Incidently, the "larynx" in this model is much like an early artificial larynx developed by the Bell Telephone Company to provide a voice for patients who had undergone surgical removal of the larynx (a *laryngectomy*). The principal difference is that the vibrator for laryngectomies was powered by the patient's own breath and the resulting sound led into his mouth by a tube outside the body. A model more like the human speech mechanism in appearance is shown in Figure 4-2. It has the same three basic components: a bellows mechanism for driving air through a tube (corresponding to the trachea), a constriction in the tube something like the con-

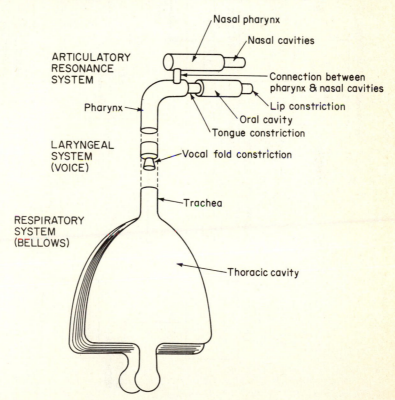

Figure 4-2   Diagramatic model of human speech mechanism, with a bellows "lung," a constriction in the airway simulating the larynx, and a complex set of cavity resonators corresponding to the pharyngeal, oral, and nasal cavities.

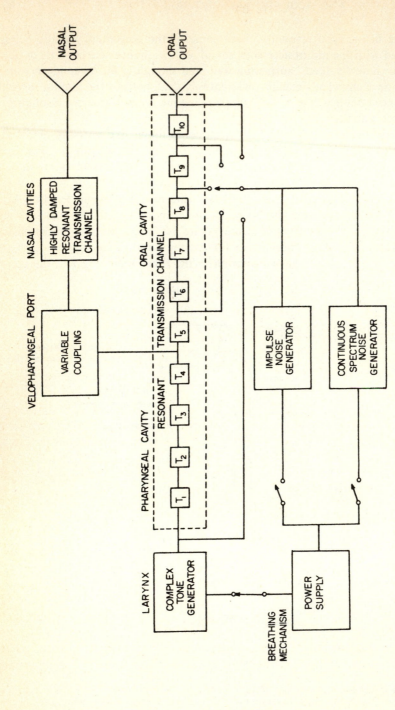

Figure 4-3 Block diagram of a hypothetical electrical speech-synthesizing system which illustrates by analogy certain fundamental principles and relationships of the speech generation processes. (Figure and caption from J. F. Curtis, in D. C. Spriestersbach and D. Sherman (eds.), *Cleft Palate and Communication*, New York: Academic Press, Inc., 1968. By permission.)

striction in the human larynx, and a series of resonance tubes comparable to the human pharynx and oral and nasal cavities for the purpose of giving different qualities or features to the artificial speech sounds.

Modern technology has made it possible to produce remarkably lifelike speech by generating its acoustic features electronically. Among the earliest of these devices was the Vocoder exhibited by the Bell Telephone Company in the 1930s, mainly as a scientific curiosity, but since that time many highly sophisticated systems have been developed. A block diagram of one hypothetical electronic speech synthesizer is shown in Figure 4-3. In a superficial sense, such electronic models are poorer analogs to speech than the early talking machines of von Kempelen and others, but they have proved more useful in the investigation of many theoretical and practical problems related to speech.[1]

With this overview as an introduction we can turn now to a more extended description of the structure and function of the speech system, organizing the discussion around its three subsystems mentioned earlier: (1) *respiratory*, (2) *phonatory*, and (3) *resonance-articulation*. These matters must be understood in some detail for a full appreciation of speech behavior, although we shall try to avoid needless particulars.

THE RESPIRATORY SYSTEM

Breathing in and out (*inhalation* and *exhalation*) is an aerodynamic process which depends on creating a difference between air pressure within the *thoracic* (chest) *cavity* and atmospheric air pressure outside the body. When pressure in the thorax is less than that in the atmosphere, air flows into the lungs; when the situation is reversed, air flows outward. During any single inhalation-exhalation cycle, this inward or outward flow of air will continue until the *intrapulmonic* and atmospheric pressures are equalized.

Anatomical Features

The major anatomical features of the respiratory system are shown in Figure 4-4. The two lungs lie in the thoracic cavity and communicate with the atmosphere ouside the body by way of the respiratory tract. Starting at the top, successive sections of the airway include (1) the *nasal passages–nasopharynx* and the *oral (buccal) cavity*, either or both of which may serve as the entry-exit port for the breath stream; (2) the *pharynx*, or throat cavity; (3) the *larynx*; and (4) the *trachea* or "windpipe." The latter divides, at a point called the *bifurcation*, into two *bronchi* (bronchial tubes), each leading to a lung. The section of the breathing passage lying above the trachea is often referred to

---

[1] For more information about early and modern artificial speech systems consult Dudley and Tarnoczy (1950), Flanagan (1972), and David (1957). Paget (1930) also discusses some aspects of artificial speech.

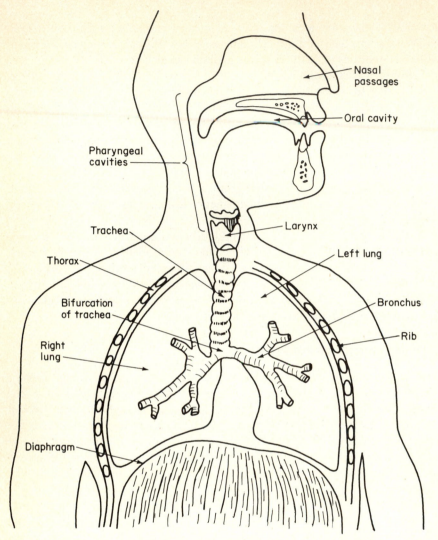

Figure 4-4 Anatomical features of the upper respiratory tract, showing in semi-diagrammatic form some of the major respiratory, phonatory, and resonance structures.

as the *upper respiratory tract*, as distinguished from the *lower respiratory tract*, which is the inferior section of the airway. When the focus of interest is on speech and voice production, the respiratory tract is alternatively referred to as the *vocal tract*.

The lungs need not be described in detail, except to note that they are porous sacs which, except for some degree of elasticity, have no significant capacity for movement except as they are inflated and deflated by changes

in air pressures.   The curious notion tends to persist that it is the lungs themselves which somehow "suck in" and "push out" air. This is not true, of
course, since the lungs are essentially passive structures which can be changed
in volume only by means of movement of other structures.

Within the lungs the bronchi undergo a series of treelike branchings
(*arborization*) whose final divisions are the minute air cells called *alveoli*.
It is through the membranous walls of these that the oxygen–carbon dioxide
exchange with the blood takes place. The trachea (and some of its first
divisions) consists of a series of incomplete cartilaginous rings connected by
membranes.

The bony framework of the chest cavity is formed by 12 pairs of curved
ribs (*costae*), and certain other bones. The ribs are articulated at the back
with *vertebrae* of the thoracic division of the spinal column in such a way
that the rib cage can be raised and lowered. The remainder of the thoracic
skeleton is made up of the two *scapulae* (shoulder blades) at the back, the
clavicles (collar bones) from which the rib cage is suspended from above, and
in front the *sternum* (breast bone), to which the upper 10 pairs of ribs are
attached either directly, or indirectly by means of interposed *costal cartilages*.

Respiratory Movements

The space within the thoracic cavity surrounding the lungs is sealed and
contains only a small amount of air, the cavity being filled principally by the
lungs and heart. Because it is airtight, after exhalation an increase in cavity
size will decrease the pressure on the outer surface of the lungs to a level
which is less than atmospheric pressure, thus creating a pressure differential
which causes air to flow into the lungs via the repiratory tract. To exhale,
cavity size is decreased, which will increase intrathoracic pressure and force
air from the lungs.

There are two major ways in which the thoracic cavity can be enlarged
for inhalation: (1) by contracting the *diaphragm* and (2) by elevating the
rib cage. The diaphragm (Figure 4-4) is a large dome-shaped muscle which
forms the floor of the thoracic cavity. When relaxed, the diaphragm arches
upward into the chest cavity; when its fibres contract, the diaphragm flattens
and so increases the vertical dimension of the thoracic cavity. Since this
downward movement displaces viscera lying under the diaphragm, some dis-
tension of the abdominal wall just beneath the level of the lower ribs can
usually be noted. Breathing of this type is often called *abdominal* or *diaphragmatic*.

Elevation of the rib cage with resulting chest expansion is accomplished
by a complex group of inspiratory muscles which need not be identified here.
At rest, when exhalation is complete, the ribs slant downward; if they are
raised, the front-to-back dimension of the thoracic cavity will increase as the
angle of the ribs becomes less acute. The same action will rotate the ribs

upward and outward on their vertebral articulations, somewhat as a bird's wings lift, thus increasing the side-to-side dimension of the chest cavity. Breathing in which rib cage action predominates is usually termed *thoracic* or *chest*. When diaphragmatic and rib cage movement occur together, the thoracic cavity size is increased simultaneously in all dimensions, providing the possibility of inhalation of the maximum volume of air.

Although there are some differences of opinion, exhalation during quiet nonspeech breathing can be regarded as a largely passive process. If so, gravity and the elasticity of tissue would account for lowering of the rib cage and return of the diaphragm to a resting position. The elasticity of the lungs probably aids in expelling air. When the respiratory rate increases because of exercise or for some other reason, exhalation becomes a more active process. In this case, certain muscles which can depress the rib cage are brought into play. Abdominal muscles also contract to press viscera against the diaphragm, forcing it upward. Exhalation to initiate speech is a process which will be discussed in the following section.

Speech Initiation

Nothing further need be said about respiration to maintain life, but we must review in some detail the way breathing movements are modified to initiate and maintain speech. There are several important differences between the two modes of respiration. First is a contrast in the duration of the inhalation-exhalation phases of the breathing cycle. In quiet life breathing, the inhalation-exhalation time intervals are about equal, the ratio being about 1.5 to 1.0. During speech, however, we inhale more quickly—normally during pauses—but expend the breath over a much longer period; under this condition the time ratio of exhalation to inhalation may be 20 or more to 1, depending largely on the manner and content of the speaker's utterance. Exhalation for quiet conversational speech requires but little expiratory effort but loud speech and the supported tone of singers calls for active use of the rib depressors and certain abdominal muscles.

Next, several parameters of speech require fine regulation of the outgoing breath stream, including particularly vocal pitch and loudness. While the details of these complicated pitch and loudness mechanisms need not concern us, it should be appreciated that the respiratory system plays a critical role in determining some of the pitch and loudness fluctuations of speech and voice.[1] That syllabification may depend upon arresting action of the respiratory muscles was mentioned earlier. Finally, regulation of the breath stream is critical for production of the fricative and stop sounds, which are the so-called *pressure consonants*, or *obstruents*.

[1] For a more extensive discussion of this aspect of speech physiology see Stetson (1951) and Lieberman (1967).

Among the languages of the world, energy for speech is generated in a variety of different ways, called *initiatory types*. By far the commonest is the *pulmonic egressive* type, which utilizes air forced from the lungs in the manner described above as the energy source. With only a few exceptions, the English speech we hear daily is initiated in this way. A *pulmonic ingressive* mode of initiation is used for some phones in certain languages, but is unusual in English. However, an English speaker might occasionally talk on inhalation under some special circumstance, as when he wished to continue counting aloud without missing a beat, or give a fillip to some emotional phrase or interjection. Certain nonverbal but meaningful sounds—various kinds of groans and gasps—are frequently of the pulmonic ingressive type.

Other initiatory types are uncommon among the languages with which we are most likely to be familiar, but are somewhat more frequent in the speech of a number of non-Western cultures. Indeed, to the English ear some of these languages seem to consist of an assortment of odd clicks and other strange vocal effects. For instance, a sound can be produced by changing the position of the larynx. If it is lowered, air pressure becomes relatively greater below the vocal folds than above, leading to the potential for a *glottal egressive* initiatory type; if the larynx is raised, the pressure differential is the reverse, which could result in a *glottal ingressive* mode of initiation. Through a similar mechanism, the soft palate may generate *velar egressive* and *velar ingressive* initiatory types. Catford (1968) writes extensively about these matters in an interesting essay, "The Articulatory Possibilities of Man."

For those interested in communication disorders this discussion would be incomplete without mention of the *esophageal* initiatory type. This is used as a substitute for pulmonic egression by individuals who have been forced to undergo surgical removal of the larynx, usually for the treatment of cancer. This procedure leaves the patient with the trachea opening to the outside air in the lower part of the neck and, of course, without a larynx with which to produce vocal sounds. For *alaryngeal* or *esophageal* speech, the patient learns to inject air into the upper part of the esophagus and then to expel the air in a belchlike sound. An entirely useful substitute voice can be developed in this way. (Snidecor *et al.*, 1962, has a full discussion of all phases of alaryngeal speech.) Persons with either functional or organic disorders where motor patterns are disturbed, as in cerebral palsy or stuttering, frequently have aberrant modes of speech initiation.

THE PHONATORY SYSTEM

Voice has its origin in the vocal-fold mechanism which lies within the larynx. Both vocal-fold movements which result in a vocal note, or *cord tone*, and the air turbulences which create other kinds of laryngeal sound, such as a whisper, are powered by the respiratory system discussed in the previous section. In turn, laryngeal sounds are modified by the resonance-articulation system in ways to be described in the next section.

Basically, the larynx is a valving mechanism whose primary functions can be placed in two broad categories: (1) to protect the lower respiratory tract from the intrusion of foreign substances, a safeguard which is necessary to prevent asphyxiation and other unfortunate consequences, and (2) to create a constriction in the vocal tract which serves as a sound source for communication. In addition to protection of the airway, the larynx has several other important nonphonatory functions, which are described in detail by Negus (1929). One of them, for instance, is to hold air in the lungs and thus prevent collapse of the rib cage when strong effort is being exerted by trunk muscles.

The main anatomic features of the larynx are shown in Figure 4-5. Its framework is made up of five major cartilages: *cricoid*, *thyroid*, *epiglottis*, and two *arytenoid* cartilages. As can be seen from Figure 4-5, the cricoid, which rests on the top ring of the trachea, has a narrow bandlike portion facing to the front, but expands into an enlarged quadrilateral plate at the back. In form the cricoid is often likened to a signet ring. The thyroid is a v-shaped cartilage with two *alae* or "wings" whose anterior point we identify as our "Adam's apple."

The thyroid articulates with the cricoid by means of an *inferior cornu* on either side, the cornua being short downard projections of the posterior

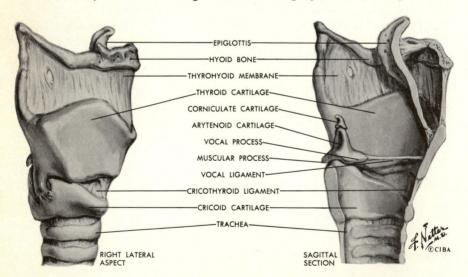

EPIGLOTTIS
HYOID BONE
THYROHYOID MEMBRANE
THYROID CARTILAGE
CORNICULATE CARTILAGE
ARYTENOID CARTILAGE
VOCAL PROCESS
MUSCULAR PROCESS
VOCAL LIGAMENT
CRICOTHYROID LIGAMENT
CRICOID CARTILAGE
TRACHEA

RIGHT LATERAL
ASPECT

SAGITTAL
SECTION

Figure 4-5 Cartilages of the larynx: right aspect with all cartilages intact; sagittal section with right half of larynx removed to show left arytenoid cartilage and vocal ligament running from thyroid to arytenoid cartilage. (© Copyright 1970 by CIBA Pharmaceutical Company, Division of CIBA-Geigy Corporation. Reproduced with permission from *Clinical Symposia*. Illustrated by Frank H. Netter, M.D. All rights reserved.)

margins of the thyroid. The crico-thyroid joint allows the thyroid to tip upward and downward, and to slide forward and backward for a limited distance. Because the vocal folds are attached in front to the inner surface of the thyroid, they can be tensed and relaxed and lengthened and shortened by these movements of the cartilage. As can been seen from the drawing, the *superior cornua* of the thyroid on either side suspend the larynx from the *hyoid bone* by means of ligaments. This bone, in turn, supports the tongue. The leaf-shaped epiglottis has a stalklike attachment to the inner surface of the thyroid in front. The epiglottis lies just under the back portion of the tongue and is part of the mechanism which closes the upper opening into the larynx.

In Figure 4-6 the vocal folds are shown as they would appear if they were opened, or *abducted*, to the normal position for inhalation and exhalation. The opening between the vocal folds is the *glottis*. Each vocal fold extends from an anterior attachment on the inner surface of the thyroid to a

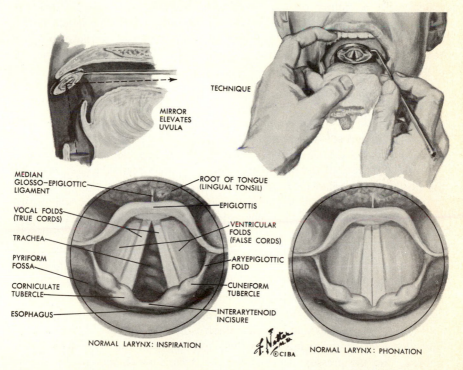

Figure 4-6 Appearance of the glottis with the vocal folds in *abducted* and *adducted* positions. Accompanying sketches show the position of the larynx in relation to the pharynx, palate, and tongue as viewed in a laryngeal mirror by an examiner using the technique of indirect laryngoscopy. (© Copyright 1970 by CIBA Pharmaceutical Company, Division of CIBA-Geigy Corporation. Reproduced with permission from *Clinical Symposia*. Illustrated by Frank H. Netter, M.D. All rights reserved.)

posterior insertion on the *vocal process* of the arytenoid cartilage on the same side. The arytenoids, which are roughly pyramidal in shape, articulate with the cricoid in such a way that they can rock or twist so as to bring their forward-projecting vocal processes toward or away from the midline; the arytenoids can also be made to glide or slide together along the upper surface of the cricoid. A combination of these movements opens and closes the glottis and to some extent helps determine the tension of the vocal folds. The edges of the vocal folds are formed by the *vocal ligaments*, and the body of the vocal fold is made up of muscle fibers running parallel to the vocal ligament.

In Figure 4-6, the vocal folds are also shown in the nearly *adducted*, or closed, position they normally assume for phonation. This change from an open to a closed position was accomplished by muscle contractions which moved the arytenoid inward so that their vocal processes came together; and by simultaneous action of other muscles, the arytenoids were brought together at the midline to close the posterior segment of the glottis. Muscles within the vocal folds and others which act on the thyroid (and hence on the vocal folds which are attached to it) serve to impart tension to the vocal folds so that they have the elasticity needed to vibrate as they do during production of a vocal note.

Phonation

An extended discussion of the physiology of phonation is not needed for our purposes. In general, voice is produced when the vocal folds are brought together and tensed to an extent which will result in their being set into motion by airflow, usually of the pulmonic egressive type. Vocal-fold vibrations are the product of a balance of forces. On the one hand, elastic forces tend to keep them in a closed position; however, in normal phonation the respiratory system applies sufficient air pressure below the glottis to overcome this force, causing the vocal folds to open. The resulting airflow through the glottis, in accordance with what is called the *Bernoulli effect*, causes a pressure drop which, together with the elasticity and inertia of the vocal folds, brings them together once more.[1] This opening and closing of the glottis occurs periodically during the production of voice.

The characteristics of vocal-fold movement influence three major aspects of voice: *pitch*, *loudness*, and *quality*. Pitch is determined by the *frequency* of fold vibration; this depends upon the mass-length of the vocal folds, their tension, and the pressure level of the air stream which actuates them. The perceived loudness of a tone is directly related to its *intensity*, which is the amount of energy generated by vocal-fold movements. Intensity varies with

[1] Detailed information about voice production will be found in Minifie, Hixon, and Williams (1973); Zemlin (1968); and Moore (1971).

the pressure level of the breath stream and the nature of the glottal constriction.

Voice quality is a much more complex matter. It is affected not only by the *pattern* of vocal-fold movement, but also by the properties of the resonance system, and the topic can best be taken up at a later point. So far as the laryngeal determinants of quality are concerned, the musculature of the larynx is capable of complex adjustments which can change the configuration of the vocal folds in such a way as to affect their form or type of vibration, even to the point of creating a condition where the vocal note is replaced by a *whisper*, which is the perceived result of turbulences in the airstream caused by laryngeal constrictions. During speech there are intricate fluctuations in pitch, loudness, and quality—the *nonsegmental features* discussed in Chapter 7—which are made possible by remarkably complex muscular adjustments in the larynx and elsewhere in the speech system.

THE RESONANCE-ARTICULATION SYSTEM

Through the actions of this subsystem the outgoing breath stream—voiced or voiceless—is manipulated to form the sounds of speech. Except for voicing, which depends on the presence of a laryngeal tone, all the distinctive features which serve to create the *network of differences* among the segmental speech sounds are imparted by the resonance-articulation system. In an appreciation of its function lies the key to an understanding of speech production.

Speech sounds can be understood most easily if we first take into account their *acoustic* composition, since this determines the way in which they are perceived by a listener, and then study next the dynamic adjustments of the articulation-resonance system which determine these distinguishing physical characteristics.

Acoustic Backgrounds

Taken simply as physical phenomena, speech sounds—or classes of sounds—may differ from one another in several respects. First, the vibrations of the sound generator may be periodic or aperiodic. A sound is said to be *periodic* if the vibrations occur at a relatively regular rate. A tuned piano string, for instance, vibrates periodically when set in motion; so do the vocal folds of a singer sustaining a musical note. Technically, the mechanics of vibrating strings and the vocal folds differ in some important respects. Vocal cords move more like the lips of a trumpet player than like the strings of a violin. As we shall explain more fully in later paragraphs, the vibratory motion for vowels and diphthongs is usually periodic. Likewise the feature *voiced*, when present in any other class of speech sound, usually reflects periodic vibrations.

In contrast, *aperiodic vibrations* are those which *do not* occur regularly. When bacon is frying in the skillet, celery is crunched, or a sheet of paper crumpled, the sound vibrations are irregular, occurring at no fixed rate. Psychologically, exposure to an aperiodic vibration gives auditors the experience of having heard what they are likely to call a "noise." As to speech sounds, the noise element of *stop* and *fricative* consonants consists physically of aperiodic vibrations whose articulatory sources will be discussed presently. If one of the latter sounds is voiced, the energy reaching the ear is a composite of periodic and aperiodic vibrations.

In addition to having the characteristic of relative periodicity or aperiodicity, sounds may differ in their acoustic composition in other ways. To explain this requires that we introduce another fact about the physics of sounds: In nature, sounds, whether periodic or aperiodic, are almost always complex. In *complex periodic sounds* the total energy delivered by the sound wave is not concentrated at a single frequency, but is divided among a greater or lesser number of frequency components which are present in the sound. Depending upon the context, these individual frequency components are spoken of as *partials*, *harmonics*, or *overtones*.

The principle here can perhaps be illustrated by likening movements of the vocal folds to those of a piano string. If struck, the string will vibrate as a whole at a frequency dependent on its mass-length and tension. These oscillations will not, however, be simple back-and-forth movements like those of a pendulum; instead, while the string is moving as a whole, sections of its total length will be vibrating, but at higher rates. These movements of the whole and by parts are the *segmental vibrations*, or *partials*.

Let us suppose that the piano string in our illustration is that for middle C on the musical scale. Its rate of vibration when set in motion will be 261.6 Hz (Hertz, or times per second). This is its *first partial*, or *fundamental* frequency, and will determine the perceived pitch when the note is played (except under special laboratory conditions). However, as the string moves as a whole, each of its halves will be vibrating at a rate twice that of the fundamental, which would be 523.2 Hz. This is the *second partial* and the *first overtone*. If analyzed, the tone will be found to contain additional segmental vibrations at progressively higher frequency rates.

Where vibrations have a regular periodicity, the frequencies of the partials have what is called a *harmonic* relationship to one another. Thus, the frequency ratio of the second and higher harmonic partials to the fundamental (which is also called the first harmonic) is, in order of progression, 2:1, 3:1, 4:1, and so on. All the partials making up a complex tone contribute some fraction of the total acoustic energy generated by the vibrator. The acoustic composition of our piano tone, to continue this comparison, is the pattern in which the total energy of the sound is distributed among its partials. This pattern reflects (1) the number of partials, (2) the frequency of each, and (3) the fraction of the total energy each partial contributes. The relation of these matters to speech sound production will presently be made clearer.

The acoustic composition of an *aperiodic* sound (the consonant *sh*, for example) differs typically in several respects from that of a periodic sound. The partials do not bear a harmonic relationship to one another, but instead have irregular modes of vibration and in general are randomly related. Aperiodic sounds of the kind encountered in speech tend to have less total energy, and less energy in the lower frequencies, than do the speech sounds which have periodicity. Characterized broadly, vowels are acoustically periodic tones and consonants aperiodic "noises," but this distinction is somewhat oversimplified since aperiodic vibrations sometimes provide important cues for the recognition of "periodic" speech sounds. Vowels, for instance, can be produced recognizably with a whispered aperiodic laryngeal noise as the energy source.

One more topic, *resonance*, remains before we can relate these facts about the physical nature of sound to the production and perception of speech sounds. Up to this point we have spoken only about the characteristics of sound generators, specifically the larynx, without taking into account the way in which complex sounds may be modified by resonators. A full explanation of resonance would introduce needless technicalities, but in general the effect of a resonance system is to *reinforce*, or "amplify," certain partials while *damping*, or not reinforcing, others. This selective effect occurs because, when the energy of the sound generator is transferred to the mass-elastic system of the resonator, the latter will be set in motion at amplitudes depending on its own natural frequencies of vibration. A common illustration of resonance is that of a parent pushing a child in a swing: If the pushes are properly timed, a small amount of energy will cause the swing to move through a wide arc; energy applied at the wrong time will be "damped."

At this point our analogy between a piano and the vocal mechanism must be abandoned, because the two systems have different types of resonators. Pianos and similar musical instruments have *sounding board* resonators which are so shaped that they will be set in motion with about equal efficiency by a wide range of frequencies. They are said to be *broadly tuned*. Vocal resonators are of the cavity type, and the air mass they contain is much more readily set into motion by some frequencies than by others. Because of this characteristic, they are said to be *sharply tuned*. Several factors determine the frequencies to which a cavity such as the vocal tract will respond, but two of the most important are *size* and *shape*. We shall later introduce some complications affecting the resonance of speech sounds which arise when two or more cavities are *coupled* together.

Depending on its characteristics, a cavity resonator system will act selectively on the partials of any complex sound introduced into it. Partials to which the resonator is tuned will be reinforced; partials to which it is not tuned will be damped, so that little or none of their energy will be transferred —the amount depending on the degree of damping. Thus, the acoustic com-

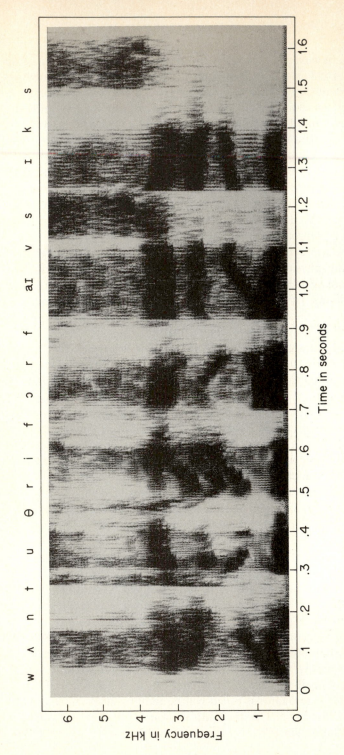

Figure 4-7 Sound spectrogram (voice print) of the spoken words, "one," "two," "three," "four," "five," "six." Vertical scale shows *frequency* in kilohertz (kHz), or thousands of cycles per second. *Time* can be read from the horizontal scale (total time of sample about 1.6 seconds). The darker the voice print mark, the greater the acoustic energy at that point in time and frequency.

position of a speech sound is determined by the manner in which the characteristics of a complex laryngeal vibratory source are modified by resonance in the vocal tract.

Perhaps the best way to visualize the acoustic patterns of speech is by means of what are popularly known as "voice prints," or, more properly, *sound spectrograms*. These are graphs which show the major variables present in the acoustic speech wave: *frequency, intensity,* and *time.* Those interested in the details of sound spectography are referred to *Visible Speech,* by Potter, Kopp, and Kopp (1966), and to *Introduction to the Spectrography of Speech,* by Pulgram (1959). A voice print of the spoken sentence "One, two, three, four, five, six" is reproduced in Figure 4-7, along with a phonetic transcription of the utterance.

In interpreting voice prints, dark areas indicate the presence of acoustic energy at some particular frequency and at some particular moment in time—the darker the shading, the greater the amount of acoustic energy. Frequency is shown on the ordinate and time on the baseline. The illustrative voice print in Figure 4-7 should be examined carefully to note certain typical characteristics of speech:

1 The differences between the "noisy" fricative and plosive sounds, with their *random* energies, and the *periodic* striations indicating voicing. Note the "noisiness" which is especially prominent for the *strident s.*

2 The dark horizontal *resonance bars* indicating the *formants* of the sonorant sounds. In particular, note the manner in which they change in time.

3 The sudden onset of energy which marks the plosive *t* and the characteristic "gaps" or drops in energy which occur at the points of consonant closure.

4 The way in which the vertical striations change from vowel to vowel. The number of vertical striations in a given period of time indicates the frequency of the fundamental glottal note, which in the illustration is highest on the word "two" and lowest on the word "six."

In Part Two of this text we shall look at typical voice prints for most of the sounds of American English, and thus be able to study their acoustic characteristics in detail. For the moment, certain important general conclusions can be drawn from the illustrative spectrogram. It can be seen that the sonorants—vowels, diphthongs, nasals, and glides—are by their nature largely *resonance phenomena,* and the same would hold true for the lateral *l* had one been included. Each has its own unique acoustic composition, with characteristic energy peaks or formants at certain frequency levels—the first two formants being the most significant features. Physically, the network of differences among vowels consists of contrasts among the resonance patterns.

Perceptually, a vowel is recognized on the basis of cues inherent in its resonance *pattern*, just as one can recognize a familiar face from its features without paying particular attention to any one of them.

Physiology of the Resonance-Articulation System

When they function as vocal resonators, the cavities of the head and neck are usually grouped into two systems: (1) the *oral pharyngeal*, or *oropharyngeal*, and (2) the *nasal*. The former consists of the mouth and throat cavities and the latter of the nasopharynx, which is that portion of the pharynx lying above the soft palate, and the nasal passages (see Figure 4-8). A *palatopharyngeal valve*, consisting of the soft palate and certain muscles of the pharynx, can partially or completely close the opening between the nasal and oropharyngeal resonators. When the cavities communicate, they are said to be *coupled*, but an explanation of the effect of this condition on resonance and a description of the valving mechanism is reserved for a later section.

Anatomically, the pharyngeal section of the oropharyngeal resonator can be seen in Figure 4-8 as a relatively large cavity, complex in shape, but roughly tubular. It can be subdivided into a lower *laryngopharynx*, into which open both the larynx and the esophagus, and a middle section, the *oropharynx*, which lies approximately opposite the mouth. The oropharynx opens into the mouth and, if the palatopharyngeal valve permits, the nasopharynx. Because of their familiarity, it does not seem necessary to describe the general features of the oral, or buccal, cavity, although some further anatomical details will be included in the explanation of consonant articulation.

In size, the nasal resonator is the smaller of the two resonance systems, and it is also more complex in shape. As will be seen from Figure 4-8, the nasopharynx is a cavity of relatively limited size. In front, at a point called the *choanae*, it opens into the nasal passages which run forward to the external openings of the nose, the *nares*. The two nasal passages are separated at the midline by certain bones of the cranium and facial skeleton, and by the *nasal septum*. Their lateral walls are marked by three scroll-like bones, the *turbinates*, creating a highly constricted and convoluted space. All these structural features greatly complicate the properties of the nasal passage–nasopharynx as a resonator.

The vocal tract is an amazing versatile resonance-articulation system because it can assume an almost unlimited number of configurations. It is because of this flexibility, of course, that we can utter the intricate flow of sound which makes up human speech. Indeed, so elaborate are the operations of the system that many details are still imperfectly understood. As a generality, however, it can be said that all sounds are produced by muscular adjustments which manipulate the size, shape, constrictions, and coupling of the vocal-tract cavities.

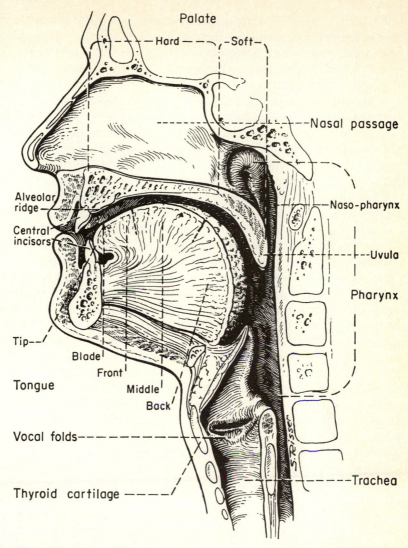

Figure 4-8 Section of the head and neck showing anatomical landmarks commonly identified in phonetic descriptions.

The Oropharyngeal Resonator The lateral and posterior surfaces of the laryngopharynx and oropharynx are formed by broad, flat, horizontally coursing muscles, the *pharyngeal constrictors*, and by other muscles which run in a generally vertical direction in the lateral walls. Action of these muscles can narrow the pharyngeal tube quite markedly. In addition, contraction of the constrictors at some levels but not at others can create a wide variety of cavity shapes. The length of the pharyngeal resonator can also be changed by muscular actions which raise and lower the larynx, with a significant effect on the resonance properties of the vocal tract. The degree of rigidity in the pharyngeal walls, which is related to muscle tonus, is also a factor in resonance. In addition to shaping the speech sounds, the pharyngeal resonator also affects vocal quality.

Tongue-jaw action is critical in determining the resonance properties of both the oral and pharyngeal cavities. If the tongue lies relaxed on the floor of the mouth, the size of this cavity can be increased by depressing the lower jaw (*mandible*). The major agent for vocal-tract change, however, is the tongue itself. Its height, degree of fronting or retraction, and shape are of paramount importance in adjusting the vocal tract for speech sound formation. Under most speaking conditions the tongue and jaw act together, and as we shall see when the vowels are discussed individually, there is a characteristic tongue-jaw posture for each of these syllabics.

In the interest of avoiding too many complications, nothing has been said up to now about the matter of *open* versus *closed* cavities and the relation of these two cavity types to resonance. All that need be said now is that the presence of an opening, and its size, will influence the frequencies to which the cavity will respond. This fact relates to both vowel and consonant production in that the size of the mouth opening tends to vary consistently for different speech sounds and is particularly characteristic for certain of the vowels. Some amount of *lip rounding* is also of significance in determining the nature of vocal-tract resonance in the formation of some sounds.

While the mouth and throat have been described as a single oropharyngeal resonator, the relationship between these two cavities is not always the same—a fact which has implications for the vocal-tract conditions which underlie the acoustic composition of some of the speech sounds, and of different vocal qualities. The change in the relationship is due primarily to variation in the dimensions of the *faucial isthmus*, which is, for ordinary purposes, the opening between the mouth and pharynx. The size and shape of this opening will depend in part on tongue posture, being smaller if the tongue has been drawn backward, or backward and upward. Also, the folds of tissue which form the sides of the opening, the *anterior* and *posterior faucial arches*, contain muscles which can reduce the aperture in speaking, as well as in swallowing.

The significance of alterations in the relationship between the "front" and "back" cavities of the vocal tract, for which tongue constriction is primarily responsible, has been considerably clarified by the classical studies of Stevens and House (1955). They found it possible to produce vowels with quite good fidelity by controlling only three variables: the *place* of the major tongue constriction in the vocal tract, the *degree* of this constriction, and the *size of the mouth opening*. In other words, the different vowel *spectra* are related principally to the relative sizes of the cavities and to the manner in which they are *coupled*. They also demonstrated (House and Stevens, 1956) that when an additional side-branching *nasal resonator* is coupled to the vocal tract some very conspicuous changes in quality (usually identified as "nasality") and also alterations of the acoustic composition of the sound result. Among the latter, they noted a shift in the first and third resonances and a lowering of the overall intensity of the vowel.

Coupling between the oropharyngeal and nasal resonators is regulated by what is commonly called the *palatopharyngeal* or *velopharyngeal* mechanism. This is a muscle complex which can contract to reduce, or close, the opening behind the soft palate. Note in Figure 4-8 that the soft palate (sometimes called the *velum* or, more properly, the *velum palatinum*) forms the posterior section of the roof of the mouth, separating the mouth cavity from the nasopharynx. When the palatopharyngeal musculature is relaxed, the *nasal port* is open, allowing the nasal and oropharyngeal resonators to be coupled. The nasal port can be partly or completely closed—with consequent alteration of coupling condition—by a sphincterlike muscular action which draws the soft palate upward and backward while certain pharyngeal muscles are simultaneously bringing the posterior wall of the pharynx forward and its lateral walls inward.

The *levator palatini*, paired muscle fibers which run from above and behind on either side to insert in the soft palate about two-thirds of the way back, are mainly responsible for the valving movements of the soft palate. Reduction of the nasal port by throat wall movement is effected by the *superior pharyngeal constrictor* and other muscles of the pharynx. The degree of nasal coupling depends upon the adjustment of the valving musculature. Valving is normally closed, or nearly so, in the formation of all English speech sounds except for the three which are classified as *nasals*.

Coupling of the nasal and oropharyngeal resonators is necessary in forming the nasal sounds, but on others the resulting nasal resonance may become adversely conspicuous. *Hypernasality* due to incomplete palatopharyngeal closure, creating abnormal coupling, is a common functional condition and is a particular problem in cases of cleft palate and paralysis of the palatal musculature. The perceptual correlates of different degrees of coupling are not yet completely understood. Within limits, the greater the size of the opening into the nasopharynx, the more prominent the nasal quality; but the relationship between the area of the opening and the perceived nasality is not linear. For those who may be interested, Curtis (1968) has an excellent review of research related to this and other aspects of coupling.

Consonant Articulation

Having considered the physiological and acoustic bases for the speech sounds which are primarily *resonance phenomena*, we can now turn our attention to the remainder of the English speech sounds. These can loosely be classified as consonants, but in an earlier section were more carefully redefined as the *nonsyllabics*. Sounds in this broad category are further divided into (1) *obstruents*, consisting of the *stops* and *fricatives;* and (2) *sonorants*, which include *nasals*, a *lateral*, and *glides*. The distinctive sounds which fall into each of these classes are shown in Table 3-2.

The physiological characteristic common to all nonsyllabic sounds is that they are produced with relatively close *constriction* at some point in the vocal tract, in contrast to vowels and diphthongs, which are shaped with the vocal tract comparatively "open." While this distinction is oversimplified in ways that will be noted at appropriate points, it will for the moment provide a convenient basis on which to discuss the so-called organs of articulation as they function to produce the nonsyllabic sounds. The *mobile* articulators which act to constrict the vocal tract include the tongue, lips, mandible, and the palatopharyngeal valve described earlier.

The Mobile Articulators

Movements and positionings of the *tongue* play the major role in the shaping for both syllabic and nonsyllabic sounds. The muscles which mediate its amazing flexibility of movement fall into two groups: *intrinsic*, which have their origin and insertion within the tongue itself; and *extrinsic*, which run between the tongue and some other point. The intricate arrangement and interrelationships among these muscles, and the way their actions can be combined, account for the almost unlimited range of fine movements the tongue can make and the variety of configurations into which it can be drawn.

The intrinsic group consists of interspersed fibers of the *longitudinal*, *transverse*, and *verticalis* lingual muscles, each named for the direction in which it runs within the tongue. Because of their arrangement, the body of the tongue can assume a wide range of postures: It can be narrowed and lengthened (transverse muscle); shortened and thickened, and thus arched toward the roof of the mouth (longitudinal muscle); made thinner and wider, and also grooved (verticalis muscle); and otherwise altered in form by a combination of these actions. Longitudinal fibers lying near the upper surface can curl the tongue front upward; similar fibers near the under surface may bring the tongue front downward. To name and describe the extrinsic muscles is unnecessary, but in general they act to extend and retract the tongue as a whole and elevate and depress its middle and back segments.

Certain parts of the tongue are specifically named for purposes of phonetic descriptions, as shown in Figure 4-8. These areas are not set off by distinct anatomic landmarks, but are more in the nature of general designations. The most anterior part of the tongue is its *tip* or *apex;* the successive areas behind this are the *blade, front, middle,* and *back.* The outer edge of the tongue is referred to simply as the *margin.* Its upper surface is the *dorsum,* although it should be noted that some phoneticians use this term to designate what we have chosen to call the *back* of the tongue. Nonsyllabic sounds formed mainly by tongue movement or posture are classified phonetically as *linguals*; if the relationship of the tongue to another structure is critical for the articulation of a sound, the form *lingua* is used for compound descriptive terms, for example, the *linguadentals* or "tongue-teeth" sounds.

Like the tongue, the lips and adjacent facial areas contain complex groups of muscles which need not be described in detail. The principal labial movements in speech are opening, closing, and rounding to various degrees. Sometimes the lips are rounded and pushed forward or *everted*, as in the possible articulation of the word "shoe"; or the corners of the mouth may be drawn back or spread, as in the pronunciation by some speakers of the vowel [i] in "see." The basic class of English consonant sounds which have lip closure or rounding as the essential articulatory feature are *labials* (or *bilabials*). The only compound word needed to identify any of the English labial sounds is *labiodental* ([f] and [v]). If needed for phonetic descriptions, the visible red portion of the lip may be referred to as the *vermilion* or *carmine border*.

As an articulator, the lower jaw, or *mandible*, acts primarily in conjunction with lip and tongue movement, and is operated by muscles of *mastication*, which need not be identified. Closure and opening of the lips during speech is usually assisted by a rise and drop in jaw position. Similarly, mandibular adjustments serve to increase and decrease the size of the mouth opening, which tends to be characteristic for each of the speech sounds, and to maintain appropriate relationships of mouth size to tongue. Note, for example, how the jaw drops progressively in speaking the vowels in the word series "beat," "bit," "bait," "bet," and "bat." Here jaw, tongue, and lip postures combine to establish appropriate relationships for shaping the sounds.

The Fixed Articulators

The hard palate and teeth play a necessary, although passive, role in articulation. The *bony palate* forms the anterior segment of the roof of the mouth, separating the oral cavity from the nasal passages. The anterior two-thirds of the hard palate (approximately) is made up of processes which project inward to the midline from the inner surface of the upper jaw, or *maxilla*. The remaining portion is formed by horizontal plates which are part of the right and left *palate bones*. The muscular soft palate or velum is continuous with the bony palate, forming the remainder of the roof of the oral cavity.

Some part of both the hard and soft palates serves as a point of contact, or near contact, for the tongue in the production of a number of speech sounds. If the constriction is at some point on the hard palate, the sound is classified as a *linguapalatal*. Descriptions can be made somewhat more precise if *back-*, *mid-*, and *front-palate* areas are distinguished. Sounds formed by tongue and soft palate are termed *linguavelars*. Even the pendant *uvula* on the posterior border of the soft palate may be a place of articulation, although this is infrequent in English speech.

As articulatory structures the teeth, upper dental arch, hard palate, and soft palate have two interrelated roles: (1) they present surfaces against which the breath stream can be channeled so as to generate the aperiodic noises of certain consonants, and (2) they provide a framework at the terminus of the vocal tract which the tongue and lips approach, or touch, in creating constriction for the speech sounds. For instance, the constriction [f] is between the under lip and the upper central teeth, usually with these structures in light contact; in making [s] the front of the tongue is held close to a point behind the upper front teeth and gums, leaving only a narrow channel through which the breath stream is forced.

The principal requirement for speech of the fixed articulators is that the dentition in the upper front region of the mouth present a relatively regular, uninterrupted surface against which the breath stream can be reflected and that there be no abnormalities in the architecture of the mouth of such severity as to interfere with either the necessary contacts between the fixed and mobile articulators or formation of the proper kind of breath channel. The part played by missing teeth, dental malocclusions, and maxillary deformities in creating deviant sounds is beyond the scope of our discussion, but a speech defect may result if the conditions mentioned above are not satisfied. There can be some deviation from completely normal anatomic relationships in the mouth without any serious effect on articulation, of course, but individual speakers vary widely in their tolerance.

Some miscellaneous details of anatomy not previously mentioned must be added, inasmuch as they are sometimes involved in phonetic descriptions. The part of the maxilla in which the teeth are rooted is the *alveolus* or *alveolar process;* in phonetic nomenclature the term *alveolar* is often used to designate a place of articulation on the gum ridge just behind the upper front teeth (*incisors*). For example, it is usually in this region that the tonguetip touches in forming [l]; hence this sound can be described as a *lingua-alveolar* (although if the contact were to be made at a different point—possibly the front palate in the case of a particular allophone of [l]—*linguapalatal* would be the correct identification). Roughly synonymous with *alveolar* in this context is *rugal*, although strictly speaking the small ridges called *rugae*, from which the term is derived, lie slightly farther back. Gum tissue is *gingiva*, and occasionally the adjective *gingival* is used in locating a point of articulation.

Summary

Summarizing, this chapter has presented in broad perspective the structure and function of the human speech system, with its three integrated subsystems: (1) *respiratory*, which is the usual source of breath flow for speech; (2) *phonatory*, which generates voice; and (3) *articulation-resonance*, which, by shaping and constricting the vocal tract, molds the outgoing breath stream to give each speech sound its identity and creates a network of differences among them.

Summarizing further, the discussion of the articulation-resonance sub-system sought to explain the fundamental physical characteristics of the speech sounds in relation to the physiological processes through which sounds are articulated. Acoustically, *vowels, diphthongs, nasals, laterals,* and *glides* were found to be *resonance phenomena*, with the identity of each as perceived by a listener depending upon its acoustic composition. Physiologically, con-sonants are produced by constrictions which are generally more radical than those through which the syllabics are shaped. These constrictions are brought about by adjusting the *mobile articulators* in juxtaposition to the *fixed artic-ulators*. Many facts about this latter group of sounds were not presented, being reserved instead for Chapter 5, which will cover the classification of speech sounds and their *distinctive features*.

EXERCISES

1 Following is a partial list of terms introduced in Chapter 4, to which you may wish to add. As before, frame a concise definition:

abdominal breathing	faucial arches
abduction (of vocal folds)	faucial isthmus
adduction (of vocal folds)	formant
alveolar	fricative
alveoli	fundamental frequency
aperiodic	gingival
apex (of tongue)	glide
articulation-resonance system	glottal egressive
back (of tongue)	glottal ingressive
Bernoulli effect	glottis
bilabials	harmonic
blade (of tongue)	Hz (Hertz)
bony palate	intensity
buccal cavity	loudness
carmine border (of lip)	labials
choanae	larynx
complex periodic motion	lingua-alveolar
cord tone	linguadental
coupling	linguapalatal
diaphragm	linguavelar
diaphragmatic breathing	mandible
dorsum (of tongue)	nares
epiglottis	nasalization

nasal resonator
obstruent
oropharyngeal resonator
oropharynx
palatopharyngeal valve
partial vibrations
periodic vibration
peripheral speech mechanism
pharynx
pitch
pressure consonants
pulmonic egressive
pulmonic ingressive
quality
resonance
resonance system

respiratory system
sonorant
sound spectrogram
stop
thoracic cavity
trachea
upper respiratory tract
velopharyngeal mechanism
velum (velum palatinum)
vermilion border
vocal folds
vocal process
vocal ligament
vocal tract
voiced

2   A number of direct observations may help you understand the discussion of
    respiration:
    a   Stand erect, preferably in front of a mirror; place your left hand on the lower
        border of your ribs somewhat to the side and your right hand on the center
        of the abdominal wall just below the ribs. Inhale as deeply as you can com-
        fortably and then exhale; repeat slowly 10 times, noting movements of the
        chest and abdominal wall. If you are average, the chest will rise and expand
        during inhalation while at the same time the abdominal wall will move out-
        ward to make room for viscera displaced by the descending diaphragm.
        During exhalation the opposite will occur: The ribs will drop while the
        abdominal wall moves inward. If your breathing does not fit this pattern,
        make an opportunity to observe the movements when you are "out of
        breath" after vigorous exercise. Also, try to breathe with chest movement
        only, then with abdominal wall movement only. (Rest for a time if you begin
        to feel dizzy while doing the first part of this exercise.)
    b   Take the same position as directed above. Take a "normal" breath and
        count aloud as though speaking to someone 20 feet away, noting the chest
        and abdominal wall movements. Next, repeat aloud several sentences from
        poetry or prose you may have memorized (or count aloud to 100), again
        noting the movements as you exhale and inhale during speech. See how high
        you can count comfortably on an ordinary inhalation, then how much higher
        if you completely exhaust your air supply. Make the same observation after
        inhaling as deeply as possible.
3   Several facts about the phonatory mechanism can be fixed in your mind by
    observation. As you do this exercise, keep the text open to Figure 4-5. Place the
    tip of your forefinger on your "Adam's apple"; this is the apex of the thyroid
    cartilage. Above, a notch can be felt in the thyroid cartilage, and above this,
    the hyoid bone (the notch and hyoid forming a kind of inverted triangle). Some
    distance below the apex of the thyroid can be felt the lower border of the thyroid
    cartilage and below this the "ring" of the cricoid cartilage, and still lower, the

upper ring of the trachea. (It helps to tilt your head back slightly for these latter observations.) Next, with your head in a normal position and your finger on the apex of the thyroid, phonate the vowel *ah* at your usual pitch; now glide upward in pitch as high as you can, then downward as far as you can, noting how the larynx rises and falls. Compare these movements with those the thyroid makes when you swallow. With your finger in the slight depression between the lower border of the thyroid and the ring of the cricoid, glide from a very low to a very high pitch, observing how these cartilages move together as you do so; this is part of the pitch change mechanism and reflects the manner in which tension is placed upon the vocal folds.

4 Early phoneticians were able to arrive at fairly accurate descriptions of articulation using only their own unaided senses; here are some of the simple but instructive kinds of observations you can make of speech sound production:

a Although you may think you are familiar with the features of your mouth, use a mirror and flashlight to examine this part of your vocal tract with care, consulting the illustrations in this book as you do so. Note particularly the appearance of the alveolar ridge, hard and soft palates, faucial arches, and tongue.

b While looking into a mirror, try all the speech sounds in order to observe tongue position or movement wherever this can be seen. (It will help to open your mouth a bit wider than usual on many sounds.) Which sounds can be observed at least fairly well this way?

c Make a specific note of lip position and movement in the same way. Pay particular attention to the lip position for vowel sounds. Learn what you can about the significance of lip position in vowel articulation by trying to produce them without lip or jaw movement. (Bite down on a match stick and freeze your lips in a smile in order to do this.)

d Another aid to learning something about the articulatory postures for speech sounds may be to feel tongue positions with your forefinger (preferably clean). As best you can, feel the tongue position for each of the vowels; note the front vowel–back vowel differences, tongue height and jaw opening, tense-lax differences, and other such details. Study as many of the consonant sounds as you can by this method.

e Combining all these methods of observation (listening, watching, feeling with the finger, and sensing position and movement by kinesthetic cues), review all the sounds for the purpose of detecting as many of their features as possible, for instance, voiced-voiceless, vowel-consonant, stop-fricative, and weak-strong contrasts; point of contact for consonants; tightness of constriction; and so on.

f As an interesting experiment which may help you to realize the significance of movement in articulation and also give you an appreciation of the possible importance of visual cues in understanding speech, try a speech-reading (lip-reading) project. With the cooperation of a friend, arrange a situation where the speaker can be seen but not heard (through a window, with the speaker at a sufficient distance to be inaudible, with your ears stopped, or with the speaker whispering or talking silently, taking care not to exaggerate movements). Recite syllable lists, word lists, and test sentences, and give commands ("Close your eyes" and so on). Which sounds can be most easily read? Which are most likely to be confused? What speech features appear to facilitate speech reading? You may be surprised at how well you can understand on the basis of visual cues.

5 The operation of the palatopharyngeal valve, which is a major factor in determining the nasal versus nonnasal feature of speech, can be observed quite readily. Using a flashlight and mirror, first study again the appearance of the hard and soft palates, and note the relation of the soft palate to the back wall of the throat. With the mouth open, alternate rather vigorous exhalations through the mouth and nose; several times try producing *ah* normally, then "through the nose" or with a great deal of nasal resonance. It should also be possible to move your soft palate voluntarily, by simulating a kind of "gag" if necessary. To get a better view, the tongue can be held somewhat forward; take hold of the tip with a square of gauze or a clean washcloth. It is easier to make these observations on another person, if you have a friend who is willing.

Chapter 5

Speech Sounds: Classification and Description; Distinctive Feature Systems

Having reviewed the anatomical, physiological, and acoustic backgrounds for speech, we are now prepared to turn more specifically in this chapter to certain fundamental characteristics of the speech sounds themselves. We shall first consider the classification, or *taxonomy*, of speech sounds, learning that they are traditionally grouped on the basis of (1) *articulatory type*, or the manner of their production, and (2) *articulatory place*, or the area of the vocal tract where the critical constriction occurs. We will next familiarize ourselves with *distinctive feature systems*, which have important implications for phonetic theory and also provide a basis on which to make detailed analyses of the sounds of speech.

ARTICULATORY TYPES

The broad classification of sounds according to *articulatory type* is indicated by the headings under which the sounds of American speech are grouped in Table 3-2, which should be examined carefully in connection with this section. As will be noted, there are two broad divisions: (1) *syllabics*, which include *vowels*, *diphthongs*, and *syllabic consonants*; and (2) *nonsyllabics*, which are of two types: (a) *obstruent consonants*, consisting of *stops* and *fricatives*, and (b) *sonorant consonants*, which are the *nasals*, *glides* and a single *lateral*. Because they may be used by American speakers, two additional articulatory possibilities called *flaps* and *trills* will be mentioned, although they are not distinctive sounds in General American speech. The characteristics of these articulatory types are covered in the following paragraphs, but additional comments applicable to individual sounds will be found when each is described in Part Two.

Vowel Production

From earlier sections it will be recalled that vowels are *resonance phenomena*; that there are usually two or more frequency regions, or *formants*, which carry a significant proportion of the total energy for each of the vowel phonemes; and that the acoustic spectrum for each vowel is determined by vocal-tract resonance. Vowel production is thus accomplished by tuning the vocal resonance system differentially for the various vowels. This tuning should be visualized as an adjustment of the *total* cavity system, and may even include typical variations in the laryngeal sound source for each of the vowels.

Because the vocal tract is so highly adjustable, the number of possible allophones in any of the vowel phonemes is in theory almost unlimited— and the number each of us uses in actual practice is undoubtedly large. Each small gradation in vowel quality implies some change in vocal-tract configuration. Nevertheless, there is still a degree of uniformity in the tongue, lip, and jaw positions which play a major role in determining vowel resonances. The three articulatory features of greatest importance in English vowel production are (1) *tongue height*, or the closeness of vocal-tract constriction; (2) *tongue fronting*, or the place of constriction within the mouth cavity; and (3) the nature of the vocal-tract opening as determined by the degree of lip *rounding* or *protrusion*, or their absence.

These three parameters of vowel articulation can be combined into *vowel diagrams* of the type shown in Figure 5-1. Although purely schematic, such charts as this are handy learning devices. The *place of constriction*, or the extent of *tongue fronting*, is noted by dividing the vowel phonemes into *front-*, *mid-* or *central-*, and *back-vowel* series. *Tongue height*, or the closeness of constriction, is shown by the location of the sound on the vertical plane of the diagram. Although a bit cumbersome, verbal designations of tongue height for the front vowels are [i] high-front, [ɪ] lower high-front, [e] higher mid-front, [ɛ] lower mid-front, and [æ] low-front. Corresponding descriptions for the back vowels are [u] high-back; [ʊ] lower high-back; [o] mid-back; [ɔ] higher low-back; and [ɑ] low-back, Lip rounding is not consistent among American speakers (and in fact is not indispensable to accurate production

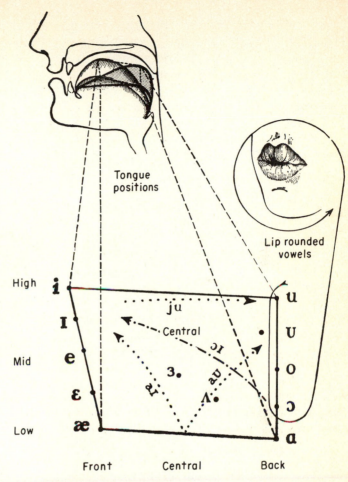

Figure 5-1 The vowel diagram and its derivation. Locations are approximate only. Arrows indicate the general direction (although not necessarily the extent) of the movement for some diphthongs.

of any vowel), but the only phonemes which normally show this feature are, from least to greatest degree of rounding [ʊ], [ɔ], [o], and [u].

It should be stressed again that the vowel diagram is schematic only, and should not be taken as representing articulation features with exactness. In Figure 5-2, however, are shown tracings of x-ray views of the articulators in the target position for the production of seven different vowels. To clarify the differences in configuration among them, they are presented in contrasting pairs. In addition to studying these tracings, it might help students become better acquainted with the vowel postures if they would watch in a mirror as they produce the sounds, trying to sense tongue position—and even placing a

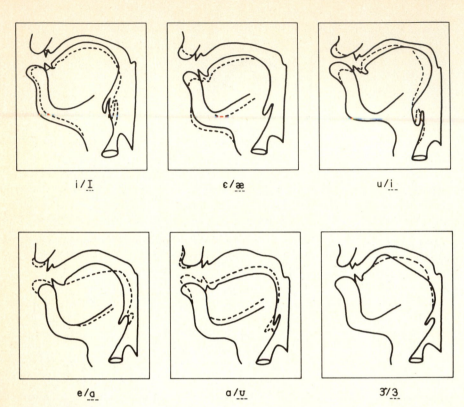

i/ɪ   ɛ/æ   u/i

e/ɑ   ɑ/ʊ   ɝ/ɜ

Figure 5-2 Vocal-tract diagrams showing tongue, lip, and jaw positions for some typical vowel productions. Data taken from x-ray tracings from a number of sources, including Delattre (1968) and Perkell (1969). Two different vowels are shown in each frame to emphasize contrasts in position.

forefinger along the dorsum of the tongue to observe the point of pressure when they shift from one sound to another. Tongue postures may prove easier to sense if the vowels are whispered. Students should also make the front and back vowels a number of times, from low to high and vice versa, to note the progressive (but not equal) steps by which the tongue rises and lowers through each series.

Diphthongs

Sounds classified as *diphthongs* are like vowels in most major respects, except that they have a more prominent *shift* of resonance, usually in the form of an off-glide, within the syllable. This is readily observed in words such as "boy," "how," and "view," if spoken with reasonable stress. Diphthongs can thus be defined as resonance sounds with *complex nuclei*. It follows that a *change* in the adjustment of the vocal tract takes place as diphthongs are uttered. Actually, however, all vowels spoken in context display some fluctuation in resonance, and under this condition there are no completely "pure" vowels. Duration and stress are the major influences which create resonance shifts, as can be illustrated by the way [e] takes on diphthongal traits when it is pronounced as a stressed sound in words such as "play," "weigh," and the like. In contrast, if the sound is of short duration and little stress, such as the [e] in "debris" or [ɪ] in "sit," it comes closest to having an unchanging resonance pattern.

There are differences of opinion about how these phenomena should be accounted for in speech analysis. Some phoneticians regard prominently diphthongized syllables as a combination of vowel-plus-glide, and include no diphthongs in their list of contrasting English sounds. It seems best to us, however, for both theoretical and practical reasons to distinguish four *distinctive diphthongs*: [aɪ] as in "file," [aʊ] as in "house," [ɔɪ] as in "boy," and [ɪʊ] or [ju] as "youth" (the latter ordinarily being an *on-glide* diphthong). Actually, the question as to which is the more defensible way to regard "diphthongs" is largely academic if one is interested mainly in the articulatory features of complex nuclei.

Figure 5-1 showing the vowel diagram also indicates the direction of shift from one vowel target to another for the distinctive diphthongs. As usual, the symbols chosen for these syllabics must be taken as indicating only a reasonable approximation of the blended resonances.

There are reasons why one might prefer either the vowel-plus-glide (for example, [aj]) or the combined vowel symbols (for instance, [ai]) in phonetic transcription. From one point of view logic favors the vowel-plus-glide notation, for the fact is irrefutable that a diphthong has glide features. This is especially true in context, where the off-glide of any diphthong tends to attach itself to a following vowel. In "I owe you," for instance, a *shift* in resonance is better indicated by [a jo ju] or [ajoju] than by [aɪ o ju], as we shall see in Chapter 6. On the other hand, the use of a vowel rather than glide symbol makes it possible to indicate in close transcription more detail about the glide target. For instance, "cow" might be variously pronounced [kau], [kaʊ], or [kao].

The fact that a ligature must occasionally be employed to indicate that two symbols stand for a diphthong rather than successive vowels is a small price to pay for the added fidelity with which the diphthong resonances are identified. In broad transcription, and when the glide has clearly taken on the function of an initiating consonant, there can be no objection to the use of a vowel-plus-glide notation. To be consistent, we have employed mainly the vowel-vowel symbolization in this text.

Consonant Production

As we shall say repeatedly, it is the fundamentally "pulselike," open-closed-open, succession of vocal-tract movements which establishes the most basic of all speech sound distinctions: *syllabic* versus *nonsyllabic*. Vowels are essentially *open* vocal-tract sounds; consonants or nonsyllabics are essentially ways in which the vocal tract is *constricted* to produce the syllabic pulses of speech. Descriptions of the consonants, therefore, are in fact specifications of the ways in which vowel sounds are started and stopped.

Obstruents: Stops and Fricatives

In manner of articulation, *obstruents* are produced with close constriction of the vocal tract, a respect in which they differ from the *sonorants*, which are made with a relatively open vocal tract. Functioning as syllable boundaries, obstruents mark a considerable drop in acoustic energy compared with that of the syllable peak. They are either *voiced* (*sonant*) or *voiceless* (*surd, unvoiced, whispered*), although voicing, when present, varies in amount with circumstances. Fricatives and stops, except for the glottal stop, can be arranged into pairs of *homophones*, which are sounds made with approximately the same articulation movements but contrasting in part on the basis of being voiced or voiceless. The pairs of homophones (with the voiceless sound first in each case) are [p]-[b], [t]-[d], [k]-[g], [f]-[v], [θ]-[ð], [s]-[z], [ʃ]-[ʒ], and [tʃ]-[dʒ].

Stops: [t]-[d], [k]-[g], [p]-[b],]tʃ]-[dʒ], [ʔ]   The central feature in the articulation of stops is a complete occlusion of the vocal tract, a cessation of breath flow, and a marked rise in breath pressure behind the point of constriction. Although stops are brief in duration and are made with continuous movements, three stages in their articulation can be distinguished: (1) the *implosion* or *fore-glide* movements leading to an occlusion; (2) a momentary *hold* in this posture; and (3) a *release* (alternatively called an *off-glide* or *after-glide*) whose nature varies with phonetic circumstances. To illustrate, in pronouncing [k] as in "keep" one can note first an upward movement of the tongue toward the roof of the mouth (*fore-glide*); next is a momentary *hold*, with the tongue in linguavelar contact, after which the tongue breaks contact, permitting a *release* of the briefly impounded air. Stop articulation is also described sometimes as consisting of *implosive* and *plosive* stages.

Mode of release determines some of the more important variations among stops. They are often *aspirated*, meaning that breath under relatively high pressure is released with an audible "puff." There are two possible sources for this noise: turbulences at the glottis which produce an "*h*-like" sound; and turbulences generated as the breath rushes through the aperture created by release of the articulatory constriction. Sounds with prominent audible release may be called *plosives* or *plosive stops*. Initial stops in stressed syllables in English words are regularly aspirated, as in "too" and "pay," but stops may also be aspirated under other phonetic conditions. The term *fortis* is sometimes applied to strong release. Prominent aspiration can, if desired, be noted in transcription by adding a small superscript *h*; for example, "pooh" might be set down as [p^{h}u]. If the breath release is weak (*lenis*), the stop may be *unaspirated*, or essentially without audible noise. Examples might be the common stop pronunciations in words such as "spot" and "cigar." Finally, stops may be *unreleased* when the break in contact is obscure. For instance, if words such as "up," "top," "back," and "hat" are spoken with an appreciable pause after each, there is a tendency for the articulators to remain briefly in the hold posture for the final stop.

An important form of release is *affrication*. In this case the release noise is produced at the point of articulatory constriction as a result of air escaping through a narrow opening under high pressure. Affricate release is sometimes indicated by the superscript symbol [']. When this form of release is among the important features of the stop, it can sometimes be noted by combining appropriate stop and fricative symbols such as [dz] and [ts]. The audible sound of fortis stops in English may be generated at both the point of articulation and the glottis, a phonetic characteristic which can be indicated by either the superscript *h* or ' symbols or both. Forgetting *suction stops*, which are not standard sounds in English, there are three characteristics which may be present in stops: (1) an abrupt onset of acoustic energy, or *plosion*; (2) a release of air through the glottis as the sound source, or *aspiration*; and (3) a release of air through the consonant constriction, or *affrication*.

Although only two English stops, [tʃ] and [dʒ], are always affricate, any stop followed by a fricative tends to have this form of release, as is the case with the *ts* cluster in words such as "pots" and "cuts." One should not be misled by the digraph form of the symbols [tʃ] and [dʒ] into supposing that the sounds indicated are combinations of an apical alveolar stop and a palatal fricative. Linguistically, physiologically, and acoustically these affricates are phone units. Thus some phoneticians have chosen single symbols, most often [č] and [ĵ], for the unvoiced and voiced palatal affricates. Others, including the authors, continue to follow IPA usage. Although not a major consideration, the digraph may possibly have some value in calling attention to the especially strong fricative release which is an essential feature of these palatals in English.

Phenomena peculiar to the *juncture*, or joining, of consonant sounds are discussed in Chapter 6, but certain features of combined consonants are of interest at this point. When consonants are doubled, as in the [k] in "black cat" or [m] in "Sam might," there are not two separate consonant releases. Instead, there is only a fore-glide, a hold, and an off-glide; the hold, however, may be considerably greater than it would have been for the production of a single sound. When two different stops occur in sequence, as do [k] and [t] in "black tomcat," there will normally be a fore-glide to the [k] position, then a hold during which the tongue shifts to the [t] contact, followed by an off-glide from the latter position. Sounds adjacent to stops may determine the manner of their release. For instance, in the phrases "stop me" or "stop now" the [p] may be released as a nasal, or as a glottal-plus-nasal, but usually no labial plosive release is heard; on the other hand, there usually is a definite plosive release of (p) when the phrase "stop and" is spoken, and in analogous situations.

To the eight distinctive stops of English listed in Table 3-2 has been added the *glottal stop* [ʔ]. Although not a contrastive phoneme, its inclusion seems justified by the frequency of its occurrence in English, particularly in certain dialects. The sound has major features of a stop, but is produced by a closure of the glottis, rather than at one of the points of articulation to be mentioned in the next section. In some dialects, it quite regularly replaces [t] in words such as "little," "bottle," and "dental." It also appears often in standard American English, for example in such contexts as the exclamations "oh, oh!" [ʔoʔo] and "huh uh" [hʌʔʌ].

Not included in Table 3-2 is another stop form, the *flap*, which is also common in much American speech. A flap is often the medial sound in words such as "water," "butter," "atom," "idiot," and so on. In these illustrative words the flap consists of a single "tap" or "bounce" at the point of articulation, rather than a hold; breath flow is interrupted, but not occluded to the point where pressure rises high enough for an audible aspirate release. Airflow acting on an elastic, flexible tonguetip probably accounts for the articulatory mechanics of such sounds. Somewhat similar are *trills*, which can be regarded as *intermittent stops*. These are not unusual in British English, but are largely absent from American speech. In manner of articulation, trills are essentially a series of rapid flaps of the order of about 20 per second. Examples of trills which may be familiar are those produced labially (a Bronx cheer!), with the tonguetip (creating a "whirring" or "purring" sound), and with the uvula. The lingua-alveolar and uvular trills are the most common. All English stops are of the *egressive* type, which is to say that the breath stream flows outward, but they may be produced with alternative modes of initiation in other languages, and occasionally in unusual forms of English utterance.[1]

Much of the foregoing information about stop articulation has immediate applications for the speech pathologist and teacher. For instance, a major problem of the cleft palate speaker may be production of defective stops because of a poorly functioning palatopharyngeal valve. Pressure levels needed for intelligible stop production are often overestimated, however. In normal English, stops are often unreleased or unaspirated. Recognition of these facts about stop articulation should prevent, in remedial training, counterproductive emphasis on attempts to develop higher levels of oral

---

[1] For a more extensive discussion of non-English stop forms see Heffner (1952).

pressure than are actually required. Subtle foreign dialect variations often center in part around relatively slight deviations from English patterns in point of contact or manner of release.

Fricatives: [f]-[v], [θ]-[ð], [s]-[z], [ʃ]-[ʒ], [h] Fricative articulation is accomplished by forcing a voiceless or voiced breath stream through a relatively narrow constriction in the vocal tract. The resulting "hissing" or "hishing" may be either a somewhat "diffuse" friction noise generated as the airstream passes along soft and hard surfaces at the point of constriction, as with [f]; or it may be a sound of more strident quality created by directing a more concentrated jet of air against hard palate and dental surfaces, as is the case in [s] articulation. Some phoneticians take cognizance of this difference by classifying [f], [v], [θ], and [ð] as *fricatives* and the more strident [s], [z], [ʃ], and [ʒ] as *sibilants*.

In manner of articulation, the movement sequence for fricatives is broadly the same as for stops: a fore-glide, hold, and release. No absolute generalities are possible to cover all phonetic contingencies, but the nature of fricatives is such that the hold is likely to be of relatively greater duration than it is in stop production. Physiologically, the length of the constriction area in the vocal tract varies considerably. Fricatives such as [f] and [θ] tend to have what is essentially a broad but limited point of constriction formed by the lower lip and teeth and the tongue and teeth, respectively, in the case of these two sounds. Others such as [ʃ] are produced with a more open broad channel along a greater length of constriction, in this instance between the tongue and palate. The term *distributed* is sometimes applied to sounds made in this manner. Sounds such as [s] are occasionally termed *concentrated*, since the jet of air is forced through a relatively narrow channel. The unique characteristics of the fricative [h] are reserved for explanation when sounds in this phoneme are discussed in Part Two.

The acoustic properties of fricatives are of interest in several respects. As mentioned before, consonants in general have lower energy values than vowels, and this observation applies particularly to some fricatives. For example, [θ] is the weakest of the English phones. Their low level of acoustic power explains why sounds in the fricative class, notably the *surds*, are in general the most difficult of all sounds for the normal listener to discriminate and are also among the sounds most likely to be misheard by persons with the commonest types of hearing loss. Acoustically, all voiceless fricatives consist of aperiodic vibrations whose energy tends to be dispersed in frequency bands above 2,000 Hz, with energy concentrations up to 8,000 Hz in the case of [s]. These are sometimes grouped as the *high-frequency* sounds. Voiced fricatives, however, because they *are* voiced, take on some of the characteristics of resonance sounds. Inability to hear high frequencies will, however, have a potential effect on their discrimination. The aperiodic noise element tends to be weaker in voiced consonants than in those which are voiceless.

These acoustic characteristics of fricatives explain in part, although not entirely, why they are so often involved in communication problems. A good many of the developmental articulation errors of children termed *infantile speech* reflect confusions among difficult-to-discriminate fricatives. The common infantile sound substitution [f] for [θ] ("fink" for "think") illustrates the point. Even relatively mild hearing losses during the child's early developmental period may interfere with accurate perception of the sounds and thus cause articulation errors. Among persons with acquired hearing loss, particularly when sensitivity to the higher frequencies is reduced, mishearing of fricative sounds is a particular problem. Structural deviations of the vocal tract in the mouth region are also much more likely to interfere with fricative articulation, especially sibilants, than with the production of vowels and other consonants.

Sonorant Consonants: Nasals, Lateral, and Glides

Acoustically and in manner of production, the *sonorants* lie somewhere between vowels and the obstruent consonants; they are, in fact, sometimes called *semivowels*. All are produced with a degree of vocal-tract constriction greater than that of adjoining vowels; they function most frequently as non-syllabics to form syllable boundaries and in these major respects have the characteristics of consonants. On the other hand, as the term *sonorant* suggests, resonance is a prominent feature of sounds in this class, and in this respect they are like vowels; indeed, some of the sonorants are at times syllabic. Only one or two exceptions to these general remarks, touching mainly on the glides, will need to be mentioned when the sounds are discussed individually.

Nasals: [m], [n], and [ŋ]; Lateral: [l]   Most of the essential acoustic information about *nasals* was covered in an earlier section (pages 84–87). As to manner of production of sounds in this class, the vocal tract is occluded either at the lips or within the mouth, but the soft palate is relaxed, allowing resonance in the nasopharynx and nasal passages. Although the vocal tract is blocked at one point, the breath stream flows outward through what has been called a *secondary aperture* consisting of the palatopharyngeal port leading to the nasal airway. Acoustically, the physical conditions which impart the perceived nasal quality to these sounds are sometimes referred to as *cul de sac* resonance, where a relatively small cavity, the nasal resonator, is coupled to a larger cavity, the oropharyngeal resonator. Some of the complexities of such resonance conditions are covered by Curtis (1968). The circumstances under which the nasals become syllabic have already been touched on briefly, but will be explained in greater detail in Part Two.

English has a single *lateral*, [l]. It is so designated because in its production the tonguetip touches in the general region of the anterior palate, but the voiced breath stream is allowed to flow laterally and outward over the sides of the tongue. Resonance quality provides the cues for recognition of the sound, although—as with all consonants—transitional movements to and from the target position are of great importance for its perception. In a syllable boundary position the movements toward and away from the point of articulation are prominent, leading some phoneticians to classify [l] as a glide.

Glides [w], [hw], [j], and [r]   Sounds of this type are called *glides* because only the movement *toward* or *away from* closure—not the closure itself —is the central feature of their articulation. In a syllable-initiating position, they function as *on-glides*; in a syllable-terminating position, as *off-glides*. In one sense, all consonants have the characteristics of glides inasmuch as they are produced with movements toward a point of articulation, a hold, and a movement away from the constriction, that is, a *fore-glide*, hold, and *off-glide*. The distinguishing characteristic of sounds classed as glides is that they are distinctive only by reason of their particular movement pattern; there is no hold. Some comments about possible fricative properties of certain glides will be made at a later point.

PLACE OF ARTICULATION

It is conventional to classify speech sounds according to their *place of articulation*, or the point or area along the vocal tract where the principal constriction occurs during their production. While a description of this kind provides at best only broad information about articulatory adjustments, it is nevertheless a useful device provided one recognizes its limitations. A place of articulation can be specified for vowels in terms of *tongue fronting* as mentioned in the previous section, but the concept is applied more often to the nonsyllabics. The IPA chart illustrates one way in which fronting or place of articulation is used as a primary feature classification (see Figure 5-3).

Possible points of articulation within the oral and pharyngeal cavities are numerous. Those which appear sufficient to describe most languages of the world are these: tonguetip in contact with lips, teeth, alveolar ridge, or hard palate; and tongue blade or dorsum in contact with hard palate, soft palate, uvula, or a pharyngeal area. Normally not all of these are employed in the production of English, but each is characteristic of sounds in some language —and of some English sounds under unusual conditions. *Nareal* articulation in the form of a nonstandard nasal fricative "snort" may be heard occasionally, particularly among cleft palate speakers and others with poor function of the palatopharyngeal valve. In *glottal* articulation it is the vocal folds

	Bi-labial	Labio-dental	Dental and Alveolar	Retroflex	Palato-alveolar	Alveolo-palatal	Palatal	Velar	Uvular	Pharyngal	Glottal
CONSONANTS											
Plosive	p b		t d	ʈ ɖ			c ɟ	k g	q ɢ		ʔ
Nasal	m	ɱ	n	ɳ			ɲ	ŋ	ɴ		
Lateral Fricative			ɬ ɮ								
Lateral Non-fricative			l	ɭ			ʎ				
Rolled			r						ʀ		
Flapped			ɾ	ɽ					ʀ		
Fricative	ɸ β	f v	θ ð s z	ʂ ʐ	ʃ ʒ	ɕ ʑ	ç ʝ	x ɣ	χ ʁ	ħ ʕ	h ɦ
Frictionless Continuants and Semi-vowels	w ɥ	ʋ	ɹ				j (ɥ)	(w)	ʁ		

	Front	Central	Back	
VOWELS				
Close	i y	ɨ ʉ	ɯ u	(y u ʉ) (ʏ ʊ)
	ɪ ʏ		ʊ	
Half-close	e ø	ɘ	ɤ o	(ø o)
		ɜ	ɤ*	
Half-open	ɛ œ	ɜ	ʌ ɔ	(œ ɔ)
	æ	ɐ		
Open	a		ɑ ɒ	(ɒ)

Secondary articulations are shown by symbols in brackets.   * The symbol ɥ is used in this book for unrounded u.

OTHER SOUNDS.—Palatalized consonants: ṭ, ḍ, etc.; palatalized ʃ, ʒ; ɕ, ʑ. Velarized or pharyngalized consonants: ɫ, d̴, z̴, etc. Ejective consonants (with simultaneous glottal stop): p', t', etc.   Implosive voiced consonants: ɓ, ɗ, etc.   ɼ fricative trill.   σ, ƍ (labialized θ, ð, or s, z).   ʅ, ʓ (labialized ʃ, ʒ).   ʇ, ʗ, ʖ (clicks, Zulu c, q, x).   ɺ (a sound between r and l).   ŋ Japanese syllabic nasal.   ʮ (combination of x and ʃ).   ʍ (voiceless w).   ɿ, ʅ, ʮ (lowered varieties of i, y, u).   ɜ (a variety of ə).   ə (a vowel between ø and o).

Affricates are normally represented by groups of two consonants (ts, tʃ, dʒ, etc.), but, when necessary, ligatures are used (ts, tʃ, dʒ, etc.), or the marks ‿ or ͡ (t͡s or t͡ʃ, etc.).   ͡ also denote synchronic articulation (m͡ŋ = simultaneous m and ŋ).   c, ɟ may occasionally be used in place of tʃ, dʒ, and ʒ, ʓ for ts, dz.   Aspirated plosives: ph, th, etc.   r-coloured vowels: ɛɹ, aɹ, ɑɹ, etc., or ɛ¹, a¹, ɔ¹, etc., or ɚ, ɐ, etc.; r-coloured ə : ɚ or ɐ¹ or ɹ or ɜ.

LENGTH, STRESS, PITCH.— ː (full length).   · (half length).   ˈ (stress, placed at beginning of the stressed syllable).   ˌ (secondary stress).   ˉ (high level pitch); ˍ (low level); ´ (high rising); ˏ (low rising); ` (high falling); ˎ (low falling); ˆ (rise-fall); ˇ (fall-rise).

MODIFIERS.— ˜ nasality.   ˳ breath (l̥ = breathed l).   ˬ voice (s̬ = z).   ʻ slight aspiration following p, t, etc.   ˷ labialization (n̫ = labialized n).   ̪ dental articulation (t̪ = dental t).   ˛ palatalization (z̧ = ʒ).   ˕ specially close vowel (e̝ = a very close e).   ˔ specially open vowel (e̞ = a rather open e).   ˔ tongue raised (e˔ or e̝ = ẹ).   ˕ tongue lowered (e˕ or e̞ = ẹ).   ˖ tongue advanced (u˖ or u̟ = an advanced u, t̟ = t̠).   ˗ or ˍ tongue retracted (i̠ or ɨ = ï, t̠ = alveolar t).   ˒ lips more rounded.   ˓ lips more spread. Central vowels: ï (= ɨ), ü (= ʉ), ë (= ə), ö (= ɵ), ɛ̈, ɔ̈.   (e.g. n̩) syllabic consonant.   ˆ consonantal vowel.   ʃ variety of ʃ resembling s, etc.

Figure 5-3   The International Phonetic Alphabet. (By permission of the International Phonetic Association.)

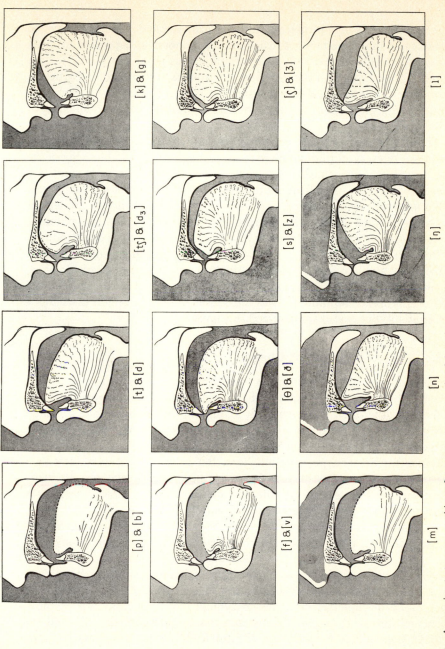

Figure 5-4 Approximate tongue positions for consonant sounds of American English.

whose adjustments may produce a stop or fricative sound. Finally, it must be kept in mind that simultaneous articulations are possible, especially in rapid contextual speech. An example is the simultaneous nasal and glottal release of "no" [?no]. Figure 5-4 shows stylized anatomical drawings of the articulations of several consonants, indicating the place of articulation for each. Readers are urged to compare these positions with their own articulation of these sounds.

Principles underlying the consonant classification chart are quite simple. In the case of every stop sound there is an essentially complete blocking of the vocal tract by the articulators; constrictions for the *continuant* consonants are created by bringing one of the mobile articulators in contact with only part of the fixed articulator surface, or near to it. This constriction, complete or partial, is specified in anatomical terms or by the use of specialized phonetic nomenclature. A *labiodental* sound ([f] or [v]), for instance, is one produced by lip-teeth constriction; [k] and [g] are *linguavelars*; and so on. Manner of articulation and the voiced-voiceless feature can also be specified; thus, [s] might be described as a *voiceless lingua-alveolar fricative* (or *sibilant*). All the appropriate terminology was introduced in the anatomical discussions in Chapter 4, but is also summarized in Figure 5-3.

A New Vowel-Consonant Chart

There have been numerous attempts to update phonetic charts to give them a sounder physiological and acoustic basis and to make possible the inclusion of features other than those which fit readily into older taxonomic schemes. One of the most logical, rigorous, and comprehensive of these charts has been prepared by Peterson and Shoup (1966). Their proposal is altogether too elaborate for detailed presentation here, but is mentioned as a matter of interest to anyone who may wish to go more extensively into phonetic taxonomy—and to emphasize the incompleteness of simpler schema. A summary of their ideas is presented in Figures 5-5 and 5-6.

The first of these figures specifies what they term *phonetic parameters;* it is an expanded and more rigorous *place-of-articulation* and *manner-of-articulation* chart which undertakes to systematize the physiological attributes of speech. Twelve secondary parameters are recognized, making possible a quite full notation of the physiological characteristics of spoken language. Their phonetic alphabet contains 86 symbols for segments, plus 69 non-segmental, prosodic, and modifying markers. In addition, they devised the matrix shown in Figure 5-6 to show the application of the secondary phonetic parameters to each of the segments of their alphabet. Although necessarily complex, the schema of Peterson and Shoup, once it is understood, provides a very useful display of information about physiological phonetics, and will repay careful study.

PHONETIC PARAMETERS

PRIMARY PARAMETERS

SECONDARY PARAMETERS

LARYNGEAL ACTION

- ○ VOICELESS 3
- △ WHISPERED 3
- ▽ BREATHY 3
- ◇ VOICED 3
- ⋀⋀ LARYNGEALIZED 3
- △ PULSATED 3
- ◁ CONSTRICTED 1
- ⌣ PHONOCONSTRICTED 1
- 2 STOPPED 1

PHARYNX SHAPE

- ⌣ OPEN 3
- ● PHARYNGEALIZED 3

TONGUE SHAPE

- N NATURAL 1
- ⌐ PALATALIZED 1
- ∼ VELARIZED 4

APEX SHAPE

- S SIMPLE 3
- ⋀⋀ RETROFLEXED 6/7

LIP SHAPE

- ⊙ SPREAD 3
- ш UNROUNDED 3
- ω ROUNDED 3

SUPPLEMENTARY NOTATION

- ⊢ ADVANCED 1
- ⊣ RETRACTED 1
- ⊤ ELEVATED 2
- ⊥ DEPRESSED 3
- □ DENTALIZED 3

- 1 = SUPERSCRIPT
- 2 = ABOVE SYMBOL
- 3 = BELOW SYMBOL
- 4 = THROUGH SYMBOL
- 5 = AFTER SYMBOL
- 6 = ATTACHED TO TOP OF SYMBOL
- 7 = ATTACHED TO BASE OF SYMBOL

AIR MECHANISM

- ⋀ PULMONIC 2
- ⋁ GLOTTIC 2
- ▽ VELIC 2
- ◇ GLOTTOPULMONIC 2
- ▽ VELOPULMONIC 2
- ◇ VELOGLOTTIC 2
- ◇ COMBINED 2

AIR DIRECTION

- → EGRESSIVE 3
- ← INGRESSIVE 3

AIR FLOW

- Z ZERO 3
- ⊓ NONFRICTIONAL 3
- ⊤ INTERMEDIATE 3
- X FRICTIONAL 3

AIR PRESSURE

- ⊐ LENIS 3
- π NORMAL 3
- ⊏ FORTIS 3

AIR RELEASE

- C CONTINUED 1
- 6 PHONOASPIRATED 1
- ʰ ASPIRATED 1
- ∪ UNASPIRATED 1
- ⊓ UNEXPLODED 1

GENERAL AIR PATH

- O ORAL 2
- ⌐ CENTRALIZED 1
- ⊶ NASALIZED 2
- ω MONORAL 2

LINGUAL AIR PATH

- ✳ NONLATERAL 1
- ⌒ UNILATERAL 3
- ⌒ BILATERAL 3

HORIZONTAL PLACE OF ARTICULATION

	BILABIAL⁺	UNILABIAL(3)	LINGUADENTAL(4)	ALVEOLAR⁺	PALATAL-1⁺	PALATAL-2⁺	PALATAL-3⁺	PALATAL-4⁺	PALATAL-5⁺	PALATOVELAR⁺	VELAR-1⁺	VELAR-2⁺	UVULAR		
NASAL	m ɯ			n			ɲ				ŋ		N	CLOSED	
STOP(1)	p b			t d			c ɟ				k g		q G	VERY CLOSE	
FLAP	ʙ			ɾ									ʀ	CLOSE	HIGH-3⁺⁺
TRILL(2)	B			r									R		HIGH-2⁺⁺
SIBILANT				s z	ʃ ʒ		ç				x ɣ				HIGH-1⁺⁺
FRICATIVE	ʍ φ β	f v	θ ð				ç ʝ				x ɣ	χ ʁ		MID-2⁺⁺	
SONORANT	w ɥ	ʋ		ɹ l	ɪ y	ɨ ʉ	ɯ				ɯ u			MID-1⁺⁺	
VOWEL					i y	ɨ ʉ	e ø	ɛ œ ɜ ɞ	æ ɐ	ɑ ɒ	ɤ o	ʌ ɔ	ɐ	LOW-3⁺⁺	
											a	a ɒ	ʔ ɦ	PHARYNGEAL⁺⁺	
													Q G 2 2	GLOTTAL	

VERTICAL PLACE OF ARTICULATION

MANNER OF ARTICULATION

(1) PARAMETER VALUES
- | PLOSIVE 1
- ˡ EJECTIVE 1
- ↿ IMPLOSIVE 1
- ⊶ CLICK 1

(2) FRACTIONAL PARAMETER VALUES
- -2 TRILL-2 5
- -3 TRILL-3 5
- -4 TRILL-4 5
- -m TRILL-m 5

(3) PARAMETER VALUES
- ⌐ LABIODENTAL⁺
- ∟ LINGUALABIAL 3⁺

(4) PARAMETER VALUES
- ⌐ INTERDENTAL 3⁺
- DENTAL⁺

⁺ FRACTIONAL PARAMETER VALUES
- < FRONT 1
- ▫ CENTRAL 1
- > BACK 1

⁺⁺ FRACTIONAL PARAMETER VALUES
- ⋀ RAISED 1
- ⌐ CENTERED 1
- ⋁ LOWERED 1

PROSODIC PARAMETERS

PHONETIC DURATION   AVERAGE LARYNGEAL FREQUENCY   AVERAGE SPEECH PRODUCTION POWER

The Physiological Speech Parameters.

Figure 5-5 Phonetic parameter chart of Peterson and Shoup (1966). (By permission of the authors and the *Journal of Speech and Hearing Research*.)

	PULMONIC	EGRESSIVE	NONFRICTIONAL INTERMEDIATE FRICTIONAL	NORMAL	CONTINUED UNASPIRATED	ORAL NONORAL	NONLATERAL BILATERAL	VOICELESS WHISPERED BREATHY VOICED	CONSTRICTED PHONOCONSTRICTED STOPPED	OPEN PHARYNGEALIZED	NATURAL PALATALIZED VELARIZED	SIMPLE RETROFLEXED	UNROUNDED ROUNDED
iɨ ʉ ɯ ɪ ɛ ɜ ə / æ ɐ ʌ ɤ ɑ ɒ / ɐɾ ɑ ʁ / BɾR/ʁɟɐ	•	•	•	•	•	•	•	•		•	•	•	•
yʉ ʏ ɤ ø ʊ œ ɞ ə / ɔ ɔ ɒ	•	•	•	•	•	•	•	•		•	•	•	•
w	•	•	•	•	•	•	•	•		•	•	•	•
ɥ	•	•	•	•	•	•	•	•		•	•	•	•
ʋ ɹ	•	•	•	•	•	•	•	•		•	•	•	•
l	•	•	•	•	•	•	•	•		•	•	•	•
r	•	•	•	•	•	•	•	•		•	•	•	•
j	•	•	•	•	•	•	•	•		•	•	•	•
ʎ	•	•	•	•	•	•	•	•		•	•	•	•
ʍ	•	•	•	•	•	•	•	•		•	•	•	•
ɸ f θ ç x χ/s ʃ	•	•	•	•	•	•	•	•		•	•	•	•
β v ð ɣ ʁ/z ʒ	•	•	•	•	•	•	•	•		•	•	•	•
ħ	•	•	•	•	•	•	•		•	• •		•	•
ʕ	•	•	•	•	•	•	•		• •			•	•
h	•	•	•	•	•	•	•	• •		•	•	•	•
ɦ	•	•	•	•	•	•	•	• •		•	•	•	•
ɕ	•	•	•	•	•	•	•	•		•	•	• •	•
ʑ	•	•	•	•	•	•	•	•		•	•	•	•
ʔ	•	•	•	•	•	•	•		• •			•	•
p t c k q	•	•	•	•	•	•	•	•		•	•	•	•
b d ɟ g ɢ	•	•	•	•	•	•	•	•		•	•	•	•
Q	•	•	•	•	•	•	•		•		• •	•	•
ɢ	•	•	•	•	•	•	•		•		• •	•	•
ʔ	•	•	•	•	•	•	•		• •			•	•
m ɱ n ɲ ŋ N	•	•	•	•	•	•	• •	•		•	•	•	•

Secondary Parameter Values Implicit in the Primary Phonetic Symbols.

Figure 5-6   Secondary phonetic parameter chart of Peterson and Shoup (1966). (By permission of the authors and the *Journal of Speech and Hearing Research*.)

DISTINCTIVE FEATURES

As an approach to the description and analysis of spoken language, distinctive feature theory has gained wide currency in contemporary phonology and general linguistics, and seems also to be coming into increasing use in such applied fields as the correction of communication disorders and language teaching. In broadest outline, the theory holds that (1) the sounds of speech are bundles of *distinctive* articulatory and acoustic *features*, (2) that it is the feature and *not* the phoneme which is the ultimate discrete unit into which speech can be analyzed, and (3) that the recognition of any given speech sound depends on a set of *binary* (either-or) judgments as to the presence or absence of those features which are distinctive to it. A basic goal of linguistic scholars utilizing this approach has been to devise a set of features which would have universal applicability to the analysis of spoken languages. Many of them have also been interested in such important collateral questions as what it is that children learn when they speak and acquire language.

Among the early seekers after a universal set of distinctive features, and certainly the most influential, were Jakobsen, Fant, and Halle, who, in their classical *Preliminaries to Speech Analysis* (1951), made these observations:

> Any minimal distinction carried by the message confronts the listener with a two-choice situation. Within a given language each of these oppositions has a specific property which differentiates it from all others. . . . The choice between the two opposites may be termed a *distinctive feature*. The distinctive features are the ultimate distinctive entities of the language since no one of them can be broken down into smaller linguistic units [p. 3].

There are several points to be made about distinctive features. Regardless of whether or not they are considered the "ultimate" contrasting units of speech, the concept of distinctive features provides a valuable method for the description of speech sounds, and one which goes beyond older systems. The latter have their uses, but they are also wanting in several respects. They suggest that type and place of articulation are of paramount concern, which may or may not be the case, and they fail to make provision for noting characteristics of speech sounds which do not fit conveniently into a three-dimensional *type-place-voicing* classification.

There is no doubt, of course, that phones can be said to have features. If these can be specified, the description, classification, and patterning of speech can be noted with greater validity than would otherwise be possible. As to the status of distinctive feature theory, there is as yet no strong consensus as to whether phonemes or features are the more authentic perceptual units for the analysis of speech. Although the distinctive feature approach to speech analysis is widely followed, there are still great differences in thinking about what is the most valid set of distinctive features, as will be brought out in this section.

The original set of distinctive features proposed by Jakobsen, Fant, and Halle, while no longer commanding the attention once given it by linguists, still has much to tell us about one possible way of conceptualizing the problem of phonetic analysis, in this case on the basis of a set of features which are primarily *acoustic*. The critical choices between language oppositions are to be made, in the view of the authors of the *Preliminaries*, on the basis of the acoustic traits of the speech signal because, they reasoned, what one perceives is an auditory pattern, not a succession of articulatory movements. As they put the matter, "The closer we are in our investigation to the destination of the message (i.e., its perception by the receiver), the more accurately we can gage [*sic*] the information conveyed by its sound shape [p. 12]."

Whether or not such reasoning is completely acceptable is a question we need not discuss here (we think it may not be). The fact remains that acoustically oriented distinctive features were accounted valid in the past by many phoneticians, and are still so regarded by a few. Certainly they are of sufficient importance historically to merit their being understood by students of phonetics; and the thesis that the important characteristics of speech sounds are best described in terms of their acoustic properties must still be given serious consideration. The original set of distinctive features proposed by Jakobsen, Fant, and Halle is therefore given below in a condensed and paraphrased form, presented, as is customary in most distinctive feature systems, as binary choices.[1]

Distinctive Features

As Interpreted from Jakobsen, Fant, and Halle (1951)

Fundamental Source Features
  1 *Vocalic vs. nonvocalic.* This is a feature which helps differentiate vowels from consonants, although it is not identical with the traditional vowel-consonant distinction. Vocalics are sounds which have *well-defined resonance patterns.*
  2 *Consonantal vs. nonconsonantal.* Consonantals are marked by a major drop in vocal energy.

Secondary Consonantal Source Features
  3 *Interrupted vs. continuant.* "The abrupt onset distinguishes the interrupted consonants (stops) from the continuant consonants [p. 21]."
  4 *Checked vs. unchecked.* Checked consonants have an abrupt ter-

---

[1] We will not consider here the reasoning behind the decision to express features in either-or terms, although its merits could be argued on the basis of some theories of perception. The decision was obviously influenced by information theory and by computer language.

mination, such as the glottal stop termination. This is not a distinctive feature in English.

5   *Strident vs. mellow.* Sounds that have irregular wave forms are called strident. This feature distinguishes "noisy" fricatives from sounds which do not have this characteristic.

6   *Voiced vs. voiceless.* Voiced consonants are described as "buzz" phonemes because of a tone generated at the glottal source. The pairs [b]-[p], [d]-[t], and [g]-[k] are opposed in this respect, for example.

Resonance Features

7   *Compact vs. diffuse.* Compact sounds have resonances closer together, giving a more predominant resonance in the central part of the acoustic spectrum. Said to distingish in part [o a ɛ] from [ʊ ʌ ɪ].

8   *Grave vs. acute.* Grave sounds have their predominant energy in the low part of the spectrum, as opposed to the high. This feature helps to distinguish such *grave-acute* sets as [ʊ] and [o] from [ɪ] and [ɛ].

9   *Flat vs. plain.* Flattening, it is said, manifests itself by a downward shift of a set of formants (resonances). Lip-rounded and non-lip-rounded vowels are opposed by this feature.

10 *Sharp vs. plain.* Sharp vowels are those with "a slight rise of the second formant." The acoustic effect is that produced by *palatization.* Not distinctive in English.

11 *Tense vs. lax.* Tense vowels are longer and stronger. Tense consonants are longer and have greater plosive strength. This feature helps distinguish [i] from [ɪ] and [p] from [b], for instance.

12 *Nasal vs. oral.* Nasality is characterized by typical resonances and "antiresonances." Nasal resonance is distinctive only in the case of [m], [n], and [ŋ] in English.

Hardly was the ink dry on the *Preliminaries* before extensive revision was begun on the set of distinctive features postulated by Jakobsen, Fant, and Halle. Their system was, at the outset, widely misunderstood. It was not certain exactly what was meant by a number of the acoustical terms, several sounds did not seem to be uniquely described by the suggested set of features, and it was unclear to many whether the system ought to be used specifically to describe speech sounds, or for labeling more or less abstract categories of decision making which were thought to underlie the process of language discrimination. In retrospect, it seems that the significance of this formulation was not that it took any great step forward in actual information about the properties of speech sounds, but instead that it proposed an important hypothesis about language, and about the kinds of decisions about sound patterns which may be critical for the perception of speech.

More recently, distinctive feature theory and traditional phonetic taxonomy seem to have been drawing closer together. The set of features proposed by Chomsky and Halle (1968), which currently is the most influential and widely accepted, appears to move in this direction. In their book *Sound Patterns of English* these authors make the point that a total set of features is "identical with the set of phonetic properties than can in principle be controlled in speech; they represent the phonetic capabilities of man and, we would assume, are therefore the same for all languages [pp. 294–295]."

With this principle in mind, Chomsky and Halle undertook to sketch a universal and primarily physiologically motivated set of phonetic features adequate to cover all languages. In *Sound Patterns* they arrived at 33 features (including prosodic features), expressed as binary oppositions. Although generally considered an advance over earlier schemes, it still is not altogether easy to interpret some of the Chomsky and Halle features, and certainly they must be regarded as tentative in their nomenclature, completeness, relevance, and validity.

Those features in their system which seem to apply most clearly to English have heavily influenced the distinctive feature system which we describe below. The major departure of the following system from that of Chomsky and Halle is in the use of the opposition *syllabic versus nonsyllabic* in place of their two oppositions *vocalic versus nonvocalic* and *consonantal versus nonconsonantal*. This change is thought to make the Chomsky and Halle schema even more consistent with recent general phonetic theory, and certainly with the usages recommended in this text. The descriptions are not necessarily those of Chomsky and Halle, but have been freely paraphrased and modified to reflect interpretations of the present authors.

Distinctive Features

As Interpreted from Chomsky and Halle (1968)

Major Class Features
1 *Syllabic vs. nonsyllabic*. Syllabics are segments comprising a syllabic peak or "loop" as opposed to a nonsyllabic node or "valley."
2 *Sonorant vs. obstruent*. Sonorants are open vocal-tract sounds, and in English include vowels, nasals, lateral, and glides. Obstruents are produced with vocal-tract constrictions which tend to shut off the airflow, and may produce turbulent noises or affricative releases. This feature characterizes stops and fricatives of English.

Cavity Features
3 *Coronal* vs. *noncoronal*. Sounds having the coronal feature are produced with the tongue blade raised as opposed to sounds where

this is not the case. Coronal sounds in English are the dentals, alveolars, and palatals (but not velars). The sounds [t] and [k] illustrate the coronal vs. noncoronal opposition.

4 *Anterior vs. nonanterior*. Anteriors are produced with the major constriction forward of the palatoalveolar region. In English these are typically the labials, dentals, and alveolars. The sounds [m] and [ŋ] illustrate the anterior vs. nonanterior opposition.

5 *High vs. nonhigh*. This feature applies to the position of the *tongue body*. The feature *high* is defined as indicating that the sound is produced with the tongue raised above a "neutral" position—approximately that of the English [ɜ]. This opposition applies primarily to vowels and some sonorant consonants. The vowels [i] and [e] illustrate the high-nonhigh opposition.

6 *Low vs. nonlow*. Low sounds are those made with the tongue body below the neutral position. Examples of low vowels are [æ], [ʌ], [ɔ], and [ɑ].

7 *Back vs. nonback*. Back sounds are made with the tongue retracted from its neutral position. English back vowels are [ɑ], [ɔ], [o], [ʊ], and [u].

8 *Front vs. nonfront*. This is not among the Chomsky and Halle features. It becomes necessary, it seems to us, in distinguishing most easily the central vowels [ɝ], [ɜ], and [ʌ], which are quite readily defined in terms of a *front vs. nonfront* distinction. There are other ways of handling these oppositions in a system which recognizes only front and back vowels, but not well, we feel.

9 *Rounded vs. nonrounded*. This feature refers to lip rounding or constriction of the lip opening in speech sound production. In typical English speech the lip-rounded vowels are [u], [ʊ], [o], and [ɔ], and consonants are [w] and [hw].

10 *Distributed vs. nondistributed*. Distributed sounds may be defined as those with a constriction which seems to extend for more than an assumed average distance along the vocal tract. Chomsky and Halle do not regard this as a significant feature in English speech. It is included here, however, because it seems to permit a distinction between certain palatal sounds which have a wide area of constriction and others which do not. The sounds [tʃ], [dʒ], [ʃ], and [ʒ] can be considered *distributed*, as opposed, for example, to [t], [d], [s], and [z].

Secondary Aperture Features

11 *Nasal vs. nonnasal*. Nasal sounds, as explained earlier, are made with the palatopharyngeal port sufficiently opened to produce a significant amount of nasal resonance. English nasals are [m], [n],

and [ŋ]. Nasalization may be a characteristic of interest in the production of English vowels, but is not a contrastive feature among vowels in this language.

12 *Lateral vs. nonlateral.* Laterals are produced with the tongue positioned to create a midline obstruction, but allowing for an open lateral airflow path around one or both sides of the tongue. This opposition is significant only for [l] in English, but other languages and variants of English may also have lateralized stops and fricatives.

Manner of Articulation Features

13 *Stop vs. nonstop.* In *Sound Patterns* a related feature is expressed as *continuant vs. noncontinuant.* The opposition is that between articulatory adjustments which effectively block the airstream as earlier described for stops and those which do not. This feature distinguishes between stops and, in general, all *sustainable* consonants and glides.

14 *Tense vs. lax.* Chomsky and Halle describe a tense sound as "a deliberate, accurate, maximally distinct gesture that involves considerable muscular effort [p. 324]." Lax sounds are produced with less effort, greater rapidity, and less audible noise. English vowels for which *tense* may be a feature are [i], [e], [æ], [o], and [u]; consonants are [p], [t], [tʃ], [dʒ], [k], [f], [θ], [s], and [ʃ].

Source Features

15 *Voiced vs. voiceless.* Voiced sounds are usually said to be marked by glottal vibrations of a periodic (tonal) or quasi-periodic type. Voiced English consonants are [b], [d], [dʒ], [g], [v], [ð], [ʒ], [z], [m], [n], [ŋ], [l], [r], [w], and [j]. English vowels are conventionally classified as voiced. However, it is not a significant feature of English vowels, which may be voiced or whispered.

16 *Strident vs. nonstrident.* Strident sounds are characterized by prominent turbulent noise of the kind resulting from a constricted airflow directed against an articulatory obstruction. English strident sounds are usually listed either as [tʃ], [dʒ], [s], and [z] after the usage of Jakobsen, Fant, and Halle, or as [f], [v], [ʃ], [ʒ], [tʃ], [dʒ], [s], and [z], in accordance with the description of Chomsky and Halle (pp. 176–177).

Application of Distinctive Feature Systems

Using for a base the modified Chomsky-Halle features which are applicable to English, we can now turn to the use of the system. First, however, this kind of analysis should be placed in perspective with other methods of describing the sounds of speech. As we earlier noted, *phonemic analysis* limits itself broadly to a specification of the contrastive classes known to occur in the language uttered by a particular speaker; *phonemic transcription* uses an agreed-upon group of symbols to represent these phonemes. *Phonetic analysis* undertakes to identify what the auditor takes to be the segments of an actual utterance; *phonetic transcription*—within the limits of what is desired and what is possible—attempts to record all those details of a speech sample under study which the transcriber perceives to be important. For this purpose the transcriber utilizes an appropriate symbol system such as that of the IPA, together with its modifying marks and symbols for nonsegmental features. Again, phonemic analysis is confined to the enumeration of the contrastive sound categories required of a speaker; phonetic analysis is carried out within the scope of the perceptually distinct categories available to the listener.

Feature analysis proceeds on the assumption that distinctive features are the best units for the analysis of spoken language; phonetic symbols are employed simply as informal abbreviations for feature bundles. In the abstract, distinctive feature analysis leads to a determined list of features presumed to embrace the characteristics of all spoken languages, but not all of which necessarily occur in any one language. Applied to a given language, such as English, distinctive feature analysis particularizes those features thought to be critical in making the decisions necessary for the perception of that language. In what may as well be called *distinctive feature transcription* or *feature transcription*, the transcriber records the features observed in actual samples, or at least those features of interest.

All the theoretical formulations which have been presented up to this point are important, but it will be seen at once that *phonetic analysis transcription* and *feature analysis transcription* have a common goal; they merely proceed from different theoretical assumptions, although even some of these are shared. Both call for the same refined listening skills. Regardless of the analytical and descriptive method, phoneticians need to know the presumed typical characteristics for each of the *canonical* or "standard" sounds of the language with which they are concerned, and they must be able to perceive and describe deviations therefrom which characterize new, unexpected, or nonstandard forms. Thus, phonetic analysis and feature analysis as we have defined them are complementary and overlapping approaches. Anyone interested in applied problems of the kind we have alluded to at several points will find both methods valuable.

Feature Matrices With respect to the specific procedures for distinctive feature analysis, it is customary to present the findings in the form of a matrix, with the phone identified at the head of each column (using IPA symbols in our illustrations) and the features arranged in rows, as in Tables 5-1 and 5-2.

Table 5-1   Feature Matrix for Vowels

Features	Front					Central		Back				
	i	ɪ	e	ɛ	æ	ʌ	ɝ	ɑ	ɔ	o	ʊ	u
Syllabic	+	+	+	+	+	+	+	+	+	+	+	+
Sonorant	+	+	+	+	+	+	+	+	+	+	+	+
High	+	+	−	−	−	−	−	−	−	−	+	+
Low	−	−	−	−	+	+	−	+	+	−	−	−
Back	−	−	−	−	−	−	−	+	+	+	+	+
Front	+	+	+	+	+	−	−	−	−	−	−	−
Rounded	−	−	−	−	−	−	−	−	+	+	+	+
Tense	+	−	+	−	+	−	+	−	−	+	−	+

It is also customary to note the presence or absence of features by entering a plus or minus symbol (+ or −) on each row under the phonetic symbol. Where a feature is redundant, not applicable, or in free variation, the usual practice is either to leave the cell blank or to enter both a plus and minus sign (±). Which course is followed may depend on whether the analysis is meant to specify the distinctive features theoretically attributed to the "idealized" form of the sound or is intended to describe some particular utterance. In the latter case, each feature must obviously have some state, if only neutral, and it is usually desirable to indicate what this is.

Two typical matrices, one for consonants and the other for vowels, are presented in Tables 5-1 and 5-2. Reading the matrix is simple. For example, in the consonant matrix a verbal description based on the features of [ŋ] would be *nonsyllabic, sonorant, noncoronal, nonanterior, high, back, nontense, nonstrident, voiced, nasal*. Lip rounding is not relevant. In contrast, in a *type place-voicing* analysis [ŋ] would be designated as a *linguavelar voiced nasal*. Both types of description will be given for each sound when they are discussed individually in Part Two.

It is easy to lay too much stress on the plus-minus notation, and on the necessity of a matrix form for presenting feature analyses. In strictly phonetic descriptions there is no need to be limited to two-value decisions about the features. As speech is actually uttered, for instance, the lips are capable of more than two postures, *rounded* and *unrounded*. Some features such as *stop versus nonstop* do lend themselves quite well to binary choices, but others such as *high* and *low* do not. Particularly where one is attempting to analyze nonstandard speech forms, such as the misarticulations of defective speech, a flexible methodology for analysis will usually serve best.

Because distinctive feature theory has made substantial contributions in the past and is a promising line of inquiry for the future, distinctive feature analysis has come into wide use. A word of caution to the beginning student of phonetics seems indicated. No set of features proposed up to this date,

Table 5-2 Feature Matrix for Consonants

| | Obstruent | | | | | | | | | | | | | | | | | Sonorant | | | | | | | |
| | Stops | | | | | | | | Fricatives | | | | | | | | | Nasals | | | | Glides | | | |
Features	p	b	t	d	tʃ	dʒ	k	g	f	v	θ	ð	s	z	ʃ	ʒ	h	m	n	ŋ	l	r	w	hw	j
Syllabic	−	−	−	−	−	−	−	−	−	−	−	−	−	−	−	−	−	−	−	−	−	−	−	−	−
Sonorant	−	−	−	−	−	−	−	−	−	−	−	−	−	−	−	−	−	+	+	+	+	+	+	+	+
Coronal	−	−	+	+	+	+	−	−	−	−	+	+	+	+	+	+	−	−	+	−	+	+	−	−	−
Anterior	+	+	+	+	−	−	−	−	+	+	+	+	+	+	−	−	−	+	+	−	+	+	−	−	−
High	−	−	−	−	+	+	+	+	−	−	−	−	−	−	+	+	−	−	−	+	−	−	+	+	+
Low	−	−	−	−	−	−	−	−	−	−	−	−	−	−	−	−	+	−	−	−	−	−	−	−	−
Back	−	−	−	−	−	−	+	+	−	−	−	−	−	−	−	−	−	−	−	+	−	−	+	+	−
Rounded	−	−	−	−	−	−	−	−	−	−	−	−	−	−	−	−	−	−	−	−	−	−	+	+	−
Nasal	−	−	−	−	−	−	−	−	−	−	−	−	−	−	−	−	±	+	+	+	−	−	−	−	−
Lateral	−	−	−	−	−	−	−	−	−	−	−	−	−	−	−	−	−	−	−	−	+	−	−	−	−
Stop	+	+	+	+	+	+	+	+	−	−	−	−	−	−	−	−	−	+	+	+	−	−	−	−	−
Tense	+	−	+	−	+	−	+	−	+	−	+	−	+	−	+	−	−	−	−	−	−	−	−	−	−
Voiced	−	+	−	+	−	+	−	+	−	+	−	+	−	+	−	+	±	+	+	+	+	+	+	−	+
Strident	−	±	−	±	+	+	−	−	+	+	−	−	+	+	+	+	±	−	−	−	−	−	−	−	−

119

either in this text or elsewhere, is guaranteed to be of proven validity or or to constitute the final sought-after universal set. Indeed, on the basis of present information, the probabilities are in the opposite direction. The problem is not so much that the variables of human speech cannot be labeled, but rather that we do not as yet know with any real confidence what are the fundamental decision-making units in either speech production or speech perception.

There are many areas of uncertainty. We are not sure, for instance, whether present feature sets are larger than need be to represent the minimum number required for speech analysis, or whether they are too small to describe accurately the salient facts of speech behavior. Much more needs to be learned about the processing of speech signals before the critical features of speech can be defined. It may well be that new ways will be found to delineate the physiological and acoustic traits which determine speech perception or that new concepts of analysis not now forseen may emerge. For the moment, of course, we must navigate as best we can with the available charts and instruments, making certain that they are used with the greatest skill possible.

As an example of the kinds of changes in feature systems which have been recently proposed, Halle and Stevens (1969) have suggested the features "advanced tongue root" and "constricted pharynx" as replacements for the features "low" and "tense." In their system [u], [i], [o], and [e] would be considered as advanced-tongue-root vowels while [ɔ], [æ] and [ɑ] would be constricted-pharynx vowels. The vowel feature specification which they propose is as follows:

Feature	[u]	[ʊ]	[i]	[ɪ]	[o]	[ɔ]	[e]	[ɛ]	[æ]	[a]	[ʌ]
High	+	+	+	+	−	−	−	−	−	−	−
Back	+	+	−	−	+	+	−	−	−	+	+
Advanced tongue root	+	−	+	−	+	−	+	−	−	−	−
Constricted pharynx	−	−	−	−	−	+	−	−	+	+	−

PRIME FEATURES

Recently Ladefoged (1972, 1975) has suggested that a distinction should be made between phonetic features which are definable in terms of physical phenomena varying along a single continuum (high-low, front-back, for example), and features which are "cover terms" for complex processes which cannot be so measured (for example, coronal and tense). The first, more basic, group of features he terms *primes* or *prime features*.[1] The following is a

[1] For a discussion of the senses in which they are more basic, see Ladefoged (1972).

list of some of those prime features of special interest in the description of English sound patterns, as they are listed by Ladefoged (1972) in *multivalued*, as opposed to *binary* terms. Both the features themselves and the abandonment of the binary notion point, as Ladefoged suggests, to the ease with which "many traditional IPA notions can be adapted for use in current generative phonologies [p. 11]."

> *Voice onset:* voiced, voiceless unaspirated, aspirated
> *Glottal stricture:* creaky voice, stiff voice, voice, slack voice, breathy voice, voiceless
> *Nasality:* oral, nasal
> *Articulatory place:* bilabial, labiodental, dental, alveolar, postalveolar, palatal, velar, uvular, glottal, labial-velar, labial-alveolar
> *Apicality:* apical, laminal
> *Stop:* no closure, closure
> *Fricative:* no turbulence, turbulent airstream
> *Vibration:* no vibration, trill
> *Rate:* ballistic, normal, long, extra long
> *Laterality:* central, lateral
> *Height:* high, mid-high, mid-low, low
> *Backness:* front, central, back
> *Width:* pharyngealized, neutral, advanced tongue root
> *Rounding:* spread lips, neutral lips, rounded lips
> *Sibilance:* no sibilance, high pitch turbulence
> *Gravity:* high-frequency energy, low-frequency energy

As we conclude this chapter, we feel we should emphasize again that systems of phonologic classification, whether on the basis of the feature, phone, phoneme, cognitive category, or some as-yet-unmentioned unit, can be no more complete or valid than our incomplete knowledge of speech behavior will allow. It is possible that before this book is in print some new manner of expressing the fascinating logic of speech production and reception will be suggested. We would venture the guess that the future will see more *dynamic* systems of analysis, perhaps focusing upon the rate, time, and rhythmical characteristics of the speech system. However, one need not wait for the best system before doing anything. Each way of looking at speech behavior has its value, particularly for those who wish primarily to raise their own level of awareness of speech behavior and their understanding of the communications problems and possibilities of those whom they may wish to help.

EXERCISES

1 Following is a partial list of terms from this chapter that should be in your glossary; add others you will need to remember, and frame a concise definition of each:

affrication	homophone
after-glide	intermittent stop
aspirate release	juncture
binary features	lenis
broad channel	nareal
canonical	narrow channel
complex nucleus	off-glide
consonant chart	place of articulation
consonant doubling	plosive
continuant	release
diphthong	rounding
distinctive feature	secondary aperture
distributed channel	semivowel
distributed contact	surd
feature matrix	strength of articulation
flap	tongue fronting
fore-glide	tongue height
fortis	trill
fricative	type of articulation
glide	vowel diagram

2 Add to your glossary definitions of the following proposed distinctive features:

acute	low
anterior	mellow
back	nasal
checked	obstruent
compact	plain
continuant	rounded
coronal	sharp
diffuse	sonorant
distributed	stop
flat	strident
front	syllabic
grave	tense
high	vocalic
lateral	voiced
lax	

3 Construct simplified vowel and consonant charts showing only the major sounds common in your own dialect. Use any system which you believe would be most useful and informative for your purposes.

4 Construct a binary feature matrix for the analysis of "he sings bad" (as pronounced [hi sĭŋz bɛd]). Use the following features: *syllabic, sonorant, high, low back, front, rounded, coronal, anterior, nasal, stop, tense, voiced*, and *strident*.

5 List each English speech sound customarily thought to be in each of the following classes: high vowels, central vowels, low vowels, lax vowels, lip-rounded vowels, fricatives, stops, sonorants, nasals, laterals, glides, trills, glottals, continuants, secondary aperture sounds, coronals, stridents, tense vowels, and tense stops.

6 Compare the feature system of Jakobsen, Fant, and Halle with that adapted from Chomsky and Halle. Attempt to identify in each system (1) the features which are unclear or seemingly illogical; (2) the features which are not consistently either acoustic or physiological within the system. What seem to you to be the strengths and weaknesses of each of the four systems presented in this chapter?

7 For each of the stop consonants of English, attempt to produce the following variants: unreleased stop, plosive release only, aspirate plus affricate release, aspirate release only, affricate release only. When you are ready, try them out on your instructor. Are some of these release mechanisms impossible for certain stops?

Chapter 6

Dynamics of
Articulatory Movements

From previous chapters emerge five fundamental facts about speech:
(1) it is pulselike, or *syllabic*, in nature; (2) the *open* or *closed* state
of the vocal tract during these pulsations forms the basis for the most
important distinctive feature of speech sounds: *syllabic or nonsyllabic
(vowel or consonant)*; (3) in the syllabic pulses of spoken language,
vowels and consonants are inseparably bound together; (4) while
individual speech sounds can and should be described in terms of
their *target positions*, in the dynamic context of ongoing speech
they are better thought of as *movements*; and (5) within such a
context, variation among the sounds within each phoneme, or speech
sound class, is a rule, not the exception.

These generalizations make it clear that the essential nature of
spoken language can be grasped only in terms of the dynamics of
articulatory movements as they are found in ongoing speech, which
is the topic to which we turn in the present chapter. After first examining
certain fundamental characteristics of *speech movements*, we shall
consider next the articulation of speech sounds in context, and finally,
some of the major phonetic features which are unique to ongoing

speech. All facets of speech dynamics are interrelated, but for discussion purposes thay are presented under the following separate headings: (1) *transitions*, (2) *juncture and related phenomena*, (3) *coarticulation*, (4) *assimilation*, (5) *vowel reduction*, (6) *ellipsis*, and (7) *rhythm*.

THE NATURE OF SPEECH MOVEMENTS

As a starting point for exploring the dynamics of articulation, we should become aware that speaking movements, like those of any body part, can be of three primary types: *fixed*, *guided*, and *ballistic*, with the latter predominating in articulation. It will help in our explanations if we mention first that in terms of their function, muscles or muscle groups are designated as opposing *agonists* and *antagonists*. Thus, when we "make a fist," muscles which curl the fingers (*flexors*) are agonists and those which straighten the fingers (*extensors*) are antagonists. With regard to the neural sensory-motor circuits which mediate all types of movement, we can say here only that they are exceedingly complicated and involve every level of the nervous system. One prominent speech disorder, *dysarthria*, results when these circuits are disrupted by accident or disease.

In *fixed* "movement" or positioning, the body part is held in a certain attitude by a suitably equalized contraction of agonist-antagonist muscle groups. So long as one is remaining still, for example, the body is maintained in its position by this mechanism, with the postural muscles in balanced contraction. A simpler example would be the opposing agonist-antagonist action needed to hold the arm raised at shoulder height. To the extent that movable articulators remain for a time in one position, which is actually very little, speech may have fixed movements. If a continuant were to be unusually prolonged, as in the interjection "aaah!" the syllable would be produced with fixed movement.

Many skilled actions are mediated by *guided* movement. Here the agonist muscle actions are controlled by a kind of "governor" function of the antagonists, much as one might use the left hand to guide and steady the right in order to make an exceedingly fine accurate movement. Thus, if you wished to touch a certain word on this page, agonist muscles which extend the arm would come into play, but the pointing movement would be kept on target by a "braking" action of other muscles—with the brain utilizing visual and movement-sense (*kinesthetic*) cues to determine any corrections needed in the direction and extent of arm movement.[1]

Some of the neuromuscular responses in speaking are of the guided type.

[1] For more information about disorders of movement which may affect speech see McDonald and Chance (1964). Additional technical references will be found in their bibliography.

It is generally taught, for instance, that the fine control of the outgoing breath stream during speaking and singing is accomplished by opposed contraction of muscles of inhalation, principally the diaphragm, and those of exhalation, with the latter exerting the greater pressure. Broad pitch and loudness modulations probably fall into this category, as may the movements underlying the shifts in resonance which are a feature of diphthongs. Conceivably syllables which are significantly longer than normal in duration, particularly if they are initiated or terminated by any of the nonsyllabic glides, may also have the characteristics of guided movements.

The third type, *ballistic movement*, predominates in the normal articulation of speech sounds, however, and is the basis for understanding many of the phenomena of connected speech. The nature of ballistic movement can be illustrated by such a movement as flicking water off the fingers after washing one's hands. The action is begun by an abrupt strong contraction of agonist muscles; but once the hands are set in motion, contraction in these muscles subsides. The hands have been "thrown," so to speak—toward no really definite target in this case. A dart player tosses darts toward the bull's eye ballistically; most syllabic pulses are analogous.

Much is yet to be learned about the details of ballistic articulation movements, but speech physiologists agree generally on their major characteristics. The action is started by what Stetson (1951) has called a *beat stroke*, this being a rapid contraction of the agonist muscle complex which propels the movable articulators toward their *articulatory target*.[1] This, of course, is whatever occlusion or constriction is characteristic for the phone in question. The agonist muscle group should be visualized as including those which effect respiratory and phonatory movements, as well as the muscles which act on the tongue, lips, and so on.

Subsequent to the beat stroke, one of several events may follow, depending on the nature of the utterance. The agonist muscles may relax, allowing the articulators to return to their point of rest through the influence of gravity or tissue elasticity; or the articulators may be withdrawn from their target posture by antagonist muscles in an action sometimes called a *back stroke*. Alternatively, the articulators may be arrested at the target position for a momentary hold before releasing. However, when syllables follow one another in rapid succession as they do in speech, the beat stroke of one syllable may overlap the releasing movements of its predecessor in time, a fact related to coarticulation and other phonetic features of connected speech. Because of this overlap, individual segments are fused into uninterrupted articulatory units which do not necessarily correspond to word, phrasal, or sentence divisions.

[1] For an especially interesting account of Stetson's views on speech dynamics, see his earlier work, *Bases of Phonology* (1945).

Time Factors in Articulation

Some interesting observations about *time* factors in articulation grow out of the fact that speech movements are predominantly ballistic. As we know, the greater the inertia of any body, the more the force required to set it into motion in a given length of time or bring it to a stop after it has been set in motion, or—if equal force is applied—the longer it will take to move the body a given distance. This familiar principle has a direct bearing on the velocities of movement characterizing certain kinds of articulation since each of the articulators—jaw, lips, soft palate, tonguetip, tongue body—has an inherent inertia which gives it a kind of "time constant."

There is, of course, a neurophysiological limit to the rate at which any series of muscle movements can be executed, and this restricts the rate of articulation. Within this limit, the speed at which speech sounds can be uttered is dependent upon a variety of factors, including the mass and elasticity of the articulatory structure itself, the extent to which its movement is impeded by muscular tensions, and the distance it must be moved. In addition, tongue and lip movements can be assisted by the airstream, as in the articulation of plosive consonants. If other factors are held constant, increased effort can compensate for the relatively greater inertia inherent in some articulatory adjustments, but only within distinct limits.

Some of these facts can be illustrated quite simply. Try repeating the syllable series "tahtahtah . . ." as rapidly as possible. Note that there is a definite upper limit (about seven per second?) and that as this is approached, the movements tend to become slurred. Next try the series "gahgahgah . . .," and you may be able to observe that your maximum syllabic rate is either slightly slower or produced with noticeably greater effort. The relatively greater inertia which must be overcome to lift the entire tongue body for "gah" instead of the tonguetip for "tah" is presumably one reason for this. The distance the tongue must travel to reach the vowel target is, of course, a related variable. Note how much easier it is to sustain a long string of "geegeegee . . ." syllables at maximum rate than to sustain "gahgahgah . . ." syllables at the same rate.

Successive syllables do not, of course, always involve repetitive movements by the same articulator. Articulation can be greatly speeded when articulators alternate in their action. The neuromuscular problem is quite different in the articulation of "tuhtuhtuh . . ." than of "puhtuhpuh . . . ." One of the authors was able to articulate a "tuhtuh . . ." series at a maximum rate of about 9 per second, while his maximum for "puhtuh . . ." was about 13 per second.[1]

---

[1] These figures should not be taken as standardized "norms," but simply illustrate a single isolated case, for the purposes of making a general point about articulatory dynamics. The interested student might wish to consult Hudgins and Stetson (1937) or the more recent study of Siguard (1973).

The number of individual sounds which can be produced in a given time interval will vary with articulatory conditions and is, of course, different from the syllable frequency. Taking the condition of "tuhtuh . . ." as spoken by the author, and counting two sounds per syllable, the maximum rate was about 18 phones per second. It might be supposed that syllabic rate would drop as the consonant structure became more complex, and this does prove to be the case. The author's articulation of "stuhstuhstuh . . ." was at a maximum rate of only about 6 syllables per second, and his articulation of "sluhfsluhf . . ." was only 4.5 syllables per second. However, a little calculation will show that in all three cases the *phones*-per-second rate was 18.

From the above discussion we see that articulation rate and timing is a more complex matter than appears at first glance and that, obviously, a number of factors are involved, including articulator inertia and elasticity, movement path, movement amplitude, movement complexity, and neuro-muscular control. It also seems likely that the phones-per-second rate will reach its maximum at somewhere in the vicinity of 15 to 20 per second depending upon the nature of the measurement and the tolerance for "slurring."

With the foregoing information about the nature of movement in speech as a background, the way is now open for a consideration of the phenomena of connected speech and the dynamics of speech sounds in context, organizing the discussion under the topic headings listed at the beginning of this chapter.

TRANSITIONS

We have already spoken of *glides* as a class of speech sounds which consist of a movement *to* or *from* a syllabic nucleus. The acoustic cue from which the glide is identified lies solely in the manner in which resonance changes in time. We must now emphasize that *all* consonants are glides in the sense that such a resonance change always takes place when consonants combine with vowels to form syllables. The movement from one segment to another cannot occur in zero time; there is always a crucially important *transition* period. This is not something which is simply incidental to the articulation of sounds in sequence, for *within* the transition is much of the "place of articulation" information upon which our perception of the consonant depends. The duration of the transition may be brief, often only a few hundredths of a second, but it still may suffice.

There have been many experiments demonstrating the importance of transition information to speech recognition, but none is more conclusive than the work with vocal-tract analogs, or artificial talking devices. Such systems have been programmed to change the formant frequencies of vowels at certain rates and, if desired, to add plosive and fricative noises as well. It has been discovered that merely by manipulating the frequencies of two or three vowel resonances at appropriate rates it becomes possible to "hear" the intended consonant sound, even without the usually expected noise components for the fricative or stop in question (see Minifie, et al., 1973, for a more detailed discussion of experimental findings).

To be sure, speech produced without the normal consonant noises may not always sound quite natural, and occasionally words are ambiguous, but the truly astonishing fact is that so little intelligibility is lost. On the other hand, if an attempt is made to reproduce speech without transitions, even though all the appropriate consonant noises are included, the resulting utterance is nearly unintelligible, as Harris (1953) and others have shown. One can demonstrate that [p], [t], and [k] can be "heard" on the basis of transitions alone by asking someone to pronounce the syllables [æp], [æt], and [æk] *without* consonant release, and with the lips concealed. There should be little difficulty in identifying the syllables correctly, although the distinctions among them may not be as clear-cut as they would be under normal speaking conditions.

JUNCTURE

Blending of syllables in the words and phrases of connected speech is termed *juncture*, which may be either of two types: *closed* or *open*. Inasmuch as syllables are the basic units of speaking, it follows that the manner in which they are joined is among the details which need to be noted in any full analysis of speech, and certainly must be taken into account in applying phonetic theory to speech improvement.

When syllables are spoken as isolated forms, that is, without being followed immediately by another syllable, those with a vowel (*open*) arrest are by far the least common type. Under these circumstances even monosyllabic words which seem to end with a vowel resonance actually are terminated by an off-glide consonant in most cases. Thus, "how" usually has a [w] off-glide ([haw]) and "be" a [j] off-glide ([bij]). Whether or not an off-glide is indicated in transcription under these circumstances is a matter of choice (see page 57); the point relevant to juncture is the infrequency with which isolated syllables are spoken with open arrest. Few words in isolation end with simple, lax vowels which would therefore have no off-glides; are there, for instance, any ending in [ɛ], [ʌ], or [ʊ]?

The situation is mostly reversed in contextual speech, where one syllable is immediately followed by another except at the point of perceptible pauses. The factor of *timing* leads to a situation where there is a strong tendency for consonants to be perceived as regularly *starting*, but rarely terminating, syllables. At syllable rates in excess of about 2.5 to 4 per second, terminating consonants become, in effect, initiating consonants for the next syllable, or at least are positioned at the syllable *interface* in such a way that they share the function of terminating one syllable while simultaneously initiating the next.[1]

The process whereby the vowel-consonant relationship may change in contextual speech can be demonstrated easily, as Stetson (1951) and others before him have noted. Say the word "eat" (a VC syllable) at a rate of no more than twice per second; little or no variation is observed. Then gradually increase the rate to about four or five per second. As timing is speeded "eat-eat-eat . . ." first changes perceptually to a somewhat ambiguous "eateateat . . ." but ultimately shifts to a "tea-tea-tea . . ." (a CV syllable). The reversal can be delayed somewhat through the exercise of greater than usual care in articulation, but at the higher rate of repetition "eat" becomes "tea" regardless of the effort taken to prevent this change.

Many complications surround juncture, but a broad distinction can be drawn between *closed* and *open* types. In line with previous explanations, at customary speech rates all syllables, whether CV or VC, are usually joined together as a series of consonant-vowel forms. This has been termed a *normal transition*, or a *closed* juncture. Where syllables are not joined in this manner, that is, where an effort has been made to retain a consonant ending or VC form for the first of two adjacent syllables, we may say that the juncture is *open*, or that the transition has been *interrupted*. Illustrations of this distinction will be provided later by means of transcribed speech samples.

Full exploration of reasons why closed juncture is the usual mode of transition between syllables cannot be undertaken here, but a brief comment is called for. Physiological considerations seem to favor a CV form of syllable pulsing at customary speech rates. Pulsing occurs when there is a major node, or point of maximum energy drop, between syllables. This node is created by a consonant closure, or by the most constricted consonant of a cluster. The acoustic energy level of the speech flow is significantly reduced by the consonant constriction and is lowest at the instant of maximum constriction. However, the pressure vector of the pulmonic air is in the direction of breath flow, and back pressure which has built up behind the point of constriction aids in—or may even provide the impulse for—consonant release. All these factors combine to create a closed-open pulse, or a CVCVCV . . . series.

Junctural Ambiguity

Type of juncture—closed or open—reflects intended meanings; hence our tendency toward CV syllables in speaking raises the possibility of what may be called *junctural ambiguity*. For example, what is meant by [aɪskrim]? An answer can be given only if the speaker does something to make it clear that the two words are "ice cream" or "I scream," whichever the case may be.

---

[1] This is a considerable simplification of a complex phenomenon. The interested student should turn for amplification to Stetson (1951) or Lehiste (1960).

There is also the illustration provided by the time-worn story of the child who returned from the first visit to Sunday school to report that they sang a song about "Gladly, the cross-eyed bear." Context supplies the clues to meaning more often than not, but there are cases where ambiguity is to be avoided only by opening the juncture—usually by changing the timing in some way by pausing, by holding the sound for a longer period of time, by inserting an additional sound such as a glottal stop, or by a marked change in stress.

Doubled Consonants

There is a special juncture condition when the final consonant of one word is the same as the initial consonant of the following word. The phrases "take care," "Jane needed," and "Jim made" are examples. In contextual speech, English speakers almost never release both consonants of the abutting pair, often treating the doublet as a single consonant. Our illustrative phrases are customarily pronounced [tekɛr] ("take care"); [dʒenidəd] ("Jane needed"); and [dʒɪmed] ("Jim made"). This is analogous to the fact that we pronounce only one [l] in "fellow," one [t] in "better," and one [d] in "ladder" even though all three are spelled with double consonants. Similar conditions exist with *homorganic abutting consonants*. These are consonants made with similar articulatory movements and which therefore present a comparable kind of blending problem. Examples of homorganic pairs are [t]-[d], [p]-[b], and [s]-[z].

Several abutting consonant blends occur in Example 5 below in the transcriptions which have been prepared to illustrate juncture. Note the way in which "Was stabbed," "Tom made," and "Hal left" were pronounced by the speaker. Although the blend "Tom's happy" in the same sample does not involve homorganic or identical abutting consonants, it illustrates the necessity for a juncture which avoids the unfortunate "Tom's sappy."

Linking and Intrusive Sounds

Where vowel sounds join in adjacent words, there occur some interesting phenomena which lead to *linking* or *intrusive* sounds. This has been mentioned indirectly before, but needs some further comment. Consider the phrase "who under," which is usually pronounced [huwʌndɚ] in conversational speech. The glide [w] may be an intrinsic feature of the complex vowel [u], but it may also arise, or be exaggerated, as an adventitious sound linking [u] with [ʌndɚ]. As a purely phonetic phenomenon the [w] is acting in much the same way as the [j] of [aj] ([aɪ]) in the linking of [a] with [æm] in "I am" [ajæm]. If the latter phrase were to be spoken with a distinct break between the words, an intervening glottal [ʔ] might be used to distinguish "I am" from "ah yam." The [ʔ] might in this case be considered "linking."

An especially interesting case of linking and intrusive sounds can be found in the case of linking *r*. Often in the speech of persons who do not otherwise use a final or "post vocalic" *r* (as in [hɪə] for "here" and [bɛə] for "bear") the *r* will nevertheless be used to link syllables in the case of such phrases as "here I am" [hɪ ra jæm] and "bear up" [bɛ rʌp]. An even more interesting case is the so-called intrusive *r* which may be used to link two syllables neither of which would normally contain the sound [r] in an *r* pronouncing dialect. An example is [ði ajdiərʌvət] for "the idea of it."

Transcribing Juncture

In phonetic transcription it is often desirable to indicate whether a juncture is open or closed and if open, how the opening is accomplished. Absence of a notation is usually taken to mean that the transition was normal or *closed* (or that the transcriber was not interested in this feature). The common symbol for open juncture is [⁺], but the manner of opening can be shown by the length symbol [:] or the pause symbol [‖] or by indicating an intervening glottal stop [ʔ] or other linking sound. Here are four ways "keep on" might be recorded to indicate open juncture between the words: [kip⁺ən], [kip:ən], [kip‖ən], and [kipʔən]. All imply a change of timing between the syllables. Another problem in recording contextual speech can sometimes be handled by using the symbol [⁻] to indicate that a consonant is unreleased, or by employing other symbols which indicate some aspirate, affricate, or other release mechanism. Thus, "picked two" might be transcribed [pɪk'tu] if the type of juncture was such that [k] and [t] were both released, but [pɪk⁻tu] if the consonant combination between [ɪ] and [u] was stopped and released only once, that is to say, stopped as [k] but released as [t].

Let us now observe some examples of the types of juncture. In the first two examples which follow, an effort has been made to transcribe a short excerpt from Shakespeare's *Hamlet* so that each syllable is written as though it were isolated from its neighbor and so that each consonant or consonant blend is transcribed with the syllable to which it seems most clearly to belong. This is not a normal way to transcribe, but it will enable us to observe the shifts of consonants from terminating to initiating positions. The first transcription indicates the way the passage might sound if rendered slowly and with great care. The second represents a rapid, conversational delivery:

> [spik⁺ ðə spitʃ,⁺ aɪ pre ju,⁺ æz⁺ aɪ prə naunst⁺
> 1 "Speak the speech, I pray you, as I pronounced
>
> ɪt⁺ tu ju,—tri pɪŋ lɪ⁺ ən ðə tʌŋ]
> it to you,—trippingly on the tongue. . . ."
>
> [spi kθə spi tʃaɪ pre ju, ʔæ zaɪ prə naun stɪ
> 2 "Speak the speech, I pray you, as I pronounced

tu ju,—trɪ pɪŋ lɪ jən ðə tʌŋ]
it to you,—trippingly on the tongue. . . ."

Example 2 may possibly show more marked blending than would occur in careful, cultivated diction, but on the whole such a reading would not be abnormal for a conversational speech rate. Observe that the only exceptions to the consonant-vowel succession within the syllable occur with the [n] and [ŋ], both *semivowels*. Note also that at phrase endings, where pauses normally occur, the juncture is typically open. This can usually be taken for granted at the end of sentences and need not be marked in phonetic transcription.

Let us now consider some more examples of blending, transcribed in the manner of the two previous examples:

[aɪ θɪŋ kaɪ bɛ tə go tə klæs.+ ʃu dwɪ ji tæ ftə
3 "I think I better go to class. Should we eat after

ðə mi tɪ ŋə ʃu dwi go tə lʌn tʃæ ftə klæs?]
the meeting or should we go to lunch after class?"

[a jəm go wɪ ŋə we+ i stə tə kə lɛ ksəm de tə ʔə bau
4 "I am going away Easter to collect some data about

ʔma juθ. aɪ pɪ ktʃuə taun tə staə tɪn.]
my youth. I picked your town to start in."

[hi wə stæ bdu rɪ ŋə faɪ ʔlæ snaɪt.   tɑm+
5 "He was stabbed during a fight last night. Tom

med de zi+ i vən mɔ ræŋ gri hwɛn hæl+ lɛft. ha wɛ və
made Daisy even more angry when Hal left. However,

tɑmz+ hæ pɪ nau tə ki ʔm̩ mə thom.]
Tom's happy now to keep them at home."

COARTICULATION

We have alluded several times to the fact that the sounds of a word do not simply follow one another like printed letters and that, unlike letters, spoken sounds fall partially on one another in such a way as to "overlap." This characteristic of articulation is called *coarticulation*, a term apparently coined by German phoneticians.[1] As the articulators are in the process of forming one sound, their pattern of adjustment prepares them for the sound which is to follow. In the terminology of Stetson (1951), sounds may occur consecutively at a tempo which causes the *beat stroke* of one to overtake the

---

[1] For an early discussion of this phenomenon see Menzerath and deLacerda (1933). Öhman (1966) also presents background material.

back stroke of its predecessor. From a physiological point of view, coarticulation is a feature which is unique to the blending of sounds in contextual speech.

That coarticulation occurs is a remarkable characteristic of the neuro-muscular coordinations of connected utterance. It will be remembered from the earlier section on speech movements that some articulations are inherently slower than others, and thus take more time to start and stop. This means that the motor circuits of the brain cannot be programmed to produce individual sounds as it might conceivably produce individual letters. Instead, if articulation is to be normally synchronized, information about differences in response latency among the articulators must be part of the neural "memory traces" for an almost infinite number of speech sound configurations. How this is accomplished cannot as yet be satisfactorily explained.

Some of the more obvious manifestations of coarticulation can be illustrated quite easily. For instance, in speaking the word "two" one can notice that movement of the lips toward a lip-rounded [u] begins at or before the consonant [t] is released. Hence, parts of [t] and [u] overlap in time, with the result that a lip-rounded [t] is produced in the context of [tu]; if the word were "tea," there would have been no lip rounding. An example of coarticulation more difficult to observe is what happens in pronouncing the phrase "it will end." Here the relatively slow response of the velar mechanism makes it necessary to "anticipate" the nasal feature by lowering the soft palate well before the [n] target is reached, probably before the midpoint of the [ɛ] segment. As a consequence, the vowel takes on nasal resonance. Because of coarticulation, a nasal quality may pervade all phones in a word such as "minimal" or "memory."

To generalize about the phenomena of coarticulation, articulatory features do not parallel exactly in time the phonetic segments which these figures are presumed to generate. An illustration of the kind of relationship which does exist is shown graphically in Figure 6-1. It follows that there are no invariant or "universal" speech sound segments in either a strict physiological or acoustic sense. Speech sounds *influence*, and are influenced by, other sounds within a phonetic environment. It also becomes obvious that actual phonetic events can be specified only in terms of changing sets of features whose characteristics at any point in time depend upon the whole articulatory context.

Two significant practical applications grow from the preceding account. First, it must be understood that because speech sounds cannot be invariant, a canonical or "standard" pronunciation for each is only an abstraction, although one which has its legitimate uses. Second, successful techniques of speech improvement cannot consist simply of learning and practicing target positions for misarticulated sounds, although this has a place, but must include exercises in the dynamic motion sequences of speech. No amount of

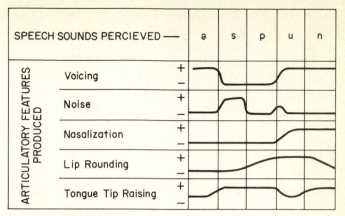

Figure 6-1   Coarticulation of features in the spoken phrase "a spoon."

rehearsal of sounds "in isolation" will enable the speaker to solve complex ballistic and timing problems; practice must also incorporate performance in a wide variety of contexts. This principle is now generally accepted in speech pathology, and has been developed by McDonald (1964) and others.

ASSIMILATION

The term *assimilation* refers generally to the influence one sound may have on another when the two are contiguous in time, as a result of coarticulation. Assimilative changes are those which alter the phonetic characteristics of sounds; coarticulation is the physiological basis for these changes. There are three major types of assimilation: *regressive*, *progressive*, and *reciprocal*. Assimilations may be *partial* or *complete*, which is a matter of degree; and *consonant* or *vowel*, with the consonant generally exerting the greater influence.

   In *regressive assimilation* a particular sound influences the one immediately preceding. For instance, the word "inquest" is commonly heard as [ɪŋkwɛst] rather than [ɪnkwɛst]. This pronunciation can be attributed to the fact that the nasal [n] has taken on some of the palatal characteristics of the following linguapalatal consonant, thus converting [n] to [ŋ]. The same influence causes "income" to become [ɪŋkʌm]. These particular pronunciations happen not to be dictionary-approved, but some analogous usages which have received sanction are the usual sound given "congress," "ink," "think," and so on.

   If a given sound produces changes in the one which follows next, the assimilation is *progressive*. For example, the phrase "Miss Doan" may be pronounced [mɪston] through assimilation of a voiceless feature from [s] into the ordinarily voiced [d]. The humorist P. G. Wodehouse has one of

his characters return a damaged hat to its owner with an observation something like, "Here's yer rat; that tat is not the yat it uster be." Some of this
is, incidently, *complete* assimilation.

Reciprocal assimilation refers to the mutual influence of two sounds to
produce a single sound which is something other than the standard pronunciation of either. For example, "picked your," which by canon is [pɪkt jʊr],
in rapid speech (which is the "normal" case) becomes [pɪktʃɚ], an instance
where [t] plus [j] merge to create [tʃ]. The palatal and alveolar are combined
into a more simply articulated alveolar-palatal or palatal-affricate stop-
plosive.

All these facts about blending seem to imply a kind of "law of least
effort" through which speaking is made simpler and quicker by arranging
that articulatory features be shared. This is, after all, a characteristic of any
skilled motor response. Historically, assimilation has been of major importance in the evolutionary changes in pronunciation which have taken place
in the past and still go on. One of the principal differences between formal
and conversational speech styles is that the latter displays natural assimilative
blendings. On the other hand, assimilation may be responsible for usages
which must be considered nonstandard by any reasonable criterion—as when
"gee chet" stands for "Did you eat yet?" and "grotch" is the place where
automobiles are kept.

ELLIPSIS

We have already alluded to the fact that informal, conversational speech is
marked by the omission of elements which are present in a full formal style
of utterance. Having now considered the way sounds are blended in context,
perhaps we can better understand why such *ellipsis* is natural at conversational
speech rates; forced to choose between a faster rate and phonetic detail, the
speaker makes a choice in favor of timing. Only when the speaker consciously
or unconsciously senses the need, will the detail which is typical of a full
form be included.

There are numerous causes for ellipsis: exigencies of conversational rate
and rhythm, use of informal grammatical constructions such as contractions,
assimilation, the occurrence of consonant clusters which are difficult to pronounce, and others. Linguistic habit and physiological conditions such as
neuromuscular disease may underlie elliptical forms which are beyond the
normal. What is left out in elliptical speech? Elements at several levels:
words, syllables, segments, nonsegmental variations, and articulatory features.
Although most of these have been touched on in previous sections, some
further examples might be of interest.

The word elisions of "telegraphic speech" are more lexical than phonetic.
For those who may be interested, Vygotsky (1962) has gone extensively into

the subject in his *Thought and Language*. He has a particularly interesting analysis (p. 143) of a scene from Dostoevski's *Diary of a Writer* where six drunken men carry on a conversation consisting exclusively of a single obscenity which each utters in his turn—all with perfect understanding among them. Our common practice of talking in single words and abbreviated sentences is too familiar to require discussion. Telegraphic speech is among the language abnormalities in the disorder called *dysphasia* from which many brain-injured individuals suffer (see Weisenburg and McBride, 1935). Syllable elisions are also a familiar feature of everyday speech. Many are the result of simplified phonetic constructions such as "can't," "don't," and "isn't" which have found their way into the dictionary, and thus have become canonical forms. Others which it might be argued are equally logical have received no such sanction, even though they are often used by educated speakers. Examples are "hist'ry," "prob'ly," "'cause" for "because," "'specially" for "especially," "'long" for "along," and so on. In obviously nonstandard speech, examples of aggravated syllable elision are not hard to find: "Wuncha?" "prolly" for "probably," "pearnly" for "apparently," and the like.

A host of terms have been applied to different kinds of elisions and assimilations. *Syncope* and *haplology*,[1] for instance, refer to certain pervasive forms of elision, among which are "o'er," "e'er," and "ne'er," for "over," "ever," and "never," often used for rhythmic effect in poetic language. Even among educated speakers the deletion of difficult consonant combinations is frequent. For instance, [ɑrktɪk] for "arctic," [kloz] for "clothes," and even [æst] for "asked" may be commoner than the so-called normal forms. However, analogous forms such as [laɪbɛri] for "library" and [lɛtʃɚ] for "lecture" are often obtrusive to the sensitive ear. Clusters such as [stl] and [sts] may be awkward because of the tongue shifts which would be required for complete articulation; hence one regularly hears pronunciations such as [kɔsli] for "costly," [væsli] for "vastly," and [pos] for "posts." Note the almost unavoidable fusion of segments in such combinations as "forced choices" and "bunched children."

The omission of features is quite common, although such elisions do not ordinarily fall within the definition of the term *ellipsis*. However, in the detailed analysis of speech which is often desirable, they may be of significance. The voiced feature is absent in whispered speech and other forms of unvoicing; poor palatal function may interfere with the nasal-nonnasal distinction; vowel reduction may obscure height, fronting, and tense-lax distinctions among vowels; and in many other ways the articulatory characteristics of speech

---

[1] *Syncope* is "loss of a medial vowel, due generally to stress accent elsewhere," and *haplology* is "an omission in speech of one or two consecutive identical or similar sounds or groups" (Pei, 1966).

may be affected. As a matter of fact, the analysis of actual speech as opposed
to "expected" speech essentially takes the form of a determination of the
effects elisions, coarticulation, assimilation, and other blending phenomena
have upon canonical usages.

We should not like to leave this discussion of blending on a note which
could be construed as advice that "anything goes" in speaking or with an
implication that, in the authors' view, a standard of speech should not be a
legitimate goal. We tried to make clear at the outset that society—not the
phonetician—sets up whatever criteria there are for acceptable speech. As a
realistic value judgment, it seems to us that clearly articulated speech con-
forming to a thoughtfully chosen standard is indeed important to the individual. If so, it follows that the lawful phenomena of blending not only are
of interest to the scholar, but also are useful to any who seek to guide either
themselves or others away from those practices which might defeat this
purpose.

VOWEL REDUCTION

A peculiarity of English vowel production is the frequency of their *reduction*
to a shorter or weaker form as a result of rate, stress, and rhythm conditions.
Properties of this weakened form of the segment will depend primarily on
the time allowed it by the exigencies of speech rhythm, but in general the vowel
tends to become shorter, simpler, weaker, and more central when compared
with longer and more tense vowel resonances. The exact resonance will be
consistent with a tongue posture which can be achieved in the shortened
interval. Sometimes, but not always, the reduced vowels may resemble in
quality a shortened [ʌ] or [ɜ].

The phonetic symbol used to indicate a *markedly* reduced vowel is the
schwa [ə]. This "murmured" or "indefinite" vowel, as it has been called,
may be the remnant of any "definite" vowel which has been sufficiently unstressed by reason of articulatory conditions. In such cases the vowel resonance
is largely assimilated from its surrounding consonant context. There may or
may not be any semblance of the resonance of the sound of which [ə] is a
reduced version. The schwa is a syllabic which functions only as a transition
from one consonant to another in keeping with the characteristic cadences
of English speech. (See also pages 221–224 in Chapter 10.)

RHYTHM

Because it is syllabic, speech is perceived as a stimulus series, and as a series
it tends to be perceived as *rhythmical*. Woodrow, writing in the *Handbook of
Experimental Psychology* (1951), says that "by rhythm, in the psychological
sense, is meant the perception of a series of stimuli as a series of groups of

stimuli [p. 1232]." An interesting fact about this tendency to impose a rhythmical pattern upon a series—musical notes, for example—is that it seems to occur even in the total absence of any objective physical marker which might identify group boundaries. There seem no obvious reasons why one should, for example, speak a list of numbers in certain groupings as opposed to certain others, or why we should conceptualize them in such a manner when we wish to memorize them. Nevertheless, we all know that it is easier to memorize "*six* eight/*two* three/*one* five" than it is to memorize the same set of digits without a rhythmical grouping.

But perhaps an even more interesting fact to phoneticians is the tendency for the stimuli of a series to "induce in the subject a rhythmical series of actions on his part [Woodrow, 1951, p. 1233]." We not only perceive speech rhythmically, we also tend to produce it in the same way. From these facts it would appear that, as Martin (1972) has expressed it, "speaking and listening are dynamically coupled rhythmic activities [p. 489]." He has proposed that there is an underlying fundamental structure to speech rhythms, that these are based upon the simple unstressed-stressed pattern, and that the rhythm patterns of an utterance by themselves carry a significant amount of phonetic information.

This is not to say that all speech is of the simple *iambic meter* (short-long). Martin does propose that the iambic is a kind of basic, underlying form, transformations of which appear as patterns of considerable complexity in actual speech performance. Of course, we do not need to accept this particular simplifying hypothesis about speech to recognize that to one degree or another, and in some form, rhythm is to be found in speech and may be of greater influence than is sometimes appreciated.

It may help us to become more aware of speech rhythms to note a few of the common metric forms as they might appear in some short speech samples. Using the "long" (*macron*) symbol ($^-$) and the "short" (*breve*) symbol ($^\cup$) to indicate stressed and unstressed syllables respectively—a common practice—here are a few common formal or regular metric structures:

Iambic ($^\cup$$^-$):   Collapsed upon the pickle bush.

Trochaic ($^-$$^\cup$):   Frankie Dinkle thwarted Bessy.

Anapestic ($^\cup$$^\cup$$^-$):   It's a fact that he talks to himself all the time.

Dactylic ($^-$$^\cup$$^\cup$):   Corpulent Cadillacs padded in chrome.

Like the student who was so pleased to discover that he was "speaking in prose," phoneticians are beginning to be impressed by the possibility that we are all "speaking in poetry," at least in the sense that all speech has an important rhythmic component. If this is true, and it appears a quite plausible notion, then the segmental speech sounds need to be understood as being produced within a rhythmical syllabic matrix which has the potential for exerting considerable influence upon the stress and timing, and hence upon the nature of the sounds themselves.

The idea that a rhythmic structure requires that stressed syllables be more or less regularly spaced within an utterance is by no means a new one. Many phoneticians have observed the tendency of English to be *isochronous*, in the sense that stress groups appear to fall at regular intervals of time (see Lehiste, 1973). English has also been described as a "stress-timed" language as opposed to a "syllable-timed" language.

There is a considerable disagreement among phoneticians as to the details of the rhythmical structure of English, but the tendency toward a constant rhythmical pattern is one plausible explanation for the tendency for English to reduce or omit its unstressed syllables in certain contexts and at certain rates. It can perhaps best be seen in counting, which tends by its very nature to stress the rhythmical nature of speech. As we count, we tend to "beat time," and the beat tends to fall on each number at the same interval of time regardless of whether the word contains a single syllable as in "one," or three syllables, as in "twenty-one." Of course, there is an opposing tendency to preserve the necessary information in the utterance, but it is obvious that in poetry, and perhaps in much prose also, rhythm can influence pronunciation.

It would seem, a priori, probable that in normal, less obviously metered speech, the lexical and phonological structures of a language would predispose it toward certain rhythms, so that a normal sentence in English might set up certain metric "expectations" in listener and speaker. For example, in the following it is obvious that when the meter is "broken" there is a tendency to want to collapse the word "visited."

$$— \cup \quad — \cup \quad — \cup \quad — \qquad \cup \quad — \qquad \cup \quad — \qquad \cup \quad —$$
Mary had a little lamb. It's fleece was white as snow,
$$\cup \quad — \cup \quad — \quad — \cup \cup \cup \quad — \qquad \cup \quad — \cup \quad —$$
And everywhere that Mary visited, the lamb was sure to go.

Note that the otherwise regular alteration of short and long syllables is broken by the injection of three unstressed syllables in a row in "visited the lamb." For that reason we might expect "visited" to be realized in the spoken metric pattern as something closer to [vɪzd], a reduced form which would preserve the pattern which had been established—one which could be said now to have "poetic license." On the other hand, in the context "Mary Lou Halihan visited town" the long-short pattern fits perfectly, the context itself suggesting the "full form" of the word "visited." Exactly how much influence the rhythms of speech have upon pronunciation is a matter about which very little has been written. It is enough at this point to indicate the possibilities, and to suggest that the phonetician ought to become sensitive to this aspect of articulatory dynamics.

There is an old and well-known limerick which has gone the rounds for many years. Its origins are lost, but it has been read to generations of students to make points about rhythm and style. We quote it now as a suitable way to end this chapter and to help make our point about the significance of rhythmical structure in speech.

A certain young man of Japan

Wrote verses that never would scan;

And when they asked why,

He replied, "Because I

Always try to get as many words in the very last line as I possibly
   can."

EXERCISES

1 The following terms may be used as a guide to your review of this chapter or as a list to be added to your continuing glossary of technical terms:

abutting consonants	fixed movement
agonists	flexors
anapestic meter	guided movement
antagonists	haplology
articulatory target	homorganic
assimilation:	iambic meter
complete	intrusive sounds
partial	isochronous
progressive	junctural ambiguity
reciprocal	juncture
regressive	kinesthetic cues
back stroke	linking sounds
ballistic movement	macron
beat stroke	open juncture
breve	rhythm
closed juncture	syllabic
coarticulation	syncope
dactylic meter	transitions
ellipsis	trochaic meter
extensors	vowel reduction

2 Investigate the nature of the syllable in English by having each of several un-trained native speakers count the syllables in the passage below, as it appears in print.

> The fire department choir sang with flowers on the day the sailor went to jail for acquiring a flowering quince.

Next ask the speakers to tell you how they accomplished this task, and explain to them your definition of the syllable in speech. Then ask them to count the number of syllables again, as they think they would speak the passage. Finally ask the subjects to read the passage while you count the number of syllables. Report the results of the study, explaining the nature and possible reasons for disagreement among your various measures.

3 If you have the equipment available to do it, try to replicate the rate experiment reported on pages 127 and 128, in which the author compared his maximum rates for [tʌtʌtʌ . . .], [pʌpʌpʌ . . .], [stʌstʌstʌ . . .], and [slʌfslʌfslʌf . . .]. Calculate your own rates and those of several other persons. Report and discuss the significance of the differences which you find.

4 Ask several persons to repeat the following words at a rate of about one per second, then to gradually increase the rate of repetition until they are going about as fast as they can: "ape" [ep], "eye" [aɪ], "eat" [it], and "ant" [ænt]. Say nothing about your reason for asking them to do this, but note the rate at which the VC syllable begins to sound like a CV syllable ("pay," "yah," "tea." "tan") or becomes ambiguous. Then ask them simply to report their own observations. Finally, tell them what it is that you are trying to observe and ask them to do the task again, this time taking care to *not* make the "ape" sound like "pay," etc. Report and discuss your results as they apply to the discussion of juncture.

5 At normal speech rates the "rule" is closed juncture. That is to say, all syllables begin with consonants and end with vowels unless a special opening rule is applied. The sentences below are CV syllable transcriptions. Read them at normal rates. They should sound quite natural, although perhaps ambiguous at times. Place open-juncture symbols and double the consonants where you think opening and consonant doubling occur in more careful, unambiguous pronunciations of the same sentences. (Answers will be found in Appendix E.)

1 [spi kθə spi tʃaɪ pre ju trɪ pɪŋ li jɔn ðə tʌŋ]
2 [aɪ θɪŋ kaɪ bɛ tɚ go tə klæ sun]
3 [ʃʊ dwi go tə lʌn tʃæ ftə rə hwaɪl]
4 [hi wə stæ bdʊ rɪ ŋə faɪ tlæ stnaɪt]
5 [kə mɑ no və ræn dhæ vlʌn tʃwɪ θmi]

6 Construct some of your own junctural pairs after the fashion of those discussed on page 130 ("ice cream"/"I scream," "key pawn"/"keep on," etc.). From these, construct practice sentences, fashioned in such a way that the entire sentence will be ambiguous unless the juncture is made clear. For example: [kipɔn ɪn ðə tʃɛs gem] or [hwɛn ɪt gɛtstuhɑt aɪskrim ən lɛmənəd wɪl bi sɝvd]. Have someone read your sentences and observe what it is he or she does to clarify the sentence, if anything. Inform a second subject of the ambiguous words and ask him or her to read the sentences with both interpretations. Observe the manner in which each reader handles the junctures. Report and discuss.

7 The following "slurvianisms" (see Tiffany, 1963) have two possible and quite divergent meanings, as they are *pronounced*, depending in part upon the location of an open juncture or a consonant doubling. For example, "bugs pray" and "bug spray" are usually not phonetically distinguishable except for an

open juncture which may be placed either between [g] and [s] or between [s] and [p]. Try to discover juncture pairs in the examples below, by finding the "second sense" of the utterance. (Translations will be found in Appendix E.)

Youth inks owe	I scream
Key pawn	Bat a lax
Sick shears	Heath ought
Cast a royal	Waddle pick hum offer
Pipe late able	Cry doubt
Ike wit aching	Bile awe
Known ooze	Note I'm

8 The phenomenon of coarticulatory nasality may be easily demonstrated by obtaining a small flexible tube with an inside diameter about the size of a drinking straw and using it as a nasality "sensor." With one end of the tube in your ear and one end in your nostril say the sentence "She helped her pick up sticks." Unless you have a habitual tendency toward nasality, you should hear nothing from the tube. Now say, "She helped her pick up sticks and some new marbles." This time you will note that at or before the [n] of "and" a loud buzz will be emitted from the tube, indicating the palate opening and the consequent transfer of vibratory energy into the tube and to your ear. Now test for the assimilative effects of the nasal sounds on the vowels by attempting to say "a hand," "can," and "soon" without letting the nasal resonance influence the vowel. Try also the words "man" and "moon." You will note that it is very difficult, and perhaps impossible, to prevent nasal resonance on at least some part of the vowel.

9 The elision of sound segments is common at normal speech rates, especially in complex consonant combinations. For example, the word "arctic" is usually elided to the form [ɑrtɪk], presumably owing to the awkwardness of the complex consonant sequence. Words ending in -st, such as "cost" and "vast," frequently lose [t] when the -ly is suffixed. [kɑsli] and [væsli] are by no means confined to "substandard" speech. These are but a few isolated examples. At normal rates of speech many segments will be elided in the interests of simplicity and rapidity of articulation. Such strings are, for example, found in "squelched Charles," "bunched screaming," "forced choices," and other "tongue twisters." Try to find other such examples and note the manner in which speakers simplify them. Can you formulate any consonant elision rules which you think would explain your observations?

10 In the passage below count the maximum number of syllables in which a reduced vowel would be appropriate in casual conversation. Count as reduced vowels any instances in which the schwa, schwar, or a syllabic consonant might appear. Now count them again as you would expect them to occur in natural-sounding but *formal* speech. Use these results as part of a paper on the nature and frequency of vowel reduction. Here is the practice passage: "The book was about American educational policy experiments, the effects of the generation gap, and the possibility of inappropriate government influence upon community actions."

11 Select at random from the newspaper a sample of prose about 100 syllables long. Mark its rhythm, using the macron and breve symbols, with the [||] symbol to indicate the end of a phrase. Have at least one other person do the same thing. Analyze the patterns in terms of (1) total number of syllables, (2) number of stressed and unstressed syllables, (3) number of instances where one, two, three, or more *unstressed* syllables follow one another, (4) number of instances where one, two, three, or more *stressed* syllables follow one another, and (5) number of times when short-long, long-short, or any other type of pattern is repeated twice in succession, three times in succession, etc. Can you generalize any rules from your result? Report and discuss.

12 Find some poetry with regular meter and look for instances where the normal pronunciation of a word needs to be changed in order to meet the demands of the metric plan of the poem. Make a list of these words (try to find at least five) and phonetically transcribe both the canonical pronunciation and the "poetic" pronunciation. Discuss your findings.

Chapter 7

Nonsegmental Features
of Speech

Until now our discussion has been concerned primarily with *segmental* phonetics, or the nature of individual speech sounds. It is now time to emphasize that not all the meaning of a spoken message is encoded in the contrasting segments; on the contrary, there are significant *nonsegmental* (a term we prefer to *suprasegmental*) contrasts in speech to which we turn our attention in this chapter. These are the melodic or *prosodic* elements in the flow of spoken language whose complex characteristics and interactions will be discussed under five headings: (1) *pitch*, (2) *time*, (3) *loudness*, (4) *stress*, and (5) *vocal quality*.

The flow of acoustic energy on which the phones are carried, is one marked by fluctuations in power, and in the pitch and quality of the vocal tone; likewise, the rate at which speech sounds are uttered varies greatly and in subtle ways, as do the "silences" or pauses between sound sequences which have been grouped into words or phrases. Thus, during speech two kinds of variation go on simultaneously, and to some degree independently: changes in the segments being spoken, and an ebb and flow in the nonsegmental configurations. Occurring somewhat more slowly than segmental rates, the nonsegmental fluctuations not only "punctuate" units of syllable, word, or phrase size, but may also carry much of the meaning of what is being said—and sometimes its only true meaning.

When one considers the relation between sound and meaning, even if only from a common sense point of view, it becomes evident, as Crystal (1969) has pointed out, that the components which contribute to the meaning of a communicative situation are of at least three kinds (1) "segmental and verbal," (2) nonlexical "verbalizations" which are not words in the restricted sense (a sigh would be one example), and (3) *prosodic features* which, he says, are those "nonsegmental characteristics of speech referable to variations in pitch, loudness, and silence duration [p. 140]." Vocal quality must also be added to this list of prosodic features.

The combined prosodic features of speech are sometimes said to constitute a *paralanguage*, or to be *extralinguistic*. This must not be taken to mean that they are somehow a less fundamental part of language code than segmental contrasts, although it is true that they have been studied less extensively and therefore are more poorly understood. There have, however, been a relatively large number of quite recent works on prosody, suprasegmentals, and the communication of emotion, including the work of Crystal (1969), Lehiste (1970), and Ostwald (1969).

FUNCTIONS OF PROSODY

Before undertaking a detailed treatment of nonsegmental features, we should make some further points about their contribution to the communication of information. The prosodic parameters of speech do serve as "punctuation," but a closer examination seems to leave no doubt that the most important impressions they convey relate to the speaker's identity, attitudes, and emotional states, and perhaps most significant of all, the speaker's evaluation of what he or she is saying. Abercrombie (1967) calls these the *indexical functions* of speech. Three of those he mentions, the *sociosyncratic, idiosyncratic*, and *nonce indices*, are sufficiently interesting to call for discussion.

Sociosyncratic Indices

When sources of variation were reviewed in an earlier section, a number of comments were offered about the way in which speech traits may lead to inferences about the status and social class of a speaker. Such judgments are by no means conditioned solely by pronunciation, vocabulary, and syntax, however, for the rhythms of an individual's utterances may do quite as much —or even more—to influence our perceptions of him. Tarone (1972) for instance, has suggested that the differences in melody patterns between inner-city Black dialects and those heard elsewhere may be a potentially serious source of cultural misunderstanding. Certain intonations tend to be associated with a number of rural subcultures (rural Vermont and the Tennessee mountains, for example) as they do also with urban dialects such as "Brooklynese." British English has a distinctive melody, particularly when such patterns as RP and Cockney are analyzed.

Idiosyncratic Indices

Our speech melodies carry many cues about us. There are truly personal features of speech which identify us as individuals or as members of a family. Our individuality, as others perceive us, probably depends as much on manner of talking as on any other single attribute of behavior. As mentioned earlier, age and sex can be reliably estimated on the basis of vocal cues alone; and when the sex of an individual is not consistent with the nonsegmental cues in the voice, unfavorable evaluations may be the consequence. If the conscious or unconscious motivations are present, the "sexy" voice carries powerful signals. No one has as yet troubled to analyze the human mating call scientifically, but there is little doubt its most compelling language is nonsegmental. Many forms of deviant speech and voice have prominent nonsegmental features, of course.

Nonce Indices

One of the most noteworthy kinds of information carried by speech concerns our *nonce* or "*immediate*" state, both physical and emotional. Consciously or unconsciously, we consistently utilize these cues in making personal judgments. Physical states are readily sensed, both from the vigorous, "alive" speech of one who feels in top form and from the subtle changes which take place when the individual is at low ebb. The latter may show particularly in voice timbre— the "sick" voice— but are evidenced also by a reduction of the vigor and energy of respiratory and articulatory movements. The tendency of speech to reflect physical states is so persistent that even conscious efforts to dissemble are likely to be unconvincing to a perceptive listener. Speech symptoms of physical vigor or some degree of debility are doubtless among the cues on which a speaker's age is estimated.

The nonsegmental features of an individual's speech are perhaps the most revealing of all indicators of feelings and attitudes. This is so self-evident that a discussion of the fact may seem needless, yet we sometimes fail to appreciate its importance in interpersonal relationships. The general point is put well by the phonetician R–M. S. Heffner (1952): "What one says in English is probably never contingent upon the melody of one's utterance, but what one thinks about what he says is often implicit in the tune to which one says it, and frequently this, rather than the literal sense of the speech form, is the real gist of an utterance [p. 217]."

One student of voice disorders, Moses (1954), has devoted a book, *The Voice of Neurosis*, to the thesis that emotional states can be diagnosed reliably from nonsegmental features. Helmick (1968) has recently demonstated the remarkable efficiency a speaker may have in communicating attitudes toward an utterance which in itself was basically noncommittal. He had three experienced speakers read a simple five-word declarative sentence in ways intended to reveal to listeners that the speaker was "assured," in "disagreement," "indifferent," "surprised," or "uncertain." The five samples differed only in nonsegmental features, yet listeners were able to identify the five mental states with up to 94 percent accuracy.

We have yet to comment on the significant fact that there are considerable individual differences among speakers in their command of the language of prosody. There can be wide gaps between what one is able to sense in the speech of others and what one can transmit. Helmick (1968) demonstrated this when he asked both trained and untrained speakers to express and detect different emotional connotations in speaking and listening to a sentence whose verbal content was neutral. In agreement with other studies, his subjects recognized the emotions intended by trained speakers with about 80 percent success. However, auditors did no better than 40 percent on the sentences uttered by untrained speakers. While this study is not conclusive, it suggests that the language of prosody may be of a special sort, and quite possibly depends on mechanisms of perception and learning which differ from those of other kinds of verbal behavior.

PITCH VARIABLES

Pitch modulations contribute substantially to the nonsegmental features of all languages. The topic is a difficult one to discuss for several reasons: There seemingly are few really firm generalizations that can be made about pitch usages in English, the subject is at best a complex one, and the systematic research studies on pitch prosody are comparatively few in number. Among the major points of interest, however, are the following: (1) the role of pitch in the communication of meaning, (2) the contribution of pitch modulation to the expression of subjective states, (3) the relationship between pitch and stress, (4) the variations in fundamental voice pitch and pitch flexibility, and (5) problems of pitch notation in phonetic transcription.

Pitch and Language

Much remains to be learned about the manner in which pitch prosody varies from language to language. Given a phonatory system which is uniform through the species, one might expect that to some degree pitch modulations would be uniform among the languages of the world. To the extent that forms of emotional expression have a correspondingly uniform physiological basis, this expectation is probably realized. On the other hand, cross-linguistic comparisons must be made with great caution, for pitch movements are heavily conditioned by culture and language rules.

Unlike English, in certain *tone languages* pitch is used as part of the segmental linguistic code, and it may be pitch alone which is the feature responsible for significant contrasts between phonemes. In a restricted sense, this is true of English, where inflection may determine shades of meaning. For instance, "yah" with a falling inflection is an answer; with a rising inflection, it is a question. English does not, however, employ tone systems in the way that Vietnamese or Chinese do, for example. The latter languages contain many words which are contrasted in meaning by a pitch-level feature in the same way that English uses such features as voicing or tongue height. The two English "yahs" are nonlexical "empty" forms to which significance is given by pitch modulation, but in our language pitch is not regularly phonetic, only prosodic. That English is not a tone language in the segmental sense is evident from the fact that little or no lexical confusion results if speech is monopitched, such as that which may be generated by an electronic synthesizer. It may be monotonous, not lifelike, and lacking in any emotional tone, but its lexical significance is not greatly affected.

Pitch does have some linguistic functions, of course, particularly as an important syntactic marker. It may signal phrase boundaries, differentiate didactic statements from questions, denote incompleteness or uncertainty, and convey the relative importance of one speech fragment in relation to another. Examples of pitch modulations which accomplish such functions are presented in Figure 7-1. These *melody curves* represent the speech of one of the authors recorded with the use of a fundamental frequency analyzer. Elapsed time is indicated on the horizontal axis of the graph, frequency on the vertical axis.

Note that when the words "one," "two," "three" were spoken in series, a rising inflection is repeated until the final unit of the set, which is a typical intonation pattern for a series. Observe also that "Oh?" and "Oh!" show pitch movements in opposite directions: upward for the question, downward for the statement. This commonly accepted rule that questions are signified by an upward inflection holds for typical instances but cannot be generalized for all cases. In the short sentence is seen a typical English phrase pattern, with pitch rising toward the stressed word of the phrase and falling away at the phrase ending. A range of about two octaves on the musical scale is covered. There are, however, great individual differences in all aspects of pitch usage.

Pitch and Affective States

A general statement about nonsegmental features as indicators of feeling and emotion was made during the discussion of the *nonce indices*, but the contribution of pitch modulations to this function needs further examination.

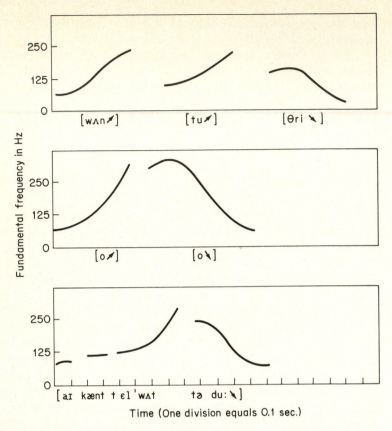

Figure 7-1 Fundamental frequency graphs ("melody curves") of three sets of utterances by one of the authors: "One, two, three." "Oh? Oh!" and "I can't tell *what* to do!"

Lieberman and Michaels (1962) isolated the pitch feature from a series of recorded speeches which had previously been identified by listeners as having "bored," "confidential," "doubting," and other such subjective qualities. Using only the pitch signal, they constructed musical "tunes" which had no segmental phonetic information, but did have the same music as the original speech samples. These content-free melodies were then presented to subjects who were asked to identify the emotions they conveyed. The results provided a convincing demonstration of the importance of pitch prosody in the transmission of information about the speakers' affective states.

A study by Fairbanks (1940) earlier had provided evidence that prosodic cues reveal subjective states. He asked trained actors to read five different passages depicting the emotions of anger, grief, fear, indifference, and contempt. An identical sentence was buried within the context of each. This was removed from a phonograph recording of each sample and presented out of

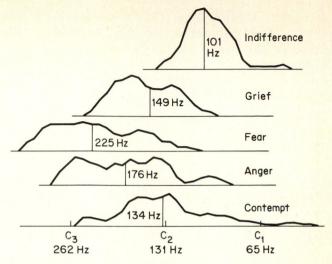

Figure 7-2 Pitch distribution curves of Fairbanks (1940). These indicate the frequency with which certain pitches are used in utterances said to be typical of portrayal of five different emotions. The average speech frequency is also indicated in each instance. (By permission.)

any context to observers who were asked to identify the emotion expressed in each of the five identical sentences. The level of success was generally good, ranging from a low of 78 percent correct identifications for "anger" to a high of 94 percent for "contempt" and "grief." Some pitch distribution curves prepared by Fairbanks are found in Figure 7-2. These show the characteristic differences in modulation, and in average pitch, as he determined these for his samples of the various affective states. Much more research will be needed before generalizations can be formulated about the prosody of emotional expression, but even now the conclusion is inescapable that this critical information is encoded in speech in ways which are fundamentally lawful.

Pitch and Stress

Stress is essential to the grammar and syntax of a language, functioning to mark or give prominence to elements of an oral sentence or paragraph. It signals that a speaker is reacting more strongly at some point in the discourse or that some significant relationship exists between parts of a sentence, phrase, or word. Since stress is so much involved in the dynamics of speech sounds in context, it has been discussed in Chapter 6. At this point we should note the part played in stressing by pitch factors.

There appears to be general agreement among phoneticians that while stress is a composite of several features, including pitch, duration, and loudness, the most salient factor is pitch, and nearly always a *rise* in pitch. To

Table 7-1 Comparison of Fundamental Frequency and Duration of Selected Vowels in Words Emphatically Stressed and in the Same Context in Words not Emphatically Stressed

Vowel	Frequency, Hz		Duration, sec	
	Emphatic	Nonemphatic	Emphatic	Nonemphatic
[i]	190	131	0.161	0.109
[ɪ]	168	127	0.161	0.126
[e]	179	139	0.181	0.137
[ɛ]	170	120	0.115	0.104
[æ]	195	134	0.155	0.126
[o]	153	136	0.186	0.144
[ʊ]	176	116	0.141	0.096
[u]	195	123	0.174	0.115
[ɑ]	137	97	0.264	0.243
[ʌ]	141	103	0.179	0.166
Mean:	170	122	0.172	0.137

produce emphasis, pitch must depart from some anticipated base level, and the specific nature of the stress pitch change will thus depend on the characteristics of the pitch contour of the phrase.[1] No specific figures can be given for the amount of change.

To illustrate the kinds of pitch (and durational) changes which operate in stressing, the results of a study of emphatic stress by Tiffany (1959) are presented in Table 7-1. Twenty speakers were asked to read sentences, giving emphatic stress to certain selected words under one condition, but no special stress under another. The frequencies of 10 different vowels were determined for both conditions.[2] As can be seen from the table, the stressed vowels were spoken at pitches several tones higher than those given no special stress; specifically, the average frequencies of the stressed and not-stressed vowels were 170 Hz and 122 Hz, respectively. Although not included in the tabulation, the minimally stressed *schwa* syllables were found to have an even lower pitch of the order of 100 Hz or less. It is true that under some conditions an unvarying pitch level may give a particular emphasis—as in the stern warning, "Don't you do that!"—but this may be only a special case of a rule that *departure* from an expected pitch modulation is the critical emphasis factor.

[1] For a fuller comment on this point see Lieberman (1967).
[2] A number of writers such as Peterson and Barney (1952) have noted that the vowels themselves have characteristically different durations and pitches.

Voice Pitch and Pitch Flexibility

Figures for average vocal pitches are not too meaningful because of wide individual differences. The mean for adult male voices is usually given as about one octave below middle C on the musical scale, or a bit lower, while the adult female voice averages about four tones to an octave higher. Voice pitch is among the secondary sexual characteristics and is taken also as an indication of emotional states. Marked deviations from what are deemed pitch levels appropriate to the age and sex of the speaker may lead to judgments—correct or incorrect—in these areas.

Although greatly influenced by habit and affective states, a speaker's vocal pitch is basically determined by physical factors, including the size of the larynx and the mass-length of the vocal folds. Theoretically, this *physiological pitch* is also the *optimum pitch*, or the level around which the speaker should be expected to range if there are no conditions which prevent. Physiological pitch is often located by first determining the lowest and highest tones the speaker can produce (including falsetto); the physiological pitch is then fixed at a point about one-fourth of the distance up from the bottom, or about one-third of the way up if the falsetto is not included in the range. Thus, a male with a 16-tone range with falsetto would have an optimum pitch four or five tones above the lowest point of his range.

However, the fundamental vocal pitch around which an individual speaks is less important for pitch prosody than are the patterns of pitch variation. Average animated reading by speakers not inhibited by emotional stress or habit have been found to cover a range of an octave or more, although individual differences are marked. A nearly monopitched speaking voice is not unusual, doubtless for a variety of reasons. Little has been learned about the constraints which language and speech style place on pitch variations, but there are obviously limits: too little variation is likely to impair the use of expressive prosody; too great variation tends to violate canons of emotive style which are undefined, but to which we unconsciously expect "normal" speakers to adhere.

Age and Sex Pitch Differences

Significant changes in the fundamental pitch of the voice occur at different periods during the life span. During the pubertal change of voice or *mutation* the male vocal pitch shifts downward—as a result of changes in the size and shape of the larynx—about one octave in a comparatively short interval of time to reach a final average level of about 100 to 125 Hz. Girls also undergo a voice change, but the typical drop is as few as two or three notes. Data on pitch trends (Figure 7-3) show that pitch continues to drop slightly during middle life, but rises again in the senile decades. As Shakespeare said:

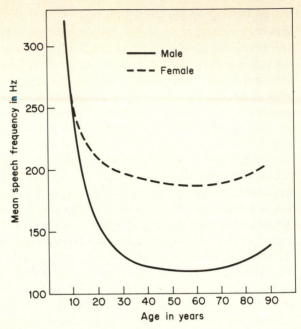

Figure 7-3 Curves showing the change in speech fundamental frequency as a function of age. From data abstracted from about twenty different studies.

The sixth age shifts
Into the lean and slipper'd pantaloon,
With spectacles on nose and pouch on side,
His youthful hose, well sav'd, a world too wide
For his shrunk shank; and his manly voice,
Turning again toward childish treble, pipes
And whistles in his sound. . . .
                    (Shakespeare, *As You Like It*)

Phonetic Pitch Symbols

It may have been noticed that in none of the remarks about the analysis of speech thus far has there been provision for phonetic recording of pitch, except for certain pitch symbols included as part of the IPA chart in Figure 5-3. These, which are repeated below for convenience, were designed primarily to indicate the kinds of pitch level or movement found to characterize segmental units individually. The symbols are:

[‾] High pitch level   ['] High falling pitch
[_] Low pitch level   [ˎ] Low falling pitch
['] High rising pitch   [^] Rise-fall pitch
[ˏ] Low rising pitch   [˅] Fall-rise pitch

As can be seen from Figure 7-1, however, pitch changes extend over many segments and appear in the form of continuous *profiles* or *contours*. The IPA symbols therefore are not adapted to a phonetic analysis of pitch, since they refer to individual segments, although they may be useful in transcribing tone languages. What is required for the analysis of the pitch prosody otherwise is a system of notation which is not bound to individual segments, but will permit the recording of both pitch levels and direction of movement in word, phrase, and sentence units. Ideally, such a system would be sufficiently precise to record the prosodic pitch distinctions which carry the important nonsegmental information about the speaker's attitudes and feelings.

As a matter of practical fact, however, no system has been commonly accepted for everyday use outside the laboratory. For an exact determination of the fundamental frequency of speech signals, electronic instrumentation is necessary. With its use, pitch contours such as those in Figure 7-1 can be drawn and are of great value in studying pitch movements. *Impressionistic* analyses are also of use, however, such as a trained musician might be able to accomplish on the basis of an ear for pitch. The accuracy of such analyses will depend entirely on the listening skills of the transcriber, of course, and this may well prove a serious limitation for all but a few.

At this stage a simpler system of pitch notation is recommended. It is still an open question among phoneticians as to how many levels of pitch need to be specified in order to indicate the necessary speech "tunes," but most agree that for most purposes it is sufficient to indicate four levels. In using this system, the speaker's average voice level may be symbolized by [^{2}], a low level by [^{1}], a high level by [^{3}], and an extra high level by [^{4}]. In this system "He *did* it!" might be transcribed [^{2}hi^{4}dɪd^{1}ɪt], and "He did it?" [^{1}hi^{2}dɪd^{3}ɪt]. A simple declarative statement "He did it" might perhaps be adequately represented by [^{2}hi dɪd^{1}ɪt]. Symbols need be used only where a change in pitch is observed. The numbers used to designate pitches indicate only *relative* levels in terms of a particular speaker's average pitch and thus make no provision for recording absolute pitches on a musical scale. This is at best only an approximate method of transcribing intonation, but will probably suffice for most transcription.

It is important to consider not only the pitch level of each syllable but also the inflection, particularly at phrase terminals.[1] Inflection may be indicated by the symbols [↗], [↘], and [→], depending upon whether the voice at the end of the phrase rises in pitch, falls off in pitch, or remains level. Thus, [mi↗] contrasts with [mi↘], the first being a question, the second

---

[1] The definition of what constitutes a phrase involves complexities which cannot be discussed fully here. It is sufficient for our purposes to state that a phonetic phrase is similar to a grammatical phrase, which the speaker of a language will recognize intuitively and which the speech student may have been taught is roughly equivalent to the *thought unit*.

being an answer. Compare [wɛl→aɪ dont no↗] (a statement marked by con-
templation, incompleteness, or possibly a lack of assurance) with [wɛl↘aɪ
nevə↘] (a statement of disgusted surprise). It is, of course, not often that
both pitch-level and pitch-inflection symbols are required in the same transcription. Ordinarily the symbols for level are quite sufficient for indicating
pitch changes for native speakers. In certain instances, however, both types
of symbols, or even the inflection symbols alone, may be more useful.

Here is an example of pitch notation which employs symbols for both
pitch level and terminal inflections:

[²hwʌt dɪd ju¹se↗ ²aɪ dɪdnt³hɪr²ju↘
³o kʌm ɔn²nau↘ ¹ju³rili²dɪdnt du³ ðæt²↘
²ju↘ ³tʃɑrl¹i↘ ³gɛt⁴ aut² əv¹hɪr↘]

Other intonational marking systems often employ *contour lines*, the
height of which indicate the pitch level, as in the example below. In many
ways this system is more simple to use than the index system used above. It
is, of course, more difficult to adapt to type.

[aɪ kænt tɛl/hwʌt tə du ̮əbaut ət
hwʌt dɪd hi ̮du hwaɪl aɪ ̮wəz/əwe
hwɛr ̮ðə/bɔl ̮ɪts/ðɛr ̮ovə/ðɛr ̮]

A Feature System for Pitch

To summarize the discussion so far relative to the pitch features, we have
suggested that they are of at least three types: *level*, *contour*, and *range*. While
there is neither the carefully worked out theoretical framework for a "pitch
distinctive feature system" nor as much data on pitch as we need (especially
relative to the perception of phrase contours), the strictly phonetic features
might be systematized to a first approximation like this:

Pitch-Level Features	*Pitch-Contour Features*
Low	Level
Mid	Rising
High	Falling
Markedly High	Rise-fall
	Fall-rise

Pitch-Range Features
Monopitch
Narrow
Normal
Markedly wide

TIME

As a significant nonsegmental feature, the time variable of speech has been of great interest to phoneticians. At a somewhat superficial level the rate of speaking measured in words per minute has been found to average about 170 for oral reading, but for a broader range of speaking situations is reported to vary from about 80 to nearly 200 words per minute. It is obvious at the outset that how fast one talks depends on such a wide range of influences—habit and temperament, the nature of the situation, speech content, attitudes and feelings, and so on—that such a gross measure as words per minute, especially average rates, is insufficient for any particularly meaningful analysis of the temporal aspects of speaking.

The timing of speech is, in fact, a composite of several factors, some inherent in the segments themselves and others of a nonsegmental prosodic nature. Articulation itself is a set of movements in time, and the overall rate of speaking is necessarily related to the duration of the segments of which it is composed. Duration appears to be one of the distinguishing features of segments, although one which is more important to some than to others. Liberman, et al. (1956) found, for instance, that a syllable-initiating [b] could be changed into [w] simply by decreasing instrumentally the rate of onset of the following vowel. The explanation which could be offered is that [b] is a fast-onset labial consonant while [w] is a relatively slow-onset labial consonant, and for this reason the rate of onset influences perceptual identification. To cite additional illustrations of durational characteristics, tense vowels tend to be longer than lax vowels, vowels before voiced consonants are longer than those which precede voiceless consonants, fricative noise has greater duration than plosive noise, and so on.

With respect to the prosodic features of speech timing, three appear to be of major importance: (1) *syllable length*, (2) *rate* or *tempo* of utterance, and (3) *pausing*, which may be either a silent interval or what will be termed a *filled pause*. The concept of *rhythm* encompasses all these.

Syllable Length

Syllable length is influenced primarily by the duration of its vowel nucleus. Some idea of the average length of vowels can be gained from Table 7-1, taken from the study by Tiffany (1959) cited earlier in connection with the discussion of pitch-stress relationships. On the basis of his normative data, the duration of emphatic vowels averaged 0.17 second and of nonemphatic vowels 0.14 second in the speech of 20 subjects. Among these vowels, [ɑ] was the longest and [ɛ] the shortest. Shortest of all were the unstressed schwa vowels, not included in the tabulation, whose duration was found to be as brief as 0.03 second. While variation was observed among speakers, there is nothing in the data which casts serious doubt on the conclusion that these averages represent a "typical" vowel length. Syllables with complex prominently diphthongized nuclei tend to be longer than the values given above. At the upper end of the continuum one may occasionally hear a vowel well over a second in length in such a form as "ahhh!"

Exactly how and for what purposes the feature of syllable length is used is not altogether clear. Constraints on syllable length are imposed by phonological rules of English, or whatever language is being spoken. One important function, mentioned earlier, is the contribution to stressing made by pitch, duration, and loudness in combination. Although many points about the relationship between these three variables remain obscure, it is clear that durations are consistently longer in stressed syllables. Duration obviously is subject to the same rhythmic, prosodic alterations as are the other nonsegmental features of speech. For general descriptive purposes, the terms *short*, *normal*, *half-long*, and *long* are suggested, although these are subject to the same limitations that were noted for the pitch-level designations discussed earlier.

Tempo

Measurements of speech rate indicate that the average is about four syllables per second, with some variation to be expected because of the influence of segmental structure, stress patterns, and prosodic considerations. In a study by Bennett and Tiffany (1970), the average syllabic rate for the reading of speech samples consisting entirely of monosyllabic words was somewhat slower, specifically 2.9 per second, but for polysyllabic prose samples (averaging two syllables per word) the rate was 3.7 syllables per second. Under other conditions both slower and faster rates may be observed, but the averages given can probably be considered typical.

There are some remarkable facts about speech tempo. First of these is the apparent stability of each individual's rate of utterance. In the study just cited, subjects were asked to read a prose passage four times in succession in any way they wished. The elapsed times for the successive readings were astonishingly similar, rarely varying by more than 2 percent. For the 40 subjects as a group, average times for the four readings were 69.9, 68.9, 68.6, and 68.2 seconds, respectively. Considered individually, each of the subjects evidenced a comparable consistency in rate of utterance.

While speakers differ in the agility with which they can manipulate their articulatory musculature, there is an upper limit imposed by human physiology.[1] Within this limitation speakers *can*, of course, change rate even if they tend not to do so. But when subjects in the study were asked to read "twice as fast" and "half as fast," it was discovered that they were, on the whole,

---

[1] In this connection a term often used is *diadokokinesis*, which is the maximum speed with which reciprocal muscle movements can be executed. This is among the diagnostic tests administered to individuals with certain types of speech disorders.

quite unable to do so; in fact, the average amount of change amounted to no more than 15 percent, and most of this was the result of lengthening or shortening pauses. When highly trained speakers were given this same task, a few were found who could reduce their rate by approximately 50 percent, but no such increase was possible. It was a subjective impression that most individuals habitually speak about as rapidly as they can without sacrificing accuracy of articulation.

As a matter of common observation, changes in rate do take place, both in the number of syllables per second and in the form of accelerations and decelerations at different time points within samples of spoken language; these are the cadences of normally expressive speech. As such, they make up a set of prosodic features which communicate much the same kind of information as do the nonsegmental pitch variables. As an aside, certain kinds of *dysprosody*, found principally among individuals with central nervous system impairment, are characterized by a monotonous "scanning" type of speech in which there is little fluctuation in rate (or in pitch and loudness). It does seem apparent, however, that except for pausing, rate of utterance per se may be less variable than are other nonsegmental features. Quite possibly the magnitude of *perceived* changes in rate is mostly the result of pausing and articulatory changes rather than in speech rate as such.

Work which has been done by communication engineers on *time compression* of speech may have implications for timing as one of its nonsegmental features. By use of electronic and electromechanical instrumentation it is possible to increase the rate of speech without any alteration in the relative durational relationships among sounds and phrases; that is, by a reduction of the total elapsed time in a way which a human speaker cannot. When speech is thus processed, a compression of as much as 30 percent is hardly noticeable—only an added "crispness" is perceived. Even a 50 percent compression, to a rate of approximately 300 words per minute, is still highly intelligible, provided the original was accurately articulated.

Pausing

Although one of the most unobtrusive facets of timing, *pauses* are critical to the prosody of speech. They allow time for replenishing the supply of breath with which to speak, and may be used to formulate the verbalizations which are to follow. They also exercise an important linguistic function by indicating the groupings into which the words and phrases must fall if the logical meanings, and the relationships among them, are to be brought out in the way intended by the speaker. Pauses are the closest of the nonsegmental features of speech to the commas, semicolons, and periods with which we punctuate written language. Although not a stress feature per se, appropriate pausing may nevertheless do much to emphasize ideas. The number and length of pauses necessary to implement these aspects of speech prosody are not known, but as a working basis we suggest three lengths : *short, long,* and *extended.*

What may not be fully appreciated is the relatively large proportion of total speaking time ordinarily occupied by these periods of silence. In the study of Bennett and Tiffany mentioned previously, about 35 percent of the total time for some readings was taken up by pauses—a percentage which was reduced substantially when subjects were asked to read "twice as fast." It can be estimated that pauses can occupy as much as one-third of the speaking time without making one appear hesitant, unsure of oneself or of what one wishes to say, or unnatural in any other way. As another aside, the conspicuous non-fluencies of stutterers often are not so much in the pauses themselves, as they might be perceived by listeners, but more in the stut- terers' reactions to their own lapses in fluency.

Goldman-Eisler (1968) has contributed substantially to our understand- ing of the phenomena of pausing. She has demonstrated, for example, that the pauses of spontaneous speech and those which occur in oral reading appear to obey quite different rules. In reading, pauses tend to appear in places that would be predicted on the basis of a knowledge of English gram- matical structure—at the ends of sentences, for instance. In spontaneous speech, however, she found that 45 percent of all pauses occurred in "non- grammatical" places. These she termed "hesitation pauses." Such pauses proved to be surprisingly long, occupying between 35 and 67 percent of the cumulative speaking time for different individuals. The number of hesitation pauses was smallest when the content consisted of highly learned, carefully planned, or stereotyped utterances, and greatest under the opposite con- ditions.

In summarizing the behavior of hesitations in speech, Goldman-Eisler has this advice most pertinent to our understanding of normal human speech timing: "Spontaneous speech was shown to be a highly fragmented and dis- continuous activity. When even at its most fluent, two-thirds of spoken lan- guage comes in chunks of less than six words, the attribute of flow and fluency in spontaneous speech must be judged an illusion [p. 31]." As far as the question as to what constitutes the "best" pausing, there is obviously no simple answer. Hesitations are apparently evidences that speakers are thinking and planning as they go. Lack of such hesitations may reveal either that they are not thinking or that they have already done their thinking. The lis- tener is free to choose.

Pause Types   It seems of some value to propose a classification of types of pauses as nonsegmental features of speech. A first type would, of course, be a genuine interval of silence, which can be termed an *unfilled pause.* It is a matter of common observation, however, that not all pauses are of this char- acter; another type can, in general, be called *filled pauses,* which are of three kinds. *Adventitious fills* consist of nonlexical vocalizations ("uh, uh, uh," for example) or largely irrelevant verbalization. An illustration of the latter is such a phrase as "you know," which has become annoyingly common as this is being written. *Repetition fills*, as the name suggests, occur when words or phrases are repeated, as in, "Now, I'd like, I'd like, I'd like to say. . . ." A *steady fill* is one in which the pause is continuously vocalized, as when a speaker says, "mmmmmmm don't know for sure." The latter might be considered a variant of the *adventitious fill*. All these types of filled pauses will be heard daily, and must be considered a characteristic mode of pausing—desirable or not.

Phonetic Time Symbols

The manner of indicating pause and length in phonetic transcription is fairly uniform. A sound of slightly greater than average length may be followed by [·], sometimes called the *half-long* notation. A sound which is pronounced with considerably more than average length may be followed by [:], sometimes called the *full-long* notation. Contrast, for example, the British pronunciations of "cot" [kɑt] and "cart" [kɑːt]. This notation system may easily be extended by adding further colons.

For indicating *pauses* many phoneticians rely on conventional English punctuation marks, such as commas, semicolons, and periods, just as they would if the speech were written in conventional spelling. However, we must realize that punctuation marks are linguistic, not phonetic, devices. For silent pauses the ordinary phonetic symbols are a single vertical bar to mark a shorter pause, and a double bar to mark longer pauses (or more bars to indicate greater length, if desired). The following example shows how the vertical bars might be used in a short transcription:

[wɛl|hwʌt də ju θɪŋk‖aɪ min raɪt nau‖ wɛl↗]

There are no standard phonetic symbols for tempo other than the usual musical notations. These have the rough time equivalents, in beats per minute, of the following: *largo*, 60; *largetto*, 90; *adagio*, 120; *andante*, 140; *allegro*, 170; and *presto*, 190. Considering that syllabic rate is on the average close to 240 beats per minute and that even the timing of stressed syllables is close to 180, human beings ordinarily speak *molto presto*! Musical tempo rates are obviously better adapted to a kind of phrase tempo. In any case it is doubtful whether phoneticians need to distinguish more than about three or four degrees of tempo, say *slow*, *normal*, and *fast*.

A Feature System for Time

Syllabic Duration Features

Short	Half-Long
Normal	Long

Pause Features

  Short   Long   Extended

Tempo Features *Pause Fill Features*
  Slow   Adventitious fill
  Normal   Repetition fill
  Fast   Steady fill
        Unfilled

LOUDNESS

As a term for one of the nonsegmental features of speech, *loudness* has its ordinary meaning, that is, the strength of the auditory experience. In colloquial language we mean much the same thing when we speak of *force*, *volume*, or *intensity*, although these are less suitable terms. The information transmitted by loudness as a nonsegmental feature centers primarily around the contribution it may make to stressing, but this in turn relates in many ways to the expression of the intellectual and affective content of speech.

Strictly defined, loudness is an auditory *sensation* whose magnitude depends primarily on the *intensity* of the speech signal, roughly its acoustic energy or power. The latter may be measured and expressed in a number of ways which need not be discussed here,[1] although some of the facts about speech energies and their relation to sensation level will help to understand loudness as a nonsegmental feature. In actuality, the absolute amount of power in any of the phones is exceedingly small; hence communication engineers commonly find it convenient to express such values in a unit called the *microwatt*, which is one-millionth of a watt.

There are astonishing variations in power in the speech stimuli to which we are exposed. A loud voice may have 100 times the power of an average conversational voice, which, in turn, may have 100 times as much power as a soft voice. The human auditory system is even more remarkable in its ability to respond to an exceedingly wide range of energies, so that at some frequencies the ratio between a just-audible sound and one which is uncomfortably loud may be as much as 1 to 10,000,000,000 or more. If our range of vision were as great, we should have very little need for either microscopes or field glasses. The energy ratios such as those mentioned are customarily expressed in units called *decibels*, abbreviated dB. Taking the energy level of a just-audible sound as the 0 point from which sensation level measurements may be made, the sensation level of a nearby conversational voice might be about 65 dB, while a loud voice could reach a 75 to 85-dB level.

---

[1] For anyone interested in the technical aspects of speech power and its measurement an excellent reference would be Denes and Pinson (1963), Ladefoged (1962), or Small (in Minifie et al., 1973).

Prosodic Functions

Loudness modulations make obvious contributions to speech prosody by helping to indicate one's, thoughts and feelings. For example, a rather marked variation in power has been found to be characteristic of "superior" speech, as judged by critical listeners. In one early study of the basic aspects of effective speech (Murray and Tiffin, 1934), "good" voices were reported to have 21 percent greater variation in intensity than did "poor" voices. In another study (Lewis and Tiffin, 1934) it was found that speakers who received low ratings by listeners were those who used relatively less loudness contrast between articles and prepositions, on the one hand, and the more important sense-carrying words, such as nouns and verbs, on the other.

Contrary to what may be a general impression, however, loudness by itself is usually not the most important element in stressing. This point will be developed further in the next section, when the factors which do determine emphasis will be considered in some detail. For the moment it will be sufficient to say that pitch and durational cues are significantly more important to stress and that alterations in speech power nearly always are accompanied by variations in pitch, voice quality, and duration; and it is upon these, especially pitch, which we depend for most of our perception of rhythm and stress.

This can easily be demonstrated by recording a sample of loud speech, then another of soft speech. Listen to the recordings with the volume control adjusted to give them equal loudness during the playback; under these conditions the "loud" and "soft" samples can readily be identified even though they are actually heard at the same intensity.

There are no phonetic symbols for loudness as such, apart from stress marks, and their absence is probably not greatly missed in transcription. If one did wish to note loudness features, probably the best expedient would be to designate four broadly impressionistic levels: *soft, conversational, loud,* and *shout.* To define these levels specifically in terms of speech power is quite impossible for a number of reasons, some of them obvious. Rough approximations, however (if the speaker is 3 feet distant), would be *soft,* 50 to 65 dB; *conversational,* 65 to 75 dB; *loud,* 75 to 85 dB; and *shout,* above 85 dB.

EMPHASIS

Having given a separate treatment to pitch, duration, and loudness—the determinants of emphasis—it is now possible to draw together facts about the elements of these three features which contribute to stress, and to discuss its function in speech more specifically. Physiologically, stressing is the result of an increased articulatory effort of some kind which gives relatively greater prominence to some portions of an utterance than to others, creating thereby a nonsegmental signal which is critical for the communication of both lexical and affective meanings. Two kinds of stressing are often distinguished: (1) *phrasal*, or sentence, stress and (2) *word* stress. These have already been discussed in relation to speech *rhythm*, but they also exercise certain communicative functions which should be noted.

The composite nature of stress has been mentioned several times, and the interdependence of pitch, duration, and loudness in giving prominence to syllables and phrases is probably clear already. The results of a study by Tiffin and Steer (1937) may serve to reinforce the point. After comparing stressed and unstressed versions of the same words, they reached the following conclusions: (1) In 98 percent of the cases, stressed words were longer; (2) in 84 percent, stressed words were more highly inflected; (3) in 75 percent, they reached a higher pitch; (4) in 74 percent, they were more intense; and (5) in 71 percent, they reached a lower pitch. As we have indicated, however, the order in which these factors are listed may not necessarily be the order of their relative influence in determining emphasis. For further information on this point we suggest Bolinger's "A Theory of Pitch Accent in English" (1958).

Phrasal Stress

This kind of stress, also known as *sentence stress*, which we use intuitively from the time we begin to talk, is best understood by means of an example. Obviously the command "Give me the book" has different meanings, depending on whether one says "*Give* me the book," "Give *me* the book," "Give me the *book*," or even "Give me *the* book." There is a constant rise and fall of stress within the phrase during most ongoing speech. In this way we establish meaningful relationships among the words of a phrase, giving prominence to some by stressing and subordinating others by unstressing. Phrases within a sentence may be treated in the same way, and there are even broader patterns of emphasis in longer utterances.

Word Stress

It is often extremely important to establish the primacy of one syllable over another in any multisyllabic word. Hence the notion of *word stress*, which involves gradations of force on syllables within a word.[1] Phrasal stress is a baseline upon which word stress is superimposed, somewhat as small hillocks may change the outline of a mountain slope. Word stress may have a special grammatical function when it contrasts the meaning of words which otherwise could sound alike. Note, for example, forms such as the noun-verb

[1] This has also been called *syllable* stress, because the stress is placed upon the syllable, rather than the whole word. However, the logic more often used is that the stress type indicates the unit *within which* stress establishes relationships. The minimum domain of stress is probably always the syllable, regardless of the function of the stressing.

pairs "*con*flict" and "con*flict*," "*add*ress" and "ad*dress*," and *sub*ject" and "sub*ject*." Also, without a stress signal one could not, for instance, differentiate "telephone" from "tell a phone," except by contexts which are sometimes ambiguous.[1]

Phonetic Transcription of Stress

In this text we suggest that four degrees of stress are useful for the accurate description of speech:[2] (1) *primary stress*, to which the symbol [ˈ] is assigned; (2) *secondary stress*, marked by [ˌ]; (3) *tertiary stress*, for which there is usually no special symbol (such a syllable is ordinarily considered simply *unmarked*); and (4) markedly *weak stress*, to which the symbol [◡], the *breve*, is sometimes assigned. However, because weak syllables tend to become *indefinite*, they are often best described with the schwa [ə] or schwar [ɚ] symbols. It is worth noting here that in English some syllabic consonants come about as a result of marked syllable weakening. Note for example the weak syllables of "puddle" [pʌdl̩] and "cup and saucer" [kʌpm̩sɔsɚ]. The symbols for primary and secondary stress are placed *before* the syllable, not *after*.

Primary stress needs little explanation. It is the heaviest emphasis given monosyllabic words when they are spoken in isolation or placed on the most important syllable of an important word in context. In the sentence "*An*swer the *tele*phone" the first and fourth syllables may both receive primary stress. *Secondary stress* is of a perceptibly lesser degree but is still great enough to constitute stressing. Take the example "telephone." Both "tel" and "phone" are stressed and thus are strong syllables, but the "phone" is usually subordinate to "tel"; this would be symbolized by transcribing the word [ˈtɛləˌfon]. Other illustrations would be "applejack" [ˈæpəlˌdʒæk], "cupcake" [ˈkʌpˌkek], "hatrack" [ˈhætˌræk], and so on.

Tertiary stress is not quite so easy to define because we get here into somewhat more subtle distinctions as to what constitutes unmarked stress. Briefly, tertiary stress is the amount of emphasis needed to preserve normal vowel quality without, on the one hand, giving it the attention-getting emphasis of primary or secondary stress or, on the other hand, allowing it to be weakened to the point where the vowel becomes indefinite. For an illustration of tertiary stress, compare "syntax" [ˈsɪntæks] with "sin tax" [ˈsɪn ˌtæks]. The second syllable of "syntax" has tertiary stress. The same condition is found in "potash" and "pot ash," and "hardware" and "hard wear." The final syllables in "syntax" and "hardware" need not receive

---

[1] For more information on the phonetic correlates and linguistic functions of stress see Lehiste (1970).

[2] Perceptual analysis is not as simple as it might seem, and experts disagree about whether or not listeners can perceive and transcribe more than two or three levels. Three degrees of stress can usually be discerned in *words*, but we believe that the fourth degree recommended in our notation is desirable at the level of the *phrase*.

secondary stress as the words are customarily spoken; yet the final syllables are not weak, else the words would be heard as (ˈsɪntəks] and [ˈhɑrdwɚ].[1]

Weak stress will be mentioned again when the schwa and schwar syllables are discussed, but something of its characteristics may be described in a preliminary way. As was brought out in the treatment of *rhythm* (pages 138 to 141), the cadences of speech are such that strong and weak syllables tend to alternate, the latter often having the lightest of emphases. The most easily noted evidence of this unstressing is its effect on the vowel quality, length, and pitch; such syllables are short, often low in pitch, and indefinite in quality, leading to a low-central lax vowel. Thus, by definition, the weak syllable becomes [ə] although [ɚ] and the syllabic consonants [m̩], [n̩], and [l̩] also usually appear in weak syllables only.

It must be admitted that there may be some deficiencies in this system of stress notation, but it works reasonably well for most purposes. The more observant student may have detected that, strictly speaking, all weak syllables do not have the same vowel quality as the use of a single symbol [ə] might imply. We will discuss this matter further in Part Two. Some weak syllables seem to have a quality which is sufficiently definite to disqualify them as schwas, yet have less than tertiary stress. The symbol [˘] can be used in these cases, although this practice is not followed in the examples given in this text.

A Feature System for Prominence

General Loudness Level Features	Stress Features
Soft	Primary
Conversational	Secondary
Loud	Tertiary (unmarked)
Shout	Weak

VOICE QUALITY

As a nonsegmental which may transmit information of consequence, particularly about a speaker's health and affective reactions, voice quality may possibly have been given less attention than it deserves. No systematic feature system for the parameters of vocal quality can be found in phonetic literature, despite the promise one might hold for a comprehensive description of spoken language. We are, therefore, proposing such a system, couched in primarily physiological terms. It divides the principal features into those of *source* and *resonance* or *filter*, that is, into those features which originate in the laryngeal and resonance systems, respectively.

Quality is the attribute of voice which is most difficult of all to describe

---

[1] The so-called spondee word, often used in tests of hearing, has two stressed syllables ("toothbrush" and "blackboard" are examples), but they are almost never equally stressed. One syllable will have primary, the other secondary or tertiary stress.

verbally, although the meaning of the term is probably well understood by most readers. A rather awkward way to define quality is to say that it is that aspect of voice which is independent of pitch, loudness, or duration; it is the remaining cue which enables us to differentiate two tones if the other three acoustic variables are held constant. Thus, we have no difficulty distinguishing the notes of a violin and a clarinet, even though they sound tones of the same pitch, intensity, and duration, for they differ in quality. The quality of a tone is sometimes called its *tone color* or *timbre*.

The quality of voice is a subjective experience, just as are its pitch and loudness. The physical *anlage* for perceived voice quality lies in the acoustic composition of the tone, as it does for *vowel quality* as well. A fuller explanation of the relation between quality, a *sensation*, and its *stimulus*, the acoustic spectrum, was given in Chapter 4, and if necessary should be reviewed. If the distinction between voice quality and vowel quality is confusing, bear in mind that voice quality is an overall perceptual experience conditioned by the form of the wave generated in the larynx but modified by cavity resonance. Vowel quality depends primarily on the patterning of the first two or three major resonances, or *formants*, for which tongue height and fronting are mainly responsible. It may help to remember that whispered vowels without voice are perfectly intelligible.

Source Features: Periodicity

It has been customary for musicians and teachers to describe vocal quality impressionistically as "thin," "shrill," "harsh," "rough," "guttural," "hoarse," and so on. Such terms may have some artistic or pedagogical applications, but their ambiguity and lack of system make them unsatisfactory. The question of what is satisfactory cannot be answered fully, but the attribute of periodicity or aperiodicity of vocal-fold vibration underlies at least some of the important perceptual attributes of voice.

Specifically, if the vocal note arises from vibrations which are sufficiently regular, or *periodic* (see page 79), it will usually be free of those qualities impressionistically described as "rough," "hoarse," "harsh," and so on. It obviously does not follow that the total experience will be necessarily aesthetically pleasing, of course, since this may depend on a number of other considerations. Certain departures from a relatively regular periodicity will tend to impart those qualities listed above, to the degree that the wave form is irregular. The resulting vocal characteristics, when sufficiently prominent, include one major category of voice disorders for which there is a wide variety of functional and organic causes.[1] Upward and downward *pitch breaks* are also a product of aperiodicity and in general arise from the same kinds of causes.

[1] For discussion of these see Moore (1971).

Source Features: Voice Register

The importance of voice *register* as an element of vocal quality has not been widely discussed in the speech literature, nor have the mechanisms of the registers themselves been understood until recently. We do not have the space here to explain the matter fully, but it is becoming clear that register changes are more important in the speaking voice than we had hitherto realized, and should be considered in any discussion of vocal theory or practice.

To understand the concept of the vocal register, we need only to be aware that as the pitch of the voice changes there is ordinarily an accompanying change in voice quality, particularly at the higher and lower ends of the pitch range. This change in quality is a result of the fact that as the mass-elastic structure of the larynx changes to produce alterations of pitch, the *form* of vibration of the vocal folds also changes.

One of the chief changes in vibratory form which occurs is a change in the relative proportion of time within the vibratory cycle during which the vocal folds remain closed. In normal phonation, at the "comfortable" voice frequencies (*modal register*), the pattern of movement is as follows: a rapid opening, followed directly by an even more rapid closing, with the closed part of the cycle occupying an appreciable length of time. This kind of movement generates an acoustic signal which is very complex—rich in harmonic partials. However, as the voice pitch begins to reach the upper end of its comfortable pitch range, there is a tendency—which can be avoided to only a limited extent—for the vibration to become not only more rapid but also more simple in its form (*falsetto register*). This "simplicity" in part takes the form of a shortening of the proportionate time of the cycle during which the glottis is closed. The resulting acoustic signal has less of its energy in the harmonics, and sounds less "full" or less "rich" in harmonic overtones.

At the lower end of a speaker's pitch range lies the *pulse register*. Here the laryngeal adjustment is such that the vocal folds become thicker and more lax than they are in the production of tones in higher registers. For this and other reasons their pattern of vibration has two characteristics which distinguish the pulse register: (1) frequency of vibration is low; and (2) the proportion of time during a total cycle when the glottis is open is relatively brief. The result is a low-pitched vocal note in which a series of individual vibrations can be sensed. If one's perception is analyzed introspectively, such a tone tends to have a pulsing or intermittent—rather than even—tonal characteristic. The individual pulses are sometimes described, although imperfectly, as "popping" or "frying" noises, and may be particularly noticeable in the lower ranges of the register.[1]

---

[1] For additional information on the register question, consult Vennard (1967), Van Den Berg (1968), and Hollien (1974).

Not everyone agrees on the names to be applied to the different registers, or even upon how many types of registers ought to be distinguished, but most would agree that at least the above three should be identified: the *modal*, also called *chest* or *midrange register*; the *falsetto*, also called *head* or *upper register*; and the lowest register called variously the *pulse register*, *vocal fry*, *glottal fry*, or *creaky voice*.

Possibly the most important thing to emphasize about these registers is that each is a normal part of the phonation pattern for most speakers. An exception is perhaps the rarity of the pulse register in young women and children. None of the above registers can be called abnormal when appropriately correlated with voice pitch. However, unskilled use of any one of them must be counted a vocal defect.[1] For example, the falsetto register is normal at the high end of the pitch range, but habitual use of falsetto is abnormal, especially in males. On the other hand, to maintain modal register conditions in the high pitch range is normal only in singing. Total avoidance of pulse register is, if not exactly a "defect," at least not typical male speech. In the very relaxed, quiet, low-pitched male voice the low-frequency popping quality is common. Normally, most phonation will, of course, be in the midrange and in the modal register. Precisely how we use register changes in normal speech and the differences in their use in female and male speakers are matters about which little is known at present.

Movement between the lower and the upper registers requires a change in muscular set which, if unskillfully accomplished, can result in a register *break*, a kind of sudden change of pitch akin to the *yodel*. Excessive tensions may also result in falsetto tones which instead of sounding "simple" or "pure" may instead sound "shrill," "piercing," "tight," "thin," "strident," and the like. Similarly the pulse register can be misused, and in this register speech may sound "harsh," "grating," "guttural," or "rough." It should be noted that speaking either below or above one's comfortable register may under certain conditions induce vocal tensions or, alternatively, be a result of such tensions, with accompanying unpleasant vocal features. Both abnormally high and abnormally low speech are sometimes related to what the voice pathologist calls *hyperkinetic phonation*. It is generally believed that the trained speaker or singer can phonate without vocal abuse over a wider pitch range than the average untrained individual.

Source Features: Vocal Noise

This source feature is made up of friction-like noises usually arising at the glottis. They are due not to periodic vocal-fold movements, but rather to the random turbulent motions of the airstream itself, as it is forced through a constricted glottal opening. What we impressionistically call a "breathy"

---

[1] For treatment of registers in relation to voice disorders, see Brodnitz (1967).

voice consists of some relatively periodic vocal tone with an admixture of "hishing" which is the result of incomplete closure of the glottis. The breathy quality may be minimal or so prominent as to approach a total loss of vocal note. An effortful *hoarse whisper* combines aperiodic vocal-fold movement with vocal-tract noise. Typical *hoarseness* acoustically and physiologically resembles a hoarse whisper. While many of these noise source phenomena are of more concern to the speech pathologist than to the phonetician, there are occasions when the latter may wish to note them, for from time to time they may be heard in the voices of perfectly normal speakers.

Source Features: Vibrato

A final vocal source feature is *vibrato*, which assumes the form of a *tremolo* in special cases. As a feature of "normal" voices, vibrato is a fluctuation in pitch of about a semitone on the musical scale occurring at a regular rate of about six times per second. A vibrato is easily noted as a kind of "pulsing" in any sustained musical tone and is usually thought to be a mark of musical artistry. In what singers may call a *straight* tone there may be a virtual absence of vibrato. A very pronounced fluctuation in the vibrato "amplitude," perhaps greater than a tone in extent, or a pronounced intensity fluctuation, may be called a *tremolo*. Impressionistically this is a component of what we may mean by a "quavering" voice. Tremulous voices are often a variation which signals age and physical debility. Although vibrato is a major feature in singing quality, its significance for speaking is debatable, since the speaker does not ordinarily sustain a tone as long as even two vibrato cycles. It is, however, at least a minor feature of speech quality.

Resonance Features: Cavity Coupling

It will be recalled from the discussion of the speech system (Chapter 4, pages 86 to 87) that under certain conditions the resonance system will impart a quality called *nasality* to vocal tones. Acoustically, the condition necessary for this is *cavity coupling*; physiologically, the most frequent condition is relaxation of the soft palate to allow communication between the nasal and oropharyngeal resonators.

Except for three *nasals*, nasality is not in theory a characteristic of English resonant sounds; hence its presence is a voice quality feature one may wish to note. In the feature system outlined at the end of this section, it has seemed more convenient to use the impressionistic term *nasality* in place of the resonance system condition, *coupling*, which is responsible for this vocal quality.

A further remark should be made about what is implied when a notation of this voice quality feature is included in the description of speech samples. Nasality is noteworthy only when present in sounds which in theory should have a *normal oral* feature. As a matter of fact, English speakers may evidence considerable nasality, without loss of intelligibility, for the feature is not distinctive in our vowel system. If nasality is considered sufficiently prominent, the symbol [~] can be used. Logic would seem to indicate that provision should be made for indicating *denasalization* of nasal sounds, but this does not often occur to a significant degree among "normal" speakers.

In classifying the nasality feature on the basis of the various resonance cavity conditions from which it may arise, we have gone only so far as to indicate two types: *open and closed.* The first of these, *open* nasality, is a resonance which develops when the soft palate is relaxed and the nasal passages are free from abnormal obstruction. *Closed* nasality has a similar but more pronounced tone color and occurs when there is a blocking or construction of the nasal passages which leaves an aperture substantially smaller than the palatopharyngeal opening. Such cavity characteristics are found mainly when there is some pathology or deformity in the nasal passages. Actually, open and closed nasality cannot be differentiated without some moderately sophisticated diagnostic examination, and the type of nasality may be of more interest to the speech pathologist than to the general phonetician. The term *twang* or *whang* is sometimes applied to nasal-sounding resonances presumed due to constriction of the vocal tract rather than coupling of the nasal and oropharyngeal resonators.

Resonance Features: Cavity Length

This feature and the one to be discussed next, *cavity constriction*, have a critical influence on voice quality. They are not, however, easy to determine, since this requires close observation of the pattern of muscular adjustment the speaker assumes during phonation. This may be so difficult, in fact, that in many cases a judgment about the vocal-tract configurations will have to depend on inferences drawn from the perceived voice characteristics as much as from direct observation of the speaker. Nevertheless, the variables of cavity length and constriction must be taken into account as fully as possible by anyone who is attempting to appraise voice quality features in detail.

Cavity length is important to voice timbre because it is one of the prime factors which determine the resonant frequencies to which the cavity system will respond. As might be inferred, the greater the cavity length, the lower the frequencies to which it will be tuned. The average length of the male vocal tract has been calculated as 17 centimetres, but normal variability in length is of greater interest, of course. Children's voices, for example, are "thinner" not only because they are pitched higher than most adult voices of the same sex, but also because they are resonated in relatively shorter vocal tracts. As a matter of fact, the attributes which underlie our classification of voices into bass, baritone, tenor, and so on, are based on resonance properties related to vocal-tract length, as well as upon the pitch range of the singer or speaker.

Obviously any individual can shorten and lengthen the vocal tract only within distinct limits, but the possible extent of such variation may be greater then commonly supposed—and in any event it is sufficient to cause perceptible changes in voice quality. The most easily observed indication of changes in cavity length is the position of the larynx in relation to its point of rest. As the larynx moves upward, the vocal tract is shortened; if it is lowered, cavity length is increased. Some elevation and depression of the larynx is a natural accompaniment to pitch fluctuations within the speaker's customary range, but these are not sufficient to cause marked quality changes. When the larynx is drawn toward extreme high or low positions, however, cavity length may be altered to the extent of introducing resonance patterns which result in voice qualities that attract unusual attention.

In the feature system, notation of cavity length as *normal* refers, of course, to conditions of phonation in which laryngeal position, and hence cavity length, varies for the most part only within limits consistent with the speaker's physiologically normal range; *lengthened* and *shortened* are descriptive terms employed for what are judged to be significant departures therefrom.

Resonance Features: Cavity Constriction

While the speech sounds are formed by various constrictions of the vocal tract, the configurations into which it is drawn also play a significant role in creating the resonances which determine voice quality. This whole subject is altogether too broad and complex for discussion here at any length, but the relevant point is that, for each individual, there tends to be a habitual pattern of muscular adjustment which affects vocal-tract resonance and which can be described, in part, in terms of vocal-tract constrictions.

Point of constriction, like some of the other voice features that have been mentioned, is probably most important in the analysis of abnormal voice qualities. In many abnormally resonant voices the voice specialist may be able to identify *foci of tension*, or points in the vocal tract at which "distortions" of the cavity system are to be found. Incidentally, it is important to recognize that the cavity constrictions which need to be noted regularly go along with *lengthened* and *shortened* cavity length. In the descriptive feature system, *normal* implies an absence of noteworthy constrictions at any point in the vocal tract, although each individual has habitual modes of phonation.

It is something of an oversimplification to locate a point of constriction at any one place, because the excessive muscular contractions tend to be generalized. There are, nevertheless, certain regions of the vocal tract where constriction is typical, or is at least more marked. These we have designated as *oral-front*, *oral-back*, and *pharyngeal*. The voice characteristics associated with each are covered best in the literature on disorders of phonation. (See, for instance, Boone, 1971.)

Oral-front constrictions center around the lips and associated facial muscles. Size of mouth opening tends to be restricted, partly because the jaw also is likely to be "clenched." *Oral-back* may also be characterized by abnormal tension in the jaw muscles, but may involve hypertonicity in the intrinsic and extrinsic muscles of the tongue which draw it abnormally backwards, and perhaps upwards. *Pharyngeal* constrictions are found at a lower point, and in the majority of cases probably affect the laryngeal muscles as well as those of the pharynx. It seems wise to warn again that constrictions are usually generalized, that they occur in many configurations, and that the three constriction features given here are adequate only for broad descriptions.

Preverbal Vocalizations

Although not included among voice quality features, our discussion would be incomplete without mention of certain kinds of vocal output not part of speech prosody in the usual sense, but which are by no means not without linguistic significance. These are sounds such as crying, laughter, sighing, and a host of other inarticulate but meaningful sounds. Some of these are emotional interjections, uttered automatically; others, such as the meaningful cough or throat clearing, are derived from reflexive vocal-tract behavior having a physiological purpose. To call them prelinguistic implies that these sounds were the forerunners of verbal communication, as they are to some extent in the child who has not yet learned to talk. Whatever, their nature, however, they may take on functions peculiar to a genuine speech code.[1]

Phonetic Symbols for Voice Quality

The problem of devising an adequate set of phonetic symbols to represent the different voice qualities has never been fully solved, for a satisfactory theory of voice quality has not yet been developed. The long-term voice quality "sets" may be indicated simply by a descriptive footnote to the phonetic transcription. Where a quality is used prosodically or extends over relatively short spans of one of a few syllables, then phonetic symbols are helpful. The following are those which have some sanction of usage and can be recommended as partially standardized at this time. Some are taken from the work of Peterson and Shoup (1966), some from the IPA. All symbols are placed below the vowel except as noted.

[ₒ]   *Voiceless*. This symbol stands for a source featured by an open glottis, allowing a relatively free airflow without vocal-fold vibration. Peterson and Shoup distinguish this condition from [ᴧ], which stands for *whispered* sounds produced with a constricted glottis.

---

[1] For a recent account of the origins of speech and its relation to prelinguistic "sign stimuli," see Mattingly (1972).

[ᵥ]   *Voiced.* The source tone is regularly periodic, or relatively so.

[◻]   *Breathy voice.* The addition of turbulent noise to a voiced periodic signal.

[ᴡ]   *Irregular periodic.* Typical of harshness or hoarseness in vocal quality.
        Termed *laryngealized* by Peterson and Shoup.

[ᴧ]   *Pulse register.* Also termed *glottal fry* or *creaky voice.*

[~]   *Nasalized.* Characterized by nasal resonance. (Modifier is placed above
        the phonetic symbol.)

A Summary of Voice Quality Features
Source Features

Periodicity Features	*Register Features*
Periodic	Modal register
Irregular	Falsetto register
Upward break	Pulse register
Downward break	

Noise Features	*Vibrato Extent*
Normal	Straight
Breathy	Moderate
Whisper	Wide
	Tremolo

Vibrato Rate	*Vibrato Regularity*
Slow	Regular
Normal	Irregular
Fast	

Filter Features

Nasality	*Cavity Length*
Normal oral	Normal
Open nasal	Lengthened
Closed nasal	Shortened

Cavity Constriction
   Normal
   Oral-front
   Oral-back
   Pharyngeal

EXERCISES

1 Following are suggested glossary terms; add others you wish to remember
   and frame a concise definition of each:

breve
cavity constriction features
cavity coupling
cavity length features
creaky voice
denasalization
dysprosody
emphasis
  phrasal
  sentence
  syllable
  word
empty forms
extralinguistic
filter features
full-long
fry register
half-long
hesitation pauses
hoarseness
hyperkinetic phonation
indexical functions
  idiosyncratic
  nonce
  sociosyncratic
intensity
irregular periodic
loudness
macron
melody curves
nasality features
nonsegmentals
nonlexical verbalization
optimum pitch
paralanguage
periodicity features

physiological pitch
pitch features
  contour
  level
  range
prominence features
  loudness
  stress
prosody
registers
  falsetto
  modal
  pulse
stress
  emphatic
  primary
  secondary
  tertiary
  unmarked
  weak
suprasegmentals
rhythm of speech
sources features
terminal inflections
timbre
time features
  duration
  pause
  pause fill
  tempo
vocal quality
vibrato
vocal noise features
  breathy
  normal
  whisper

2 Read the following as a surprised question, a simple statement, a highly emphatic statement, and as an incomplete sentence. Then assign pitch contours to each so that a reader of your pitch transcription would know which of the above was intended. The italicized word is to be given emphatic stress.

Oh.
They came to *town.*
Helen started to *laugh.*
Final exams are *canceled.*

Did *he* go fast.
Everyone in class gets an A.

Here is an example of what you should do, using the sentence " The boy went *home*," and employing the four-level, three-terminal system discussed in this chapter:

Question: ¹the ²boy ²went ³home⁴↗ .
Statement: ¹the ²boy ²went ²home¹↘ .

3 Try to determine your own average speaking pitch, your pitch range normally used in reading and speaking, your maximum pitch range including falsetto, and your optimum pitch. Your instructor will help you with this, or see Fairbanks (1940, p. 122). Discuss your results in the light of the discussions of this chapter.

4 Attempt to read in a complete monotone. Then gradually increase your range to an octave or more. Try to do this without sounding unnatural. Try to analyze what effect there is on the meaning and emotive tone of the pitch-range expansion. If your reading sounds unnatural, can you explain why? You may need help with this!

5 Read each of the following (tape your reading if possible), timing yourself as accurately as possible as you read in three different ways: (1) in a natural conversational manner, (2) at a rate which seems only half the rate of the normal reading, and (3) at a rate which seems to you twice as fast. When you have finished timing each reading, compare your measurements with the norms given in Appendix E, in words per second, syllables per second, and sounds per second.

> *Multisyllabic passage:* 28 words, 88 syllables, about 213 speech sounds
> Notice the complications of configuration distinguishing articulatory patterning among dialect areas. Listeners certainly perceive divergent usages among anterior explosive consonants. Assimilative changes particularly characterize numerous exotic regionalisms.

> *Monosyllabic passage:* 58 words, 58 syllables, about 179 speech sounds
> Please see the way folks from a far place use their speech, and note that they don't make sounds as you and I do. You can hear some quite new ways that stop sounds are made in the front of the mouth. How sounds are left out or changed is one more thing to note in strange speech.

6 Tape record the paragraphs above and analyze them for pausing and phrasing. Phonetically transcribe the readings, using single and double vertical lines to indicate pausing. Practice reading these paragraphs with both a lengthening and a shortening of the pauses you initially employed, and also with additioned pauses at which you believe to be logical locations. Record these readings and analyze their timing, comparing them with the results obtained in the above exercises.

7 Record a lecture by one of your instructors. Make a typescript of a few minutes of the lecture. Mark it for pauses. For all pauses of over about 1 second indicate the nature of the pause, its type of fill, if any, and its approximate duration. Comment in the light of what we have said about pausing in this chapter.

8 Read the following, carefully observing the pause and length notations:

> [ɑ::‖so:|aɪ θɔ·t hi wəz gonə se ðæt‖ɑ̃:::::|
> jə si. wijustə god|ʌtʃ ðɛr|bət|bət|wɛl ‖‖ jə si:‖
> wi gɑt kaɪnə taɪrdəvət‖so:: m̩:::‖hwʌtļ wi du·]

8 Pronounce the following two-syllable words and phrases as both strong-weak and weak-strong patterns. Which stress patterns are nonsense? Which words or phrases have their meanings changed? To what? Why?

1	compress	6	conflict	11	rebel
2	reject	7	subject	12	safeguard
3	reward	8	blackbird	13	white house
4	a tall	9	sailing	14	permit
5	inter	10	relay	15	object

10 Pronounce the following three-syllable words or phrases in five different ways: ‾ᵕ‾, ᵕ‾ᵕ, ‾‾ᵕ, ᵕ‾‾, and ᵕᵕ‾. Which pattern is best for each?

1	telephone	5	a ball game	9	confuse me
2	castigate	6	good looking	10	psychosis
3	confuses	7	rectify	11	uniform
4	Long Island	8	repair parts	12	unhappy

11 The following two-syllable words and phrases are generally pronounced with one strong and one weak syllable. The strong syllable usually has primary stress, although this would depend upon sentence context. The weak syllable is ordinarily [ə], [ɚ], [m̩], [n̩], or [l̩], but this also could vary in connected speech. Which syllable is strong when the words are spoken in isolation? Transcribe the words, using stress marks, and practice saying them in such a way that each word has a primary and a weak syllable. Then check yourself with a pronouncing dictionary.

able	causes	enter	notice	second
about	certain	father	people	service
a boy	colors	fired	percent	standard
alone	chorus	German	profit	suppose
a man	correct	human	promote	the boy
better	cotten	idle	pupil	the man
business	doctor	mental	return	woman
button	dollar	nation	science	women

12   The following three-syllable words and phrases are ordinarily pronounced with two degrees of stress. Most of these pronunciations, if not all, require one stressed and two weak (or a weak and a tertiary) syllables. Transcribe these words with stress marks. Turn to a pronouncing dictionary for confirmation if you are unsure in any case.

a camper	connection	mineral	remover
a sadness	delicate	mistaken	stamina
camera	delicious	palaces	the circus
caresses	feminine	optimum	the saddle
companion	intimate	poisonous	together
condition	Iowa	potato	

13   The following three-syllable words and phrases usually require three different degrees of stress. In most examples there is a primary stress, a secondary stress, and a weak stress. In some cases, however, two primary (or two secondary) stresses and one weak or tertiary stress might be satisfactory. Transcribe these words with stress marks. When in doubt, consult the dictionary.

abdicate	exercise	medicate	penalize
Birmingham	harmonize	memorize	persevere
carpetbag	holiday	now complain	put it there
cavalier	introduce	operate	some ice cream
civilize	lemonade	overlook	telephone
elevate	magazine	pearly gate	

14   In the following four- and five-syllable words two, three, or four degrees of stress may be employed. Transcribe them phonetically with stress marks, then check a pronouncing dictionary for verification.

additional	elementary	indoctrination	personality
anniversary	elimination	intelligence	possibility
apparently	environment	international	qualitatively
civilization	especially	manufacturer	requirements
composition	examination	mechanical	situation
consideration	experiment	nationally	specialization
cooperation	generation	necessarily	superintendents
curriculum	immediately	opportunity	syllabification
educational	individual	particularly	university

15   In any normal, informal prose text, search out the following words and observe their stress in your own or someone else's pronunciation (in informal contexts). Which of the four stress levels is most frequent? Phonetically transcribe the weak form of each. See answers in Appendix E.

1	a	**5**	but	**9**	some
2	an	**6**	for	**10**	if
3	the	**7**	at	**11**	so
4	of	**8**	to	**12**	or

16 Using the stress system described in this text, mark the following sentences in such a way as to indicate that the italicized word has emphatic stress in its sentence, while also preserving appropriate stress balance in the remainder of the sentence. See Appendix E for the authors' transcription.

1 "How do I do? How do *you* do?"
2 "It's *impossible* for me to go."
3 "It's impossible for *me* to go."
4 "It's impossible for me to *go*."

17 Read the following to someone who has an unmarked script, written in normal paragraph form. Tell the listener to place parentheses around *soft* passages, no marks on normal-level passages, a line under loud passages, and a double line under very loud or shouted passages. Try to follow the loudness level and phrasing instructions given below, attempting to contrast phrases sufficiently well that your listener will succeed in underlining according to your intent. Try to make the contrasts clear while at the same time making your reading flow naturally and sensibly. That will, of course, require some art as well as phonetic skill.

Speak the speech, (I pray you,) as I pronounced it to you, (trippingly on the tongue); but if you mouth it, as many of your players do, (I had as lief the town crier spoke my lines). Nor do not saw the air too much with your hands, (thus); but use all (gently). . . .

(Shakespeare, *Hamlet*)

Part Two

Applications

Chapter 8

Introduction to the Sounds of American English

It will be our purpose in the remaining chapters to consider each of the major classes of American speech sounds in detail, toward the ultimate goal of pointing a way toward the application of some of the theoretical formulations from previous chapters to problems of speech analysis and speech improvement. There will be no attempt to catalogue all the facts about standard and nonstandard American English, for this would be an impossible task; neither will we undertake to offer prescriptions for "good" speech. Instead, notes on the individual sounds and the accompanying exercises which make up Part Two should be thought of as *directions for listening* which, if followed systematically, can lead to the development of those *phonetic skills* which are an indispensable complement to a grasp of *phonetic theory* in the study, analysis, and use of speech.

For purposes of speech analysis, *listening* is a very special technique. As we observed in Chapter 1, one can comprehend the meaning of spoken language without specific attention to its phonetic characteristics. On those occasions when we do become aware of such details, it takes no special expertise to tell whether or not speech is intelligible, is "our kind," or is serving the speaker's purposes effectively. It is quite a different matter to listen *analytically;* to be able to distinguish exactly the segments and articulatory features of an utterance one needs to study. The objective of the following sections, then, is to direct attention to the articulatory behavior of American English speakers as an aid to analytical listening. Bear in mind that it helps greatly in making accurate observations if one first knows the articulatory possibilities; therefore, effective listening is a matter of knowing to what one should listen.

The "attention directing" materials which will be found in the following chapters include the following: (1) voice prints, or spectrograms of the sounds discussed; (2) examples of the different English spellings of each sound; (3) analyses of the normal articulatory features of the sounds; (4) discussions of some major sources and types of variation in the use of each sound in American speech; (5) a practice paragraph loaded with the sound under study; (6) lists of common or relatively common English words which may employ the sound (although it must be remembered that because of dialect factors the words may not always be pronounced with the sound under study by speakers you may hear); (7) lists of minimal pair contrasts, spelled conventionally and also transcribed phonetically; and (8) relatively broad phonetic transcriptions of a pronunciation of the practice paragraphs. An appendix which follows these chapters on the individual sounds contains additional phonetic transcriptions which can be used for practice.

NOTES ON THE VOICE PRINTS

It may be recalled from Chapter 4 (pages 79 to 84 and Figure 4-7) that speech sounds are complex organizations of acoustic energy in time. These acoustic patterns may be made visible as *voice prints*, or *sound spectrograms*. Each of the chapters to follow will be headed by a series of spectrograms of all or most of the sounds to be discussed in that section, as they were carefully pronounced by one of the authors. They should help give you a special appreciation of the dynamic characteristics of the sounds as they vary in time and as they may influence one another in context. Take particular note of the following: (1) the manner in which the resonance "bars" change from vowel to vowel, and within the vowel, taking special note of the diphthongal characteristics of some vowels, and the pronounced changes of resonance in those sounds classified as diphthongs; (2) the different influences which consonants have on the vowel, as indicated by a bending of the resonance bars at the consonant boundaries; (3) the nature of the silent interval or "gap" typical of the consonants; (4) the different appearance of the "fill" within these gaps, whether by indications of voicing, noise, or different kinds of resonance or simply by an interval of silence.

NOTES ON THE LOADED PARAGRAPHS

The short paragraph exercises were written to provide a context which could include a wide variety of allophones of the sound under study, particularly those which seem to offer perceptual problems and problems in phonetic transcription. It is suggested that you practice transcribing these paragraphs as you believe you personally would speak them and in addition have someone else read them for you to transcribe. It may also be a useful exercise simply to identify each occurrence of the sound as you believe it would appear in standard conversational American speech—whatever dialect you choose. Then you may turn to the last paragraph in the same section to compare your transcription with that of one of the authors. The two transcriptions will be different, of course, but the differences should be explainable on the basis of your knowledge of the permissible variants of that sound. Finding the differences and rationalizing them will constitute a valuable exercise in speech and language perception. Recall that the authors speak with a General American dialect. They also have their own *idiolects*.

NOTES ON THE TRANSCRIPTIONS

The transcriptions in the exercise sections have employed the following conventions which may be helpful to you in explaining any variations between your transcriptions and ours: (1) For the most part Americanized IPA symbolization is used, including the use of [tʃ] and [dʒ] (rather than [č] and [ǰ]) and [ʃ] and [ʒ] (rather than [š] and [ž]); (2) we have distinguished only two low-back vowels, [ɑ] and [ɔ], in the broad transcriptions; (3) with a few exceptions we have generally employed [i], [u], [o], and [e] for both the diphthongal and nondiphthongal allophones of these vowels; (4) the major diphthongs [aɪ], [aʊ], and [ɔɪ] use the vowel-plus-vowel form; and (5) normal punctuation is used.

From the above you will realize that the phonetic transcriptions in all but a few of the appendix transcriptions are what we would call "broad," for the most part using only the major phonemic class symbols, plus schwa, schwar, syllabic consonants, and glottal stop. Special note should be taken of these, however, in view of the importance of vowel reduction in American English.

NOTES ON THE WORD LISTS

The lists of example words may be of help to you, particularly in identifying the various spellings of the sound and in drawing attention to some usages which may be at variance with your own. The list of vowel examples include nearly all the words in two sources: *The One Thousand Most Frequently Spoken Words* (Voelker, 1942) and the 1,000 most common words in the count of Thorndike and Lorge (1944). Read our examples aloud, not only to sense the similarities among the sounds they have in common, but also to identify the differences among the various allophones represented.

NOTES ON THE MINIMAL PAIRS

In addition to the practice paragraphs and word lists you will find for each sound groups of contrasting *minimal pairs*. Such pairs differ with respect to only a single phone. You may read them aloud, listening and analyzing the nature of the feature differences which underlie the contrasts. You may also use them to test the ability of others to recognize or produce the appropriate distinctions. The lists can be made the basis for an effective "intelligibility" test.

NOTES ON THE ANALYSES

Vowels

The articulatory characteristic common to all vowels is the feature *syllabic*. Therefore it may be of help to you, before you begin to study the vowels in detail, to review what has been said so far about the vowels and about syllables in general (Chapters 4 to 6, especially pages 96 to 99). Recall that the syllabic is the articulatory event featuring an open vocal tract and a peak of resonant acoustic energy. The vowel *target* is a particular tongue, lip, and jaw posture which determines the cavity resonance.

We suggest that at this time you consult again Figures 5-1 and 5-2, which depict some of the characteristic shapes taken by the tongue, lips, and jaw. It will help you to become better acquainted with the postures if you observe the contrasts in the diagrams, and also in yourself, as you produce each of the vowels and diphthongs in a context and as sustained "sung" vowels. Note, if you can, the differences in tongue height, or closeness of the vocal-tract constriction, jaw opening, tongue fronting (place of articulation), and lip rounding. Other features pertaining to vowel articulation should also be reviewed from the diagrams of Figures 5-3, 5-5, and 5-6, and Table 5-1.

Diphthongs

We have previously (see pages 98 to 99) defined the diphthong as a class of sounds in which *two* resonances could be perceived as occurring within the space of a single syllable or, alternatively, a speech event consisting of a nuclear vowel part and a glide part. If the latter point of view were to be stressed, we could, of course, easily eliminate the diphthong classification entirely, simply treating such events as combinations of vowel plus consonant. This is a perfectly feasible approach. [aɪ] is a back vowel plus a high-front off-glide, [aʊ] is a back vowel plus a back or labial off-glide. The transcription of these diphthongs as [aj] and [aw] is perfectly logical.

It is helpful in our understanding of some of the more frequently encountered classes of diphthongs to classify them in three ways. The first is to distinguish among front, back and centering diphthongs. The front diphthongs include the [aɪ], [ɔɪ], [eɪ], and [ɪi]. The back diphthongs include the [aʊ], [oʊ], and [ʊu] ([uw]). The centering diphthongs include the [ɪə], [ɛə], [æə], [ɑə], [ɔə], [ʊə], and their *r*-colored counterparts [ɪr], [ɛr], etc.

The second way in which diphthongs may be classified is to distinguish the on-glide from the off-glide diphthongs. The only on-glide diphthong which we will discuss is the [ju], which behaves like the other diphthongs, probably because it is a variant of the form [ɪu].

The third way in which diphthongs may be classified is in terms of whether or not the diphthongization is *significant*. In [eɪ], [oʊ], [ɪi], and [ʊu] it is not significant, in the important sense that these complex diphthongal vowels do not contrast phonemically with their nondiphthongal counterparts [e], [o], [i], and [u]. The significant diphthongs [aʊ], [aɪ], [ɔɪ], and [ju], do contrast with other nondiphthongal vowels. We will comment at some length about diphthongization of the tense vowels under the appropriate vowel categories in Chapters 9 through 11. The significant diphthongs will be considered separately in Chapter 12, where we will also consider some centering diphthongs, the [ɪr] ([ɪə]), [ɛr] ([ɛə]), [ɑr] ([ɑə]), [ɔr] ([ɔə]), and [ʊr] ([ʊə]).

Stop Consonants

You may recall from Chapter 5 that the stops are characterized by a complete obstruction of the airflow. The acoustic result is a silent interval of varying length, depending in part upon whether or not the air pressure remains adequate for continued voicing into the closed cavity. This closed-cavity voicing obviously cannot be long sustained, but the fact that glottal vibration can be preserved for varying amounts of time during a vocal-tract closure makes possible the voice-voiceless distinction among stops.

As airflow continues into the closed oropharyngeal cavity, pressure is built up behind the constriction, to a degree dependent mostly upon the force of articulation. The *release* of this consonant "dam" therefore will vary markedly in terms of the noise which may be generated by the eventual escape of the impounded air. Generally speaking, the greater the pressure behind the dam, the noisier the release. A study of the voice prints of Figure 13-1 will indicate the presence of these variations among the different stops of American English. As you read the sections on the stops, you should be especially attentive to these facts concerning voicing and consonant release, in addition to noting the cues to place of articulation.

Fricative Consonants

The class of obstruent consonants termed *fricative* is characterized by an incomplete or "leaky" obstruction of the airstream (they have been called "leaky stops.") The result is an interval of time more or less filled by noise. This fill varies markedly in a number of ways, including the frequency characteristics, voicing, and timing of the noise. These can in part be studied in Figure 14-1, but you should seek good models to sharpen your awareness of the subtleties which distinguish the fricatives from one another.

Nasal and Lateral Consonants

The feature common to these sounds is that all are formed by the introduction of a *secondary aperture* (see page 104). The voice prints of Figure 15-1 illustrate the highly characteristic acoustic patterns and dynamic properties of these sounds. Note that in each of these the "gap" between the vowels is filled, not by silence as in the stops, or by noise, as in the fricatives, but by another formant pattern, radically and abruptly changed from that of the vowel, but still vowellike in nature. Instead of a significant drop in energy at the consonant we see here a significant *change* in the energy pattern.

Glides

All consonants are in some respects glides, from a more closed to a more open position or vice versa. In the case of the glides per se, however, the *back stroke* of the consonant reverses the consonantal movement before an actual consonant obstruction occurs (see page 105). The result is that the air pressure change is usually quite insufficient to interfere with the continuous production of resonant tone, and so the consonant becomes not a radical drop of acoustic energy, nor an abrupt change, but rather a gliding change in resonance. The voice prints of Figure 16-1 show the typical pattern.

STUDYING THE SOUNDS OF SPEECH

While it is necessary to study the sounds of speech as isolated phones, strictly speaking the so-called individual sounds cannot be produced in isolation, since the syllable, as we have learned, is the irreducible unit of speech behavior. Even syllabics must be started and stopped in some way. Attempts to produce them without consonants usually result in producing the vowel with a glottal attack and an aspirate release. Any vowel or continuant consonant can, however, be prolonged in some of its features sufficiently well to permit study and practice. Certain other sounds—the stops, glides, and affricates—cannot become syllabic; hence they can be produced in "isolation" only if some vowel is provided, perhaps a voiceless neutral vowel which will not distract the attention from the features of the consonant. Whether or not a certain consonant can be isolated often will depend on which particular feature of that consonant is being studied. If the dynamic movement pattern is the important thing, as it usually is, then consonants simply cannot be pronounced by themselves. The pedagogical device of "isolating" a phone may nevertheless be an important way of developing adequate speech sound discrimination.

Auditory Cues

The first and most important rule in mastering the sounds is *learn to listen perceptively*. This is a matter of practice and of adopting certain listening attitudes. When we ourselves are talking, or when someone is talking to us, our natural inclination, obviously, is to pay attention to *what* is being said, not to the *how* of it. This behavior is so deeply rooted and so nearly unconscious that the average person without phonetic training makes only the grossest discrimination of sounds, and then only in terms of word meanings. In consequence a speaker may be quite unaware of conspicuous deviations in articulation and pronunciation, particularly in the case of habitual errors. The speaker has simply not been listening to himself or herself, or to others, or both. One hears oneself much more perceptively when speech is recorded and played back, and this is an excellent technique for practice.

To develop a good phonetic attitude, follow the basic principle of listening to speech as if it were only a certain kind of sound. For purposes of analysis ignore the meaning. Most especially, be sure you have not been thinking in terms of conventional word spellings. From the earlier discussions and from your own experience you know that printed words are regularly not pronounced the way they are spelled. Unfortunately, however, many persons seem to be "visual-minded" with respect to language, because in their school experience they have studied language almost exclusively in terms of reading and writing. Now it is essential to learn to hear words in terms of auditory and articulatory images.

The extent to which students must become familiar with the articulation movements or positions for each of the distinctive sounds may depend to a degree on their interests, but for almost every purpose this information is desirable. Certainly the teacher who undertakes to help others must be thoroughly familiar with the physiology of sound production. Students who have acquired a trained perception may be able to make correct speech sounds without much conscious awareness of the exact mechanics of their own speech, simply by "trial-and-error" learning—providing, of course, that they have someone who can pinpoint their errors. Even so, a good knowledge of speech sound production can help shortcut the learning process when properly applied.

Visual Cues

Visual cues often may help. Movements can be observed by watching the lips and, to some extent, the tongue of another person as he or she speaks. Watch yourself in a mirror. Visible movements or positions are particularly important for the labial and dental sounds, and for some other sounds such as the lip-rounded vowels. Even when the movement or adjustment for a sound is not readily seen in actual speech, one can nevertheless get supplemental help from visual stimuli. For instance, one can produce [1] and hold the tongue in position while the mouth is opened wide enough so that the adjustment can be observed. Visual cues are especially important in instructing the deaf and hard-of-hearing.

Tactual and Kinesthetic Cues

Touch, or *tactual* cues, may provide a great deal of information about the way sounds are made. Many of the consonants require some contact between the tongue or lower lip and some other structure. Where this is the case, it is possible to sense the position through touch. In making [f], for instance, one can feel that the lower lip is in contact with the cutting edge of the upper teeth. In a similar way one can sense that the tongue is in contact with the roof of the mouth behind the upper front teeth for such sounds as [t] or [l]. A great number of the consonant and semivowel sounds offer tactual cues of which one can learn to be aware.

Kinesthetic cues can be widely used, although they may at first be more difficult to identify than visual, tactual, or auditory sensations. Kinesthetic sensations enable us to judge the position of the tongue, lips, and soft palate and also to recognize the direction and extent of movement. These sensations are the result of impulses carried to sensory areas of the brain by nerves whose endings are in the joints and muscles. We depend to a great extent upon kinesthesis to control posture and movement, including speech movements. In most circumstances we are not consciously aware of such sensations, but we can learn to be. To do so, pronounce the speech sound being learned many times and in many contexts, focusing attention specifically on the position of the articulators or their pattern of movement. Conscious monitoring of speech movements may then be facilitated by a sensitivity to kinesthetic cues.

We have now reached the point in our study of phonetics where it becomes essential for the student to begin working with phonetic transcription. This technique, which is basic to all kinds of phonetic study, can make an important contribution to speech improvement, particularly as a necessary first step in the process of speech analysis. If you have not already begun to record your speech perceptions in the form of phonetic transcriptions, we suggest a reading (or rereading) of the comments on this subject in Chapter 3, pages 60 to 65.

Chapter 9

Front Vowels

[i], [ɪ], [e], [ɛ], [æ]

[i]
*E*VEN S*EE*M WH*EA*T DEC*EI*VE F*IE*LD
RAV*I*NE P*EO*PLE AM*O*EBA C*AE*SAR QU*A*Y

ANALYSIS

The [i] is the highest of the front vowels, in terms of both tongue position and resonance frequency (see Figure 9-1). In many cases the tongue nearly touches the hard palate, with an approximation so close that a fricative sound is often heard. The lower jaw is raised, and the teeth are nearly in occlusion. The lips are not rounded, and may be noticeably drawn back. The [i] is one of the complex, diphthongal, *tense* vowels. This tension is usually reflected in a lengthening of [i] (relative to [ɪ], its lax counterpart), its diphthongization, and a drawing forward of the back of the tongue (see x-rays of Figure 5-2).

The amount of diphthongization of [i] varies considerably, but when present results from a tongue movement from a lower to a higher and more

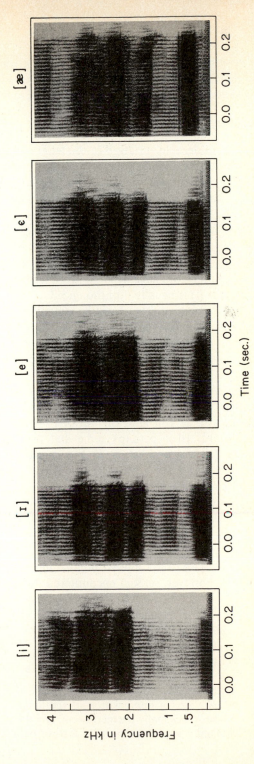

Figure 9-1 Sound spectrogram of [i], [ɪ], [e], [ɛ], and [æ].

193

tense position. The [ɪi], [ɪj], or [ij] symbols are sometimes used to represent this complex tongue movement. The feature classification for [i] is *high, front, tense, sonorant,* and *syllabic* in most distinctive feature systems.

VARIATION

There is considerable variation in the length and diphthongization of sounds of the [i] category, depending, of course, upon the context, rate, and stress. In words such as "see" and "scream," as strongly pronounced, the pattern is usually such that [i] could be quite accurately transcribed as a diphthong; [ɪj] or [ɪi]. When the vowel is stressed but not diphthongized, the sound may seem vaguely "foreign" to an American listener. However [i] is not always conspicuously diphthongized in our speech, even in stressed words. For example, words such as "teak," "seat," and "meter" may, as a result of the terminating stop, have little diphthongization. On the other hand, in final positions the [i] is usually diphthongized.

As with most vowels [i] will become "reduced" in unstressed positions. In the first syllable of such a word as "revise," for example, the lessened stress may result in pronunciations of [rɪvaɪz] or even [rəvaɪz]. Such pronunciations would, in fact, be the rule rather than the exception in informal speech.

Final weak '*y* sounds' vary rather markedly, from [ij] to the weaker [ɪ], or perhaps even [ə], in words such as "city" or "twenty." This variation will strike you as you read the various phonetic transcriptions in this text. In such words [ɪ] is perhaps somewhat more common in British English, while final [ij] is more likely to be heard in New Zealand. A somewhat more lax and simple [i] (yet not exactly the [ɪ] of "bit") is probably more or less the rule in General American.

[i] is seldom heard as a tense vowel before [r] in most American speech. In the General American "beer" and "we're," the usual pronunciation is best represented by the transcriptions [bɪr] and [wɪr].

Other variants of [i] are the centralized variety, symbolized by the "barred *i*" [ɨ] and the rounded high-front vowel, the [y]. Lip-rounded front vowels are, however, seldom encountered in English, as they are in Swedish, for example.

EXERCISES

1 Practice paragraph for [i]:

There are many reasons why the study of speech sounds would give each of us a keener appreciation of the language we speak. Our information is sometimes really meager. Seemingly the obvious reason is that we deem spelling the most important feature of a word, when this may not be exactly true. Needless to say, there must be no tendency to become too easygoing about orthography. But even the most pedantic teacher would be obliged to agree that ordinary devices of spelling constitute a very ineffective means of recording, with any real accuracy, the precise details of the language we hear when someone is speaking. Editors of dictionaries would be pleased, if it became even remotely feasible, to replace our present ineffective procedure for recording pronunciation. Various schemes have been devised for alleviating some of the agonies created by inconsistencies in spelling, but these ideas, although ingenious and appealing in some respects, are neither practical nor realistic.

2   Word list:

be	feel	keep	read	speak
being	feet	least	realized	speech
believe	field	leave	reason	speed
between	fifteen	machine	receive	street
complete	fourteen	me	sea	teacher
each	free	meal	seal	these
ease	green	mean	seam	thirteen
easily	Greek	meet	season	three
easy	he	need	see	tree
economics	heating	nineteen	seem	we
eighteen	idea	people	seen	weak
either	increase	piece	seventeen	week
evening	indeed	reach	sixteen	Z

3   Minimal pairs:

[i]—[ɪ]

each [itʃ]	itch [ɪtʃ]
feel [fil]	fill [fɪl]
feet [fit]	fit [fɪt]
green [grin]	grin [grɪn]
lead [lid]	lid [lɪd]
least [list]	list [lɪst]
meal [mil]	mill [mɪl]
meet [mit]	mitt [mɪt]
read [rid]	rid [rɪd]
week [wik]	wick [wɪk]

[i]—[ɛ]

bead [bid]	bed [bɛd]
beast [bist]	best [bɛst]
each [itʃ]	etch [ɛtʃ]
heed [hid]	head [hɛd]
lease [lis]	less [lɛs]
mean [min]	men [mɛn]
read [rid]	red [rɛd]
seal [sil]	sell [sɛl]
seat [sit]	set [sɛt]
seed [sid]	said [sɛd]

[i]—[e]

be [bi]	bay [be]
ease [iz]	A's [ez]
feel [fil]	fail [fel]
feet [fit]	fate [fet]
free [fri]	fray [fre]

he [hi]   hay [he]
least [list]   laced [lest]
me [mi]   may [me]
see [si]   say [se]
we [wi]   way [we]

4 Phonetic transcription. Criticize the following version of the paragraph in Exercise 1. A few intentional errors in transcription have been included. These would call for highly improbable pronunciations. There are supposed to be fewer than 12 but more than 4. How many can you find? Are you sure they are *errors?* Or are they simply acceptable alternatives?

[ðɛr ɑr ˈmɛnɪ rizənz hwaɪ ðə ˈstʌdi əv spitʃ saundz wʊd gɪv itʃ əv əs ə kinə əˌprɪʃɪˈeʃən əv ðə ˈlɪŋgwɪdʒ wi spik. ɑr ɪnfəˈmeʃən ɪz ˈsʌmˌtaɪmz ˈrili migɚ. ˈsimɪŋlɪ ðɪ ˈɑbviəs rizən ɪz ðət wi dim spɛlɪŋ ðə most ɪmˈpɑtn̩t fitʃɚ əv ə wɚd, hwɛn ðɪs me nɑt bi ɛgˈzæktlɪ tru. nɪdləs tə se ðɛr mʌs bi no ˈtɛndənsi tə bɪˈkʌm tu izɪgoɪŋ əbaut ɔrˈθɑgrəfɪ. bət ivən ðə mos pəˈdæntɪk titʃɚ wʊd be oˈblidʒd tu əgri ðət ˈɔrdɪnɛrɪ dɪˈvaɪsəz əv ˈspɛlɪŋ ˈkɑnstətut ə vɛrɪ ˌɪnɪˈfɛktɪv minz əv rɪˈkɑrdɪŋ, wɪð ɛnɪ riəl ækjərəsɪ, ðə prɪˈsaɪs dɪˈteəlz əv ðə læŋgowɪdʒ wi hir hwɛn sʌmwən əz ˈspikɪŋ. ɛdətəz əv ˈdɪkʃəˈnɛriz wʊd bi plizd, ɪf ɪt bɪkem ivən rɪˈmotlɪ fizəbl̩, tu rɪples aʊr prɛzənt ɪnɪˈfɛktɪv prəsidʒɚ fɔr rɪˈkɔrdɪŋ prəˌnʌnsɪˈeʃən. ˈvɛriəs skimz həv bɪn dɪˈvaɪzd fɚ əˈliviˌetɪŋ sʌm ə ðɪ ˈægənɪz kriˈetəd baɪ ˌɪnkənˈsɪstənsɪz ɪn ˈspɛlɪŋ, bət ðiz aɪˈdiəz, ɔlˈðo ɪnˈdʒinjəs æn əˈpilɪŋ ɪn sʌm rɪˈspɛkts, ɑr niðɚ ˈpræktɪkl̩ nɔr ˌriəˈlɪstɪk.]

[ɪ]
H*I*T   H*Y*MN   B*UI*LD   H*E*RE   B*U*SY
D*EA*R   D*EE*R   P*IE*RCE   W*O*MEN

ANALYSIS

The [ɪ] is probably the most frequently occurring of all stressed vowels in American English. In terms of the classical vowel tongue position diagram it lies between [i] and [e] in tongue height, with jaw somewhat lower than [i] and with lips more lax, slightly more open and unrounded. Acoustically [ɪ] tends to be a more simple (less diphthongal) and shorter vowel than [i], its tense counterpart. As the x-ray tracings of Figure 5-2 will show, in both [i] and [ɪ] the tongue body is forward, producing a markedly constricted front cavity compared with the much larger back cavity. This configuration gives to both of these vowels their characteristic high-frequency resonance. Figure 9-1 shows these typically high second-formant positions in the speech of one of the authors.

The distinctive feature classification usually given for [ɪ] is *high, front, lax, sonorant,* and *syllabic.* It is nonlabialized and ordinarily nonnasal.

VARIATION

The major distinction between such pairs of words as "bit" and "beet" is that of the tense/lax feature according to some phoneticians. Because of this, considerable variation in the pronunciation of either of these vowels is found as a result of contextual variations influencing stress or tongue height. The varieties of "final-*y*" pronunciations have already been cited (see [i]). Even in stressed words, one encounters variations between [i] and [ɪ]—in [ziro] versus [zɪro], for example, or [siŋ] versus [sɪŋ]. The influence of [ŋ] typically imparts to the vowel of "ing" a quality which is more "tense" than that found in "in." This is simply one typical example of the contextual influences discussed in Chapter 6.

In certain unstressed syllables there may be considerable alternation between [ɪ] and [ə] in certain words. Either [hæbɪt] or [hæbət], may be heard and indeed the latter pronunciation is the more likely in informal General American speech. Interesting variations may be heard resulting from *vowel reduction* in "ing" words, from the tense [iŋ] to [ɪŋ], [ɪn], [ən], and finally a vowel that is "lost" altogether. For example "putting" may be [putiŋ], [putɪŋ], [putɪn], [putən], or [putn̩].

For many non-English speakers the distinction [i]/[ɪ] is a difficult one to make, inasmuch as many languages do not make such a tense/lax distinction. In Italian and Mexican dialects of English, for example, a sound higher than [ɪ], but shorter and less tense than [i] may be used for both "sheep" and "ship." You should try to learn to produce this simple high-front variant.

Other allophones of /ɪ/ of special interest are the [ĩ], the nasalized high-front vowel; the [ɨ], the "barred ɪ" heard, for example, in most pronunciations of "just" used as an American adverb; and the [Y], the lip-rounded variant heard in the German "glück." [ɪ˔] and [ɪ˕] are raised and lowered versions, respectively, the former being a vowel with resonance toward [i] and the latter representing sound closer to [e].

EXERCISES

1 Practice paragraph for [ɪ]:

> By this time the beginner will find that the seeming intricacies of phonetic transcription should be resolving themselves into certain relatively simple principles which enable him to begin spelling with sounds instead of less meaningful letters. As this ability improves, an important skill will begin developing: the capacity to distinguish the different sounds in the myriad

familiar words we hear repeatedly, and to notice what has hitherto been missed. Bit by bit, listening facility is being acquired in easy but effective ways. It is within the realm of possibility for nearly every individual to become so proficient that he can, without seeming design, get a vivid impression of the pronunciation of English. Learning the diction of a language will appear increasingly simple if the novice makes it his business to consider words as sounds fitted together in a close-knit mosaic.

2 Word list:

a Illustrative words using [ɪ] in stressed syllables:

ability	different	increase	miniatures	simple
activity	dishes	Indian	miss	since
appear	district	individual	Mr.	situation
been	efficient	industry	Mrs.	six
begin	exist	information	official	still
bill	fifteen	instant	opinion	system
bit	figure	institution	particularly	this
build	fill	isn't	permit	thrift
built	finish	instrument	physical	until
business	give	insurance	physics	visit
children	given	intelligent	picture	which
city	him	international	political	will
civilization	his	interpret	position	wind
committee	history	introduce	possibility	window
composition	illustrate	killed	principle	wish
condition	imply	liquor	quick	with
consider	importance	little	religion	within
continue	impossible	live	rich	without
criminal	include	milk	river	women
did	income	million	ship	written

b Illustrative words using [ɪ] in unstressed, or relatively unstressed, syllables (pronunciation may vary among [i], [ɪ], [ɛ], and [ə]):

accomplish	begin	divide	expression	receive
advantage	believe	drastic	extent	remain
always	benefit	economics	furnish	remember
article	between	enjoy	if	represent
audience	college	enough	in	reserve
average	decide	entirely	is	result
became	degree	employ	it	return
because	demand	examination	knowledge	subject
become	department	example	language	the
before	describe	except	percentage	topic
began	design	experiment	public	various

c Illustrative *ing* words:

being	doing	going	resulting	think
bring	during	king	single	training
coming	English	putting	thing	trying

d Illustrative [ɪr] words:

appears	dear	hear	merely	serious
beard	experience	here	near	spirit
clear	fear	material	period	year

e Illustrative final-*y* words (pronunciation may vary between [ɪ] and [i]):

ability	company	fifty	ninety	scarcely
activity	country	finally	opportunity	seventy
actually	duty	forty	party	sixty
already	early	Friday	personality	study
any	easily	happy	philosophy	Sunday
apparently	easy	heavy	poetry	thirty
army	eighty	history	policy	Thursday
body	elementary	immediately	possibility	Tuesday
carry	entirely	industry	practically	twenty
century	especially	lady	pretty	university
city	every	Monday	primarily	usually
committee	exactly	money	probably	variety
community	family	necessary	Saturday	very

3 Minimal pairs:

[ɪ]—[i]		[ɪ]—[æ]	
been [bɪn]	bean [bin]	begin [bɪgɪn]	began [bɪgæn]
bid [bɪd]	bead [bid]	bit [bɪt]	bat [bæt]
did [dɪd]	deed [did]	did [dɪd]	dad [dæd]
dim [dɪm]	deem [dim]	fist [fɪst]	fast [fæst]
is [ɪz]	ease [iz]	him [hɪm]	ham [hæm]
live [lɪv]	leave [liv]	his [hɪz]	has [hæz]
rich [rɪtʃ]	reach [ritʃ]	in [ɪn]	an [æn]
rill [rɪl]	real [ril]	miss [mɪs]	mass [mæs]
ship [ʃɪp]	sheep [ʃip]	mister [mɪstɚ]	master [mæstɚ]
sin [sɪn]	seen [sin]	sit [sɪt]	sat [sæt]

[ɪ]—[ɛ]	
bill [bɪl]	bell [bɛl]
bit [bɪt]	bet [bɛt]
bitter [bɪtɚ]	better [bɛtɚ]
fear [fɪr]	fair [fɛr]

here [hɪr]	hair [hɛr]
in [ɪn]	N [ɛn]
knit [nɪt]	net [nɛt]
lift [lɪft]	left [lɛft]
wrist [rɪst]	rest [rɛst]
sit [sɪt]	set [sɛt]

4 Phonetic transcription. Here is a transcription of the material in Exercise 1. Criticize and compare your own pronunciation with that of the author. In which ways do you differ?

[baɪ ðɪs taɪm ðə bɪˈgɪnɚ wɪl faɪnd ðæt ðə ˈsimɪŋ ˈɪntrəkəsiz əv fəˈnɛtɪk ˌtrænˈskrɪpʃən ʃəd bi rɪˈzɑlvɪŋ ðɛmˈsɛlvz ɪntə sɝtn̩ ˈrɛlətɪvli sɪmpl̩ prɪnsəpl̩z hwɪtʃ ənebl̩ hɪm tə bɪˈgɪn ˈspɛlɪŋ wɪθ saundz ɪnˈstɛd əv lɛs ˈmɪnɪŋfəl lɛtɚz. æz ðɪs əbɪləti ɪmˈpruvz, æn ɪmˈpɔrtn̩t skɪl wɪl bɪˈgɪn dɪˈvɛləpɪŋ: ðə kəpæsəti tə dɪsˈtɪŋgwɪʃ ðə dɪfrənt saundz ɪn ðə ˈmɪriəd fəmɪljɚ wɝdz wi hɪr rɪˈpitədlɪ, æn tə notəs hwʌt həz ˌhɪðɚˈtu bɪn mɪst. bɪt baɪ bɪt, ˈlɪsənɪŋ fəˈsɪləti ɪz ˈbiɪŋ əkwaɪɚd ɪn ɪzi bət ɪˈfɛktɪv wez. ɪt ɪz wɪˈðɪn ðə rɛlm əv ˌpɑsəˈbɪləti fɔr nɪrli ɛvri ˌɪndəˈvɪdʒəwəl tu bɪˈkʌm so prəfɪʃənt ðət hi kæn, wɪˈðaut ˈsimɪŋ dɪˈzaɪn, gɛt ə vɪvəd ɪmˈprɛʃən əv ðə prəˌnʌnsiˈeʃən əv ˈɪŋglɪʃ. ˈlɝnɪŋ ðə dɪkʃən əv ə ˈlæŋgwɪdʒ wɪl əpɪr ɪnˈkrisɪŋli sɪmpl̩ ɪf ðə nɑvəs meks ət ɪz bɪznəs tə kənsɪdɚ wɝdz æz saundz fɪtəd təgɛðɚ ɪn ə klos nɪt moˈzeɪk.]

[e]
LATE RAIN SAY STEAK THEY
MESA GAUGE CHALET

ANALYSIS

As pronounced in standard American speech the [e] is *front* but slightly lower than the [ɪ] or the [i]. In comparison with the other front vowels, both [e] and [ɛ] are in an approximately "neutral" or *mid-front* position with respect to tongue height. As a consequence, a somewhat larger front cavity is formed than for [i] or [ɪ], and there is about a 100-Hz shift in some of the major acoustic resonances. The [e] articulation is described as *tense*. a fact which is probably related to a number of features which characterize this sound: an increased muscular effort, a drawing forward of the root of the tongue, a tendency toward diphthongization, and an increased length. In this sense [e] is to its lax counterpart [ɛ] as [i] is to [ɪ]. Perceptually the [e] is "brighter" in quality than the [ɛ].

Perhaps the most important aspect of the [e] as it contrasts with the lower-front vowels is its prominent diphthongal quality—the shift from a more lax [ɛ]-like quality toward a more tense [i]-like quality. For this reason this sound is often classified as a diphthong and represented by such transcriptions as [eɪ], [ɛɪ], [ej], and [ɛj]. In distinctive feature terms [e] is *front*, *tense*, *unrounded*, *nonhigh*, *nonlow*, *sonorant*, and *syllabic*.

VARIATION

Differences in characteristic tension may be responsible for most of the major [e] variants within American dialects. In less stressed syllables between certain consonants [e] is relatively monophthongal and short. On the other hand, [e] in stressed word-final position may be clearly perceived as [ej] (as in [təˈdej]). In "cake" the pronunciation [kek] may freely alternate with [kejk]. In dialects spoken by persons whose native language does not distinguish between [e] and [ɛ]—a language in which the feature tense-lax is not significant in the vowel system—a high but short and monophthongal vowel may be heard in both [ɛ] and [e] words. "He's late" may thus be perceived by an American ear as "his let." The shortening of this vowel is, of course, not the only dialect variant. An interesting lower and diphthongal variant, much like American [aɪ], is a common form in some English and Australian dialects. "Take it today," in these dialects is much like "tike it to die" [taɪk ət tədaɪ].

In native pronunciations of [e] one occasionally encounters short allophones of [e], or such *relic* pronunciations as [ɛt] and [nɛkəd] for "ate" and "naked." Interesting variants on [e] may be found in pronunciations of the days of the week, which vary, according to stress and style, from [sundej] to [sʌnde] to [sʌndi] to [sʌndɪ].

Allophones of [e] which should perhaps be given special mention are these: [e], [ɛj], [ej], [e̞], [eᴛ], the nasalized allophone [ẽ], and the labialized (lip-rounded) [ø] such as may be heard in the German pronunciation of the word *hören*.

EXERCISES

1   Practice paragraph for [e]:

> Good taste in speech will repay one daily for such small effort as it may
> entail. Basically, the way in which we talk is taken as a measure of our
> personality traits, our education and culture. It can be claimed, with considerable persuasive force, that too much stress can be placed on slavish
> concern for pronunciation rules. The practiced ease of a good speaker,
> however, is mainly a painstakingly cultivated "feel" for the ryhthm and
> style of spoken language. In the main, he will favor plain and straightforward ways of saying what he has to convey, and will not deign to lay on,
> like a cape, the presumed elegancies of stage diction or some other strained

or ornate manner. He will thus be related to his listener in a communicative way, but ostentation and seeming display will play no part in his speech behavior.

2 Word list:

able	education	late	pay	station
afraid	eight	lay	phase	stay
age	eighth	made	place	straight
aid	escape	main	play	strange
always	explain	maintain	race	Sunday
away	face	major	radio	taste
baby	famous	make	rain	take
based	Friday	making	raise	taken
basis	gain	may	remain	taxation
bay	game	maybe	safe	Thursday
became	gate	Monday	sale	today
break	gave	name	same	trade
came	generation	nation	Saturday	train
case	graduate	nature	save	Tuesday
change	gray	neighbors	say	wait
contain	great	occasion	shape	wave
create	illustrate	page	space	way
date	labor	paint	stage	Wednesday
day	laid	paid	state	weight
educate	lake	paper		

3 Minimal pairs:

[e]—[ɪ]

ale [el]	ill [ɪl]	aid [ed]	Ed [ɛd]
break [brek]	brick [brɪk]	bale [bel]	bell [bɛl]
case [kes]	kiss [kɪs]	laid [led]	led [lɛd]
eight [et]	it [ɪt]	laced [lest]	lest [lɛst]
gave [gev]	give [gɪv]	paced [pest]	pest [pɛst]
laid [led]	lid [lɪd]	paint [pent]	pent [pɛnt]
lake [lek]	lick [lɪk]	phase [fez]	fez [fɛz]
pain [pen]	pin [pɪn]	taste [test]	test [tɛst]
stake [stek]	stick [stɪk]	rain [ren]	wren [rɛn]
tape [tep]	tip [tɪp]	wait [wet]	wet [wɛt]

[e]—[i]

great [gret]	greet [grit]
laid [led]	lead [lid]
lake [lek]	leak [lik]
male [mel]	meal [mil]
main [men]	mean [min]

pace [pes]   peace [pis]
shape [ʃep]   sheep [ʃip]
way [we]   we [wi]
wake [wek]   week [wik]
wave [wev]   weave [wiv]

4 Phonetic Transcription. Study the following phonetic transcription of the paragraph in Exercise 1. Compare your pronunciation with that of the author, keep-in mind that the author's pronunciation illustrates only *one* of many which would have been acceptable. This pronunciation is informal colloquial. What changes would occur in a formal style?

[gud test ɪn spitʃ wɪl rɪˈpe wʌn delɪ fɚ sʌtʃ smɔl ɛfɚt əz ɪt me əntel. ˈbesɪklɪ
ðə we ɪn hwɪtʃ wi tɔk ɪz tekən əz ə mɛʒɚ əv aur pɚsəˈnælətɪ trets, aur
ɛdʒɚˈkeʃən ən kʌltʃɚ. ɪt kən bi klemd, wɪθ kənsɪdərəbl̩ pɚˈswesɪv fɔrs, ðət
tu mʌtʃ strɛs kən bi plest ɑn ˈslevɪʃ kənsɚn fɔr prənʌnsiˈeʃən rulz. ðə
præktəst ɪz əv ə gud spikɚ, hauˈɛvɚ, ɪz menlɪ ə ˈpenz tekɪŋlɪ ˈkʌltəvetəd
fiəl fɔr ðə rɪðəm ən staɪəl əv spokən ˈlæŋgwɪdʒ. ɪn ðə men hi wəl fevɚ plen ən
ˈstretˈfɔrwɚd wez əv seɪŋ hwʌt hi hæz tə kənve, ænd wəl nɑt den tə le ɑn,
laɪk ə kep, ðə prɪˈzumd ˈɛləgənsiz əv stedʒ dɪkʃən ɔr sʌm ʌðɚ strend ɚ ɔrˈnet
mænɚ. hi wəl ðʌs bi rɪˈletəd tu ɪz lɪsnɚ ɪn ə kəmˈjunəketɪv we, bət ɔstənˈteʃən
ən ˈsimɪŋ dɪsˈple wɪl ple no pɑrt ɪn hɪz spitʃ bɪˈhevjɚ.]

[ɛ]
GET MANY HEAD AGAIN GUESS BURY SAYS HEIFER LEONARD

ANALYSIS

This extremely common sound, ranking about fourth in frequency of usage among American vowels, calls for a tongue position somewhat lower than that for the [e], with the root of the tongue perhaps slightly further back, and with slightly more open lips and lowered jaw. This *lower-mid-front* vowel is lax, short, and ordinarily undiphthongized. The feature description customarily applied to [ɛ] is *front, nonhigh, nonlow, lax, unrounded, sonorant,* and *syllabic.*

VARIATION

As with other vowels, the precise feature composition of [ɛ] may be considerably altered as a result of the influence of context, rate, stress, and other factors. When [ɛ] is followed by certain tongue-body consonants, assimilative change may result in an [e]-like vowel. Hence, perhaps, the tendency in some dialects for words like "fresh" and "egg" to be [freʃ] and [eg]. On the other hand, when unstressed, phonemic /ɛ/ may be reduced to a lax central vowel in such words as "letter" [lɛtɚ], "evident" [ɛvədənt], or "interpret" [ɪntɝprət].

In certain areas one may encounter interesting variations in the pronunciation of a number of words in which a nasal is normally preceded by [ɛ] in standard speech. Perhaps owing to Southern and Midland dialect influences, students in our classes are sometimes almost evenly divided between [ɛ] and [ɪ] in the words "pen" and "many" and a number of other words of similar vowel-nasal construction. Most dictionaries do not sanction [pɪn] and [mɪnɪ] for these words, but these pronunciations are frequent.

Substitutions of [æ] for [ɛ] are frequently encountered in a number of foreign dialects. A common burlesque of Russian may be [læt mi sæl də pænsəlz] for "let me sell the pencils." In other dialects a more tense and high variant may be heard (see [e]).

In some Southern speech a variant of [ɛ] may be heard which takes the form of a diphthongization which has been transcribed as [ɛə], or in some cases, [ɛjə]. This is a speech sound variant which is paralleled by other forms (often termed a "drawl"—Wise, 1957) such as [ɪjə] for [ɪ], [æjə] for [æ], and [uwə] for [u]. Such forms are nonstandard, even in "typical" Southern speech according to Wise.

In listening for [ɛ], you should be aware that like most other "open" vowels it never appears in the final position in words.

To review and add to the above list of variants, the major allophones of [ɛ] are these: [ɛ˔]-raised, [ɛ˕]-lowered, [ɛə]-low off-glide, [ɛjə]-drawled, [ɛ̃]-nasalized, [œ]-lip rounded, as in German *wörter*.

EXERCISES

1 Practice paragraph for [ɛ]:

> The discerning student of speech will have many occasions to speculate on the relation between voice and personality. Unless he is completely insensitive to what is said in his presence—and to how it is said—he may note that such things as tension in the voice and certain patterns of inflection may sometimes allow him to make fairly correct guesses about the personality, education, or place of residence of the speaker. This matter of the relation between voice and personality has been studied many times by various investigators, apparently with somewhat disparate results. There is one very important fact that has emerged from all of these attempts to clarify the situation: whether we like it or not, people do get a picture of us from the sound of our voice alone. This picture is not necessarily a true one, but it is very often a reliable one. This means that the effect spread

by our voices is one listeners agree upon, even though it may not be the same as the effect spread by other kinds of behavior. We should remember these lessons as we prepare to be better speakers.

2 Word list:

again	eleven	intelligent	primarily	step
against	else	itself	process	strength
ahead	end	kept	protect	success
already	energy	left	question	tell
amendment	enter	less	read	ten
America	ever	let	red	test
any	every	letter	remember	their
attempt	evidently	many	represent	them
attention	expression	measure	rest	themselves
benefit	fair	men	said	then
best	February	mental	scarcely	there
better	federal	mention	second	twenty
century	fellow	met	self	unless
correct	forget	method	sell	very
death	French	necessary	sense	wears
debt	friend	never	separate	Wednesday
December	general	next	September	well
definite	generation	November	send	went
depend	get	pen	sentence	when
develop	hair	percentage	set	where
direct	head	personnel	seven	whether
education	heavy	prepare	specialize	yellow
effect	held	present	spend	yes
egg	help	president	spent	yet
element	however			

3 Minimal pairs:

[ɛ]—[e]		[ɛ]—[æ]	
best [bɛst]	based [best]	any [ɛni]	Annie [æni]
debt [dɛt]	date [det]	bet [bɛt]	bat [bæt]
edge [ɛdʒ]	age [edʒ]	head [hɛd]	had [hæd]
get [gɛt]	gate [get]	left [lɛft]	laughed [læft]
let [lɛt]	late [let]	less [lɛs]	lass [læs]
M [ɛm]	aim [em]	letter [lɛtɚ]	latter [lætɚ]
men [mɛn]	main [men]	met [mɛt]	mat [mæt]
sell [sɛl]	sale [sel]	pen [pɛn]	pan [pæn]
west [wɛst]	waste [west]	sell [sɛl]	Sal [sæl]
wreck [rɛk]	rake [rek]	then [ðɛn]	than [ðæn]

[ɛ]—[ɪ]

head [hɛd]   hid [hɪd]
letter [lɛtɚ]   litter [lɪtɚ]
met [mɛt]   mitt [mɪt]
pen [pɛn]   pin [pɪn]
red [rɛd]   rid [rɪd]
said [sɛd]   Sid [sɪd]
sell [sɛl]   sill [sɪl]
tell [tɛl]   till [tɪl]
ten [tɛn]   tin [tɪn]
well [wɛl]   will [wɪl]

4 Phonetic transcription. In the following phonetic transcription of the paragraph in Exercise 1, most of the [ɛ] words appear in accented syllables, and their pronunciation is fairly uniform. This is not always the case, however. Which of the following [ɛ] sounds might be pronounced with an [ɪ] quality by some speakers? Which might be pronounced with [æ] rather than [ɛ]?

[ðə dɪ'zɝnɪŋ studn̩t əv spitʃ wɪl hæv mɛni əkeʒənz tə 'spɛkjəˌlet ɔn ðə rɪ'lɛʃən bɪ'twin vɔis ən ˌpɝsə'nælət. ʌn'lɛs hi ɪz kəmplitli ɪn'sɛnsətɪv tə hwʌt ɪz sɛd ɪn hɪz prɛzəns—æn tə hau ɪt ɪz sɛd—hi me nɑt ðət sʌtʃ θɪŋz əz tɛnʃən ɪn ðə vɔis ən sɝtn̩ pætənz əv ɪn'flɛkʃən me 'sʌm'taɪmz əlau hɪm tə mek fɛrli kərɛkt gɛsəz əbaut ðə ˌpɝsə'nælət, ˌɛdʒə'keʃən, ɔr plɛs əv rɛzədəns əv ðə spikɚ. ðɪs mætɚ əv ðə rɪ'lɛʃən bɪ'twin vɔis ən ˌpɝsə'nælət hæz bɪn 'stʌdɪd 'mɛni taɪmz baɪ 'vɛriəs ɪn'vɛstəˌgetɚz, əpɛrəntli wɪθ 'sʌm'hwʌt dɪspərət rɪ'zʌlts. ðɛr ɪz wʌn vɛri ɪm'pɔrtn̩t fækt ðət hæz ɪ'mɝdʒd frəm ɔl ə ðiz ətɛmps tə 'klɛrəˌfaɪ ðə ˌsɪtʃə'weʃən: hwɛðɚ wi laɪk ɪt ɔr nɑt, pipl̩ du gɛt ə pɪktʃɚ əv ʌs frʌm ðə saund əv aur vɔis əlon. ðɪs pɪktʃɚ ɪz nɑt ˌnɛsə'sɛrəli ə tru wʌn, bʌt ɪt ɪz vɛri ɔfən ə rɪ'laɪəbl̩ wʌn. ðɪs minz ðət ði əfɛkt sprɛd baɪ aur vɔisəz ɪz wʌn lɪsənəz əgri əpɑn, ivən ðo ɪt me nɑt bi ðə sem æz ði əfɛkt sprɛd baɪ ʌðɚ kaɪndz əv bɪ'hevjɚ. wi ʃəd rɪ'mɛmbɚ ðiz lɛsənz æz wi prɪ'pɛr tu bi bɛtɚ spikɚz.]

[æ]
HĂT ĂUNT PLAĬD

ANALYSIS

The [æ] has the distinction of being the most consistently spelled of the vowels, and it is the lowest of the front-vowel series. Its articulation is similar to that of [ɛ] except for a substantially greater jaw lowering and lip opening. [æ] represents a pronounced departure from the articulatory "neutral" position. The tongue body is forward but usually described as a bit back of the other front vowels. See Figure 5-2 for the typical x-ray tongue diagram.

The [æ] is often classed as a tense vowel. This tension is variable and redundant, however. The sound is long, yet it is normally considered a simple syllabic. It does not appear in word-final positions. The feature analysis of a strong, stressed, canonical General American pronunciation is *low*, *front*, *unrounded*, *tense*, *sonorant*, and *syllabic*.

VARIATION

A rather wide range of pronunciations is characteristic of this family of speech sounds—variations in the tension, height, diphthongization, and nasality, for the most part. Before high-back consonants and sometimes in other contexts as well [æ] may have a higher, more tense sound. For example, "hang" may become something like [hɛŋ] or [heŋ]. Like any other vowel, [æ] can easily assimilate nasality from adjacent nasal consonants. In addition, the low tongue position appears in some speakers to invite a nasalization of this sound even in the absence of an adjacent nasal consonant.

American [æ] does not appear with significant regularity in modern European languages, with the consequence that a variant, usually a sound similar to [ɑ] or [a], may be heard in French, Italian, and Spanish dialects of English. In a French dialect, for example, we may hear [ajamapi] for "I am happy." On the other hand, a German may come closer with a raised [æ⊥] (or lowered [ɛт]). It is, however, the variants spoken by English-speaking persons which are especially interesting to most native students. For some speakers the use of the so-called broad *A*, actually [a] or [ɑ], is typical in a group of some 150 or so words which are pronounced with [æ] in General American.[1] These are words in which [æ] precedes [f], [s], [θ], and [n] plus a consonant. Examples are "laugh" [laf], "mast" [mast], and "can't" [kant] as spoken by a few Easterners, many British, and occasionally other Americans with pretensions to "culture."

Perhaps more frequent than the British [a] in America are the diphthongal Southern variants [æɪ] and [æjə], and the [ɛə] of Yiddish and perhaps some other New York City dialects. Examples are the Southern [a:kæjənt] for "I can't," and the Yiddish [fɛənsɪdðɛət] for "fancy that."

A summary of some of the more important allophones and dialectal variant of [æ] is as follows: [a], the retracted "compromise" vowel between [æ] and [ɑ]; [æ̃], the nasalized variant; [æ⊥], the higher, more tense [ɛ]-like variant; [æə] or [æjə], the "drawled" diphthongal variants.

---

[1] For a discussion of British versus American *ah*-vowel usage, see Kenyon (1946).

EXERCISES

1 Practice paragraph for [æ]:

Good speech habits, in the last analysis, do not demand any special aptitude. Drill must be carried out after the fashion of trial-and-error learning,
so that speech has exactly the sound demanded by acceptable standards of
pronunciation. It is necessary to give careful attention to the pattern of
sound, and to practice until one is satisfied that he has actually mastered
an accurate standard. When the capacity to catch fine distinctions between
sounds has at last been mastered, there will be ample reward for past effort,
and the battle for good speech will have been half won. One must ask,
"How should it sound?" Then marry academic theory to practical accom-
plishment.

a Illustrative words using [æ] in stressed syllables:

accident	camp	hand	practically
act	captain	happen	practice
action	catch	happy	ran
activity	contact	hat	sat
actually	drastic	land	stamp
add	exactly	Latin	stand
animal	examination	man	standard
average	fact	manner	taxation
back	factory	mathematics	taxes
bad	family	matter	traveling
bag	glad	national	understand
balance	graduate	natural	valley
battle	grammar	perhaps	value
began	grass	plan	

b Illustrative words pronounced [æ] or, in Eastern speech, [a] or [ɑ]:

advance	chance	France	master
advantage	class	glass	past
after	command	grant	pass
afternoon	dance	half	plant
answer	demand	last	rather
ask	drama	laugh	slant
can't	fast		

c Illustrative [ær] words, in which either [æ] or [ɛ] is commonly heard:

apparently	carry	marry	various
care	character	share	

d Illustrative unaccented [æ] words, usually pronounced in connected speech with [ə]:

an	at	had	than
and	can	has	that
as	cannot	have	

e Illustrative [æŋ] words:

bank	hang	sank	rang
crank	language	tank	thank

3 Minimal pairs:

[æ]—[ɛ]

		[æ]—[ɑ]	
and [ænd]	end [ɛnd]	add [æd]	odd [ɑd]
back [bæk]	beck [bɛk]	ax [æks]	ox [ɑks]
bad [bæd]	bed [bɛd]	bag [bæg]	bog [bɑg]
bag [bæg]	beg [bɛg]	battle [bætl̩]	bottle [bɑtl̩]
land [lænd]	lend [lɛnd]	cat [kæt]	cot [kɑt]
man [mæn]	men [mɛn]	hat [hæt]	hot [hɑt]
pat [pæt]	pet [pɛt]	lack [læk]	lock [lɑk]
sad [sæd]	said [sɛd]	pat [pæt]	pot [pɑt]
sat [sæt]	set [sɛt]	sap [sæp]	sop [sɑp]
tan [tæn]	ten [tɛn]	valley [vælɪ]	volley [vɑlɪ]

[æ]—[ɔ]

Al [æl]	all [ɔl]
at [æt]	ought [ɔt]
cast [kæst]	cost [kɔst]
crass [kræs]	cross [krɔs]
lag [læg]	log [lɔg]
lass [læs]	loss [lɔs]
last [læst]	lost [lɔst]
rang [ræŋ]	wrong [rɔŋ]
sang [sæŋ]	song [sɔŋ]
tat [tæt]	taught [tɔt]

4 Phonetic transcription. The following is a phonetic transcription of the paragraph given in Exercise 1, as it was spoken in a conversational manner by one of the authors. You should compare this pronunciation with your own, checking on your conclusions with regard to the pronunciations of the [æ] words in particular. It should be emphasized at this point that this is not the only way this paragraph could be correctly pronounced— or even, possibly, the best way for your own particular purposes or locality. It is spoken in what we call a General American dialect—roughly synonymous with that spoken in the West and North, as opposed to the Eastern and Southern regions.

[gʊd spitʃ hæbəts, ɪn ðə læst ənæləsəs, du nɑt dɪˈmænd ɛnɪ spɛʃəl ˈæptəˌtud.
drɪl mʌst bi ˈkɛrɪd aʊt æftə ðə fæʃən əv traɪəl ən ɛrə ˈlɜnɪŋ, so ðət spitʃ
hæz ɛgˈzæktlɪ ðə saʊnd dɪˈmændəd baɪ ækˈsɛptəbl̩ stændədz əv prəˌnʌnsiˈeʃn̩.
ɪt ɪz ˈnɛsəˌsɛrɪ tə gɪv kɛrfəl ətɛnʃən tə ðə pætən əv saʊnd, æn tə præktəs
əntɪl wʌn ɪz ˈsætəsˌfaɪd ðət hi əz ˈæktʃəwəlɪ mæstəd ən ækjərət stændəd.
hwɛn ðə kəpæsətɪ tə kætʃ faɪn dɪˈstɪŋkʃənz bɪˈtwin saʊndz hæz ət læst bɪn
mæstəd, ðɛr wəl bi æmpl̩ rɪˈwɔrd fɔr pæst ɛfət, ænd ðə hæbl̩ fɔr gʊd spitʃ
wɪl həv bɪn hæf wʌn. wʌn mʌst æsk, "haʊ ʃʊd ɪt saʊnd?" ðɛn ˈmɛri
ˌækəˈdɛmɪk ˈθɪrɪ tʊ ˈpræktɪkl̩ əˈkɑmplɪʃmənt.]

Chapter 10

Central and
Reduced Vowels

[ʌ], [ɜ], [ɝ], [ə], [ɚ]

[ʌ]
CUP SOME COUPLE DOES FLOOD

ANALYSIS

There is some doubt as to exactly how the American [ʌ] should be described. The International Phonetic Association used the symbol [ʌ] to stand for a *back* vowel which was an unrounded counterpart of [ɔ]. Taking their lead, Heffner (1952) and many others also describe [ʌ] as a back vowel. However, still other phoneticians, such as Francis (1958) and Kenyon (1946), describe [ʌ] as *mid-central*. These disagreements probably have arisen because of the distinctions between British and American pronunciations of low-mid and back vowels.

British pronunciation of words such as "love" and "above" do indeed use a more backed vowel than the American. Kenyon's description may be the best: "lower mid-central retracted." The x-ray evidence, however, is not clear, there being no good x-rays available which could be unambiguously

211

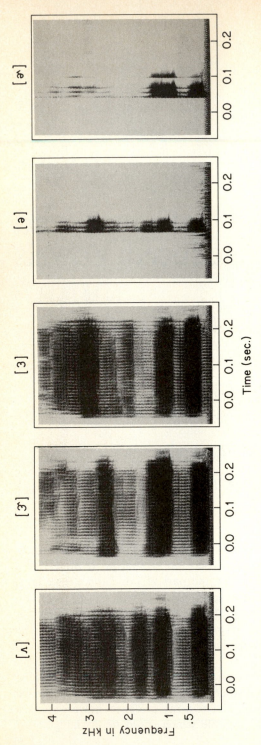

Figure 10-1   Sound spectrogram of [ʌ], [ɜ], [ɝ], [ə], and [ɚ].

related to a "typical" American [ʌ]. We can say, however, that the vowel is low and lax and short. It is possibly the most lax of the American vowels and comes fairly close in quality and tongue position to the "neutral" [ɜ]. However, as we shall learn, [ʌ] is not simply a stressed version of the neutral or schwa vowel.

The distinctive feature classification of [ʌ] which seems to account for most of its significant properties is *nonhigh*, *nonfront*, *nonround*, *lax*, and *syllabic*.

VARIATION

The [ʌ] is a fairly frequently used vowel in English, coming sixth among the vowels in the Dewey word count (Miller, 1951) and third in Moser (1960). The greatest source of observable dialectal variation is the notable British backing and lowering of the sound compared with American. This [ɑ]-like variant is also heard in certain Eastern and Southern American English dialects and may be transcribed [ʌ˕˖] or [ɑ˔˗]. In addition there are many other variants to be found in other English dialects and foreign dialects of English, for generally, with the possible exception of Russian, the sound is not part of the sound systems of modern European languages. Note the following examples of [ʌ] pronunciations in ten different English and foreign dialects to obtain some idea of how variable is the pronunciation of this sound.[1]

Cockney:	[ɑ] in "mother"
Scottish:	[ɪ] in "mother"
Irish:	[ʊ] in "rub"
New York:	[ɑ] in "come"
Appalachia:	[ɛ] in "touch"
French:	[ɑ] in "must"
German:	[u] in "just"
Norwegian:	[ɑ] in "but"
Italian:	[a] in "but"
Spanish:	[ɑ] in "cut"

One final note should be made concerning the extremely common adverb "just." This word illustrates well the effects of vowel reduction and assimilation. Stressed, it may be pronounced [dʒʌst], but spoken quickly in such a phrase as "It's just a shame," the vowel becomes centralized and higher—

[1] It should not be supposed, of course, that all American [ʌ] words will be pronounced in these ways by speakers of the indicated dialects. For amplification see Wise (1957), from whose work these examples were taken.

better transcribed as [dʒɨst], where the vowel is the "barred ɨ" standing for a short high-central unrounded allophone of [ʌ].

A summary of some of the more important allophones of [ʌ] is as follows: [ʌ⊤ʟ]-backed and *ah*-like; [ʌ⊥˧]-raised and fronted and [ɜ]-like; [ɨ]-high-central variant.

EXERCISES

1 Practice paragraph for [ʌ]:

> One exercise the serious student might someday undertake is the study of why it is that some dialects have greater social status than do others. He might try to understand, for example, why the American is more tolerant of Standard British (sometimes with a kind of grudging admiration) than is our English cousin of the American dialects. In a number of words (perhaps hundreds) where no good phonetic reason can be found to favor the pronunciation of one country over another the educated Britisher will have something of a feeling that the American word, no matter how carefully articulated by us, is somehow substandard or undesirable. On the other hand, the equally well-educated American will often show a kind of unconscious snobbishness in reverse in his willingness to accept as superior, or just as good, the different British pronunciation. However, the reasons for the muddle are likely to be normal historic-linguistic-phonetic ones. None is likely to stem from any innate perversity, snobbishness, or linguistic superiority for either tongue.

2 Word List

a Words using [ʌ] in stressed syllables:

above	cup	husband	once	such
among	cut	income	other	sudden
another	done	judge	production	suffer
blood	double	lover	public	sun
brother	dull	Monday	result	Sunday
club	enough	money	run	thus
color	front	month	rush	trouble
come	fund	mother	something	trust
coming	government	much	son	uncle
company	gum	none	stuck	under
country	gun	nothing	study	wonderful
cover	hundred	number	subject	young

b Words in which the [ʌ] syllable is commonly unstressed to [ə] or some other pronunciation:

anyone	does	must	some	up
but	from	one	unless	us
difficult	just	product		

3 Minimal pairs:

[ʌ]—[ɑ]		[ʌ]—[ʊ]	
color [kʌlə˞]	collar [kɑlə˞]	bucking [bʌkɪŋ]	booking [bʊkɪŋ]
done [dʌn]	Don [dɑn]	crux [krʌks]	crooks [krʊks]
dull [dʌl]	doll [dɑl]	huck [hʌk]	hook [hʊk]
gun [gʌn]	gone [gɑn]	huff [hʌf]	hoof [hʊf] or [huf]
none [nʌn]	non- [nɑn]	lucky [lʌkɪ]	"looky" [lʊkɪ]
puck [pʌk]	pock [pɑk]	lux [lʌks]	looks [lʊks]
pup [pʌp]	pop [pɑp]	putt [pʌt]	put [pʊt]
stuck [stʌk]	stock [stɑk]	rough [rʌf]	roof [rʊf] or [ruf]
sup [sʌp]	sop [sɑp]	ruck [rʌk]	rook [rʊk]
un- [ʌn]	on [ɑn]	shuck [ʃʌk]	shook [ʃʊk]

[ʌ]—[ɔ]	
but [bʌt]	bought [bɔt]
cussed [kʌst]	cost [kɔst]
cut [kʌt]	caught [kɔt]
done [dʌn]	dawn [dɔn]
fun [fʌn]	fawn [fɔn]
lung [lʌŋ]	long [lɔŋ]
ruckus [rʌkəs]	raucous [rɔkəs]
rung [rʌŋ]	wrong [rɔŋ]
stuck [stʌk]	stalk [stɔk]
sung [sʌŋ]	song [sɔŋ]

4 Phonetic transcription. The following is a phonetic transcription of the paragraph in Exercise 1 as it might be spoken in GA. Compare this transcription with your own and comment on the differences.

[wʌn ˈɛksə˞ˌsaɪz ðə ˈsɪrɪəs ˈstjudn̩t maɪt ˈsʌmde ˌʌndə˞ˈtek ɪz ðə stʌdɪ əv hwaɪ ət ɪz ðət sʌm ˈdaɪəlɛkts hæv gretə˞ ˈsoʃəl stetəs ðən du ʌðə˞z. hi maɪt traɪ tu ʌndə˞stænd, fɔr ɛgˈzæmpl̩, hwaɪ ðɪ əˈmɛrəkən ɪz mɔr ˈtɑlərənt əv ˈstændəd ˈbrɪtɪʃ (ˈsʌmˌtaɪmz wɪð ə kaɪnd əv ˈgrʌdʒɪŋ ˌædməˈreʃən) ðən ɪz aʊr ˈɪŋglɪʃ kʌzən əv ðɪ əˈmɛrəkən ˈdaɪəlɛkts. ɪn ə ˈnʌmbə˞ əv wɜ˞dz (pə˞ˈhæps ˈhʌndrədz) hwɛr no gʊd fəˈnɛtɪk rizən kən bi faʊnd tə ˈfevə˞ ðə prənʌnsɪˈeʃən əv wʌn kʌntrɪ ovə˞ əˈnʌðə˞ ðɪ ˈɛdʒuketəd ˈbrɪtɪʃə˞ wɪl hæv ˈsʌmθɪŋ əv ə filɪŋ ðət ðɪ əˈmɛrəkən wɜ˞d, no mætə˞ haʊ ˈkɛrfəlɪ ˌɑrˈtɪkjuletəd baɪ ʌs, ɪz ˈsʌmˌhaʊ ˈsʌbstændəd ɔr ˌʌndɪˈzaɪrəbl̩. ɔn ðɪ ʌðə˞ hænd ðɪ ˈikwəlɪ wɛl ɛdʒuketəd əˈmɛrəkən wɪl ɔfn̩ ʃo ə kaɪnd əv ʌnkɑnʃəs ˈsnɑbɪʃnəs ɪn rɪˈvɝs ɪn hɪz ˈwɪlɪŋnəs tu æk̍ˈsɛpt əz səˈpɪriɚ, ɔr dʒʌst əz gud, ðə dɪfrənt ˈbrɪtɪʃ prənʌnsɪˈeʃən. hauɛvɚ, ðə rizənz fɔr ðə mʌdl̩ ɑr laɪklɪ tə bi nɔrməl hɪsˈtɔrɪk lɪŋˈgwɪstɪk fəˈnɛtɪk wʌnz. nʌn ɪz laɪklɪ tə stɛm frəm ɛni ɪnet ˌpɚˈvɝsətɪ, ˈsnɑbɪʃnəs, ɔr ˌlɪŋˈgwɪstɪk səpɪriˈɔrəti fɔr ˈiðɚ tʌŋ.]

[ɝ] and [ɜ]

TERM HURT STIR WORD EARN COURAGE
MYRTLE COLONEL

ANALYSIS

Two different *mid-central* vowels are common in English speech. The [ɝ] is generally described as mid-central, tense, and produced with moderate jaw opening and some degree of lip rounding. There has been a considerable amount of uncertainty as to how the tongue position ought to be described, whether with a "curling back" of the tongue (the *retroflex* position) or an arching of the body of the tongue toward the palate. Recent research (see Delattre and Freeman, 1968) has shown that a better description of tongue shape is "bunched," or arched toward the palate. In addition, the back of the tongue provides a second constriction of the vocal tract so that the oropharyngeal cavity is "doubly constricted." There is, however, a wide variation in tongue posture used in *r*-sound production, and the interested student should consult the above reference for further details.

The second major mid-central vowel is that used by "non-*r*-pronouncing" speakers. This [ɜ] vowel is more lax, and the vocal tract is without the obvious tongue constrictions of the [ɝ], giving the vocal tract the form of a relatively unconstricted tube. The [ɜ] has been termed by some a "neutral" vowel. It also may be described as mid-central. It is obviously neither back, front, high, low, or tense. It is suggested that at this point you turn back to Figure 5-2 and consult the x-ray diagrams presented there which compare *r*-colored and non-*r*-colored vowels. Remember that these represent only two of many slightly different kinds of postures, all of which can give the same general vowel quality. Perceptually, of course, the *r* and the non-*r* vowels are quite different.

In the symbol system employed in this text the [ɝ] designates only the stressed syllables having a very definite *r* quality and should be reserved to indicate such sounds. A similar resonance appearing as the major syllabic element in unstressed and partially reduced syllables is transcribed [ɚ]. It should be emphasized that the symbol [ɝ] designates a vowel and therefore is used only to represent the major resonance of the syllable. The resemblance between [ɝ] and [ɚ], which are vowels, and the glide [r], which is a consonant, will be discussed presently.

VARIATION

Most native speakers of American English are quite likely to need some instruction and practice before they are able to analyze the differences among the various *r* sounds. In general, pronunciation problems centering around [ɝ] arise first because of the confusion occasioned by the fact that *r* resonance is a feature of both syllabic [ɝ] and nonsyllabic [r] and second, because of the somewhat marked difference in usage of the *r* sounds in various dialect regions of the United States and England. In this last connection, the difference between the [ɝ] and the [ɜ] must be understood.

For the most part, it is not difficult to differentiate [ɝ] and [r] as they occur in American speech. As will be brought out in more detail later (see Chapter 17), the glide [r] either initiates or terminates a syllable, as in the words "remark" [rɪmark] and "archive" [ɑrkaɪv]; but it does not make up the major resonance or *nucleus* of the syllable to which it belongs. On the other hand, in the words "early" [ɝli] and "burden" [bɝdn̩], the sound clearly makes up the major resonance of the syllable.

The way in which the various *r* vowels are used makes up one of the most distinctive differences between dialect regions in the United States and between American and British speech. In ordinary language, Americans say that certain persons "drop their *r*'s." In general, those who use Eastern or Southern American speech or who follow British drop their *r*'s, but General American speakers pronounce theirs. This means, of course, that the two vowel qualities are different, not that any speech sound has actually been dropped out or retained.

In the speech of about three-fourths or more of all American speakers, the pronunciation symbolized by [ɝ] is used for all syllables which could, because they have an *r* spelling, contain *r* "coloring." Geographically, this is the typical speech of the General American area. In certain dialects of Southern American, Eastern American, and Great Britain [ɝ] is replaced by [ɜ]. To the untrained General American speaker the latter sound may seem to resemble a somewhat prolonged [ʌ] or [ʊ].

Without going into all the rules for pronouncing *r* sounds, we may note that the speaker who replaces [ɝ] with [ɜ] may also use [ə] instead of [ɚ]. Typical pronunciations of those who drop their *r*'s would be [mɜmə] instead of [mɝmɚ] for "murmer" and [rɪfɜ] instead of [rɪfɝ] for "refer."

Persons who are phonetically and liguistically naïve may have a good many mistaken notions about "proper" usage for the various *r* sounds. To be sure, any one of these sounds may be too tense or too nasal or may be pronounced with an exaggerated *r* coloring. This so-called "twang" should be avoided, where it may call attention to itself. On the other hand, there is positively nothing objectionable about pronouncing one's *r* sounds where this practice is consistent with the general dialect characteristics of one's speech, as it is for the General American speaker. Indeed, the most grievous error occurs when the self-conscious person with a false idea of what constitutes cultured speech tries to emulate a supposedly superior Eastern or British dialect. If one wishes to do so, one is entitled to adopt such standards *in toto*, but one's speech becomes a caricature if only the *r*'s are dropped.

The [ɝ] appears to be one of the most easily recognized vowels in the English sound system. Nevertheless it is typically the last to be learned by children and often gives them great difficulty. It is one of the most difficult to teach to those who lack the sound. Children sometimes have the greatest trouble with the consonant [r], and often substitute [w]. However, the characteristic substitution of either [ɜ] or [ə] for [ɝ] or [ɚ] is only a little less common and may even be more so in the North and West. Often children substitute a "labialized," or lip-rounded, vowel, something like a rounded [ʊ] or [ʌ] in their attempts to pronounce [ɝ], and it is likely that most *r* distortions in infantile speech are of this type. Such labialization leads to rounded, nonstandard [ɝ] vowels and consonantal [r] sounds which are very close to [w]. The *r* dialects are most affected by this kind of distortion, but non-*r* dialects are also disturbed because of the consonant [r] problem.

Another type of *r* distortion often heard in the speech of children, and also of adults, is in the direction of the high-front vowels. The [ɝ] may take on an [i]-ish quality, and the [r] may sound something like [j].

In teaching correct *r* quality to children and adults, *ear training* must be relied upon heavily, and trial-and-error learning plays a major part in drills and exercises. It is helpful sometimes, of course, to draw attention to the lip position, the feel of the border of the tongue along the teeth, and the position of the tongue.

The diphthong [ɜɪ] may be heard in [ɝ] words in the Deep South and in New York City areas, but is is considered too much a localism to be accepted as fully standard. It is this diphthong which gives the impression that [ɔɪ] has been "hoid" and provides the stereotype for the Brooklyn dialect. It should be pointed out, of course, that the [ɜɪ] is a variant of [ɜ] rather than of [ɝ] directly.

Sometimes the [ɝ] (or [ɜ]) vowel is confused with a vowel-plus-[r] diphthong—[ɪr], [ɛr], [ær], [ɑr], [ɔr], or [ʊr]. The substitution of [ɝ] for one of these diphthongs is occasionally heard and is often considered nonstandard; it is involved in such confusing pronunciations as [hɝ] for "here" [hɪr] or [fɝ] for "far" [fɑr]. Unacceptable substitutions of one of the vowel-plus-[r] diphthongs in place of [ɝ] may also be heard, as in [lɑrn] for "learn" [lɝn] and [hɪrd] for "heard" [hɝd]. Such pronunciations, of course, are to be avoided as narrowly dialectal or nonstandard. On the other hand, in some words, notably in words like "hurry" and "worry," either the diphthong or the *r*-colored vowel may be correct, depending upon the dialect region. Compare [hʌrɪ] with [hɜɪ], [wʌrɪ] with [wɜɪ], and [sɪrəp] with [sɝəp] (in the words "hurry," "worry," and "syrup"). This problem of variation in *r* usage may be better understood after the discussion of the consonant [r] in Chapter 16. The numerous difficulties of the foreign speaker with this sound can also be discussed more conveniently in the section on the consonant [r].

EXERCISES

1 Practice paragraph for [ɜ]:

> Work is variously a curse and a blessing, depending upon the circumstances one is forced to meet. Certainly, a world in which there were no daily tasks to be performed, no new opportunities for the pursuit of truth, or no earth to be turned by the farmer's plow would indeed be a sterile place. Nevertheless, there are times in the life of every person when he dreams of the vast delights that would surely be his if he were a millionaire, freed of the burdens of earning a living or performing any task for which he had no fancy. He is prone, in intervals such as these, to regard himself as a kind of poor serf, forced by an unfriendly world to concern himself with matters for which he has no taste, merely to fatten a lean purse. Yet there are few persons who would not, if brought face to face with stern reality, admit, perhaps grudgingly, that they are happier by virtue of the fact that they have been furnished an opportunity to carry out some productive labor. Man can learn true happiness only if he is creative, whether his achievement is great or small. There is a pride in such accomplishment which goes far beyond any material reward the worker may receive; it is the satisfaction of knowing that to a greater or lesser degree he has served, that he has in at least some small measure made the earth on which he lives a better place.

2 Word list:

a Words using [ɝ] or [ɜ] in stressed syllables:

bird	curve	herself	reserve	Thursday
burn	dirt	hurt	return	turn
clerk	early	jerk	serve	university
church	earnest	learn	service	urge
circle	earth	occur	shirk	verse
certain	fur	person	skirt	were
certainly	furnish	personality	squirt	word
commercial	further	personnel	stir	work
concern	German	purpose	term	world
concerning	heard	purse	third	worst
curse	her	research	thirty	worth

b   Words using [ɝ] or a vowel-plus-[r] diphthong:

courage   hurry   syrup   worry

3   Minimal pairs:

[ɝ]—[ʌ]		[ɝ]—[ɔɪ]	
bird [bɝd]	bud [bʌd]	burl [bɝl]	boil [bɔɪl]
burn [bɝn]	bun [bʌn]	burrs [bɝz]	boys [bɔɪz]
circle [sɝkl̩]	suckle [sʌkl̩]	curl [kɝl]	coil [kɔɪl]
earn [ɝn]	un [ʌn]	earl [ɝl]	oil [ɔɪl]
girl [gɝl]	gull [gʌl]	early [ɝli]	oily [ɔɪlɪ]
hurt [hɝt]	hut [hʌt]	hurt [hɝt]	Hoyt [hɔɪt]
pert [pɝt]	putt [pʌt]	learn [lɝn]	loin [lɔɪn]
stern [stɝn]	stun [stʌn]	sir [sɝ]	soy [sɔɪ]
third [θɝd]	thud [θʌd]	verge [vɝdʒ]	voyage [vɔɪdʒ]
turn [tɝn]	ton [tʌn]	verse [vɝs]	voice [vɔɪs]

[ɝ]—[ɛr] (or [ær])	
burr [bɝ]	bare [bɛr]–[bær]
cur [kɝ]	care [kɛr]–[kær]
err [ɝ]	air [ɛr]–[ær]
fir [fɝ]	fair [fɛr]–[fær]
her [hɝ]	hair [hɛr]–[hær]
hurry [hɝɪ]	Harry [hɛrɪ]–[hærɪ]
purr [pɝ]	pair [pɛr]–[pær]
spur [spɝ]	spare [spɛr]–[spær]
stir [stɝ]	stair [stɛr]–[stær]
were [wɝ]	wear [wɛr]–[wær]

4   Phonetic transcription. The following transcription of the paragraph in Exercise 1 represents a General American pronunciation:

[wɝk ɪz ˈvɛrɪəsˌlɪ ə kɝs ænd ə ˈblɛsɪŋ, dɪˈpɛndɪŋ əˈpɑn ðə ˈsɝkəmˌstænsəz wʌn ɪz fɝst tə mit. ˈsɝtənlɪ, ə wɝld ɪn hwɪtʃ ðɛr wɝ no delɪ tæsks tə bi pɝˈfɔrmd, no nu ɑpɝˈtunətɪz fɔr ðə pɝsut əv truθ, ɔr no ɝθ tə bi ˈtɝnd baɪ ðə ˈfɑrmɝz plau wud ɪnˈdid bi ə ˈstɛrəl ples. ˌnɛvɝðəˈlɛs ðɛr ɑr taɪmz ɪn ðə laɪf əv ɛvrɪ pɝsn̩ hwɛn hi drimz əv ðə væst dɪˈlaɪts ðət wud ʃurlɪ bi hɪz ɪf hi wɝ ə ˈmɪljənɝ, frid əv ðə bɝdənz əv ɝnɪŋ ə lɪvɪŋ ɔr pɝfɔrmɪŋ ɛnɪ tæsk fɝ hwɪtʃ hi hæd no fænsɪ. hi ɪz pron, ɪn ɪntɝvəlz sʌtʃ əz ðiz, tə rɪˈgɑrd hɪmsɛlf æz ə kaɪnd əv pur sɝf, fɔrst baɪ ən ʌnˈfrɛndlɪ wɝld tu kənˈsɝn hɪmsɛlf wɪð mætɝz fɝ hwɪtʃ hi hæz no test, mɪrlɪ tə fætn̩ ə lin pɝs. jɛt ðɛr ɑr fju pɝsənz hu wud nɑt, ɪf brɔt fes tə fes wɪθ stɝn rɪˈælətɪ, ədmɪt, pɝˈhæps grʌdʒɪŋlɪ, ðət ðe ɑr hæpiɝ baɪ vɝtʃu əv ðə fækt ðət ðe həv bɪn fɝnɪʃt ən ɑpɝˈtunətɪ tə kɛrɪ aut sʌm prəˈdʌktɪv lebɝ. mæn kən lɝn tru ˈhæpɪnəs onlɪ ɪf hi ɪz kriˈetɪv, hwɛðɝ hɪz ətʃivmənt ɪz gret ɔr smɔl. ðɛr ɪz ə praɪd ɪn sʌtʃ əˈkɑmplɪʃmənt hwɪtʃ goz fɑr bɪjɑnd ɛnɪ məˈtɪrɪəl riwɔrd ðə wɝkɝ me rɪˈsiv; ɪt ɪz ðə sætəsˈfækʃən əv

noıŋ ðət tu ə gretɚ ɔr lɛsɚ dıgri hi hæz sɝvd, ðət hi həz ın ət list ın sʌm smɔl
mɛʒɚ med ðı ɝθ ɔn hwıtʃ hi lıvz ə bɛtɚ ples.]

[ə] and [ɚ]
*A*BOUT OP*E*N *A*BILITY COMM*O*N *U*PON
AF*TE*R LAB*O*R STAND*A*RD MEAS*U*RE

ANALYSIS

There has been much disagreement among phoneticians concerning the status of the speech sound known as the schwa, in part for the reason that its *phonemic* status is quite dubious. One cannot, for example, fit this "indefinite" vowel into a contrast network such as that illustrated in Table 2-1. But while [ə] is not contrastive in the same way that [i] contrasts with [u], the symbol [ə] does represent a kind of speech behavior of great significance.

As you may recall from the discussion of vowel reduction in Chapter 6, there is a significant interaction between stress and vowel quality. In unstressed syllables there is often such a marked reduction in the duration and energy of the syllable that the vowel tends to lose its characteristic resonance. As a kind of "minimal syllabic" it then retains only that resonance which is allowed by the transition from one consonant to another, which in turn will depend primarily upon the tongue-body position of the adjacent speech sounds. The schwa symbol is, then, a way of indicating that a vowel has been reduced to the status of an indefinite transition. The syllable is still there; the vowel, in its definite contrastive sense, is gone.

VARIATION

Given the above description of the nature of that phenomenon called schwa, it is obvious that there is no single articulatory position or resonance which can be described for it. It is simply the reduced allophone of some other vowel. Most decidedly it is not simply an unstressed [ʌ] as some have described it. Like [ʌ], [ɜ], and [ɨ], it tends to be central and lax. The fundamental feature which describes it, however, should probably be only the feature *reduced*. The voice print of [ə] in Figure 10-1 shows the typically reduced length of a schwa—to about 0.03 to 0.05 second—but the resonance pattern of schwa may vary widely from that illustrated.

When the reduced vowel is followed by a final sonorant, [m], [n], [l], or [r], for example, the consonant itself may become syllabic, as in [bʌtn̩] instead of [bʌtən] for "button," or in the case of [r] the vowel may assimilate some of the quality of the glide. This is especially notable in the vowel-plus-*r* syllables such as those of "better" or "color," where there may be heard an *r*-colored schwa, or schwar [ɚ]. The hook on the schwa is an indication of the remnants of the strong *r* palatization which remains in the otherwise reduced vowel.

Phoneticians differ considerably in their employment of the symbol [ɚ]. We would use it to symbolize the reduced *r*-colored final vowel of informally pronounced words such as "color" [kʌlɚ]. Some ignore the reduction by using the symbol [ɝ] in this context; others ignore the shortness and simplicity of the syllabic by transcribing it [or], [ɝr], etc. Still others will transcribe the same event as [ər], choosing to consider the event as a reduced vowel plus a glide, which perhaps it may sometimes be. We believe the use of [ɚ] enables us to symbolize better the perceptual facts of speech, but we recognize that some of these distinctions are extremely fine ones.

Problems in the use of [ə], and incidental difficulties in phonetic analysis and transcription, center to a large extent on a seeming unawareness of the frequency with which vowel reduction occurs in English. So far as transcription is concerned, the commonest mistake is to think that some definite vowel resonance ought to be recorded, usually the one with which the spelling of the word is most often associated. For instance "system" may be misheard and incorrectly transcribed as [sɪstɛm]. It is possible, of course, that the word was spoken with the vowel [ɛ] rather than [ə] in the final syllable, but this is most unlikely even in formal speech. If students grasp this point, they will soon be able to recognize in the speech around them innumerable instances where [ə] is used instead of the definite vowel suggested by the spelling. One difference between formal pronunciations listed by the average dictionary and the way words are heard in everyday speech grows out of the frequency with which the definite vowels marked in the dictionary are replaced by [ə].

When students begin to study their own speech and lack the assurance which comes with a trained ear, they are likely to have the impulse to shun the indefinite vowel in favor of some more definite vowel resonance—again, the sound suggested by spelling or listed by the dictionary as "correct." But it can be shown that it is not at all unusual to obscure more than one-third of the syllables in conversational pronunciation. In one 94-syllable passage from Mark Twain the authors counted 35 syllables which could have been correctly pronounced [ə].

To give an accented, definite pronunciation to vowels in most unaccented syllables in English is to distort the overall rhythm of the spoken language and to produce a pedantic and unnatural-sounding articulation. This is particularly true in English speech because of the marked tendency toward alternation of stressed and unstressed syllables that is so typical of its rhythm pattern. Thus, the pronunciation of two definite vowels in words such as "again," "correct," "science," and "given" is certain to result in an unnatural or even an unintelligible pronunciation, particularly if there is any effort to pronounce the word as it is spelled.

The phenomenon of alternation of stress and the replacement of some definite vowel with [ə] is particularly noteworthy in connected speech, as compared with the pronunciation of words in isolation. The emphasis of "content" words as a way of making meaning clear tends to knock out the accentuation of the relatively unimportant "helping" words. For instance, in context, words such as "a," "an," "the," "but," "of," and "at" are almost always [ə], [ən], [ðə], [bət], [əv], and [ət]. Any effort to use the appropriate definite vowel which these words would have if they were stressed is quite artificial, unless, of course, the sense of the sentence requires that these words be emphasized. Note how sense stress would change the pro-nunciation of "should" in the natural expression of the sentence "You should always emphasize the word *should*" [ju ʃəd əlwɪz ɛmfəsaɪz ðə wɝd ʃud].

A somewhat minor, but sometimes substandard, usage grows out of the process known as *restressing*. Here a syllable which has been obscured from a definite (and historically older) vowel pronunciation is restressed and given an [ʌ] pronunciation instead of the resonance from which [ə] developed through unstressing. The central-vowel characteristics of the indefinite vowel are retained. The sentence "I said *a* boy, not *the* boy" would, for purposes of making sense, lead to restressing of the two words "a" and "the." A speaker restressing a central vowel would say [ʌ] for "a" and [ðʌ] for "the," but in most cases it would be better to restore the original vowels, [e] and [i]. In a similar way "ascending" is usually pronounced [əsɛndɪŋ], but if the sense of the sentence made it natural to emphasize the initial sound of the word, as in "*a*scending, not *de*scending," it might be pronounced [esɛndɪŋ] rather than [ʌsɛndɪŋ].

In certain words, and when the speech is relatively formal or careful, the sound used in unstressed or relatively unstressed syllables may hover between [ə] and [ɪ] or [ʊ]. For example, "remark" is commonly either [rəmɑrk] or [rɪmɑrk], and "demand" may be either [dəmænd] or [dɪmænd]. In such words either pronunciation is quite acceptable.

As the speech grows more formal, the tendency is naturally to come closer to a full restoration of the vowel quality, and it is difficult to define the point where this tendency should be checked if overprecise and pedantic speech is to be avoided. If the sentence "Just the same, he should go" is spoken as [dʒʌst ðə sem, he ʃud go] instead of [dʒəst ðə sem, hi ʃəd go], the speaker certainly has not been guilty of overpronunciation. On the other hand, the sentence "As he remarked today, the reason is good enough" would probably sound somewhat stilted if restressing led to [æz hi rimɑrkt tude, ði rizən ɪz gud inʌf]. One must remain aware of the fact that the person who yields too readily to unstressing may end up with careless and underpronounced speech. Attentive listening will provide many examples of this common fault, so that one illustration will suffice: [sə fjə gənə ənsɪst, əl hæf tə]. ("So if you're going to insist, I'll have to.")

The discrimination between [ɚ] and other *r* sounds may not be easy for the unsophisticated listener. To understand the distinction between [ɝ] and [ɚ], which is largely a matter of stress, the earlier discussion of this point, in connection with the description of [ɝ], should be reviewed. It was explained then that [ɝ] is always *stressed*, whereas [ɚ] is always *unstressed*.

It is somewhat more difficult, at least in many phonetic contexts, to tell whether the speaker has used an *r*-colored vowel ([ɚ] or [ɝ]) or the consonant [r]. The beginner cannot be blamed for confusion when [ɚ] follows a vowel, for even experts disagree in many instances about whether the *r* coloring should be considered part of a diphthong, and thus transcribed with the vowel symbol [ɚ], or whether it should be regarded as a glide, which would call for the consonant symbol [r]. For example, in the word "terrific," do we hear the pronunciation [tɚɪfɪk] or [tərɪfɪk]?

Some of the argument about [r] versus [ɚ] in instances such as those just mentioned can be considered a mere debate over terminology. The difference between [ɚ] and [r] in the above examples is certainly not phonemic in the sense that meaning would be affected by either pronunciation. Practically speaking, students will not be seriously wrong if they use either notation in broad transcription. Nevertheless, in many cases the careful and experienced listener can transcribe most accurately when making the fine distinction between [ɚ] and vowel plus [r].

There can be no real justification for the transcription practice of using [r] when the *r* coloring is the major resonance of the syllable, whether the syllable is stressed or unstressed. Nor does the transcription [ər], as occasionally used in such a word as "better" [bɛtər], ordinarily serve as well as [ɚ] ([bɛtɚ]). The transcription [bɛtər] would indicate a neutral vowel followed by a glide, whereas characteristically only a single resonance is present for this syllable. This is not to say, however, that [ər] cannot be heard instead of [ɚ] in some cases where the syllable on which the *r* coloring rests is in question, for it can. "Mirage," for example, may be heard as [mɚɑʒ] or [mərɑʒ], depending upon very subtle temporal cues. Here again the difference is not distinctive and need not be considered important by the student just beginning the study of speech analysis.

In general, the comments about [ɝ] in connection with dialect differences also apply to [ɚ]. Thus, in words spelled with the letter *r*, those persons who pronounce their *r*'s will say [ɚ] as the *r* resonance for unstressed syllables and [ɝ] for the *r* resonance in stressed syllables. Those who do not pronounce their *r*'s will, of course, substitute [ə] for [ɚ].

Because [ɚ] tends to lose its *r* coloring more easily than [ɝ], an occasional speaker who habitually uses [ɝ] in the accented position will nonetheless use [ə] in unstressed syllables. In Eastern American, for example, "further" might be heard as [fɝðə], though [fɝðə] would be more frequent.

EXERCISES FOR [ə]

1   Practice paragraph for [ə]:

> The principles and facts concerning speech sound production which we learn in a study of phonetics are a great deal more than mere mental exercises. They will be found to be very useful notions, capable of helping us to be better speakers in a more practical way. For example, the seemingly obscure observation that the vowel in an unstressed syllable tends to become indefinite in quality, short in duration, and low in pitch, even in highly cultivated speech, may help us to avoid a number of errors in pronunciation. It may prevent our speech from becoming conspicuous and overpronounced as we work for more precise and acceptable articulation. Finally, if we are foreigners, it may help us to obtain a rhythm pattern more typical of American speech, with its heavy and marked alternation of stressed and unstressed syllables.

2   Word list:

a   Words with [ə] in the initial position:

about	against	allowed	apply	enough
above	ago	among	around	essential
accomplish	ahead	amount	attempt	occasion
across	alone	another	attention	occur
advance	along	appear	away	upon
again				

b   Words with [ə] in the initial syllable:

before	community	continue	produce (v.)	supply
believe	complete	control	project (v.)	reserve
between	compose	correct	protect	suppose
combine (v.)	concern	machine	provide	today
commercial	consider	prepare	receive	together
committee	consumer	present (v.)		

c   Words with [ə] in a middle syllable:

activity	difficult	illustrate	policy
benefit	economics	immediately	primarily
company	educate	industry	probably

d Words with [ə] in the final syllable:

April	expression	individual	movement	purpose
audience	foreign	instant	Mrs.	reason
balance	German	insurance	nation	science
basis	given	interest	natural	second
cases	government	interpret	normal	seven
children	graduate (n.)	isn't	often	several
common	greatest	judges	open	system
dishes	happen	material	opera	taken
different	human	mention	parents	thousand
environment	hundred	million	period	Washington
even	husband	minutes	problem	woman
experience	idea	moment	profit	

e Words with [ə] in more than one syllable:

ability	condition	essential	national	possibility
accident	department	evidently	occasion	president
amendment	develop	examination	official	principle
American	education	experiment	opposite	production
beautiful	efficient	experiment	philosophy	protection
commercial	element	intelligent	political	requirements
composition	especially	generation	population	

f Words whose weak form uses the vowel [ə] (or drops the vowel entirely):

a	can	is	on	then
am	could	it	shall	to
an	from	its	than	us
and	had	just	that	was
as	has	must	the	what
at	have	my	them	you
but	in	of		

3 Although the same kinds of minimal pairs cannot be listed for the [ə] that were listed for the definite vowels, the pairs given below do indicate the very important and practical kind of distinction which the [ə] represents. Practice these pairs, noting specifically the part played by stress.

[ə]—[ʌ]

instance [ɪnstənts]	in stunts [ɪn stʌnts]
lettuce [lɛtəs]	let us [lɛt ʌs]
mention [mɛnʃən]	men shun [mɛn ʃʌn]
Washington [waʃɪŋtən]	washing ton [waʃɪŋ tʌn]

[ə]—[ɛ]

greatest [gretəst]	gray test [gre tɛst]
hundred [hʌndrəd]	hun dread [hʌn drɛd]
material [mətɪriəl]	materiel [mətɪriɛl]
shortest [ʃɔrtəst]	shore test [ʃɔr tɛst]

[ə]—[ɚ]

Hi ya [haɪə]	higher [haɪɚ]
manna [mænə]	manner [mænɚ]
panda [pændə]	pander [pændɚ]
seven [sɛvən]	Severn [sɛvɚn]

[ə]—[ɪ]

foreign [fɔrən]	four in [fɔr ɪn]
given [gɪvən]	give in [gɪv ɪn]
judges [dʒʌdʒəz]	judge is [dʒʌdʒ ɪz]
license [laɪsəns]	lie since [laɪ sɪns]

[ə]—[ɑ]

German [dʒɝmən]	germ on [dʒɝm ɑn]
often [ɔfən]	off on [ɔf ɑn]
produce (v.) [prədjus]	produce (n.) [prɑdjus]
project (v.) [prədʒɛkt]	project (n.) [prɑdʒɛkt]

[ə]—[æ]

human [hjumən]	hue man [hju mæn]
insurance [ɪnʃurənts]	insure ants [ɪnʃur ænts]
normal [nɔrməl]	Norm, Al [nɔrm æl]
parents [pɛrənts]	pair ants [pɛr ænts]

4 Phonetic transcription. Compare the following informal colloquial GA pronunciation of the paragraph from Exercise 1 with your own pronunciation. Try to account for any differences on the basis of the discussion of the sound [ə].

[ðə prɪnsəplz ən fækts kənˈsɝnɪŋ spitʃ saund prəˈdʌkʃən hwitʃ wi lɝn ɪn ə stʌdi əv fəˈnɛtiks ɑr ə gret dil mɔr ðən mɪr mɛntəl ˈɛksəsaɪzəz. ðe wɪl bi faund tə bɪ vɛri jusfəl noʃənz, ˈkepəbl̩ əv ˈhelpɪŋ əs tə bi bɛtɚ spikɚz ɪn ə mɔr ˈpræktəkl̩ we. fɚ ɛgˈzæmpl̩, ðə ˈsimɪŋli əbˈskjur ˌabzɚˈveʃən ðət ðə vaul ɪn ən ˈʌnstrest siləbl̩ tɛndz tə bɪkʌm ɪnˈdɛfənət ɪn ˈkwɑləti, ʃɔrt ɪn duˈreʃən, ən lo ɪn pɪtʃ, ivən ɪn haɪli ˈkʌltəvetəd spitʃ, me help əs tu əvɔɪd ə ˈnʌmbɚ əv ɛrəz ɪn prənʌnsiˈeʃən. ɪt me prəˈvent aur spitʃ frəm bɪkʌmɪŋ kənˈspɪkjuəs ən ˌovɚprəˈnaunst æz wi wɝk fɚ mɔr priˈsais ən ækˈseptəbl̩ ɑrtikjəˈleʃən. ˈfaɪnəli, if wi ɑr ˈfɔrənɚz ɪt me help əs tu əbˈten ə rɪðəm pætən mɔr ˈtɪpɪkl̩ əv əˈmɛrəkən spitʃ wɪð ɪts hɛvi ən mɑrkt ɔltɚˈneʃən əv strest ən ˈʌnstrest ˈsiləblz̩.]

EXERCISES FOR [ɚ]

1 Practice paragraph for [ɚ]:

The question as to how one determines whether a pronunciation is standard is rather difficult to answer. It certainly depends on a great number of factors. Among these the speaker should consider the nature of the subject, together with the nature of the occasion and the factors involving the dialect region in which the speaking is done. After all, what is thoroughly acceptable in Denver may be considered entirely substandard in a finishing school in Vermont. On the other hand, grammar and pronunciation which are thoroughly permissible around the family dinner table may not be permissible from the lips of a radio announcer. It is almost certain, however, that if one ceases to worry about what is "proper" or popular and asks himself only what is most efficient and contributes most to better and quicker communication, he will not fail to discover the better answer to the problem in the greater number of cases.

2 Word list:

a Words using [ɚ] in General American and [ə] in Eastern speech:

after	figure	modern	proper
another	finger	mother	rather
answer	flower	nature	remember
better	further	neighbors	river
brother	future	never	Saturday
center	gather	November	shoulder
character	government	number	smaller
color	grammar	October	soldier
consider	greater	offer	speaker
corner	higher	officer	standard
cover	however	older	suffer
daughter	information	opportunity	sugar
December	international	order	summer
desire	junior	other	superintendent
dinner	labor	outer	surprise
discover	later	over	teacher
doctor	letter	paper	together
dollar	liquor	particularly	under
effort	lower	percent	understand
either	major	perform	weather
energy	manner	perhaps	whether
enter	manufacturer	permit	winter
ever	matter	picture	wonder
farther	measure	pleasure	worker
father	mister	popular	

b [ɚ] triphthongs, which may be one- or two-syllable words:

entire	hour	power
environment	iron	require
fire	our	tire

c Sometimes pronounced [ɚ], sometimes [ər]:

centering	difference	generation	opera
consideration	factory	interest	separate
cooperate	general	natural	several

d [ɚ] or [ə] only when unstressed (as is usually the case):

are	her	there	your
for	herself	were	yourself
forget	nor	where	

3 Because the [ɚ] is not phonemically distinct from [ɜ] in quite the same way as are the other stressed vowels, it is not possible to produce lists of minimal pairs of exactly the same type. The following pairs will however, indicate the importance of the stress difference between [ɜ] and [ɚ] as a matter of practical pronunciation (or between [ɜ] and [ə], if that is your choice).

[ɜ]—[ɚ]

back word [bækwɜd]	backward [bækwəd]
cub bird [kʌbɜd]	cupboard [kʌbəd]
fed early [fɛdɜlɪ]	Fedderly [fɛdəlɪ]
great err [grɛtɜ]	greater [grɛtə]
I earn [aɪɜn]	iron [aɪən]
lay burr [lebɜ]	labor [lebə]
man erring [mænɜɪŋ]	Mannering [mænəɪŋ]
neigh burrs [nebɜz]	neighbors [nebəz]
pay purr [pepɜ]	paper [pepə]
some myrrh [sʌmɜ]	summer [sʌmə]

4 Phonetic transcription. Practice the following paragraph, comparing the author's pronunciation with your own. Where you find [ə], try substituting [ɜ], [ɜ], and [ə] to observe the effect that this has on the pronunciation and rhythm of the passage.

[ðə kwɛstʃən æz tu hau wʌn dɪˈtɜmənz hwɛðɚ ə prənʌnsɪˈeʃən ɪz stændəd ɪz rɛðɚ ˈdɪfəˌkʌlt tu ænsɚ. ɪt sɜtənlɪ dɪˈpɛndz ɑn ə gret nʌmbɚ əv ˈfæktɚz. əmʌŋ ðiz ðə spikɚ ʃud kənsɪdɚ ðə netʃɚ əv ðə ˈsʌbdʒɪkt təˈgɛðɚ wɪθ ðə netʃɚ əv ði əˈkeʒən ænd ðə fæktɚz ɪnvɑlvɪŋ ðə daɪəlɛkt rɪdʒən ɪn hwɪtʃ ðə spikɪŋ ɪz dʌn. æftɚ ɔl, hwʌt ɪz ˈθɜəlɪ ækˈsɛptəbl̩ ɪn dɛnvɚ me bi kənsɪdɚd ɛnˈtaɪrlɪ

ˈsʌbstændəd ɪn ə ˈfɪnɪʃɪŋ skul ɪn vəˈmɑnt. ɔn ðɪ ʌðə hænd, græmə ən prənʌnsɪˈeʃən hwɪtʃ ɑr θɜəlɪ pəmɪsəbḷ əraund ðə fæmlɪ dɪnə tebḷ me nɑt bi pəˈmɪsəbḷ frəm ðə lɪps əv ə redio əˈnaunsə. ɪt ɪz ɔlmost sɜtən, hauɛvə, ðət ɪf wʌn sisəz tə wɜɪ əbaut hwʌt ɪz prɑpə ɔr ˈpɑpjulə ænd æsks hɪmsɛlf onlɪ hwʌt ɪz most ɪˈfɪʃənt ænd ˌkənˈtrɪbjuts most tə bɛtə ən kwɪkə kəmjunəˈkeʃən, hi wɪl nɑt fel tə dɪˈskʌvə ðə bɛtə ænsə tə ðə prɑbləm ɪn ðə gretə nʌmbə əv kɔsəz.]

Chapter 11

Back Vowels

[u], [ʊ], [o], [ə], [ɑ]

[u]
BOOT RULE MOVE GROUP DUE FRUIT THROUGH
RENDEZVOUS TWO SHOE

ANALYSIS

The [u] is the highest and most rounded of the back vowels. In its production the lips are often almost "puckered." The combination of the backing of the tongue body, the drawing forward of the base of the tongue (typical in most tense vowels), and the small lip opening gives to the [u] its special "low" resonance, seen in Figure 11-1. The American English [u] is also described as tense, long, and is ordinarily diphthongized, particularly in stressed and word-final positions. In terms of tongue tension the relationship of [u] to [ʊ] is analogous to the relationship between [i] and [ɪ]. In summary, the feature classification of this sound is *high, back, tense, rounded, sonorant,* and *syllabic.* (See Figs. 5-1 and 5-2).

231

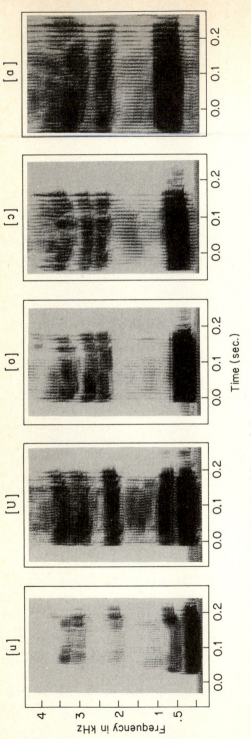

Figure 11-1 Sound spectrogram of [u], [ʊ], [o], [ɔ], and [ɑ].

VARIATION

With the exception of a few words such as "oops," "ooze," and "oolong," this tense back vowel is heard only in medial and final positions in English words, seldom in unaccented syllables or before [ŋ] or [r]. In common with other "long" vowels, [u] often has diphthonglike characteristics, but since these are not distinctive in the same way that they are for [aɪ], [aʊ], and [ɔɪ], we classify this sound as a vowel. In much the same manner that [i] is often more accurately transcribed [ij], so [u] is often more accurately represented by [uw] (or [ʊu]). Vowel quality and stress are always interrelated, and it is interesting to note how the strength of articulation influences the quality of this high-back vowel. As stress changes from maximum to minimum, the character of the sound changes from [uw] to [u] to [ʊ] and to [ə], and then may finally disappear entirely. As an illustration of this, carefully compare the pronunciations of the following:

I have *too* much. (Maximum stress: [uw])
The numbers six *two* five. (Secondary stress: [u])
A score of six *to* one. (Tertiary stress: [ʊ])
I have *to* go. (Reduced, schwa: [ə])
What t'do. (Omitted: [t'du])

One of the most obvious variants of [u] in American English occurs in a group of words following alveolar, and sometimes velar, consonants. Compare, for example, [studn̩t], [nuz], and [tun] with [stjudn̩t], [njuz], and [tjun]. The typical form for most General American speakers is probably [u] rather than [ju], but in some speech forms, such as stage diction, a few Eastern dialects, and Southern British, the [ju] is heard or alternates with [u]. One's native intuitions should be followed, for the "rules" for [ju] are complex. [mjun], for example, would certainly be an unacceptable pronunciation for the word "moon."

In another group of words there is considerable variation in usage between the [u] and [ʊ]. Over the country as a whole, cultivated colloquial pronunciation seems to be surprisingly evenly divided between these two sounds in words such as "roof," "hoop," and "soot." Again, the habitual practices of experienced speakers may be relied upon for the pronunciation of "oo" words; the most frequent pronunciation is [u].[1]

In certain foreign dialects of English there are encountered other interesting variations of [u]: the centralized [ʉ] of some Scottish, Cockney, and

---

[1] In an analysis of the [u] and [ʊ] words in American English, Hanna et al. (1966) found that 28 percent of the [u] words were spelled *oo*; 31 percent of [ʊ] words were spelled *oo*. In his list *One Syllable Words*, Moser (1957) found the *oo* spelling in 238 [u] words and in 63 [ʊ] words.

Norwegian pronunciations, for example; the fronted [Y] also heard in some Scottish; and a long [u:] heard in some German words. The most notable problem for most foreign speakers, however, is a failure to diphthongize this vowel appropriately.

To summarize, some of the more interesting allophones of /u/ are simple [u], complex [uw], centralized [ʉ], weak or short [ŭⱦ], an unrounded [ɯ], and off-glides [uə] and [uwə].

EXERCISES

1   Practice paragraph for [u]:

> Anyone who has ever been to school knows all too well of the importance of phonetic rules in learning to read and write. Although schoolteachers who are interested in such rules choose to call their subject *phonics*, the study really uses nothing new to the student of phonetics. Loosely speaking, phonics is the application to the language-learning problem of just such principles as are outlined in this book. This is especially true with regard to the correlation, or lack of it, between audible events (sounds, syllables) and visual cues (letters and letter groups). In its simplest (perhaps too simple) form it involves introducing to the student the root notion that, loosely speaking, it is possible to "sound out" words through the process of associating with each letter, and with some letter groups, a certain kind of sound. Of course it would not only be foolish but also would surely prove to be impossible that this notion could be carried to its logical conclusion. A completely phonetic approach is doomed from the start because English neither looks nor sounds like a phonetic language. Nevertheless, as most would agree, phonetic knowledge is a useful tool in language learning.

2   Word list:

a   Words pronounced [u] by most speakers:

afternoon	fruit	mood	root	too
blue	goose	moon	route	two
choose	grew	moose	rule	who
cool	group	move	school	whom
do	include	movement	soon	whose
doing	into	noon	soup	zoo
doom	loop	prove	through	
food	loose	room	to	
fool	lose	roost		

b [u] words which may be heard with [ju] or [ɪu]:

attitude	institution	knew	produce
consumer	introduce	new	shoe
due	June	news	Tuesday
duty	junior	opportunity	tune

3 Minimal pairs:

[u]—[ju]		[u]—[ʊ]	
boot [but]	butte [bjut]	booer [buɚ]	boor [bʊr]
booty [butɪ]	beauty [bjutɪ]	cooed [kud]	could [kʊd]
coot [kut]	cute [kjut]	fool [ful]	full [fʊl]
food [fud]	feud [fjud]	gooed [gud]	good [gʊd]
fool [ful]	fuel [fjul]	Luke [luk]	look [lʊk]
moos [muz]	muse [mjuz]	pool [pul]	pull [pʊl]
moot [mut]	mute [mjut]	shoed [ʃud]	should [ʃʊd]
ooze [uz]	use [juz]	stewed [stud]	stood [stʊd]
who [hu]	Hugh [hju]	who'd [hud]	hood [hʊd]
whose [huz]	hews [hjuz]	wooed [wud]	would [wʊd]

[u]—[ʌ]	
boost [bust]	bust [bʌst]
doom [dum]	dumb [dʌm]
mood [mud]	mud [mʌd]
moose [mus]	muss [mʌs]
whom [hum]	hum [hʌm]
roost [rust]	rust [rʌst]
root [rut]	rut [rʌt]
school [skul]	skull [skʌl]
soon [sun]	sun [sʌn]
soup [sup]	sup [sʌp]

4 Phonetic transcription. The following phonetic transcription of the paragraph in Exercise 1 represents the pronunciation of one of the authors. Compare your pronunciation with his. Does your pronunciation of the [u] words differ? Note the uses of [ju] and [ʊ].

[ˈɛnɪwʌn hu hæz ɛvɚ bɪn tə skul noz ɔl tu wɛl əv ðɪ ɪmˈpɔrtəns əv fəˈnɛtɪk rulz ɪn ˈlɜnɪŋ tə rid n̩ rait. ɔlðo skultitʃɚz hu ɑr ɪntərɛstəd ɪn sʌtʃ rulz tʃuz tə kɔl ðɛr ˈsʌbdʒɪkt ˈfɑnɪks, ðə stʌdɪ rɪlɪ juzəz nʌθɪŋ nju tə ðə studn̩t əv fəˈnɛtɪks. luslɪ ˈspikɪŋ, ˈfɑnɪks ɪz ði ˌæpləˈkeʃən tə ðə ˈlæŋgwɪdʒ ˈlɜnɪŋ prabləm əv dʒʌst sʌtʃ prɪnsəpl̩z æz ɑr ˈautˌlaɪnd ɪn ðɪs buk. ðɪs ɪz əspeʃəlɪ tru wɪθ rɪˈgɑrd tə ðə ˌkɔrəˈləʃen, ɔr læk əv ət, bɪtwin ɔdəbl̩ ɪˈvɛnts (saundz, sɪləbl̩z) ən ˈvɪʒuəl kjuz (lɛtɚz ən lɛtɚ grups). ɪn ɪts sɪmpləst (pɚˈhæps tu sɪmpl̩) fɔrm ɪt ɪnˈvalvz ɪntrəˈdusɪŋ tə ðə studn̩t ðə rut noʃən ðət, ˈluslɪˈspikɪŋ, ɪt ɪz

pasəbl̩ tə saʊnd aʊt wɝdz θru ðə ˈpraɪsɛs əv əˈsoʃietɪŋ wɪð itʃ lɛtɚ, æn wɪθ
sʌm lɛtɚ grups, ə sɝtn̩ kaɪnd əv saʊnd. əv kɔrs ɪt wəd nɑt onlɪ bi ˈfulɪʃ bət
ˈɔlso wʊd ʃʊrlɪ pruv tə bi ɪmˈpɑsəbl̩ ðət ðɪs noʃən kəd bi kɛrɪd tu ɪts ˈlɑdʒɪkəl
kənˈkluʒən. ə kəmˈplitlɪ fəˈnɛtɪk əprotʃ ɪz dumd frəm ðə stɑrt bɪkɔz ˈɪŋglɪʃ
niðɚ lʊks nɔr saʊndz laɪk ə fəˈnɛtɪk ˈlæŋgwɪdʒ. ˈnɛvɚðəlɛs, æz most wʊd
əgri, fəˈnɛtɪk ˈnɑlɪdʒ ɪz ə jusfəl tul ɪn ˈlæŋgwɪdʒ ˈlɝnɪŋ.]

[ʊ]
BO*OK* PULL C*OULD* WOMAN

ANALYSIS

The vowel [ʊ] stands just below [u] in the vowel diagram and is therefore
usually classified as a lower high-back vowel. The single most important
feature which distinguishes these two vowels appears to be tension, as re-
vealed by change in vowel quality, length, and diphthongization. [ʊ] sounds
less "low" in its resonance, is characteristically the shortest of the accented
vowels, and is not diphthongal. In addition, [ʊ] is less lip rounded, is lax,
and appears to have a characteristically less retracted tongue base and a
lower tongue height. The feature classification is *high*, *back*, *lax*, *rounded*,
sonorant, and *syllabic* (Figs. 5-1 and 5-2).

VARIATION

This vowel seems to present difficulties far out of proportion to its frequency
of use, both in attempting to achieve acceptable pronunciation and in learning
to listen analytically. It is astonishing how many persons do not recognize
that [ʊ] is a vowel distinct from [u], even though they may use it properly
in their own speech. This is possibly the result of the fact that [ʊ] appears
fewer times than any other stressed vowel in American speech. Linguists
would say that the vowel doesn't carry much of a "functional load." Like
the letter *q* in spelling, it could probably be dropped without too much damage
to the language.

Before *r*, and in unstressed syllables, the historical tendency has been
for [u] to change to the [ʊ]. Restoring the [u] in such cases often results in
such dialectal pronunciations as [pur] instead of [pʊr] for "poor" and
[lur] instead of [lʊr] for "lure." The [u] may be occasionally substituted
for [ʊ] in other types of words as well in certain American dialects (see [u]),
or a sound close to [ʌ] may be heard, especially in reduced or inaccurate
articulation, as [wʌd] for [wʊd] and [ʃʌd] for [ʃʊd]. The [ju], which was
shown to be an occasional variant pronunciation of [u] words, may also be

found as an occasional variant in some [ʊ] words. For example, the word "during" may be heard as [djʊrɪŋ] or [dʊrɪŋ] with equal acceptability.

Foreign speakers often have conspicuous difficulty with [ʊ]. In most foreign languages no phonemic distinction is made between [u] and [ʊ], with the result that [u] is substituted or the two sounds are confused; [puʃəmʌp] instead of [pʊʃəmʌp] would be a possible dialectal version of "push him up." The substitution of [u] for [ʊ] may also occur in certain regional dialects in America, as in [puʃ] for "push."

The dependence of vowel quality on stress is nowhere more evident than in the pronunciation of the [ʊ] words. A very large proportion of these words, such as those listed in the exercises of this section, may be quite acceptably pronounced [ə] where stress is minimal, as it often is in context. Examples include "would," "should," and "could." Shifts among [u], [ʊ], and [ə] can be heard in such words as "to," "you," and "education." Lowering of [ʊ] to [ə], as in [aɪ ʃər du] for "I sure do," is a common nonstandard dialect usage.

EXERCISES

1 Practice paragraph for [ʊ]:

> Sometimes we find that individuals have poor speech and a drab speech manner which could be improved simply by putting more energy into the task. As any good speech book will tell us, successful oral communication requires full participation during the speech act, and this full participation should mean that the man or woman doing the speaking should actually be working harder. Slovenly speech and "butchered" articulation can be cured only by those who would apply this principle to their speech training program. Why should it be assumed that an efficient oral output ought to be easy? It isn't, and the student who is looking for an effective speech education should be prepared to foot the bill.

2 Word list:

a Words nearly always pronounced with the [ʊ]:

book	hood	poor	sugar
bull	hook	pull	sure
cook	insurance	put	took
could	look	putting	woman
foot	looking	shook	wood
full	nook	should	would
good	output	stood	

b Words in which [ʊ] or some variant may be heard:

actually	education	situation	yourself
beautiful	Europe	to	
cure	individual	you	
during	roof	your	

3 Minimal pairs:

[ʊ]—[ʌ]		[ʊ]—[u]	
book [bʊk]	buck [bʌk]	boor [bʊr]	booer [bur]
could [kʊd]	cud [kʌd]	could [kʊd]	cooed [kud]
look [lʊk]	luck [lʌk]	full [fʊl]	fool [ful]
puss [pʊs]	pus [pʌs]	good [gʊd]	gooed [gud]
put [pʊt]	putt [pʌt]	hood [hʊd]	who'd [hud]
puts [pʊts]	putts [pʌts]	look [lʊk]	Luke [luk]
roof [rʊf]	rough [rʌf]	pull [pʊl]	pool [pul]
shook [ʃʊk]	shuck [ʃʌk]	should [ʃʊd]	shoed [ʃud]
stood [stʊd]	stud [stʌd]	stood [stʊd]	stewed [stud]
took [tʊk]	tuck [tʌk]	wood [wʊd]	wooed [wud]

[ʊ]—[ɝ]	
book [bʊk]	Burke [bɝk]
could [kʊd]	curd [kɝd]
hood [hʊd]	heard [hɝd]
look [lʊk]	lurk [lɝk]
pull [pʊl]	pearl [pɝl]
put [pʊt]	pert [pɝt]
shook [ʃʊk]	shirk [ʃɝk]
stood [stʊd]	stirred [stɝd]
took [tʊk]	Turk [tɝk]
wood [wʊd]	word [wɝd]

4 Phonetic transcription. Study the following phonetic transcription, paying particular attention to the pronunciation of [ʊ] words. This transcription shows the way one of the authors read the paragraph in Exercise 1. Compare your own pronunciation.

[ˈsʌmtaɪmz wi faɪnd ðət ɪndɪˈvɪdʒuwəlz hæv pʊr spitʃ ən ə dræb spitʃ ˈmænɚ hwɪtʃ kəd bi ɪmˈpruvd ˈsɪmplɪ baɪ pʊtɪŋ mɔr ˈɛnədʒi ˈɪntʊ ðə tæsk. æz ɛni gʊd spitʃ bʊk wɪl tɛl əs, səkˈsɛsfəl ɔrəl kəmjunəˈkeʃən rɪˈkwaɪrz fʊl pətɪsə-ˈpeʃən dʊrɪŋ ðə spitʃ ækt, ənd ðɪs fʊl pətɪsəˈpeʃən ʃʊd min ðət ðə mæn ɔr wʊmən dʊɪŋ ðə spikɪŋ ʃʊd ˈækʃʊəlɪ bi wɝkɪŋ hɑrdɚ. ˈslʌvənlɪ spitʃ ən bʊtʃɚd ɑrtɪkjəˈleʃən kæn bi kjurd onlɪ baɪ ðoz hu wʊd əˈplaɪ ðɪs ˈprɪnsəpḷ tu ðɛr spitʃ trenɪŋ ˈprogræm. hwaɪ ʃʊd ət bi əˈsumd ðət ən ɪˈfɪʃənt ɔrəl aʊtpʊt ɔt tə bi izɪ? ɪt ˈɪznt̩, ænd ðə ˈstʊdnt hu ɪz ˈlʊkɪŋ fɔr ən ɪˈfɛktɪv spitʃ ɛdʒəˈkeʃən ʃʊd bi prɪˈpɛrd tə fʊt ðə bɪl.]

[o]
NOTE COAT TOW TOE OH OWE SEW THOUGH
SOUL BEAU HAUT YEOMAN BROOCH APROPOS

ANALYSIS

The [o], next below [ʊ] on the vowel diagram, is typically described as a
mid-back vowel. It is characteristically tense, and has a strong lip rounding.
More important, it is a complex vowel, diphthongized to the extent that a
symbol such as [ow] or [oʊ] is often appropriate for the phonetic transcription
of the typical American pronunciation, especially in stressed and final positions. During the production of [o] the tendency is for the tongue to move
to a higher position, near [u] or [ʊ], and for the lips to round more markedly.
Those phoneticians who class [e] as a diphthong do so also in the case of the
[o]. The usual distinctive feature classification is *nonhigh*, *nonlow*, *back*, *tense*,
rounded, *sonorant*, and *syllabic*. See Figures 5-1, 5-2, and 11-1 for the vowel
placement diagram and voice print pattern.

VARIATION

When [o] occurs in the final position, and when it is prolonged or stressed,
the tendency to diphthongize is particularly strong in American speech. In
such contexts failure to give the typical lip-rounding (or tongue-backing)
off-glide will result in a "foreign" sound—the more simple nondiphthongal
[o] of Italian, French, and German, for example, or perhaps like the [ɔ] of
Norwegian or Russian. This is not to say that the American [o] is invariably
diphthongal. This is often not the case, for example, in some rapid and unstressed contexts and between some stops. "Token," for example, would
likely have a more pure [o] in conversational speech.

    The above comments should serve to explain why it is necessary in
detailed phonetic analysis to be aware of the many diphthongal and other
variants characteristic of the tense vowels. A common manner of symbolizing
the diphthongization is to follow [o] with the labial glide [w]. In some cases,
however, where the glide target is of interest, the vowel-plus-vowel symbolization will enable one to distinguish the more strongly rounded [ou] from
the less strong [oʊ]. In more broad phonetic transcription [oʊ], [ou], and
[ow] would all be adequate for symbolizing the diphthongal allophones
of [o].

    Several other variants of the [o] (or [ow]) sound are heard in English
and American speech. Before *r* the [o] is usually a more lax sound—more
like [ɔ], so that students should be careful that what they expect to hear as
[or] is not actually closer to [ɔr]. For example, "horse" is [hɔrs] in most
(but not all) American speech. In some dialects "horse" is distinguished

from "hoarse" [hors], but such distinctions appear to be disappearing in America.

There are other variants of, and substitutions for, [o] which would be considered nonstandard or dialectal by Americans. Among them perhaps the most notable are [ɜʊ] and [ɛʊ] as heard in some British pronunciations. Another is a variety of short [o] approaching [ə] or [ʌ] which is sometimes heard in lax and unrounded or centralized pronunciations in rapid, elliptic speech. [ɣ] is a symbol often used to stand for an unrounded mid-back vowel. The substitution of [ə] for [o] in final *ow* words is sometimes considered rather too informal; [ðə fɛlə faləd], for "the fellow followed," is an example. The Southern drawled version [owə] is, of course a perfectly normal variant form, in its own area. In Cockney one can also hear an interesting diphthongal variant of [o], a sound which may be heard as [ʌʊ] or [aʊ].

A summary of some of the more common English allophones of /o/ is as follows: [o], [oʊ], [ou], [ɜʊ], [owə], [ə˔], [oᴛ], and [ɣ].

EXERCISES

1   Practice paragraph for [o]:

> So-called loaded passages of prose or poetry, which are supposed to contain heroic doses of a single sound for the neophyte to pore over in his efforts to master pronunciation, have been the favorite device of professors of diction since time immemorial. The composers of this opus are loath to forgo this custom. Because the vowel [o] is noteworthy for the role it plays in English words, the authors are going along with their fellow tutors. There have been, of course, some notable and often quoted examples of such sentences, liberally sprinkled with such old familiar words as "alone," "blow," "gold," "cold," "soul," and so on. Actually, those who will devote a few moments to such material in practice at home can hope before long that their own pronunciation has grown more nearly correct. Fine differences in the sounds must be noted, of course, if the novice is to progress as he is supposed to; he need not be bored with the proposal that he force himself to go through such a procedure.

2   Word list:

a   Words employing [o] in a first or non-final syllable:

almost	chosen	control	grown	known
alone	close	cooperate	hold	lower
boat	coal	don't	holds	moment
bonus	coat	goes	hole	most
broke	cold	gold	home	motor
broken	compose	golden	hope	nose

note	open	program	smoke	suppose
notice	over	prose	sold	those
ocean	own	road	soldier	told
old	owned	robe	soul	tones
older	poetry	role	spoke	whole
only	post	rose	stone	won't

b Words employing [o], or [ou] in a final stressed syllable:

ago	blow	know	O	so
although	go	low	oh	though
below	grow	Negro	snow	

c Words in which pronunciation may vary between [o] or [ə], depending upon stress, dialect, formality, and other factors:

Chicago	opinion	pronunciation	so
fellow	potato	protection	tobacco
follow	project (v.)	provide	tomorrow

d [or] words, which are sometimes pronounced with [or] but in some dialects with [ɔr]:

before	course	floor	more	sport
board	court	force	report	store
chorus	door	four	shore	

3 Minimal pairs:

[o]—[ɔ]		[o]—[ʌ]	
bole [bol]	ball [bɔl]	boat [bot]	but [bʌt]
coal [kol]	call [kɔl]	bone [bon]	bun [bʌn]
coast [kost]	cost [kɔst]	coal [kol]	cull [kʌl]
goes [goz]	gauze [gɔz]	hole [hol]	hull [hʌl]
hole [hol]	hall [hɔl]	home [hom]	hum [hʌm]
know [no]	gnaw [nɔ]	known [non]	none [nʌn]
low [lo]	law [lɔ]	note [not]	nut [nʌt]
oh [o]	awe [ɔ]	robe [rob]	rub [rʌb]
pole [pol]	Paul (pɔl)	stone [ston]	stun [stʌn]
row [ro]	raw [rɔ]	tones [tonz]	tons [tʌnz]

[o]—[ɑ]	
coat [kot]	cot [kɑt]
dole [dol]	doll [dɑl]
hope [hop]	hop [hɑp]

known [non]	non [nɑn]
note [not]	not [nɑt]
own [on]	on [ɑn]
road [rod]	rod [rɑd]
soak [sok]	sock [sɑk]
tome [tom]	Tom [tɑm]
wrote [rot]	rot [rɑt]

4 Phonetic transcription. Compare the pronunciation indicated by this transcription of the paragraph in Exercise 1 with your own pronunciation and explain any differences on the basis of the discussions in this chapter.

[so kɔld ˈlodəd ˈpæsɪdʒəz əv proz ɚ ˈpoətrɪ, hwɪtʃ ɑr səˈpozd tə kənˈten hɪˈroɪk dosəz əv ə sɪŋgl̩ saʊnd fɚ ðə ˈniəˌfaɪt tə pɔr ovɚ ɪn hɪz ɛfɚrts tə mæstɚ prəˌnʌnsiˈeʃən, hæv bɪn ðə fevərət dɪˈvaɪs əv prəˈfɛsəz əv dɪkʃən sɪns taɪm ˌɪməˈmɔrɪəl. ðə kəmˈpozəz əv ðɪs opəs ɑr loθ tə fɔrgo ðɪs kʌstəm. bɪkɔz ðə vaʊl o ɪz ˈnotwɚði fɔr ðə rol ɪt plez ɪn ˈɪŋglɪʃ wɚdz, ði ɔθɚz ɑr goɪŋ əloŋ wɪð ðɛr fɛlo tutɚz. ðɛr həv bɪn, əv kɔrs, səm ˈnotəbl̩ ən ɔfən kwotəd ɪgˈzæmpl̩z əv sʌtʃ sɛntənsəz, ˈlɪbrəli sprɪŋkəld wɪθ sʌtʃ old fəˈmɪljɚ wɚdz æz əlon, blo, gold, kold, sol, ænd so ɔn. ˈæktʃuəli, ðoz hu wɪl dɪˈvot ə fju ˈmomənts tə sʌtʃ məˈtɪrɪəl ɪn præktəs ət hom kən hop bɪfɔr lɔŋ ðət ðɛr on prənənsiˈeʃən hæz gron mɔr ˈnɪrli kəˈrɛkt. faɪn ˈdɪfrənsəz ɪn ðə saʊndz məst bi notəd, əv kɔrs, ɪf ðə ˈnavəs ɪz tə prəˈgrɛs æz hi ɪz səˈpozd tu; hi nid nɑt bi bɔrd wɪð:ə prəˈpozəl ðət hi fɔrs hɪmsɛlf tə go θru sʌtʃ ə prəˈsidʒɚ.]

[ɔ]
SOFT BALL FAULT JAW OUGHT UTAH BROAD TALK

ANALYSIS

The higher low-back rounded vowel [ɔ] is characterized by a tongue height which is between the positions for [o] and [ɑ]. As [ɔ] is pronounced by the typical American speaker, its chief distinguishing characteristic (setting it apart from [ɑ]) is its lip rounding. Although some speakers are able to produce an acceptable [ɔ] with little or no lip rounding, a broadly rounded and everted lip position is typical. The resonances which characterize the [ɔ] quality are usually about 100 to 200 Hz lower than those for [ɑ]. [ɔ] even when lengthened is not ordinarily diphthongal. The feature analysis may be summarized as *low, back, round, lax, sonorant,* and *syllabic.* (Figs. 5-1, 5-2).

VARIATION

The [ɔ] is one of a somewhat varied and complex group of sounds which may be called the *ah* vowels. The two major sound families within this group are usually represented by the symbols /ɔ/ and /ɑ/. The normal practice among speakers of General American dialects is to distinguish only one or two significant variants among the possible articulations which lie in the "articulatory space" between [æ] and [o]. If each of the words "mad" "mod," "Maude," and "mowed" constitute a set of minimally contrasting forms for you, then obviously two phonemes appear in the low-back area, and two symbols are required in traditional phonemic transcription. The symbols usually chosen represent phonetically the higher low-back rounded [ɔ] and the low-back unrounded [ɑ]. If you do not distinguish "mod" from "Maude," then obviously a single phonemic symbol is sufficient to represent the needs of your sound system. However, for a more detailed transcription we are presenting here both symbols, in order to account for the phonemic facts in some dialects of American English, and in order to provide symbols for distinguishing among important allophones in all dialects. In the various dialects of English one may hear the following vowel variants between [æ] and [o]:

[a] A backed variant of [æ] heard in British "path" and already described above (see [æ]).
[ɑ] The low-back unrounded vowel normally heard in Eastern New England "hot" (see [ɑ]), and also in Scottish.
[ɒ] A sound perceived as between [ɑ] and [ɔ], frequently encountered in General American dialects in which "mod" and "Maude" are pronounced alike. It may be described as an unrounded [ɔ].
[ɔ] The sound described above in the "Analysis."
[ɔ⊥] A higher and more tense back vowel used in many words in Southern British, in New York City dialect, and as an allophone of [o].

In many, if not most, General American dialects the above variants are simply allophones of a single low-back vowel. In the transcriptions in this text you will find American speech transcribed with two varieties of low-back vowel, broadly symbolized by [ɑ] and [ɔ]. The serious student may, however, wish to learn to distinguish all the above variants. However, it seems fruitless to attempt to describe the distinctions among them verbally. They must be heard to be learned.

If the lists of common [ɔ] and [ɑ] words found in the exercises are consulted for examples of *ah*-word pronunciations, certain interesting generalizations can be made. Note, for example, that whenever [ɑ] occurs in a stressed syllable it is spelled with the letter *o*. Note also that all the common stressed [ɑr] pronunciations are spelled *ar* or *ear*. On the other hand, observe that only eight of the words using [ɔ] in a stressed syllable are spelled with an *o*. Note also that the common words pronounced [ɔr] are mostly spelled *o*, *oa*, or *ou*. Finally, note that most of the exceptions to these rules occur in words beginning with a [w] sound, which would normally be expected to exert an influence toward lip rounding.

A very few additional comments about dialectal variations may be helpful. Some interesting diphthongal varieties of the low-back vowels occur, for instance the Southern [ɔo] or [ɔʊ], as in [tɔok] and [kɔofɪ] for "talk" and "coffee." In a few words even [ou] may be used. In New York City speech a diphthongal [ɔ⊥ə] may be heard in "coffee" and in a wide range of other *ah* words. Finally, in some regions [ər] and [ɔɪ] may be heard in some words—[wərʃ] for "wash" is an example, or [wɔɪʃɪŋtən] for "Washington."

EXERCISES

1 Practice paragraph for [ɔ]:

> If you will think about it a short time you will doubtless recall many instances of what might be called speech snobbery caused by mistaken notions as to what is thought to be correct pronunciation. Many people who would not ordinarily want to be thought of as " culture conscious " often display a kind of self-taught haughtiness in their speech. They nearly always do this when they try to mimic a dialect not their own, for the laudable but wrongly directed purpose of becoming more cultivated and effective in their speech habits. Most experts have taught that although a discussion of pronunciation logically belongs in a speech course it is the clarity and precision of formation of the sounds which is of the strongest importance, not the choice of sounds as such. Not only will the adoption of certain foreign or regional pronunciations fail to improve speech but also it will almost always cause the speech to sound tawdry and draw attention to itself.

2 Word list:

a Words using [ɔ] in the stressed syllable:

across	brought	long	saw
almost	call	loss	soft
already	cause	lost	tall
also	cost	off	taught
although	daughter	often	thought
always	draw	ought	walk
ball	hall	salt	wall
belong	law		

b Unaccented [ɔ] words, which are sometimes pronounced with [ɚ]:

for   nor

c Words usually pronounced with [ɔr] but sometimes with [or]:

before	force	horse	sort
board	form	lord	sport
born	forth	more	store
chorus	forty	morning	storm
corner	forward	north	story
course	four	shore	war
court	George	short	warm

d Words varying between [ɔ] and [ɑ]:

along	offer	tomorrow	watch
foreign	officer	want	water
log	song	wash	wrong
long	strong	Washington	

3 Minimal pairs:

[ɔ]—[ɑ]		[ɔ]—[ʌ]	
aught [ɔt]	Ott [ɑt]	bawdy [bɔdɪ]	buddy [bʌdɪ]
caught [kɔt]	cot [kɑt]	call [kɔl]	cull [kʌl]
core [kɔr]	car [kɑr]	caught [kɔt]	cut [kʌt]
for [fɔr]	far [fɑr]	log [lɔg]	lug [lʌg]
law [lɔ]	lah [lɑ]	long [lɔŋ]	lung [lʌŋ]
naught [nɔt]	not [nɑt]	lost [lɔst]	lust [lʌst]
pawed [pɔd]	pod [pɑd]	naught [nɔt]	nut [nʌt]
sought [sɔt]	sot [sɑt]	pawn [pɔn]	pun [pʌn]
taught [tɔt]	tot [tɑt]	taught [tɔt]	tut [tʌt]
wrought [rɔt]	rot [rɑt]	wrought [rɔt]	rut [rʌt]

[ɔ]—[o]	
awning [ɔnɪŋ]	owning [onɪŋ]
called [kɔld]	cold [kold]
caught [kɔt]	coat [kot]
clause [klɔz]	close [kloz]
daunt [dɔnt]	don't [dont]
gnaws [nɔz]	nose [noz]
hauled [hɔld]	hold [hold]
lawn [lɔn]	lone [lon]
naught [nɔt]	note [not]
Raleigh [rɔlɪ]	rolly [rolɪ]

4 Phonetic Transcription. This transcription represents the pronunciation of one of the authors as he read the paragraph in Exercise 1. It may differ considerably from yours, and these variations should be noted. Do you find any unacceptable pronunciations in his reading of the passage or in yours?

[ɪf ju wɪl θɪŋk əbaut ɪt ə ʃɔrt taɪm ju wɪl ˈdautləs rɪˈkɔl mɛni ˈɪnstənsəz əv hwʌt maɪt bi kɔld ˈspɪtʃ ˈsnabəri kɔzd baɪ məˈstekən noʃənz æz tə hwʌt ɪz θɔt tə bi kəˈrɛkt prənʌnsiˈeʃən. mɛni pipḷ hu wud nat ordənˈɛrəli want tə bi θɔt ʌv æz ˈkʌltʃɚ ˈkantʃəs ofən dɪsple ə kaɪnd əv ˈsɛlf ˈtɔt ˈhotɪnəs ɪn ðɛr spɪtʃ. ðe nɪrli ˈɔlwɪz du ðɪs hwɛn ðe traɪ tə ˈmɪmɪk ə ˈdaɪələkt nat ðɛr on, fɔr ðə ˈlodəbḷ bət rɔŋli dəˈrɛktəd pɝpəs əv bɪkʌmɪŋ mɔr ˈkʌltəvetəd ænd ɪˈfɛktɪv ɪn ðɛr spɪtʃ hæbəts. most ˈɛkspɝts hæv tɔt ðət ɔlðo ə dɪsˈkʌʃən əv prənʌnsiˈeʃən ˈladʒɪkli bɪˈlɔŋz ɪn ə spɪtʃ kɔrs ɪt ɪz ðə ˈklɛrəti ən prɪˈsɪʒən əv ˈfɔrmeʃən əv ðə saundzhwɪtʃ ɪz əv ðə ˈstrɔŋgəst ɪmˈpɔrtəns, nat ðə tʃɔɪs əv saundz æz sʌtʃ. nat onli wɪl ði əˈdapʃən əv sɝtṇ forən ɔr ˈrɪdʒənəl prənʌnsiˈeʃənz fel tu ɪmpruv spɪtʃ bət ɔlso ɪt wɪl ɔlmost ɔlwɪz kɔz ðə spɪtʃ tə saund ˈtɔdrɪ ən drɔ əˈtɛnʃən tu ɪtsɛlf.]

[ɑ]
COT FATHER CALM *AH!* SERGEANT
GUARD HONEST HEARTH

ANALYSIS

The [ɑ] is the lowest of the back vowels. As the x-ray figures show, the tongue may be quite close to the back wall of the pharynx, producing a narrow and constricted back cavity and a large front cavity—almost the opposite of the [i]. The other highly noteworthy feature of [ɑ] is the lack of lip rounding. Characteristically it is the only unrounded back vowel in English. It is lax, there is relatively wide mouth opening, and it is a relatively *long* vowel. It is not ordinarily diphthongal. The feature summary for [ɑ] is *low, back, lax, unrounded, sonorant,* and *syllabic* (Figs. 5-1, 5-2).

VARIATION

After the previous discussion of the similarities and differences among the various members of the *ah* group of vowels, there is little more that need be said about the pronunciation of [ɑ]. Despite the difficulties often encountered in distinguishing among various *ah* sounds, the native American speaker is unlikely to have any difficulty producing some acceptable sound from this group, and the [ɑ]–[ɔ] confusions rarely render speech substandard.

Occasionally, to be sure, nonstandard dialect usages replace [ɑ]. One instance of this may be heard in the diphthong [ɑr] which may frequently, in some regions, be heard as [ɔr], thereby leading to potential confusion between such pairs of words as "card"–"cord" and "barn"–"born." Another instance is the substitution of [æ] for [ɑ], although this is not frequent. "Calm," for example, may become more nearly [kæm]—which was standard in colonial times in America but is no longer.

The situation with respect to the so-called *broad a* has been touched upon in the section on [æ]. Since the broad *a* is such a well-known distinction between American and Standard British speech, it is perhaps desirable to add a few more comments.

In general, the whole group of *ah* vowels is pronounced differently in Southern British and American speech, and the same set of phonetic symbols do not represent accurately allophones in the two dialects. However, the specific pronunciations which lead to the popular feeling that British and Eastern American speakers use a broad *a* occur mostly in a limited group of words like "ask" and "aunt." These are pronounced [ɑ] or [a] in Southern British and some Eastern American speech. Most of the more common words in this category, which are pronounced with an [æ] by the majority of American speakers, are included in the exercises of this chapter.

EXERCISES

1   Practice paragraph for [ɑ]:

> If the student has followed the text closely and observed its counsel, he should by this time have accomplished at least some modest improvement in his own speech. It is almost never possible, of course, to describe effective speech simply; one must take cognizance of the fact that the whole matter is far too complex. It would also be hard to say what qualities are the best mark of a good speaker. One can be certain that good speech is honest; it follows that the speaker himself must have a sincere interest in the topic or content of his utterance. Good speech is the offspring of honest convictions, a stock of logical ideas, and a genuine desire to communicate them to his auditor. Beyond this, the job of speaking well involves a mastery of the language and a proper respect for its usage. Many of the bars to effective communication lie far below the surface, and one must seek constantly to take stock of himself and his true feelings and beliefs. The gain has been large when even a modicum of self-understanding has been reached. Good speech is an art, but it starts from within.

2 Word list:

a Words using [ɑ] in a stressed syllable:

accomplish	father	October	profit
beyond	follow	opera	project (n.)
body	god	opposite	promise
bomb	honor	popular	proper
box	hot	population	rock
college	job	possible	shop
common	John	possibility	shot
doctor	logical	probably	spot
dollar	lot	problem	stock
drop	modern	process	top
economics	not	product	topic

b Unaccented [ɑ] words, which may be pronounced with [ə] or, in some cases, with [ɚ]:

are	of	was
got	on	what

c Words pronounced with [ɑr]:

arm	artist	farmer	part
army	car	hard	party
art	charge	heart	star
Arthur	far	March	start
article	farm	mark	yard

d Some common words pronounced [ɑ] or [a] in British and some Eastern American speech and [æ] in General American speech:

Vowels preceding [s]

ask	disaster	last	past
basket	fast	mast	plaster
blast	fasten	master	rasp
cast	glass	nasty	task
class	grass	pass	

Vowels preceding [f] and [θ]

after	craft	half	raft
bath	draft	laugh	shaft
calf	graft	path	staff

Vowels preceding [m] and [n]

advance	branch	dance	glance
advantage	can't	demand	grant
answer	chance	example	plant
aunt	command	France	sample

3 Minimal pairs:

[ɑ]—[ɔ]		[ɑ]—[ʌ]	
are [ɑr]	or [ɔr]	cop [kɑp]	cup [kʌp]
body [bɑdɪ]	bawdy [bɔdɪ]	cot [kɑt]	cut [kʌt]
car [kɑr]	core [kɔr]	got [gɑt]	gut [gʌt]
collar [kɑlɚ]	caller [kɔlɚ]	hot [hɑt]	hut [hʌt]
farm [fɑrm]	form [fɔrm]	lock [lɑk]	luck [lʌk]
hock [hɑk]	hawk [hɔk]	not [nɑt]	nut [nʌt]
Moll [mɑl]	maul [mɔl]	rot [rɑt]	rut [rʌt]
popper [pɑpɚ]	pauper [pɔpɚ]	shot [ʃɑt]	shut [ʃʌt]
rah [rɑ]	raw [rɔ]	spotter [spɑtɚ]	sputter [spʌtɚ)
star [stɑr]	store [stɔr]	sock [sɑk]	suck [sʌk]

[ɑ]—[æ]	
box [bɑks]	backs [bæks]
job [dʒɑb]	jab [dʒæb]
lost [lɑst]	last [læst]
not [nɑt]	gnat [næt]
possible [pɑsəbl̩]	passible [pæsəbl̩]
rock [rɑk]	rack [ræk]
sot [sɑt]	sat [sæt]
spot [spɑt]	spat [spæt]
stock [stɑk]	stack [stæk]
top [tɑp]	tap [tæp]

4 Phonetic transcription. The following is a transcription of a GA pronunciation of the paragraph in Exercise 1.

[ɪf ðə studn̩t həz fɑlod ðə tɛkst ˈklosli ænd əbˈzɝvd ɪts kaunsəl, hi ʃud baɪ ðɪs taɪm həv əˈklamplɪʃt ət list sʌm madəst ɪmˈpruvmənt ɪn ɪz on spɪtʃ. ɪt ɪz ɔlmost nɛvɚ pasəbl̩, əv kɔrs, tə dɪsˈkraɪb ɪˈfɛktɪv spɪtʃ sɪmpli; wʌn məst tek ˈkagnəzəns əv ðə fækt ðət ðə hol mætɚ ɪz fɑr tu kamˈplɛks. ɪt wud ɔlso bi hard tə se hwʌt ˈkwɑlətɪz ɑr ðə bɛst mɑrk əv ə gud spikʌ. wʌn kən bi sɝtn̩ ðət gud spɪtʃ ɪz anəst; ɪt fɑloz ðət ðə spikɚ hɪmˈsɛlf mʌst hæv ə sɪnˈsɪr ˈɪntərəst ɪn ðə ˈtɑpɪk ɔr ˈkantɛnt əv ɪz ˈʌtərəns. gud spɪtʃ ɪz ði ˈɔfsprɪŋ əv ˈanəst ˈkənvɪkʃənz, ə stɑk əv ˈladʒɪkl̩ aɪˈdɪəz, ænd ə ˈdʒɛnjəwən dɪˈzaɪr tu kəˈmjunəket ðəm tu hɪz ˈɔdətɚ. biand ðɪs ðə dʒɑb əv spikɪŋ wɛl ɪnvalvz ə mæstəri əv ðə ˈlæŋˌgwɪdʒ ənd ə prapɚ rɪˈspɛkt fɔr ɪts ˈjusɪdʒ. mɛni əv ðə bɑrz tu ɪˈfɛktɪv kəmjunəˈkeʃən laɪ fɑr bɪlo ðə ˈsɝfəs, ænd wʌn məst sik ˈkanstəntli tə tek stɑk əv himsɛlf ənd hɪz tru ˈfilɪŋz ən bɪˈlifs. ðə gen həz bɪn lardʒ hwɛn ivən ə ˈmadəkəm əv sɛlf ʌndɚˈstændɪŋ həz bɪn rɪtʃt. gud spɪtʃ ɪz ən art, bət ɪt starts frəm wɪðˈɪn.]

Chapter 12

Diphthongs

[aɪ], [aʊ], [ɔɪ], [ju], [ɪr], [ɛr], [ɑr], [ɔr], [ʊr]

[aɪ] [aj]
F*I*ND P*IE* B*Y* H*IGH* A*I*SLE *A*YE *E*YE BU*Y* L*Y*E
GU*I*DE H*EIGH*T *I*SLAND GE*Y*SER

ANALYSIS

The diphthongal movement of [aɪ] proceeds from a position near that for the [ɑ] to a position near [ɪ] or [i]. In the usual General American production of the sound the tongue may be somewhat farther forward than for the vowel [ɑ] of "hot." This has influenced the choice of symbol, so that [a] is probably more commonly used to represent the initial resonance. In gliding toward the high-front position, the tongue probably never reaches a point quite as high as it does for [i]. Beyond mention of this fact, however, no exact statement can be made about the final resonance of this off-glide. It is variable, although it is always in the direction of [i]. The symbol [ɪ] has been chosen as the best representation of this resonance.

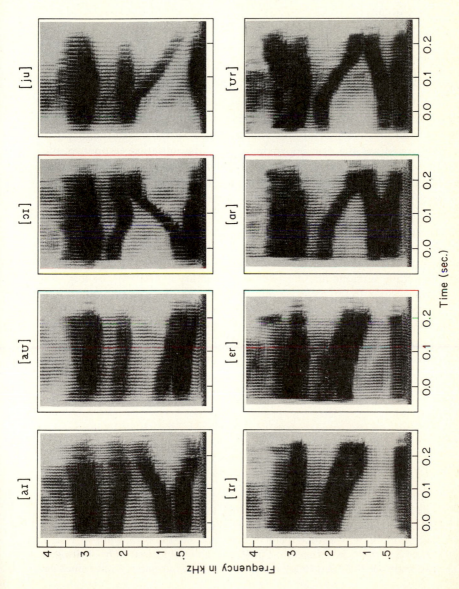

Figure 12-1 Sound spectrogram of [aɪ], [aʊ], [ɔɪ], [ju], [ɪr], [ɛr], [ɑr], and [ʊr].

In the production of the [aɪ], the gliding toward [ɪ] is rapid and smooth, occurring in the space of a single syllable. The first element of the diphthong is given more prominence, with the energy diminishing as the resonance proceeds to the [ɪ]. The essential inseparable nature of this vowel plus glide combination can be demonstrated by trying to sustain the sound as a sung tone. When this is attempted, it will become apparent that in order to produce [aɪ] rather than some other distinctively different sound ([a] or [ɪ]) a resonance *change* must occur.

VARIATION

In the pronunciation of [aɪ], like that of most diphthongs, the direction and rate of movement are much more stable properties of the phoneme than are the precise locations of the terminating and initiating resonances. The exact quality of the first element of this sound is also variable. Although [a] is generally considered the best approximation of the initiating resonance, the [ɑɪ] is a common and perfectly acceptable variant in some areas, perhaps more often in the South. Another version, also frequently heard in the South, may be represented by the symbol [a:], where the [:] indicates increased length. Thus, in this pronunciation a drawn-out, or "drawled," vowel replaces the diphthong. A Southern pronunciation of "nice smile" might be transcribed [na:s sma:l]. This usage would be considered dialectal outside of the South. Still other dialectal pronunciations may be encountered for this diphthong, including versions tending toward the quality of [ɔɪ], [ʌɪ], or [eɪ].

When words with [aɪ] receive a minimum amount of stress, the diphthong may be replaced by the neutral vowel [ə]. This often occurs, for example, in the pronunciation of "I" or "I'm." In rapid colloquial speech "I don't know what I'm going to do" might be heard [ə dont no hwʌt əm goən tə du]. This is not necessarily substandard. On the other hand, an overprecise pronunciation of [aɪ] may result in a two-syllable sound. In this case [taɪm] would become [ta·ɪm].

EXERCISES

1   Practice paragraph for [aɪ]:

> After we had climbed about a mile in the rising sunshine of that bright July day, we turned to look at the sky line, as it lay far away over our right shoulders. As far as the eye could see, the horizon was afire with the glow of the morning. We stood there, our eyes glued to the sight, while we rested, tired and quite out of breath. Finally our guide surprised us by inviting us to untie our lines and to lay our packs on the white snow. I have since de-

cided, in the light of later events, that he decided at that time to take the entire party over the ice field and to fight on to the summit before we realized that danger as well as beauty was in the climb; and that we would try it right after this last respite.

2 Word list:

a Words in which [aɪ] appears in the initial or medial position:

arrive	fight	island	outside	surprise
behind	finally	I've	price	time
beside	find	kind	primarily	tire
bright	fine	knight	provide	tired
child	fire	life	realize	tried
combine	five	light	require	type
crime	Friday	like	ride	united
decide	guide	line	right	variety
define	high	live (adj.)	rise	while
describe	higher	might	side	white
design	height	mile	sight	wide
desire	ice	mind	sign	wife
divide	idea	mine	size	wild
drive	idle	mite	smile	wind (v.)
entire	I'll	nice	society	wise
environment	iron	night	specialize	write

b Words in which [aɪ] appears in the final position:

buy	die	I	lie	tie
by	eye	imply	my	try
cry	fly	July	sky	why

3 Minimal pairs:

[aɪ]—[ɔɪ]		[aɪ]—[ɑ]	
buy [baɪ]	boy]bɔɪ]	fire [faɪr]	far [far]
fire [faɪr]	foyer [fɔɪr]	guide [gaɪd]	God [gɑd]
fried [fraɪd]	Freud [frɔɪd]	high [haɪ]	hah [hɑ]
imply [ɪmplaɪ]	employ [ɪmplɔɪ]	light [laɪt]	lot [lɑt]
ire [aɪr]	oyer [ɔɪr]	like [laɪk]	lock [lɑk]
rye [raɪ]	Roy [rɔɪ]	mile [maɪl]	moll [mɑl]
sigh [saɪ]	soy [sɔɪ]	night [naɪt]	not [nɑt]
tie [taɪ]	toy [tɔɪ]	ride [raɪd]	rod [rɑd]
tile [taɪl]	toil [tɔɪl]	side [saɪd]	sod [sɑd]
try [traɪ]	Troy [trɔɪ]	time [taɪm]	Tom [tɑm]

[aɪ]—[e]

fight [faɪt]	fate [fet]
high [haɪ]	hay [he]
ice [aɪs]	ace [es]
I'll [aɪl]	ale [el]
light [laɪt]	late [let]
like [laɪk]	lake [lek]
mine [maɪn]	mane [men]
ride [raɪd]	raid [red]
time [taɪm]	tame [tem]
wise [waɪz]	ways [wez]

4 Phonetic transcription. Count the [aɪ] diphthongs in the following transcription of the paragraph in Exercise 1; then read the passage aloud and note the variations that may occur within the phoneme.

[æftɚ wi həd klaɪmd əˈbaut ə maɪl ɪn ðə ˈraɪzɪŋ ˈsʌnˌʃaɪn əv ðæt braɪt dʒulaɪ de, wi tɜnd tə lʊk ət ðə ˈskaɪˌlaɪn æz ɪt le far əwe ovɚ aur raɪt ˈʃoldɚz. əz far əz ði aɪ kəd si, ðə həˈraɪzən wəz əˈfaɪr wɪðːə glo əv ðə ˈmɔrnɪŋ. wi stud ðɛr, aur aɪz glud tə ðə saɪt, hwaɪl wi rɛstəd, taɪrd ən kwaɪt aut əv brɛθ. ˈfaɪnlɪ aur gaɪd səˈpraɪzd əs baɪ ɪnˈvaɪtɪŋ ʌs tu ʌntaɪ aur laɪnz æn tə le aur pæks ɔn ðə hwaɪt sno. aɪ həv sɪns dɪˈsaɪdəd, ɪn ðə laɪt əv ˈletɚ ɪvɛnts, ðət hi dɪˈsaɪdəd ət ðæt taɪm tə tek ði ɛnˈtaɪr partɪ ovɚ ði aɪs fild æn tə faɪt ɔn tə ðə sʌmət bɪˌfɔr wi ˌriəlaɪzd ðət dendʒɚ əz wɛl əz bjutɪ wəz ɪn ðə klaɪm; ænd ðət wi wud traɪ ɪt raɪt æftɚ ðɪs læst ˈrɛspət.]

[ɔɪ] [ɔj]
BOY OIL FREUD

ANALYSIS

The change which produces the diphthong [ɔɪ] is from a low-back vowel [ɔ] to a high-front vowel near [i] or [ɪ]. Since the extent of the off-glide in [ɔɪ] is perhaps greater than for any other diphthong, the second half of this sound is somewhat more prominent than the corresponding resonance in other diphthongs; hence the [ɔɪ] rather easily breaks into two separate vowels. Thus, there seems to be less difference between [ɔɪ] and [ɔ·ɪ] than between, for example, [aʊ] and [a·ʊ]. Nevertheless, the sound is ordinarily classified and pronounced as an off-glide diphthong.

VARIATION

In native American speech there do not appear to be many difficulties with this sound. The pronunciation may vary normally somewhat toward the [oɪ] or [oi], but unless the variation is marked, this is not necessarily substandard. In some dialects, [aɪ] may be substituted for [ɔɪ] in such words as "hoist" and "boil," so that they are pronounced [haɪst] and [baɪl]. These usages are historically logical but are usually considered substandard or old-fashioned today.

In some dialects the substitution [ɜɪ] may be heard. This fact, together with the use of [ɜɪ] for [ɝ] can make for confusion between [ɝ] and [ɔɪ]. This is common in New York City. Professor John Black of Ohio State University (personal communication) states that "'berl' for 'boil' is common enough in southern Indiana; 'terlet' for 'toilet' pops up in central Ohio." McDavid (1958) notes the use of [ɜɪ] in New York City, the Hudson Valley area, New Orleans, and the South Carolina–Georgia low country.

EXERCISES

1 Practice paragraph for [ɔɪ]:

> Although it is true that voice quality may vary within widely acceptable limits without annoyance, most people would join me in expressing a dislike for the quality known as nasality, at least in its more unalloyed forms. Why it is that by choice most of us avoid the voice with strong nasal resonance is not clear. The fact which should be pointed out, however, is that we do. The employment of excessive nasality has often spoiled what would otherwise be an enjoyable and effective speech quality. The correction of the annoying quality involves the avoidance of certain faults of palate movement and the direction of the tone through the mouth instead of the nose. To coin a phrase, we might enjoin the speaker to use his head and not to get nosey.

2 Word list:

alloy	coin	join	pointing	spoil
annoy	convoy	joy	poison	toil
boil	destroy	noise	Roy	toy
boy	employ	oil	soil	voice
choice	enjoy	point	soy	void

3 Minimal pairs:

[ɔɪ]—[aɪ]		[ɔɪ]—[ɝ]	
boil [bɔɪl]	bile [baɪl]	avoid [əvɔɪd]	averred [əvɝd]
coin [kɔɪn]	kine [kaɪn]	boy [bɔɪ]	burr [bɝ]
foil [fɔɪl]	file [faɪl]	Boyd [bɔɪd]	bird [bɝd]
lawyer [lɔɪɚ]	liar [laɪɚ]	coy [kɔɪ]	cur [kɝ]
Lloyd [lɔɪd]	lied [laɪd]	foil [fɔɪl]	furl [fɝl]
loin [lɔɪn]	line [laɪn]	foist [fɔɪst	first [fɝst]

oil [ɔɪl]	isle [aɪl]	hoist [hɔɪst]	Hurst [hɝst]
poi [pɔɪ]	pie [paɪ]	noil [nɔɪl]	knurl [nɝl]
point [pɔɪnt]	pint [paɪnt]	poi [pɔɪ]	purr [pɝ]
voice [vɔɪs]	vice [vaɪs]	voiced [vɔɪst]	versed [vɝst]

[ɔɪ]—[ɔ]

boil [bɔɪl]	ball [bɔl]
coil [kɔɪl]	call [kɔl]
joy [dʒɔɪ]	jaw [dʒɔ]
loin [lɔɪn]	lawn [lɔn]
noise [nɔɪz]	gnaws [nɔz]
oil [ɔɪl]	awl [ɔl]
poi [pɔɪ]	paw [pɔ]
Roy [rɔɪ]	raw [rɔ]
soy [sɔɪ]	saw [sɔ]
toil [tɔɪl]	tall [tɔl]

4 Phonetic transcription. The following is a phonetic transcription of the paragraph in Exercise 1:

[ɔlðo ɪt ɪz tru ðət vɔɪs ˈkwɑlətɪ me vɛrɪ wɪðɪn ˈwaɪdlɪ æk ˈsɛptəbļ lɪməts wɪðaut ə ˈnɔɪəns, most pipḷ wʊd dʒɔɪn mi ɪn ɛks ˈprɛsɪŋ ədɪsˌlaɪk fɔr ðə ˈkwɑlətɪ nɔn æz ne ˈzælətɪ, ət list ɪn ɪts mɔr ˌʌn ˈəlɔɪd fɔrms. hwaɪ ɪt ɪz ðət baɪ tʃɔɪs most əv əs ə ˈvɔɪd ðə vɔɪs wɪθ strɔŋ nezəl ˈrɛzənəns ɪz nɑt klɪr. ðə fækt hwɪtʃ ʃud bi pɔɪntəd aut, hauɛvɚ, ɪz ðət wi du. ðɪ em ˈplɔɪmənt əv ɛk ˈsɛsɪv ne ˈzælətɪ həz ɔfən spɔɪld hwʌt wʊd ˈʌðɚˌwaɪz bi ən ɛn ˈdʒɔɪəbļ ænd ɪ ˈfɛktɪv spɪtʃ ˈkwɑlətɪ. ðə kə ˈrɛkʃən əv ðɪ ə ˈnɔɪɪŋ ˈkwɑlətɪ ɪn ˈvalvz ðɪ ə ˈvɔɪdəns əv sɝtṇ fɔlts əv ˈpælət muvmənt ænd ðə də ˈrɛkʃən əv ðə ton θru ðə mauθ ɪnstɛd əv ðə noz. tə kɔɪn ə frez, wi maɪt ɛn ˈdʒɔɪn ðə spikɚ tə juz hɪz hɛd ənd nɑt tə gɛt nozɪ.]

[aʊ], [aw]
HOW LOUD KRAUT BOUGH HOUR

ANALYSIS

The [aʊ] is an off-glide diphthong which proceeds from the relatively more stable resonance of the [a] or [ɑ] and glides off toward the vowel quality of [ʊ], though perhaps not always reaching that point. The amount of resonance change is often very small, perhaps less than occurs in any other distinctive diphthong discussed in this chapter.

VARIATION

The precise quality represented by the first element of the digraph [aʊ] may vary considerably from one English dialect region to another. Probably the most frequent pronunciation in the General American dialect is [a]—a vowel quality between the [ɑ] and [æ]. In many regions the more retracted vowel quality of the [ɑ] in "father" is frequently heard and, unless exaggerated, is not considered unusual or substandard.

In addition to [aʊ] and [ɑʊ], both of which are widely accepted, the pronunciation [æʊ] may be heard in parts of the East and South, but this usage has less general acceptance and is usually considered nonstandard by speakers of General American. In parts of the East and Canada several other variations are heard for this diphthong in some contexts. The most frequent are [ɜʊ], [ɛʊ], and [ʌʊ], although even [oʊ] and [ʊʊ], may be heard in some localities and contexts.

In some American speech there seems to be a distinct tendency to neglect the second element of this diphthong, so that words like "house" and "cloud" come to sound like [hɑs] and [klɑd]. Although it is normal for this diphthong to have a weaker glide than the [aɪ], [ɔɪ], or [ju], for example, such a tendency may reach the point of being obtrusive.

EXERCISES

1 Practice paragraph for [aʊ]:

It is possible to analyze vowel production much more exhaustively than we have found it desirable to do in this text. Some authors list more than forty sounds of the vowel category, without counting those listed as semivowels or diphthongs. We may, of course, break down vowel quality however we wish, the only real limitation being the usefulness of the breakdown. Now it goes without saying that the student should be aware of many degrees of difference among vowels. There are thousands, almost countless, distinctions which could be made. But it is doubtful whether any very powerful arguments can be found for applying phonetic labels to all of these unless some specific interest calls for such labeling. The important thing for the student of speech is that he have as good a grounding as possible in the functionally important differences among sounds in his language and an understanding of how those sounds vary and influence one another.

2 Word list:

about	cloud	found	mount	outer
account	count	ground	mountain	output
allowed	crowd	hour	mouth	outside
amount	doubt	house	now	pound
around	down	how	our	power
brown	flower	however	out	round

shout   south   thousand   town
sound   thou   throughout   without

3 Minimal pairs:

[aʊ]—[ɑ]		[aʊ]—[ɔ]	
cloud [klaʊd]	clod [klɑd]	brown [braʊn]	brawn [brɔn]
doubt [daʊt]	dot [dɑt]	cloud [klaʊd]	clawed [klɔd]
down [daʊn]	don [dɑn]	down [daʊn]	dawn [dɔn]
hour [aʊr]	are [ɑr]	found [faʊnd]	fawned [fɔnd]
how [haʊ]	hah [hɑ]	howl [haʊl]	haul [hɔl]
lout [laʊt]	lot [lɑt]	louse [laʊs]	loss [lɔs]
our [aʊr]	are [ɑr]	now [naʊ]	gnaw [nɔ]
outer [aʊtɚ]	otter [ɑtɚ]	out [aʊt]	ought [ɔt]
pound [paʊnd]	pond [pɑnd]	owl [aʊl]	awl [ɔl]
shout [ʃaʊt]	shot [ʃɑt]	town [taʊn]	tawn [tɔn]

[aʊ]—[o]	
about [əbaʊt]	a boat [əbot]
couch [kaʊtʃ]	coach [kotʃ]
crowd [kraʊd]	crowed [krod]
ground [graʊnd]	groaned [grond]
how [haʊ]	hoe [ho]
noun [naʊn]	known [non]
now [naʊ]	know [no]
shout [ʃaʊt]	shoat [ʃot]
thou [ðaʊ]	though [ðo]
town [taʊn]	tone [ton]

4 Phonetic transcription. The following transcription represents the pronunciation
of one of the authors as he read the paragraph in Exercise 1:

[ɪt ɪz ˈpɑsəbl̩ tu ˈænəlaɪz vaʊl prəˈdʌkʃən mʌtʃ mɔr ɛgˈzɔstɪvlɪ ðən wi həv
faʊnd ɪt dɪˈzaɪrəbl̩ tə du ɪn ðɪs tɛkst. sʌm ɔθɚz lɪst mɔr ðən ˈfɔrtɪ saʊndz əv
ðə vaʊl ˈkætəgɔrɪ wɪðaʊt ˈkaʊntɪŋ ðoz lɪstəd æz ˈsɛmaɪˌvaʊlz ɔr ˈdɪfθɔŋz. wi
me, əv kɔrs, brek daʊn vaʊl ˈkwɑlətɪ haʊɛvɚ wi wɪʃ, ðɪ onlɪ rɪl lɪməˈteʃən
biŋ ðə ˈjusfəlnəs əv ðə ˈbrekˌdaʊn. naʊ ɪt goz wɪðaʊt seɪŋ ðət ðə studənt ʃud
bi əwɛr əv mɛni dɪˈgriz əv ˈdɪfrəns əmʌŋ vaʊlz. ðɛr ɑr ˈθaʊzəndz, ɔlmost
ˈkaʊntləs, dɪˈstɪŋkʃənz hwɪtʃ kʊd bi med. bʌt ɪt ɪz ˈdaʊtfəl hwɛðɚ ɛni vɛri
paʊrfəl ˈɑrgjumənts kən bi faʊnd fɔr əˈplaɪŋ foˈnɛtɪk ˈlebəlz tu ɔl əv ðiz
ənlɛs sʌm spəˈsɪfɪk ˈɪntərəst kɔlz fɔr sʌtʃ ˈlebəlɪŋ. ðɪ ɪmˈpɔrtənt θɪŋ fɔr ðə
studənt əv spɪtʃ ɪz ðət hi hæv æz gud ə ˈgraʊndɪŋ əz ˈpɑsəbl̩ ɪn ðə ˈfʌŋkʃənəli
ɪmˈpɔrtənt ˈdɪfrənsəz əmʌŋ saʊndz ɪn hɪz ˈlæŋgwɪdʒ ænd ən ʌndɚˈstændɪŋ
əv haʊ ðoz saʊndz vɛri ənd ˈɪnfluəns wʌn ənʌðɚ.]

[ju]

*U*NIT *V*I*EW CUE YOU* F*EU'*D B*EAU*TY *YU'*LE *YEW*
H*U*G*H*

ANALYSIS

The [ju] is the only distinctive diphthong which may be produced with an *on-glide* rather than an off-glide change of resonance. For this reason we often call [ju] a *rising*, as distinguished from a *diminishing*, diphthong. The syllabic energy rises rapidly to a more stable resonance in this diphthong. In [aɪ], [ɔɪ], and [aʊ], on the other hand, the energy falls off *from* a more stable resonance. Although the starting point for this glide is approximately the tongue position of the [i] or [ɪ], the consonant symbol [j] is used to draw attention to the on-glide function of the initial resonance. Phonetically the glide performs the same function it does with many consonant-vowel combinations, like "yet" [jɛt] and "yawn" [jɔn].

VARIATION

A common variant of this diphthong within and at the end of words can be transcribed [ɪu], [ɪʊ], or [ɪw], as in "ridicule" [rɪdəkɪul] or "beauty" [bɪutɪ]. These symbols indicate a pronunciation in which the first sound has relatively more stress or prominence than it does in the [ju]. Such a diphthong is diminishing, but not usually to the degree that characterizes other diphthongs. The tongue position for the [u] of this diphthong is often influenced in such a way that the vowel is farther forward than the [u] of such a word as "fool." The vowel quality of the [u] probably lies somewhere midway between the typical [i] and [u] of stressed syllables. This distinction can be made in phonetic transcription, if necessary, with the symbol [ʉ].

For the most part, the [ju] sound heard in American speech is that of the rising diphthong. The off-glide variety symbolized by [ɪu] is, however, neither infrequent nor, in most cases, substandard. This pronunciation may be heard in words such as "museum" [mɪuzɪəm] (or [mɪuzɪəm]) and "confuse" [kənfɪuz]. It is interesting to note that [ɪu] is probably the historically older pronunciation, which later developed into the [ju] variety (see Sweet, 1888, pp. 210–218).

In positions of less than maximum stress the [ju] may frequently weaken to [jʊ] or even [jə]. For example, "immunize" may be heard correctly as [ɪmjunaɪz], [ɪmjʊnaɪz], or [ɪmjənaɪz]. In some cases, however, the [jə] could be nonstandard. For example, [kəntɪnjə] and [menjə] for "continue" and "menu" would be close to the border line of acceptability.

EXERCISES

1 Practice paragraph for [ju]:

> It is interesting to speculate on what will happen to the dialects of the United States in the future. Will there continue to be the same kinds of change we have seen in the past? Will the new patterns used by the youth of today prevail to become the accepted standards utilized by adults and taught in your schools tomorrow? If we could review the future dialects from some fourth-dimensional vantage point, would we view the new as more or less beautiful than the old? Will speech become more or less efficient from the viewpoint of communication? We can't say, but as sure as we are human beings our speech will continue to change in the future. It will continue to improve so long as those who use it are not more interested in speech for its own sake than as a tool to be used toward the end of more useful and effective social cooperation.

2 Word list:

a

amuse	cute	mule	unit	usually
beautiful	few	music	united	utilize
beauty	fuse	musical	university	value
community	future	refuse	use	view
continue	huge	review	used	you
cube	human	union	uses	youth

b For words pronounced with [u] by some speakers, [ju] by others, see list **b** under sound [u].

3 Minimal pairs:

[ju]—[u]	
Butte [bjut]	boot [but]
beauty [bjutɪ]	booty [butɪ]
cute [kjut]	coot [kut]
feud [fjud]	food [fud]
fuel [fjul]	fool [ful]
hews [hjuz]	whose [huz]
Hugh [hju]	who [hu]
muse [mjuz]	moos [muz]
mute [mjut]	moot [mut]
use [juz]	ooze [uz]

4 Phonetic transcription. The following phonetic transcription of the paragraph in Exercise 1 represents the pronunciation of one of the authors:

[ɪt ɪz ˈɪntərɛstɪŋ tə ˈspɛkjəlet ɔn hwʌt wɪl hæpən tu ðə ˈdɪaəlɛkts əv ðə juˈnaɪtəd stets ɪn ðə ˈfjutʃɚ. wɪl ðɛr kənˈtɪnju tə bi ðə sem kaɪndz əv tʃendʒ wi həv sin ɪn ðə pæst? wɪl ðə nu ˈpætənz juzd baɪ ðə juθ əv təˈde prəˈvel tə bɪkʌm ðɪ ækˈsɛptəd ˈstændɚdz ˈjutəˌlaɪzd baɪ əˈdʌlts ən tɔt ɪn jɔr skulz təˈmɑro? ɪf wi kʊd rɪˈvju ðə ˈfjutʃɚ ˈdaɪəlɛkts frəm sʌm ˈfɔrθ dɪˈmɛnʃənəl ˈvæntɪdʒ pɔɪnt, wʊd wi vju ðə nu æz ˈmɔr ɔr ˈlɛs ˈbjutəfəl ðæn ðɪ old? wɪl spitʃ bɪkʌm ˈmɔr ɔr ˈlɛs ɪˈfɪʃənt frəm ðə ˈvjupɔɪnt əv kəmjunəˈkeʃən? wi kænt se, bət əz ʃur əz wi ɑr hjumən biɪŋz aʊr spitʃ wɪl kənˈtɪnju tə tʃendʒ in ðə ˈfjutʃɚ. ɪt wɪl kənˈtɪnju tu ɪmˈpruv so lɔŋ æz ðoz hu juz ɪt ɑr nɑt mɔr ˈɪntərɛstəd ɪn spitʃ fɔr ɪts on sek ðæn æz ə tul tə bi juzd tɔrd ðɪ ɛnd əv mɔr ˈjusfəl ənd ɪˈfɛktɪv ˈsoʃəl koɑpəˈreʃən.]

[ɪr] (or [ɪə]) and [ɪə]

*H*E*AR* S*T*E*ER H*E*RE* P*ER*IOD P*IER* SP*IR*IT W*EIR*

ANALYSIS

This diphthong combines an off-glide from a relatively stable vowel near [ɪ]. The off-glide may be toward the resonance of [ɝ] or, in some Eastern and Southern dialects, toward the resonance of [ɜ]. The accepted phonetic symbol for the former is [ɪr] or [ɪɚ]. In the latter case the accepted symbol is [ɪə].

VARIATION

There is some variation in the resonance of the stable portion of this diphthong. Ordinarily the tongue glides from the lower high-front position, but the pronunciation [ir] may also be heard, and this difference may constitute a significant change in some regions. Those who distinguish in pronunciation between "we're" and "weir," without making a two-syllable word of "we're," may have both [ɪr] and [ir] diphthongs in their phonetic vocabulary. This is not likely, however. In any event, the differences are not very important for the average native speaker.

Whether one says [ɪr] or [ɪə] is generally determined by one's dialect region. If the *r*-colored vowels are used habitually, the pronunciation is likely to be [ɪr]. If not, [ɪə] is a more natural choice. Either is "correct," of course, so long as it is consistent with the rest of the speaker's dialect pattern.

With the [ɪr] or [ɪə], as well as with the other diphthongs, the pronunciation may be slightly different when the sound is followed by a vowel rather than by a consonant. When [ɪr] is followed by a consonant (as in "beard" [bɪrd]), there is little question that the sound should be classified as a diphthong, which may be transcribed equally well as [ɪr] or [ɪɚ]. When [ɪr] is followed by a vowel, however (as in "leering" [lɪrɪŋ]), there is a strong tendency for the off-glide to become an on-glide for the next syllable, so that it can best be classified as a consonant. Thus [lɪ·rɪŋ] may be a somewhat more appropriate phonetic transcription than [lɪɚɪŋ]. For the most part, of course, this is a hairsplitting argument. The glide separates two syllables, with an off-glide from one and an on-glide to the other. In the *r*-less dialects [ɪə] changes to [ɪr] when followed by a vowel. To give an example of this, the Easterner who normally says [hɪə] for "hear" will nevertheless say [hɪrɪŋ] for "hearing." For further information on this point turn to Chapters 6 and 16.

EXERCISES

1 Practice paragraph for [ɪr]

> The job of classifying speech sounds appears to be nearly impossible, unless we clearly specify the type of speech to be analyzed, the audience for whom we're writing, and the purpose of the classification. If we are to steer clear of serious errors here, we must realize that none of these factors is irrelevant.

2 Word list:

a Words with [ɪr] in a final position or followed by a consonant:

appears	dear	here	nearly
beard	fear	mere	steer
beer	gear	merely	we're
cheer	hear	near	year
clear			

b Words with [ɪr] followed by a vowel:

appearing	material	period	spirit
fearing	miracle	serious	steering

3 Minimal pairs:

[ɪr]—[ɛr]		[ɪr]—[ɪ]	
[ɪə]—[ɛə]		[ɪə]—[ɪ]	
cheer [tʒɪr]	chair [tʃɛr]	beard [bɪrd]	bid [bɪd]
dear [dɪr]	dare [dɛr]	leered [lɪrd]	lid [lɪd]
fear [fɪr]	fair [fɛr]	reared [rɪrd]	rid [rɪd]
here [hɪr]	hair [hɛr]	seared [sɪrd]	Sid [sɪd]
steer [stɪr]	stair [stɛr]	tears [tɪrz]	'tis [tɪz]

4 Phonetic Transcription. The following is a phonetic transcription of the author's pronunciation of the paragraph in Exercise 1. The alternative transcriptions shown in parentheses are possibilities for a hypothetical Eastern dialect. These have been given only for [ɪr] diphthongs.

[ðə dʒɑb əv ˈklæsəfaɪŋ spitʃ saundz əˈpɪrz (əˈpɪəz) tə biˈ nɪrlɪ (ˈnɪəlɪ) ɪmˈpɑsəbl̩ ənlɛs wi ˈklɪrlɪ (ˈklɪəlɪ) ˈspɛsəˌfaɪ ðə taɪp əv spitʃ tə bi ˈænəlaɪzd, ðɪ ˈɔdiəns fɔr (fɔə) hum wɪr (wɪə) ˈraɪtɪŋ, ænd ðə ˈpɜpəs əv ðə klæsəfəˈkeʃən. ɪf wi ɑr tə stɪr (stɪə) klɪr (klɪə) əv ˈsɪriəs ˈɛrərz hɪr (hɪə), wi məst ˈriəlaɪz ðət nʌn əv ðiz ˈfæktəz ɪz ɪˈrɛləvənt.]

[ɛr] (or [ɛɚ]) and [ɛə]
VERY BERRY WEAR MARY MARRY CARE
PAIR THERE THEIR

ANALYSIS

The sounds of this class are centering diphthongs, where the glide moves from a relatively stable resonance near [ɛ] or [æ] toward a central-vowel position resembling [ɚ] for those who pronounce *r* and toward [ə] for those who do not pronounce *r*. In actual speech one may hear a whole range of slightly different resonances from [ɛ] to [æ] for the start of these diphthongs, but there is no practical reason for listing them.

VARIATION

The distinctions among these diphthongs are so fine and the usage so varied that it seems impossible to formulate any rule about when each is (or should be) used. The usual practice in General American is to employ [ɛr] or its approximate equivalent. In other dialects, perhaps most commonly in Eastern American, a distinction may be made—although not necessarily with any consistency. Where this practice is followed, one may hear such distinctions as [vɛrɪ]–[værɪ] for "very"–"vary," [kɛrɪ]–[kærɪ] for "Kerry"–"carry," and [mɛrɪ]–[mærɪ] for "merry"–"marry."

Another infrequent variation from [ɛr] is the use of [er]. For instance, the phrase "they are" when contracted to "they're" becomes [ðer]. Not many Americans make such a distinction. Pronunciations such as [wer] for "wear" and [ker] for "care" are dialectal, but not necessarily objectionable. In words like "they're" the [er] diphthong tends to break down into two syllables, becoming [ðe ɚ].

EXERCISES

1   Practice paragraph for [ɛr]:

It may interest you to discover whether or not all of these *ar* and *er* words in the following nonsense sentence share the same pronunciation in your vocabulary: "One very merry Christmas evening Mary narrowly escaped being married to a fair-haired boy named Jerry, a librarian who had come there from Gary."

2   Word list:

air	dare	narrow	share	vary
bare	fair	necessary	spare	very
care	hair	pair	square	wear
carry	marry	prepare	stare	where
character	merry	primarily	their	
chair	Mary	scarcely	there	

—and other words with stressed -*ery* or -*ary* syllables.

3   Minimal pairs:

[ɛr]—[ɝ]

air [ɛr]	err [ɝ]
bare [bɛr]	burr [bɝ]
carry [kɛrɪ]	curry [kɝɪ]
fair [fɛr]	fir [fɝ]
merry [mɛrɪ]	Murray [mɝɪ]
pair [pɛr]	purr [pɝ]
spare [spɛr]	spur [spɝ]
stare [stɛr]	stir [stɝ]
wear [wɛr]	were [wɝ]

4   Phonetic transcription. The following is a phonetic transcription of the paragraph in Exercise 1. The pronunciation recorded represents a Western dialect. Compare this pronunciation with your own.

[ɪt ˌme ˈɪntərɛst ju tə dɪsˈkʌvɚ ˈhwɛðɚ ɔr nɑt ˌɔl əv ðiz ˈeˌɑr ən ˈiˌɑr ˌwɝdz ɪn ðə ˈfɑloɪŋ ˈnɑnsɛns ˈsɛntəns ʃɛr ðə sem prəˌnʌnsɪˈeʃən ɪn jɔr voˈkæbjulɛrɪ: ˈwʌn ˈvɛrɪ ˈmɛrɪ ˈkrɪsməs ˈivnɪŋ ˈmɛrɪ ˈnɛrolɪ əsˈkept ˌbiɪŋ ˈmɛrɪd tu ə ˈfɛr ˈhɛrd bɔɪ ˌnemd ˈdʒɛrɪ, ə ˌlaɪˈbrɛrɪən hu həd ˌkʌm ˌðɛr frəm ˈgɛrɪ.]

[ɑr] (or [ɑɝ]) and [ɑə]
ART HEART SERGEANT GUARD

ANALYSIS

The [ɑr] diphthong features an off-glide from the relatively stable low-back [ɑ] to the central-vowel position for [ɝ] or [ɜ]. Among those who do not pronounce their *r*'s the glide is either toward [ɜ] or virtually absent. In the latter case the *monophthong* [ɑ] is increased in length and "farther" would be distinguished from the [ɑ] of "father" in this way. The symbol for this long monophthong is [ɑ:].

VARIATION

The historical development of the [ɑr] pronunciation has led to some interesting dialect differences and spelling inconsistencies. A detailed discussion of these points would, however, be beyond the scope of this book, although the student might enjoy reading more about these and other historical changes in the works of Kenyon (1946), Krapp (1909), Bloomfield (1933), Sweet (1888), and others. Attention is drawn to the British pronunciations of "clerk" and "derby" as [klɑːk] and [dɑːbɪ] and to the dialect pronunciations of a few words like "certain" and "learning" as [sɑrtṇ] and [lɑrnən]. Such pronunciations as these are nonstandard or dialectal in American speech.

Occasionally substitutions of [ɔr] for [ɑr] are found among native speakers and may be nonstandard. Some variation within the range [a]–[ɑ]–[ɔ]–[o] is, of course, to be expected. For example, one hears either [hors] or [hɔrs] for "horse." On the other hand, [hɑrs] for "horse," [fɔrmɚ] for "farmer," and [dɔrk] for "dark" are clearly nonstandard.

Among Eastern and Southern speakers a common variant of [ɑr] is a prolonged [ɑ], transcribed [ɑ:], as in "car" [kɑ:] and "bar" [bɑ:]. In these dialects "pot" [pɑt] and "part" [pɑːt] are distinguished largely by the lengthening of the vowel in the latter word. The diphthong [ɑə] instead of [ɑr] is, of course, regularly heard among Eastern and Southern speakers, since they may not pronounce *r*.

There are some interesting variations in pronunciation between [ɑ] and [ɔ] in what are sometimes called the *for* words. Examples of words which might contain either sound are "forest," "forehead," and "foreign." Either pronunciation must be considered acceptable, with [ɔr] tending to predominate in General American.

EXERCISES

1   Practice paragraph for [ɑr]:

> It is never very hard to start an argument about pronunciation. It is far
> more difficult to win. Take a word like "forest" for example. Part of the
> population may insist on rhyming the first syllable with "far," while others
> will insist on rhyming it with "four." Both groups are partly right and
> partly wrong. They are right in their pronunciations but wrong in their
> insistence.

2   Word list:

a   Words nearly always pronounced with [ɑr] rather than [ɔr]:

are	bargain	far	hard	star
army	bark	farm	heart	start
article	card	farmer	large	
artist	dark	farther	market	
bar	department	guard	part	

b   Words which may be pronounced with [ɑr] or [ɔr]:

borrow	foreign	moral	tomorrow	warrant
forehead	forest	sorrow	torrid	Warren

3   Minimal pairs:

[ɑr]—[ɑ]		[ɑr]—[ɔr]	
card [kɑrd]	cod [kɑd]	bar [bɑr]	bore [bɔr]
dark [dɑrk]	dock [dɑk]	card [kɑrd]	[cord [kɔrd]
far [fɑr]	fah [fɑ]	far [fɑr]	four [fɔr]
farther [fɑrðɚ]	father [fɑðɚ]	lard [lɑrd]	lord [lɔrd]
lark [lɑrk]	lock [lɑk]	mar [mɑr]	more [mɔr]
part [pɑrt]	pot [pɑt]	part [pɑrt]	port [pɔrt]
shark [ʃɑrk]	shock [ʃɑk]	star [stɑr]	store [stɔr]

4   Phonetic transcription. The following is a phonetic transcription of the paragraph in Exercise 1. It is in the General American dialect of one of the authors.
What changes would be made in the [ɑr] sounds in Eastern or Southern dialect?

> [ɪt ɪz ˈnɛvɚ ˌvɛrɪ ˈhɑrd tə ˈstɑrt ən ˈɑrgjəmənt əˌbaut prəˌnʌnsiˈeʃən. ɪt ɪz
> ˈfɑr ˌmɔr ˈdɪfəkəlt tə ˈwɪn. ˌtek ə ˌwɜrd ˌlaɪk ˈfɔrəst fɔr ɪgˈzæmpl̩. ˈpɑrt əv ðə
> ˌpɑpjəˈleʃən me ɪnˈsɪst ɑn ˌraɪmɪŋ ðə ˌfɜrst ˈsɪləbl̩ wɪð ˈfɑr, hwaɪl ˈʌðɚz wɪl
> ɪnˈsɪst ɑn ˌraɪmɪŋ ət wɪð fɔr. ˈboθ ˌgrups ɑr ˈpɑrtlɪ ˈraɪt ən ˈpɑrtlɪ ˈrɔŋ. ˌðe
> ɑr ˈraɪt ɪn ðɛr prəˌnʌnsiˈeʃənz bət ˈrɔŋ ɪn ˌðɛr ɪnˈsɪstəns.]

[ɔr] (or [ɔɚ]) and [ɔə]
OR COURT WARM OAR GEORGE

ANALYSIS

In this diphthong the gliding is from the more stable resonance of a back vowel near [ɔ] or [o] toward the position of the central vowel [ɝ] or [ɜ].

VARIATION

It is a very real question whether the [or] and [ɔr] should be considered distinctive diphthongs or simply important variations of a single phoneme. Here [or] and [ɔr] are treated as variations of a single sound, since this seems the best way to describe the usage of most speakers of General American. For a significant number of people, however, the difference between [ɔr] and [or] does serve to differentiate some words. Common examples are such pairs of words as "mourning" and "morning," "hoarse" and "horse," "oar" and "or." Those distinguishing between these pairs must use both sets of symbols. Those who do not differentiate these pairs will find that one symbol will suffice for phonetic transcriptions of their own speech. The serious student will, of course, wish to develop a sensitivity to the distinction between such usages as [hors] and [hɔrs].

The substitution of the sound [ɑr] for [ɔr] or [or] is often encountered. In most words this pronunciation becomes somewhat conspicuous and might be considered nonstandard in the General American dialect region. This would hold particularly for those words where the [ɔr]–[ɑr] distinction is important to the meaning. Thus "born in a barn" should not sound like [bɑrn ɪn ə bɑrn] or [bɑrn ɪn ə bɔrn]. The picture is somewhat complicated by that group of words in which usage varies *normally* between [ɑr] and [ɔr], as in the pronunciation of "foreign," "forest," and other words in which the diphthong [ɔr] or [ɑr] is followed directly by an unstressed vowel.

In Eastern and Southern speech, of course, the [ɔə] and [oə] replace the [ɔr] and [or]. In some Southern dialects a long monophthongal [o:] is used in place of the diphthong. The phrase "board up the door," for example, might be heard [bo:d ʌp ðə do:].

EXERCISES

1 Practice paragraph for [ɔr]:

In the morning we boarded the foreign ship from the wharf at the foot of Fourth Street. Going forward toward what we supposed was our cabin, I was thrown into a mortal panic to discover that my passport and tickets were not in the portfolio or the pocket where I was certain I had placed them before the quarrel with Horace. After a few moments of mental torture, and a show of concern I would normally abhor, I was fortunate to find the missing documents.

2   Word list:

a   Words ordinarily pronounced only with [ɔr] in most dialects:

born	form	lord	order	sort
cord	forward	morning	ordinary	storm
corner	George	normal	organized	war
course	horse	north	perform	warm
for	important	or	short	

b   Words for which both [or] and [ɔr] pronunciations are acceptable (according to Kenyon and Knott, 1953):

before	court	forty	port	tore
board	force	fourth	sport	torn
chorus	ford	hoarse	store	toward
course	forth	more	story	

c   Words for which either [ɔr] or [ɑr] may be acceptable (according to Kenyon and Knott, 1953):

borrow	forest	quarrel	torrent	Warren
forehead	Horace	sorrow	torrid	warrent
foreign	moral	tomorrow		

d   Words for which either [ɔr] or [ɚ] may be correct, depending upon stress:

for   nor   or

3   Minimal pairs:

[ɔr]—[o]		[ɔr]—[ɔ]	
board [bɔrd]	bowed [bod]	board]bɔrd]	bawd [bɔd]
court [kɔrt]	coat [kot]	court [kɔrt]	caught [kɔt]
more [mɔr]	mow [mo]	lord [lɔrd]	laud [lɔd]
store [stɔr]	stow [sto]	more [mɔr]	maw [mɔ]
toward [tɔrd]	toad [tod]	tore [tɔr]	taw [tɔ]

[ɔr]—[ɑr]	
board [bɔrd]	bard [bɑrd]
core [kɔr]	car [kɑr]

pour [pɔr]   par [pɑr]
shored [ʃɔrd]   shard [ʃɑrd]
tore [tɔr]   tar [tɑr]

4 Phonetic transcription. The following is a phonetic transcription of the paragraph in Exercise 1. The words "boarded," "Fourth," "toward," "passport," "portfolio," and "before," could also be pronounced with [or]. The use of [ɑr] would be equally acceptable for the words "foreign," "Horace," and "quarrel." The word "or" could be pronounced with [ɚ]:

[ɪn ðə ˈmɔrnɪŋ wi ˈbɔrdəd ðə ˈfɔrən ˈʃɪp frəm ðə ˌwɔrf ət ðə ˌfut ə ˈfɔrθ ˌstrit. ˌgoɪŋ ˌfɔrwəd tɔrd hwʌt wi səˈpozd wəz aur ˈkæbən, aɪ wəz ˌθron ɪntu ə ˈmɔrtəl ˈpænɪk tu dɪsˈkʌvɚ ðət maɪˈpæsˌpɔrt æn ˈtɪkəts wɚ nɑt ɪn ðə pɔrtˈfolio ɔr ðə ˈpɑkət hwɛr aɪ wəz ˈsɜtən aɪ həd ˌplest ðəm bɪˈfɔr ðə ˈkwɔrəl wɪθ ˈhɔrəs. æftɚ ə ˌfju ˈmomonths əv ˈmɛntəl ˈtɔrtʃɚ ænd ə ˌʃo əv kənsɜn aɪ wud ˈnɔrməlɪ əbˈhɔr, aɪ wəz ˈfɔrtʃənət tə ˌfaɪnd ðə ˌmɪsɪŋ ˈdɑkjəmənts.]

[ur] (or [uɚ]) and [uə]
POOR, TOUR, SURE

ANALYSIS

The more stable portion of this diphthong is usually produced as a lower high-back vowel near [u], although it may vary in some pronunciations toward the [u] or the [o] position. As in the other central diphthongs, the off-glide is toward the [ɚ] or [ə], depending upon the dialect spoken.

VARIATION

Although [ur] may occasionally be substituted for [ur], as in [pur] for "poor," this pronunciation is common only in some subregional dialects. When this usage does occur, the tendency is for the diphthong to break down into two syllables so that [ur] becomes [u·ɚ]. A more frequent variation in the pronunciation of [ur] involves a lowering of the tongue to the point where the pronunciation becomes [or], or perhaps even [ɔr], so that "poor" [pur] becomes more like "pour" [pɔr]. Such a pronunciation would generally be considered nonstandard in General American, although in some regional dialects and in some words it is common.

One rather prominent characteristic of some Southern speech is the substitution of [oə] for the Northern [ur] or [uə]. For example, in the sentence "He sure was a poor man," we may hear [hi ʃoə wʌz ə poə mæn]. Although this is dialectal, it may not be noticeable in some regions. The substitution of a long monophthong [oː] may also be heard in the South, as in [hi ʃoː wʌz poː]. This is considered nonstandard in almost any case.

In many words [ɚ] or [ɝ] may be substituted for [ʊr], as in [ʃɝ] instead of [ʃʊr] for "sure." With the possible exception of [jɚ] for "your," which is acceptable where the word is not stressed, this usage is not standard in cultivated speech. Pronunciations such as [ʃɝ] and [kjɝ] for "sure" and "cure" are, however, common in everyday speech.

EXERCISES

1 Practice paragraph for [ʊr]:

> One sure way to do poorly in phonetic transcription is to write furiously without listening carefully. During the period when your mastery of the symbols is so limited that you do not feel secure, permit nothing to lure your attention from the sounds the speaker makes. It is a curious fact that it may go against your nature to ignore his meaning, but the skills of listening will endure, once they are mastered, and will be a form of real insurance against bad speech form.

2 Word list:

    a Words using [ʊr] in the final position or preceding a consonant:

allure	lure	spoor
boor	moor	sure
cure	poor	tour

    b Words using [ʊr] (sometimes [ɝ]) followed by a vowel:

bureau	during	fury	mural
curious	Europe	insurance	rural

3 Minimal pairs:

[ʊr]—[ɔr]		[ʊr]—[o]	
lure [lʊr]	lore [lɔr]	lure [lʊr]	low [lo]
moor [mʊr]	more [mɔr]	poor [pʊr]	Poe [po]
poor [pʊr]	pour [pɔr]	sure [ʃʊr]	show [ʃo]
your [jʊr]	yore [jɔr]	tour [tʊr]	tow [to]

[ʊr]—[uɚ]	
cure [kjʊr]	cue'er [kjuɚ]
moor [mʊr]	mooer [muɚ]
poor [pʊr]	"pooer" [puɚ]
sure [ʃʊr]	shoer [ʃuɚ]

4 Phonetic transcription. Compare the following phonetic transcription of the paragraph in Exercise 1 with your own pronunciation. Do any of the differences indicate nonstandard usages in your speech?

[ˈwʌn ˈʃur we tə du ˈpurli ɪn fəˈnɛtɪk trænsˈkrɪpʃən ɪz tə ˌraɪt ˈfjuriəslɪ wɪðˌaut ˈlɪsənɪŋ ˌkɛrfəlɪ. ˈdurɪŋ ðə ˈpɪriəd hwɛn jur ˈmæstrɪ ə ðə ˈsɪmbəlz ɪz so ˈlɪmətəd ðət ju du ˈnɑt ˈfil sɪˈkjur, pəˌmɪt ˈnʌθɪŋ tə lur jə əˈtɛnʃən frəm ðə ˈsaundz ðə ˌspikɚ ˈmeks. ɪt ɪz ə ˈkjuriəs ˈfækt ðət ɪt ˌme ˌgo əˈgɛnst jur ˈnetʃɚ tu ɪgˈnɔr hɪz ˈminɪŋ, bət ðə ˌskɪlz əv ˈlɪsənɪŋ wɪl ɛnˈdur, ˈwʌns ðe ɑr ˈmæstəd, ænd wɪl ˌbi ə ˌfɔrm əv ˈriəl ɪnˈʃurəns əˈgɛnst, bæd spitʃ fɔrm.]

Chapter 13

Stops

[p], [b], [t], [d], [tʃ], [dʒ], [k], [g]

[p]
*PA*PER *A*PPLY SHE*P*HERD HICCOU*GH*

ANALYSIS

[p] is classically described as a *voiceless bilabial* (or simply *labial*) stop. It is a *nonsyllabic obstruent*, and in distinctive feature terminology is also *anterior, tense, noncoronal*, and *nonsonorant*. To produce this sound, the unvoiced breath stream is impounded by a more or less firm closure of the lips; pressure is built up behind this closure during a "hold" or "stop gap" phase of the articulation (a short period of silence of the order of 0.1 second) and is then released by opening the lips to the position for the following sound, or to a neutral position if [p] occurs as a final consonant. Velopharyngeal closure is complete or nearly so in normal production (Fig. 5-4).

Inasmuch as [p] is a "plosive" in its function as an initial releasing consonant, it has the releasing characteristics of most stops, that is, a tendency

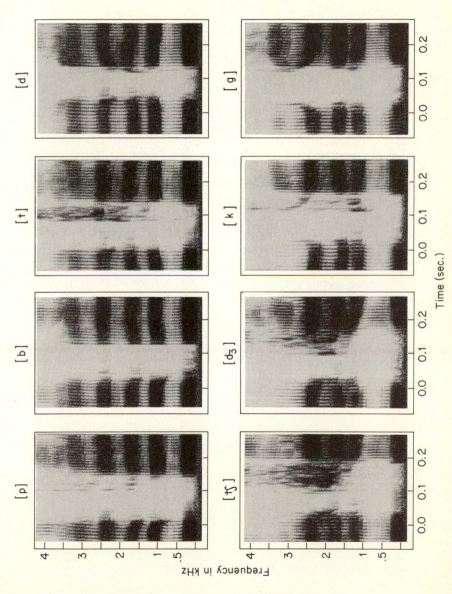

Figure 13-1 Sound spectrogram of [p], [b], [t], [d], [tʃ], [dʒ], [k], and [g].

toward some degree of aspirate and affricate noise accompanying an abrupt onset of the following syllable. However, the [p] is the weakest of the voiceless stops in the stridency of its release. Little if any affrication is heard except in the most vigorous articulation.

VARIATION

Many of the variants of [p], and of some other stops as well, occur as a result of the manner in which the sound is released into the following syllable. Thus we may encounter an extremely strongly released (*fortis*) variant prior to some especially strong syllables, with both aspirate (p^h] and affricate [p'] varieties, or both [p'^h]. On the other hand, it is not unusual, particularly with [p], to encounter a sound with very weak release, a variant which to an English ear may sound much like a [b], and for which such symbols as [p̣], [ḅ], or [b] may be used.

As a general rule, English voiceless stops will be more strongly released than their voiced counterparts. However, in the case of certain blends, such as the [sp] of "spin" and as the initiating consonant of an unstressed vowel, the [p] release is almost never strident, neither aspirate nor affricate. Variation from this rule will, of course, sound "foreign."

There are still other interesting variations in consonant release mechanisms in certain other sound combinations. For example, when [p] is followed by [m̩] or [l̩], nasal or lateral releases are common. In the nasal release, as in "keep'm" [kip^mm] the lips remain closed and the pressure is released nasally. In the lateral release, as in "grapple" [græp^Ll], [p] is released as an [l]. The tongue assumes the lateral position (see page 105) simultaneously with the bilabial opening.

In Chapter 6, the general characteristics of doubled stops were discussed, and these remarks of course apply to [p]. Note, for example, that in the typical pronunciation of such a phrase as "lamp post" only one stop-plosive occurs. There may be, however, a perceptible hold between the stop at the end of the word "lamp" and the plosive release which initiates the word "post." This pronunciation can be transcribed either as [læmp¯post], [læmp⁺post] or [lamp:ost], with the symbol [:] designating a distinctive lengthening of the [p] stop. The person who consciously tries to release two contiguous identical stops in casual speech is at best guilty of conspicuous "overpronunciation." For further discussion of this problem of joining sounds in adjacent syllables or words, you may consult the section on *juncture* in Chapter 6.

Several other facets of the articulation of [p] should also be noted. When [m] is followed by certain other sounds, particularly by [t], [k], [f], [θ], [s], or [ʃ], an "intrusive" [p] may occur when the lips open from the [m] position to the following unvoiced sound. Historically this has led to the adoption of the letter *p* as a spelling convention in words such as "preempt," "bumpkin," "exempt," and "glimpse." In many cases, however, this natural phonetic tendency is not recognized in spelling. A [p] is usually heard in "something" [sʌmpθɪŋ], "comfort" [kʌmpfɚt], "warmth" [wɔrmpθ], and other words of similar construction.

A question sometimes is raised as to whether or not the careful speaker should take pains, on the one hand always to pronounce [p] in situations where it is sanctioned by spelling and, on the other, not to let it intrude where it is not called for by spelling. "Something" [sʌmpθɪŋ] or [sʌmθɪŋ] may serve as an example. As a matter of common sense the question cannot be considered particularly important except as an illustration of the way in which we can become confused by failing to realize that it is the spoken language which is basic to the written rather than the reverse.

In some speech disorders, particularly those associated with disease of, or injury to, the central nervous system, there may be weakness in the labial musculature or difficulty with its control. Also, anyone who has had a generous injection of a local anesthetic near the lips can testify to the effect of sensory deadening of the lips on articulation of [p]. The [p] may become a kind of bilabial glide or even a weak bilabial fricative [ɸ]. Certain dental malocclusions, which fortunately are not common, involve abnormal relationships between the upper and lower teeth which are so marked that it may be difficult for the speaker to bring the lips together. In this case the [p] will often be made as a labiodental [p̪].

In common with all the obstruents the [p] requires a buildup of intraoral air pressure behind the articulation. In cleft palate speech this may be impossible because of the lack of velopharyngeal closure. The nasal escape of air may, particularly if the subject sees the problem as one of producing a "plosive," result in a noisy nasal fricative, or, failing that, the use of the glottal stop, either as a substitute for or in addition to the labial articulation.

Notwithstanding the necessity for this somewhat extended discussion of [p], it is after all an easy sound, in the sense of being early learned, universal among language systems (so far as we know), easily observed, and in speakers with normal lips and palates is relatively easily changed.

Among the common voiceless labial stop variants are these: aspirate [pʰ], affricate [p'], unreleased [p⁻], glottalized [pˀ], dentalized [p̪], bilabial voiceless fricative [ɸ], laterally released [pᴸ], and nasally released [p̚ᴹ].

EXERCISES

1   Practice paragraph for [p]:

Perhaps one of the most remarkable examples of animal performance is to be found in the perfectly trained sheep dogs who help the shepherd tend his flock. The sheep dog apparently has bred into him an aptitude for his work and an understanding of sheep psychology which far surpasses that of the people who are supposed to be his superiors. The mountain traveler will sometimes come upon a sheepherder, camped in some alpine meadow and presumably guarding the flock. More probably he will be found perched on a convenient rock, sopping up the warmth of the sun, and peering at something just beyond the empty horizon. His dog, however, poised and vigilant, allows nothing to escape him. If a sheep strays too far, he leaps and plunges into instant motion. The sheep dog is happy only when he is working; he is not to be pampered or petted. He and others of his corps are indeed the philosophers and psychologists of the sheep raising industry.

2 Word list:

Initiating consonant: pat, pay, pie, pill
Terminating consonant: ape, rope, up, weep
Initiating and terminating: pep, pipe, pop, Pope
Strong consonant: apart, appeal, comply, repair
Weak consonant: copper, happen, open, stopping
Initial blends: [sp] space, speech; [pr] pray, prize; [pl] place, plead; [spr] spring, spry; [spl] splash, splay
Final blends: [ps] rips, tops; [pt] kept, wrapped; [mp] damp, stump; [mps] bumps, lamps; [mpt] prompt, stamped

3 Minimal pairs:

	[p]—[b]		[p]—[t]	
cop [kɑp]	cob [kɑb]	flap [flæp]	flat [flæt]
pat [pæt]	bat [bæt]	flapper [flæpɚ]	flatter [flætɚ]
pay [pe]	bay [be]	grape [grep]	great [gret]
pie [paɪ]	by [baɪ]	hip [hɪp]	hit [hɪt]
pill [pɪl]	bill [bɪl]	P [pi]	T [ti]
pin [pɪn]	been [bɪn]	pen [pɛn]	ten [tɛn]
rip [rɪp]	rib [rɪb]	pile [paɪl]	tile [taɪl]
ripping [rɪpɪŋ]	ribbing [rɪbɪŋ]	pipe [paɪp]	type [taɪp]
rope [rop]	robe [rob]	pun [pʌn]	ton [tʌn]
staple [stepḷ]	stable [stebḷ]	top [tɑp]	tot [tɑt]

	[p]—[k]	
ape [ep]	ache [ek]
lip [lɪp]	lick [lɪk]
open [opən]	oaken [okən]
P [pi]	key [ki]
past [pæst]	cast [kæst]
pay [pe]	K [ke]
play [ple]	clay [kle]
purr [pɝ]	cur [kɝ]

supper [sʌpɚ]   sucker [sʌkɚ]
stop [stɑp]   stock [stɑk]

4 Phonetic transcription:

[pɚhæps wʌn əv ðə most rɪˈmɑrkəbḷ ɛgˈzæmpḷz əv ænəməl pɚˈfɔrməns ɪz tə bi faʊnd ɪn ðə ˈpɝfɪktlɪ trend ʃip dɔgz hu hɛlp ðə ʃɛpɚd tɛnd ɪz flɑk. ðə ʃip dɔg əˈpɛrəntlɪ hæz brɛd ˈɪntu hɪm ən ˈæptəˌtud fɔr hɪz wɝk ænd ən ˌʌndɚˈstændɪŋ əv ʃip saɪˌkɑlədʒɪ hwɪtʃ fɑr sɚˈpæsəz ðæt əv ðə pipḷ hu ɑr səˈpozd tə bi hɪz səˈpɪriɚz. ðə maʊntṇ trævəlɚ wɪl ˈsʌmˌtaɪmz kʌm əpɔn ə ˈʃipˌhɝdɚ, kæmpt ɪn sʌm ˈælpaɪn mɛdo ən prɪˈzuməblɪ ˈgɑrdɪŋ ðə flɑk. mɔr prɑbəblɪ hi wɪl bi faʊnd pɝtʃt ɔn ə kənˈvɪnjənt rɑk, ˈsɑpɪŋ ʌp ðə wɔrmpθ əv ðə sʌn, ən ˈpɪrɪŋ ət sʌmpθɪŋ dʒʌst biˈɑnd ðɪ ɛmptɪ həˈraɪzən. hɪz dɔg, hawɛvɚ, pɔɪzd ən ˈvɪdʒələnt, əlauz ˈnʌθɪŋ tu əskep hɪm. ɪf ə ʃip strɛz tu fɑr, hi lips ən plʌndʒəz ɪntu ˈɪnstənt ˈmoʃən. ðə ʃip dɔg ɪz hæpi onlɪ hwɛn hi ɪz ˈwɝkɪŋ; hi ɪz nɑt tə bi pæmpɚd ɚ pɛtəd. hi ən ʌðɚz əv ɪz kɔr ɑr ɪnˈdid ðə fəˈlɑsəfɚz ən ˌsaɪˈkɑlədʒəsts əv ðə ʃip ˈrezɪŋ ɪndəstrɪ.]

[b]
BOY BU**BB**LE

ANALYSIS

The [b] is an obstruent usually classified as a *voiced bilabial* stop. The articulatory features significant to [b] are about the same as for [p], except that *voice* has been added. This "addition," however, is not always a simple matter to analyze. Sometimes it means that the vocal cords will continue to vibrate right on through the stop and into the next syllable, without cessation. At other times there is a silent interval, but one which is short relative to that of a voiceless consonant. As Figure 13-1 shows, the silent interval is typically shorter for the voiced sounds (see also Fig. 5-4).

Because of the decreased airflow in voiced, as opposed to voiceless, stops, the voiced sounds are also weaker and less likely to be "noisy." The [b] is typically described as *lax*. Although some degree of aspiration or affrication is occasionally present in stressed syllables, it is characteristically less than in the corresponding voiceless stop. Except for voicing and reduced tension, the feature analysis is essentially the same as for [p].

VARIATION

Although much of the discussion concerning the pronunciation of [p] is applicable to [b], certain additional considerations should be mentioned. Since [b] is voiced, there is less or no aspiration on the plosive release of this sound. In extremely vigorous plosives, however, affrication may be heard.

In final position there may also be heard a kind of schwa or "release vowel," as in [stæbᵊ] for "stab."

In numerous non-English languages voiced stops may have rather different dynamics from those described. A weakened form of [p] may be perceived, for example, when a native German speaker says words such as "about" and "stab." English [b] becomes [p]-like. One way to transcribe this "devoiced" variant is [b̥]. In the case of the final voiced consonant the transcription [bp] may be appropriate, as in [stæbp] for "stab." Normal English voicing of stops is sometimes surprisingly difficult for some foreign speakers who, in their native languages, do not prolong vocal-cord vibration into a closed cavity in producing such sounds.

Another interesting variant of [b] is the fricative variety [β], the bilabial fricative of Spanish, related to [b] approximately as [p] is related to [ɸ].

Finally, there are many release variants of [b], comparable to those discussed for [p] except that affricate release variants are extremely rare in English speech.

To summarize, some of the variant pronunciations of [b] are aspirate [bʰ], affricate [b'], nasal release [bᴹ], lateral [bᴸ], unreleased [b⁻], partial devoiced [b̥] or [bp], labial fricative [β], dentalized [b̪]. There is no agreed-upon manner of indicating the nasal frication air release heard in cleft palate speech. The nasal aspirate [h̃] is suggested as a suitable symbol for the cleft palate fricative which is often a characteristic of this form of defective speech.

EXERCISES

1   Practice paragraph for [b]:

> There is sometimes a curious snobbery about good speech. Many who write ably and who would doubtless be greatly troubled by shabby writing seem to be quite oblivious to the basic need to make themselves understood. There seems to be a subtle belief that the habits of good writing and good speaking bear no resemblance, and in consequence unnumbered good and useful thoughts lie as buried as in the tomb. Such a basically false concept of speech will rob both the speaker and the listener of any benefits which might be theirs. These observations are no invitation for anyone to clamber onto a platform, bent on rabble-rousing, but thrice-blest will be he who obeys our plea that he content himself neither with dumb show nor unrecognizable babbling.

2   Word list:

> *Initiating consonant:* bay, bee, bow, boy
> *Terminating consonant:* Abe, rob, rub, web

Initiating and terminating: babe, bib, bob, boob
Strong consonant: above, about, imbibe, rebuff
Weak consonant: habit, robber, rubbing, stubborn
Initial blends: [br] break, brown; [bl] black, blue
Final blends: [bz] clubs, rubs; [bd] clubbed, stubbed

3   Minimal pairs:

[b]—[p]		[b]—[d]	
Abe [eb]	ape [ep]	Abe [eb]	aid [ed]
about [əbaut]	a pout [ə paut]	about [əbaut]	a doubt [ə daut]
ball [bɔl]	pall [pɔl]	B [bi]	D [di]
bee [bi]	p [pi]	bon [bɑn]	don [dɑn]
bet [bɛt]	pet [pɛt]	bet [bɛt]	debt [dɛt]
bill [bɪl]	pill [pɪl]	bill [bɪl]	dill [dɪl]
lab [læb]	lap [læp]	buy [baɪ]	die [daɪ]
rib [rɪb]	rip [rɪp]	lab [læb]	lad [læd]
sob [sɑb]	sop [sɑp]	rib [rɪb]	rid [rɪd]
sobbing [sɑbɪŋ]	sopping [sɑpɪŋ]	sob [sɑb]	sod [sɑd]

[b]—[m]	
bat [bæt]	mat [mæt]
bay [be]	may [me]
bee [bi]	me [mi]
bet [bɛt]	met [mɛt]
bill [bɪl]	mill [mɪl]
bob [bɑb]	bomb [bɑm]
buy [baɪ]	my [maɪ]
cob [kɑb]	calm [kɑm]
lab [læb]	lamb [læm]
rib [rɪb]	rim [rɪm]

4   Phonetic transcription:

[ðɛr ɪz ˈsʌmˌtaɪmz ə ˈkjurɪəs snɑbəri əbaut gud spitʃ. mɛnɪ hu raɪt eblɪ ən
hu wud dautləs bi gretlɪ trʌbḷd baɪ ʃæbɪ raɪtɪŋ sim tə bi kwaɪt əˈblɪvɪəs tə
ðə ˈbesɪk nid tə mek ðəmsɛlvz ʌndəˈstud. ðɛr simz tə bi ə sʌtḷ bɪˈlif ðət ðə
hæbəts əv gud ˈraɪtɪŋ ən gud ˈspikɪŋ bɛr no rɪˈzɛmbləns, ænd ɪn ˈkɑnsəˌkwɛns
ˌʌnˈnʌmbəd gud n̩ jusfḷ θɔts laɪ əz bɛrɪd əz ɪn ðə tum. sʌtʃ ə besɪklɪ fɔls
ˈkɑnsɛpt əv spitʃ wɪl rɑb boθ ðə spikɚ ən ðə ˈlɪsənɚ əv ɛnɪ ˈbɛnəfɪts hwɪtʃ
maɪt bi ðɛrz. ðiz ˌɑbzɚˈveʃənz ɑr no ˌɪnvəˈteʃn̩ fɔr ˈɛnɪ wʌn tə klæmɚ ɔntu
ə ˈplætfɔrm, bɛnt ɔn ˈræblˌrauzɪŋ, bət θraɪs blɛst wɪl bi hi hu əbez aur pli
ðət hi kəntɛnt ɪmsɛlf niðɚ wɪθ dʌm ʃo nɔr ʌnˈrɛkəgˌnaɪzəbḷ ˈbæblɪŋ.]

[t]
TO A*TT*END ASK*ED* INDI*CT*
*TH*YME *PHTH*ISIC

ANALYSIS

The [t] is classically described as an *unvoiced lingua-alveolar stop* consonant, and in distinctive feature terms as *anterior, coronal, tense, unvoiced, obstruent,* and *stop.* In articulating this sound the tonguetip and blade are in contact with the alveolar ridge behind the upper central teeth, with the lateral margins of the tongue in contact with the teeth and gums in such a way as to form an airtight closure. Breath pressure is ordinarily built up behind this closure, then released as the tongue moves either to the next sound or, if there is no following sound, to a neutral position. The canonical stressed [t] is strong, plosive, aspirate, and usually affricate as well. That is, noise is produced by the airstream turbulence at both the glottis and the alveolar contact. Velopharyngeal closure is complete or nearly so (Fig. 5-4).

VARIATION

The sounds within the [t] class vary considerably, and there are some interesting differences in pronunciation to be considered. For the most part these variations are heard in other stop consonants as well. They may be classified as follows: (1) variants in *place* of articulation resulting from assimilation, elision, consonant clustering, and dialect; (2) variants in articulatory *tension* or force which result from differences in stress, rhythm, and juncture; (3) variants in release mechanisms, related to stress and context; and (4) variants of articulatory *type*, largely related to stress and rhythm.

Some variability among [t] sounds grows out of differences in the exact point of tongue contact, as influenced by phonetic context. Sometimes, but not often among native English speakers, [t] is made as a linguadental sound, with the tonguetip in contact with the teeth rather than with the alveolar ridge. Such a dental sound may be heard in the usual pronunciation of the word "eighth" [eṱθ] or in a phrase such as "at them" [æṱθəm]. In these cases [t] has obviously been influenced by the fact that the following sound is a linguadental. Where [t] is followed by a front vowel, as in "Tim" [tɪm] and "tea" [ti], the tonguetip may be placed very nearly at the point where the teeth and gums meet, in which case the sound is sometimes referred to as *gingival.* If a gingival [t] does not occur in these circumstances, the point of articulation is at least more likely to be forward, as compared, for example with the [t] of words such as "Tom" and "top." As with other stops, a nasal after [t] may lead to a nasal release, a lateral to a lateral release. "Button" [bʌtⁿn̩] and "bottle" [bɔtˡl̩] are examples.

In some foreign dialects the coronal anterior stop is customarily dental, and it is common to hear this variant carried into all English contexts, sometimes as an *interdental* stop which may be transcribed [tθ].

In stressed syllables English [t] is often quite strong (fortis), especially in initial positions, where the stridency may be particularly noticeable. On the other hand, it is also normal for the [t] to become quite weak in unstressed syllables. Compare, for example the [t] sounds of "attack" [ət'æk] and "attic" [ætɪk]. Notice how much less stridency there is in the latter context.

When [t] comes at the end of a word, particularly after an obstruent, it may differ appreciably from the initial sound, and there is the familiar tendency toward weak release, such as in "act" [ækt]. Indeed further weakening of the final stop in certain clusters may result in its complete omission. Thus "act" may approach the nonstandard [æk], and such words as "ghosts" and "cost" may become [gos] and [kɔs]. [t]s which are respectively plosive, unreleased, aspirate, and affricate may be transcribed as follows: [t], [t⁻], [tʰ], and [t'].

In some junctures the influence of a preceding or following segment reduces the extent to which [t] is aspirated, or affects the manner in which aspiration takes place. Thus, in conversational speech the phrase "last night" [læstnaɪt] may be spoken with no release of breath on [t]; the result might be a nasal release, or perhaps the [t] might be eliminated and the pronunciation [læsnaɪt] result. This normal articulatory behavior results since the tongue is already in the position for the following [n]; hence it is "natural" to make the shift by lowering the soft palate while the tongue is in the [t] (and [n]) position. The same phenomenon can be found in such a phrase as "past me" [pæsmi], where the lips may be closed for [m] before the breath is released. The doubled [t] has the same characteristics as other doubled stops. When [t] is followed by a different stop, as in "that dog" "that cat," or "that paper," the phonetic situation is comparable. There is a consonant closure which is alveolar, but only a single consonant release, which is from the position of the second consonant. Double releases are very uncommon, and in general sound overprecise.

In casual style such pronunciations as [sɪdaun] for "sit down," [ðæʔdɔg] for "that dog," and [ðæpepɚ] for "that paper" are marks of informality rather than of illiteracy, provided, of course, that they occur at appropriate articulatory pacing and in an appropriate social setting.

One variant of [t] found principally in reduced syllables calls for special discussion. In most dialects of General American the [t] of words such as "butter," "water," and "what a man" will be pronounced as a much more weak and brief sound than the one appearing in a context such as "attend" or "return." Such a weak [t] will often be a *flap*, the phonetic symbol for which is the [ɾ] (see Chapter 5). Not all English speech is alike in this. In some Eastern dialects, and in British English, the stop, with its more strident release, will be preserved in such contexts.

There is also a tendency to voice [t] when it occurs before reduced vowels, although it is usually possible with more careful listening to detect a difference between a flap [t] and a [d], even though to a casual observer they might sound the same. The difference between the weak flap [t] of "matter," and the voiced [d] of "madder" is slight, but it can be significant.

A kind of "intrusive" [t] exists in English in much the same way that we have an intrusive [p] (discussed in a preceding section). Note the tendency to add [t] in the words "dance," "tense," "prance," and "pence." Such pronunciations as [dænts] and [tɛnts] are perfectly normal and usually wholly unobtrusive in American English. "Tense" and "tents" are normally identical in their pronunciation.

An interesting and usually conspicuous dialectal variant of [t], and of many other stops as well, is the glottal stop [ʔ]. Its use is particularly notable in Cockney English and, in some contexts, in New York City speech. In Cockney one might hear "with a little bit of luck" as [wɪʔə lɪʔlbɪʔə lʌʔ], for example.

Among those who have physical defects affecting their speech, persons with a cleft palate are particularly prone to use the glottal, often as a substitute for any stop, often as a stop produced simultaneously with the standard articulation. "Take time," in cleft palate might be transcribed as [ʔh̃tẽʔh̃tãɪm] (using [h̃] to symbolize the nareal fricative).

To summarize, the allophones of [t] discussed in this chapter are plosive [t], aspirate [tʰ], affricate [tˢ], unreleased [t⁻], dental [t̪], flap [ɾ], and glottal stop [ʔ].

EXERCISES

1 Practice paragraph for [t]:

> Good taste in speech, as in all one's habits, will truly stand each of us in good stead. Training in natural, communicative diction should, it seems apparent, be a part of everyone's education. There is certainly no truth to the notion that such an attitude as we have expressed will result in superficiality. Good speech provides the best possible guarantee of sympathetic attention to one's thoughts. The best time to learn is while one still thinks of himself as a student. Ofttimes the question is asked, "Why can't everyone be taught to speak clearly and effectively?" The answer is, of course, that teaching these skills is not too difficult a process; it wants only better acceptance as an important part of the educational process.

2 Word list:

Initiating consonant: tea, tie, toe, two
Terminating consonant: at, ate, eat, ought
Initiating and terminating: Tate, taught, tight, toot
Strong consonant: atone, attach, between, esteem
Weak consonant: better, bottle, bottom, butter
Initial blends: [st] stand, stay; [tr] train, try; [str] straight, string; [tw] twelve,
          twin
Final blends: [ts] lets, puts; [st] lost, past; [pt] kept, stopped; [ft] laughed, sift;
          [nt] rent, want; [nts] pants, tents; [ʃt] cashed, pushed; [mpt]
          lumped, stamped; [ŋkt] honked, ranked; [rt] part, start; [ntʃt]
          pinched, wrenched; [rts] carts, parts; [nst] fenced, glanced

3 Minimal pairs:

[t]—[d]		[t]—[k]	
at [æt]	add [æd]	ate [et]	ache [ek]
ate [et]	aid [ed]	batter [bætɚ]	backer [bækɚ]
boat [bot]	bowed [bod]	late [let]	lake [lek]
cart [kɑrt]	card [kɑrd]	lot [lɑt]	lock [lɑk]
matter [mætɚ]	madder [mædɚ]	mate [met]	make [mek]
patter [pætɚ]	padder [pædɚ]	rater [retɚ]	raker [rekɚ]
T [ti]	D [di]	tall [tɔl]	call [kɔl]
ten [tɛn]	den [dɛn]	tame [tem]	came [kem]
tick [tɪk]	Dick [dɪk]	tea [ti]	key [ki]
two [tu]	do [du]	toy [tɔɪ]	coy [kɔɪ]

[t]—[p]		[t]—[θ]	
ate [et]	ape [ep]	Bert [bɝt]	birth [bɝθ]
cotter [kɑtɚ]	copper [kɑpɚ]	boat [bot]	both [boθ]
Kate [ket]	cape [kep]	pat [pæt]	path [pæθ]
matter [mætɚ]	mapper [mæpɚ]	rat [ræt]	wrath [ræθ]
sheet [ʃit]	sheep [ʃip]	sheet [ʃit]	sheath [ʃiθ]
tack [tæk]	pack [pæk]	team [tim]	theme [θim]
tea [ti]	P [pi]	tick [tɪk]	thick [θɪk]
tie [taɪ]	pie [paɪ]	tie [taɪ]	thigh [θaɪ]
toe [to]	Poe [po]	tread [trɛd]	thread [θrɛd]
ton [tʌn]	pun [pʌn]	tree [tri]	three [θri]

4 Phonetic transcription:

[gʊd test ɪn spɪtʃ, æz ɪn ɔl wʌnz hæbəts, wɪl trulɪ stænd ɪtʃ əv əs ɪn gʊd stɛd.
ˈtrenɪŋ ɪn ˈnætʃərəl, kəˈmjunəˌketɪv dɪkʃən ʃʊd, ɪt simz əˈpɛrənt, bi ə pɑrt
əv ˈɛvrɪˌwʌnz ˌɛdʒəˈkeʃən. ðɛr ɪz ˈsɝtənlɪ no truθ tə ðə noʃən ðət sʌtʃ ən
ˈætətud əz wi həv ɛkˈsprɛst wɪl rɪˈzʌlt ɪn ˌsupɚˌfɪʃɪˈælətɪ. gʊd spɪtʃ prəvaɪdz
ðə bɛst pɑsəbļ ˌgɛrənˈti əv ˌsɪmpəˈθɛtɪk əˈtɛnʃən tə wʌnz θɔts. ðə bɛs taɪm

tə lɜn ɪz hwaɪl wʌn stɪl θɪŋks əv ɪmsɛlf əz ə studn̩t. ˈɔfˈtaɪmz ðə ˈkwɛstʃən
ɪz æskt, hwaɪ kænt ˈɛvrɪ͵wʌn bi tɔt tə spik klɪrli ənd ɪˈfɛktɪvlɪ? ði ænsɚ iz,
əv kɔrs, ðət titʃɪŋ ðiz skɪlz ɪz nɑt tu ˈdɪfə͵kʌlt ə prɑsɛs; ɪt wɔnts onlɪ bɛtɚ
ək'sɛptəns æz ən ɪmˈpɔrtənt part əv ði ͵ɛdʒəˈkeʃənəl ˈprɑsɛs.]

[d]
*D*ISH   ADD

ANALYSIS

The [d] is classified traditionally as a *voiced lingua-alveolar stop* (or stop-plosive) and in distinctive feature terms as *stop, anterior, coronal, lax*, and *obstruent*. It tends to be significantly more weak than the corresponding voiceless alveolar [t]. Essentially it is made in the same manner as the [t] except for voicing and related features. As with the other voiced stops in English, the glottal vibration continues to be prolonged into the closed cavity during a part, if not for the entire duration of the consonant occlusion. Any previous vowel is likely to be lengthened, and the release of the [d] is less likely to be either aspirate or affricate (see Fig. 5-4).

VARIATION

The varieties of sounds within the [d] category are to a large extent comparable to those described in the discussion of [t]. This certainly applies to the place of tongue contact, which may range from a dental to a palatal location. As usual, these variations are mainly the result of phonetic context, so that the point of the contact tends to be forward in such a word as "width" [wɪdθ] and farther back in such words as "dog" [dɔg] and "heard," where the [d] is followed or preceded by a backed or palatalized tongue position.

[d] is often weakened substantially in colloquial elliptic speech and prior to unstressed syllables, sometimes becoming a flap, as in "rudder," [rʌɾɚ], an allophone of /d/ which phonetically may be exactly the same as the flap allophone of /t/ discussed in the preceding section. Further weakening can produce a kind of lingua-alveolar fricative or even glide.

In nonstandard speech the [d] is sometimes omitted altogether, as for example in cases where [d] is followed by the contraction of "not," giving [wʊnt] and [ʃʊnt] for "wouldn't" and "shouldn't." Likewise [d] may be missing from certain consonant clusters in any situation where either the preceding or following sound has a similar articulatory position. Examples include [stæn ʌp] for "stand up," [ol bɔɪ] for "old boy," [hænl̩] for "handle," [frɛnli] for "friendly," and [saʊnz] or [sãʊ̃z] for "sounds." Which of these would you consider substandard in good informal English?

Weakening of the consonant [d] is, of course, related to variations in consonant release mechanisms. This may vary with [d] in much the same way that they do with [t], except that a strongly aspirated or affricated [d] is more rare.

Strong release of a final stop consonant, whether it is a [d] or some other stop, may result in the addition of an extra syllable. We usually remain unaware of this final vowel unless it becomes overstrong, too frequently used, or employed in a nonfinal context. [stændə] for "stand" may go unnoticed at the end of a phrase, but [stændəhɪr] for "stand here" would sound "foreign" to us. In many foreign dialects all syllables end in vowels, with the result that all consonants in final position may have an added vowel. [ɪtsədə raɪtə tɪŋə tə du].

It is interesting to note in passing that a number of words which now contain the letter *d* once were spelled without it, so that "thunder" and "sound," for example, have developed from "thunor" and "soun" (see Kenyon, 1946, p. 124). The often heard addition of [d] to the word "drown" makes it "drownd," with the past tense "drownded." In this case the addition of [d], while not rare, is not yet acceptable.

A number of foreign dialect pronunciations of *d* words generally parallel those variants found for [t]. Possibly the most common is the use of a dentalized [d̪], usually employed by the same speaker who has a dental [t̪]. In some dialects the sound thus produced may have a strong affricate release or even be a fricative, and as a consequence may resemble the sounds [ð] or [d̪ð]. Also, in some foreign dialects of English voicing may be the major problem, giving rise to confusion between [d] and [t], and sentences which sound like this: [tæt hæt ə pɪkɚ tək] for "dad had a bigger dog."

To summarize, the allophones of /d/ described above are aspirate [dʰ], affricate [d'], unvoiced or partially unvoiced [d̥], dentalized [d̪] or [d̪ð], flap [ɾ], palatized [d̩], nasal release [dᴺ], lateral release [dᴸ], and strong vowel release [dᵊ].

EXERCISES

1 Practice paragraph for [d]:

You should now and then seek out individuals who can serve as models for your own diction, for speech is a living thing, better to be heard than read about. Those individuals whom we encounter in daily life who speak the language of the educated man can provide us with the needed examples. Of course a good deal of bad diction and decidedly careless articulation is certain to be heard, for many of us have become addicted to a mode of speech which is far below what a modern standard should be. Radio diction is not too reliable a guide, since the speech is often too studied and thus robbed of its naturalness. Formal public addresses, likewise, often produce a tendency toward formal usage. Speech of cultured persons in animated conversation affords a good opportunity for study since the odds are great that none of the speakers will use stilted pronunciations—but at the same time, bad usages will not be condoned.

2 Word list:

Initiating consonant: day, die, do, dough
Terminating consonant: add, aid, eyed, odd
Initiating and terminating: dad, dead, deed, did
Stronger consonant: condone, produce, reduce, today
Weaker consonant: indicate, model, modern, study
Initial blends: [dr] draw, dress
Final blends: [nd] end, round; [ld] called, cold; [dz] beads, loads; [rd] card, ford; [md] calmed, tamed; [gd] bagged, rigged; [zd] pleased, raised; [bd] robbed, stabbed; [vd] behaved, starved; [dʒd] caged, judged; [ŋd] hanged, wronged; [rdz] birds, boards; [ndʒd] hinged, impinged; [ðd] bathed, soothed

3 Minimal pairs:

[d]—[t]		[d]—[b]	
bad [bæd]	bat [bæt]	cad [kæd]	cab [kæb]
bed [bɛd]	bet [bɛt]	dad [dæd]	dab [dæb]
bedding [bɛdɪŋ]	betting [bɛtɪŋ]	Dan [dæn]	ban [bæn]
died [daɪd]	tied [taɪd]	darn [dɑrn]	barn [bɑrn]
do [du]	too [tu]	dead [dɛd]	bed [bɛd]
dough [do]	toe [to]	deed [did]	bead [bid]
had [hæd]	hat [hæt]	died [daɪd]	bide [baɪd]
leader [lidɚ]	liter [litɚ]	did [dɪd]	bid [bɪd]
made [med]	mate [met]	din [dɪn]	bin [bɪn]
wader [wedɚ]	waiter [wetɚ]	dressed [drɛst]	breast [brɛst]

[d]—[n]		[d]—[ð]	
bead [bid]	bean [bin]	breeding [bridɪŋ]	breathing [briðɪŋ]
bed [bɛd]	Ben [bɛn]	D [di]	thee [ði]
cad [kæd]	can [kæn]	Dan [dæn]	than [ðæn]
D [di]	knee [ni]	dare [dɛr]	there [ðɛr]
debt [dɛt]	net [nɛt]	die [daɪ]	thy [ðaɪ]
deed [did]	need [nid]	dine [daɪn]	thine [ðaɪn]
dot [dɑt]	not [nɑt]	dough [do]	though [ðo]
dough [do]	no [no]	fodder [fɑdɚ]	father [fɑðɚ]

leader [lidɚ]	leaner [linɚ]	read [rid]	wreathe [rið]
made [med]	main [men]	ride [raɪd]	writhe [raɪð]

4 Phonetic transcription

[ju ʃud nau ənd ðɛn sik aut ɪndə'vɪdʒuwəlz hu kən sɝv əz madl̩z fɚ jɚ on dɪkʃn̩, fɚ spitʃ ɪz ə 'lɪvɪŋ θɪŋ, bɛtɚ tə bi hɝd ðən rɛd əbaut. ðoz ɪndə vɪdʒəwəlz hum wi ɛnkauntɚ ɪn dɛli laɪf hu spik ðə 'læŋgwɪdʒ əv ði 'ɛdʒəˌketəd mæn kən prə'vaɪd ʌs wɪð ðə nidəd ɛg'zæmpl̩z. əv kɔrs ə gud diəl əv 'bæd 'dɪkʃən ən dɪ'saɪdədlɪ kɛrləs ɑrtɪkjə'leʃən ɪz sɝtən tə bi hɝd, fɚ mɛni əv əs hæv bɪ'kʌm ə'dɪktəd tu ə mod əv spitʃ hwɪtʃ ɪz fɑr bilo hwʌt ə madən stændɚd ʃud bi. 'redio dikʃən ɪz nɑt tu rɪ'laɪəbl̩ ə gaɪd, sɪns ðə spitʃ ɪz ɔfən tu 'stʌdid ən ðʌs rɑbd əv ɪts 'nætʃərəlnəs. fɔrməl pʌblɪk ə'drɛsəz 'laɪkˌwaɪz ɔfən prə'dus ə tɛndənsɪ tɔrd fɔrməl 'jusɪdʒ. spitʃ əv 'kʌltʃəd pɝsənz ɪn 'ænəmetəd kɑnvɚ'seʃən əfɔrdz ə gud əpɚ'tunəti fɚ stʌdi sɪns ði ɑdz ɚ gret ðət nʌn əv ðə spikɚz wɪl juz stɪltəd prəˌnʌnsɪ'eʃənz—bʌt ət ðə sem taɪm, bæd 'jusɪdʒəz wɪl nɑt bi kən'dond.]

[tʃ] or [č]
*CH*ANGE WA*TCH* NA*TURE* *CELLO*

ANALYSIS

Before going on to our analysis of [tʃ], a few general facts about affricates should be emphasized. First, do not be misled by the digraph [tʃ] into supposing that [tʃ] and [dʒ] are fundamentally different kinds of sounds uniquely different from other stops.[1] The combination [t] plus [ʃ] as in "put shoes" [put ʃuz] represents a pronunciation in which an alveolar is followed by a palatal. However, the digraphs [tʃ] and [dʒ] are single affricated *stops* (often called *affricates*), not alveolars plus palatals.

Ordinarily in broad transcription it would not be a serious compromise to use [tʃ] to represent both the consonant combination and the single palatal. However, in a more narrow phonetic transcription care should be taken to differentiate between them, in order that such a pair as "ought shoe" [ət ʃu] may be differentiated from "aw chew" [ətʃu]. In line with these arguments many phoneticians prefer the use of the symbols [č] and [j] instead of the IPA ligatured forms. Others, including the present authors, have elected to continue the traditional usage. Although more awkward, it has the sanction of usage and may have some value in calling special attention to the strong affrication which is typical of the English palatal stop.

[1] The exigencies of typesetting make it difficult to use the ligature. [tʃ] can stand for either a combination or a single palatal. Context will usually clarify ambiguities.

The [tʃ] is usually classified as an *unvoiced palatal* or *palato-alveolar affricated stop*, or sometimes *affricate* for short. In some distinctive feature systems it is also described as *nonanterior, tense,* and *strident*. The sound is produced by placing the blade and body of the tongue in a broadly distributed contact with the hard palate, not infrequently including the alveolar ridge. The margins of the tongue are in contact with the teeth and gums laterally. The breath stream thus impounded is released to create a distinctly affricate [ʃ]-like release, which in English is nearly always of considerable power and length. Velopharyngeal closure is complete, or nearly so. Unlike the other stops this one has no weak or nonaffricate allophone in standard English. (For approximate tongue position see Fig. 5-4.)

The production of [tʃ] may be much misunderstood by anyone who fails to examine its articulation carefully. In general outline the starting tongue posture resembles the position for [ʃ], except that it is a stop rather than a fricative. It involves a broad area of contact by the blade and body of the tongue. The [ʃ]-like release is the indication that the stop position is actually palatal and not alveolar. There may be some lip rounding of [tʃ] comparable to that for [ʃ]. Finally, [tʃ] is not doubled as are the other stops. When two [tʃ] sounds abut, there are nearly always two releases. In other words, it is very distinctively strong and strident.

VARIATION

Note that the tongue position for [tʃ] is in many respects not unlike that for [j]. Kenyon (1946) points out that during the Early Modern period (1500 to 1700) [tʃ] evolved from [tj] in a number of words. Without going into the details of these changes, the results can be indicated by the following alterations: "question" has changed from [kwɛstjən] to [kwɛstʃən] and "adventure" has changed from [ædvɛntjur] to [ædvɛntʃɚ]. Such changes continue to occur, so that when a linguapalatal glide such as [j] follows [t] the new [tʃ] may emerge.

A comparable phenomenon occurs often when a word which would end with the [t] if pronounced alone is followed by another which in isolation would begin with [j] or [ʃ]. For instance, the words "that" and "you" in sequence will, by reciprocal assimilation ordinarily be pronounced in informal American speech as [ðætʃu]. Such pronunciations are entirely acceptable and, indeed, efforts to retain a separate [t] followed by [j] may result in stilted, unnatural-sounding pronunciation.

Sounds within this class do not appear to be particularly hard for the foreign speaker to master, although some may employ the nonaffricated sound or may substitute a less broadly distributed tongue contact sound, for which [c] and [ɟ] are the IPA symbols (voiceless and voiced, respectively). The French have no palatal or alveolopalatal plosive in their sound system and so will find this sound difficult. A French person might be expected to pronounce [tʃ] and [dʒ] as [ʃ] and [ʒ], as in [ʃarli] for "Charlie." The digraph *ch* is, of course, uniformly [ʃ] in French.

Errors associated with failure to learn [tʃ] are heard with a fair degree of regularity in children with developmental speech delay. They usually take the form of substitution of [ʃ] and occasionally [ts]. When this happens, such a word as "church" may take the form of [ʃɝʃ] or [tsɝts]. These two variants can also be occasioned by foreign dialect interference, as can the substitution of the palatal [c] or the [ʃ]. As you may well predict, [tʃ] may be grossly distorted by persons with a cleft palate. In these cases one may often hear a glottal or pharyngeal stop followed by a nareal fricative release.

Before going on to [dʒ] we should note that although [tʃ] and [dʒ] are the only English sounds formally classified as affricates, there are other sound combinations which have typical affricate dynamics. One is the [t̪θ], as in "eighth" [et̪θ]. Here the glide from a stop to a fricative is, as we have discussed it in the section on [t], a combination in which the [t] has become a dental in most contexts. Phonetically this sound is also an affricate, although we do not so classify it for linguistic (phonological) reasons. Similar affricate pronunciations are heard in [t̪s] as in "outside," and the [d̪z] in "adds."

A summary of some of the major allophones and dialect variants of [tʃ] is as follows: alveolar-plus-palatal [tʃ], alveolar-plus-glide [tj], weaker or less distributed palatal [c], fricative [ʃ], and alveolar [ts].

EXERCISES

1 Practice paragraph for [tʃ]:

> Choices of all sorts face you as a college student, and you are indeed fortunate if you reach a wise decision half the time. To mention a few: you must first learn to choose the kind of work into which you propose to put your energies and talents for, perhaps, the remainder of your life. The amount of attention given to vocational counseling has not shown much change for a long time, which is most unfortunate. All too often, students make a selection without a chance to ask the kind of questions that should be answered before a decision is reached. You bet your life, so to speak, without watching the odds. The chap with an itch for learning has an enchanting vista before him, and a challenge to achieve. He cheats himself, really, if he does not range widely in the field of knowledge—not so much in search of "culture," but because time so spent will purchase something of lasting value.

2 Word list:

> *Initiating consonant:* chair, chill, chore, chow
> *Terminating consonant:* each, etch, itch, ouch

Initiating and terminating: church
Stronger consonant: perchance, recharge, unchanged, unchecked
Weaker consonant: picture, pitcher, purchase, urchin
Final blends: [ntʃ] bench, ranch; [ntʃt] launched, punched

3   Minimal pairs:

[tʃ]—[dʒ]		[tʃ]—[ʃ]	
beseech [bɪsitʃ]	beseige [bɪsidʒ]	batch [bætʃ]	bash [bæʃ]
chain [tʃen]	Jane [dʒen]	catch [kætʃ]	cash [kæʃ]
char [tʃɑr]	jar [dʒɑr]	cheap [tʃip]	sheep [ʃip]
chin [tʃɪn]	gin [dʒɪn]	cheer [tʃɪr]	sheer [ʃɪr]
chive [tʃaɪv]	jive [dʒaɪv]	chin [tʃɪn]	shin [ʃɪn]
chumps [tʃʌmps]	jumps [dʒʌmps]	choose [tʃuz]	shoes [ʃuz]
chunk [tʃʌŋk]	junk [dʒʌŋk]	ditch [dɪtʃ]	dish [dɪʃ]
match [mætʃ]	Madge [mædʒ]	match [mætʃ]	mash [mæʃ]
perch [pɝtʃ]	purge [pɝdʒ]	matching [mætʃɪŋ]	mashing [mæʃɪŋ]
search [sɝtʃ]	serge [sɝdʒ]	watching [wɑtʃɪŋ]	washing [wɑʃɪŋ]

[tʃ]—[t]		[tʃ]—[k]	
batch [bætʃ]	bat [bæt]	chain [tʃen]	cane [ken]
catch [kætʃ]	cat [kæt]	char [tʃɑr]	car [kɑr]
cheer [tʃɪr]	tear [tɪr]	cheap [tʃip]	keep [kip]
chew [tʃu]	too [tu]	chick [tʃɪk]	kick [kɪk]
chick [tʃɪk]	tick [tɪk]	chin [tʃɪn]	kin [kɪn]
chin [tʃɪn]	tin [tɪn]	ditch [dɪtʃ]	Dick [dɪk]
match [mætʃ]	mat [mæt]	latch [lætʃ]	lack [læk]
matching [mætʃɪŋ]	matting [mætɪŋ]	patch [pætʃ]	pack [pæk]
patch [pætʃ]	pat [pæt]	patcher [pætʃɚ]	packer [pækɚ]
patcher [pætʃɚ]	patter [pætɚ]	watching [wɑtʃɪŋ]	walking [wɑkɪŋ]

4   Phonetic transcription:

[tʃɔɪsəz əv ɔl sɔrts fes ju æz ə kɑlɪdʒ studn̩t, ənd ju ɚ ɪnˈdid fɔrtʃənət ɪf ju ritʃ ə waɪz dɪˈsɪʒən hæf ðə taɪm. tə mentʃən ə fju: ju məst fɝst lɝn tə tʃuz ðə kaɪnd əv wɝk ɪntə hwɪtʃ ju prəˈpoz tu pʌt jɔr ˈenɚdʒɪz ən tælənts fɔr, pəhæps, ðə rɪˈmendɚ əv jɔr laɪf. ði əmaunt əv əˈtenʃən gɪvən tu voˈkeʃənəl ˈkaunsəlɪŋ həz nat ʃon mʌtʃ tʃendʒ fɔr ə lɔŋ taɪm, hwɪtʃ ɪz most ʌnˈfɔrtʃənət. ɔl tu ɔfən, studn̩ts mek ə səˈlekʃən wɪˈðaut ə tʃænts tə æsk ðə kaɪnd əv ˈkwestʃənz ðət ʃud bi ænsɚd bɪˈfɔr ə dɪˈsɪʒən ɪz ritʃt. ju betʃɔr laɪf, so tə spik, wɪˈðaut wɑtʃɪŋ ði ædz. ðə tʃæp wɪð ən ɪtʃ fɚ ˈlɝnɪŋ hæz ən enˈtʃæntɪŋ vɪstə bɪˈfɔr ɪm, ənd ə ˈtʃæləndʒ tu əˈtʃiv. hi tʃits hɪmself, riəlɪ, ɪf hi dəz nat rendʒ waɪdlɪ ɪn ðə fild əv ˈnɑlɪdʒ—nat so mʌtʃ ɪn sɝtʃ əv ˈkʌltʃɚ, bət bɪˈkɔz taɪm so spent wɪl pɝtʃəs ˈsʌmpθɪŋ əv læstɪŋ vælju.]

[dʒ] or [ĵ]
*J*UNE A*GE* E*DGE* A*DJ*UST SOL*D*IER EXA*GG*ERATE

ANALYSIS

The [dʒ] may be classified as a *voiced linguapalatal* (or *linguapalato-alveolar*) affricated *stop*, and as *nonanterior, tense,* and *strident*. The coronal feature is questionable in both [tʃ] and [dʒ]. Tongue contact is perhaps better described as *distributed*. Details of articulation are essentially the same as those described for [tʃ], except that [dʒ] is voiced (Fig. 5-4).

VARIATION

As with the other pairs of unvoiced-voiced stops, the voiced [dʒ] usually is articulated with somewhat less force than the voiceless [tʃ], although [dʒ] is still strongly affricate and strident. The [dʒ] shows the same characteristic variation of sounds within the palatal stop class and has all the other attributes of [tʃ] variation discussed in the preceding section.

The problems of the native speaker in pronouncing [dʒ] resemble those encountered with [tʃ]. Thus, words which might have been spoken with [dj] have quite generally acquired the pronunciation [dʒ], although this is not always the case, as illustrated by the nonstandard pronunciation of "Indian" [ɪndɪjən] or [ɪndjən] as [ɪndʒən] and of "India" [ɪndɪjə] as [ɪndʒə]. The shift of [dj] to [dʒ] in connected speech is perfectly natural in American English in such instances as "did you" [dɪdʒu] and "would you" [wʊdʒu]. In some cases [dj] might incur the risk of sounding pedantic.

Among young children those who have not learned [tʃ] usually cannot say [dʒ]. In adult American speakers one may hear an overly weak allophone of [dʒ] as the fricative [ʒ], for example in the nonstandard anesthetized, "drunken" sound of [aɪ pɛʒəlizə̃s] for "I pledge allegiance." In such a case many other sounds may be similarly affected. "That's alright, Chuck" may sound like [æsʌraɪʃʌʔ], for example. There are some instances, however, where a variation among [dʒ] and [ʒ] usages is normal in native dialects. In the [ndʒ] cluster, for example, [nʒ] may be a quite common variant, for example in "orange," which may be either [ɔrnʒ] or [ɔrndʒ].

In some foreign dialects the nonaffricate palatal stop [ɟ] may be heard, and indeed this sound may be encountered in the speech of native children. German dialects of English tend to omit or weaken the voicing feature of [dʒ] and other voiced stops. A similarity to some German dialects of American English may be heard in this phrase: [aɪ ɝtʃ ju tə tʃʌtʃ hɪs etʃ] for "I urge you to judge his age." Foreign speakers have, of course, the usual troubles with English spelling. As is well known, the letter *j* has the value [j] in some languages and for this reason the Swede, for instance, may give words such as "jump" and "joke" an initial [j], as in [jʌmp] and [jok]. The French native who is learning English is likely to retain [ʒ] in places where the customary English form is [dʒ]. Examples are the pronunciations [ʒʌst] and [ʒɑk] for "just" and "Jack."

The previous summary of variants (see [tʃ]) is appropriate for this section also, except we are dealing here with the voiced versions: [dʒ], [dj], [ɫ], [ʒ], and [dz].

EXERCISES

1 Practice paragraph for [dʒ]:

> The importance of regional speech usages in the United States has probably been exaggerated, if one can judge from the amount of heat generated by arguments on the subject. Generally speaking, genuine and major deviations from region to region are, at least to some degree, more imaginary than real. It seems to us poor pedagogy to badger students with suggestions that they reject what are, at the worst, only marginal usages. The average person is not unfavorably judged if he adjusts his speech reasonably well to the pronunciations he hears most often around him. To be practical, we must budge just a bit from the rigid positions we sometimes take. It is almost always safe to urge that the student be intelligible, but the barrage of criticisms sometimes laid down quite often verges on the ridiculous.

2 Word list:

Initiating consonant: jaw, jay, Joe, joy
Terminating consonant: age, edge, ridge, urge
Initiating and terminating: George, judge
Stronger consonant: adjudicate, adjust, digest (v.), rejuvenate
Weaker consonant: major, paging, region, Roger
Final blends: [dʒd] judged, raged; [ndʒ] orange, range; [ndʒd] ranged, tinged

3 Minimal pairs:

[dʒ]—[tʃ]		[dʒ]—[d] and [dz]	
age [edʒ]	H [etʃ]	age [edʒ]	aid [ed]
badge [bædʒ]	batch [bætʃ]	badge [bædʒ]	bad [bæd]
edge [ɛdʒ]	etch [ɛtʃ]	jeep [dʒip]	deep [dip]
jeep [dʒip]	cheep [tʃip]	jeer [dʒɪr]	dear [dɪr]
jeer [dʒɪr]	cheer [tʃɪr]	ridge [rɪdʒ]	rid [rɪd]
Jews [dʒuz]	choose [tʃuz]	age [edʒ]	aids [edz]
Jill [dʒɪl]	chill [tʃɪl]	budge [bʌdʒ]	buds [bʌdz]
joke [dʒok]	choke [tʃok]	edge [ɛdʒ]	Ed's [ɛdz]
ridge [rɪdʒ]	rich [rɪtʃ]	hedge [hɛdʒ]	heads [hɛdz]
surge [sɝdʒ]	search [sɝtʃ]	ledge [lɛdʒ]	leads [lɛdz]

[dʒ]—[g]

badge [bædʒ]	bag [bæg]
budge [bʌdʒ]	bug [bʌg]
edge [ɛdʒ]	egg [ɛg]
jail [dʒel]	gale [gel]
James [dʒemz]	games [gemz]
jeer [dʒɪr]	gear [gɪr]
jet [dʒɛt]	get [gɛt]
Joe [dʒo]	go [go]
ledge [lɛdʒ]	leg [lɛg]
ridge [rɪdʒ]	rig [rɪg]

4 Phonetic transcription:

[ði ɪmˈpɔrtəns əv ˈrɪdʒənəl spitʃ ˈjusɪdʒəz ɪn ði juˈnaɪtəd stets hæz ˈprɑbəblɪ
bɪn ɛgˈzædʒəretəd, ɪf wʌn kən dʒʌdʒ frəm ði əmaunt əv hit ˈdʒɛnəˌretəd
baɪ ˈɑrgjuments ɔn ðə ˈsʌbdʒɪkt. ˈdʒɛnrəlɪ ˈspikɪŋ, ˈdʒɛnjəwən ənd ˈmedʒɚ
ˌdivɪˈeʃənz frəm rɪdʒən tə rɪdʒən ɑr, ət list tə sʌm dɪˈgri, mɔr əmædʒənɛrɪ
ðən riəl. ɪt simz təwʌs ˈpur ˈpɛdəgodʒɪ tə bædʒɚ studn̩ts wɪθ səˈdʒɛstʃənz
ðət ðe riˈdʒɛkt hwʌt ɑr, æt ðə wɝst, onlɪ ˈmɑrdʒənəl ˈjusɪdʒəz. ði ˈævrɪdʒ
pɝsən ɪz nɑt ʌnˈfevərəblɪ dʒʌdʒd ɪf hi əˈdʒʌsts ɪz spitʃ ˈrizənəblɪ wɛl tə ðə
prəˌnʌnsɪˈeʃənz hi hɪrz most ɔfən əraund hɪm. tə bi ˈpræktɪkl̩, wi mʌst
bʌdʒ dʒʌst ə bɪt frəm ðə rɪdʒəd pəˈzɪʃənz wi ˈsʌmˌtaɪmz tek. ɪt ɪz ˈɔlmost
ˈɔlwez sef təwɝdʒ ðət ðə studn̩t bi ɪnˈtɛlədʒəbl̩, bət ðə bəˈrɑʒ əv ˈkrɪtəˌsizəmz
ˈsʌmˌtaɪmz led daun kwaɪt ɔfən vɝdʒəz ɔn ðə rɪˈdɪkjələs.]

[k]

CAT *KEEP* BA*CK* E*CH*O PI*CK* A*CC*OUNT *KH*AKI BO*X*
*QU*ICK

ANALYSIS

The [k] is ordinarily classified as an unvoiced velar (linguavelar) stop, or in
some feature systems as *stop, tense, nonanterior, noncoronal, nonvoiced,* and
nonsyllabic. To make this sound, the back of the tongue is placed in contact
with the soft palate; breath pressure is built up behind this closure and then
released as the tongue moves to the position for the following sound or to a
neutral position. Velopharyngeal closure is complete, or nearly so.

When [k] is made as a plosive, what is heard is not only a result of the
influence of the [k] upon the surrounding vowels, but also the friction noise
of the released breath stream. As with other stops there are three potential
"noise" sources: (1) the rapid plosive impulse, (2) the turbulent noise of a

narrowed airstream escaping from the tongue-palate closure, and (3) the release of air through the glottis in a kind of whisper (the *aspiration*) (Fig. 5-4).

VARIATION

The [k] group of sounds is one of those which contain a relatively large number of important variants in English, principally because the exact point of articulation is so often strongly influenced by the sounds which precede and follow. The reason for this is that the [k] is a *tongue-body* consonant. Thus, unlike the anterior stops we have discussed, it uses the same tongue structure to produce the consonant as is used to produce the vowels. For this reason [k] and [g] are markedly influenced by the vowels on either side. For instance, if [k] is followed by a front vowel, as in "keep" [kip] and "keen" [kin], the contact which stops the breath is quite far forward, perhaps even on the hard palate, rather than on the velum. On the other hand, when words like "car" [kɑr] and "cook" [kʊk] are pronounced in the usual way, the contact is much farther back, since in each case the sound following [k] is from the back-vowel group.

There is considerable variation in the amount of affricate or aspirate noise given the [k] release in English speech, as is true of most plosives. Where [k] precedes a stressed vowel, there is almost always considerable noise, compared, for example, with the unstressed release in such words as "broker" [brokɚ] and "taking" [tekɪŋ].

As with other stops, [k] may have a variety of release mechanisms other than the one used in simple CV syllables. A lateral release may often be heard in instances where [k] is followed by [l], for example in "buckle" [bʌkˡl]. The phenomena associated with doubled stops occur also with [k], of course (see the discussion of [p] and the section on juncture in Chapter 6).

As with other stops, [k] release may be weak in some complex consonant combinations, and may be unreleased, or released from a different position when followed by some other stop. Note for example that in "pick Tim" the stop is velar but the release is alveolar. Note also that the release of [k] in the word "key" is much stronger than it is in the word "ski." The [k] may be even weaker in flaccid or in "drunk" speech to the point of a fricative [x].

Sounds in the /k/ class are involved in certain foreign dialect errors. Some German speakers, for example, may sometimes appear to substitute a weaker or voiced stop. Often nonnative speakers may give [k] somewhat less aspiration than would be normal for English, just as the other voiceless stops are weaker in many languages than in English. In some dialects the palatal [c] or postvelar (*uvular*) [q] may be used as substitutes for [k]. Even a glottal [ʔ] may be heard, sometimes in standard American in some contexts, as for example "back and forth" in its reduced form [bæʔŋfɔrθ].

Occasionally English speakers will preserve the [x] sound in many German words, especially in proper names. "Bach," for example will often be heard as [bɑx] even though other *ch* words taken from the German are anglicized.

For reasons that are not entirely clear, [k] seems to be among the English sounds that are relatively difficult for children. Many children are late in learning this sound, and the substitution of a [t]-like sound for [k] is frequently heard in infantile speech. [dɪv mijə tʊti] for "give me a cookie" is an example. [k] also presents marked difficulties for cleft palate speakers, or for the individual who has inadequate velopharyngeal closure for any reason. In these cases [k] may be weak and distorted by nasal fricative release or may be replaced by some glottal or pharyngeal stop.

To summarize, the variants presented above are fronted [k˧], backed [k˩], unreleased [k⁻], aspirate [kʰ], affricate [k'], voiced or partially voiced [ḵ], palatal [c], pharyngeal [q], and velar fricative [x].

EXERCISES

1 Practice paragraph for [k]:

> A pleasant vocal quality is an aspect of cultured speech which ranks high in importance, although necessary facts about voice production cannot be included in this text. Voice and personality are connected in a unique way, and the key to an accurate appraisal of what most persons are really like can often be found in voice cues. Strength of character will be reflected by a manner of talking which is honest and forthright. If the voice is timid and weak, we account it no accident that a lack of courage lies back of this manner of talking. If one's thinking is chaotic and unclear, this laxity is certain to become known through vocal inflections; think clearly, and the groundwork has been laid for effective communication. There is little extra difficulty required in taking care that one's vocal skills are adequate to his needs and that his voice does not weaken his chances of success.

2 Word list:

Initiating consonant: coo, cur, Kay, key
Terminating consonant: ache, irk, oak, Ike
Initiating and terminating: cake, coke, cook, kick
Stronger consonant: become, income, recount, request
Weaker consonant: backer, bucket, taken, vacant
Initial blends: [sk] school, sky; [kr] crown, cry; [kl] clay, clip; [kw] queen, quite; [skr] scratch, screen; [skw] squash, squire
Final blends: [ks] backs, six; [kt] looked, parked; [ŋk] sank, think; [ŋks] honks, thanks; [ŋkt] linked, thanked; [sk] ask, risk; [rk] fork, park

3 Minimal pairs:

[k]—[g]		[k]—[t]	
back [bæk]	bag [bæg]	back [bæk]	bat [bæt]
backer [bækɚ]	bagger [bægɚ]	backer [bækɚ]	batter [bætɚ]
came [kem]	game [gem]	cone [kon]	tone [ton]
come [kʌm]	gum [gʌm]	cool [kul]	tool [tul]
could [kʊd]	good [gʊd]	knock [nɑk]	not [nɑt]
Kay [ke]	gay [ge]	lick [lɪk]	lit [lɪt]
lock [lɑk]	log [lɑg]	neck [nɛk]	net [nɛt]
locker [lɑkɚ]	logger [lɑgɚ]	pack [pæk]	pat [pæt]
pick [pɪk]	pig [pɪg]	pick [pɪk]	pit [pɪt]
racks [ræks]	rags [rægz]	racks [ræks]	rats [ræts]

[k]—[tʃ]	
ache [ek]	H [etʃ]
back [bæk]	batch [bætʃ]
cat [kæt]	chat [tʃæt]
Dick [dɪk]	ditch [dɪtʃ]
kill [kɪl]	chill [tʃɪl]
knock [nɑk]	notch [nɑtʃ]
pack [pæk]	patch [pætʃ]
pick [pɪk]	pitch [pɪtʃ]
racket [rækət]	ratchet [rætʃət]
suck [sʌk]	such [sʌtʃ]

4 Phonetic transcription:

[ə plɛzənt vokəl ˈkwɑlətɪ ɪz ən ˈæspɛkt əv ˈkʌltʃəd spitʃ hwɪtʃ ræŋks haɪ ɪn ɪmˈpɔrn̩s, ɔlðo ˈnɛsəsɛrɪ fækts əbaut vɔɪs prəˈdʌkʃən kəˈnɑt bi ɪnˈkludəd ɪn ðɪs tɛkst. vɔɪs ən ˌpɝsəˈnælətɪ ɑr kənɛktəd ɪn ə junik we, ænd ðə ki tu ən ˈækjurət əˈprezəl əv hwʌt most pɝsənz ɑr rili laɪk kən ɔfən bi faund ɪn vɔɪs kjuz. strɛŋθ əv ˈkɛrɪktɚ wɪl bi rɪˈflɛktəd baɪ ə mænɚ əv tɔkɪŋ hwɪtʃ əz ˈɑnəst ən ˈfɔrˌθɪraɪt. ɪf ðə vɔɪs ɪz tɪməd ən wik, wi əkaunt ət no ˈæksədənt ðət ə læk əv ˈkɝɪdʒ laɪz bæk əv ðɪs mænɚ əv tɔkɪŋ. ɪf wʌnz ˈθɪŋkɪŋ ɪz keˈɑtɪk ænd ˌʌnˈklɪr, ðɪs læksətɪ ɪz sɝtən tə bɪˈkʌm non θru vokəl ɪnˈflɛkʃənz; ˈθɪŋk ˈklɪrlɪ, æn ðə graund wɝk həz bɪn led fɔr ɪˈfɛktɪv kəˌmjunəˈkeʃən. ðɛr ɪz lɪtl̩ ɛkstrə ˌdɪfəˈkʌltɪ rɪˈkwaɪrd ɪn tekɪŋ kɛr ðət wʌnz vokəl skɪlz ɑr ˈædəkwət tu ɪz nidz æn ðət ɪz vɔɪs dəz nɑt wikən hɪz tʃænsəz əv səkˈsɛs.]

[g]
GO BE*GG*AR *GH*ETTO E*X*AM

ANALYSIS

The [g] may be classified as a *voiced velar stop*. It is produced like [k] insofar as place of articulation and tongue shape is concerned, but it is voiced.

Distinctive features are usually described as *nonsyllabic, stop, nonanterior, noncoronal, lax,* and *voiced.* Like other voiced stops in English, [g] tends to have less force of articulation than its unvoiced counterpart, and as a consequence less aspiration and affricate release (Fig. 5-4).

VARIATION

Notes on the pronunciation of [g] parallel those for [k]. As one might expect, the exact place of articulation will vary from a distinctively forward position to one well back on the soft palate. These extremes are approximated in the words "geese" [gis], where the front vowel leads to a forward position, and "gong" [gɑŋ], in which [g] is followed by a low-back vowel.

The release mechanisms for [g] vary similarly to those of other stops. Nasal, lateral, aspirate, affricate, and unreleased forms are common. Sometimes [g] may be so weakened, or "slurred" that it becomes a velar fricative [ɣ].

Both [k] and [g] are involved in common infantile speech errors, and the typical substitution of [d] for [g] is usually heard among children who also substitute [t] for [k]. [dʊd] for "good" is an example.

Voicing confusions are also common in the velars, usually as a result of foreign dialect influences. In some German dialects [g] may be partially or wholly unvoiced, "big dog" sounding to an American ear as "bic dock." Foreign dialect influences may also be responsible for a weakening of the articulatory contact toward the fricative [ɣ], or may result in a palatal [ɫ] or uvular [ɢ].

To summarize, common [g] variants are unreleased [g¯], affricate [g'], aspirate [gʰ], fronted [g⊣], backed [g⊢], unvoiced [g̥], palatal [ɫ], uvular [ɢ], and velar fricative [ɣ].

EXERCISES

1   Practice paragraph:

> The emergence of speech in an infant is a great and wonderful thing. Psychologists recognize its beginning in what is sometimes called the pre-linguistic period of growth. In the early months of growth adults should make a big game of the gurglings and cooings which are actually the genesis of articulation. The little beggar will then acquire agility in tongue and lip movements which later will be guided into recognizable words. The sounds he exhibits at this period beggar description, and the attempt to make an exact catalogue has exhausted observers who have made this attempt. Much early communication is by gesture, but as time goes by one must expect to get from the child stronger efforts to show true linguistic behavior in the form of recognizable words. One cannot exaggerate the great importance of motivation, for the biggest gains are made by the child who is in a stimulating world.

2 Word list:

Initiating consonant: gay, go, goo, guy
Terminating consonant: egg, erg, hog, ugh
Initiating and terminating: gag, gig, Greg, Grieg
Stronger consonant: ago, began, forget, regret
Weaker consonant: bargain, begger, biggest, struggle
Initial blends: [gr] green, grow; [gl] glass, glue
Final blends: [gz] bags, digs; [gd] bagged, logged

3 Minimal pairs:

[g]—[k]		[g]—[dʒ]	
bagging [bægɪŋ]	backing [bækɪŋ]	bag [bæg]	badge [bædʒ]
gall [gɔl]	call [kɔl]	bagger [bægɚ]	badger [bædʒɚ]
gap [gæp]	cap [kæp]	egg [ɛg]	edge [ɛdʒ]
gate [get]	Kate [ket]	gain [gen]	Jane [dʒen]
gauge [gedʒ]	cage [kedʒ]	gig [gɪg]	jig [dʒɪg]
ghost [gost]	coast [kost]	go [go]	Joe [dʒo]
guild [gɪld]	killed [kɪld]	goon [gun]	June [dʒun]
gum [gʌm]	come [kʌm]	gust [gʌst]	just [dʒʌst]
lag [læg]	lack [læk]	log [lɑg]	lodge [lɑdʒ]
rig [rɪg]	rick [rɪk]	slug [slʌg]	sludge [slʌdʒ]

[g]—[ŋ]		[g]—[d]	
bag [bæg]	bang [bæŋ]	beg [bɛg]	bed [bɛd]
bagging [bægɪŋ]	banging [bæŋɪŋ]	big [bɪg]	bid [bɪd]
big [bɪg]	Bing [bɪŋ]	gad [gæd]	dad [dæd]
hug [hʌg]	hung [hʌŋ]	gain [gen]	deign [den]
log [lɑg]	long [lɑŋ]	go [go]	dough [do]
rig [rɪg]	ring [rɪŋ]	goal [gol]	dole [dol]
rigger [rɪgɚ]	ringer [rɪŋɚ]	God [gɑd]	Dodd [dɑd]
rug [rʌg]	rung [rʌŋ]	grain [gren]	drain [dren]
sag [sæg]	sang [sæŋ]	lag [læg]	lad [læd]
slug [slʌg]	slung [slʌŋ]	tag [tæg]	tad [tæd]

4 Phonetic transcription:

[ði ə'mɝdʒəns əv spitʃ ɪn ən ɪnfənt ɪz ə 'gret ænd 'wʌndɚfəl θɪŋ. saɪ'kɑlədʒəsts 'rɛkəgˌnaɪz ɪts bɪ'gɪnɪŋ ɪn hwʌt ɪz 'sʌmˌtaɪmz kɔld ðə 'prilɪn'gwɪstɪk 'pɪriəd əv groθ. ɪn ði ɝlɪ mʌnθs əv groθ ədʌlts ʃud mek ə 'bɪg 'gem əv ðə 'gɝglɪŋz ənd kuwɪŋz hwɪtʃ ɑr 'ækʃuəli ðə 'dʒɛnəsəs əv artɪkjə'leʃən. ðə lɪtl̩ bɛgɚ wɪl ðɛn ə'kwaɪr ə'dʒɪləti ɪn tʌŋ ənd lɪp ˌmuvmənts hwɪtʃ letɚ wɪl bi gaɪdəd ɪntu 'rɛkəgnaɪzəbl̩ wɝdz. ðə saundz hi ɛg'zɪbəts æt ðɪs 'pɪriəd bɛgɚ

dɪˈskrɪpʃən, ənd ðɪ ətɛmpt tə mek ən ɛgˈzækt ˈkætələg həz ɛgˈzɔstəd
əbˈzɜˑvəz hu həv med ðɪs ətɛmpt. mʌtʃ ɜˑlɪ kəˌmjunəˈkeʃən ɪz baɪ ˈdʒɛstʃɚ,
bət əz taɪm goz baɪ wʌn məst ɛkˈspɛkt tə gɛt frəm ðə tʃaɪld strɔŋɡɚ ɛfəts
tə ʃo tru lɪnˈgwɪstɪk bɪˈhevjɚ ɪn ðə fɔrm əv ˈrɛkəgnaɪzəbl̩ wɜˑdz. wʌn ˈkænɑt
ɛgˈzædʒəret ðə gret ɪmˈpɔrtəns əv motəˈveʃən, fɔr ðə bɪgəst genz ɑr med
baɪ ðə tʃaɪld hu ɪz ɪn ə ˈstɪmjuletɪŋ wɜˑld.]

Chapter 14

Fricatives

[f], [v], [θ], [ð], [s], [z], [ʃ], [ʒ], [h]

[f]
FOR HALF STAFF PHONE LAUGH

ANALYSIS

The distinctive features of [f] are sometimes described as *consonantal, anterior, voiceless, nonsonarant, nonstrident and coronal*. In more common terms [f] is a *voiceless labiodental fricative*. It is also often classified among the *continuants*, in recognition of the fact that it is possible to prolong the frication noise. Commonly in its articulation the inner border of the lower lip is raised into a close approximation to the cutting edge of the upper central incisors. An unvoiced breath stream is passed through the light contact, creating the friction noise which is one of the characteristics of sounds of this class. Velopharyngeal closure is complete, or nearly so.

One significant fact about this sound is the relative weakness of its "stridency." The [f] noise is so weak, in fact, that it often cannot be heard in even moderately noisy environments without considerable exaggeration

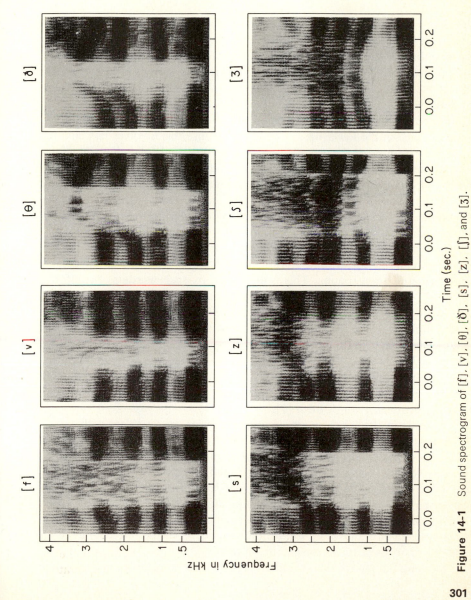

Figure 14-1 Sound spectrogram of [f], [v], [θ], [ð], [s], [z], [ʃ], and [ʒ].

by the speaker. Even when it can be heard, the noise of [f] is very much like the noise of [θ]. Obviously we must depend to a significant degree upon the effect of the consonant on the surrounding vowels as a means of establishing its identity (see Fig. 5.4).

VARIATION

Because fricatives are dependent upon the nature of a constricted airflow, and its resultant turbulence, for the precise quality of their "noise" element, wide variations are encountered in some of the fricatives (see [s]). However, there is relatively little variation with the [f] group of sounds in native speech. When the sound is deliberately pronounced in isolation, the teeth may be in contact with a point fairly well out on the carmine border of the lip. In connected speech, however, the teeth more often touch the upper part of the inner surface of the lower lip, presumably because this involves less contrast with the positions of the articulators for preceding and following sounds.

There is no special tongue position for [f], with the result that [f] and surrounding vowels will be strongly coarticulated. The lip-rounding feature of adjacent vowels, for example, will influence the exact position of dental-lip contact, as one can easily demonstrate by comparing the articulations of "feel" and "fool."

When [f] follows a bilabial sound, it may become a kind of bilabial fricative, with the lips tending to form a constriction which is like or replaces the labiodental constriction. This is illustrated by such words as "comfort," "cupful," and "cabfare." A more accurate transcription of these may employ the *labial* fricative, as in [kʌpɸul] or [kæbɸɛr]. The word "comfort" also is an example of a case in which [f] may be pronounced as an affricate [pf] or [pɸ]. All these tend to be normal allophonic variants in the appropriate contexts, but may be conspicuous deviations in inappropriate contexts.

In abnormally weak articulations of [f] the difference between [f] and [ɸ] may become negligible. Hence some weak allophones of both [p] and [f] may be identical, both of them [ɸ].

Sounds in the [f] class are among the easier ones to deal with in any kind of speech improvement program. Native speakers rarely have any conspicuous errors of pronunciation or articulation involving [f], presumably because the articulatory pattern for the sound is relatively simple, and there are good visual and tactile cues. The speech pathologist may occasionally encounter an individual who finds it difficult to make the necessary labiodental contact because of a dental malocclusion. Children are more likely to choose [f] as a substitute for another sound, as in the interchange of [f] and [θ], than they are to replace or omit it.

Among foreign speakers failure to produce an acceptable approximation of standard American [f] is not usually a problem, although the bilabial fricative [ɸ] is not uncommon, and the German [f] may sometimes be a little weaker than the American.

EXERCISES

1   Practice paragraph for [f]:

> The idea of a phonetic alphabet to facilitate the recording of pronunciation with the greatest possible fidelity occurred to orthographers as early as the eleventh or twelfth century. One of the first was Orme, who formulated a system using single consonants after short vowels and doubled consonants following long vowels. Fortunately for a fuller understanding of early fashions in speech, his early manuscripts make it possible to determine, at least in a fairly rough way, many features of early speech. Philadelphia's own Ben Franklin afforded himself an excursion into spelling reform by offering a phonetic alphabet in 1768. His efforts did not weigh heavily enough, however, to affect the established philosophy of spelling. Such spelling changes will have to wait for a more favorable day. In the future phoneticians will not have to rely as fully on written language, since the recording of human speech by means of the phonograph will provide a far more accurate foundation for historical studies.

2   Word list:

Initiating consonant: Fay, fee, fir, few
Terminating consonant: if, off, oaf, wife
Initiating and terminating: fife, fluff
Stronger consonant: affirm, conform, perform, refuse (v.)
Weaker consonant: laughing, offer, suffer, taffy
Initial blends: [fl] flap, fly,; [fr] free, front
Final blends: [ft] laughed, left; [fs] laughs, stuffs

3   Minimal pairs:

[f]—[v]		[f]—[θ]	
face [fes]	vase [ves]	deaf [dɛf]	death [dɛθ]
fast [fæst]	vast [væst]	fin [fɪn]	thin [θɪn]
feel [fiəl]	veal [viəl]	first [fɝst]	thirst [θɝst]
few [fju]	view [vju]	fought [fɔt]	thought [θɔt]
fine [faɪn]	vine [vaɪn]	free [fri]	three [θri]
half [hæf]	have [hæv]	fret [frɛt]	threat [θrɛt]
proof [pruf]	prove [pruv]	Goff [gɑf]	Goth [gɑθ]
safe [sef]	save [sev]	half [hæf]	hath [hæθ]

[f]—[v]		[f]—[θ]	
serf [sɝf]	serve [sɝv]	miff [mɪf]	myth [mɪθ]
thief [θif]	thieve [θiv]	offer [ɔfɚ]	author [ɔθɚ]

[f]—[p]		[f]—[s]	
face [fes]	pace [pes]	after [æftɚ]	aster [æstɚ]
fact [fækt]	pact [pækt]	fame [fem]	same [sem]
fair [fɛr]	pair [pɛr]	fed [fɛd]	said [sɛd]
far [far]	par [par]	feel [fiəl]	seal [siəl]
fast [fæst]	past [pæst]	feet [fit]	seat [sit]
feel [fiəl]	peal [piəl]	fine [faɪn]	sign [saɪn]
feet [fit]	peat [pit]	fought [fɔt]	sought [sɔt]
fine [faɪn]	pine [paɪn]	fun [fʌn]	son [sʌn]
laugh [læf]	lap [læp]	gaff [gæf]	gas [gæs]
suffer [sʌfɚ]	supper [sʌpɚ]	laugh [læf]	lass [læs]

4 Phonetic transcription:

[ðɪ aɪdɪə əv ə fəˈnɛtɪk ˈælfəbɛt tə fəˈsɪlətet ðə rɪˈkɔrdɪŋ əv prəˈnʌnsɪˈeʃən wɪð
ðə gretəst pasəbḷ fəˈdɛlətɪ əkɝd tu ɔrˈθɔgrəfəz əz əli əz ði ɪˈlɛvənθ ɔr twɛlfθ
ˈsɛntʃɛrɪ. wʌn əv ðə fɝst wəz ɔrm, hu ˈfɔrmjəˌletəd ə sɪstəm juzɪŋ sɪŋgḷ kʌnsənənts æftɚ ʃɔrt vauɛlz ən dʌbḷd kʌnsənənts ˈfalowɪŋ lɔŋ vauɛlz. ˈfɔrtʃənətlɪ
fɔr ə fulɚ ʌndɚˈstændɪŋ əv ɝlɪ fæʃənz ɪn spitʃ, hɪz ɝlɪ ˈmænjuskrɪpts mek ət
ˈpasəbḷ tə dɪˈtɝmən, æt list ɪn ə fɛrlɪ rʌf we, mɛnɪ fitʃəz əv ɝlɪ spitʃ. fɪləˈdɛlfɪəz
on bɛn fræŋklən əfɔrdəd hɪmsɛlf ən ɛkˈskɝʒən ɪntə spɛlɪŋ rɪˈfɔrm baɪ ɔfərɪŋ
ə fəˈnɛtɪk ˈælfəbɛt ɪn sɛvəntin sɪksti et. hɪz ɛfəts dɪd nat we hɛvəlɪ ənʌf,
hauɛvɚ, tu əfɛkt ði əˈstæblɪʃt fəlasəfi əv ˈspɛlɪŋ. sʌtʃ ˈspɛlɪŋ tʃɛndʒəz wɪl
hæf tə wet fɔr ə mɔr ˈfevrəbḷ de. ɪn ðə fjutʃɚ, fonəˈtɪʃənz wɪl nat hæf tə rɪˈlaɪ
əz fulɪ ɔn rɪtṇ ˈlæŋgwɪdʒ sɪns ðə rɪˈkɔrdɪŋz əv hjumən spitʃ baɪ minz əv ðə
fonəgræf wɪl prəvaɪd ə far mɔr ækjərət faunˈdeʃən fɔr hɪˈstɔrɪkḷ ˈstʌdɪz.]

[v]

VERY FLIVVER STEPHEN

ANALYSIS

The [v] is the cognate of [f]; hence it may be described as a *voiced nonsyllabic,
anterior, strident* or as a *voiced linguadental fricative*. It is also *continuant*.
In common with other voiced cognates [v] is a more lax and less strident
sound than [f]. In fact, in many contexts [v] is not really strident in the
purely phonetic sense of the term. Any noise component present is frequently
masked by environmental noise. The voice print of Figure 14-1 is of a strong,
stressed, intervocalic [v]. Compare it with the [f] and other fricatives shown

in this same figure. Aside from voicing and the typically related changes in force, articulation is essentially the same for [v] as for [f] (see Fig. 5-4).

VARIATION

The general remarks made about variations in the production of [f] also hold true for [v]. Thus, there may be some deviations from what one might describe as a "standard" position of articulation because the tongue and lips tend to assume the positions dictated by contextual and rhythmical influences.

When [v] is in a final position or when it is followed by an unvoiced sound, as in "I have to go" [aɪ hæf tə go], voicing is often reduced or absent. Where the [v] is in a relatively weak position (as an initiating consonant for an unstressed syllable, for example) friction noise may be less strong than when the syllable is stressed. Compare, for example, the fricative hiss of [v] in "revert" [rɪˈvɝt] with the [v] sound in "lover" [lʌvɚ].

Nonnative speakers of English may occasionally pronounce [v] as a voiced bilabial [β]. Also they may produce a more obstruent variant similar to [b̞], or they may produce a less voiced variant close to, or identical with, English [f]. Spanish is often cited as a language in which bilabial [β] is common. An example is [həβanə] for "Havana."

EXERCISES

1   Practice paragraph for [v]:

> The vast majority of Americans have never viewed spoken language with the same concern they have shown for writing and reading. Nevertheless, if the modern vogue in education continues, it is very likely that the language arts curriculum will stress spoken communication to a greater degree. It has always been a matter of grave concern that, save in a few schools, so little time has been devoted to speech. The more obvious deviations have been given over to the speech therapist, but the average child has never enjoyed the advantages that training in speech could give. The inevitable consequence, which could have been predicted by anyone with vision, has been that the greatest poverty in the use of language has been in its everyday use in speaking. If we should sever our ties with tradition and revive an interest in our native tongue, there would be much that would prove of value to the child which would result from such a revision of the language arts curriculum.

2   Word list:

> *Initiating consonant:* V, vie, view, vow
> *Terminating consonant:* eve, Irv, I've, you've

Initiating and terminating: verve, valve
Stronger consonant: convex, convey, review, revolt
Weaker consonant: braver, given, having, river
Final blends: [vd] starved, waved; [vz] saves, stoves

3 Minimal pairs:

[v]—[f]

believe [bɪliv]	belief [bɪlif]
five [faɪv]	fife [faɪf]
leave [liv]	leaf [lif]
live [laɪv]	life [laɪf]
save [sev]	safe [sef]
vault [vɔlt]	fault [fɔlt]
versed [vɜst]	first [fɜst]
very [vɛrɪ]	fairy [fɛrɪ]
vile [vaɪl]	file [faɪl]
vine [vaɪn]	fine [faɪn]

[v]—[b]

rove [rov]	robe [rob]
thieves [θivz]	Thebes [θibz]
V [vi]	B [bi]
vase [ves]	base [bes]
vat [væt]	bat [bæt]
versed [vɜst]	burst [bɜst]
very [vɛrɪ]	berry [bɛrɪ]
vet [vɛt]	bet [bɛt]
vie [vaɪ]	buy [baɪ]
vile [vaɪl]	bile [baɪl]

[v]—[ð]

breve [briv]	breathe [brið]
clove [klov]	clothe [kloð]
lave [lev]	lathe [leð]
loaves [lovz]	loathes [loðz]
V [vi]	thee [ði]
van [væn]	than [ðæn]
vat [væt]	that [ðæt]
vie [vaɪ]	thy [ðaɪ]
vine [vaɪn]	thine [ðaɪn]
vow [vaʊ]	thou [ðaʊ]

[v]—[z]

brave [brev]	braize [brez]
clove [klov]	clove [kloz]
grave [grev]	graze [grez]
have [hæv]	has [hæz]
live [laɪv]	lies [laɪz]
pave [pev]	pays [pez]
rove [rov]	rose [roz]
V [vi]	Z [zɪ]
veal [vil]	zeal [zil]
wave [wev]	ways [wez]

4 Phonetic transcription:

[ðə væst məˈdʒɔrətɪ əv əˈmɛrəkənz həv nɛvɚ vjud spokən ˈlæŋgwɪdʒ wɪθ ðə sem kənsɚn ðe həv ʃon fɔr raɪtɪŋ ən ˈrɪdɪŋ. ˌnɛvɚðəˈlɛs, ɪf ðə madən vog ɪn ɛdʒəˈkeʃən kənˈtɪnjuz, ɪt əz vɛrɪ laɪklɪ ðət ðə ˈlæŋgwɪdʒ arts kərɪkjələm wɪl strɛs spokən kəmjunəˈkeʃən tu ə gretɚ dɪˈgri. ɪt həz ˈɔlwɪz bɪn ə mætɚ əv grev kənsɚn ðæt, sev ɪn ə fju skulz, so lɪtḷ taɪm həz bɪn dɪˈvotəd tə spɪtʃ. ðə mɔr ˈabvɪəs divɪˈeʃənz həv bɪn gɪvən ovɚ tu ðə spɪtʃ θɛrəpəst, bət ðɪ ˈævrɪdʒ tʃaɪld həz nɛvɚ ənˈdʒɔɪd ðɪ ədˈvæntɪdʒəz ðət ˈtrenɪŋ ɪn spɪtʃ kʊd gɪv. ðɪ ɪnɛvətəbḷ ˈkansɪkwɛns, hwɪtʃ kʊd əv bɪn prɪˈdɪktəd baɪ ˈɛnɪwʌn wɪð vɪʒən, həz bɪn ðət ðə gretəst pavɚtɪ ɪn ðə jus əv ˈlæŋgwɪdʒ həz bɪn ɪn ɪts ˈɛvrɪde jus ɪn ˈspikɪŋ. ɪf wi ʃud sevɚ aʊr taɪz wɪθ trədɪʃən ænd rɪˈvaɪv ən ɪntrəst ɪn aʊr ˈnetɪv tʌŋ, ðɛr wʊd bi mʌtʃ ðət wʊd pruv əv ˈvælju tu ðə tʃaɪld hwɪtʃ wəd rɪˈzʌlt frəm sʌtʃ ə rɪˈvɪʒən əv ðə ˈlæŋgwɪdʒ arts kərɪkjələm.]

[θ]
*TH*INK

ANALYSIS

The [θ] is classified as a *nonsyllabic, unvoiced dental* (or linguadental) fricative, Other feature descriptions of this sound are *coronal, anterior, tense, non-strident,* and *continuant.* The sound may be made by placing the flattened tip of the tongue on, or very close to, the cutting edge of the upper central teeth and by directing an unvoiced breath stream through the close but broad gap between tongue and teeth. The lower teeth may touch the undersurface of the tonguetip. Velopharyngeal closure is complete or nearly so. The friction sound created by passage of the airstream between tongue and teeth may or may not be heard in actual speech, for the noise is weak (the weakest of all the fricatives except possibly the [ð]) and easily masked. The character of the noise itself, in terms of power and frequency composition is very close to that of the [f]. From this we see the possibility for confusion between these two sounds and the special need for syllabic cues to consonant identification in the case of [θ] (see, for example, Miller and Nicely, 1955; for articulatory position see Fig. 5-4).

VARIATION

Both articulatory place and articulatory type variations may be heard among allophones and dialectal variants of [θ]. There is, of course, a marked similarity between fricative [θ] and the dental stop [t̪], and one of the more common variants of [θ] is the dental affricate [t̪θ]. It is a common variant, not necessarily an error, in certain contexts. However, an overstrong affricate, or a substitution of the alveolar affricate or stop is, in most dialects, counted as nonstandard, or indeed, *sub*standard. "Tink" for "think," and "dese" and "dose" for "these" and "those" may be a kind of *class* marker in English, almost a *shibboleth* (see Judges, 12:4–6].

There are some slight differences in the exact place of [θ] articulation among American speakers, and these too should be noted. The [θ] can be described as an interdental sound, with the tonguetip between the teeth, and it is convenient to use this position when it becomes necessary to demonstrate an articulation posture for the sound. Occasionally the tongue will protrude 1/4 inch or more beyond the teeth. Although [θ] may be produced this way in connected speech by some persons, the tongue-teeth contact is also more often on the lower portion of the back surface of the upper teeth, behind and above the cutting edge. This adjustment creates acoustic conditions which, for practical purposes, are equivalent to those for the interdental articulation.

Th words often present problems to nonnative speakers not only because of the possibility of the lack of appropriate dentalization or voicing, but also because there is no way to symbolize the difference between [θ] and [ð] in English. Both are spelled *th*. It is perhaps futile to enumerate the rules governing a choice between [θ] and [ð] in standard speech. The differences between these sounds are often slight, and distinctions in meaning do not often depend upon whether one says [θ] or [ð]. There are such wide variations in the amount of voicing on these sounds that in conversational speech it is often nearly impossible to say whether a given sound should be considered voiced or voiceless. Phonetic context naturally has a great effect. Take, for example, the word "with," which may be either [wɪð] or [wɪθ] in the phrase "with us," but would more likely be [wɪθ] in the phrase "with Sam."

The [θ] sound is often involved in nonstandard speech errors of children. One of the commonest defects in infantile speech is some sort of substitution for [θ], very frequently [f], as in [fɪŋk] for "think." Presumably the relative difficulty in hearing the sound accounts for the fact that it is so often missing from the child's repertoire of sounds. Fortunately, once recognized, the [θ] usually proves relatively easy to learn.

Substitution of [t̪] for [θ] is heard in some kinds of dialect speech, as we have pointed out above. Foreign speakers often have difficulty acquiring an English [θ], usually because they may have no comparable contrast between dental and alveolar fricative in their own language. Some persons may substitute [s], so that "think" becomes "sink"; less often [f] may be used in place of [θ], the notable case being Cockney English [fɜtifri] for "thirty-three."

In summary, the most common variants of [θ] are the voiced [θ̬] or [ð], the affricate [t̪θ], or in some dialects the substitution of [t] or [f].

EXERCISES

1 Practice paragraph for [θ]:

> The earliest months of a child's life are rather important for his later growth in speech and language. One can think of the infant's birth cry, sounded as he draws his first breath, as the first thing he has done to prepare for speaking. By the third month, he will have begun to express many kinds of information through sound, although only Mother is likely to understand that one means that he is thirsty, another that he thinks the time has come for a change. Without conscious tutoring, he will learn the sounds of speech, and the pathways thus formed will be with him always. Later, by perhaps between the ninth or tenth and the twelfth month, he may have spoken his first word—an indescribably thrilling thing for both Father and Mother. Though the way will not always be smooth, through patience and understanding the child can be set upon the path which will lead to a full realization of his capabilities.

2 Word list:

Initiating consonant: thaw, thigh, thing, threw
Terminating consonant: earth, oath, wrath, youth
Stronger consonant: cathedral, pathetic, unthankful, unthinkable
Weaker consonant: author, birthday, healthy, nothing
Initial blends: [θr] thread, through
Final blends: [θs] births, youth's

3 Minimal pairs:

[θ]—[ð]

ether [iθɚ]	either [iðɚ]
loath [loθ]	loathe [loð]
mouth (n.) [mauθ]	mouth (v.) [mauð]
sheath [ʃiθ]	sheathe [ʃið]
sooth [suθ]	soothe [suð]
teeth [tiθ]	teethe [tið]
thigh [θaɪ]	thy [ðaɪ]
wreath [riθ]	wreathe [rið]

[θ]—[f]

author [ɔθɚ]	offer [ɔfɚ]
death [dɛθ]	deaf [dɛf]
oath [oθ]	oaf [of]
sheaths [ʃiθs]	sheafs [ʃifs]
thigh [θaɪ]	fie [faɪ]
thin [θɪn]	fin [fɪn]
thread [θrɛd]	Fred [frɛd]
threat [θrɛt]	fret [frɛt]
three [θri]	free [fri]
wreath [riθ]	reef [rif]

[θ]—[t]

death [dɛθ]	debt [dɛt]
hath [hæθ]	hat [hæt]
myth [mɪθ]	mitt [mɪt]
themes [θimz]	teams [timz]
thigh [θaɪ]	tie [taɪ]
thin [θɪn]	tin [tɪn]
thought [θɔt]	taught [tɔt]
thread [θrɛd]	tread [trɛd]
three [θri]	tree [tri]
through [θru]	true [tru]

[θ]—[s]

mouth (n.) [mauθ]	mouse [maus]
myth [mɪθ]	miss [mɪs]
themes [θimz]	seems [simz]
thigh [θaɪ]	sigh [saɪ]
thin [θɪn]	sin [sɪn]
thing [θɪŋ]	sing [sɪŋ]
think [θɪŋk]	sink [sɪŋk]
thong [θɔŋ]	song [sɔŋ]
thought [θɔt]	sought [sɔt]
thumb [θʌm]	some [sʌm]

4 Phonetic transcription:

[ði ɝliəst mʌnθs əv ə tʃaɪldz laɪf ɑr ræðɚ ɪmˈpɔrtənt fɔr hɪz letɚ groθ in spitʃ
ən ˈlæŋgwɪdʒ. wʌn kən θɪŋk əv ði ɪnfənts bɝθ kraɪ, saʊndəd əz hi drɔz ɪz
fɝst brɛθ, æz ðə fɝst θɪŋ hi əz dʌn tə prɪˈpɛr fɚ spikɪŋ. baɪ ðə θɝd mʌnθ hi
wɪl həv bɪˈgʌn tu ɛkˈsprɛs mɛni kaɪndz əv ɪnfɚˈmeʃən θru saund, ɔlðo onli
mʌðɚ ɪz laɪkli tu ʌndɚˈstænd ðət ˈwʌn minz ðət hi ɪz θɝsti, ənʌðɚ ðət hi
θɪŋks ðə taɪm həz kʌm fɚ ə tʃɛndʒ. wɪˈðaut kɑnʃəs ˈtutərɪŋ, hi wɪl lɝn
ðə saundz əv spitʃ, ænd ðə ˈpæθwez ðʌs fɔrmd wɪl bi wɪθ hɪm ˈɔlwez. letɚ, baɪ
pəhæps bɪˈtwin ðə naɪntθ ɚ tɛntθ ænd ðə twɛlfθ mʌntθ, hi me həv spokən
hɪz fɝst wɝd—æn ɪndəˈskraɪbəblɪ θrɪlɪŋ θɪŋ fɔr boθ faðɚ ən mʌðɚ. ðo ðə we
wɪl nat ˈɔlwɪz bi smuð, θru peʃəns ən ʌndɚˈstændɪŋ ðə tʃaɪld kən bi sɛt əpɑn
ðə pæθ hwɪtʃ wəl lid tu ə ful riələˈzeʃən əv hɪz kepəˈbɪlətɪz.]

[ð]
THAT BA*THE*

ANALYSIS

The common classification of [ð] is identical to that for [θ] except for the features of tension and voicing. [ð] is lax, and consequently even less likely to be strident. From this it can be appreciated that the linguadental influence upon the adjacent vowels is often the only acoustic cue to the identification of this sound. In common with other voiced consonants it is usually distinguished from its voiceless counterpart by a lengthening of the preceding vowel (see Fig. 5-4).

VARIATION

Most of the variations discussed for the sound [θ] have their analog in the voiced [ð]. For example, the dentalized affricate [d̪ð] or the alveolar stop [d̪] may often be heard in [ð] words, not only in foreign dialect speech but also in many nonstandard English forms, such as [diz] and [doz] for "these" and "those."

Minor place variants such as those discussed in the previous section are if anything even less noticeable in the case of [ð], and assimilative changes are quite common in American English speech. Two extremely common forms are [ɪzætso] and [wʌzɛr] for the phrases "is that so" and "was there." Other common dialectal forms include the substitution of [θ], [z], and [v], as in [wɛθɚ] for "weather," [ze] for "they," and [mʌvɚ] for "mother." The last example will be recognized as especially common in the speech of children.

EXERCISES

1   Practice paragraph for [f]:

> Those of us who are fast oxidizing, as some heathen has scathingly put it, look back on the healthy days of our childhood growth as without a doubt the most glorious period in American history. Life did not always go smoothly to be sure, and there were many tribulations that faced the youths of this bygone day. I think they must have been made of sterner stuff, for instance, to have withstood the medication that was the order of the day. It bothered my brother not at all, but as I watched my father measure out a generous spoonful of thick and loathsome castor oil, knowing that another would be mine, I remember I would literally writhe in expectant agony, and perspiration would bathe my brow. On these occasions my

thoughtful mother was quick to show the white feather; she could not watch in comfort, so prudently withdrew. Later she would soothe me as best she could. I do not know whether this nostrum is still being ladled out or not, but if it is, then all the orchids that have been thrust at the feet of medical scientists should have been left to wither on their vines.

2   Word list:

Initiating consonant: thee, they, thou, though
Terminating consonant: bathe, clothe, smooth, soothe
Stronger consonant: although, to these, to them, without
Weaker consonant: bother, breathing, other, rather
Final blends: [ðz] bathes, breathes; [ðd] clothed, soothed

3   Minimal pairs:

[ð]—[d]		[ð]—[z]	
bathe [beð]	bayed [bed]	bathe [beð]	bays [bez]
breathe [brið]	breed [brid]	breathe [brið]	breeze [briz]
father [fɑðɚ]	fodder [fɑdɚ]	clothe [kloð]	close [kloz]
lathe [leð]	laid [led]	lathe [leð]	lays [lez]
loathe [loð]	load [lod]	seethe [sið]	sees [siz]
their [ðɛr]	dare [dɛr]	sheathe [ʃið]	she's [ʃiz]
they [ðe]	day [de]	teethe [tið]	tease [tiz]
thine [ðaɪn]	dine [daɪn]	thee [ði]	Z [zi]
thy [ðaɪ]	die [daɪ]	tithe [taɪð]	ties [taɪz]
wreathe [rið]	read [rid]	writhe [raɪð]	rise [raɪz]

[ð]—[θ]	[ð]—[v]
See [θ]–[ð].	See [v]–[ð].

4   Phonetic transcription:

[ðoz əv ʌs hu ɑr fæst ˈaksəˌdaɪzɪŋ, æz sʌm hiðən həz ˈskeðɪŋlɪ pʌt ɪt, luk bæk ɔn ðə hɛlθɪ dez əv aur ˈtʃaɪldhud groθ æz wɪˈðaut ə daut ðə most ˈglɔrɪəs ˈpɪrɪəd ɪn əˈmɛrəkən hɪstərɪ. laɪf dɪd nat ˈɔlwɪz go so ˈsmuðlɪ tə bi ʃur, æn ðɚ wɚ mɛnɪ ˌtrɪbjuˈleʃənz ðət fest ðə juðz əv ðɪs ˈbaɪgɔn de. aɪ θɪŋk ðe mʌst əv bɪn med əv stɚnɚ stʌf, fɔr ɪnstəns, tə həv wɪθˈstud ðə mɛdəˈkeʃən ðət wəz ði ɔrdɚ əv ðə de. ɪt bɑðəd maɪ brʌðɚ nat ə tɔl, bət æz aɪ watʃt maɪ fɑðɚ mɛʒɚ aut ə dʒɛnərəs ˈspunful əv ðə θɪk ən loðsəm kæstɚ ɔɪl, noɪŋ ðət ənʌðɚ wəd bi maɪn, aɪ rɪˈmɛmbɚ aɪ wəd ˈlɪtərlɪ raɪð ɪn ɛkˈspɛktənt ˈægənɪ, æn pɚspəˈreʃən wud beð maɪ brau. ɔn ðiz əkeʒənz maɪ θɔtfəl mʌðɚ wəz kwɪk tə ʃo ðə hwaɪt feðɚ; ʃi kəd nat watʃ ɪn kʌmfət, so prudəntlɪ wɪθˈdru. letɚ ʃi wəd suð mi əz best ʃi kud. aɪ du nat no hwɛðɚ ðɪs nastrəm ɪz stɪl biɪŋ ledld aut ɚ nat, bət ɪf ɪt ɪz, ðɛn ɔl ðə ɔrkədz ðət həv bɪn θrʌst æt ðə fit əv ˈmɛdɪkl̩ ˈsaɪəntəsts ʃud həv bɪn lɛft tə wɪðɚ ɔn ðɛr vaɪnz.]

[s]
*S*EE CLA*SS* *S*CENE CYCLE *S*CHIZM *PS*YCHIC

ANALYSIS

The [s] is most commonly classified as an *unvoiced lingua-alveolar* fricative. In other feature terminology it is also *coronal, anterior, tense, strident,* and *continuant.* Along with [z], [ʃ], and [ʒ] it is frequently referred to as a *sibilant.* In producing [s] the margin of the tongue is typically in contact with the teeth and gums laterally, with the blade of the tongue near, but not touching, the alveolar ridge. This position forms a narrow breath channel at the midline of the tongue between the tongue and the anterior part of the hard palate. [s] has been called a *narrow-channel fricative* in contrast to [ʃ], a broad-channel fricative. Velopharyngeal closure is complete, or nearly so. The sound is made as the unvoiced breath stream is forced through the narrow channel between the grooved blade of the tongue and the roof of the mouth. Noise is produced as the breath stream becomes turbulent upon its release from the narrow constriction.

It is important to emphasize here that the frictionlike noises of all speech sounds are caused by an airflow directed through a relatively constricted opening. The nature of the noise is thought to be dependent upon a number of factors, including the following: (1) the air pressure and flow rate, (2) the degree of constriction of the airflow, (3) the shape of the constriction (broad versus narrow channel), (4) the nature of the obstructions within and in front of the air channel (rugal ridges of the palate and teeth, for example), (5) the presence of an air cavity forward of the air turbulence which might act as a high-frequency resonator, and (6) the resonance frequency of that air cavity.

The [s] is often referred to as a "high-frequency" sound. The basis for this is that very little acoustic energy in the noise is present below about 4,000 Hz. There is also usually an especially prominent peak of energy in the noise at about 6,000 Hz. It should also be noted that [s] has one of the highest *frequencies of occurrence* of any of the consonants of English and appears in a very large number of consonant blends (see fig. 5-4).

VARIATION

There is commonly a considerable variability in the manner of producing [s], much of which is a result of variations in the posture of the tonguetip and blade and differences in tongue grooving and dentition. Some individuals make [s] with the tonguetip behind the lower teeth, and others pronounce the sound with the tip at various levels between this placement and a point behind the alveolar ridge. Lip positions for [s] may also vary considerably, with the result that a forward cavity resonance may color the [s] slightly when [s] is labialized, as in the word "Sue" [su]. Such variations are acceptable in appropriate phonetic contexts. However a lip-rounded [s] would not be anticipated preceding a nonrounded vowel. In any case the appropriate channeling must be accomplished.

The standard [s] articulation places some rather special demands upon the speech production system which are probably responsible for this sound figuring so prominently in disorders of articulation. The tongue must be properly placed and adequately grooved. The airstream must be placed under proper pressure and directed over the appropriate turbulence-producing obstructions. It is also especially important that the hearing mechanism of the speaker be capable of receiving the very high frequencies typical of [s], 4,000 to 7,000 Hz. If [s] is to be appropriately produced, it must be appropriately received. Absence of this feedback will seriously impair requisition of this sound. In view of all these requirements it comes as no surprise that there are many different kinds of lisps.

Defective [s] sounds are usually classified as one of the following varieties: (1) weak [s], of roughly appropriate type but low in energy; (2) "hishy" or [ʃ]-like sound produced by retracted placement of the tongue, a too broad channel of air emission, improper air pressure, or some combination of these, as in [ðæʃɑraɪt] for "that's all right"; (3) an *interdental* lisp, in essence a kind of [θ] substitution, as the "baby talk" [θuði θɔ θæm] for "Susie saw Sam"; (4) a *lateral* lisp, in which the ungrooved tongue occludes the airway at the midline while the air is directed laterally—around one or both sides of the tongue (for this sound there is a "voiceless lateral" [ɬ] symbol which may be used); (5) a *whistle* such as is occasionally heard as a result of new dentures or missing teeth; (6) an affricative [ts], sometimes heard in children and in the hard-of-hearing; (7) a nasal-oral-fricative combination typical of cleft palate speech; and (8) a *strident* or overly "hissed" [s].

In the field of speech disorders, defective articulation of [s] is quite frequently associated with a dental malocclusion. Since the fricative noise for [s] depends in part on directing the breath stream against the upper central teeth, any deformity which disturbs the dentition may make it difficult for the speaker to produce the sound; an underbite, overbite, irregular teeth, or an abnormal opening in the bite are common conditions.

[s] sounds are among the last to be learned by many children; hence omissions of, and substitutions for, the sound are very common in infantile speech. The pronunciation of "see" as [θi] instead of [si] is typical, but other voiceless sounds, such as [h], [f], or even [t] may be used. There are doubtless some reasonably complex factors which account for the frequency with which [s], and to a lesser extent other sibilants, present learning difficulties for children.

Foreign speakers of English may have some problems with [s] although alveolar fricatives are common in the languages of the world. A more anterier and more strongly aspirated [s] may color the English pronunciation of those whose native language is German, for example. This is also true of French, but to a less marked degree. Still other languages have varieties of [s] which may sound strange when transferred to English diction. Voicing or weakening of the sound so that it may approximate [z] also occurs.

Perhaps attention would be called to the way in which a [sj] combination, when it occurs in connected speech, may bring about a change in what would otherwise be [s]. Thus, although "kiss" ends in [s] when it is spoken alone and in most contexts, the phrase "kiss you" in conversational speech is usually [kɪʃu] in American English; it seems quite unnatural, in fact, for the speaker to make any effort to retain [s]. The phrase "pass you" [pæʃu] illustrates the same operation of reciprocal assimilation, as does [vɪʃəs] as a pronunciation of "vicious" ([nætjurəl əsɪmələesjən ɪz ði ɪsju]).

EXERCISES

1 Practice paragraph for [s]:

It is interesting how certainly a listener can sense the emotional reactions of a speaker through the nuances of his vocal quality and inflection. No trained phychologist is necessary to advise us that someone we chance to meet is passionately opposed to an idea that may come under discussion. Nor are we likely to miss the fact that his feelings have been hurt by a fancied snub or slight, no matter how earnestly he may seek to dissemble. There is perhaps no better or more scientific way to assess emotions than through voice, for the speaker quite unconsciously reveals his true feelings in this way. Most psychiatrists would tell us that they can fix with considerable accuracy the intensity of a neurosis by observing the patient's voice.

2 Word list:

Initiating consonant: saw, say, see, sir
Terminating consonant: ace, ice, us, use (n)
Initiating and terminating: cease, sass, source, souse
Stronger consonant: concern, consist, instead, restore
Weaker consonant: fasten, lesson, passing, possible
Initial blends: [sk] scare, sky; [skr] scream, screw; [skw] square, squeak; [sl] slant, slip; [sm] smoke, smooth; [sn] snake, snow; [sp] spare, spoil; [spl] splash, split; [spr] sprain, spring; [st] stay, stop; [str] straight, street; [sw] sway, swell
Final blends: [fs] cuffs, staffs; [ks] lacks, talks; [lts] belts, wilts; [mps] bumps, stamps; [nts] once, plants; [ŋks] tanks, thinks; [ps] lips, tops; [rs] farce, force; [rts] arts, forts; [st] first, past; [sts] lasts, posts; [ts] hits, lets; [θs] deaths, growths; [ntst] bounced, fenced; [sk] bask, mask

3 Minimal pairs:

	[s]—[z]		[s]—[ʃ]
base [bes]	bays [bez]	class [klæs]	clash [klæʃ]
close (adj.) [klos]	close (v.) [kloz]	close (adj.) [klos]	cloche [kloʃ]
lace [les]	lays [lez]	lass [læs]	lash [læʃ]
lice [laɪs]	lies [laɪz]	mass [mæs]	mash [mæʃ]
race [res]	rays [rez]	same [sem]	shame [ʃem]
rice [raɪs]	rise [raɪz]	see [si]	she [ʃi]
seal [sil]	zeal [zil]	sin [sɪn]	shin [ʃɪn]
see [si]	Z [zi]	so [so]	show [ʃo]
sink [sɪŋk]	zinc [zɪŋk]	son [sʌn]	shun [ʃʌn]
use (n.) [jus]	use (v.) [juz]	sore [sɔr]	shore [ʃɔr]

	[s]—[t]		[s]—[θ]
base [bes]	bait [bet]	Goss [gɑs]	Goth [gɑθ]
lice [laɪs]	light [laɪt]	lass [læs]	lath [læθ]
mass [mæs]	mat [mæt]	mass [mæs]	math [mæθ]
pass [pæs]	pat [pæt]	moss [mɑs]	moth [mɑθ]
race [res]	rate [ret]	pass [pæs]	path [pæθ]
rice [raɪs]	right [raɪt]	race [res]	wraithe [reθ]
same [sem]	tame [tem]	sick [sɪk]	thick [θɪk]
see [si]	T [ti]	sinking [sɪŋkɪn]	thinking [θɪŋkɪn]
sick [sɪk]	tick [tɪk]	souse [saʊs]	south [saʊθ]
so [so]	toe [to]	use (n.) [jus]	youth [juθ]

4 Phonetic transcription:

[ɪt ɪz ɪntərɛstɪŋ haʊ sɜtənlɪ ə lɪsənɚ kən sɛns ði ɪmoʃənəl riˈækʃənz əv ə spikɚ
θru ðə ˈnuɑnsəz əv ɪz vokəl ˈkwɑlətɪ ən ɪnˈflɛkʃən. no trend saɪˈkɑlədʒəst ɪz
ˈnɛsəsɛrɪ tu ədvaɪz ʌs ðət ˈsʌmwʌn wi tʃæns tə mit ɪz ˈpæʃənətlɪ əpozd tu ən
aɪˈdɪə ðət me kʌm ʌndɚ dɪsˈkʌʃən. nɔr ɑr wi laɪklɪ tə mɪs ðə fækt ðət ɪz filɪŋz
həv bɪn hɜt baɪ ə ˈfænsɪd snʌb ɔr slaɪt, no mætɚ haʊ ɜnəstlɪ hi me sik tu
dɪˈsɛmbl̩. ðɛr ɪz pɚhæps no bɛtɚ ɔr mɔr saɪənˈtɪfɪk we tu əsɛs iˈmoʃənz ðæn
θru vɔɪs, fɔr ðə spikɚ kwaɪt ʌnˈkɑnʃəslɪ rɪˈvilz hɪz tru ˈfilɪŋz ɪn ðɪs we. most
səkaɪətrəsts wʊd tɛl əs ðət ðe kən fɪks wɪð kənˈsɪdərəbl̩ ækjərəsɪ ði ɪnˈtɛnsətɪ
əv ə nurosəs baɪ əbˈzɜvɪŋ ðə peʃənts vɔɪs.]

[z]
HIS ZERO JAZZ XYLOPHONE

ANALYSIS

This consonant is commonly classified as a *voiced lingua-alveolar* fricative,
and as *coronal, anterior, lax, strident,* and *continuant.* The details of articulation described for [s] also apply to [z] except for the addition of voicing

with a resultant weakening of the fricative noise, and the added length of the preceding vowel.

VARIATION

After the rather extended treatment of [s], the discussion of [z] can be relatively short. The preceding remarks on the variability of tongue and lip positions are pertinent to both [s] and [z]. Perhaps the somewhat less forceable articulation of [z] makes its limits of acceptable pronunciation somewhat broader than for [s], however. The tongue posture employed by any given speaker for [s] is likely to be duplicated for [z] sounds, although this is not always the case.

Special note should be taken of the tendency to unvoice [z], particularly in syllable-final positions, but sometimes in initial positions as well. In the final position the tendency is to cut off voicing very shortly after the friction noise begins. Consequently, for much of the duration of the sound the friction may be unaccompanied by voice, even though the total voicing length is such as to give sufficient cue to the fact that the [z], not [s], is being produced. It is, of course, important that the notion of "final position" be understood. This refers to *phrase* final, not simply word final; ". . . his" contains a final [z], but in "his apple" the [z] is *not* final except in unusual circumstances.

Partial devoicing of final [z] may be indicated in phonetic transcription by [z̧] or [zz̧]. Seldom is voicing present all the way up to the point of release except in intervocalic position. One does occasionally hear such a form as [plez°] for "plays," with a release vowel, but this is normally not recognized in phonetic transcription. Devoicing of [z] can be an outstanding dialect feature, as anyone knows who has listened to strong German dialects of English. [hi fros hɪs nos] for "he froze his nose" is an example.

EXERCISES

1 Practice paragraph for [z]:

> Modern jazz music has both its devotees and its detractors. Where it originated is not certain, although many think its characteristic syncopated rhythms arose in the alleys and byways of New Orleans as a cousin to folk melodies. Chicago and its environs became the jazz capital of the world in the 1920s, an age which was in all ways an amazing period in contemporary American history. The argument as to whether such music is a kind of disease or a genuine art form still rages, and the strains of swing or the exaggerated beat of "rock" continue to dismay or please the listener, depending on his fancies.

2 Word list:

Initiating consonant: xi, zee, Zoe, zoo
Terminating consonant: as, ease, eyes, is
Initiating and terminating: Czars, Z's, Zoe's, zoos
Stronger consonant: deserve, disaster, nasality, resign
Weaker consonant: dozen, easy, pleasant, using
Final blends: [bz] jobs, rubs; [dz] beds, fords; [gz] bags, digs; [lz] bells, fills;
[mz] comes, swims; [nz] or [ndz] hands, winds; [ŋz] brings, sings;
[rz] hears, wears; [rdz] boards, beards; [ðz] bathes, breathes; [vz]
saves, stoves; [zd] caused, used

3 Minimal pairs:

[z]—[s]		[z]—[d]	
braize [brez]	brace [bres]	has [hæz]	had [hæd]
curs [kɜz]	curse [kɜs]	his [hɪz]	hid [hɪd]
hers [hɜz]	hearse [hɜs]	lays [lez]	laid [led]
his [hɪz]	hiss [hɪs]	pays [pez]	paid [ped]
maize [mez]	mace [mes]	phase [fez]	fade [fed]
Jews [dʒuz]	juice [dʒus]	rays [rez]	raid [red]
pays [pez]	pace [pes]	rise [raɪz]	ride [raɪd]
rays [rez]	race [res]	ways [wez]	wade [wed]
trays [trez]	trace [tres]	Z [zi]	D [di]
zoot [zut]	suit [sut]	zoo [zu]	do [du]

[z]—[v]	
arise [əraɪz]	arrive [əraɪv]
close (v.) [kloz]	clove [klov]
dies [daɪz]	dive [daɪv]
does [dʌz]	dove [duv]
has [hæz]	have [hæv]
highs [haɪz]	hive [haɪv]
lays [lez]	lave [lev]
pays [pez]	pave [pev]
rays [rez]	rave [rev]
ways [wez]	wave [wev]

[z]—[ʒ]	
bays [bez]	beige [beʒ]
composer [kəmpozɚ]	composure [kəmpoʒɚ]
incloser [ɪnklozɚ]	inclosure [ɪnkloʒɚ]
ruse [ruz]	rouge [ruʒ]
Caesar [sizɚ]	seizure [siʒɚ]

4 Phonetic transcription:

[madən ˈdʒæz ˈmjuzɪk hæz boθ ɪts dɛvəˈtiz ænd ɪts dɪˈtræktɚz. hwɛr ɪt
əˈrɪdʒənetəd ɪz nɑt sɜtṇ, ɔlðo mɛnɪ θɪŋk ɪts ˌkɛrɪktɚˈɪstɪk ˈsɪŋkəˌpetəd rɪðəmz

ɚoz ɪn ði æliz ən ˈbaɪˌwez əv ˌnuˈɔrliənz æz ə kʌzən tə fok ˈmɛlodɪz. ʃəˈkɔgo
ən ɪts ɛnˈvaɪrənz bɪkem ðə dʒæz kæpətl̩ əv ðə wɜ˞ld ɪn ðə ˈnaɪnˈtin ˈtwɛntɪz,
ən edʒ hwɪtʃ wəz ɪn ɔl wez ən əˈmezɪŋ ˈpɪriəd ɪn kənˈtɛmpərɛrɪ əˈmɛrəkən
hɪstərɪ. ði ˈɑrgjəmənt æz tə hwɛðɚ sʌtʃ ˈmjuzɪk ɪz ə kaɪnd əv dɪˈzɪz ɔr ə
dʒɛnjəwən ɑrt fɔrm stɪl redʒəz, ænd ðə strenz əv swɪŋ ænd ði ɛgˈzædʒəretəd
bit əv rɑk kənˈtɪnju tʊ dɪsˈme ɔr pliz ðə lɪsənɚ, dɪˈpɛndɪŋ ɔn hɪz ˈfænsɪz.]

[ʃ]
SHOE PASSION VACATION CHICAGO SUGAR
CONSCIOUS PSHAW

ANALYSIS

The [ʃ] is sometimes classified as an *unvoiced linguapalatal fricative* but is
referred to by the IPA as a *palatoalveolar* fricative. In other feature terms it
is a *coronal, nonanterior, tense, strident* obstruent. A standard [ʃ] is typically
produced with the sides of the tongue in contact with the teeth and gums in
such a way that lateral escape of breath is prevented; the tip and blade of
the tongue are raised toward, but do not touch the alveolar ridge and front
part of the palate; with the tongue held in this position, an unvoiced breath
stream is directed against the palate and alveolar ridge. The tongue is adjusted
in such a way that a relatively broad breath channel is formed between the
tongue and roof of the mouth (Fig. 5-4).

The articulation of [ʃ] involves a large portion of the tongue body, with
the result that the obstruction between tongue and palate is distributed over
a considerably greater portion of the palatal length than is the case with the
anterior tonguetip and blade sounds. The tongue position closely resembles
that for the [tʃ], and it could thus be called a *distributed* sound. [ʃ] has also
been termed a *broad-channel* fricative because of ·the broader area through
which the air flows, in contrast with the narrow [s]. The [s] airstream is
concentrated and produces a "hiss," while the [ʃ] is diffuse and the sound is
a "hish." In addition, the [ʃ] is colored by a larger resonance chamber in
front of the noise source, which may be made even larger by a characteristic
rounding and moving forward of the lips. Generally the lip position for [ʃ]
is assimilated from the adjacent vowels and is not distinctive to [ʃ]. There
does appear, however, to be a tendency to round [ʃ] more often than the
coarticulatory effects might predict. Characteristically when Americans are
asked to produce an isolated [s]—a "hiss"—they will not round, and perhaps
may even spread, the lips; but when asked to produce a "shhh," they tend
to produce a quite obvious lip rounding.

Acoustically [ʃ] is the strongest of the fricatives, with more acoustic
power at lower frequencies than is the case with the other fricatives—down

to about 1600 Hz. It is also the longest, as will be seen from the characteristic voice print pattern of Figure 14-1 (see also Fig. 5-4).

VARIATION

The sound [ʃ] is not often involved in nonstandard English speech. It may be underpronounced or weakened, of course, but even this is not a particularly common problem. The sound is, however, subject to some of the same kinds of defects that are associated with [s]. It is sometimes lateralized by children or distorted as a result of severe dental malocclusions. It can be overly weak, partially or completely voiced [ʃ̬] or [ʒ], laterally emitted [ʃˡ], or made as an affricate [tʃ] or [ts]. In addition, spelling pronunciations may result in a substitution of [sj] for [ʃ] (see [s]).

Both hissing [s:::] and hishing [ʃ:::] have interesting nonverbal functions in our language and others as well: To urge quiet, we use [ʃ:], to show disapproval we say [s::]. According to Professor John Black of Ohio State University (personal comment), "A variation [of ʃ] would be used in Italian opera houses. It lies somewhere between [ʃ] and [s]. The [s] is used to show disapproval of a performer; the high-frequency [ʃ] is used to quiet a balcony."

Foreign speakers may mispronounce [ʃ] in their English speech, but the sound does not usually prove difficult to learn. It should be noted in this connection that English is notably short on nonanterior fricatives. The IPA alphabet provides symbols for retroflex [s], palatoalveolar [ʃ], alveolopalatal [ɕ], palatal [ç], velar [x], uvular [χ], pharyngeal [ħ], and glottal [h]. Of these only the [ʃ] and [h] are canonical in English, although some of the others are commonly encountered allophones and foreign dialect variants.

EXERCISES

1   Practice paragraph for [ʃ]:

> It is no longer as fashionable to pursue the topic of speech gestures as it was in the days of the elocution teachers. However, it is surely not a case of mere devotion to the pressure of custom to point out that we usually (and unashamedly) show some emotion both by facial and bodily expression as part of the total communication process. In fact, although we may not be conscious of it, we are disturbed if the speaker's countenance displays a response which is out of keeping with his professions. Harsh words with a bashful expression, expressions of shyness with a grimace of grim determination, or words of high resolve issuing from a face showing only a "deadpan" are a shock to the audience. The reaction is likely to be rejection of the speaker's efforts as mere sham and show, no matter how passionately he has argued.

2 Word list:

Initiating consonant: she, shoe, show, shy
Terminating consonant: ash, rash, wash, wish
Stronger consonant: ashamed, cashier, insure, machine
Weaker consonant: fashion, motion, washer, wishing
Initial blends: [ʃr] shrewd, shrink
Final blends: [ʃt] pushed, rushed

3 Minimal pairs:

[ʃ]—[tʃ]

cashing [kæʃɪŋ]	catching [kætʃɪŋ]	leash [liʃ]	lease [lis]
lash [læʃ]	latch [lætʃ]	push [pʊʃ]	puss [pʊs]
mash [mæʃ]	match [mætʃ]	sash [sæʃ]	sass [sæs]
shin [ʃɪn]	chin [tʃɪn]	shall [ʃæl]	Sal [sæl]
ship [ʃɪp]	chip [tʃɪp]	sheen [ʃin]	seen [sin]
shoe [ʃu]	chew [tʃu]	shelf [ʃɛlf]	self [sɛlf]
shore [ʃɔr]	chore [tʃɔr]	shell [ʃɛl]	sell [sɛl]
wash [waʃ]	watch [watʃ]	ship [ʃɪp]	sip [sɪp]
washer [waʃɚ]	watcher [watʃɚ]	shoe [ʃu]	sue [su]
wish [wɪʃ]	witch [wɪtʃ]	short [ʃɔrt]	sort [sɔrt]

[ʃ]—[θ]

hash [hæʃ]	hath [hæθ]
rash [ræʃ]	wrath [ræθ]
shank [ʃæŋk]	thank [θæŋk]
sheaf [ʃif]	thief [θif]
shin [ʃɪn]	thin [θɪn]
shore [ʃɔr]	Thor [θɔr]
shorn [ʃɔrn]	thorn [θɔrn]
shrew [ʃru]	through [θru]
shrift [ʃrɪft]	thrift [θrɪft]
shy [ʃaɪ]	thigh [θaɪ]

[ʃ]—[ʒ]

Aleutian [əluʃən]	allusion [əluʒən]
Asher [æʃɚ]	azure [æʒɚ]
Confucian [kənfjuʃən]	confusion [kənfjuʒən]
glacier [gleʃɚ]	glazier [gleʒɚ]
mesher [mɛʃɚ]	measure [mɛʒɚ]
ruche [ruʃ]	rouge [ruʒ]

4 Phonetic transcription:

[ɪt ɪz no lɔŋgɚ æz ˈfæʃənəbl̩ tə pɚˈsu ðə ˈtɑpɪk əv spitʃ dʒɛʃtʃɚz æz ɪt wʌz ɪn ðə
dez əv ði ˌɛləˈkjuʃən titʃɚz. haʊɛvɚ, ɪt ɪz ˈʃurlɪ nat ə kes əv mɪr dɪˈvoʃən tə ðə
prɛʃɚ əv kʌstəm tə pɔɪnt aʊt ðət wi ˈjuʒʊəlɪ ænd ʌnəˈʃemədlɪ ʃo sʌm iˈmoʃən

boθ baɪ feʃəl æn ˈbadəlɪ ɛkˈsprɛʃən æz part əv ðə totḷ kəˌmjunəˈkeʃən ˈprasɛs. ɪn fækt, ɔlˈðo wi me nat be kanʃəs əv ət, wi ar dɪˈstɜbd ɪf ðə ˈspikəz ˈkauntənəns dɪˈsplez ə rɪˈspans hwɪtʃ ɪz aut əv ˈkipɪŋ wɪθ hɪz prəˈfɛʃənz. harʃ wɜdz wɪð ə bæʃʃəl ɛkˈspreʃan, ɛkˈsprɛʃənz əv ʃainəs wɪð ə grɪˈmes əv grɪm dɪˌtɜmənˈeʃən, ɔr wɜdz əv haɪ rɪˈzalv ˈɪʃuɪŋ frəm ə fes ˈʃowɪŋ ˈonlɪ ə dɛdpæn ar ə ʃak tə ði ˈodɪəns. ðə riˈækʃən ɪz laɪklɪ tə bi rɪˈdʒɛkʃən əv ðə spikəz ɛfəts æz mɪr ʃæm ən ʃo, no mætɚ hau ˈpæʃənetlɪ hi hæz ˈargjud.]

[ʒ]
MEASURE ROUGE AZURE

ANALYSIS

The [ʒ] is commonly classified as a *voiced palatoalveolar fricative* or *sibilant*, and it is *coronal, nonanterior, lax, strident,* and *obstruent* in some feature systems. The description of the articulation for [ʃ] also applies to [ʒ], except, of course, that [ʒ] is lax and voiced. As might be anticipated, many of the earlier comments on the production of [ʃ] pertain to [ʒ] as well. It is generally the case that [ʒ] is articulated with less breath pressure than [ʃ], but in other respects the patterns of production are similar (see Fig. 5-4).

VARIATION

The nature of the variability of voicing of [ʒ] can be understood by consulting the discussions on some of the other voiced fricatives. It is common for the voicing not to continue through to the termination of the fricative noise in the final consonant position at the end of a phrase. Overstressing of the voicing feature can produce a form such as [beʒᵊ] for "beige." On the other hand the voicing must be adequate, the aspirate noise weak enough, and the preceding vowel long enough; otherwise [ʒ] will be preceived as [ʃ], and pairs such as "glacier" and "glazier" might become ambiguous.

That [ʒ] presents so few problems to English speakers is in part a result of its low incidence in the language. Moser (1957) lists only three words ending with [ʒ] in his count of all the one-syllable words, and none beginning with [ʒ]. All those listed are of French origin. The other origin of [ʒ] is assimilative change, which parallels that discussed in the previous section on [ʃ]. Such assimilations are those in which [zj] has become [ʒ], such as "pleasure," "azure," and "closure," which in most American English are [plɛʒɚ], [æʒɚ] and [kloʒɚ]. The pronunciations [æzjur] and [klozjɚ] would generally sound pedantic to most Americans. It is also normal, except in more formal and careful speech, to allow this assimilated form to occur in such a phrase as "close your door as you're leaving" [kloʒɚ dɔr æʒɚ livɪŋ]. An anglicized [dʒ] is occasionally heard as a spelling pronunciation in the few words where French [ʒ] is spelled with the letter *g*, and indeed the word "garage" is often heard with either [dʒ] or [ʒ], the former being only marginally nonstandard.

We may again point out that English is short on nonanterior fricatives. Those voiced fricatives analogous to the foreign variants presented in the previous section are these: retroflex [ʐ], alveolopalatal [ʑ], palatal [j], velar [ɣ], uvular [ʁ], pharyngeal [ʕ], and glottal [ɦ].

EXERCISES

1 Practice paragraph for [ʒ]:

> Intrusions into our privacy through the usual hidden persuaders in television and radio and other advertising media are held to be an enemy invasion of one of our most basic human dignities. These seizures of our sacred privacy and leisure time are camouflaged as pleasurable visual and auditory illusions. The resulting lesions in character and erosion of the will are passed off with persiflage and evasion by the huckster who envisions the treasure and prestige resulting from the rape of the public mind.

2 Word list:

> *Terminating consonant:* beige, corsage, garage, mirage, prestige, rouge
> *Stronger consonant:* negligee, regime, Roget
> *Weaker consonant:* casual, pleasure, usual, vision
> *Final blends:* [ʒd] camouflaged, rouged

3 Minimal pairs:

> [ʒ]—[dʒ]
>
> lesion [liʒən]   legion [lidʒən]
> version [vɝʒən]   virgin [vɝdʒən]
> pleasure [plɛʒɚ]   pledger [plɛdʒɚ]

4 Phonetic transcription:

> [ɪnˈtruʒənz ɪntu aur praɪvəsɪ θru ði ˈjuʒuwəl hɪdn̩ pəˈswedɚz ɪn ˈtɛləvɪʒən ən ˈredɪo ənd ʌðɚ ˈædvɚˌtaɪzɪŋ mɪdɪə ar hɛld tə bi ən ˈɛnəmɪ ɪnˈveʒən əv wʌn əv aur most ˈbesɪk hjumən ˈdɪgnətɪz. ðiz siʒəz əv aur ˈsekrəd ˈpraɪvəsɪ ən liʒɚ taɪm ar ˈkæməˌflɑʒd əz ˈplɛʒərəbl̩ ˈvɪʒəwəl ənd ˈɔdətɔrɪ ɪˈluʒənz. ði rɪˈzʌltɪŋ liʒənz ɪn ˈkɛrɪktɚ ænd ɪˈroʒən əv ðə wɪl ar pæst ɔf wɪθ ˈpɝsəˌflɑʒ ənd iˈveʒən baɪ ðə hʌkstɚ hu ɛnˈvɪʒənz ðə treʒɚ ən prɛˈstiʒ rɪˈzʌltɪŋ frəm ðə rep əv ðə pʌblɪk maɪnd.]

[h]
HAT WHO

ANALYSIS

The [h] is generally classified as an *unvoiced laryngeal* or *glottal fricative* (or *aspirate*) consonant. It has been frequently described as a sound in which a fricative noise is generated by a glottal constriction. Such a description is appropriate for the glottal fricatives of some languages, but in English the glottal "constriction" is usually absent or very slight, with the result that glottal friction is of low power and often inaudible.[1] It therefore seems better to describe [h] as a sound which is produced by a relatively unimpeded air flow through the glottis. This flow does, of course, produce friction noise, but the glottally produced noise may be of relatively slight consequence compared with the sound produced by other constrictions in the vocal tract. Such constrictions are those which result from the articulatory positions for following speech sounds. As Kenyon (1946) puts it, "Remember that *h* always assumes the mouth shape of the following sound [p. 47]."

Perhaps the most fruitful way of thinking of about [h] is to consider it a kind of *breathed*, or *voiceless* onset of a vowel, an onset which is completely coarticulated with the vowel. For example, [hi] is a syllable in which a voiceless [i̯] is followed by a voiced [i]. [hɑ] is a syllable in which the voiceless [ɑ̯] is followed by a voiced [ɑ].

Whether or not significant noise is generated at the *glottis* in the production of [h], it is clear that there are as many different [h]'s as there are vowels. The reason for this is that the nature of any fricative sound which does accompany [h] will be determined by the vocal tract constrictions, either acting to resonate the glottally produced sound or acting to produce additional noise as a result of the closeness of the tongue or other constriction which may be present.

Another way in which [h] differs from other fricatives in English is that it has no contrastive voiced cognate. A voiced [h] has been described in most systematic phonetic treatments and is symbolized in the IPA alphabet with the symbol [ɦ] to stand for a voiced glottal fricative, which of course would have to imply both glottal aspiration and voicing being produced concomitantly. This is, as we have learned in Chapter 7, the same as a breathy voice quality.

---

[1] Heffner (1952) states that "no audible sound is produced by the air as it passes through the larynx [p. 120]." Jones (1940) says that the "air is emitted through the wide open glottis [p. 186]." Bronstein (1960) describes a "slight degree of friction [p. 94]." Wise (1957) notes that the vocal bands are "almost closed [p. 139]." Obviously [h] has been a bone of contention among phoneticians.

VARIATION

Typically in words such as "huge" [hjudʒ], for example, the fricative sound is often stronger at the tongue-palate constriction than at the glottal. In this case the palatal fricative [ç] is produced. Where [h] occurs with [u], the lip-rounding constriction may produce the allophone [ɸ], so that "who" may be transcribed as [ɸu]. In strongly backed vowels, fricatives may be heard which approximate the velar [x], the uvular [χ], or the pharyngeal [ħ].

While [h] occurs only in word-initial position, this does not imply that glottal fricative release of vowels does not also occur. It is in fact highly likely that a final *unchecked* vowel (without terminating consonant) will have some degree of aspirate release, inasmuch as voicing may stop before glottal airflow. The *phonetic* transcription of "hah" might appropriately be [hɑh] or, as the aspirate release is often written, [hɑʰ].

The [h] sound may be considerably weakened or even lost in connected speech. Initial sounds are quite commonly obliterated in conversational speech when they occur in unstressed positions in words and phrases, as in "Hello," which is often [ɛlo], or "How are you?" which may be heard as [aʊ ɑr ju]. This is not necessarily substandard. Within words *h* frequently becomes silent in unstressed positions, as in "shepherd" [ʃɛpɚd], "forehead" [fɔrəd] or [fɔrhɛd], or "vehement" [viəmənt]. The same kind of change takes place with great regularity in connected speech, particularly with the *h* pronouns. In the following examples, which represent perfectly acceptable colloquial pronunciation, a clear [h] would risk becoming overprecise: "it's to his credit" [ɪts tu ɪz krɛdət], "if he will" [ɪf i wɪl]. Pronunciation, of course, changes under the influence of stress. The sentence "I have none," if spoken as a simple declarative statement, will probably be [aɪ əv nʌn]; if, however, the meaning is "I *had*, but no longer *have*," the pronunciation is likely to be [aɪ hæv nʌn]. Note that [h] tends to remain in stressed positions, as in the words "enhance" [ɛnhæns] and "inhibit" [ɪnhɪbət].

Kenyon (1946) makes some interesting comments about the supposed tendency of those who speak certain English dialects to drop [h] from words where it might appear, as in [ɪr naʊ] for "here now," and add the sound where it should not be, as in [haɪ se] for "I say." This is not, he believes, a uniform practice, but a change which takes place haphazardly as a result of the fact that [h] is no longer a speech sound in these dialects. The tendency is to use [h] on strongly emphatic words, although this is not always done. He also notes that the common [hɪt] for [ɪt] in some Southern American speech corresponds to the pronunciation of this pronoun in earlier English.

Aside from dialect errors or failure to deal with [h] in conformity with the principles mentioned in earlier paragraphs, there are not likely to be any difficulties arising from misarticulation of the sound by native speakers. In foreign dialect the errors are somewhat more numerous. The [h] may be

omitted, as in typical French dialect, or a non-English variant may be substituted, such as the velar fricative [x] or the [ç] of German.

EXERCISES

1 Practice paragraph for [h]:

> How can the English alphabet be overhauled so as to hold a more highly
> consistent relationship to the speech it is somehow supposed to represent?
> He who has hitherto had hardly any experience with phonetics will perhaps
> have held no honest convictions on the subject. But even half-taught phone-
> ticians will usually be happy to help you out by having you hear their
> well-rehearsed plans for an overall overhaul of an alphabet which they
> consider wholly outmoded and in general behind the times. The public,
> however, is highly successful in hiding its zeal for committing any hasty
> mayhem on its ABC's and generally behaves with habitual indifference
> toward its academic hecklers, no matter how high their scholarly honors.

Initiating consonant: half, hay, he, heard, him, horse, hoe, who
Stronger consonant: ahead, ahoy, behave, behind, enhance, perhaps, rehearse,
unhook
Weak or lost consonant: forehead, mayhem, vehicle, vehement

3 Minimal pairs:

[h]—without [h]		[h]—[f]	
had [hæd]	add [æd]	had [hæd]	fad [fæd]
hair [hɛr]	air [ɛr]	hair [hɛr]	fair [fɛr]
hand [hænd]	and [ænd]	hat [hæt]	fat [fæt]
has [hæz]	as [æz]	head [hɛd]	fed [fɛd]
hat [hæt]	at [æt]	he [hi]	fee [fi]
her [hɝ]	err [ɝ]	her [hɝ]	fur [fɝ]
here [hɪr]	ear [ɪr]	here [hɪr]	fear [fɪr]
his [hɪz]	is [ɪz]	hill [hɪl]	fill [fɪl]
high [haɪ]	eye [aɪ]	hit [hɪt]	fit [fɪt]
hold [hold]	old [old]	hold [hold]	fold [fold]

[h]—[s]		[h]—[θ]	
had [hæd]	sad [sæd]	Hank [hæŋk]	thank [θæŋk]
halt [hɔlt]	salt [sɔlt]	hatch [hætʃ]	thatch [θætʃ]
hand [hænd]	sand [sænd]	heard [hɝd]	third [θɝd]
hat [hæt]	sat [sæt]	hermit [hɝmət]	Thermit [θɝmət]
he [hi]	see [si]	hick [hɪk]	thick [θɪk]
head [hɛd]	said [sɛd]	high [haɪ]	thigh [θaɪ]
her [hɝ]	sir [sɝ]	hill [hɪl]	thill [θɪl]

[h]—without [h]		[h]—[f]	
high [haɪ]	sigh [saɪ]	Hong [hɔŋ]	thong [θɔŋ]
hold [hold]	sold [sold]	horn [hɔrn]	thorn [θɔrn]
hope [hop]	soap [sop]	hump [hʌmp]	thump [θʌmp]

4 Phonetic transcription:

[hau kən ði ˈɪŋglɪʃ ˈælfəbɛt bi ˌovəˈhold so æz tə hold ə mɔr haɪlɪ kənsɪstənt
rɪˈleʃənʃɪp tə ðə spitʃ ɪt ɪz ˈsʌmˌhau səpozd tə ˌrɛprɪˈzɛnt? hi hu həz ˈhɪðətu
hæd hɑrdlɪ ɛnɪ ɛkˈspɪrɪəns wɪθ fəˈnɛtɪks wɪl pəhæps həv hɛld no ɑnəst
kənˈvɪkʃənz ɔn ðə sʌbdʒɪkt. bʌt ivən hæf tɔt ˌfonəˈtɪʃənz wɪl ˈjuʒuəlɪ bi hæpɪ
tə hɛlp ju aut baɪ hævɪŋ ju hɪr ðɛr wɛl rɪˈhɝst plænz fɔr ən ˈovəɔl ˈovəˌhɔl
əv ən ˈælfəbɛt hwɪtʃ ðe kənsɪdə holɪ ˌautˈmodəd ænd ɪn dʒɛnərəl bɪˈhaɪnd
ðə taɪmz. ðə ˈpʌblɪk, hauɛvə, ɪz haɪlɪ səkˈsɛsfəl ɪn ˈhaɪdɪŋ ɪts zil fɔr kəˈmɪtɪŋ
ɛnɪ hɛstɪ ˈmɛhɛm ɔn ɪts ˈeˈbiˈsiz æn dʒɛnərəlɪ bihevz wɪθ həˈbɪtʃuwəl ɪnˈdɪfrəns
tɔrd ɪts ˌækəˈdɛmɪk hɛkləz, no mætə hau haɪ ðɛr ˈskɑləlɪ ɑnəz.]

Chapter 15

Nasals and Lateral

[m], [n], [ŋ], [l]

[m]
ME COMMENT CALM LIMB PHLEGM HYMN

ANALYSIS

The [m] is classed as a *voiced labial* (or *bilabial*) *nasal*. It is also *noncoronal*, *anterior*, and *sonorant* in distinctive feature terminology. In making a standard English [m] the lips are closed and the breath stream is emitted through a resonance system which includes both oral and nasopharyngeal resonators. The tongue position has little significant effect on [m], tending to take the position of the preceding or following vowel (see Fig. 5-4).

[m] is one of three English nasals, the others being [n] and [ŋ]. The nasal quality for all three is imparted to the tone as a result of relaxing, or otherwise lowering the soft palate. This action serves to couple the nasopharynx to the oropharynx, thereby producing the typical sound of nasality (see Chapters 4 and 5). This coupling action through the velopharyngeal aperture gives rise to the terminology *secondary aperture*, sometimes applied to the nasals and the lateral.

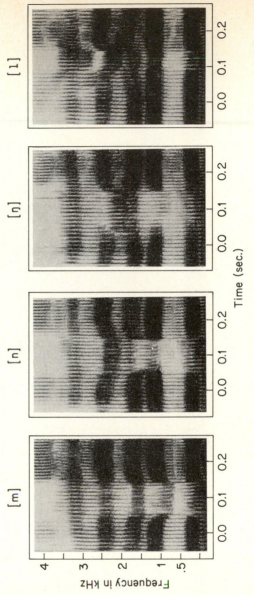

Figure 15-1   Sound spectrogram of [m], [n], [ŋ], and [l].

The function of the nasopharynx vis-à-vis the nasal passages themselves is sometimes misunderstood. It is the *nasopharynx* which is the primary resonator involved. Because of their constricted and convoluted shape, the *nasal cavities* themselves act primarily to dampen the resonance system.

An important characteristic of velar action is its relative sluggishness. The result of this sluggishness is that the normal nasal resonance of [m], [n], and [ŋ] may in many cases be assimilated by surrounding vowels.

VARIATION

Like other nasals and the lateral, the [m] is often syllabic as well as non-syllabic, in which case the symbol [m̩] is used in phonetic transcription. A ready example is the common conversational pronunciation of the phrase "keep them" as [kipm̩]. The tendency to reduce the schwa plus [m] or [n]

the syllabic [m̩] is extremely common following bilabial stops. Examples

kʌpm̩sɔsɚ] for "cup and saucer" and [opm̩ʌp] for "open up." These

mples of informal, but not necessarily substandard, speech.

nglish there is little variation among the sounds in this class. Rarely

fail to learn and use [m] appropriately, perhaps because of the

licity of the articulatory adjustment. Persons with a foreign

ground likewise experience little trouble with the sound.

or shortening of [m] may deprive speech of a certain sonority,

ach a critical point in the speech of most physically normal

uld be any pathological condition which tends to block

nasal pharynx (hypertrophied tonsils or adenoids, for

a lack of adequate nasal resonance, may be a con-

ad cold can give the same results.

an articulation defect rather than a change of

owel sounds in English are normally nonnasal

in the sense of any abnormality of resonance.

, denasality will result in the radical change

consonants. Inability to open the velo-

nasal to its homorganic stop: [m] will

] will become [g]. The sentence "Some

ld be transmuted into [sʌb bɛd bek

s spreads to adjacent sounds, the

his occurs to a degree wherever

remely common. One almos

pearing between two nas

"moon."

constitutes a seriou

stamp;
m, storm

æs]
[kʌnɪŋ]
[fonɪ]
on]
[nil]
[nɪt]
nɛt]
t [naɪt]
[ræn]
n [sʌn]

EXERCISES

1 Practice paragraph for [m]:

H. L. Mencken was a man whose journalistic writings never are damned with faint praise. Readers tend either to sing high hymns of admiration and deem him one of the immortal wits or else they condemn him as monstrous and wish the Lord would have struck him dumb. Among English scholars he commands immense respect for his volume *The American Language*, which is really a monumental commentary on American usage. For many years a newspaper reporter in a clamourous political age, he maintained a keen interest in oratory. He had great admiration for William Jennings Bryan, in a sort of reverse English manner, and took delight in the Great Commoner's "immortal declaration that man is not a mammal." He has this to say of him: "The average impromptu speech taken down by a stenographer, is found to be a bedlam of puerile cliches, thumping nonsequiturs and limping, unfinished sentences. But Jennings emitted English that was clear, flowing and sometimes not a little elegant, in the best sense of the word. Every sentence had a beginning, a middle and an end. The argument, three times out of four, was idiotic, but at least it hung together."

2 Word list:

Initiating consonant: may, me, moo, my
Terminating consonant: aim, am, arm, him
Initiating and terminating: maim, mam, Maugham, mom
Stronger consonant: admire, amass, commence, remit
Weaker consonant: coming, hamlet, rumor, stammer
Initial Blends: [sm] smell, smoke
Final blends: [mz] comes, tombs; [md] blamed, bombed; [mp] lump
        [mps] stamps, thumps; [mpt] clamped, stamped; [rm] a

3 Minimal pairs:

[m]—[b]		[m]—[n]	
bomb [bɑm]	bob [bɑb]	a mass [əmæs]	an ass [ə
mat [mæt]	bat [bæt]	coming [kʌmɪŋ]	cunning
may [me]	bay [be]	foamy [fomɪ]	phoney
meet [mit]	beat [bit]	home [hom]	hone
met [mɛt]	bet [bɛt]	meal [mil]	kneel
might [maɪt]	bight [baɪt]	meat [mit]	neat
moss [mɔs]	boss [bɔs]	met [mɛt]	net
must [mʌst]	bust [bʌst]	might [maɪt]	nig
ım [rʌm]	rub [rʌb]	ram [ræm]	ra
ne [sʌm]	sub [sʌb]	some [sʌm]	sʏ

The function of the nasopharynx vis-à-vis the nasal passages themselves is sometimes misunderstood. It is the *nasopharynx* which is the primary resonator involved. Because of their constricted and convoluted shape, the *nasal cavities* themselves act primarily to dampen the resonance system.

An important characteristic of velar action is its relative sluggishness. The result of this sluggishness is that the normal nasal resonance of [m], [n], and [ŋ] may in many cases be assimilated by surrounding vowels.

VARIATION

Like other nasals and the lateral, the [m] is often syllabic as well as non-syllabic, in which case the symbol [m̩] is used in phonetic transcription. A ready example is the common conversational pronunciation of the phrase "keep them" as [kipm̩]. The tendency to reduce the schwa plus [m] or [n] to the syllabic [m̩] is extremely common following bilabial stops. Examples are [kʌpm̩sɔsɚ] for "cup and saucer" and [opm̩ʌp] for "open up." These are examples of informal, but not necessarily substandard, speech.

In English there is little variation among the sounds in this class. Rarely do children fail to learn and use [m] appropriately, perhaps because of the relative simplicity of the articulatory adjustment. Persons with a foreign language background likewise experience little trouble with the sound.

Weakening or shortening of [m] may deprive speech of a certain sonority, but this does not reach a critical point in the speech of most physically normal persons. If there should be any pathological condition which tends to block the opening into the nasal pharynx (hypertrophied tonsils or adenoids, for example), *denasality*, or a lack of adequate nasal resonance, may be a consequence. A full-blown head cold can give the same results.

Denasality is ordinarily an articulation defect rather than a change of voice quality. By definition, vowel sounds in English are normally nonnasal and cannot therefore be denasal in the sense of any abnormality of resonance. As an articulation defect, however, denasality will result in the radical change of all nasals from sonorant to stop consonants. Inability to open the velopharyngeal valve will change each nasal to its homorganic stop: [m] will become [b], [n] will become [d], and [ŋ] will become [g]. The sentence "Some men make new songs for a living" would be transmuted into [sʌb bɛd bek du sɔgz fɔr ə lɪvɪg].

When resonance from one of the nasals spreads to adjacent sounds, the phenomenon is called *assimilation nasality*. This occurs to a degree wherever a nasal is found. In American English it is extremely common. One almost always hears a nasal allophone of any vowel appearing between two nasal consonants, as in [mæn] and [mũn] for "man" and "moon."

Dentalized [m̪] is often encountered but seldom constitutes a serious or even noticeable change.

EXERCISES

1   Practice paragraph for [m]:

H. L. Mencken was a man whose journalistic writings never are damned
with faint praise. Readers tend either to sing high hymns of admiration
and deem him one of the immortal wits or else they condemn him as monstrous and wish the Lord would have struck him dumb. Among English
scholars he commands immense respect for his volume *The American Language*, which is really a monumental commentary on American usage. For
many years a newspaper reporter in a clamourous political age, he maintained a keen interest in oratory. He had great admiration for William
Jennings Bryan, in a sort of reverse English manner, and took delight in the
Great Commoner's "immortal declaration that man is not a mammal."
He has this to say of him: "The average impromptu speech taken down by
a stenographer, is found to be a bedlam of puerile cliches, thumping nonsequiturs and limping, unfinished sentences. But Jennings emitted English
that was clear, flowing and sometimes not a little elegant, in the best
sense of the word. Every sentence had a beginning, a middle and an end.
The argument, three times out of four, was idiotic, but at least it hung
together."

2   Word list:

Initiating consonant: may, me, moo, my
Terminating consonant: aim, am, arm, him
Initiating and terminating: maim, mam, Maugham, mom
Stronger consonant: admire, amass, commence, remit
Weaker consonant: coming, hamlet, rumor, stammer
Initial Blends: [sm] smell, smoke
Final blends: [mz] comes, tombs; [md] blamed, bombed; [mp] lump, stamp;
            [mps] stamps, thumps; [mpt] clamped, stamped; [rm] arm, storm

3   Minimal pairs:

[m]—[b]		[m]—[n]	
bomb [bɑm]	bob [bɑb]	a mass [əmæs]	an ass [ənæs]
mat [mæt]	bat [bæt]	coming [kʌmɪŋ]	cunning [kʌnɪŋ]
may [me]	bay [be]	foamy [fomɪ]	phoney [fonɪ]
meet [mit]	beat [bit]	home [hom]	hone [hon]
met [mɛt]	bet [bɛt]	meal [mil]	kneel [nil]
might [maɪt]	bight [baɪt]	meat [mit]	neat [nit]
moss [mɔs]	boss [bɔs]	met [mɛt]	net [nɛt]
must [mʌst]	bust [bʌst]	might [maɪt]	night [naɪt]
rum [rʌm]	rub [rʌb]	ram [ræm]	ran [ræn]
some [sʌm]	sub [sʌb]	some [sʌm]	sun [sʌn]

[m]—[ŋ]

bomb [bɑm]	bong [bɑŋ]
dim [dɪm]	ding [dɪŋ]
gum [gʌm]	gung [gʌŋ]
hum [hʌm]	hung [hʌŋ]
ram [ræm]	rang [ræŋ]
rim [rɪm]	ring [rɪŋ]
rum [rʌm]	rung [rʌŋ]
Sam [sæm]	sang [sæŋ]
slam [slæm]	slang [slæŋ]
some [sʌm]	sung [sʌŋ]

Phonetic transcription:

[etʃ ɛl mɛŋkən wəz ə mæn huz ˌdʒɜːnəˈlɪstɪk ˈraɪtɪŋz nɛvɚ ɑr dæmd wɪð fent
prez. rɪdɚz tɛnd ɪðɚ tə sɪŋ haɪ hɪmz əv ˌædməˈreʃən ən dim ɪm wʌn əv ði
ɪˈmɔrtəl wɪts ɔr ɛls ðe kənˈdɛm ɪm əz ˈmʌnstrəs ən wɪʃ ðə lɔrd wud əv strʌk
ɪm dʌm. əmʌŋ ˈɪŋglɪʃ skaləz hi kəˈmændz əmɛns rɪˈspɛkt fɚ ɪz valjəm, ði
əˈmɛrəkən ˈlæŋgwɪdʒ, hwɪtʃ ɪz rili ə ˈmʌnjəˌmɛntḷ ˈkʌmənteri ɔn əˈmɛrəkən
ˈjusɪdʒ. fɔr mɛni jɪrz ə ˈnuzpepɚ rɪˈpɔrtɚ ɪn ə ˈklæmərəs ˈpəlitɪkḷ edʒ, hi
ˈmentend ə kin ɪntrəst ɪn ˈɔrətɔri. hi hæd ə gret ædməˈreʃən fɚ ˈwɪljəm
ˈdʒɛnɪŋz braɪən, ɪn ə sɔrt əv rɪˈvɜːs ˈɪŋglɪʃ mænɚ, ən tʊk dɪˈlaɪt ɪn ðə gret
ˈkʌmənəz ˈɪmɔrtḷ dɛkləˈreʃən ðət mæn ɪz nɑt ə ˈmæməl. hi hæz ðɪs tə se əv
ɪm: ði ˈævrɪdʒ ˌɪmˈprɑmtu spɪtʃ, tekən daʊn baɪ ə stəˈnɔgrəfɚ, ɪz faʊnd tə
bi ə ˈbɛdləm əv pjʊrəl kliˈʃez, θʌmpɪŋ nɑn ˈsɛkwətəz ən ˈlɪmpɪŋ ʌnˌfɪnɪʃt
ˈsɛntṇsəz. bət ˈdʒɛnɪŋz iˈmɪtəd ˈɪŋglɪʃ ðət wəz klɪr, ˈflowɪŋ ən ˈsʌmˌtaɪmz nɑt
ə lɪtḷ ˈɛləgənt, ɪn ðə bɛst sɛns əv ðə wɜːd. ɛvrɪ ˈsɛntṇs hæd ə bɪˈgɪnɪŋ, ə mɪdḷ
ænd ən ɛnd. ði ˈɑrgjəmənt, θri taɪmz aʊt əv fɔr, wəz ɪdiatɪk, bət ət lɪst ɪt
hʌŋ təˈgɛðɚ.]

[n]
NO A*NN*OY *GN*AT *KN*OW *PN*EUMONIA *MN*EMONIC

ANALYSIS

The [n] is classified as a *voiced alveolar nasal*. It is also *coronal, anterior,* and
sonorant. To make this sound, the tip and blade of the tongue are placed on
the alveolar ridge, with the sides of the tongue in contact with the upper
teeth and gums. The soft palate is relaxed. With the tongue and palate in this
position the voiced (or sometimes whispered) breath stream is resonated in
the nasal pharynx as well as in the oral and pharyngeal cavities. The basic
tongue adjustment corresponds to that for the plosives [t] and [d]. For further
information on [n] as a secondary aperture sound, and the importance of
nasal resonance see Chapters 4, 5, and 8, and Fig. 5-4.

VARIATION

The [n] is another of the consonants which can become syllabic, and it does so more often than either [m] or [l]. The syllabic sound is transcribed [n̩]. Examples are the usual pronunciations of such words as "fasten" [fæsn̩], "cotton," [katn̩], and "written" [rɪtn̩]. Because the nasal vowel may be initiated with a glottal attack in some contexts, it may sometimes be more accurate to transcribe these words as [kaʔn̩] and [rɪtʔn̩]. A syllabic [n̩] pronunciation for the word "and" is fully standard in contexts where "and" follows an alveolar obstruent in conversational speech. The phrases "pot and pan" [patn̩pæn] and "Pat and Mike" [pætn̩maɪk] illustrate the point.

There is considerable assimilative variation among sounds in the /n/ class. For instance the [n] in "knee" may be more forward (perhaps dentalized to [n̪]) than the sound in "gnaw," because of the influence of adjacent vowels.

Another assimilative change merits a word of comment. When followed by a velar [k] or [g], the [n] may be replaced by [ŋ] in a way that sometimes is and sometimes is not standard. Assimilations of this sort which are now sanctioned include "conquer" [kaŋkɚ], "ink" [ɪŋk], and many other *nk* words. On the other hand, [ɪŋkʌm] for "income" and [ɪŋkwɛst] for "inquest" may not be accepted as standard in any but rapid informal speech.

Notice also the curious phenomenon which occurs when [n] precedes or follows a bilabial [p] or [b]. A phrase such as "on purpose" may often be [əmpɝpəs], "open" may be pronounced [opm̩], and "grandpa" may be [græmpa]—and so on. This change from [n] to [m] is nonstandard in theory, but it happens so regularly that most of these usages must be accepted.

Other variants of /n/ may be the voiceless or fricative nasal [n̥] or glottalized [ʔn̩] of the cleft palate speaker. Retroflexed [ɳ] may also be heard in dialectal speech and as allophones of /n/ in English. The [ɲ] is the palatal pronunciation of Spanish [maɲanə], often pronounced by speakers of English as [manjanə]. The comments on denasality, made in the previous section, apply also to [n].

EXERCISES

1   Practice paragraph for [n]:

> Fortunately for the peace of mind of many of us, current fads and fancies in teen-age talk are certain to change eventually, after the manner of all fashions. Since time has kindly drawn a mantle over our own postadolescent diction, our inclination is to maintain it could never have held a candle to the zany slang, for instance, of the hot rodder. This machine, of course, is a stripped-down car. An innocent appearing hot rod is a sleeper. Whitewall tires are snowballs. Hubcaps are spinners, a double ignition system is

known as a flame thrower, chrome ornaments are goodies, and the engine is the mill. Should some mechanical breakdown happen which the genius behind the wheel cannot identify, he solemnly and knowingly explains, "The Johnson rod broke," and all other informed passengers understand what he means. Should they chance to stop for a snack, pancakes are collision mats. A profound thinker has static in his attic, while a maiden who is chronically dizzy is a mixed chick. A dance is a drag, but this also is the name for a kind of nonsensical and insane race. And so on, ad infinitum. We are inclined to say, "Twenty-three skiddoo!"

2   Word list:

Initiating consonant: gnaw, knee, nay, no
Terminating consonant: an, earn, in, on
Initiating and terminating: known, nine, non-, none
Stronger consonant: annoy, canoe, enough, renew
Weaker consonant: any, banner, earning, many
Syllabic consonant: button, cotton, fatten, hat 'n coat
Initial blends: [sn] sneeze, snow
Final blends: [nz] bones, hens; [nd] burned, ground; [nt] bent, count; [nts] or
            [ns] once, rents; [ntʃ] bunch, ranch; [ntʃt] or [nʃt] benched,
            wrenched; [ndʒ] mange, orange; [rn] barn, torn; [ndʒd] or [nʒd]
            hinged, ranged; [nst] or [ntst] bounced, fenced

3   Minimal pairs:

[n]—[d]		[n]—[m]	
can [kæn]	cad [kæd]	can [kæn]	cam [kæm]
kneel [nil]	deal [dil]	gain [gen]	game [gem]
man [mæn]	mad [mæd]	gun [gʌn]	gum [gʌm]
near [nɪr]	dear [dɪr]	near [nɪr]	mere [mɪr]
nearly [nɪrlɪ]	dearly [dɪrlɪ]	neigh [ne]	may [me]
neigh [ne]	day [de]	nice [naɪs]	mice [maɪs]
net [nɛt]	debt [dɛt]	nicks [nɪks]	mix [mɪks]
nice [naɪs]	dice [daɪs]	no [no]	mow [mo]
no [no]	dough [do]	Norman [nɔrmən]	Mormon [mɔrmən]
pan [pæn]	pad [pæd]	sane [sen]	same [sem]

[n]—[ŋ]	
ban [bæn]	bang [bæŋ]
bun [bʌn]	bung [bʌŋ]
pan [pæn]	pang [pæŋ]
ran [ræn]	rang [ræŋ]
run [rʌn]	rung [rʌŋ]
sinner [sɪnɚ]	singer [sɪŋɚ]
tan [tæn]	tang [tæŋ]
thin [θɪn]	thing [θɪŋ]

ton [tʌn]   tongue [tʌŋ]
win [wɪn]   wing [wɪŋ]

4 Phonetic transcription:

[ˈfɔrtʃənətlɪ fɚ ðə pis əv maɪnd əv mɛnɪ əv əs, ˈkʌrənt fædz ən ˈfænsɪz ɪn tin
edʒ tɔk ɑr sɝtn̩ tə tʃendʒ iˈvɛntʃuəlɪ, æftɚ ðə mænɚ əv ɔl fæʃənz. sɪns taɪm
həz kaɪndlɪ drɔn ə mæntl̩ ovɚ aur on postædəˈlɛsənt ˈdɪkʃən, aur ɪnklənˈeʃən
ɪz tə ˌmɛnˈten ɪt kəd nɛvɚ həv hɛld ə kændl̩ tə ðə ˈzɛnɪ slæŋ, fɚ ˈɪnstəns, əv
ðə hɑt radɚ. ðɪs məˈʃin, əv kɔrs, ɪz ə strɪpt daun kɑr. ən ˈɪnəsənt əˈpɪrɪŋ hɑt
rad ɪz ə slɪpɚ. hwaɪt wɔl taɪrz ɑr ˈsnoˌbɔlz. hʌbkæps ɑr spɪnɚz; ə dʌbl̩
ɪgˈnɪʃən sɪstəm ɪz non əz ə flɛm θroɚ; krom ˈɔrnəmənts ɑr ˈgudɪz, ən ði
ɛndʒən ɪz ðə mɪl. ʃud sʌm məˈkænɪkl̩ ˈbrekˌdaun hæpən hwɪtʃ ðə ˈdʒinjəs
bɪˈhaɪnd ðə hwil kəˈnɑt aɪˈdɛntəfaɪ, hi ˈsaləmli ən ˈnowɪŋli ɪkˈsplɛnz, ðə
ˈdʒʌnsən rad brok, ənd ɔl ʌðɚ ɪnˈfɔrmd ˈpæsəndʒɚz ʌndɚˈstænd hwʌt i
mɪnz. ʃud ðe tʃænts tə stap fɚ ə snæk, ˈpænkeks ɑr kəˈliʒən mæts. ə prəˈ-
faund ˈθɪŋkɚ hæz ˈstætɪk ɪn ɪz ˈætɪk, hwaɪl ə medn̩ hu əz ˈkrɑnɪklɪ ˈdɪzɪ ɪz ə
mɪkst tʃɪk. ə dæns ɪz ə dræg, bət ðɪs ɔlso əz ðə nem fɚ ə kaɪnd əv ˌnɑnˈsɛnsɪkl̩
ənd ɪnˈsen res. ən sowɔn, æd ˌɪnfənˈaɪtəm. wi ɑr ɪnˈklaɪnd tə se, ˈtwɛntɪ θri
skɪˈdu!]

[ŋ]
THI*N*K BRI*NG*

ANALYSIS

The [ŋ] is classified as a *voiced linguavelar nasal*, and as a *high*, *back*, *non-coronal sonorant*. To make this sound, the tongue body is brought into contact with the lowered soft palate. With the tongue in this position, the breath stream is emitted through the nose, having been resonated primarily in the pharyngeal cavities, including the nasopharynx. Little oral cavity resonance is possible, for the tongue position, which is roughly that for [k] and [g] (see Fig. 5-4), blocks off most if not all of the oral cavity.

VARIATION

The existence of the [ŋ] sound is curiously unrecognized by most persons who speak English, even though they may use it uncounted times a day. The reason is obvious, of course. There is no letter of our alphabet which unambiguously symbolizes this sound. The digraph *ng* often stands for [ŋ], of course, but not consistently, as testified by such words as "finger," where it stands for [ŋg], "vangard," where it is pronounced [ng], and "singer," where the digraph is pronounced [ŋ]. It is obvious that in some combinations [ŋ] is a velarized allophone of /n/, and its status as a distinctive sound goes unnoticed. In this regard, notice that [ŋ] is never found in an initial position in a word.

From the above one can understand why spelling-pronunciation inconsistencies of *ng* sometimes cause confusion. The historically older [ŋg] pronunciation has been retained in some words, such as "jungle" [dʒʌŋgl], but it has been dropped at the end of most words, and within some. This has led to [rɪŋ] for "ring" and [sæŋ] for "sang," and so on. When followed by [k] or [g] the letter *n* is, as we have said, usually [ŋ]. More literal spelling pronunciations, such as [θɪnk] for "think" and [fɪngɚ] for "finger" tend to sound stilted and pedantic on the very rare occasions where they are heard. There is, unfortunately, no simple rule of spelling for the student to apply in determining when to choose any one of the three possible pronunciations for the *ng*: [ŋ], [ŋg] or [ng].

The physiological explanation for the tendency of [n] to become [ŋ] before velar sounds is a simple one. [ŋ] is a tongue-body consonant; that is, it uses the same part of the tongue which is used to form [k], [g], and the vowels. We would therefore expect considerable coarticulation among these sounds, with the assimilation of features of one to the others.

Foreign dialect errors are not frequent, although they are occasionally noted. In a few dialects (Yiddish for example) final [ŋ] may have an added stop—as in the pronunciation of [goɪŋk] for "going." Nasals resembling [n] are sometimes carried into English from another language, or may be heard as more or less rare allophones of /ŋ/. A fronted, or palatized, [ɲ] or a uvular [N] are not standard in English, but may be heard as variants. The previous discussion of inadequate nasal resonance (see [m]) applies also to [ŋ].

EXERCISES

1 Practice paragraph for [ŋ]:

> Thanks to an astonishing brain mechanism, talking is a singularly unconscious form of behavior. We can keep on expressing ideas without much searching for words; they spring forth with surprisingly little conscious thought. Incoming words are understood, although fleetingly heard. Had not speech increased in keeping with other forms of behavior the brain would look much different, for man's imposing frontal development serves the language function. In contrast, the sloping forehead of the ape is that of a species without linguistic capacity. Brain injury carries a danger to speech, and there is distinct reason to be anxious in such a situation. As the understanding of brain function increases, added knowledge may bring hope for those with such defects.

2 Word list:

Terminating consonant: long, rang, ring, wrong
Weaker consonant: hanger, longing, ringing, singer
[ŋg] *words:* English, finger, longer, single
[ŋk] *words:* blanket, conquer, sink, thank
[nk] *and* [ng] *words:* income, ingrate, inquest, vanguard
Other blends: [ŋks] honks, thinks; [ŋz] things, wrongs; [ŋkt] junked, thanked;
              [ŋd] hanged, wronged

3 Minimal pairs

[ŋ]—[g]		[ŋ]—[n]	
banger [bæŋɚ]	bagger [bægɚ]	banger [bæŋɚ]	banner [bænɚ]
ding [dɪŋ]	dig [dɪg]	clang [klæŋ]	clan [klæn]
dung [dʌŋ]	dug [dʌg]	ding [dɪŋ]	din [dɪn]
Hong [hɔŋ]	hog [hɔg]	gong [gɔŋ]	gone [gɔn]
hung [hʌŋ]	hug [hʌg]	gung [gʌŋ]	gun [gʌn]
long [lɔŋ]	log [lɔg]	hung [hʌŋ]	Hun [hʌn]
ping [pɪŋ]	pig [pɪg]	king [kɪŋ]	kin [kɪn]
ring [rɪŋ]	rig [rɪg]	ping [pɪŋ]	pin [pɪn]
tongue [tʌŋ]	tug [tʌg]	sing [sɪŋ]	sin [sɪn]
wringing [rɪŋɪŋ]	rigging [rɪgɪŋ]	sung [sʌŋ]	sun [sʌn]

[ŋ]—[ŋk]	
clang [klæŋ]	clank [klæŋk]
dingy [dɪŋɪ]	dinky [dɪŋkɪ]
dung [dʌŋ]	dunk [dʌŋk]
Hong [hɔŋ]	honk [hɔŋk]
hung [hʌŋ]	hunk [hʌŋk]
ring [rɪŋ]	rink [rɪŋk]
sing [sɪŋ]	sink [sɪŋk]
singer [sɪŋɚ]	sinker [sɪŋkɚ]
slung [slʌŋ]	slunk [slʌŋk]
sung [sʌŋ]	sunk [sʌŋk]

4 Phonetic transcription:

[ðæŋks tu ən əˈstanɪʃɪŋ bren ˈmɛkənɪzm̩, ˈtɔkɪŋ ɪz ə ˈsɪŋgjulɚlɪ, ʌnˈkantʃəs
fɔrm əv bɪˈhevjɚ. wi kən kip ən ɛkˈsprɛsɪŋ aɪˈdɪəz wɪˈðaut mʌtʃ ˈsɝtʃɪŋ fɚ
wɝdz; ðe sprɪŋ fɔrθ wɪθ sɚˈpraɪzɪŋlɪ lɪtl̩ kanʃəs θɔt. ˈɪnkʌmɪŋ wɝdz ar ʌndɚ
stud, ɔlðo ˈflitɪŋlɪ hɝd. hæd nat spitʃ ɪnˈkrist ɪn ˈkipɪŋ wɪθ ʌðɚ fɔrmz əv
bɪˈhevjɚ ðə bren wəd luk mʌtʃ dɪfrənt, fɔr mænz ɪmˈpozɪŋ frʌntl̩ dɪˈvɛləp-
mənt sɝvz ðə ˈlæŋgwɪdʒ ˈfʌŋkʃən. ɪn ˈkantræst, ðə ˈslopɪŋ fɔrəd əv ði ep ɪz
ðæt əv ə ˈspiʃiz wɪˈðaut lɪŋˈgwɪstɪk kəˈpæsətɪ. bren ˈɪndʒərɪ ˈkɛrɪz ə dendʒɚ
tə spitʃ, ənd ðɛr ɪz dɪˈstɪŋkt rizən tə bi ˈæŋkʃəs ɪn sʌtʃ ə ˌsɪtʃəˈweʃən. æz ði
ʌndɚˈstændɪŋ əv bren ˈfʌŋkʃən ɪnˈkrisəz, ædəd ˈnɑlɪdʒ me brɪŋ hop fɚ ðoz
wɪθ sʌtʃ dɪˈfɛkts.]

[l]
LOOK   WILL

ANALYSIS

The [l] is classified as a *voiced lingua-alveolar lateral*, and as *anterior, coronal*, and *sonorant*. The standard target position is described as tonguetip against alveolar ridge, with the tongue adjusted so that its margins do not touch the teeth and palate at the sides. With the tongue held in this position, lateral *secondary apertures* are created in the oral cavity which have a strong influence upon the resonance pattern of this sonorant. It is normally nonnasal. The [l] has sometimes been called a glide, but as a comparison of the voiceprints of Figures 15-1 and 16-1 will show, [l] is dynamically more like the nasals than the glides (see also Figure 5-4).

VARIATION

Although [l] usually fulfills the function of a consonant by initiating or terminating a syllable (and in this role is *nonsyllabic*), there are phonetic circumstances in which it serves as a separate syllable, and hence becomes *syllabic*. When this occurs, the proper symbol is [l̩]. Examples include "wrestle" [rɛsl̩], "camel" [kæml̩], and "fatal" [fetl̩]. Such words need not be spoken with a syllabic [l̩] ([əl] may also be heard), but in common patterns of American speech the [l̩] is probably more frequent than [əl] in such contexts.

A number of different variants within the class of [l] sounds can be heard in American speech, inasmuch as preceding and following sounds exert a strong influence on [l], and there is considerable dialectal and idiosyncratic variation in the pronunciation of this sound. In words like "lip" [lɪp] and "fling" [flɪŋ], and others where [l] is influenced by front tongue placement, the tongue is forward on the alveolar ridge. It may even be dental or *gingival* (at the junction of the gums and teeth). When a back vowel follows, as in "law" [lɔ], "look" [lʊk], and "load" [lod], or precedes, as in "awl" [ɔl], the contact is often much further back. A voiceless [l̥] is standard following voiceless stops in English. [kl̥ɪp] and [pl̥et] for "clip" and "plate" are the expected forms.

It is not only in terms of the apex position that the tongue shape may vary, but in tongue-body position as well. The forward tongue-body position gives a lighter or [ɪ]-like quality to [l], while a retracted tongue body gives a more [ʊ]-like, or darker quality. The *light* [l] is perhaps more typical of German than is the *dark*. American English in quite variable with respect to light and dark [l], although an overdark [ɫ] is nonstandard in many contexts.

In American English a type of palatal glide [ʎ] may be found in contexts where [l] is followed by [j], as in "million" and "William." Often, however, the sound will become [j], so that "million" becomes [mɪjən] and "William" becomes [wɪjəm]. This is a nonstandard usage, viewed by some speech clinicians as in the "defect" category.

Still another nonstandard variant is the labialized [l̫], a sound which comes close to [w] perceptually. The result is that such a word as "yellow" [jɛlo] may become phonetically indistinguishable from [jɛwo]. Because of the strong association of such labialized, overdark, or glide variants with the typical patterns of infantile speech, they represent a considerable speech handicap in the speech of an adult.

In children the [l] may often appear to be missing entirely, and they may say [ɪto] for "little" and [aɪk] for "like." Also, various vowels, principally the [ʊ], [ʌ], [ɛ], [o], and [ə], may be substituted for a final [l] by children. [jɪtʌ] for "little" is a reasonably typical example. The general term *lalling* is sometimes applied to failure to make a standard [l].

It is frequently the case, even in adult speech, that the lateral will be nonstandard as a syllabic or a final off-glide, even where the initial [l] is reasonably accurate. This may be understandable if you will note how much the dark [ɫ] resembles the [ʊ] when each is produced as a sung vowel. [bɑtʊ] is not so very different from [bɑtl̩], although [ʊɛt] is perceptually very different from [lɛt]. Nevertheless, the glide or back-vowel substitution for any [l] is usually perceived as a dialectal variant or speech defect by most American listeners.

We now summarize some of the above and add a few of the more important modifications of this highly variable class of speech sounds:

[l̪]   Dental [l], usually of a "brighter" quality.
[l]   Alveolar [l], variable in English, but perhaps less "clear" or "bright" than the [ɪ]-ish light [l] of German.
[ɫ]   Dark [l], with typical back-vowel coloring. More [ʊ]-like.
[ɬ]   This symbol is used to stand for the voiceless lateral fricative heard in Welsh. Also marked [l̥].
[l̫]   Labialized or lip-rounded.
[ɭ]   Retroflexed (palatalized).
[ʎ]   Palatal glide variant. May be heard in English in some [lj] contexts.
[ɺ]   A sound between [l] and [r] in Japanese, for example. Also may be symbolized as [rl]. To the American ear a Japanese speaker seems to substitute [r] for [l] and vice versa.

EXERCISES

1   Practice paragraph for [l]

One of the lesser and more useless literary diversions to while away a dull hour is compiling a list of the most beautiful words in the English language.

This was popular as a pastime several years ago, culminating in a poll of a number of leading authors. Although our own favorite all-time choice is Camay, words with a liberal sprinkling of *l* sounds walked off with the honors. Among the nominations were such mellifluous sound melodies as "Lillian," "Laura," "lingering," "yellow," "mellow," "low," "ulnar," and even "tintinnabulation," the latter doubtless brought to mind by Edgar Allen Poe's "tintinnabulation of the bells, bells, bells." It is hard to say why these liquid notes are so pleasing to the sensibilities of these literary folk; the gentle murmur of *m* sends us much faster. We recall also that Sinclair Lewis described the mock melodiousness of one of his female characters with something like "her *l*'s were like the trilling of thrushes."

2　Word list:

Initiating consonant: lay, lee, lie, low
Terminating consonant: ale, awl, earl, eel
Initiating and terminating: Lill, loll, Lowell, lull
Sronger consonant: alarm, asleep, hello, rely
Weaker consonant: ability, careless, pulling, solid
Syllabic consonant: battle, bottle, gable, saddle
Initial blends: [kl] claim, cloth; [sl] slick, slow; [fl] flower, fly; [bl] black, blue;
　　　　　　[pl] plan, play; [gl] gleam, glue
Final blends: [lz] fills, holes; [ld] called, pulled; [lt] belt, wilt; [lts] colts, halts;
　　　　　　[ldz] holds, molds; [lk] hulk, milk; [lp] help, kelp; [lm] film, helm

3　Minimal pairs:

[l]—[r]		[l]—[j]	
later [letɚ]	rater [retɚ]	clue [klu]	cue [kju]
law [lɔ]	raw [rɔ]	lack [læk]	yak [jæk]
lay [le]	ray [re]	lamb [læm]	yam [jæm]
lie [laɪ]	rye [raɪ]	lay [le]	yea [je]
light [laɪt]	right [raɪt]	let [lɛt]	yet [jɛt]
line [laɪn]	Rhine [raɪn]	local [lokəl]	yokel [jokəl]
long [lɔŋ]	wrong [rɔŋ]	long [lɔŋ]	Yong [jɔŋ]
lower [loɚ]	rower [roɚ]	loose [lus]	use (n.) [jus]
mill [mɪl]	mere [mɪr]	lore [lɔr]	yore [jɔr]
pull [pʊl]	poor [pʊr]	lung [lʌŋ]	young [jʌŋ]

[l]—[w]	
lake [lek]	wake [wek]
later [letɚ]	waiter [wetɚ]
lay [le]	way [we]
led [lɛd]	wed [wɛd]
let [lɛt]	wet [wɛt]
lie [laɪ]	Y [waɪ]
line [laɪn]	wine [waɪn]
long [lɔŋ]	Wong [wɔŋ]

lore [lɔr]   wore [wɔr]
low [lo]   woe [wo]

4 Phonetic transcription:

[wʌn əv ðə lɛsɚ ən mɔr ˈjusləs ˈlɪtəˌrɛrɪ dɪˈvɝʒənz tə hwaɪl əwe ə dʌl aʊr ɪz
kəmˈpaɪlɪŋ ə lɪst əv ðə most ˈbjutəfəl wɝdz ɪn ði ɪŋglɪʃ ˈlæŋgwɪdʒ. ðɪs wəz
ˈpɑpjəlɚ əz ə ˈpæsˌtaɪm ˈsɛvrəl jɪrz əgo, ˈkʌlmənetɪŋ ɪn ə pol əv ə nʌmbɚ əv
ˈlidɪŋ ɔθɚz. ɔlðo aʊr on fevrət ɔl taɪm tʃɔɪs ɪz kæme, wɝdz wɪð əlɪbrəl ˈsprɪŋklɪŋ
əv ɛl saʊndz wɔkt ɔf wɪθ ði ɑnɚz. əmʌŋ ðə ˌnɑməˈnɛʃənz wɚ sʌtʃ məˈ-
lɪfluwəs saʊnd ˈmɛlədɪz əz ˈlɪliən, ˈlɔrʌ, ˈlɪŋgɚɪŋ, ˈjɛlo, ˈmɛlo, lo, ˈʌlnɑr, ænd
ivən ˌtɪntɪnæbjuˈlɛʃən, ðə lætɚ dautləs brɔt tə maɪnd baɪ ɛdgɚ ælən poz
ˌtɪntɪnæbjuˈlɛʃən əv ðə ˈbɛlz, ˈbɛlz, ˈbɛlz. ɪt əz hɑrd tə se hwaɪ ðiz lɪkwəd
nots ɑr so ˈplizɪŋ tə ðə ˌsɛnsəˈbɪlətɪz əv ðiz ˈlɪtərɛrɪ fok; ðə ˈdʒɛntl̩ ˈmɝmɚ
əv ɛm sɛndz ʌs mʌtʃ fæstɚ. wi rɪˈkɔl ɔlso ðət ˈsɪnˌklɛr luəs dɪˈskraɪbd ðə mɑk
məˈlodiəsnəs əv wʌn əv ɪz ˈfimel ˈkɛrɪktɚz wɪð sʌmpθɪŋ laɪk "hɚ ɛlz wɚ laɪk
ðə ˈtrɪlɪŋ əv θrʌʃəz."]

Chapter 16

Glides

[j], [r], [w], [hw]

[j] (or [y])
UNION   YET   UNITE   HALLELUJAH

ANALYSIS

The [j] (alternate symbol [y]) is classified as a *voiced linguapalatal glide*. It is also *nonsyllabic*, *high*, *front*, and *sonorant*. The on-glide is begun with the front of the tongue raised toward the anterior part of the hard palate, in the approximate position for [ɪ] or [i]. The glide is made as the tongue moves to the position for the following vowel. The closeness of the articulation will occasionally give [j] a slight friction noise. Resonance *change* is, of course, the most distinctive major feature of this sound. What has been said about glides in general (see Chapters 5 and 8) has application to an understanding of the nature of [j].

If one is familiar with the articulation of the [i] and [ɪ], the glide should be readily identified, since the starting (or terminating) position of the articulators is, for all practical purposes, the same as for these vowels. This can

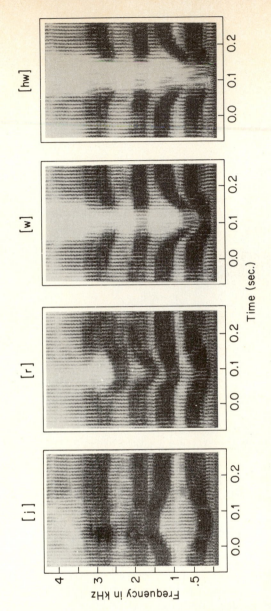

Figure 16-1 Sound spectrogram of [j]. [r]. [w]. and [hw].

342

be easily demonstrated by first pronouncing [i] and [u] as adjacent blended syllables, then cutting off the "steady-state" portion of [i]. A good approximation of [ju] will be the result.

VARIATION

The high-front glide may be found in a number of different contexts: as an *on-glide* in such words as "yellow," "yet," and "beyond" (it is customarily the pronunciation of the letter *y*); as an *off-glide* in the diphthongs of "buy" and "boy"; and sometimes as the terminal diphthongization in the front tense vowels, as in "day" [dej] and "bee" [bij].[1]

There is considerable variation in the pronunciation of [j] which is related both to dialect and stress differences. In both on- and off-glides the consonant target is sometimes quite high and front (closer to [i]), sometimes considerably lower and more central (perhaps closer to [ɪ]). "Bye bye" may vary all the way from a very tense [bai bai] to a near monophthong. There is some evidence to show that the General American target may, on the average, come closer to [ɪ] than to [i]. Where [j] is followed by a high-front vowel, it may become more tense or the following vowel may be changed, as in [jɪj] instead of [ji] for "ye."

Satisfactory production of [j] does not ordinarily offer much of a problem in any kind of speech improvement work. It is very common among the major modern language sound systems. Foreign speakers may often mistakenly confuse the [j] and [dʒ] sounds because of the peculiarities of English spelling, but this is a spelling-pronunciation problem rather than a problem of articulation. Children learn the sound readily, although they may omit it in words like "yes" and "you," so that "Oh, yes you are" may be [o ɛs u ɑr] in infantile speech.

EXERCISES

1 Practice paragraph for [j]:

> We have always been fascinated by yoga, although we have yet to accumulate any ability to use this unique art. How useful, though, to a tutor of youth would be the curious power to keep the young pupils in view through a new but hidden eye. Meanwhile, we could with impunity pursue our fancies or commune with beautiful nature, yet be ready for the usual moment of punitive retribution. Millions of other valuable uses could be found. The power to transmute the body to another place without the nuisance of

---

[1] In this text we have usually adhered to the common practice of recording off-glide diphthongs as [aɪ], [eɪ], etc., while using the symbol [j] for on-glides.

actual travel would be nice. But there are drawbacks; few of us could endure the singularly uncomfortable posture which seems a purely preliminary measure for communicants, although we might eventually become inured to it. Certainly we would be accused of behavior unsuited to a mature man and there might be considerable furious abuse of a secular nature.

2 Word list:

Initiating consonant: year, yore, you, your
Terminating "consonant": A, I, Ray, Roy
Stronger consonant: accuse, beyond, yanking, yesterday
Weaker consonant: accurate, argument, familiar, volume
Initial blends: [kj] cure, cute; [pj] puny, pure; [hj] hew, human; [fj] few, fuse;
          [mj] mew, mule; [vj] view, viewed

3 Minimal pairs:

[j]—[r]		[j]—[dʒ]	
use [juz]	ruse [ruz]	use (v.) [juz]	Jews [dʒuz]
Yale [jel]	rail [rel]	use (n.) [jus]	juice [dʒus]
yak [jæk]	rack [ræk]	yak [jæk]	Jack [dʒæk]
yen [jɛn]	wren [rɛn]	Yale [jel]	jail [dʒel]
yip [jɪp]	rip [rɪp]	yaw [jɔ]	jaw [dʒɔ]
yo [jo]	row [ro]	yell [jɛl]	jell [dʒɛl]
you'd [jud]	rude [rud]	yessed [jɛst]	jest [dʒɛst]
you'll [jul]	rule [rul]	yo [jo]	Joe [dʒo]
your [jʊr]	Ruhr [rʊr]	yolk [jok]	joke [dʒok]
"yum" [jʌm]	rum [rʌm]	you'll [juəl]	jewel [dʒuəl]

[j]—without [j]		[j]—[l]	
use [juz]	ooze [uz]	few [fju]	flew [flu]
Yale [jel]	ale [el]	use [jus]	loose [lus]
yawl [jɔl]	awl [ɔl]	yacht [jɑt]	lot [lɑt]
yea [je]	A [e]	yaw [jɔ]	law [lɔ]
year [jɪr]	ear [ɪr]	yea [je]	lay [le]
yearn [jɝn]	earn [ɝn]	year [jɪr]	leer [lɪr]
yegg [jɛg]	egg [ɛg]	yegg [jɛg]	leg [lɛg]
yell [jɛl]	L [ɛl]	yip [jɪp]	lip [lɪp]
yo [jo]	owe [o]	yo [jo]	low [lo]
yolk [jok]	oak [ok]	your [jʊr]	lure [lʊr]

4 Phonetic transcription:

[wi həv ˈɔlwɪz bɪn ˈfæsənetəd baɪ ˈjogə, ɔlˈðo wi həv jɛt tu əˈkjumjələt ɛni əˈbɪləti tə juz ðɪs juˈnik ɑrt. haʊ jusfəl, ðo, tu ə tutɚ əv juθ wəd bi ðə kjʊriəs paʊr tə kip ðə jʌŋ pjupəlz ɪn vju θru ə nu bət hɪdn̩ aɪ. ˈminˌhwaɪl, wi kʊd wɪθ

ɪmˈpjunəti pɚsu aur ˈfænsɪz ɔr kəˈmjun wɪð ˈbjutəfəl netʃɚ, jɛt bi rɛdɪ
fɚ ðə ˈjuʒjəwəl momənt əv ˈpjunətɪv ˌrɛtrəˈbjuʃən. ˈmɪljənz əv ʌðɚ ˈvæljəbl̩
jusəz kəd bi faund. ðə paur tə trænzˈmjut ðə bɑdɪ tu ənʌðɚ ples wɪθˈaut ðə
ˈnusəns əv ˈæktʃuwəl trævl̩ wəd bi naɪs. bət ðɛr ɑr ˈdrɔˌbæks; fju əv əs kəd
ɪnˈdjur ðə ˈsɪŋgjələlɪ ʌnˈkʌmftɚbl̩ pɑstʃɚ hwɪtʃ simz ə ˈpjurli prɪˈlɪmənɛrɪ
mɛʒɚ fɚ kəˈmjunəkənts, ɔlˈðo wi maɪt iˈvɛntʃuwəlɪ bɪˈkʌm ɪˈnjurd tu ət.
ˈsɚtənlɪ wi wəd bi əkjuzd əv bɪˈhevjɚ ʌnˈsutəd tu ə məˈtjur mæn ən ðɛr maɪt
bi kənˈsɪdərəbl̩ fjurɪəs abjus əvə ˈsɛkjələ netʃɚ.]

[r]
RUN   CARROT   RHYME   WRITE

ANALYSIS

The American [r] is classified as a *voiced linguapalatal glide*. In other feature
terms it is usually *anterior* and *sonorant*, and sometimes as both *back* and
coronal. Like other glide consonants it is characterized mainly by change of
resonance, produced by a gliding movement of the organs of articulation
involved in its production. As a resonant consonant the important articulatory
target is a vocal-tract posture which is similar to, if not identical with, the
vocal-tract configuration for the American *r*-colored vowel [ɝ] (see Chapter
10).

When the [r] is an on-glide, and thus initiates a syllable, the tongue
moves from the [ɝ] position to that for the following vowel. If [r] terminates
a syllable, as an off-glide, the tongue moves from some other vowel to or
toward the vowel [ɝ]. The essence of the sound is movement, either toward
or away, with little or no static "hold" position (see Figure 16-1).

The [r] is often termed a "retroflex" and described as being made with
a "curling back" of the anterior portion of the tongue toward the palate.
For a discussion of this oversimplification see [ɝ].

VARIATION

[r] sounds have been transcribed in such a variety of ways, and with such a
variety of phonetic symbols, that the student cannot be blamed for being
confused by practices in phonetic transcription. For one thing, American
phoneticians have used the IPA *r* symbol for the sonorant glide (rather than
the rolled or trilled version for which [r] was the IPA symbol). Also, as with
other glides, it has sometimes been used for either on- or off-glides (as in
[pɪr] and [rɪp]) and at other times used for only the on-glide.

But the above matters are only questions of form. A more important
variation is the real distinction which can (with difficulty) be made between

the vowel [ɜ] and such centering diphthongs as [ər] and [ɜr]. Either may be heard in American speech. However, we believe that in General American [ɚ] and [ɜ] more accurately describe the *r* syllable of such words as [bʌtɚ] and [tɜn] (for "butter" and "turn"). [bʌtər] and [tɜrn] are probably for the most part indistinguishable variants to all except highly trained listeners.

Although within the *r* group of sounds there is a rather wide range of perfectly acceptable forms (depending upon such factors as stress and context), nonstandard pronunciations are also heard with great frequency, and what is standard varies markedly among American dialects. The curious notion, rather less widespread than a generation ago, that dropping one's *r*'s is more "cultivated," probably grew out of the persistence in America of certain British speech forms through the influence of the stage, and as a result of the great fondness of the British themselves for their Received Pronunciation. The notion that there is something disagreeable or "low class" about *r* glides or vowel [ɜ] has, apparently, died a natural and well-earned death in America. It is hoped that it will not be replaced by an opposite insistence on the use of *r* coloring as a kind of class status marker. There is, by the way, a highly retracted variety of [ɜ] and [r] which one occasionally hears in burlesques of American speech.

Foreign speakers have a multitude of problems with the *r* sounds. A principal reason is that many modern languages have *r*'s that differ conspicuously from the American. When the foreign sound is carried into English, the result may be a very prominent dialect feature. The fact that the foreigner's native sound bears some general resemblance to American [r] may make earning the [r] all the more difficult.

One of the greatest difficulties seems to be teaching the foreign speaker to treat [r] as a glide, rather than as a fricative, tap, or trill—sounds which are also characteristically represented by the letter *r* in many languages. The learner of American as a second language should be taught that the tongue must not touch the roof of the mouth. The case of the Oriental [l] has been mentioned. This glide is something like an [r] and something like a [l]. It represents a very serious stumbling block in teaching standard American pronunciation to Japanese, for example.

For reasons that are not entirely clear, [r] and the *r*-colored vowels appear to be among the most difficult sounds for native children to learn. Sounds within these classes are typically the last to be acquired during the developmental period, and one of the most common characteristics of infantile speech is the use of labialized [r] or [w] in *r* words. In speech of this sort the sentence "First read the story about Peter Rabbit" might be spoken [fɜst wid ðə təwi baut pitə wæbət]. Children can usually overcome this fault most readily if they are first taught the *r*-colored vowels, then introduced to [r] as a sound that begins with the adjustment learned for the [ɜ].

Among American dialects *r* usage differs characteristically. When the

consonant [r] is an on-glide, as in "run" or "red" there occur only a few
distinguishing differences among the dialect regions. There are, however,
many phonetic situations where the General American speaker uses [r] as
an off-glide but where the typical New Englander or Southerner "drops"
the sound or uses a non-r-colored glide. The word "car," for instance, would
be [kɑr] in GA but might be [kɑ:] in some other regions. Note that the vowel
is characteristically lengthened in this case. Other examples are [pɑrdən]–
[pɑ:dən] and [wɔr]–[wɔ:]. Where r follows a vowel other than [ə] or [ɑ],
however, some speakers glide off to the non-r-colored neutral vowel. For
example, the "beer" [bɪr] and "care" [kɛr] of the Middle Westerner or
Westerner may be replaced by [bɪə] and [kɛə] in Boston.

An important exception to the foregoing statements is the New England
treatment of the *linking r*. In words where r is followed by a vowel, the sound
[r] may be restored as an on-glide or releasing consonant for the following
syllable. For example, although the word "mar" is pronounced [mɑ:],
"marring" may be heard as [mɑrɪŋ] or as [mɑɾɪŋ] (with the flapped r). As
another example, the New Englander who habitually says [hɪə] and [fɑ:]
when these words come at the end of a phrase (or are followed by a word
beginning with a consonant) restores the [r] when a vowel follows, as in the
phrase "here I am" [hɪrajæm] or "far away" [fɑrəwe]. Note the common
"over and over" [ovə rən dovə], which has first a linking r and then a final [ə].

An *intrusive r* is often heard in some dialects because of the tendency
to supply a *linking r* after vowels where the spelling does not call for it. A
typical example is the pronunciation [ði aɪdiər əv ɪt] for "the idea of it."
In such cases the linking r is not particularly conspicuous. When the analogy
is carried to the point where "idea" is [aɪdiər] in a nonlinked position—as
in [gʊd aɪdiər] for "good idea"—then the usage is nonstandard and conspicuous to most American ears.

One of the distinctive differences in pronunciation among the dialect
regions of the United States is the way in which certain vowels are spoken
before r. The full details of these variations are too complex to be discussed
here, but a few examples will be given to show the kinds of pronunciations
which may be heard. Many of the distinctive usages will be overlooked by
the average listener, and in this sense are not conspicuous dialect traits. The
words "hurry" and "worry," for example, are pronounced [hɝi] and [wɝi]
in GA but may also be heard as [hʌri] and [wʌri]. In still another group of
words such typical General American pronunciations as [kɛrət] for "carrot"
and [bɛrən] for "barren" are [kærət] and [bærən] in some areas.

Because r sounds are so common among modern languages, and because
several varieties may be heard within a given language, many symbols are
necessary for these sounds in any phonetic alphabet. The explanation of even
the major r sounds of other languages would be impossible in this text. A
few of the symbols for such sounds should, however, be introduced.

The [r] as it ordinarily appears in lower-case form is the symbol originally chosen by the IPA to stand for the rolled or trilled *r*, made with the tip and blade of the tongue trilling against the alveolar ridge. The obvious reason for this choice was that the European scholars who compiled the alphabet were more familiar with this pronunciation. In American treatises on speech sounds, however, it has become conventional to employ [r] to designate the glide. When this is done, the symbol assigned to the trilled *r* is the upside-down [ɹ].

To summarize the varieties of *r* discussed so far, and with a couple of additions: [ɾ] flapped or single-tapped sound; [ɹ] alveolar trill; [ʀ] uvular rolled *r*; [ʁ] uvular fricative *r*; [ɭ] Japanese sound between [r] and [l]; [r] glide *r*.

The explanation for the complexity of *r* is probably that American [r] and [ɝ] represent an evolutionary weakening of a strong trilled sound believed to be the forerunner of the present glide. The historically older sound, still standard in many languages and dialects, has weakened to a single tap in certain British dialects and to no obstruction at all in most American dialects.

EXERCISES

1 Practice paragraph for [r]:

> The birth cry marks the origin of speech, we are told. Here for the first time the nerve pathways necessary for articulation are brought into play. Presently the rapidly growing baby will arrive at a period when true rehearsal for speech begins. This is described as vocal play, when a remarkable and varied repertoire of random sounds emerges. Baby and parent both appear to derive great gratification. Whereas early screams and cries reflect primary responses to body states, later use of sounds is aroused by the presence of others, and a true but primitive interaction with persons in the surrounding environment has been brought about. Various curious sounds he may apparently have borrowed from another world now rapidly drop out; he begins to prefer sounds he hears. Random babbling becomes more nearly purposive. Increasing use is made of sound in the second and third three-month periods. As he draws nearer and nearer to the first birthday the first word will probably be heard, and greeted, you may be sure, with praise and approval. The preparatory period is now largely over; crowing and gurgling are replaced by true verbalization.

2 Word list:

Initiating consonant: raw, ray, row, rye
Terminating consonant: air, are, ire, oar

Initiating and terminating: rare, rear, roar, Ruhr
Stronger consonant: arouse, arrive, bereave, caress
Weaker consonant: bearing, borrow, hearing, wearing
Initial blends: [kr] crack, cry; [br] breathe, brown; [gr] group, grow; [tr] train, try; [dr] draw, drive; [pr] pray, press; [fr] friend, fry; [str] strain, street; [skr] scream, screw; [θr] threw, thrust
Final blends: [rz] fears, wears; [rd] beard, board; [rt] cart, court; [rts] hearts, parts; [rdz] boards, cards; [rn] barn, horn; [rk] bark, cork; [rks] corks, marks

3   Minimal pairs:

[r]—[w]

array [əre]	away [əwe]
crack [kræk]	quack [kwæk]
rain [ren]	Wayne [wen]
rate [ret]	wait [wet]
read [rid]	weed [wid]
red [rɛd]	wed [wɛd]
rent [rɛnt]	went [wɛnt]
rest [rɛst]	west [wɛst]
run [rʌn]	one [wʌn]
train [tren]	twain [twen]

[r]—[j]

a cruise [əkruz]	accuse [əkjuz]
crew [kru]	cue [kju]
ram [ræm]	yam [jæm]
raw [rɔ]	yaw [jɔ]
rear [rɪr]	year [jɪr]
roar [rɔr]	yore [jɔr]
rot [rɑt]	yacht [jɑt]
rue [ru]	you [ju]
rung [rʌŋ]	young [jʌŋ]
Ruth [ruθ]	youth [juθ]

[r]—[l]

array [əre]	allay [əle]
bear [bɛr]	bell [bɛl]
correct [kərɛkt]	collect [kəlɛkt]
hear [hɪr]	hill [hɪl]
rain [ren]	lain [len]
ram [ræm]	lamb [læm]
rate [ret]	late [let]
raw [rɔ]	law [lɔ]
read [rid]	lead [lid]
rot [rɑt]	lot [lɑt]

[r]—without [r]

far [fɑr]	fah [fɑ]
lore [lɔr]	law [lɔ]
rat [ræt]	at [æt]
rate [ret]	ate [et]
reach [ritʃ]	each [itʃ]
red [rɛd]	Ed [ɛd]
real [ril]	eel [il]
rich [rɪtʃ]	itch [ɪtʃ]
spar [spɑr]	spa [spɑ]
wrought [rɔt]	ought [ɔt]

4   Phonetic transcription:

[ðə bɝθ kraɪ mɑrks ðə ˈɔrədʒən əv spitʃ, wi ɝ told. hɪr fɚ ðə fɝst taɪm ðə nɝv pæθwez ˈnɛsəsɛrɪ fɔr ɑrtɪkjəˈleʃən ɑr brɔt ɪntə ple. ˈprɛzəntlɪ ðə ˈræpədlɪ ˈgrowɪŋ ˈbebɪ wɪl əraɪv ət ə ˈpɪrɪəd hwən tru rɪˈhɝsəl fɔr spitʃ bɪˈgɪnz. ðɪs ɪz dɪˈskraɪbd əz vokl̩ ple, hwən ə rɪˈmɑrkəbl̩ ən ˈvɛrɪd ˈrɛpəˌtwɔr əv rændəm saundz iˈmɝdʒəz. ˈbebɪ ən pɛrənt boθ əpɪr tə dɪˈraɪv gret grætəfəˈkeʃən. ˈhwɛræz ɝlɪ skrimz ən kraɪz rɪˈflɛkt ˈpraɪmɛrɪ rɪˈspɑnsəz tə bɑdɪ stets, letɚ jus əv saundz ɪz əˈrauzd baɪ ðə ˈprɛzəns əv ʌðɚz, ənd ə tru bət ˈprɪmətɪv ɪntɚˈækʃən wɪθ pɝsənz ɪn ðə səˈraundɪŋ ɛnˈvaɪrnmənt həz bɪn brɔt əbaut. vɛrɪəs ˈkjurɪəs saundz hi me əˈpɛrəntlɪ həv ˈbɑrod frəm ənʌðɚ wɝld nau

ˈræpədlɪ drɑp aʊt; hi bɪˈgɪnz tə prɪˈfɝ saʊndz i hɪrz. ˈrændəm ˈbæblɪŋ
bɪˈkʌmz mɔr ˈnɪrlɪ ˈpɝpəsɪv. ɪnˈkrisɪŋ jus ɪz med əv saʊnd ɪn ðə sɛkənd ən
θɝd θri mʌnθ ˈpɪrɪədz. æz i drɔz nɪrɚ ən nɪrɚ tə ðə fɝst ˈbɝθˌide ðə fɝst
wɝd wɪl ˈprɑbəblɪ bi hɝd, ən gritəd, ju me bi ʃur, wɪθ prez ən əˈpruvl̩. ðə
prəˈpɛrətɔrɪ ˈpɪrɪəd ɪz naʊ ˈlɑrdʒlɪ ovɚ; ˈkrowɪŋ ən ˈgɝglɪŋ ɑr rɪˈplest baɪ
trу vɝbələˈzeʃən.]

[w]
*W*E QUITE *O*NCE *CH*OIR

ANALYSIS

The [w] may be classified as a *voiced labial* or *bilabial* glide. It is also sometimes classed as *high*, *back*, *noncoronal*, and *sonorant*. It is articulated primarily by rounding the lips and then moving them to the position for the
following vowel. The major class feature is, of course, *nonsyllabic*. In a sense
this sound could also be classified as a linguapalatal glide, for it can be made
by moving from the approximate position of the high-back [ʊ] or [u] to the
adjustment for the following vowel. Both lip and tongue movements may
occur, but the lip movement for this glide appears to be more prominent
than the tongue movement, and the [w] is bilabial because of the rapid
rounding or unrounding of the lips which takes place during its production.
The [w] is related to [u] in somewhat the same way that [j] is related to [i]
and that [r] is related to [ɝ]. To verify this, note that the word "way" [we]
can be closely approximated by blending [u] and [e] rapidly.

VARIATION

Although [w] may seem to be a relatively stable sound with little or no
variation in speech, this is not the case in a strictly acoustic or physiological
sense. A number of variations can be heard if one listens very carefully. In
"woo" and "woe," for example, relatively little lip *un*rounding is possible
because both the vowel and the consonant are fairly strongly rounded sounds.
In these circumstances [w] may have extremely close lip rounding, even taking
on a fricativelike quality. In other circumstances the [w] may influence the
following vowel, so that "woo" would be phonetically transcribed as [wʊuw]
rather than [wu] or [wuw]. In any case the [w] would be quite different from
one which preceded [i], as in [wi] "we."
    Closeness of rounding in [w] will also be a function of stress and timing.
An example is the manner in which "toward" has changed from [tuwərd],

to [twərd] and finally to [tɔrd]. In informal and reduced speech the lip-rounding or tongue-backing gesture may become very slight.

Like [j] and [r], the [w] may be either an on-glide or an off-glide, but it must not be supposed that [wɑ] is exactly the reverse of [ɑw] or [ɑʊ]. In the latter kind of final off-glide the articulation may be considerably less "close" than canonical stressed initial [w].

Except for some spelling-pronunciation problems, such as the German use of [v] for [w], in a word such as German "wagen" for example, the back glides present few problems in either the classroom or the speech clinic.

EXERCISES

1 Practice paragraph for [w]:

> How language began will always remain a qualified mystery. One theory is that words were first acquired by imitation of sounds made by birds and animals or fashioned after the noises in nature. We sometimes call this the onomatopoetic theory. Words like "swish" and "buzz" would possibly have begun this way; however, this theory is quite inadequate, for it in nowise accounts for the complexities of language, and there must have been subsequent influences. Language grew as words were acquired by subsequent use. We do not know what was the first language. The first evidences with which scholars are acquainted date back only to about 4000 B.C. There is no question but that newer language grew out of older, but the situation is that no records of these exist. Fewer than six languages can be followed back as far as 1800 B.C. Few are aware of the large number of languages that have existed; American Indians alone had more than 350, which were grouped into 25 families. The consequence of communication problems in our multilingual world has been to point up the need for one tongue.

2 Word list:

Initiating consonant: way, we, woe, Y
Terminating "consonant": cow, low, new, owe
Stronger consonant: away, bewail, request, reward
Weaker consonant: cower, going, Howard, lower
Initial blends: [sw] sway, swing; [kw] question, quick; [skw] squeak, squelch;
          [tw] twenty, twin; [dw] Duane, dwell

3 Minimal pairs:

[w]—[r]		[w]—[hw]	
quack [kwæk]	crack [kræk]	way [we]	whey [hwe]
quest [kwɛst]	crest [krɛst]	wear [wɛr]	where [hwɛr]

twill [twɪl]	trill [trɪl]	wen [wɛnɟ]	when [hwɛn]
wave [wev]	rave [rev]	were [wɝ]	whirr [hwɝ]
way [we]	ray [re]	wet [wɛt]	whet [hwɛt]
ways [wez]	raise [rez]	wile [waɪl]	while [hwaɪl]
week [wik]	reek [rik]	wine [waɪn]	whine [hwaɪn]
went [wɛnt]	rent [rɛnt]	witch [wɪtʃ]	which [hwɪtʃ]
wife [waɪf]	rife [raɪf]	world [wɝld]	whirled [hwɝld]
will [wɪl]	rill [rɪl]	Y [waɪ]	why [hwaɪɟ]

[w]—[v]

wane [wen]	vane [ven]
want [wɔnt]	vaunt [vɔnt]
weep [wip]	"veep" [vip]
went [wɛnt]	vent [vɛnt]
west [wɛst]	vest [vɛst]
wet [wɛt]	vet [vɛt]
wine [waɪn]	vine [vaɪn]
worse [wɝs]	verse [vɝs]
wow [waʊ]	vow [vaʊ]
Y [waɪ]	vie [vaɪ]

[w]—[f]

way [we]	fey [fe]
wear [wɛr]	fair [fɛr]
were [wɝ]	fir [fɝ]
wife [waɪf]	fife [faɪf]
wile [waɪl]	file [faɪl]
will [wɪl]	fill [fɪl]
wine [waɪn]	fine [faɪn]
witch [wɪtʃ]	Fitch [fɪtʃ]
world [wɝld]	furled [fɝld]
Y [waɪ]	fie [faɪ]

4 Phonetic transcription:

[haʊ ˈlæŋgwɪdʒ bɪˈgæn wɪl ˈɔlwɪz rɪˈmen ə ˈkwɑləfaɪd ˈmɪstrɪ. wʌn ˈθiərɪ ɪz ðæt wɝdz wɚ fɝst əˈkwaɪrd baɪ ɪməˈteʃən əv saʊndz med baɪ bɝdz ən ænəməlz ɔr fæʃn̩d æftɚ ðə nɔɪzəz ɪn netʃɚ. wi ˈsʌmˌtaɪmz kɔl ðɪs ðə ˌɑnəmɑtəpoˈwetɪk ˈθiərɪ. wɝdz laɪk swɪʃ ən bʌz wəd ˈpɑsəblɪ həv bɪˈgʌn ðɪs we; haʊˈɛvɚ, ðɪs ˈθiərɪ ɪz kwaɪt ɪnˈædəkwət, fɔr ɪt ɪn ˈnoˌwaɪz əkaʊnts fɚ ðə kəmˈplɛksətɪz əv ˈlæŋgwɪdʒ, ənd ðɛr mʌst əv bɪn ˈsʌbsəkwənt ˈɪnfluwənsəz. ˈlæŋgwɪdʒ gru æz wɝdz wɚ əˈkwaɪrd baɪ ˈsʌbsəkwənt jus. wi du nɑt no hwʌt wəz ðə fɝst læŋgwɪdʒ. ðə fɝst ˈɛvədənsəz wɪð hwɪtʃ skɑlɚz ɑr əˈkwɛntəd det bæk onlɪ tu əbaʊt fɔr ˈθaʊzənd bi si. ðɚ ɪz no ˈkwɛstʃən bət ðət nuwɚ ˈlæŋgwɪdʒ gru aʊt əv oldɚ, bət ðə sɪtʃəˈweʃən ɪz ðət no rɛkɚdz əv ðɪz ɛgˈzɪst. fjuwɚ ðən sɪks ˈlæŋgwɪdʒəz kən bi ˈfɑlod bæk əz fɑr əz eˈtin hʌndrəd bi si. fju ɑr əwɛr əv ðə lɑrdʒ nʌmbɚ əv ˈlæŋgwɪdʒəz ðət əv ɛgˈzɪstəd; əˈmɛrəkən ɪndɪjənz əlon hæd mɔr ðən θri hʌndrəd ən fɪftɪ, hwɪtʃ wɚ grupt ɪntu ˈtwɛntɪ faɪv ˈfæmlɪz. ðə ˈkɑnsəkwɛns əv kəˈmjunəkeʃən prɑbləmz ɪn aʊr ˈmʌltəˌlɪŋgwəl wɝld həz bɪn tə pɔɪnt ʌp ðə nid fɔr wʌn tʌŋ.]

[hw] or [ʍ]
WHICH

ANALYSIS

The [hw] is commonly classified as an *unvoiced labial* (or *bilabial*) *glide*, and as a *high-back rounded, noncoronal, nonanterior sonorant*. It is a sound very much like the unvoiced labial fricative [ɸ]. To articulate [hw], the lips are rounded as in [w], then opened to the position of the following vowel, but with a delayed voice onset. It is, of course, classed as *nonsyllabic*. In addition some tongue backing and raising may occur, as discussed in the preceding section. The major difference between [w] and [hw] is in the feature of voicing. As Figure 16-1 will show, the voice print of [hw] has the "silent" interval, typical of voiceless consonants, but without the plosive or aspirate release of the obstruents. There is also present during the voiceless interval in [hw] some rather weak aspirate noise energy. In some cases this appears to be produced in part at the lips, in part at the glottis.

There has been some considerable misunderstanding of the dynamics of [hw], in part because of the digraph symbolization, which seems to imply that this is a voiceless glottal fricative followed by a voiced glide. It is possible to produce such a sequence, and the impression is not unlike the usual voiceless glide, but neither is it the best description of the common articulation of this sound in American English, as Figure 16-1 will show. Nevertheless we will use [hw] in our transcriptions as a convenient expedient. However, the symbol [ʍ] is often used for sounds in this class and may be less misleading. The symbol [w̥] may be even better for logic and convenience.

The sound of the *wh* consonant has also been described as a bilabial fricative. As we have explained, it is in part characterized by some weak frication noise. However, it is not the same as the close and more fricative [ɸ].

VARIATION

The [hw] is one of the relatively few sounds in English that has a virtually consistent spelling; hence there are not often spelling-pronunciation errors. A cursory search of the dictionaries in common use turned up only the following words where an initial *wh* calls for [h] rather than [hw] (derivatives should be included): "who," "whole," "whore," and "whoop." The word "whoa" is variously [hwo], [wo], and [ho].

Considerable energy seems to have been expended uselessly on the matter of [hw] versus [w] in words such as "when," "where," and "what." Although these words are marked *hw* in most dictionaries, the aspirate quality and unvoicing may be sharply reduced, or entirely absent, in context. "Wear" and "where" are usually indistinguishable in informal speech in most American dialects. Great stress is sometimes laid on the desirability of making certain that this does not happen, but in most phonetic situations [hw] can move toward [w] without rendering the pronunciation seriously substandard. To be sure, such phrases as "which witch?" "what watt?" and "weigh whey" require a fuller and more formal pronunciation if they are not to be ambiguous, but in much American speech these pairs would be homophones. If the usage of the authors' students is any criterion, the [w]/[hw] contrast is in the process of being lost—at least in Seattle speech.

To summarize, the likely variants of the *wh* pronunciations are voiced [w]; bilabial fricative [ɸ]; consonant combination [h] plus [w]; dialectal [v] or [f] (as in German dialects of English); and of course the more or less "standard" [w̥], [ʍ], or [hw].

EXERCISES

1   Practice paragraph for [hw]:

> Phonetic transcription can be practiced anywhere with whatever samples of speech come along. When we first became intrigued with phonetics we whiled away a good deal of time which probably should have been spent otherwise recording the professor, who candidly was not the best speaker we have heard. After a while it was possible to turn out what proved very readable notes, although whenever a classmate observed the hen scratches he either became overwhelmed by curiosity or dismissed us as a whimsical fellow. "Odd ball" was the way he often put it in a whispered aside. Whetted by these small successes, we were wholly delighted to discover the amazing variety of dialects that could be heard on the elevated train. Somewhat later in what is sometimes called a whistle-stop town we tried to help with a dialect study, which was made by recording samples of the speech of persons who came into the whitewashed office of the county clerk. If you are seriously interested, do the same kind of thing; transcribe whenever and wherever you can.

2   Word list:

Initiating consonant: what, when, where, whey, which, whirr, whoa, why
Stronger consonant: awhirl, awhile, anywhere, somewhere

3   Minimal pairs:

[hw]—[w]		[hw]—[v]	
whacks [hwæks]	wax [wæks]	whale [hwel]	vale [vel]
whale [hwel]	wale [wel]	whee [hwi]	V [vi]
whee [hwi]	we [wi]	wheel [hwil]	veal [vil]
wheel [hwil]	weal [wil]	wheeze [hwiz]	V's [viz]
wheyed [hwed]	weighed [wed]	wherry [hwɛrɪ]	very [vɛrɪ]
whig [hwɪg]	wig [wɪg]	whet [hwɛt]	vet [vɛt]
while [hwaɪl]	wile [waɪl]	while [hwaɪl]	vile [vaɪl]
whist [hwɪst]	wist [wɪst]	whine [hwaɪn]	vine [vaɪn]
white [hwaɪt]	wight [waɪt]	why [hwaɪ]	vie [vaɪ]
whys [hwaɪz]	wise [waɪz]	whys [hwaɪz]	vies [vaɪz]

[hw]—[f]

whale [hwel]	fail [fel]
whee [hwi]	fee [fi]
wheel [hwil]	feel [fil]
wherry [hwɛrɪ]	ferry [fɛrɪ]
whig [hwɪg]	fig [fɪg]
while [hwaɪl]	file [faɪl]
whine [hwaɪn]	fine [faɪn]
whist [hwɪst]	fist [fɪst]
white [hwaɪt]	fight [faɪt]
why [hwaɪ]	fie [faɪ]

4 Phonetic transcription:

[fəˈnɛtɪk trænˈskrɪpʃən kən bi ˈpræktəst ˈɛnɪhwer wɪð hwʌtˈɛvɚ sæmpl̩z əv spitʃ kʌm əlɔŋ. hwɛn wi fɜst bɪˈkem ɪnˈtrigd wɪθ fəˈnɛtɪks wi hwaɪld əwe ə gud dil əv taɪm hwɪtʃ ˈprɑbəblɪ ʃud əv bɪn spɛnt ˈʌðɚwaɪz rɪˈkɔrdɪŋ ðə prəˈfɛsɚ, hu ˈkændədlɪ wəz nɑt ðə bɛst spikɚ wi həv hɜd. æftɚ ə hwaɪl ɪt wəz pɑsəbl̩ tə tɜn aut hwʌt pruvd tə bi vɛrɪ ridəbl̩ nots, ɔlðo hwənˈɛvɚ ə ˈklæsˌmet əbˈzɜvd ðə ˈhɛn ˌskrætʃəz hi iðɚ bɪˈkem ovɚˈhwɛlmd baɪ ˌkjurɪˈɑsətɪ ɔr dɪsˈmɪst ʌs æz ə ˈhwɪmzɪkl̩ fɛlo. ɑd bʌl wəz ðə we hi ɔfən put ət ɪn ə ˈhwɪspəd əsaɪd. hwɛtəd baɪ ðiz smɔl səkˈsɛsəz, wi wɚ holɪ dɪˈlaɪtəd tə dɪˈskʌvɚ ði əˈmezɪŋ vəˈraɪətɪ əv ˈdaɪəlɛkts ðət kəd bi hɜd ɔn ðɪ ˈɛləvetəd tren. ˈsʌmhwʌt letɚ ɪn hwʌt ɪz ˈsʌmˌtaɪmz kɔld ə hwɪsl̩ stɑp taun wi traɪd tə hɛlp wɪð ə ˈdaɪəlɛkt stʌdɪ, hwɪtʃ wəz med baɪ rɪˈkɔrdɪŋ sæmpl̩z əv ðə spitʃ əv pɜsənz hu kem ɪntə ðə ˈhwaɪtwɔʃt ɔfəs əv ðə ˈkauntɪ klɜk. ɪf ju ɚ ˈsɪrɪəsli ˈɪntərɛstəd, du ðə sem kaɪnd əv θɪŋ; trænˈskraɪb hwɛnɛvɚ ən hwɛrɛvɚ jə kæn.]

REFERENCES

Abercrombie, D.: *Studies in Phonetics and Linguistics*, London, Oxford University Press, 1965.

———: *Elements of General Phonetics*, Edinburgh: University Press, 1967.

Barnhart, C. L. (ed.): *The American College Dictionary*, text ed., New York: Harper & Brothers, 1948.

Baugh, A. C.: *A History of the English Language*, 2d ed., New York: Appleton-Century-Crofts, Inc., 1957.

Bell, A. M.: *Visible Speech—The Science of Universal Alphabets*, New York: D. Van Nostrand Company, Inc., 1867.

Bennett, D. N., and W. R. Tiffany: *A Study of Some Constraints on Changes in Speech Rate*, Seattle, Laboratory Report Series B., No. 405, University of Washington Speech Science Laboratories, 1970.

Berg, J. van den: "Mechanism of the Larynx and the Laryngeal Vibrations," in B. Malmberg, *Manual of Phonetics*, Amsterdam: North-Holland Publishing Company, 1968.

Bloomfield, L.: *Language*, New York: Henry Holt and Company, Inc., 1933.

Bolinger, D. L.: "A Theory of Pitch Accent in English," *Word*, **14**:109–149, 1958.

———: *Aspects of Language*, New York: Harcourt, Brace & World, Inc., 1968.

Boone, D. R.: *The Voice and Voice Therapy*. Englewood Cliffs, N.J.: Prentice-Hall, Inc., 1971.

Brodnitz, F. S.: *Vocal Rehabilitation*, Rochester, Minn.: Whiting Press, 1967.

Bronstein, A. J.: *The Pronunciation of American English*, New York: Appleton-Century-Crofts, 1960.

Brown, R.: *Words and Things*, New York: The Free Press, 1958.

Catford, J. C.: "The Articulatory Possibilities of Man," in B. Malmberg (ed.), *Manual of Phonetics*, Amsterdam: North-Holland Publishing Company, 1968.

Chomsky, N., and M. Halle: *The Sound Patterns of English*, New York: Harper & Row, 1968.

Crystal, D.: *Prosodic Systems and Intonation in English*, London: Cambridge University Press, 1969.

Curtis, J. F., "Acoustics of Speech Sound Production," in D. C. Spriestersbach and D. Sherman (eds.), *Cleft Palate and Communication*, New York: Academic Press, Inc., 1968.

David, E. E., Jr.: "Voice-actuated Machines: Problems and Possibilities," *Bell Laboratories Record*, **35**:281–286, 1957.

Delattre, P., and D. C. Freeman: "A Dialect Study of American R's by X-Ray Motion Pictures," *Linguistics*, **44**:29–68, 1968.

Denes, P. B., and E. N. Pinson: *The Speech Chain*, Bell Telephone Laboratories, Inc., 1963, and Anchor Press, Doubleday, Garden City, N.Y., 1973.

Dudley, H., and T. H. Tarnoczy: "The Speaking Machine of Wolfgang von Kempelen," *Journal of the Acoustical Society of America*, **22**:151–166, 1950.

Fairbanks, G.: "Recent Experimental Investigations of Vocal Pitch in Speech," *Journal of the Acoustical Society of America*, **11**:457–466, 1940.

Flanagan, J. L.: "The Synthesis of Speech," *Scientific American*, **226**:48–61, February 1972.

Francis, W. N.: *The Structure of American English*, New York: The Ronald Press Company, 1958.

Goldman-Eisler, F.: *Psycholinguistics: Experiments in Spontaneous Speech*, New York: Academic Press, Inc., 1968.

Hall, R. A., Jr.: *Leave Your Language Alone!*, Ithaca, N.Y.: Linguistica, 1950.

Halle, M. and K. N. Stevens: "On the Feature 'Advanced Tongue Root'" *Quarterly Progress Report No.. 94*, M.I.T. Research Laboratory of Electronics, Cambridge, Mass., July 15, 1969.

Hanna, P. R., J. S. Hanna, R. E. Hodges, and E. H. Rudorf: *Phoneme-Grapheme Correspondences as Clues to Spelling Improvement*, U.S. Department of Health, Education, and Welfare, 1966, Document OE-32008.

Harris, C. M.: "A Study of the Building Blocks in Speech," *Journal of the Acoustical Society of America*, **25**:962–969, 1953.

Heffner, R-M. S.: *General Phonetics*, Madison: The University of Wisconsin Press, 1952.

Helmick, J. W. "An Analysis of Speaker-Listener Competencies in the Communication of Selected Connotative Meanings Dependent upon Surprasegmental Phenomena," unpublished Doctoral Dissertation, University of Washington, Seattle, 1968.

Hockett, C. F.: *A Course in Modern Linguistics*, New York: The Macmillan Company. 1958.

Hollien, H.: "On Vocal Registers," *Journal of Phonetics*, **2**:125–143, 1974.

House, A. S., and K. N. Stevens: "Analog Studies of the Nasalization of Vowels," *Journal of Speech and Hearing Disorders*, **20**:208–232, 1956.

Hudgins, C. H., and R. H. Stetson: "Relative Speed of Articulatory Movements," *Arch. Néer. Phonetique Exp.*, **30**:85–94, 1937.

Jakobsen, R., C. G. M. Fant, and M. Halle: *Preliminaries to Speech Analysis*, Cambridge, Mass. The M.I.T. Press, 1951.

Jones, D.: *An Outline of English Phonetics*, New York: E. P. Dutton & Co., Inc., 1940.

Joos, M.: *The Five Clocks*, New York: Harcourt, Brace & World, Inc., 1967.

Kenyon, J. S.: *American Pronunciation*, 9th ed., Ann Arbor, Mich.: George Wahr Publishing Company, 1946.

———— and T. A. Knott: *A Pronouncing Dictionary of American English*, Springfield, Mass.: G. & C. Merriam Company, 1953.

Krapp, G. P.: *Modern English, Its Growth and Present Use*, New York: Charles Scribner's Sons, 1909.

Labov, W.: *The Study of Nonstandard English*, Champaign, Ill.: National Council of Teachers of English, 1970.

Ladefoged, P.: *Elements of Acoustic Phonetics*, Chicago: The University of Chicago Press, 1962.

————: *Three Areas of Experimental Phonetics*, London: Oxford University Press, 1967.

————: "Phonological Features and their Phonetic Correlates," *Journal of the International Phonetic Association*, **2**:2–12, 1972.

————: *A Course in Phonetics*, New York: Harcourt Brace Jovanovich, Inc., 1975.

Leeper, R.: "A Study of a Neglected Portion of the Field of Learning—The Development of Sensory Organization," *Journal of Genetic Psychology*, **46**:41–75, 1935.

Lehiste, I.: "An Acoustic-Phonetic Study of Open Juncture," *Phonetica*, **5** (Suppl.): 1–54, 1960.

————: *Suprasegmentals*, Cambridge, Mass.: The M.I.T. Press, 1970.

————: "Rhythmic Units and Syntactic Units in Production and Perception," *Journal of the Acoustical Society of America*, **54**:1228–1234, 1973.

Lenneberg, E. H.: *Biological Foundations of Language*, New York: John Wiley & Sons, Inc., 1967.

Lewis, D., and J. Tiffin: "A Psychophysical Study of Individual Differences in Speaking Ability," *Archives of Speech*, **1**:43–60, 1934.

Liberman, A. M., P. C. Delattre, L. J. Gerstman, and F. S. Cooper: "Tempo of Frequency Change as a Cue for Distinguishing Classes of Speech Sounds," *Journal of Experimental Psychology*, **52**:127–137, 1956.

————, Cooper, F. S., D. P. Shankweiler, and M. Studdert-Kennedy: "Perception of the Speech Code," *Psychological Review*, **74**:431–461, 1967.

Lieberman, P.: *Intonation, Perception, and Language*, Cambridge, Mass.: The M.I.T. Press, 1967.

————: *The Speech of Primates*, The Hague, Mouton, 1972.

—— and E. S. Crelin: "On the Speech of Neanderthal Man," *Linguistic Inquiry*, **2**:203–222, 1971.

—— and S. B. Michaels: "Some Aspects of Fundamental Frequency Envelope Amplitude, as Related to the Emotional Content of Speech," *Journal of the Acoustical Society of America*, **34**:922–927, 1962.

Malmberg, B.: *Manual of Phonetics*, Amsterdam: North-Holland Publishing Company, 1968.

Martin, J.: "Rhythmic (Hierarchical) Versus Serial Structure in Speech and Other Behavior," *Psychological Review*, **79**:487–509, 1972.

Mattingly, I.: "Speech Cues and Sign Stimuli," *American Scientist*, **60**:327–337, 1972.

McDavid, R.: "The Dialects of American English," in W. N. Francis, *The Structure of American English*, New York: The Ronald Press, 1958.

——: "Sense and Nonsense about American Dialects," *PMLA*, May 1966, as reprinted in R. M. Aderman, and E. M. Kerr, *Aspects of American English*, 2d ed., New York: Harcourt Brace Jovanovich, Inc., 1971.

McDonald, E.: *Articulation Testing and Treatment: A Sensory-Motor Approach*, Pittsburgh, Pa.: Stanwix House, Inc., 1964.

—— and B. Chance, Jr.: *Cerebral Palsy*, Englewood Cliffs, N.J.: Prentice-Hall, Inc., 1964.

Mencken, H. L.: *The American Language*, revised by Ravin I. McDavid, Jr., New York: Alfred A. Knopf, Inc., 1963.

Menzerath, A., and A. de Lacerda: *Koartikulation, Steuerung und Lautabrenzung*, Berlin: Fred. Dümnlers Verlag, 1933.

Miller, G. A.: *Language and Communication*, New York: McGraw-Hill Book Company, 1951.

—— and P. E. Nicely: "An Analysis of Perceptual Confusions among English Consonants," *Journal of the Acoustical Society of America*, **27**:338–352, 1955.

Minifie, F. D., T. J. Hixson and F. Williams (eds.): *Normal Aspects of Speech, Hearing and Language*, Englewood Cliffs, N.J.: Prentice-Hall, Inc., 1973.

Moore, G. P.: *Organic Voice Disorders*, Englewood Cliffs, N.J.: Prentice-Hall, Inc., 1971.

Moser, H. M.: *One Syllable Words—Revised and Arranged by Ending Sounds*, Technical Report 53, RF Project 882, AFCCDD TN 60–58, Columbus: Ohio State University Research Foundation, 1960.

Moses, P. J.: *The Voice of Neurosis*, New York: Grune & Stratton, Inc., 1954.

Murray, E., and J. Tiffin: "An Analysis of Some Basic Aspects of Effective Speech," *Archives of Speech*, **1**:61–83, 1934.

Negus, V. E.: *The Mechanism of the Larynx*, London: William Heinemann, Ltd., 1929.

——: *The Comparative Anatomy and Physiology of the Larynx*, rev. ed., New York: Grune & Stratton, Inc., 1949.

Neisser, U.: *Cognitive Psychology*, New York: Appleton-Century-Crofts, Inc., 1967.

Nist, J.: *A Structural History of English*, New York: St. Martin's Press, Inc., Macmillan & Co., Ltd., 1966.

Öhman, S. A.: "Coarticulation in VCV Utterances: Spectrographic Measurements," *Journal of the Acoustical Society of America*, **39**:151–168, 1966.

Ostwald, P. F.: *Soundmaking: The Acoustic Communication of Emotion*, Springfield, Ill.: Charles C Thomas, Publisher, 1963.

Paget, R.: *Human Speech*, New York: Harcourt, Brace and Company, Inc., 1930; and London: Kegan Paul, Trench, Trubner & Co., Ltd., 1930.

Perkell, J. S.: *Physiology of Speech Sound Production: Results and Implications of a Quantitative Cineradiographic Study*, Cambridge, Mass.: The M.I.T. Press, 1969.

———: "Physiology and Speech Production: A Preliminary Study of Two Suggested Revisions of the Features Specifying Vowels," *Quarterly Progress Report No. 102*, M.I.T. Research Laboratory of Electronics, Cambridge, Mass., July 15, 1971.

Peterson, G. E., and H. L. Barney: "Control Methods Used in a Study of the Vowels," *Journal of the Acoustical Society of America*, **24**:175–184, 1952.

——— and J. E. Shoup: "A Physiological Theory of Phonetics," *Journal of Speech and Hearing Research*, **9**:5–67, 1966.

Pei, M.: *Glossary of Linguistic Terminology*, New York: Anchor Books, 1966.

Potter, R. K., G. A. Kopp, and H. G. Kopp: *Visible Speech*, New York: Dover Publications, Inc., 1966.

Potter, S.: *Our Language*, Baltimore: Penguin Books, Inc., 1950.

The Principles of the International Phonetic Association, London: University College, Department of Phonetics, 1949.

Pulgram, E.: *Introduction to the Spectrography of Speech*, The Hague, Mouton & Co., 1959.

Shipp, T., and H. Hollien: "Perception of the Aging Male Voice," *Journal of Speech and Hearing Research*, **12**:703–710, 1969.

Sigurd, B.: "Maximum Rate and Minimal Duration of Repeated Syllables," *Language and Speech*, **16**:373–395, 1973.

Small, A. M.: "Acoustics," in F. D., Minifie, T. J. Hixon, and F. Williams (eds.), *Normal Aspects of Speech, Hearing and Language*, Englewood Cliffs, N.J.: Prentice-Hall, Inc., 1973.

Snidecor, J. C., J. J. Pressman, E. R. Finkbeiner, E. T. Curry, A. C. Nichols, and J. O. Anderson: *Speech Rehabilitation of the Laryngectomized*, Springfield, Ill.: Charles C Thomas, Publisher, 1962.

Stetson, R. H.: *Bases of Phonology*, Oberlin, Ohio: Oberlin College, Publisher, 1945.

———: *Motor Phonetics*, Amsterdam: North-Holland Publishing Company, 1951.

Stevens, K. N., and A. S. House: "Development of a Quantitative Description of Vowel Articulation," *Journal of the Acoustical Society of America*, **27**:484–493 1955.

Sweet, H.: *A History of English Sounds*, Oxford, Clarendon Press, 1888.

Tarone, E.: "Aspects of Intonation in Vernacular White and Black English Speech," unpublished doctoral dissertation, University of Washington, Seattle, 1972.

Thorndike, E. L., and I. Lorge: *The Teacher's Handbook of 30,000 Words*, New York: Columbia University, Bureau of Publications, 1944.

Tiffany, W. R.: "Non-random Sources of Variation in Vowel Quality," *Journal of Speech and Hearing Research* **2**:305–317, 1959.

——— and D. N. Bennett: "Pronunciation: A Matter of Choice," *Laboratory Report Series B, No. 401*, Seattle, University of Washington Speech Science Laboratories, 1966.

————: "Slurvian Translation as a Speech Research Tool," *Speech Monographs*, **30**:23–30, 1963.

Tiffin, J., and M. D. Steer: "An Experimental Analysis of Emphasis," *Speech Monographs*, **4**:69–74, 1937.

Van Riper, C.: *Speech Correction Principles and Methods*, 5th ed., Englewood Cliffs, N.J.: Prentice-Hall, Inc., 1972.

Vennard, W.: *Singing: The Mechanism and the Technic*, New York: Carl Fischer, Inc., 1967.

Voelker, C. H.: "The One Thousand Most Frequently Spoken Words," *Quarterly Journal of Speech*, **28**:189–197, 1942.

Vygotsky, L. S.: *Thought and Language*, Cambridge, Mass.: The M.I.T. Press, 1962.

Warren, R. P.: "Auditory Sequence, Confusion of Patterns Other Than Speech or Music," *Science*, **164**(3879):586–587, 1969.

Webster's New International Dictionary, 2d ed., Springfield, Mass.: G. & C. Merriam Company, 1956.

Webster's New World Dictionary of the American Language, college ed., Cleveland: The World Publishing Company, 1954.

Webster's Seventh New Collegiate Dictionary, Springfield, Mass.: G. and C. Merriam Company, 1963.

Webster's Third New International Dictionary, Springfield, Mass.: G. and C. Merriam Company, 1961.

Weisenburg, T., and K. E. McBride: *Aphasia, A Clinical and Psychological Study*, The Commonwealth Fund, New York: 1935.

Wise, C. M.: *Applied Phonetics*, Englewood Cliffs, N.J.: Prentice-Hall, Inc., 1957.

Woodrow, H.: "Time Perception," in S. S. Stevens (ed.), *Handbook of Experimental Psychology*, New York: John Wiley & Sons, Inc., 1951.

Zemlin, W. R.: *Speech and Hearing Science*, Englewood Cliffs, N.J.: Prentice-Hall, Inc., 1968.

Generalized Phonetic Transcriptions

This section contains what may be called generalized phonetic transcriptions illustrating an acceptable pronunciation of the speech samples in a General American dialect. These transcriptions may serve several purposes. First of all, they can help students become familiar with the pronunciation value of the IPA symbols. As their learning progresses, they may use them as a model for transcriptions of the sort which they themselves should prepare as part of the technique for analyzing speech. Finally, the samples can serve as a basic set of transcriptions which can be used for articulation and pronunciation practice. Students will need to develop their own transcriptions for practice, of course, and should not be content with those provided by the authors.

A word should be added about the form of these generalized transcriptions. They are quite broad, and no special notations are used, except for the accent markings that seemed necessary. There are, of course, many other modifying marks that could have been inserted to bring out some of the finer features of speech. Students may wish to add some of these notations at various points, and certainly they must learn to use such marks when they are helpful in their own transcriptions. Again, the pronunciations are those that might be heard in General American speech of reasonably good quality. In view of all that has been said about speech standards in earlier parts of the book, students surely will not get the mistaken notion that these

are examples of "perfect" speech which everyone ought to imitate. The pronunciations indicated inevitably tend to be those of the author who prepared the transcriptions (or at least the pronunciations he believes he uses), and his speech is not
necessarily free of individual peculiarities. The particular prose and poetry chosen
for this purpose seemed to the authors to be suitable for reading aloud and to call for
representative degrees of informality and formality in pronunciation.

[maɪ haʊs stændz ɪn lo lænd, wɪð lɪmətəd ˈaʊtlʊk, ənd ɔn ðə skɜt əv ðə ˈvɪlɪdʒ.
bət aɪ go wɪð maɪ frend tə ðə ʃɔr əv aʊr lɪtl̩ rɪvɚ, ənd wɪð wʌn strok əv ðə pædl̩
aɪ liv ðə ˈvɪlɪdʒ ˈpɑlətɪks ən pɚsənˈælətɪz, jes, ən ðə wɜld əv ˈvɪlɪdʒəz ən pɚsən-
ˈælətɪz, bɪˈhaɪnd, ən pæs ˈɪntu ə dɛləkət rɛlm əv ˈsʌnset n̩ ˈmunlaɪt, tu braɪt
ɔlˈmost fɚ spɑtəd mæn tu entɚ wɪðˈaʊt ˌnoˈvɪʃɪet ən proˈbeʃən. wi ˈpɛnətret
ˈbɑdəlɪ ðɪs ɪnˈkrɛdəbəl ˈbjutɪ; wi dɪp aʊr hændz ɪn ðɪs pentəd ɛləmənt; aʊr aɪz
ɑr beðd ɪn ðiz laɪts ən fɔrmz . . . e rɔɪəl rɛvəl, ðə praʊdəst, most hɑrt-rɪˈdʒɔɪsɪŋ
fɛstəvəl ðət vælɚ ən ˈbjutɪ, paʊɚ ən test, ɛvɚ dɛkt ən ɛnˈdʒɔɪd, əˈstæblɪʃəz ɪtˈself
ɔn ðɪ ɪnstənt. ðiz ˈsʌnset klaʊdz, ðiz ˈdɛləkətlɪ ɪˈmɜdʒɪŋ stɑrz, wɪð ðɚ praɪvət
ən ɪnˈɛfəbəl glænsəz, ˈsɪgnəfaɪ ət ən prɔfɚ ɪt. aɪ əm tɔt ðə pɚrnəs əv aʊr ɪnˈven-
ʃən, ðɪ ˌʌglɪnəs əv taʊnz ən pæləsəz. ɑrt ən ˈlʌkʃərɪ həv ˈɜlɪ lɜnd ðətðe məst wɜk
æz ɛnˈhænsmənt ən sikwəl tu ðɪs oˈrɪdʒənəl ˈbjutɪ.]

From the essay "Nature"
By Ralph Waldo Emerson

[bivɚz kən bɪld dæmz: biz kən kənstrʌkt iˈfɪʃənt ˈdwɛlɪŋz: ðə minəst bɜd hæz
stɪl ə ʃʊrɚ ˈmɛkənˌɪzəm fɚ ˈflaɪɪŋ ənd ˈlændɪŋ ðən mæn həz jet ətʃɪvd. bət no
ʌðɚ krɪtʃɚ həz kʌm wɪˈðɪn saɪt əv mæn ɪn ðɪ ɑrts əv ˌsɪmˈbɑlɪk kəˌmjunəˈkeʃən.
ˈmenlɪ θru ˈlæŋgwɪdʒ mæn həz kriˈetəd ə sɛkənd wɜld, mɔr durəbəl ənd vaɪəbəl
ðən ðɪ ɪˈmidɪət flʌks əv ɪkˈspɪrɪəns, mɔr rɪtʃ ɪn ˌpɑsəˈbɪlətɪz ðən ðə pjʊrlɪ məˈtɪrɪəl
ˈhæbətæt əv ɛnɪ ʌðɚ krɪtʃɚ. baɪ ðə sem edʒənt, hi həz rɪˈdust ðə væstnəs ənd
ˈovɚˌpaʊrɪŋ ˌmʌltəˈplɪsətɪ əv hɪz ənˈvaɪrənmənt tu hjumən dɪˈmɛnʃənz:
ˌæbˈstræktɪŋ frəm ɪts ˌtoˈtælətɪ dʒʌst so mʌtʃ əz hi kən hændəl ən kəntrol.]

From *The Conduct of Life*
By Lewis Mumford

[saɪəns ɪn ɪts bɪˈgɪnɪŋz wəz du tə mɛn hu wɚ ɪn lʌv wɪð:ə wɜld. ðe pɚsivd ðə
ˈbjutɪ əv ðə stɑrz ənd ðə si, əv ðə wɪndz ən ðə maʊntənz. bɪˈkɔz ðe lʌvd ðem ðɛr
θɔts dwelt əpɑn ðem, ənd ðe wɪʃt tə ˌʌndɚˈstænd ðem mɔr ˈɪntəmətlɪ ðən ə mɪr
aʊtwɚd ˌkɑntəmˈpleʃən med pɑsəbl̩. "ðə wɜld," sed hɛrəˈklaɪtəs, "ɪz ən
ˈɛvɚ-ˈlɪvɪŋ faɪr, wɪθ mɛʒɚz ˈkɪndlɪŋ ən mɛʒɚz ˈgoɪŋ aʊt." ˌhɛrəˈklaɪtəs ənd ðɪ
ˌaɪˈonɪən fələsəfɚz, frəm hum kem ðə fɜst ˈɪmpʌls tu ˈsaɪənˌtɪfɪk ˈnɑlɪdʒ, felt ðə
strendʒ ˈbjutɪ əv ðə wɜld ˈɔlmost laɪk ə mædnəs ɪn ðə blʌd. ðe wɚ mɛn əv
ˌtaɪˈtænɪk pæʃənət ˈɪntəˌlɛkt, ənd frəm ðɪ ˌɪnˈtensətɪ əv ðɛr ˌɪntəˈlɛktʃuwəl pæʃən

ðə hol muvmənt əv ðə madən wɜld həz sprʌŋ. bət stɛp bai stɛp, æz saiəns həz dɪˈvɛləpt, ðɪ ˈɪmpʌls əv lʌv hwɪtʃ gev ət bɜθ həz bin ˌɪnˈkrisɪŋlɪ θwɔrtəd, hwail ðɪ ˈɪmpʌls əv paur, hwɪtʃ wəz ət fɜst ə mir kæmp ˈfalowɚ, hæz ˈgrædʒuəlɪ juˈsɜpt kəmænd ɪn ˈvɜtʃu əv its ʌnfɔrˌsin səksɛs.]

From *Scientific Outlook*
By Bertrand Russell

Reprinted by permission of W. W. Norton & Company, Inc.

[wi ˈsʌmtaimz dɪˈspjutəd, ən ˈvɛrɪ fand wi wɜ əv ˈargjəmənt ən ˈvɛrɪ dɪˈzairəs əv kənˈfjutɪŋ wʌn ənʌðɚ; hwɪtʃ ˌdɪspjuˈteʃəs tɜn, bai ðə we, ɪz æpt tə bɪˈkʌm ə ˈvɛrɪ bæd hæbət, ˈmekɪŋ pipḷ ɔfən ɪkˈstrimlɪ ˌdɪsəˈgriəbəl ɪn ˈkʌmpənɪ bai ðə kantrəˈdɪkʃən ðət ɪz ˈnɛsəsɛrɪ tə brɪŋ ɪntə præktəs; ænd ðɛnts, bɪˈsaidz ˈsaurɪŋ ən ˈspɔilɪŋ ðə ˌkanvəˈseʃən, it əz prəˈdʌktiv əv disˈgʌsts, ən pəhæps ˈɛnməˌtiz, wɪðːoz hu me hæv əkeʒən fər ˈfrɛndʃɪp. ai həd kɔt ðis bai ˈridɪŋ mai faðɚz buks əv dɪˈspjut ɔn rɪˈlidʒən. pɜsənz əv gud sɛnts, ai həv sints əbzɜvd, sɛldəm fɔl intu ət, ɛkˈsɛpt lɔjəz, ˌjunəˈvɜsətɪ mɛn, ən ˈdʒɛnrəlɪ mɛn əv ɔl sɔrts hu həv bin brɛd æt ˈɛdənbɜg.]

From the *Autobiography*
By Benjamin Franklin

[ænd nau ai spik əv ˈθæŋkɪŋ gad, ai dɪˈzair wɪð ɔl ˌhjuˈmɪlətɪ tu ækˈnalidʒ ðət ai əˈtribjut ðə mɛntʃənd ˈhæpɪnəs əv mai pæst laif tu hɪz dɪˈvain pravədəns, hwɪtʃ lɛd mi tu ðə minz ai juzd ənd gev ðə səksɛs. mai bɪˈlif əv ðis inˈdusəz mi tə hop, ðo ai məst nat prɪˈzum, ðət ðə sem gudnəs wɪl stil bi ˈɛksəsaizd tɔrd mi in kənˈtinjuɪŋ ðæt ˈhæpɪnəs ɔr ənˈeblɪŋ mi tu bɛr ə fetḷ rɪˈvɜs, hwɪtʃ ai me ik ˈspiritəns æz ʌðɚz həv dʌn; ðə kəmplɛkʃən əv mai fjutʃɚ fɔrtʃən ˈbiɪŋ non tu him ˈonlɪ in huz paur it ɪz tu blɛs ʌs, ivən in aur əflikʃənz.]

From the *Autobiography*
By Benjamin Franklin

[so far ai mʌst dɪˈfɛnd ˈpleto, æz tə plid ðət hɪz vju əv ɛdʒuˈkeʃən ən ˈstʌdiz ɪz in ðə ˈdʒɛnrəl, æz it simz tə mi, saund ənʌf, ənd fitəd fər ɔl sɔrts ən kənˈdiʃənz əv mɛn, hwʌtˈɛvɚ ðer pɜsuts me bi. "æn inˈtɛlədʒənt mæn," sɛz ˈpleto, "wil praiz ðoz ˈstʌdiz hwɪtʃ rɪˈzʌlt in hɪz sol ˈgetɪŋ ˈsobənəs, ˈraitʃəsnəs, ənd wizdəm, ənd wil lɛs ˈvælju ðɪ ʌðɚz." ai ˈkænat kənsidɚ ðæt ə bæd dɪˈskripʃən ev ðɪ em əv ɛdʒuˈkeʃən, ænd əv ðə ˈmotivz hwɪtʃ gʌvən ʌs in ðə tʃɔis əv ˈstʌdiz, hweðɚ wi ɚ prɪˈpɛrɪŋ aurˈsɛlvz fər ə həˈrɛdətˌɛri sit in ðɪ ˈɪŋglɪʃ haus əv lɔrdz ɔr fər ðə pɔrk tred in ʃəˈkɔgo.]

From the essay "Literature and Science"
By Matthew Arnold

[. . . wʌn de aur bɔrd əv ˌɛdʒəˈkeʃən tuk ə de ɔf tə θɪŋk θɪŋz ovɚ ˈkwaɪətlɪ ənd æftɚ sɛvən aurz əv ˈstɛdɪ ˈθɪŋkɪŋ dɪˈsaɪdəd tə put ˈɛvrɪ ˈpʌblɪk skul pjupəl θru ə ˈθɝo ˈfɪzɪkəl ɪgˈzæməˈneʃən tə salv, ɪf pasəbəl, ðə ˈmɪstrɪ əv hɛlθ ɪn ðə jʌŋ ɪnˈhæbətənts əv ðə slʌmz.

əˈkɔrdɪŋ tə ˌdakjəˈmɛntərɪ pruf, ˈpʌblɪʃt ən ˈtæbjəletəd, ɔl ðɪ ɪnˈhæbətənts ɔv maɪ ˈnebɚhud ʃud əv hæd ˈhædlɪ ʃept hɛdz, sʌŋkən tʃɛsts, ˈfɔltɪ bon strʌktʃɚ, ˈhalo vɔɪsəz, no ˈɛnədʒɪ, dɪsˈtɛmpɚ, ən sɪks ɚ sɛvən ʌðɚ maɪnɚ ɔrˈgænɪk dɪˈfɛkts.

əˈkɔrdɪŋ tə ðɪ ɛvədəns bɪˈfɔr ɪtʃ ˈpʌblɪk skul tɪtʃɚ, ˈhauɛvɚ, ðiz ˈrʌfiənz frəm ðə slʌmz hæd wɛl-ʃept hɛdz, saund tʃɛsts, hændsəm fɪgjɚz, laud vɔɪsəz, tu mʌtʃ ˈɛnədʒɪ, ənd ə kənˈtɪnjuəs kəmpʌlʃən tə bɪˈhev ˈmɪstʃəvəslɪ.

ˈsʌmθɪŋ wəz rɔŋ ˈsʌmhwɛr.

aur bɔrd əv ˈɛdʒəˈkeʃən dɪˈsaɪdəd tə faɪnd aut hwʌt.

ðe dɪd faɪnd aut.

ðe faund aut ðət ðə ˈpʌblɪʃt ən ˈtæbjəletəd, ˌdakjəˈmɛntərɪ pruf wəz rɔŋ.

ɪt wəz ət ðɪs taɪm ðət aɪ fɝst lɝnd wɪð dʒɔɪ ən ˈfjurɪ ðət aɪ wəz ə powət.

aɪ rɪˈmɛmbɚ ˈbiɪŋ ɪn ðə ˈsɪvɪk ˌodəˈtorɪəm əv maɪ hom taun ət haɪ nun wɪð sɪks hʌndrəd ʌðɚ fjutʃɚ stetsmən, ən aɪ rɪˈmɛmbɚ ˈhɪrɪŋ maɪ nem sʌŋ aut baɪ old mɪs ˈogəlvɪ ɪn ə klɪr hɪsˈtɛrəkəl səˈpræno.

ðə taɪm həd əraɪvd fɚ mi tə klaɪm ðə ˈsɛvəntin stɛps tə ðə stedʒ, wɔk tə ðə sɛntɚ əv ðə stedʒ, strɪp tə ðə west, ˈɪnhel, ˈɛkshel, ən bi mɛʒɚd ɔl ovɚ.

ðer wəz ə momənt əv kənfjuʒən əndˌɪndɪˈsɪʒən, ˈfalod ˈkwɪklɪ baɪ ə supɚˈhjumən ˈɪmpʌls tə bɪˈhev wɪð staɪl, hwɪtʃ aɪ dɪd, tə ðə horɚ ən bɪˈwɪldəmənt əv ðə hol bɔrd əv ˌɛdʒəˈkeʃən, θri ˈɛldəlɪ daktɚz, ə ˈhæfdʌzən ˈrɛdʒəstəd nɝsəz, ən sɪks hʌndrəd fjutʃɚ kæptənz əv ˈɪndəstrɪ.

ɪnˈsted əv ˈklaɪmɪŋ ðə ˈsɛvəntin stɛps tə ðə stedʒ, aɪ lɪpt.

aɪ rɪˈmɛmbɚ old mɪs ˈogəlvɪ ˈtɝnɪŋ tə mɪstɚ ˈrɪkənbækɚ, suprənˈtɛndənt əv skulz, ən ˈhwɪspərɪŋ ˈfɪrfəlɪ: ðɪs ɪz ˌgarogˈlɛnɪən—wʌn əv aur fjutʃɚ powəts aɪ maɪt se.

mɪstɚ ˈrɪkənbækɚ tuk wʌn kwɪk luk ət mi ən sɛd: o, aɪ si. huz i sɔr æt?

səˈsaɪətɪ, old mɪs ˈogəlvɪ sɛd.

o, aɪ si, mɪstɚ ˈrɪkenbækɚ sɛd. so əm aɪ, bət aɪl bi dæmd əf aɪ kən dʒʌmp laɪk ðæt. lɛts se no mɔr əbaut ət.

aɪ flʌŋ ɔf maɪ ʃɝt ən stud strɪpt tə ðə west, ə gud:il əv hɛr ˈbrɪslɪŋ ɔn maɪ tʃɛst.

ju si? mɪs ˈogəlvɪ sɛd. ə raɪtɚ.]

From "One Of Our Future Poets"
By William Saroyan

[ənʌðɚ klæs ðət aɪ dɪdn̩t laɪk, bət ˈsʌmhau ˈmænɪdʒd tə pæs wəz ˌikəˈnamɪks. aɪ wɛnt tə ðæt klæs stret frəm ðə ˈbatənɪ klæs, hwɪtʃ dɪdn̩t hɛlp mɪ ɛnɪ ɪn ˌʌndɚˈstændɪŋ iðɚ klæs. aɪ just tə gɛt ðəm mɪkst ʌp. bət nat əz mɪkst ʌp əz

ənʌðɚ studənt ɪn maɪ ˌikəˈnɑmɪks klæs. . . . hi wəz ə tækəl ɔn ðə ˈfutbɔl tim,
nemd ˌboˈlɛnkəwɪts. . . . ɪn ɔrdɚ tə bi ˈɛlədʒəbəl tə ple ɪt wəz ˈnɛsəsɛrɪ fɚ ɪm tə
kip ʌp ɪn ɪz ˈstʌdiz, ə ˈvɛrɪ dɪfəkəlt mætɚ, fɚ hwaɪl i wəz nɑt dʌmɚ ðən ən ɑks
hi wəz nɑt ɛnɪ smɑrtɚ. most əv ɪz prəfɛsɚz wɚ ˈliniənt n̩ hɛlpt ɪm əlɔŋ. nʌn gev
ɪm mɔr hɪnts, ɪn ˈæskɪŋ kwɛstʃənz, ɚ æskt ɪm sɪmplɚ wʌnz ðən ðɪ ˌikəˈnɑmɪks
prəfɛsɚ, ə θɪn, tɪməd mæn nemd bæsəm. wʌn de hwən wi wɚ ɔn ðə ˈsʌbdʒɪkt əv
ˌtrænspɚˈteʃən, ɪt kem bəˈlɛŋkəwɪts tɜn tə ænsɚ ə kwɛstʃən. "nem wʌn minz
əv ˌtrænspɚˈteʃən," ðə prəfɛsɚ sɛd tu ɪm. no laɪt kem ɪntə ðə bɪg tæklz aɪz.
"dʒʌst ɛni minz əv ˌtrænspɚˈteʃən," sɛd ðə prəfɛsɚ. bəˈlɛnkəwɪts sæt ˈstɛrɪŋ æt
ɪm. "ðæt ɪz," pɚsud ðə prəfɛsɚ, "ɛnɪ ˈmidiəm, ˈedʒənsɪ ɔr mɛθəd əv ˈgoɪŋ frəm
wʌn ples tu ənʌðɚ." bəˈlɛnkəwɪts hæd ðə luk əv ə mæn hu əz ˈbiɪŋ lɛd ˈɪntu ə
træp. "ju me tʃuz əmʌŋ stim, ˈhɔrs-ˌdron, ɚ əˈlɛktrɪklɪ prəpɛld ˈvihɪkl̩z," sɛd
ðɪ ɪnˈstrʌktɚ. "aɪ maɪt səgdʒɛst ðə wʌn wi tek ɪn ˈmekɪŋ lɔŋ ˈdʒɜnɪz əkrɔs lænd."
ðɛr wəz ə prəfaund saɪləns ɪn hwɪtʃ ɛvrɪwən stɜd ˌʌnˈizəlɪ, ˌɪnˈkludɪŋ bəˈlɛnkəwɪts
ən mɪstɚ bæsəm. mɪstɚ bæsəm əˈbrʌptlɪ brok ɪz saɪləns ɪn ən əˈmezɪŋ mænɚ.
"tʃu-tʃu-tʃu," hi sɛd ɪn ə lo vɔɪs, ənd ˈɪnstəntlɪ tɜnd skɑrlət. hi glænst əˈpilɪŋlɪ
əraund ðə rum. ɔl əv əs, əv kɔrs, ʃɛrd mɪstɚ bæsəmz dɪˈzaɪr ðət bəˈlɛnkəwɪts ʃəd
ste əbrɛst əv ðə klæs ɪn ˌikəˈnɑmɪks, fɚ ðə ɪləˈnɔɪ gem, wʌn əv ðə hɑrdəst n̩ most
ɪmˈpɔrtənt əv ðə sizən, wəz ˈonlɪ ə wik ɔf. "tut, tut, tu-tuːt!" sʌm studənt wɪð ə
dip vɔɪs mond, ənd wi ɔl lukt ənˈkɜɪdʒɪŋlɪ ət bəˈlɛnkəwɪts. sʌmwən ɛls gev ə faɪn
ɪməˈteʃən əv ə ˌlokəˈmotɪv ˈlɛtɪŋ ɔf stim. mɪstɚ bæsəm ɪmˈsɛlf raundəd ɔf ðə lɪtl̩
ʃo. "dɪŋ, dɔŋ, dɪŋ, dɔŋ," hi sɛd ˈhopfəlɪ. bəˈlɛnkəwɪts wəz ˈstɛrɪŋ et ðə flɔr nau,
ˈtraɪɪŋ tə θɪŋk, hɪz gret brau ˈfɜod, hɪz hjudʒ hændz ˈrʌbɪŋ təgeðɚ, hɪz fes rɛd.
  "hau dədʒu kʌm tə ˈkɑlɪdʒ ðɪs jɪr, mɪstɚ bəlɛnkəwɪts," æskt ðə prəfɛsɚ.
"tʃʌfə, tʃʌfə, tʃʌfə, tʃʌfə."
  "mə fɑðɚ sɛnt mɪ," sɛd ðə ˈfutbɔl pleɚ.
  "hwʌt ɔn," æskt bæsəm.
  "aɪ gɪt n̩ əlauwəns," sɛd ðə tækl̩ ɪn ə lo ˈhʌskɪ vɔɪs, ˈɑbvɪəslɪ ɪmˈbɛrəst.
  "no, no," sɛd bæsəm. "nem ə minz əv ˌtrænspɚˈteʃən. hwʌt dədʒu raɪd
hɪr ɔn?"
  "tren," sɛd bəˈlɛnkəwɪts.
  "kwaɪt raɪt," sɛd ðə prəfɛsɚ. "nau, mɪstɚ nudʒənt, wɪl ju tɛl əs. . . ."]

From *My Life and Hard Times*
By James Thurber

[maɪ brʌðɚ ˈtʃɑrlɪ ənd aɪ, ɪn ðə dez əv aur ˈnɑnɪdʒ, wɚ əlaud əˈfɪʃəlɪ tə ɪt ɔl ðət
wi kəd hold bət twaɪs ə jɪr. ðə fɜst əv aur tu dɪˈbɑtʃəz kem ən ðɪ ɜlɪ sprɪŋ, ðɪ
əkeʒən ˈbiɪŋ ðɪ ˈænjuəl ˈpɪknɪk əv ɛf næps ˈɪnstəˌtut . . . ; ðə sɛkənd wəz ət
krɪsməs, bɪˈgɪnɪŋ fɚ ðə sem ɔn ðə ˈmɔrnɪŋ əv ðə gret de ɪtˈsɛlf ən kənˈtɪnjuɪŋ
ˈdɔgədlɪ əntɪl aur gɪzɚdz gev aut ət læst, ən dɑktɚ zi ke ˈwaɪlɪ, ðə ˈfæməlɪ
dɑktɚ, əraɪvd tə luk ət aur tʌŋz ən plaɪ əs wɪð oliəm riˈsini.
  aur ˈrʌnɪŋ taɪm, ɪn ðɪ ˈævrɪdʒ jɪr, wəz əbaut ˈθɜtɪ-sɪks aurz, wɪð et aurz

aut fɚ ʌnˈizi slip, ˈmekɪŋ ə nɛt əv ˈtwɛnti-et. hwən wi kem ˈlipɪŋ ˌdaunˈstɛrz ɪn
aur flænəl ˈnaɪt-ˌdrɔrz ɔn krɪsməs ˈmɔrnɪŋ ðɛr wəz nat ˈonlɪ ə ˈblezɪŋ tri tə dæzḷ
əs, ənd ə pail əv gɪfts tə səpraɪz əs (əv kɔrs ˈonlɪ ɪn ˈθiərɪ, fɚ wi nu ðə kʌbəd
hwɛr sʌtʃ θɪŋz wɚ kɛpt, ənd ɔlwɪz ɪnˈvɛstəgɛtəd ət ɪn ədvæns ənd ət grɛt lɛŋθ),
bət ɔlso ə tɛbḷ lodəd wɪð ˈkændɪz, keks, rezənz, sɪtrənz, ənd ʌðɚ rɪˈfrɛʃmənts əv
ðə sizən, ɔn ɔl əv hwɪtʃ, ənd tu ɛnɪ əmaunt wi kəd əndur, wi wɚ fri tə wɝk
aur wɪkəd wɪl.

　　æt ʌðɚ taɪmz θɪŋz əv ðæt sɔrt wɚ dold aut tuwəs ɪn ə ˈvɛrɪ kɔʃəs ən ˈɔlmost
ˈnɪgədlɪ we, fɚ ðə ˈmɛdɪkəl saiəns əv ðɪ irə tɔt ðət ən ˈɛksɛs əv swits wəd ruən
ðə tiθ. bət ət krɪsməs, ʌndɚ ðɪ prɪˈvɛlɪŋ ˈbuzɪnəs ənd ˈgudˌwɪl tə mɛn, ðɪs dɛndʒɚ
wəz ɪgˈnɔrd, ənd wi wɚ pərmɪtɛd tə proˈsid ædˈlɪbɪtəm, nat ˈonlɪ ət hom, bət ɔlso
ɔn aur ˈmɔrnɪŋ vizət tə ˈgrændfɑðɚ ˈmɛŋkənz haus ɪn feˈjɛt strit. ðʌs wi wɝkt əwe
ɔl əv krɪsməs de, ˈkipɪŋ aur pakəts ful ən ˈgræbɪŋ ənʌðɚ lod ˈɛvrɪ taɪm wi kem
wɪˈðɪn armz-ritʃ əv ðɪ rɪˈzɝvz. hwən wi wɚ ɔrdəd tə bed ət læst, fɚ ə nait əv
ˌpæθəˈladʒɪkəl drimz, wi went ˈonlɪ rɪˈlʌktəntlɪ, ənd əˈmidɪətlɪ æftɚ brɛkfəst ɔn
krɪsməs ˈmʌndɪ wi rɪˈzumd ˌapəˈreʃənz. it wəz ɪn ðɪ ɝlɪ ˈivnɪŋ əv ðæt de ðət
daktɚ ˈwailɪ drov ʌp ɪn ɪz ˈbʌgɪ, hɪtʃt ɪz hɔrs tə ðə rɪŋ ɪn ðə marbəl hɔrs-blak
aut frʌnt, ən kem ɪn tə du ɪz ˈdutɪ.

　　. . . ðə daktɚ wəz ə hjuˈmen ənd ˌʌndɚˌstændɪŋ mæn, ən so i nɛvɚ ɪntrə-
ˈdust ðə ˈsʌbdʒɪkt əv ˈsʌkərɪŋ mai brʌðɚ ən mi əntɪl wi hæd ə dʌzən ɚ mɔr læst
hwæks ət ðə stʌf ɔn ðə tɛbḷ. ðɛn i wəd ˈsʌdənlɪ fɪks əs wɪð ɪz kold gre ai, kɔl fɚ
ə ˈtɛbḷspun, ən prəsid tə vju aur tʌŋz. hɪz ˈvɝdɪkt, əv kɔrs, wəz ˈɔlwɪz ðə sem.
ɪnˈdid, mai mʌðɚ ˌɪnˈvɛrɪəblɪ ˌænˈtɪsəpɛtəd it bai ˈfɛtʃɪŋ ðə ˌkæstɚ-ˈɔil batḷ
hwail i pandəd ət. tu hɔrəbəl dosəz frəm ðə sem spun, ənd wi wɚ pækt ɔf tə bed.
krɪsməs wəz ovɚ, ðo ðə tri stɪl stud, ənd sʌm əv ðə tɔiz wɚ stɪl ˌʌnˈbrokən. wi
nɛvɚ hæd mʌtʃ ˈæpəˌtait ðə de ˈfalowɪŋ.]

From *Happy Days*
By H. L. Mencken

Reprinted by permission of Alfred A. Knopf, Inc.

[læftɚ ɪz ˈprɪtɪ old stʌf. . . . stivən ˈlikak, ɪn ɪz ˈese ɔn ðə ˈsʌbdʒɪkt, sɛz ðə
lowɚ rɛndʒ əv ðə skel əv hjumɚ ɪz ˈɪləstrɛtəd bɛst bai ðə pʌn. ðə besəs əv ðə pʌn
"ɪz ðə ˌdɪsˈkʌmfətɚ əv ˈlæŋgwɪdʒ ɪtˈsɛlf, əv ˌɛgzəlˈteʃən ovɚ ðə ˈdaunfɔl əv ðə
prɪˈtɛntʃəs səˈlɛmnətɪ əv wɝdz." æz ən ɛgˈzæmpəl hi rɪˈkɔlz ðə ˈdʒɪŋglɪŋ raɪmz
əv tɔm hud (ˈetin ˌθɝtɪ-ˈfaiv tu ˈetin ˌsɛvntɪˈfɔr), ðə most feməs pʌnstɚ əv ðə
edʒəz. (hi lɪvd ə ʃɔrt laif tu əv bɪˈkʌm so feməs.) hi rot:

　　bɛn bætḷ wʌz ə soldʒɚ bold
　　ən just tə wɔrz əlarmz.
　　ə kænən bɔl tuk ɔf ɪz lɛgz
　　so hi led daun ɪz armz.

　　ˈlikak sɛz ðɪs ɪz ə ple ɔn wɝdz ən ˈnʌθɪŋ ɛls. "bət ə pʌn kəntenz ə haiɚ
ˈɛləmənt əv hjumɚ hwɛn ðə ˌkantrəˈdɪkʃən ɪn vɝbəl fɔrmz ˈkɛrɪz wɪð it ɔlso ə
ˌkantrəˈdɪkʃən ɪn ðə sɛnts," æz, fɚ ɪgˈzæmpəl:

ə drʌŋkən mæn ɪn ə ˈbɑːɹum pɪkt ʌp ə ˈsændwɪtʃ ən θru ət əgɛnst ə mɪrəd
wɔl. "ðɛrz fʊd fɚ rɪˈflɛkʃən," sɛd ə ˈbaɪstændɚ.]

From "Trade Winds" in
The Saturday Review of Literature

[ðə taurz əv zinəθ əspaɪrd əbʌv ðə ˈmɔrnɪŋ mɪst; ˈɔstɪr taurz əv stil ən səmɛnt
ən ˈlaɪmston, ˈstɝdɪ əz klɪfs ən dɛləkət əz sɪlvɚ rɑdz. ðe wɚ niðɚ ˈsɪtəˌdɛlz nɔr
tʃɝtʃəz bət ˈfræŋklɪ ən ˈbjutəflɪ ɔfəsˈbɪldɪŋz.

ðə mɪst tuk ˈpɪtɪ ɔn ðə frɛtəd strʌktʃɚz əv ɜlɪɚ ˌdʒɛnəˈreʃənz: ðə post ɔfəs
wɪð ɪts sɪŋgl tɔrtʃəd mænsəd, ðə rɛd brɪk ˌmɪnəˈrɛts əv ˈhɔlkɪn old hauzəz,
ˈfæktrɪz wɪð ˈstɪndʒɪ ən sutəd ˈwɪndoz, wudn̩ tɛnəmənts kʌləd laɪk mʌd. ðə sɪtɪ
wəz ful əv sʌtʃ ˌgroˈtɛskərɪz, bət ðə klin taurz wɚ ˈθrʌstɪŋ ðɛm frəm ðə bɪznəs
sɛntɚ, ənd ɔn ðə farðɚ hɪlz wɚ ˈʃaɪnɪŋ nu hauzəz, homz—ðe simd—fɚ læftɚ ən
ˌtrænˈkwɪlətɪ.

ovɚ ə ˈkankrit brɪdʒ fled ə ˈlɪməˌzin əv lɔŋ slik hud ən nɔɪzləs ɛndʒən. ðiz
pipl̩ ɪn ˈivnɪŋ kloz wɚ rɪˈtɝnɪŋ frəm ən ɔl-naɪt rɪˈhɝsəl əv ə lɪtl̩ θiətɚ ple, ən
arˈtɪstɪk ɑdvɛntʃɚ kənˈsɪdərəblɪ əˈlumənetəd baɪ ʃæmˈpen. bɪˈlo ðə brɪdʒ kɝvd ə
ˈrelrod, ə mez əv grin ən krɪmzən laɪts. ðə nu jork flaɪɚ bumd pæst, ən ˈtwɛntɪ
laɪnz əv ˈpɑlɪʃt stil lipt ɪntə ðə glɛr.

ɪn wʌn əv ðə ˈskaɪˌskrepɚz ðə waɪrz əv ðɪ əˈsoʃɪˌetəd prɛs wɚ ˈklozɪŋ daun.
ðə ˈtɛləˌgræf ˈɑpəretɚz ˈwɪrəlɪ rezd ðɛr ˈsɛljəˌlɔɪd aɪ-ʃedz æftɚ ə naɪt əv ˈtɔkɪŋ
wɪθ pɛrəs ən piˈkɪŋ. θru ðə ˈbɪldɪŋ krɔld ðə skrʌb-wɪmən, ˈjonɪŋ, ðɛr old ʃuz
ˈslæpɪŋ. ðə dɔn mɪst spʌn əwe. kjuz əv mɛn wɪð lʌntʃbaksəz klʌmpt tord ðɪ
əˈmɛnsətɪ əv nu ˈfæktərɪz, ʃits əv glæs ən ˈhalo taɪl, ˈglɪtərɪŋ ʃaps hwɛr faɪv
θauzənd mɛn wɝkt bɪˈniθ wʌn ruf, ˈpɔrɪŋ aut ɑnəst wɛrz ðət wəd bi sold ʌp ðɪ
juˈfretiz ənd əkrɔs ðə vɛlt. ðə hwɪsl̩z rold aut ɪn ˈgritɪŋ, ə kɔrəs tʃɪrfəl əz eprəl
dɔn; ðə sɔŋ əv lebɚ ɪn ə sɪtɪ bɪlt—ɪt simd—fɔr dʒaɪənts.]

From *Babbitt*
By Sinclair Lewis

(Manson has just been asked, "Now! Tell me about your church." He
replies:)

[aɪ əm əfred ju me nɑt kənsɪdɚ ɪt ən ɔltəˈgeðɚ ˈgrowɪŋ kənsɝn. ɪt hæs tə bi
sin ɪn ə sɝtn̩ we, ʌndɚ sɝtn̩ kəndɪʃənz. sʌm pipl̩ nɛvɚ si ɪt ətɔl. ju məst ʌndɚ-
ˈstænd, ðɪs ɪz no paɪl əv dɛd stonz ən ˈʌnˌmɪnɪŋ tɪmbɚ. ɪt ɪz ə ˈlɪvɪŋ θɪŋ. hwɛn ju
ɛntɚ ɪt ju hɪr ə saund æz əv sʌm ˈmaɪtɪ poəm tʃæntəd. lɪsən lɔŋ ənʌf ənd ju wɪl
lɝn ðət ɪt ɪz med ʌp əv ðə ˈbitɪŋ əv hjumən harts, əv ðə nemləs ˈmjuzɪk əv mɛnz
solz—ðæt ɪz, ɪf ju hæv ɪrz. ɪf ju hæv aɪz, ju wɪl ˈprezəntlɪ si ðə tʃɝtʃ ɪtˈsɛlf—ə

ˈlumɪŋ ˈmɪstərɪ əv mɛnɪ ʃeps ən ˈʃædoz, ˈlipɪŋ ʃɪr frəm flɔr tə dom. ðə wɝk əv no ˈɔrdənˌɛrɪ bɪldɚ.

ðə pɪləz ʌv ɪt go ʌp laɪk ðə ˈbrɒnɪ trʌŋks əv ˈhɪroz: ðə swit hjumən flɛʃ əv mɛn ən wɪmən ɪz moldəd əbaʊt ɪts ˈbulwɚks, strɔŋ, ˌɪmˈprɛgnəbḷ: ðə fesəz əv lɪtḷ tʃɪldrən læf aʊt frəm ˈɛvərɪ kɔrnɚ ston: ðə tɛrəbəl spænz ən artʃəz əv ɪt ar ðə dʒɔɪnd hændz əv kʌmrədz; ənd ʌp ɪn ðə haɪts ən spesəz ðɛr ar ɪnˈskraɪbd ðə nʌmbələs ˈmjuzɪŋz əv ɔl ðə drimɚz əv ðə wɝld. ɪt ɪz jɛt ˈbɪldɪŋ—ˈbɪldɪŋ ən bɪlt əpɒn. ˈsʌmˌtaɪmz ðə wɝk goz fɔrwɚd ɪn dip darknəs: ˈsʌmˌtaɪmz ɪn ˈblaɪndɪŋ laɪt: naʊ bɪˈniθ ðə bɝdṇ əv ˌʌnˈʌtərəbḷ ˈæŋgwɪʃ: naʊ tə ðə tun ev gret læftɚ ənd hɪˈrɔɪk ˈʃaʊtɪŋz laɪk ðə kraɪ əv θʌndɚ.

ˈsʌmˌtaɪmz, ɪn ðə saɪləns əv ðə ˈnaɪt:aɪm, wʌn me hɪr ðə ˈtaɪnɪ ˈhæmərɪŋz əv ðə ˈkɑmˌrædz ət wɝk ʌp ən ðə dom—ðə ˈkɑmˌrædz hu həv klaɪmd əhɛd.]

From *The Servant in the House*
By Charles Rann Kennedy

[wʌn naɪt hwaɪl wi wɚ ɪn ðɪz ˈtrɑpɪks aɪ wɛnt aʊt tə ði ɛnd əv ðə ˈflaɪɪŋ dʒɪb-bum, əpɒn sʌm dutɪ, ænd, ˈhævɪŋ ˈfɪnɪʃt ət, tɝnd əraʊnd, ənd le ovɚ ðə bum fɚ ə lɔŋ taɪm, ədˈmaɪrɪŋ ðə ˈbjutɪ əv ðə saɪt bɪˈfɔr mi. ˈbiɪŋ so far aʊt frəm ðə dɛk, aɪ kəd luk ət ðə ʃɪp, æz ət ə sepərət vesəl;—ən ðɛr roz ʌp frəm ðə watɚ, səpɔrtəd ˈonlɪ baɪ ðə smɔl hʌl, ə ˈpɪrəmɪd əv kænvəs, ˈsprɛdɪŋ aʊt far bɪˈjɑnd ðə hʌl, ən ˈtaʊrɪŋ ʌp ɔlmost, æz ət simd ɪn ði ɪndɪstɪŋkt naɪt ɛr, tə ðə klaʊdz. ðə si wəz əz stɪl əz ən ɪnlənd lek; ðə laɪt tred wɪnd wəz stʌdəd wɪð:ə ˈtrɑpɪkəl starz; ðɛr wəz no saʊnd bət ðə ˈrɪplɪŋ əv ðə watɚ ʌndɚ ðə stɝn: ənd ðə selz wɚ sprɛd aʊt, waɪd ən haɪ. . . . so kwaɪət, tu, wəz ðə si, ən so stɛdɪ ðə brɪz, ðət əf ðoz selz həd bɪn skʌlptʃɚd marbəl, ðe kəd nɑt əv bɪn mɔr moʃənləs.]

From *Two Years before the Mast*
By Richard Henry Dana, Jr.

[maɪ frɛndz: no wʌn, nɑt ɪn maɪ ˌsɪtʃuˈeʃən, kæn əˈprɪʃɪˌet maɪ ˈfilɪŋ əv sædnəs ət ðɪs ˈpartɪŋ. tu ðɪs ples, ən tu ðɪz pipḷ, aɪ o ˈɛvrɪθɪŋ. hɪr aɪ həv lɪvd ə kwɔrtɚ əv ə ˈsɛntʃərɪ, ənd həv pæst frʌm ə jʌŋ mæn tu ən old mæn. hɪr maɪ tʃɪldrən həv bɪn bɔrn, ənd wʌn laɪz ˈbɛrɪd. aɪ naʊ lɪv, nɑt ˈnoɪŋ hwɛn ɔr ɛvɚ aɪ me rɪˈtɝn, wɪð ə tæsk bɪˈfɔr mi gretɚ ðən ðæt hwɪtʃ rɛstəd ɒn ˈwɒʃɪŋtən. wɪˈðaʊt ði əsɪstəns əv ðæt dɪˈvaɪn ˈbiɪŋ hu ɛvɚ ətɛndəd hɪm, aɪ ˈkænɑt səksid. wɪð:æt əsɪstəns, aɪ ˈkænɑt fel. ˈtrʌstɪŋ ɪn hɪm hu kən go wɪð mi, ənd rɪˈmen wɪð ju, ənd bi ˈɛvrɪˌhwɛr fɔr gud, lɛt əs ˈkɑnfədəntlɪ hop ðət ɔl wɪl jɛt bi wɛl. tu hɪz kɛr kəˈmɛndɪŋ ju, æz aɪ hop ɪn jɔr prɛrz ju wɪl kəmɛnd mi, aɪ bɪd ju æn əfɛkʃənət ˈfɛrˈwɛl.]

Abraham Lincoln's Farewell Address
to the People of Springfield, Illinois, February 11, 1861

[wi mit tə ˈsɛləbret flæg de bɪˈkɔz ðɪs flæg hwɪtʃ wi ɑnɚ ənd ʌndɚ hwɪtʃ wi sɝv
ɪz ðɪ ɛmbləm əv aur ˈjunɑtɪ, aur pɑur, aur θɑt ənd pɝpəs æz ə neʃən. ɪt hæz
no ʌðɚ ˈkɛrɪktɚ ðən ðæt hwɪtʃ wi gɪv ɪt frəm ˌdʒɛnəˈreʃən tu ˌdʒɛnəˈreʃən. ðə
tʃɔɪsəz ɑr aurz. ɪt flots ɪn məˈdʒɛstɪk saɪləns əbʌv ðə hosts ðət ˈɛksəˌkjut ðoz
tʃɔɪsəz, hwɛðɚ ɪn pis ɔr ɪn wɔr. ənd jɛt, ðo saɪlənt, ɪt spiks tu əs,—spiks əv ðə
pæst, əv ðə mɛn ənd wɪmən hu wɛnt bɪˈfɔr ʌs ənd əv ðə rɛkɚdz ðe rot əpɑn ɪt.
wi ˈsɛləˌbret ðə de əv ɪts bɝθ; ənd frəm ɪts bɝθ əntɪl nau ɪt həz wɪtnəst ə
gret ˈhɪstərɪ, həz flotəd ɑn haɪ ðə sɪmbəl əv gret ɪˈvɛnts, əv ə gret plæn əv laɪf
wɝkt aut baɪ ə gret pipḷ.]

From Woodrow Wilson's Flag Day
Address, June 14, 1917

[ðə lɔrd ɪz maɪ ʃɛpɚd; aɪ ʃæl nɑt wɔnt.
hi mekəθ mi tə laɪ daun ɪn grin pæstʃɚz;
hi lidəθ mi bɪˈsaɪd ðə stɪl wɔtɚz.
hi rɪˈstɔrəθ maɪ sol;
hi lidəθ mi ɪn ðə pæðz əv raɪtʃəsnəs fɔr hɪz nemz sek.
je, ðo aɪ wɔk θru ðə ˈvælɪ əv ðə ˈʃædo əv dɛθ,
aɪ wɪl fɪr no ivəl: fɔr ðau ɑrt wɪð mi;
ðaɪ rɑd ənd ðaɪ stæf ðe kʌmfɚt mi.
ðau prɪˈpɛrəst ə tebəl bɪˈfɔr mi ɪn ðə prɛzəns əv maɪn ˈɛnəmɪz:
ðau ənɔɪntəst maɪ hɛd wɪð ɔɪl; maɪ kʌp rʌnəθ ovɚ.
ˈʃurlɪ gudnəs ənd ˈmɝsɪ ʃæl ˈfɑlo mi ɔl ðə dez əv maɪ laɪf,
ənd aɪ wəl dwɛl ɪn ðə haus əv ðə lɔrd fɔr ɛvɚ.]

Twenty-third Psalm from *The Bible*
as arranged and edited by Ernest Sutherland Bates

[ˈsʌnsɛt ənd ˈivnɪŋ stɑr,
   æ* nd wʌn klɪr kɔl fɔr mi!
ənd me ðɛr bi no ˈmonɪŋ əv ðə bɑr
   hwɛn aɪ put aut tu si,

bət sʌtʃ ə taɪd æz ˈmuvɪŋ simz əslip,
   tu ful fɔr saund ən fom,
hwɛn ðæt hwɪtʃ dru frəm aut ðə ˈbaundləs dip
   tɝnz əgɛn hom.

ˈtwaɪlaɪt ənd ˈivnɪŋ bɛl,
   ənd æftɚ ðæt ðə dɑrk!
ænd me ðɛr bi no sædnəs əv fɛrˈwɛl,
   hwɛn aɪ ɛmˈbɑrk;

fɔr ðo frʌm aut aur bɔrn əv taɪm ən ples
        ðə flʌd me bɛr mi far,
aɪ hop tʊ si maɪ paɪlət fes tu fes
        hwɛn aɪ həv krɔst ðə bar.]

"Crossing The Bar"
By Alfred, Lord Tennyson

[hwɛn aɪ kənsɪdɚ hau maɪ laɪt ɪz spɛnt
ɛr hæf maɪ dez, ɪn ðɪs dark wɜld ən waɪd,
ænd ðæt wʌn tælənt hwɪtʃ ɪz dɛθ tu haɪd
ladʒd wɪð mi jusləs, ðo maɪ sol mɔr bɛnt
tu sɜv ˈðɛrwɪð maɪ mekɚ, æn prɪˈzɛnt
maɪ tru əkaunt, lɛst hi rɪˈtɜnɪŋ tʃaɪd;
"dʌθ gad ɛgˈzækt ˈdeˌlebɚ, laɪt dɪˈnaɪd?"
aɪ ˈfɑndlɪ æsk. bʌt peʃəns, tu prɪˈvɛnt
ðæt mɜmɚ, sun rɪˈplaɪz, "gad dʌθ nat nid
iðɚ mænz wɜk ɔr hɪz on gɪfts. hu bɛst
bɛr hɪz maɪld jok, ðe sɜv hɪm bɛst. hɪz stet
ɪz ˈkɪŋlɪ: θauzəndz æt hɪz ˈbɪdɪŋ spid,
æn post ɔr lænd ənd oʃən ˈwɪðaut rɛst;
ðe ˈɔlso sɜv hu ˈonlɪ stænd ænd wet.]

"On His Blindness"
By John Milton

Appendix B

Transcriptions of Speeches of Public Figures

In this section are samples of the speech of a number of public figures, presented in broad transcription. Conventional punctuation is used instead of pause marks, and stress marks are employed sparingly. Nonphonemic and modifying symbols are used only to point out some interesting dialectal features. No attempt is made to have strict uniformity.

Some samples were taken from broadcasts, most of which originated with the Columbia Broadcasting System and were heard in the Seattle, Washington, area over KIRO; others originated with KIRO. Electrical transcriptions of the broadcasts were presented to the University of Washington by KIRO for whatever scholarly use might be made of them, and they constitute a historical collection of the School of Communications.

SECTION 1 AMERICAN DIALECTS

Dave Beck
Labor Leader

[jɛs, wɪ əv hæd ar dɪfrənsəz wɪθ ɪmplɔɪəz ɪn ar ˈɪndəstrɪ.
wi hæv fɔt ɪtʃ ʌðɚ pətɪ hard ət tɑɪmz. raɪt nau, hauɛvɚ, wɪ ar
faɪtɪŋ tugɛðɚ tu kip ar trʌks ɒn ðə rod, hɔlɪŋ ðə gudz ðæt ɚ
nidəd tə wɪn ðɪs wɔr. aɪ spik tənaɪt ˌrɛprəˈzɛntɪŋ mɔr ðən sɪks
hʌndəd θauzənd mɛmbɚz əv ðɪ ˌɪntɚˈnæʃənəl ˈbrʌðɚˌhud əv timstɚz
hwɛn aɪ ɪnˈdɔrs ðə ˈprogræm hwɪtʃ mɪstɚ ɪsmən æn mɪstɚ barjɚ
həv prɪˈzɛntəd. ar ˈmɛmbɚʃɪp ɪz ˈdiplɪ kənsɛnd wɪθːə prabləm
əv kənˈsɚvɪŋ taɪɚz ən ðə trʌks wi nau hæv. aʊr dʒab ən ðə fjutʃɚ əv ar ˈɪndəstrɪz ar ɪnˈvalvd. mɔr ðən ðæt, ar ˈkʌntrɪ ɪz
dəˈpɛndɪŋ an ʌs tə kip ðoz trʌks ˈrolɪŋ....]

Francis Biddle
U.S. Attorney General (1941–1945)

[tənaɪt aɪ prəpoz tə spik ˈbriflɪ əv sʌm ˈæˌspɛkts əv θri
pətɪkjələ məˈnɒrətɪz huz rɪˈlɛʃən tə ðə grete badɪ əv aʊə neʃən
hæz bɪn brɔt ɪntu ʃaːp fokəs baɪ tu jɪəz əv wɔə. aɪ rɪˈfɚ tə
ðə ˈdʒæpəˌnis, tə ðə dʒɚuz ænd tə ðə ˈnigroz. ɪt ɪz ə ˈkjurɪəs
ˈpærəˌdoks ðət ˈɔlˌðo ˈdjurɪŋ ðɪs wɔə sɚtn sɪvəl ˈlɪbətɪz hæv
safəd lɛs ðən ɪn ðə fɚst wɚld wɔə, ðə tɛnʃənz əˈraɪzɪŋ frəm ðə
ples əv ðiz θri reʃəl məˈnɒrətɪz ɪn ðə næʃnəl laɪf hæv ˈgretlɪ
ɪnkrist. ɪn ðə læst wɔə ðə raɪts əv eljən ˈɛnəmiz, pəˈtɪkjəlɪ
əv dʒɚmənz hu wə ˈlɪvɪŋ ɪn ə ˈkʌntrɪ, ænd əv ðoz ˈrædɪkəlz hu
əpozd ðə wɔə ænd aə ˈɛntrɪ ɪntuwɪrt, wə lɪtʃ rɪˈspɛktɪd. næʃnəl
ˈprɛdʒudɪs ðən ræn əgɛnst ˈɛnɪwʌn əv dʒɚmən ˈænsɛstrɪ no mætɚ
hau lɒŋ hi həd lɪvd hɪə ɔə hau lɔɪl i wɔz tə ʌs. fridəm əv spitʃ
wəz lɛs ˈtaləretəd ænd mɔː ˈnjuzpepəz wɚ səprɛst ɒn ðɪ graund
ðət ðe wɚ sədɪʃəs. ðɛ we ˈmɛnɪ ˌprasəˈkjuʃənz boθ stet ən fɛdrəl
ɔfən ɒn ɪl-kənˈsɪdɚd ænd pɛtɪ graʊnz. ðiz ətæks hɛv nɒt rɪˈkɚd
ɪn ðɪs wɔə--ɔr ət list tu ə faː lɛs dɪˈgri....]

Richard Kleberg
Member of U.S. Congress from Texas (1931–1945)

[aɪ səpɔrtəd ði ænti-sʌbsədi bɪl fɔr tu rizənz ɪn vɔɪsɪŋ
maɪ apəˈzɪʃən tu ə waɪd opən ˈsʌbsədi progrəm fɚ ðə pipl̩ əv ðɪ
juˈnaɪtəd stets. aɪ ˈkænɒt æn nɛvɚ wɪl brɪˈliv ðæt əmɛrəkən bɪznəs
æn ðɪ əmɛrəkən pipl̩ ar ˌɪksˈkluɪvlɪ dɪˈpɛndəndent ʌpon ðə fɛdrəl
gʌvəmənt fɔr ðɛr sælˈveʃən. ɪf ðɪs ʃɛd hæpən--gad fəbɪd ðɪs ʃɛd
evɚ bəkʌm tru--ɪt wɪl onlɪ bi bikɒz ænd hwɛn ar gʌvmənt ɪz no
lɒŋgɚ ʌ gʌvmənt hwɪtʃ əraɪzəz aʊt əv ðə pipl̩ bʌt onlɪ hwɪn ɪt
bɪˈkʌmz ə gʌvəmənt ovɚ ðə pipl̩. ðə vɛrɪ aɪdɪə ʌv dɪˈpɛndəns ɪz
ʌtɚlɪ rɪˈpʌlsɪv tu maɪ we əv ðɪŋkɪŋ bikɒz dɪˈpɛndənsɪ bɪˈgɛts

səb'sɜvjəns æn ðə mɛn æn wɪmən ðət aɪ no ænd lʌv ðæt 'kanstətjut
ðə pipḷ ʌv ðɪ ju'naɪtəd stets əv əmɛrəkə wɪl hæf tʊ tʃɛndʒ ɪ'mɛʒə‐
əbli ɪn fɔrm æn 'stætʃʊr tu bɪ'kʌm ðə 'krɔlɪŋ sɜvjɪl kritʃəz əv
sʌtʃ ə manstɚ....]

Elmer Davis
News Broadcaster and Commentator (d. 1958)

['sɪrɪəs raɪəts ɚ 'goɪŋ ɔn ɪn mɪ'læn ænd 'ɛls'hwɛr ɪn nɔrðɚn
'ɪtəlɪ ə'kɔrdɪŋ tʊ ˌɪnfɚ'meʃən 'rɪtʃɪŋ 'dɪplə,mæts ɪn ˌjugo'slavɪə
ænd rɪ'pɔrtəd baɪ ar ˌkɔrə'spandənt ɪn ˌbɛl'grad, wɪnstən bədɛt.
ðɛr simz tu hɛv bɪn sʌm sɔrt əv 'mɪlə'tɛrɪ 'raɪzɪŋ iðɚ əgɛnst ðə
fæʃəst partɪ ɔr əgɛnst ðə dʒɜmən trups hu ar rɪ'pɔrtəd əz numɚəs
ɪn nɔrðɚn ɪtəlɪ, fɚ θrɪ haɪ ɪ'tæljən afəsɚz ɚ sɛd tu hɛv bɪn
kɪld baɪ dʒɜmənz hu ˌɪntɚ'vind æn blæk ʃɛt junəts ar ə'sɪstɪŋ ðə
dʒɜmənz ɪn rɪ'prɛsɪŋ ðə ˌdɪs'ɔrdɚz. dʒɜmən soldʒɚz ɚ sɛd tu hɛv
'akjə'paɪd ðə mɛlæn 'rel,rod steʃən ən 'tɛlə,fon, 'tɛlə,græf
ænd 'rɛdɪo ɔfəsəz ænd 'ɔlso tə bi 'gardɪŋ ðə prɪnsəpəl 'fæktərɪz.
tu'rɪn ən 'vɛrɪəs ʌðɚ plɛsəz ɪn ðə po 'vælɪ ar 'ɔlso ðə sin əv
'raɪətɪŋ. ðə 'kæʒuəltɪz ar sɛd tə rʌn ʌp ɪntə ðə hʌndrədz. ðɪs
ɪnfɚ'meʃən ɪz nat jɛt kɔ'rabɚetəd frəm ʌðɚ sɔrsəz bət mɪstɚ bədɛt
ɪz ðə kɔrə'spandənt hu gat ðə fɚst njuz əv ðɪ əraɪvəl əv dʒɜmən
trups æn plɛnz ɪn 'ɪtəlɪ ænd ar ˌkɔrə'spandənt hɛrɪ 'flænərɪ rɪ‐
'pɔrtəd frʌm bɚlɪn tənaɪt ðət pepɚz ðɛr spik əv ɛndləs trɛnlodz
əv ðə dʒɜmən ɚ fɔrs æz goɪŋ θru ðə brɛnɚ pæs tɔrd ɪ'tæljən
sɔɪl....]

John Foster Dulles
U.S. Secretary of State (1953–1959)

[læst ə fraɪdi 'ivnɪŋ aɪ rɪ'tɜnd tu 'wɔʃɪŋtən æftɚ fɔr wiks
əv 'deli ˌdɪs'kʌʃən æt bɚlɪn wɪð:i farən mɪnəstɚz əf frænts, grɛt
brɪtṇ ænd ðə sov'jɛt junjən--mɪʃɚ bi'do, mɪstɚ idṇ æn mɪstɚ malə‐
tof. 'ɔlso ɔn ðə we bæk aɪ mɛt wɪθ tʃænslɚ 'ædnauɚ ə dʒɜmənɪ. aɪ
faɪnd ɔn maɪ rɪ'tɜn ət ðɛrz sʌm kənfjuʒən æz tə hwʌt rilɪ hæpənd.
ðæts nat sɚ'praɪzɪŋ. ɪts 'dɪfəkult tə græsp 'kwɪklɪ ðɪ rɪ'zʌlts
əv fɔr wiks əv dəbet ɔn 'mɛnɪ dɪfɚnt mætɚz æn ɪn'did ðə ful rɪ‐
zʌlts kænat bi 'kɪrlɪ sin fɚ mɛnɪ mʌns. aɪ kæn hauɛvɚ se ðət ðɪs
'mitɪŋ hæd tu rɪ'zʌlts hwɪtʃ wɪl pɚ'faundli 'ɪnfluwəns ðə fjutʃɚ.
fɚst, əz far əz jɚəp wəz kənsɚnd, wi brɔt mɪstɚ 'malətof tə ʃo
rʌʃəz hænd ænd ɪt wəz sin əz ə hænd ðə? hɛl fæst tə 'ɛvrɪθɪŋ ɪt
hæd, ɪn'kludɪŋ ist 'dʒɜmənɪ ænd ist ɔstrɪə ænd ɪt ɔlso sɔt tə

græb səm mɔr. æn ˈsɛkəndlɪ ɪz far əz kərɪə ænd ɪndotʃaɪnə wɚ kɛn-
ˈsɚnd wi brɔt mɪstɚ ˈmalətɔf tu ɛkˈsɛpt ə rɛzəˈluʃən hwɪtʃ spɛld
aʊt ði ˈjuˈnaɪtɛd stɛts pəzɪʃən ðæt rɛd tʃaɪnə maɪt ɪn ðɪz tu ɪn-
sənsəz bi dɛlt wɪθ hwɚ ˈnɛsəsɛrɪ, bət nɑt æz ə ɡʌvəmənt ˈrɛkɪɡ-
naɪzd baɪ ðə jənaɪtɛd stɛts....]

Guy Gillette
U.S. Senator from Iowa (1936–1945)

[ðə wɜd ˈsʌbsədɪ ɪz diˈfaɪnd æz piˈkjunɪɛri ed dəˈrɛklɪ
ɡræntɛd baɪ ə ɡʌvəmənt tu ən ˌɪndɪˈvɪdʒuwəl ɔr tu ə kəmɚʃəl
ˈɛntəpraɪz ɪn ðə pʌblɪk ˈwɛlfɚ. ˈsʌbsədɪz ɔr ˈbaʊntɪz əv ðə kaɪnd
so dɪˈfaɪnd ɑr nɑt nu æn hæv bɪn juzd ˌθruˈaʊt riˈkɔrdəd hɪstrɪ
ænd ɑr stɪl biɪŋ ɪkˈstɛnsɪvlɪ juzd ɪn ɑr neʃən. wi hæv numərəs
ˈɪnstənsɪz ɪn ɑr on iˈkɑnəmi. wi əv ped ˈsʌbsədɪz dəˈrɛklɪ tə
ˈpʌblɪk ˈkɛrɪjəz fɚ ˈtrænsˈpɔrtɪŋ mel. wi hæv ped ˈsʌbsədɪz tə bɪld,
mɛnten æn ˈɑpəret ə mɚtʃənt mərin. wi hɛv ped ˈsʌbsədɪz fɚ ðə
kənstrʌkʃən ən əpəˈreʃən əv ˈreɪrodz ən ʌðɚ taɪps ʌv pʌblɪk ˌju-
ˈtɪlətɪz. ðɪz dərɛk ˈsʌbsədɪz hæv bɪn ˈdʒʌstəfaɪd ɔn ðə preməs
ðət pʌblɪk wɪl dɪˈmænz ˈsɚtn̩ fəˈsɪlətɪz fɚ ðə neʃənz jus hwɛn
ðə prədʌkʃən ɔr ˌmɛnˈtenəns əv ðɪz fəˈsɪlətɪz dʌz nɑt əv ɪtˈsɛlf
ɡɪv əʃurəns əv səfɪʃənt ˈɪnkʌm tə ˈdʒʌstəfaɪ praɪvet kæpətəl ɪn
ˈmekɪŋ ðɪ əsɛnʃəl ɪnˈvɛsmənts fɔr iðɚ ðer kriˈeʃən ɔr ˌmɛnˈtenəns.
ðə sem ˈlɑdʒɪk əz bɪn ðə səpɔrt əv ˈmɛnɪ pɑləsɪz ʌv ɪndəˈvɪdʒuwəl
sʌbsədɪ sʌtʃ əz aʊr ˈsɛntʃərɪ old ˈpɑləsɪ əv prəˈtɛktɪv tɛrəf fɔr
ɪnfənt ˌmænjəˈfæktʃərɪŋ ˈɪndəstrɪz....]

Herbert Hoover
U.S. President (1929–1933)

[ˈvɪktərɪ ɪz naʊ ɪnˈɛvətəbəl. ðer wɛl bi mɛnɪ mɔr hɑrd mʌns,
bət ˈɛvrɪ mʌnθ brɪŋz ʌs nɪrɚ tu ðə prɑbləmz ʌv pis. ðɪ əmɛrəkən
pipl̩ ɚ əlaɪv tu ðə nid ænd ɑr dɪˈtɚmənd ðæt wi mʌst hæv ə ˈlæstɪŋ
pis ðɪs taɪm. frəm kost tə kost ju ɚ ˈθɪŋkɪŋ æn dɪsˈkʌsɪŋ ðə wez
əv pis. ju wʌnt jur sʌnz ən hʌzbəndz ən faðɚz hom. ju wɔntə mek
jur laɪvz əɡen fri frʌm ðə ˈhardʃɪps əv wɔr. bət ðə mɛθəd əv mekɪŋ
pis ɪz ɔlso ˈbiɪŋ ˈaʊrlɪ dɪsˈkʌst ɪn ðə buks ənd ɪn ðə pres ən
ovɚ ðə ˈredɪə. kɛngrɛʃənəl rɛzəˈluʃənz ən pəˈlɪtɪkəl əˈfɛnsɪvz ɑr
ɪn moʃn̩ ɔl əloŋ ðə pis frʌnt. æn ɪn ðɪs wi hæv tu skulz əv dɪ-
ˈskʌʃən. ɪn ðə fɚst skul ɑr ðoz pipəl hu ɑr ˈstraɪvɪŋ tu dɪˈstɪl
frʌm ðə wɚld ɪkˈspɪrjəns ˈsʌmθɪŋ dəfənət æn ˈpɑstɪv æn ðer hæv
bɪn ə nʌmbɚ əv ˈnotəbl̩ ˌkɑntrəˈbjuʃənz put fɔrwɚd hwɪtʃ mert ɡret

kən'sɪdəreʃən. ðə sɛkənt skul ar ðoz hu lɪv ɪn ðɪ ɪn'dɛfnət ænd
ɪn ðɪ ɪnfɪnət. ðer emz ar mæg'nɪfəsent, ðer frezəz ar sənɔrəs ənd
ðer slogənz ar ɪm'pɛlɪŋ. bət hwɪn wi sɪft ðəm lc daun ðə ə 'mostɪ
nebjələ wɜdz tə ðɪ əfɛkt ðət wi məst ko'apəret ɔr kə'læbəet wɪð:ə
wɜld tʊ prɪ'zɜv pis ænd rɪ'stɔr pras'pɛrətɪ. ðer ə lɔŋ wez frəm
haʊ tə du ət....]

H. V. Kaltenborn
Radio News Commentator (d. 1965)

[gud 'ivnɪŋ 'ɛvrɪbʌdɪ. fɔr mʌnθs pæst ðer əz bɪn ə 'kantest
əv wɪts bətwin ðə prezədent əv ðɪ ju'naɪtəd stets ænd ðə 'wɔʃɪŋtən rɪ'pɔrtəz. ðe hæv sɔt:u mek hɪm tɛl wʌt hi ɪn'tendz tə du
əbaʊt ə θɜd·tɜm. hi hæz sɔt baɪ bæntə, 'pɜsɪ,flaɜ, klɛvə ænsə,
smaɪlz ənd əkeɜənəl saɪləns nat tə tɛl hɪm. haʊ lɔŋ kæn ðæt bætʃ
əv wɪts go ɔn wɪðaʊt 'sʌmbʌdi luzɪŋ hɪz tempə? ðə prezədent ðʌs
far æz bɪn ʌn'ju:ɜuəlɪ peʃənt wɪð rɪ'spɛkt tʊ ðiz pəsɪstent ,ɪn-
'kwaɪrɪz. pəhæps hi fɪlz ðæt ðe ar ,dɜʌstəfaɪd baɪ ðə 'pʌbɪk kju-
rijasətɪ ænd pʌblɪk 'ɪntərest, bət əv kɔrs æz 'prezədent ɪf hi
wɔntəd tu hi kʊd hæv stiv ɜli tɛl ðə,bɔɪz. "naʊ ·si hɪə, no mɔr
kwestʃənz əbaʊt ðə θɜd tɜm ɔr aɪ wɪl kʌt aʊt ðə.prɛs kanfərən-
səz....]

Charles A. Lindbergh
Aviator (d. 1975)

[ɪn taɪmz əv gret ɪ'mʌdɜənsɪ men ʌv ðə sem bəlif mʌst gæðə
təgeðə fɔr 'mjutʃuəl kaʊnsəl ænd ækʃn. ɪf ðe fel tə du ðɪs ɔl
ðət ðe stænd fɔr wɪl bi lɔst aɪ spik tənʌɪt tu ðoz pipəl ɪn ðɪ
ju'naɪtəd stets əv əmerəkə hu fil ðət ðe 'dɛstənɪ ʌv ðɪs 'kʌntrɪ
dʌz nat kɔl fɔr aʊr ɪn'vɔlvmənt ɪn ,jʊrə'pɪən wɔrz. wi mʌst bænd
təgeðə tu prɪ'vent ðə lɔs ʌv mɔr ə'merəkən laɪvz ɪn ðiz ɪn'tɜnəl
stragəlz ʌv jʊrəp. wi məst kip fɔrən ,prapə'gændə frəm puʃɪŋ aʊr
'kʌntrɪ 'blaɪndlɪ 'ɪntu ənʌðə wɔr. madən wɔr wɪθ ɔl ɪts 'kansɪ-
,kwensəz ɪz tu·'trædɜɪk æn tu 'dɛvəs,tetɪŋ tə bi əprotʃt frʌm
'ɛnɪθɪŋ bʌt ə 'pjurlɪ əmerəkən 'stændpɔɪnt. wi ʃʊd nɛvə entə ə
wɔr ʌn'lɛs ət ɪz 'æbsə'lutlɪ əsentʃəl tə ðə fjutʃə 'welfer ʌv ar
neʃən. ðɪs 'kʌntrɪ wəz 'kalənaɪzd baɪ men ən wɪman frəm jʊrəp.
ðə hetrədz, ðə ,pɜsɪ'kjuʃənz, ðɪ 'ɪn,trigz ðe lɛft bɪ'haɪnd gev
ðem 'kɜɪdɜ tə krɔs ðɪ æt'læntɪk oʃən tu ə nu lænd. ðe prəfɜd ðə
wɪldənəs ænd ðɪ 'ɪndɪjənz tə ðə prabləmz əv jʊrəp. ðe wed ðə kɔst
əv fridəm frəm ðoz prabləmz ænd ðe ped ðə praɪs....]

Adlai Stevenson
American Statesman and Diplomat (d. 1965)

[....ɔlmost 'θɝtɪ jɪrz əgo æn ɪn'kwɪzətɪv jʌŋ mæn trævəld
əkrɔst jurəp, ʌp ðə blæk si ænd əkrɔs wɛstən rʌʃə æn wɛn hi gɑt
hɜʊm 'bɝstɪŋ wɪð hɪz traɪəlz ənd əd'vɛntʃɚz, 'sʌmpθɪŋ hæd gɔn
rɔŋ. ðɛr wɛz no bænd ænd no 'wɛlkəmɪŋ kə'mɪtɪ tu mit hɪm ɑn ðə
steʃən ɪn 'blumɪŋtən ˌɪlə'nɔɪ. ɪn sæd fæk ðɛr'wʌz no nʌn ət ɔl
ɛk'sɛpt æn old 'bægɪdʒ mæn ænd hɪz 'gritɪŋ wɛz, "haɪ, ædlɪ! ju
bɪn əwɛʔ" wɛl, aɪv bɪn 'trævlɪŋ əgɛn æn aɪ mʌs se ðət ðɪs wɛlkəm
kəmpɛrz kwaɪt 'fevərəblɪ wɪð:æt. aɪ əm tʌtʃt ən gritlɪ--æn diplɪ
'gretfʊl tu ðə kə'mɪtɪ...ænd tu ɔl əv ju hu hɛv kʌm hɪr tə ðə
'sɪvɪk ɒprə ðɪs 'ivnɪŋ. ju du mi gret anɚ. bət ðə trɪp ɪt'sɛlf
wɛz ə rɪ'wɔːd æn aɪ wɪʃ ðət 'ɛvrɪwʌn kənsɜnd əbaʊt hɪz 'kʌntrɪz
plɛs ɪn ðə wɜld kʊd æv hæd ðɪ ˌɑpɚ'tunətɪ aɪv hæd tu hɪr ænd tə
si, ə'spɛʃəlɪ 'ɛnɪwʌn hu dʌznt no haʊ lʌkɪ hi ɪz tu bi æn
əmɛrəkən....]

Harry S Truman
U.S. President (1945–1953)

[maɪ fɛlə 'sɪtəzənz. aɪ əm hɪr tənaɪt tə set ðə rɛkɚd stret.
aɪ əm glæd ðæt aɪ æm ebḷ tə du ðɪs ɑn mə'zɪr sɔɪl baɪ dərɛkt
kəmˌjunəkeʃən wɪθ so mɛnɪ ʌv maɪ 'fɛlo əmɛrəkənz. məzɝɪ ɪz ðə
ʃo mi stet. wɛl, aɪ ʃo ju ðə truθ. ɒn no'vɛmbɚ ðə sɪks ðə nju
əd'mɪnəˌstreʃən θru hæbət ˌbraʊnɛl dʒuŋɚ, ə fɔrmɚ tʃɝmən əv
ðə rɪ'pʌblɪkən næʃnəl kə'mɪtɪ naʊ 'sɝvɪŋ əz ə'tɝnɪ dʒɛnrəl, med ə
pɝsnəl ətæk ɔn mi. ˌbraʊ'nɛl med ðɪs ətæk ɪn ðə kɔrs ʌv ə po'lɪtɪkəl spitʃ bɪ'fɔr ə lʌntʃən klʌb ɪn ʃə'kɑgo. ðɪs ətæk ɪz wɪðaʊt
'pɛrələl aɪ bɪ'liv ɪn ðə 'hɪstrɪ əv ar 'kʌntrɪ. aɪ hæv bɪn əkjuzd
ɪn əfɛkt əv 'nowɪŋ'lɪ bɪ'treɪŋ ðɪ sɪ'kjurətɪ əv ðɪ ju'naɪtəd stets.
ðɪs tʃardʒ ɪz əv kɔrs ə 'fɔlshʊd æn ðə mæn hu med ɪt hæd ɛvrɪ
rizən tu no ɪt ɪz ə 'fɔlshʊd. ɑn 'tuzdɪ no'vɛmbɚ ðə tɛnθ æz ə
dɪ'rɛkt rɪ'zʌlt əv ðɪs tʃardʒ aɪ wɛz sɝvd wɪð ə səpinə əv ðə haʊs
kə'mɪtɪ ɒn 'Anəˌmɛrəkən æk'tɪvətɪz hwɪtʃ kɒld ɑn mi tu əpɪr bɪ-
ˌfɔr ɪt tə bi kwɛstʃənd əbaʊt maɪ 'kɑnˌdʌkt ʌv ðɪ afəs ʌv prɛzədənt əv ðɪ ju'naɪtəd stets. fɝst aɪ wɛd laɪk tə tɛl ju ðə pipəl
əv əmɛrəkə hwaɪ aɪ dɪ'klaɪnd tu əpɪr bɪˌfɔr ðæt kə'mɪtɪ. ɔn ðə
sɝfəs ɪt maɪt sim tə bi æn 'izɪ θɪŋ tə du, æn smart 'pɑlətɪks
fɚ 'hɛrɪ trumən, ə praɪvət sɪtəzən ʌv ˌɪndɪ'pɛndəns mɪ'zurɪ, tu
juz ðɪ kə'mɪtɪ əz ə fɔrəm tə 'ænsɚ ðə skɝələs tʃardʒəz hwɪtʃ
hɛv bɪn med əgɛnst mɪ. 'mɛnɪ pipəl ɝdʒd mi tə du ðæt. ɪt wɛz ən
ə'træktɪv səg'dʒɛstʃən æn əpild tə mi. bʌt əf aɪ hæd dʌn ət aɪ

wʊd əv bɪn ə ˈpartɪ wɪð ðə kəˈmɪtɪ tu ən ækʃən hwɪtʃ wʊd hæv
ˈʌndəˌmaɪnd ðə ˌkanstəˈtuʃnəl pəzɪʃən əv ðə əfəs əv ðə prɛzdənt
əv ðɪ juˈnaɪtəd stets....]

A Western college professor

[aʊr pipḷ ɪn ðə stet əv ˈwɔʃɪŋdən ar ˈmaɪtɪ praʊd foks ðɪz
dez æn wi hæv ˈɛvrɪ rizən tə bi. wihæv æn stɪl ar prəˈvaɪdɪŋ
aʊr fʊl kwotə ʌv mɛn ən wɪmən fə ðɪ arm sɜvəsəz ən ˈmɛnɪ əv
ʊɛn hæv ɔɪˈrɛdɪ med ˈɛnvɪəbəl rɛkədz ɔn ðə wɜldz ˈbætḷfiːldz. wi
hæv æn stɪl ar prəvaɪdɪŋ sʌm əv ðə most əsɛntʃəl ɪmpləmɛnts əv
wɔr...bət ˈikwəli æz ɪmˈpɔrtənt əz ɛnɪ ˌkantrəˈbjuʃən wi ar ˈmekɪŋ ɪz ðə fud hwɪtʃ ˈwɔʃɪŋtən stet farməz ar ˈgrowɪŋ ən ˈharv-
stɪŋ tə fid ar faɪtəz, wi səvɪljənz æn ar ˈælaɪz....]

Henry Wallace
Iowa Editor and U.S. Vice President (1941–1945)

[ɪn ˈtɔkɪŋ tu ðə ˈredɪo ˈbrɔdˌkæstəz aɪ wɪʃ fəst tu ɪkˈsprɛs
maɪ haɪ əˌprɪʃɪˈeʃən ʌv ic ðət ju hu wɜk ɪn ˈredɪo hæv dʌn. ju
hæv ˈkɛrɪd ðə lʌv əv gʊd ˈmjuzɪk tə ˈmɪljənz. ðə ˈlonlɪ ən sɪk ju
həv brot ˈmɛsɪdʒəz əv gʊd wɪl ænd əv med ɪt ˈpasɪbəl fə ðɛm tu
ɛnˈdʒɔɪ tʃɜtʃ sɜvəsəz ɔn ˈsʌndeɪ. təde ju ar ˈbrɪdɪŋ ˌhɛməsˈfɪr-
ɪk gʊd wɪl baɪ minz ʌv e ˈtuˈwe ˈredɪo brɪdʒ ˈkɛrɪjɪŋ əkrɔs ðə
ˈskaɪˌwez ˈprogræmz hwɪtʃ wɪl bɛtə ənˈebḷ ʌs tu əˈprɪʃɪet ðə
kʌltʃə ən ˈmjuzɪk əv lætṇ əmɛrəkə, hwaɪl ət ðə sem taɪm ar gʊd
nebəz ar ˈlənɪŋ θru ðə ˈredɪo tʊ no ʌs bɛtə. ju ar ˈpruvɪŋ ðət
ðə lætṇ kʌltʃə əv ðə saʊθ æn ðɪ ˈæŋgloˈsæksən kʌltʃə əv ðə nɔrθ
ar ˈfʌndəˌmɛntəlɪ əlaɪk bɪˈkɔz boθ ar faʊndəd ɔn bəlif ɪn də-
ˈmakrəsi æn fridəm....]

William Allen White
Kansas Editor (d. 1944)

[ɛvrɪj sæmpəlɪŋ ʌv əmɛrəkən pʌblɪk əpɪnjən rəvilz æn ovə-
ˈhwɛlmɪŋ dɪˈzaɪr ɔn ðə part əv ðə pipḷ əv ðɪ juˈnaɪtəd stets tu
kip aʊt əv wɔr; ˈɛnɪ wɔr--ðə diˈklɛrd:wɔr ɪn jʊrəp ɔr ðɪ ˈʌndɪ-
ˌklɛrd wɔr ɪn eʒə ɔr ivən ðə pasəbəl wɔr bətwin rʌʃə æn ðə ˈskæn-
dəˌnevɪjən dəˈmakrəsɪz. ɔlso, oˈpɪnjən ɪn ðɪ juˈnaɪtəd stets æz
rɪˈvild baɪ ˈɛvrɪ ˈsæmplɪŋ ʃoz frʌm ˈsɪkstɪ tu ˈnaɪntɪ pəsɛnt ʌv
ðə pipḷ hop ðə ˌdeməˈkrætɪk ˈælaɪz wɪl wɪn ɪn wɛstən jʊrəp. haʊ-
ˈevə eˈklɪr dɛfənət məˈdʒɔrətɪ əv ar pipḷ bəliv ðæt wi kæn bes

kip aut əv wɔr baɪ ˈgɪvɪŋ hwʌtevɚ ˌɛkəˈnɑmɪk ed wi kæn gɪv tu
gret brɪtn̩ ən fræns ɪn ðer ˈkɑntest wɪð ˈdʒɚmənɪ. æn əmerəkən
lidʒən pol læst wik ˈkerfəlɪ med æt ðə rɪsənt kɑnvenʃən əv ðə
lidʒən ˈɪndɪˌketəd ðæt ˈsɪkstɪ pəsent ʌv ðə ˈlidʒəners ðer dɪ-
ˈzaɪr ə tʃendʒ ɪn ðə prezənt ˌnuˈtrælətɪ lɔ. ðə lidʒən ˌreprɪ-
ˈzents æn ɑnəst krɔs sekʃən əv ðɪ əmerəkən pipl̩. ðɪ ˈnɑnˈpartə-
sən kəˈmɪtɪ fɔr pis θru ðə rɪˈvɪʒən ʌv ðɪ ˌnuˈtrælətɪ lɔ hæz ɪn-
ˈrold æn ˈovɚˌhwelmɪŋ sentəment ʌv ðɪ ˈkɑlɪdʒ prezədents əv ðɪs
ˈkʌntrɪ æz səpɔrtəz əv ðə kæʃ ən ˈkerɪ prɪnsəpəl....]

Maury Maverick
Member of U.S. Congress from Texas (1935–1939)

[frenz ən fɛlə əmerəkənz. ðɪs spitʃ ɪz bijɪŋ med frəm ðə
pəˈsɪfɪk kost ət ˈhɑlɪwud, raɪt ɪn ðə mɪdl̩ əv ðə gret ˈmuvɪ
ˈɪndəstrɪ. flaɪɪŋ hɪr əkrɔs ðə kɑntənənt, sɪɪŋ ɑː əmerəkən plenz
ən dezəts ən ˈvælɪz ən mauntənz meks wʌn ˈtrulɪ ˈrɪəlaɪz ðɪ
əˈmensəti əv ɑə ˈkʌntrɪ; ænd tə trævəl ət naɪt, tə si ðə mɪljənz
əv braɪt ˈʃanɪŋ laɪts, gɪvz wʌn ə ˈfilɪŋ əv gret saləm ˈhæpɪnəs
ðət aʊə ˈkʌntrɪ ɪz nɑt ɪn ðə ˈblækaut, ðət aʊə pipəl ɚ nɑt lɪvɪŋ
ɪn ðə hɔrə ən fɪr əv deθ frəm ðə skaɪz. ɪts faɪn æftɚ ɔl tə bi
ən əmerəkən. nau ðɪs ɪz ðə fɚstˉtaɪm aɪ əv tɔkt ɔn ə næʃnəl
ˈbrɔdkæst wɪðːi ɪkˈsepʃən əv ˌɪnfəˈmeʃən plɪz sɪns aɪ wəz dɪˈfit-
ed fɔr ˈrɪəˈlekʃən tə kɔŋgrəs ən wʌn əv ðə men rizənz ðət ɑ spik
tənaɪt ɪz tə θæŋk ðə ˈθauzəndz əv pipl̩ hu əv rɪtn̩ mi kandlɪ letəz,
ˈmenɪ əv hwɪtʃ ɑ əv faund ət ˈɪmpɑsəbl̩ tʊ ænsə. wɛl, rat sun æftɚ
ə wəz əˈlektrɪd mejɚ əv sæn əntonjə hewud ɓrun, me gad rɛst hɪz sol
ɪn pis, tol mi ðət ˈɛnɪ nɒkt aut ˈpraɪzˈfaɪtɚ hæd tə gɪt bæk
ɪn ðə rɪŋ ət wʌnts ɔ hi wʊd nevə mek ə ˈkʌmˌbæk; so ɑ gat bæk
ɪn ðə rɪŋ, nɒkt aut ðɪ old pəˈlɪtɪkəl məʃin æn kem bæk....]

Harold E. Stassen
Governor of Minnesota (1939–1943)

[....aɪ brɪŋ ju kɔrdʒəl ˈgritɪŋz æz ju əsembl̩ fɚ ðɪs faɪnl̩
seʃən əy ðə ˈfɔrtɪˈfɔrθ ænjəl kənventʃən əv ðɪ ɛn-e-e-si-pi. ən
aɪ brɪŋ ju əʃurəns ət ðɪ ˈverɪ ˈopənɪŋ ə maɪ rɪˈmarks ðət aɪ ʃəl
nɑt spik tu lɔŋ bikʌz aɪ ˈɔlso wʌnt ə hɪr ðə merənəz bɪfɔr aɪ
mʌs go ən ketʃ maɪ plen, ən bikʌz ɔlso ðə ˈmesɪdʒ ðət aɪ brɪŋ
kən bi ɪkˈsprest tə ju ˈverɪ kənˈsaɪslɪ ən ˌwɪˈðaut ˈtekɪŋ tu
menɪ mɪnəts ɪn ðɪs gret ˈklozɪŋ seʃən əv jɚ kənventʃən. me aɪ
se tə ju ˈverɪ dəˈrektlɪ æz aɪ opm̩ maɪ æˈdres ðɪs sɪmpl̩ bət ˌɪm-

'pɔrtn̩t stetmənt: ðɪ ɛn-e-e-si-pi ɪz ɪn'gedʒd ɪn e wɜk əv gret
'væju tu aʊr əmerəkə ænd tu ɔl 'mæn'kaɪnd. æz prezədən 'aɪzənhaʊr
'risəntlɪ rot--æn aɪ kwot hɪm--aɪ ʃæl kən'tɪnju tɪ di'vot maɪ
ɜnəst ɛfəts tu ədvæns boθ ðə spɪrət æz wel æz ðə fækt ʌv i'kwal-
ətɪ....]

Robert Lafollette Jr.
U.S. Senator from Wisconsin (1925–1947)

[felə 'sɪtəzənz. wʌn rizən aɪ fil so 'strɔŋli əbaʊt ðə kɔrs
an hwɪtʃ ar 'kʌntrɪ hæz ɪm'barkt ɪz ðet aɪ æv sin ðɪs 'trædʒedi
'bifɔr. aɪ fil əz ðo aɪ əd wʊkt 'ɪntu ə 'muvi 'onlɪ tu dɪ'skʌvɚ
ðet aɪ əd sin ðə pɪktʃɚ jɪrz əgo ʌndɚ ə 'sʌmhwʌt dɪfənt nem ænd
wɪð ə dɪfənt kæst. 'dʊrɪŋ 'naɪnˌtin 'sikstin 'sevənˌtin aɪ wəz
wʌn əv maɪ faðɚz 'sekrəterɪz. æz 'mænɪ əv ju rɪ'membɚ, hi fɔt tə
ðə læst dɪtʃ tu pəvent ðɪ ɪn'valvmənt əv ðə lænd hi lʌvd ɪn ðɪ
jʊrə'piən wɔr ʌv hɪz ˌdʒenə'reʃən. 'fɔrtʃənətlɪ fɔr maɪ ˌɛdʒu-
'keʃən aɪ wəz klos tu ðɪ hɪs'tɔrɪk bæt̩l hwɪtʃ redʒd ɪn 'wɔʃɪŋtən.
ɪts fʊl 'trædʒɪk 'minɪŋ bənd ɪntu mi fɔr laɪf. æz aɪ sɪt ɪn ði
ju'naɪted stets senət tede ðə wɜdz ðet ar spokən ən ðə θɪŋz ðet
ar dʌn hɪr ɪn 'wɔʃɪŋtən hæv ə 'trædʒɪk rɪŋ əv fəmɪl'jerəti. sʌm
əv ðə wɜdz ən slogənz ar dɪfənt bət ɪn spaɪt əv nu 'frezɪz kʊkt
ʌp baɪ ðə best ˌprapə'gændɪsts ɪn ðə bɪznəs wi ar 'goɪŋ step
baɪ step daʊn ðæt sem rod wi tʊk ɪn 'naɪn'tin 'sɪkˌstin 'naɪn-
'tin 'naɪn'tin 'sevənˌtin. ju ənd aɪ lʌv ar 'kʌntri. ðɪ ˌovɚ-
'hwelmɪŋ me'dʒareti ʌv əs wɔnt wɪð̄ 'ɛvri faɪbɚ əv ar 'bɪɪŋ tə
du hwʌt ɪz best fɚ ðɪs neʃən. wi sens wɪð̄ ðæt tru 'ɪnˌstɪŋkt
hwɪtʃ gad hæz gɪvən tu pipəl ɪn taɪmz əv gret kraɪsəs ðæt ðə
dɪ'siʒən wi mek wɪl bi ʌv wɜld'ʃekɪŋ ɪm'pɔrtəns....]

Helen Gahagan Douglas
Member of U.S. Congress from California (1945–1951)

[....wel. aɪ æm goɪŋ tə traɪ tə ænsɚ mɪstɚ dɚksən ɪn ðə haʊs
təmaro. mɪstɚ dɚksən left səm ɪm'preʃənz ə traɪd tu krɪ'jet səm
ɪm'preʃənz hwɪtʃ ɚ kən'fjuzɪŋ tə se ðə lɪst tu ðoz əv ʌs hu ar
nat 'ɪntemətlɪ kənəted wɪð̄ ðə fæks ɒn haʊzɪŋ...wel, mɪstɚ dɚksən
traɪd tu liv ðɪ ɪm'preʃən ðæt ɪf wi dʒʌst liv 'bɪldɪŋ tu praɪvət
'ɪndəstrɪ əlon ðət ðə wəd bi haʊzəz fə ðɪ əmerəkən pipl̩, ɔl ðə
haʊzəz ðət ðe nid ɔr kən juz æn ðət 'eniwe ðe nid ɪznt 'verɪ gret
ən ðət ju kant get 'enɪ tu əθarətɪz tu əgri ɒn hwʌt ðæt nid 'æk-
tʃulɪ ɪz. ðə bɪgəst 'haʊzɪŋ prədʌksən wəz ɪn ðə 'naɪnˌtin 'twen̄t-

ɪz, mɪstɚ dɪksən sɛz, ænd ət ðæt taɪm ðə ˈbɪldɪŋ ˈɪndəstrɪ ən ðə
riːl əstet bɔrdz wɚ lɛft əlon. ɪn ðə ˌnaɪnˌtin ˈθɝtɪz ðə ɡʌvəmənt
ɪnvɛstəd ˈtwɛntɪ bɪljən dɑlɝz ɪn ˈhaʊzɪŋ ən naʊ luk hwɛr wir æt,
mɪstə dɪksən sɛz. tə traɪ ən ʃo haʊ ˈɪnəfɛtɪv ðə ɡʌvəmənt.ɪz,
mɪstə dɪksən meks fʌn əv ðə ˈwaɪət ˌproˈɡræm ən sɛz ðæt ɪt wəz
ˈonlɪ æftɚ wi ɡat rɪd əv ðə waɪət ˌproˈɡræm ðət wi ɡat e riːl
ˈhaʊzɪŋ prədʌkʃən ˈprogræm ˈgowɪŋ ɪn ˈnaɪntin ˈfɔrtɪ sɛvən. ɪn
ʌðɚ wɝdz, mɪstə dɪksən traɪz tə liv ðɪ ɪmˈprɛʃən ðət ɪf .wi pæs
ðə ti i dʌbljə ˈhaʊzɪŋ bɪl ju nat ˈonlɪ wont get ˈɛnɪ ˈhaʊzɪŋ bʌt
ðət ˈpæsɪdʒ ə ðə bɪl.wɪl ɪnˈkris ɪnˈfleʃən....]

Harley Kilgore

U.S. Senator from West Virginia (1941–1956)

[əmɛrəkən ˈʃɪpɪŋ ɪz vaɪtəl tə ˈwɪnɪŋ ðə wɔr. ɪt kən brɪŋ ar
bɔɪz hom frəm ðə ˈbætḷ frʌnt sunɚ ɪf ɪt əz betɚ ˈmobəlaːzd. aɪm
ñat karpɪŋ hwɛn aɪ se ðət ar ˈʃɪpɪŋ kæn bi ˈmobəlaɪzd betə. e
ˈkʌntrɪ ət wɔr məst wɝk fɚ pɚfɛkʃən. wi mʌst ˈkanstəntlɪ tʃendʒ
ən tʃendʒ ən tʃendʒ ar ˈtæktɪks əntɪl wi hæv ðə bɛst məθəd tə
du ðə dʒab æn wi məst rɪˈmɛmbɚ ðət ðə dʒab ɪn ˈʃɪpɪŋ ɪz tə get
ðə gretəst pasəbəl ˈtʌnɪdʒ əv wɔr məˈtɪrɪḷz tu ðə ˈfaɪtɪŋ fɔrsəz
ət ðɪ ˈɜlɪəst ˈpasbḷ momənt. wi məst dil ɪn ˈmæksməmz; mɪnəməmz
ən ˈævrɪdʒəz hæv no ples ɪn ðə prasˈkjuʃən əv ə wɔə. ðɛə mʌs bi
no dɪˈvɝʒən əv ʃɪps ɔr ðə men ðət sel ðem frəm wɔr ˈʃɪpɪŋ ænd
ðer mʌst bi no deˈvɝʒən əv wɔr ˈʃɪpɪŋ frʌm ðə most əˈfɛktɪv jus
tu e lɛs əˈfɛktɪv jus....]

Franklin D. Roosevelt

U.S. President (1933–1945)

[maɪ ˈfɛlo əˈmɛrɪkənz: ðə sʌdn̩ krɪmənəl ətæks ˈpɝpətretɪd baɪ
ðə ˈdʒæpəˌniz ɪn ðə pəˈsɪfɪk prəvaɪd ðə ˈklaɪˌmæks ʌv ə ˈdeˌked
əv ˌɪntəˈnæʃnəl ˌɪmoˈrælətɪ. paʊəfəl ən rɪˈsɔsfəl gæŋstəz əv ˈbænd-
dɪd təgɛðʌ tə mek wɔːr əpən ðə hol hjumən res. ðɛə tʃæləndʒ həz
naʊ bɪn flʌŋ æt ðɪ juˈnaɪtəd ˈstets əv əˈmɛrəkə. ðə ˈdʒæpəˌniz
həv ˈtretʃəəslɪ ˈvaɪəletəd ðə ˌlɔŋ ˈstændɪŋ ˌpis bəˈtwin əs. mɛnɪ
əmɛrəkən ˈsoldʒəz ən ˈselɚz həv bɪn ˌkɪld baɪ ˈɛnəmɪ ˈækʃən....]

Alfred Smith

Governor of New York (1919–1921, 1923–1929)

[æt ðɪ ˈaʊtset ə maɪ rəˈmaːks lɛt mi fɝst se ðət aɪ du nat
no əv ˈɛnɪbadɪ, aɪ ˈnever iven hɝd əv ˈɛnɪbadɪ ɪn ðɪ juˈnaɪtəd
stets əv əˈmɛrɪkə hu wɒnts ðɪs ˈkʌntrɪ tə go tə wɔə. sɝtn̩lɪ aɪ

du nɑt fɔr aɪ æv θri sʌnz əv ðə ˈfaɪtɪŋ edʒ. ði oldəst əv ðəm ɪz
ɔlˈredɪ ɪn ðɪ ɑːmɪ æn wʊd bi əmʌŋ ðə fɝɪst tə liv ðɪs ˈkʌnt̬rɪ ɪn
ði əvent ðət ðɪ juˈnaɪt̬əd stets wez brɔt ˈɪntu ðɪ ˌjʊrəˈpiən
ˈstrʌgl̩. so ðɛfɔ̈ə ði ˈɑːgjəmənt æz far əz aɪm kən sɝɪnd rɪˈzɑlvz
ətself ɪntə ðɪs: hwʌt ʃəd wi du ðæt ɪz best ˈkælkjələt̬əd tə kip
ʌs aʊt̬ə wɔ̈ə? ɪn ðɪ dɪsˈkʌʃən əv ðɪs ðer ɪz no rum fɔ pɝsənælə-
tɪz̥, paːtɪz, klæsəz ɔ kridz. ɔl dɪfrənsəz mʌs bi waɪpt aʊt ɪn
ðɪs aʊr əv tʃæləndʒ. pɝsənəl ɪntrəs mʌs bi səˈbɔdənət̬əd tu ðə
kamən gʊd. wi mʌs bi ˈselfɪʃ nɑt fɔr aʊəˈselvz bʌt fə ðə hol
neʃən. aɪ wez brɔt ʌp ɪn ə tʌf pəˈlɪt̬ɪkəl skul wer fæks kaʊnt̬əd
fɔ mɔ ðən θɪrɪz. maɪ ˈtrenɪŋ hæz bɪn tu dɪˈstɪŋwɪʃ biˈtwin haɪ
saʊndɪŋ prɪnsəbəlz ænd ˈæktʃuwəl riˈzʌlts. maɪ ɛkˈspɪrɪəns hæz
tɔt mi tuˈwæsk nɑt hæz ɪt ə ˈlɔftɪ pɝpəs bʌt tu dɪˈmænd ən ænsə
tu ðə kwestʃən dʌz ət wɝɪk. ðə prezənt nuˈtrælətɪ ækt dʌz nɑt
wɝɪk....]

Douglas MacArthur

General, U.S. Army, World War II (d. 1964)

States forces in the Pacific:

[təde ðə ˌdʒæpəˈniz ɑːmd fɔːsɪz θruˈaʊt dʒəpæn kəmˈplit̬əd ðɛə
ˌdiˈmobəlzeʃən ænd sist tu ɪgˈzɪst əz sʌtʃ. ðɪz ˈfɔsɪz ɑr naʊ
kəmˈplitli əˈbɑlɪʃt. aɪ no əv no ˌdiˈmobələzeʃən ɪn ˈhɪstrɪ iðɚ
ɪn wɔr ɔr ɪn pis baɪ aʊr on ɔr baɪ ˈɛnɪ ʌðɚ ˈkʌnt̬rɪ ðæt hæz bɪn
əˈkamplɪʃt so ˈræpədlɪ ɔr so ˈfrɪkʃənləslɪ. ˈɛvriθɪŋ ˈmɪlətɛrɪ,
nevəl ɔr ɛr ɪz fɔrˈbɪdn̩ tu dʒəpæn. ðɪs endz ɪts ˈmɪlətɛrɪ maɪt,
ɪts ˈmɪlətɛrɪ ˈɪnfluwəns ɪn ɪntɚˈnæʃənəl əˈfɛrz̥. ɪt no lɔŋgɚ re-
kənz æz ə wɝld paʊɚ iðɚ lardʒ ɔr smɔl. ɪts pæθ ɪn ðə fjutʃɚ ɪf
ɪt ɪz tu sɝˈvaɪv mʌst bi kənfaɪnd tə ðə wez əv pis....]

Norman Thomas

Author and Lecturer (d. 1968)

[wi əmerəkənz hæv wʌn səprim ɪntrəst ɪn ðɪs wɝr. ɪt ɪz ðæt
ɪt ʃæl bi ˈfalod baɪ ə ˈlastɪŋ pis ˈdʊrɪŋ hwɪtʃ ɒl əv əs kən
gɪv aʊr dɪˈvoʃən tu ðə ˌjunəˈvɝsəl ˈkankwest əv ˈpavɚtɪ baɪ ðə
sem marvələs ˌtɛknəˈladʒɪk skɪlz hwɪtʃ təde ar ˈwɝkɪŋ dɪsˈtrʌk-
ʃən bɪˈjand aʊr kəˈpæsətɪ tu ˌʌndɚˈstænd. ɪt ɪz ˈprabəblɪ ə
 mɝsɪ ðæt nʌn əv ʌs kæn ˌkampriˈhend ðə harɚ ɪnˈdjʊrd baɪ ar
braðɚz æn sʌnz ɪn iwo ɔr əlɔŋ ðə raɪn ɔr baɪ ðə mɪljənz ʌv wɪmən
æn tʃɪldrən hu ˈperɪʃt ɪn ðə tot̩l̩ dɪˈstrʌkʃən ʌv gret ˈsɪtɪz.
jet wi no ənʌf tu no ðæt bæd əz ðɪs wɔr ɪz, ðə hɛks wɪl bi ˈɪn-
fənətlɪ wɝs. ðə neks taɪm wi əˈmerəkənz kænət əskep ðə ˌdəvə-

ˈsteʃən hwɪtʃ nju ˈmɛθədz əv ˈwɔrˌfɛr mek pəsəbəl, nɔr ʃæl wi
ˌɪnˈdefənətlɪ mənˈten ðɪ ɪnˈdʌstrɪəl səˌpɪrɪˈjɔrətɪ əpan hwɪtʃ
ɑr prɛzənt pɒʊr ovɚ far mɔr papjələs neʃənz ɪz bɛst....]

Neville Miller
Radio Executive

[ðiz ar nɒt nɔrməl taɪmz. ɔlˈredɪ ən ʌnˈlɪmətɪd næʃənəl əˈmɝdʒ-
ənsɪ hæz bɪn diˈklɛrd baɪ ɑr prɛzədənt æn əˈmɛrəkɚ ɪz ˈgoʊɪŋ æt
fʊl spid əheɪəd wɪθ ʌr dʒaɪˈgæntɪk næʃnəl dɪˈfɛns prʊgræm. wi
no ðət ɑr ˈkʌntrɪ hæz ˈfɪzɪkəl æn məˈtɪrɪəl ˈrɪsɔrsəz səˈpæsɪŋ
ðoz əv ˈɛnɪ neʃən ɪn ðə wɝl. wi no ðət ʃɪps æn ˈɛrplenz, gʌnz ən
æmɪˈnɪʃən ɔr ˈpɔrɪŋ aʊt əv ɑr ˈfæktrɪz æn ˈʃɪpˌjɔrdz ɛn wi no ðət
ɑr bɔɪz baɪ ðə ˈθaʊzənz ɑr ˈkraʊdɪŋ ɪntə ɔrmɪ kæmps æn ˈnevəl
besəz. bət ˈmɛnɪ ʌv ʌs du nat æz jɛt ˈrɪəlaɪz ðət ðɛr ˈɪz ə ples
fɔr ɪtʃ əv ʌs ɪn ðɪs gret næʃənəl ɛfət. ðə səksəs əv ˈɛnɪ ˈarmi
ɒr ˈnevɪ dɪˈpɛndz ɔn ðə spɪrət əv ɪts mɛn. nəˈpoljən ɪz ɔfən
kwotəd æz seɪŋ ðət ən ˈarmi trævəlz ɔn ɪts stʌmək, bət i ˈɔlso
sɛd ðɛr ɑr ˈonlɪ tu pauɚz ɪn ðə wɝl, ðə spɪrət æn ðə sɔrd. ɪn
ðə loŋ rʌn ðə sɔrd wɪl ˈɔlwez bi ˈkɒŋkəd baɪ ðə spɪrət....]

George Bender
Member of U.S. Congress from Ohio (1939–1949, 1951–1954)

[ðiz ar moˈmɛntəs dez. wi ɚ ɪn ðɪ θroz əv ˈfɔrdʃɪŋ ə nu wɝld.
wi ɚ ˈgræplɪŋ wɪð ˌdʒaɪˈgæntɪk ˈɝθ ˈʃekɪŋ ˈɪʃuz ðæt wɪl diˈtɚ-
mən ðə ˈdɛstənɪ əv ˈdʒɛnəreʃənz nat jɛt bɔrn. ɪn ðə mɪdst əv
ðɪs, sʌm ˈwɛl-ˈminɪŋ pipl æsk hwaɪ ɔl ðɪs fʌs əbaʊt ðə ˈpol ˌtæks;
hwʌt ˈdɪfɚəns dʌz ɪt mek weðɚ ðə pol tæks ɪz riˈpild ɚ nat? ðiz
ɚ ˈkwɛstʃənz ðət ɚ æskt ˈɑnɛstlɪj. tənaɪt aɪ ʃəl ətɛmpt tu ænsɚ
ðɛm wɪθikwəl ɑnəstrɪj. aɪ fɝst hɝd əbaʊt ðə pol tæks ˈmɛnɪ jɪrz
əgo æz ə bɔɪ ˈgroʊɪŋ ʌp ɪn oˈhaɪo. aɪ mʌst kənfɛs ðət maɪ fɝst
ˌriˈækʃən waz wʌn əv ˌtriˈmɛndəs ʃɒk. aɪ faʊnd ət ˈdɪfəkət tu
bəliv ðət ə grup əv stets baɪ lo ðə mesn dɪksn laɪn kʊd bi so
ˈsɪnɪkəl əbaʊt əmɛrəkən ˌdiˈmakrəsi æz tu ples ə praɪs tæg ɔn ðə
bælət, kəmˈpɛlɪŋ ðɛr ˈsɪtəzənz tə pe ə tæks baɪˈfɔr əˈlauɪŋ ðɛm
tə vot. sɪns aɪ əv bɪn ə mɛmbɚ əv kɑŋgrəs aɪv bɪn ˈtraɪɪŋ tə waɪp
aʊt ðɪs fjudəl rɛmnənt. aɪ du nat bəliv ðət ˌdiˈmakrəsi ɪz
strɛŋθənd (h)wɛn tɛn mɪljən əmɛrəkən ˈsɪtəzənz--sɛvən mɪljən waɪt
ən θri mɪljən. kʌləd pipl ɪn sɛvən sʌðɚn stets--ar kɛpt. vɔɪsləs
æn votləs....]

Following are three interesting speech samples from the radio program, Town Meeting of the Air. The dialects represented are generally Eastern American (Mr. Denny), General American (Mr. Eastman) and Southern British (Mr. Laski):

George V. Denny Jr.
Broadcaster (d. 1959)

[gʊd ˈivnɪŋ ˈnebɜz. təˈnaɪts ˈkwɛstʃən ɪz no lɔŋgɚ ˈbiɪŋ dɪsˈkʌst dʒʌst ovɚ ba:z ən bæk ˈfɛnsɪz. ɪt əz ɪndid bɪˈkʌm ə grev ɪntəˈnæʃnəl prabləm. ðæts waɪ wɪɚ dɪsˈkʌsɪŋ ɪt hɪɚ tənaɪt wɪð rɪsˈpansəbel əˈθɔrɪtɪz hu wɔnt tə du ˈɛvrɪθɪŋ ɪn ðɛɚ pɑʊɚ tu əvɔɪd ənʌðɚ wɔ:. əpɪnjənz dɪfɚ əz tə haʊ wi kən əten ðɪs goɫ....]°

Max Eastman
Author (d. 1969)

[æz θɪŋz ɑr naʊ wi ɑr kwaɪt ˈɑbvɪəslɪ hedəd fɔr wɔr wɪð rʌʃə. ðə kwɛstʃən ɪz hwɛðɚ wɪr goɪᵊn tə drɪft əhed ˈblaɪndlɪ əlɔŋ ðə sem kɔrs əntɪl wi get ðɛr, əᵑnd ðɪ ænsɚ dɪˈpendz ɑn hwɛðɚ aʊr fɔrən ˈpaləsɪ ɪz tə bi best ɑn fækt ɔr ɑn ˈsɛntəˈmentəl iˈmoʃən. sɪnts ˈnaɪnˌtin ˈfɔrtɪ wʌn ɑr ˈpaləsɪᶦ həz bɪn best ɑn ˌɪrˈæʃnəl ˈfilɪŋz, ðə ˈfilɪŋ ðət bɪˈkɔz rʌʃə wəz fɔrst ɪntə ðə wɔr ɑn aʊr saɪd ˈðɛrˈfɔr hɚ ˈgʌvɚmənt mʌst hæv sist tə bi ə toˌtælɪˈtɛrɪən ˈtɪrənɪᶦ dʒʌst æᵌz ˈæbsəˌlut æᵌz hɪtlɚz. ˈsɛvənˈtin mʌns biˈfɔr hɪtlɚ ətækt rʌʃə ˈrozəvelt stetəd ðə fækt fɔr ɔl əv ʌᵌs. ðə ˈsavɪjet junjən, æz ˈɛvrɪbʌdɪ noz hu hæz ðə ˈkɜrdʒ tu fes ðə fækts--aɪ əm ˈkwotɪŋ hɪm vɚˈbetəm-- ɪz ə ˈdɪkˌtetɚʃɪp æz ˈæbsoᵊlut æz ɛnɪ ʌðɚ ˈdɪkˌtetɚʃɪp ɪn ðə wɜrld ...rʌʃəz ˈpaləsɪ tɔrd ʌs ənd ʌðɚ ˌdeməˈkrætɪk neʃənz kʊld ɪmˈpɪrɪjələst stets ɪn ðə ˈbɔlʃəvik lɪŋgo ɪz ˈplenlɪ rɪtn̩ daʊn hwer ˈɛvrɪ mæn kæn rid ɪt. hɚ ˈpaləsɪ ɪz tə prəmot keas ɪn aʊr ˈkʌntrɪ ˌʌnˈtɪl ɪn ə kraɪsəs hɚ fɪfθ kaləm led baɪ ðə kamjənəst ˈpartɪ ænd bækt baɪ hɚ ˈmɪlɪˌtɛrɪ pɑʊɚ wɪl ˈovɚˈθro aʊr gʌvɚmənt ænd ˌriˈples aʊr ˌdeməˈkrætɪk ˌɪnstəˈtuʃənz wɪθ ə ˌtoˌtæləˈtɛrɪən stet ˈkæpɪtəlɪst ˈdɪkˌtetɚʃɪp. ðɪs kraɪsəs, ʃi bəlivz, wɪl kʌm hwɪᵋn ðə wɜrld ɪz æt wɔr. æn stælən ɪz ˈgetɪŋ redɪᶦ fɔr ðæt wɔr....]

Harold J. Laski
Economist (d. 1950)

[mɪstə ˈdɛnɪⁱ , ˈledɪz ən ˈdʒɛntəlmən: sɜtɪn θɪŋz ə boθ
klɪr ənd ˌɛlɪˈmɛntrɪ ənd aɪ hop lɛtʒ θət maɪ ol frɛn mæks ɪst-
mən wɪl kʌm bæk tʊ ðɛm. ˈfɜst ðɜ me bi pipəl ɪn gret brɪtən ɔr
ɪn ðɪ juˈnaɪtəd stets tu hum ə wɔ wɪð rʌʃə wəd bi wɛlkəm. ðɛr
ɪn ən ˌovəˈhwɛlmɪŋ ꞷaɪˈnɔrɪtɪ ɪn boθ ǃkʌntrɪz. ˈsɛkəndlɪ, ˈɛnɪ
ˈrʌᵃʃən ˈlɪdʒ wɪð ˈɛnɪ kamən sɛnts--ənd ðe ˈmostlɪ hæv ə gʊd͡lɪl
əv kamən sɛnts--noz ðət rʌʃə ɪz nɒt ɪn ə pəzɪʃən tu ɪnˈgedʒ ɪn
ə wɔ: fər ə vɛrɪ lɔŋ taɪm tə kʌᵃm, ænd θɜdlɪⁱ ˈɛnɪwʌᵈn u əz
wɒtʃt rʌᵃʃə ˈkloslɪ, ənd ivən mɔr əz dɪsˈkʌᵈst ɪts prɒbləmz
wɪð ˈkɒmjɛnɪst lɪdəz ət fɜst hænd noz haʊ raɪt mɪstə idən wɒz--
ən ə ˈtrɪbjut tə mɪstə idənz raɪtnəs frəm mɪj minz ˈsʌmθɪŋ--
wɛn ǀ ɪnˈsɪstɪd ðət ðə ˈpraɪmərɪ ˌmotɪˈveʃn̩ ɒᵊv rʌᵃʃən ˈpɒlɪsɪ
wɛz sɪkʰˈjʊrətɪ. ɪn ðə laɪt əv ðɪ ˈtwɛntɪ jɪəz sɪnts ðɪ ɒkˈtobə
revəˈluʃən ðə rʌʃənz sɜtʃ fə sɪkˈjʊrətɪ rⁱ z æᵘmplɪ ˈdʒʌstɪ-
faɪd....]

SECTION 2　OTHER DIALECTS

Winston Churchill
British Prime Minister (1940–1945, 1951–1955)

[ˈθiz suˈprim əbˌdʒɛktɪvz hæv ˈnat bin ˌlɒst. wi əv ˌgɪvən
ˌꞭə kənˈsɜvətɪv səˈpɔət tə ðə ˈmen ˈprɪnsəpəlz əv ðə ˌgʌvəmənts
ˈfaᵊrɪn ˈpɒləsɪ so ˌhwaɪl ət ðə ˌsem taɪm wi əv dɪˈplɔrd ði
əˌstanɪʃɪŋ ˈerəz hwɪtʃ həv ˈhæmpəd ɪts ˌæplɪˈkeʃən. ɪn ðɪ ˌend
haʊˌɛvʌ ɪt ɪz ðə ǀla:ˌdʒꞭə ɪsju ðət wɪl ˈkaʊnt. ˈbʌt, mɪstə
ˌtʃɛəmən, ˈhwaɪl wi aꞷ ˌso ˈbɪzɪⁱ wɪð ˌaᵊr ɪnˈtɜnəl ˈpaːtrɪ ˌkan-
trəvɜsɪz wi məst ˌnɒt fəˈgeᵗt ðə ˈgrævətɪ əv a pəˈzɪʃən ɔr ɪn-
dɪd ˈðæt ɒᵛ ðə ˈhol wɜld...ʌ bænd əv men ˈgæðəd tə ˈgɛðʌ ɪn ðə
ˈkrɛmlɪn hæz ˈrezd ɪtˌsɛlf əˈgɛnst ðə ˈwɛstən dɪˈmakrəsɪz. ðe əv
ˈædɪd tə ˌðɛə dəˈmɪnjənz ðə ˈsætɪlˌaɪt ˈstets əv ˈjurəp, ðə ˌbɔl-
tɪk stets, ˈpolənd, ˈtʃeko sloˌvækjʌᶺ, ˈhʌngərɪ, bʌlˈgerjʌᶺ, ru-
ˈmenjʌ--ən ˈɛmpaɪə n̩ ɪtˌsɛlf. ˈtito əv ˌjugoˈslavjʌᶺ hæz brokən
əˈwej; ˈgris hæz bin ˈreskjud ˌbaɪ ðɪ juˈnaɪtəd stets ˈkærɪjɪŋ
aʊt æn ˈkærɪjɪŋ ˈɒn ðə tæsk hwɪtʃ ˌwi bɪˈgæn....]

Ely Culbertson
Bridge Expert (d. 1955)

[ɪt meᵗ sim strendʒ tʊ ju, ledɪz ən dʒenəlmən, ðæt ə mæn
ʌv ə sɪstəm əv brɪdʒ ʃud biˈkʌm ˈɔlmost ovənaɪt æ mæn ʌᵛ ə
sɪstəm fər wɜld pis. æftə ɔl ɪt ɪz kwaɪt ə lip frəm ə sɪstəm

əv ˈfɪftɪ tu kɑːdz æn fɔə suts ɪntawə sɪstəm əv tu bɪljən jumən
kɑːdz æn hʌndɹəts əv suts əy neʃənz. ðɪ ˌeksplə'neʃən ɪz sɪmpl̩,
ɔlðo aɪ dɪd nɑt go ɪntu ðɪ fild əv ˌɪntə'næʃənəl ˈpɑlətɪks frʌm
ˈkɑntræk brɪdʒ. aɪ ə'rɪdʒənəlɪ wɛnt ɪntə ðə wɜld ʌv kɑrdz frʌm
maɪ ˈstʌdɪz ʌv sə'saɪətɪz ænd ɪntə'næʃənəl rɪ'leʃənz. sɪnts maɪ
ɜlɪ juθ ɪn ˈruʃɪjə æn ˌɪnsə'dɛntlɪ aɪm ði ˈonlɪ ˈnetɪv emerəkən
hu spiks raʃən wɪð'aut æn ˈæksent æn ˈɪŋlɪʃ wɪð ən ˈæksent aɪ
hev bɪ'n ˈfæsənetəd wɪð ðɪ pə'lɪtɪkəl ˈsɪstəm æn mas saɪ'kɑlə-
dʒɪr. brɪdʒ wɪl ˈɔlwɪz bi maɪ ˈhɑbɪ æn maɪ brɛt ən bʌtə bʌt ɪn
ðɪz trædʒɪk taɪmz aɪ wɔnt tə juz maɪ ˈlaɪf ˈlɔŋ ˌɪks'pɪɹɪjənts
tʊ bɪld ə nʉ kaɪnd əv e brɪdʒ, ɛ brɪdʒ ɪntu ðə fjutʃə, æ̃kɜd ɪn
ɪn ðɪ ri'æⁿlətɪz əv tu'de ovə hwɪtʃ ðɪs wɔə tɔːn hju'mænɪtɪ
kə'n krɔs ˈɪntu djuɹəbl̩ pis æn fridəm....]

Herbert Morrison
British Foreign Secretary (1951)

[....ˈʌn,laˆɪk ˈme⊥nɪ ˌdɛmə'kræ⊥tɪk ˌkɑˆntə'nentəl ˈkʌntrɪz,
aʉə ˈkʌntrɪ ɪz trə'dɪʃənəlɪ ə ˈkʌntrɪ ʌⁱv tu ˈpaːtɪz, ɒv ˈgʌvəmənt ænd ˌɑpə'zɪʃən. nə⊥ʉ ðɪs ˈprɛⱻktɪs, ðɪs ˌkɑnstə'tjuʃənəl
trə'dɪ⊥ʃən əv a⊥ʉəz ɒv hwɪtʃ ðɪ ɔðɛz a ˈrɪəlɪ ðə ˈbrɪtɪʃ ˈpipəl
ðəm'sɛlvz, ðɪs ˈpræktɪs brɪnz gret əd'væntɪdʒ⊥z ɪn ðə we əv ðɪ
ˈvɪgɜ ænd ðə stə'bɪlɪtɪ ɒˆv ə ˌpɑlə'mentrɪ ˌɪnstə'tjuʃənz, ænd
meks ɪt ˈpɒsɪbəl fə ðɪ ɪ'lɛkt ɜz tu prə'nauⁿns fɛr ənd klɪɹ ˈdʒʌ⊥-
dʒmənt, ə mɔə fɛr ɔə klɪɹ ˈdʒʌdʒmənt, ðæn wəd ˌʌðə'waˆɪz bi ðə
kʌjs. ænd ˈɪnɪˈwe, mʌtʃ tu ðɪ em'beɹəsment əv sʌm pipəl, ðer ar
ˈo⊥nlɪ tu dɪ⊥'vɪʒən ˈlɑbɪz ɪn ðə ha⊥ʉs əv ˈkamənz. sʌm wʊd laˆɪk
θri. sʌm wʊd laˆɪk faˆɪv. sʌm wʊd laˆɪk fɔː. bət hwɪn ðə ˈspɪkɜ
pʊts ðə ˈkwe stʃən frəm ðə tʃɛə ðerɪz ˈonlɪ tu θɪŋz tə du, tə
vot fɔːə ɔr ə'genst. bət ðer ɪz ə θɜd, ən ðæt ɪz nɒt tə vot ə
torl̩, ən d͡ʒæt ɪz ˈsʌm,taɪmz dʌn. bət ðe a o⊥nlɪ tu ˈlɑbɪz ɪn
ðə ha⊥ʉs əv ˈkamənz, ən ʔaɪ θɪŋk ɪt ɪz ə gʊd θɪŋ ðət ɪn ɑə
ˈkʌntrɪ wɪ ʃud hæ⊥v tu ˈpaːtɪz, ət ˈɛnɪ ret tu gret ˈpaːtɪz,
ænd ðət ðə ʃud bi ˈgʌvəmənt ɪn·ˌɑpə'zɪʃən--ðə ˈgʌvəmənt tə
gʌvən wɪð ðɪ əsent əv ðə ha⊥ʉs əv kamənz ənd ɪts səpoɹət, ɪf
ɪt kən ge⊥t ɪt, hwɪtʃ əz ɪts ˈbɪznɪs. ɪf ɪt dʌznt ðen ðə pipəl
məst dɪ'saˆɪd....]

Jan Masaryk
Foreign Minister of Czechoslovakia (1940–1948)

[aɪ wʌndɜ weðə hwɛ'nevə ɹaɪ se hʌᵋ lo tu ju foks ɪt minz̠
d͡ʒət d͡ʒɛz ɪz ə medʒɜ ˈkraɪsɪs ɑn. aɪ wʊd het tu bi ə ˈdʒonʌ,

bət əgeˑnˑɪt wʊdˑnȧ̧t bɪ̌ nàɪs əv mɪ tu riˈfjuz ə vɛɹɪ kaɪn(d)ˌɪn-
ˈvaɪt frʌm ðɪ̧ː juˈnaɪtəd stets əv əˈmɛɹɪkʌ tu tel ju haʊ ɪt
filz tu bɪ̌ ɪˑnsaɪd ə vʌᵃlgɜ ʌˈnedʒuˌketəd ˈnå̧tsɪ̌ hwel. bɪˈliv
mɪ, ɪt ɪz ə ʃakɪŋ ɪkˈspiɹɪəns æn maɪ lɪtl̩ ˈkʌntrɪ dɪˈzʌvz ɪc
ðə prez ðə disn̩t pipl̩ ʌᵊv ðə wɜld a ˈgɪvɪŋ hɜ. bət aɪ ɪnˈten
tʊ traɪ ɛˈlɪmɪˌnetɪŋ ˈtʃeko sloˈvakɪə frəm maɪ lɪtl̩ tɔk æz
mʌtʃ æz pasəbl̩ hæˑvɪŋ wʌnts əgən reˈitəˌɹetəd maɪ ˌfʌndəˈmentəl
reˈfjuzəl tu ˌakˌsept ˈmjunɪk ɔr ˈɛnɪθɪŋ ˈfalowɪŋ ˈmjunɪk ʌp tu
det. aɪ əm ˈspikɪŋ frʌm ðə sem lʌndən frʌm hwɪˑtʃ ju hɜd mɪ
hwȉn aɪ wəz ˈfaɪtɪŋ fər ˌɪntəˈnæʃənəl ˈdisənsɪ̌ ə jɪr əgo. tuˈde
aɪ m ˈfaɪtɪŋ fɔ ðə ˈvɛɹɪ sem ɪʃju bət nat æz ən əfɪʃəl pɜsən bət
æz wᴀ̇n əv ðə kauntləs mɪljənz əv əˈnanɪˑmʌs ˌrepriˈzentətɪvz̩ ʌv
ðə ˈgloɹɪjəs aɪdɪə əv ˈlɪbətɪˑ, fridəm æn raɪt ovə maɪt....]

Madame Chiang Kai-Shek
Wife of the Chinese Statesman

[ˈledɪz æn ˈdʒentəlmən: || tu ɔɪ maɪ frenz ɪn əˈmɛɹɪkʌ| ɪn-
ˈkludɪŋ ðᵊgᴜz ʌv ju hu hæv kʌm hɪə tu lɪsən tu mɪ ðɪs ˈivnɪŋ|
aɪ wɪʃ tu ɪkˈspres tᴜᵊ ju| maɪ ˈhaːtˈfelt əˌpriˈiʃjeʃən əv jᴜᵊ
kənˈsɜn fə mi| ænd jɔ̧ə ˈθɔtfl̩nɪs fɔ maɪ ˌwel ˈbiɪŋ| hwɪtʃ ju
hæv so ˈdʒenrəsli ˈdemənstrȩtɪd ɪn ˈveɹɪjəs wez| ˈdjʊɹɪŋ maɪ
ˈɪlnɪs| ænd ˌkanvəˈlesəns|| aɪ ˈwʌndʌ| weðə aɪ kən kənˈve tə
ju| haʊ ˈdiplɪ tʌtʃt aɪ æm| ðæt so ˈmenɪ pipəl| frʌm ˈevri sek-
ʃən əv əˈmeɹɪˈkʌ| hæv tekn̩ ðə taɪm æn trʌbl̩ tʊ send mi ˈmesɪdʒez
ʌv əfekʃən ænd gʊdˈwɪl||| aɪ wɪʃ aɪ kʊd ɪkˈnaɪɪdʒ| ˈevri wʌn| əv
ðə ˈmenɪ θauzənz ʌv ˈletʌz| ænd ˈteligræmz hwɪtʃ aɪ hæv rɪˈsivd||
bət sɪnts ðɪs ɪz ɪmˈpasɪbəl| wɪl ju nᴜt let mi tek ðɪs əpəˈtjun-
ɪti tu θæŋk ju| wʌn ænd ɔl ||| aɪ wɪʃ ˈtᴜ́| ðæt ɪt wə ˈpasɪbəl fə
mi tᴜ ɪkˈsept jɔr ɪnvəˈteʃənz̧| tu ˈvɪzɪt jɔə stets| ˈsɪtɪz| ˈkal-
ɪdʒez| ˈtʃɜtʃez| ænd ᴀ̇ðə ˌɔːgɪnəˈzeʃənz||....]

Thomas E. Dewey
Governor of New York (1943–1955)

[ɪn ðə sɪks jɪrz| frʌm ˈnaɪntin ˈθɜtɪˈθri| tə ðɪj ɛnd ə(v)
ˈnaɪntin ˈθɜtɪj ˈet| wi nidəd ˈθɜtɪ sɪks ˈbɪljən ˌdaləz| ˈdʒʌst
tə rɪˌples ænd tə ˌstænd ˈstɪl|| ðə græn(d) ˌtotəl əv ˈɔːl ˈkæp-
ətəl| ˌpʊt ˈɪntᴜᵊ ar prəˈdʌktɪv ˌplænt ɪn ðoz ˈjɪrz wəz ˌonlɪ
ˌtwentɪ ˌnaɪn ˌbɪljən ˈdaləz| nat ˈivən əˌnʌf tə ˌmek ˌʌp fə
ˈwer æn ˈter|| ˈseven ˈbɪljən ˈdaləz ̄ʃort ˈivən ʌv ˌholdɪŋ aʊr
ˈon| ar prədʌktɪv ˈplænt æn ɪˈkwɪpmən̩t hæv bɪn ˌrʌnɪŋ ˈdaun ət
ðə ˈhil æ̧ᵊt ðɪ ˌævrɪdʒ ˌret əˣv ˌmɔr ðən ə ˌbɪljən ˌdʊləz ə jɪr||

ˈivən ɪf wi wɚ ˌholdɪŋ ar on| ˈðæt ˌwʊdnt bi əˈnʌf|| ɪn ðə ˈlæst
dɛkˌed ˈaʊr ˌpapjəˈleʃən ɪnˈkrist| ˌnɪrlɪ ʌ³ ˈmɪljən ˈpipl ʌ³
ˈjɪr|| hæf ə ˌmɪljən nu ˈwɜkɚz ə ˌjɪr ar ˌkʌmɪŋ t̬ə məˈtʃɚətɪ|
ðæts ˌhæf ə ˌmɪljən mɔr ðən rɪˈɪ ˌtaɪr ɔr ˈdaɪ ˈɛvrɪ ˈsɪŋgəl
ˈjɪr|| ˌwi nid tu ɪksˈpænd ar plænt| ˈɛvrɪ jɪr| ˈdʒʌst t̬ə kip
ˈʌp wɪð ar ˈgroʊɪŋ ˌpapjəˈleʃən| t̬ə gɪv ðoz nju ˌwɜkɚz ˈdʒabz|
æn(d) ˈðɛn wi mʌ³st mek ɪt ˌlardʒɚ ˈjet ɪf wi ar əˈgen t̬ə rɪᶦ-
ˈzum ðə ˌstɛ̈dɪ ˌraɪz ɪn ˈaʊr ˌstændəd əv ˌlɪvɪŋ....]

Elizabeth
Queen Mother of England

[æz joə petrən| aɪ æɪm ˈvɛrɪ glæ⊥d ɪnˈdid t̬ə bi hɪ̯ɚ| t̬ə tek
paːt ɪn ðiz ˌse⊥lɪˈbreʃənz|| æ⊥nd| ɪt ɪz ən ˈædɪd pleʒɚ t̬ə mi|
t̬ə nɜɣ ðət maɪ wɜdz aː ˈbiɪŋ ˌriˈled|| nat̬ᶦ ˈɜɣnlɪ t̬ə ðə ˈfɜðɪst
paːts əv gret brɪtn| bət ˈɔlsɣ tʊ ˈmembʌz ɔn ðɪ ʌðə saɪd əv ðɪ
ətˈlæntɪk| ˌhɜɣldɪŋ ˈsɪmɪləˆˌse⊥lɪˈbreʃənz| ænd hu ɑ nɑɣ ˌlɪs-
nɪŋ|| tu ɔ⊥l| ˈmembɚz əv ðɪ əˌsosɪˈeʃən| ɪn wʌt̬ᶦ ˈevəˆpaːt̬ᶦ ə
θə wɜːld ðe me bi| aɪ send ˈgrit̬ᶦɪŋz frəm ðɪs hom|| aɪ wəd laɪk
ˈɔ⊥lsɣ t̬ə se ə speʃl wɜd əv əˈpriʃɪ⊥eʃən| t̬ə membɚz əv staf|
ænd ˈklʌbˈlidʌz bɜɣθ hɪə ænd ˈɜɣvɚˈsiz|| joɚz ɪz ðə task əv
ˈfɪt̬ᶦɪŋ juθ fɔ ðɪ rɪsˌspansəˈbɪlɪtɪ⊥z əv t̬əˈmarɣ|| fɔ³ ðɪs|
ju hæv t̬ə kip əbrest wɪθ maːdən θɔ⊥t| æ⊥nd| ət ðə sem t̬aɪm|
t̬ə gɪv ðə jʌŋ| ðæ⊥t krɪstən pɜːpəs| æn dɪˈrekʃənəl laɪf wɪ-
ˈða⊥ɣt hwɪtʃ| no rḛəl bet̬ᶦəmənt ɪz̪ ˈpasɪb||| joə task ðɛ⊥n|
ɪz bɜɣθ ə haɪ ˈprɪvɪlɪdʒ ænd ə ˌdɛdɪˈkeʃn̪....]

Transcriptions with Pausing Indicated

These transcriptions are made with pause marks, in addition to the occasional modifiers previously used. Speech samples from public figures, professional readers and actors, and student speakers are presented.

Some samples were taken from broadcasts, most of which originated with the Columbia Broadcasting System and were heard in the Seattle, Washington, area over KIRO; others originated with KIRO. Electrical transcriptions of the broadcasts were presented to the University of Washington by KIRO for whatever scholarly use might be made of them, and they constitute a historical collection with the School of Communications. Speech samples from professional readers and actors were taken from commercial records and are used through the courtesy of Caedmon Publishers.

SECTION 1   PUBLIC FIGURES (VARYING DIALECTS)

James F. Byrnes
U.S. Secretary of State (1945–1947)

[bɪˈkaʒ wi no ðæt wi kən wɪn ðɪs wɔʔ| tu ˈmɪnɪ əv əs ɑɾ
ˈæktɪŋ| æz ɪf ðə wɔɾ ɪz ˌɒlˈɾɛdɪ wʌn|| ɪt ɪz nɑ̃t|| ðə most

ˈkrɪtɪkḷ ən ðə ˈblʌdɪəst⁻bætḷz ɛv ðə wɔr| ɑr əhɛd ɛv əˈs||
aʊə bɔɪz ɛt ðə frʌnt ɑ nɒt ˈfaɪtɪŋ| æz ɪf ðə wɔr wə ɔlˈrɛdɪ
wʌn|| ðe noʊ| ðæt mʌtʃ ˈfaɪtɪŋ æn ˈdaɪːŋ mɛst kʌm| brˈfɔr ə
ˈvɪktərɪ brɪŋz pis|| ðe ɑ ˈfaɪtɪŋ hɑdɚ ðæn ɛvɚ|| wi ɒn ðə hom
frʌnt mʌst ˈɔlso faɪt hɑdɚ ðæn ɛvɚ| tu wɪn ðə wɔr ən stɒp ðə
daɪːŋ|| tu wɪn ðə pis| ænd mek ɪt ˈlæstɪŋ|| wi ɛv kʌm ə lɒŋ we
sɪns pɚl ˈhɑːbɚ|| ṇstɛd ɛv ən aɪmɪ ɛv wʌn mɪljən sɪks hʌndəd ṇ
θɝtɪ faɪv θaʊzən| tude wi hæv ən aɪmɪ ɛv sɛvən mɪljən θrɪ hʌn-
drɛd ən ˈnaɪntɪ θaʊzən|| ðæt aɪmɪ ɪz bɛtɚ iˈkwɪpt| æn bɛtɚ
trend ðæⁿn ˈɛnɪ aɪmɪ ɪn ˈhɪstrɪ|| aʊr ˈprɑgrɪs ɪn prəˈdʌktʃən|
ɪz æz ɪnˈkɝɪdʒɪŋ tu ʌs| æz ɪt ɪz ˌdɪˈskɝᴵdʒɪŋ tu aʊr ˈɛnɪmɪz||
wi prədust læsˌmʌnθ| ɔlmost əz ˈmɛnɪ ˈɛrplenz æz wi hæd ɪn aʊr
aɪmɪ ɛr fɔrs| æt ðə taɪm ɛv pɚl hɑːbɚ....]

Cordell Hull
U.S. Secretary of State (1933–1949)

[...aɪ æm əˈmɛnslɪ plizd| tə bi bæk ɪn ðɪz ˌlɛdʒəˈsletɪv
hɔlẓ| ænd tu mit| numɚs frɛnḍz| old ænd⁻nu| pəˈtɪkjələlɪ| ðoz
fɔrmə ˈkɑligẓ ɪn ðə tu haʊzəẓ| fɔr itʃ ɛv huᵛm| aɪ hæv lɒŋ
ˌɛntəˈtend ˈsɛntəmənts ʌv gretəst rɪˈspɛkt| æṇd ði most dʒɛn-
jəwən æˈfɛkʃən|| aɪ ˈpriᴵʃet ˈdiplɪ| ðə ˈkʌmplɪmənt| av bɪŋ
ɪnˈvaɪtɛd tə mit wɪθ ju təde|| bʌt aɪ ˈpriᴵʃet ivɛn mɔə| ðə
fækt| ðæt| baɪ jʊr ɪnveˈteʃən| ju hæv ˈɛmfəˌsaɪzḍ jʊr prə-
faʊnd ɪntrəst ɪn ðə ˈprɪnsəpəlz æn ˈpɑlɪsɪz| fɔ hwɪtʃ ðə ˈmas-
ˈkaʊ kanfrəns stʊd| ænd ɪn ðə progrɛs med baɪ ði pəˌtɪseˈpetɪŋ
gʌvəmənts ɪn ˈkerɪŋ ðɛm fɔwəd|| ɪn ðə maɪndz ɛv ic ʌv əs hɪə
prɛzṇt| ænd ʌv ðə mɪljənẓ ɛv ʌˈmɛrkənz ɔl ovə ðə ˈkʌntrɪ| ðɛr
ɪẓ| æn ðɛr kæn bi| æt ðɪs momənt bʌt wʌn kənˈsumɪŋ θɔt| tu dəfit
ði ˈɛnəmɪ æs⁻spidəlɪ əẓ pasəbḷ....]

Alfred M. Landon
Governor of Kansas (1933–1937)

[hwʌt ɑr ðə fjutʃɚ ˈpɑləsɪz ʌv əˈmɛrəkə?|| ðæt ɪz θə gret
kwɛstʃən| ðət ðə wɝld ɪz ˈæskɪŋ təde| ænd sɪnts ðə læst əˈlɛk-
ʃṇ| hwɪtʃ gev ðɪ rɪˈpʌblɪkən ˈpɑrtɪ| sʌtʃ e rɪˈsɝdʒəns ʌv
strɛŋθ| ðə wɝld hæz bɪn ˈæskɪŋ ɪtˈsɛlf| hwʌt ɪz ðə pəˈzɪʃən
ɛv ðɪ rɪˈpʌblɪkən ˈpɑrtɪ| ænd hwʌt ɑr ˈɪts ˈpɑləsɪz?|| ðə
ˈmɛrəkən pipḷ ɑr ˈɒlwɪz ˌɪntəˈestɛd əv ˈkɔrs| ɪn ðə næṣṇəl
ˈɪʃjuz kənˈfrʌntɪŋ ðɛm| æn ivɛn ɪn taɪm ɛv wɔr| ðe ɪnˈsɪst ɒn
ˈbiɪŋ fri| tu dɪsˈkʌs ðɪz ˈpɑləsɪz| æn tə tek ʌp əˈpozɪŋ saɪdẓ|
ɪf ðe du nɒt əgri|| təde ðɛrz wʌn ˈkwɛstʃən ɒn hwɪtʃ ðɛr ɪz
no dɪˈvɪʒən| ʌv əˈpɪnjən| ɪn əˈmɛrəkə|| wi mʌst wɪn ðə wɔr||

ar θats| ar 'enədʒi| ar welθ| ar di'votəd tə ðæt ɛn(d)|| ðer
ɪz 'skɛrslɪ e hom| ðæt hæz nat kən'trɪbjətəd| iðʌ ə sʌn| ar ə
dɑt̬ʌ| tə ðə kaz| əv ar bi'lʌved 'kʌntrɪ....]

Mrs. Eleanor Roosevelt

Wife of U.S. President Franklin D. Roosevelt (d. 1962)

[aɪ ˌθɪᴧŋk ɪt 'saʊndəd ə lɪtl 'aːbeˌtrɛrɪ ɔn 'maɪ ˌpaːt
ðət aɪd 'wɔntəˌdʒu tə ˌask 'kwɛstʃənz|| bʌt ðə 'rizən aɪ| wəd|
'laɪk tə hæv ˌpipl ask 'kwɛstʃənz| ˌɪz ðət 'frikwəntlɪj| hweᴵn
wi tɔk ə'baʊt ðiᴧ ju'naɪtəd 'neʃənz|| ðə vɛrɪ θɪŋz ðæt 'sʌmˌwʌn
ɪn ən ˌɔdiəns wəd ˌlaɪk tə hɪr əˌbaʊt| a ˌnevə 'menʃənd|| ænd
ˌso| aɪ ˌɔlwez ˌfil ðət ðə 'kwɛstʃən ˌpɪrɪəd 'ɔftən ˌbrɪŋz 'aʊt|
ðə θɪŋz ðət ar əv pə'tɪkjələ 'ɪntrəst| tu ði 'ɛrɪə| hwɪtʃ ju me
bi 'ɪn|| ənd aɪm 'kwaɪt ˌʃʊe ðət ˌhɪə 'ɪn ðə ˌnɔθˌwest| hwɛə ju
a ˌdʊrɪŋ ə 'gret 'diəl| ˌfɔːə| ðiᴵ ju'naɪtəd ˌneʃənz ɪn ˌjɔ
'skulz| ənd ɪn jɔə 'æktɪv ˌɔgənɪ'zeʃənz|| ðə 'mʌst ˌbi ˌkwɛs-
tʃnz| ðæt 'ju wʊd 'laɪk tə hæv ˌænsəd| ˌɪf| ˌwi no ðɪ 'ansəz|
ən əz ˌlɔŋzɪ hæv mɪstə 'aɪkəlˌbɛgə tu| ˌansə hwɛn aɪ 'dont no
ðɪ ˌansɜ| aɪ fil ˌkwaɪt ˌsef ɪn sə'dʒɛstɪŋ| ðət ju 'ask ðə
'kwɛstʃənz|| ˌnaʊ| ˌaɪm tə tɔk əbaʊt ðiᴵ ju'naɪtəd ˌneʃənz ˌænd
'ju| ænd ˌðæt 'taɪtl əv ˌkɔəs ɪz ˌgɪvən| bə'kɔːz| ˌso 'menɪᵻ əv
ʌs 'fil ðət ði ju'naɪtəd ˌneʃənz ɪz ˌsʌmθɪŋ 'far ə'wej| frʌm
'ʌs əz ˌɪndə'vɪdʒwəlz| ˌoʊ 'jes ets 'hedˌkwɔtez ɔrɪn nu ˌjɔːk|
ænd ə| wi ˌhɪr ə gʊd ˌdil əˌbaʊt 'ræŋlɪŋ ðæt ˌgoz ˌɔn ɪn ðə
sɪˌkjʊrɪtɪ 'kaʊnsəl|| ˌbʌt| 'wi lid aʊr ˌɔn 'laɪvz ən ˌwi ˌdont
ˌsi ðət ðɪ ju'naɪtəd ˌneʃənz 'riəlɪ əfɛks əs ˌvɛrɪ ˌmʌtʃ....]

Wendell Willkie

American Politician from Indiana (d. 1944)

[gʌvənɚ 'duwɪ| mædəm dʒɑŋ| (Madame Chiang) maɪ fɛlo əmærə-
əkənz|| aɪm diˣ'laɪt̬əd| tu ri'sɪprəˌket| ən ˌɪntəᵻ'dʌkʃən tu
ən ə'mærəkən ɔdjənts| əv mædəm dʒɑŋ| far ʃi| ɪnəᵻ'dust mi| tə
sɛvrəl tʃaɪ'niz 'ɔdjənsəz dʒʌst ə fju mʌns əgo|| ɪt ɪz bɪn maɪ
'apəˌtunət̬ɪ| tu əv sin| æn t̬əv dɪ'skʌst| mæt̬əz| əv ðə prezənt
de wɜld| wɪθ ðə lidəʒ əv 'menɪ əv ðə 'kʌntrɪz əv ðɪs wɜld| ɪn
ðə 'tereˌtɔrɪz ɪn wɪtʃ ðe 'aperet| ənd aɪ θɪᴧŋk aɪ kən 'se ət|
wɪˌðaʊt ɛnɪ 'ɪnəᵻ'proprɪət| kʌm'pærəsənz| ðət ðə gest əv anɚ hɪr
ðɪs 'ivnɪŋ| ɪz ðə most 'fæsənɛt̬ɪŋ ˌwʌn əv ðɛm 'ɔl||| me aɪ 'ɔlso
'se ðæt ʃi ɪz ðə most 'pɝsnlɪ bi'lʌvd| baɪ ðə 'pipəl əv hɚ 'kʌn-
trɪ|| ɪt ɪz əv kɔrs 'supɚ'abvɪəs tə spik əv ɚ wɪt| ənd ɚ tʃaɪm
æn ɚ gres æn ɚ 'bjut̬ɪᵻ| bʌtʃu mɪs ðə pɜpəs əv ɚ laɪf æn ɚ
'kɛrɪt̬ə| ɪf ju 'θɪŋk ʃi ɪz 'dʒʌst ən endʒəl| ʃi me bi wʌn bʌt
ʃiz ən ə'vendʒɪŋ endʒəl|| fɔr ʃi muvz wɪð ə pɜpəs| æn ʃi muvz

wɪð ə maɪnd‖ ɪt wəz tʃaɪnə‖ ðət nat əlon fɝst wɪθstud‖ ðɪ
esɔlt əv ðɪ ɛgrɛsəz‖ bʌt ɪt wəz tʃaɪnʌ ðət fɝst ʌndəstud ðə
tru netʃə əv ðɪs wɔr....]

Mrs. Robert Taft
Wife of U.S. Senator from Ohio

[aɪ æm glæd tə hæv ə paːrt ɪn ðɪs ˈbrɔdˌkæst‖ ən ðə ˈsʌbdʒɪkt əv ðə ˈples əv ðə ˈlig əv wɪmən votɚz‖ ɪn ðə pəˈlɪtɪkəl
ˈfild‖ aɪ həv bɪn ə sɪnˈsɪr bəˈlivɚ ɪn ðə lig aɪˈdɪə‖ ɛvɚ
sɪns ðɪs ˌɔrgənəˈzeʃən wəz ˌlantʃt‖ sun æftɚ ˌwɪmɪn wɚ ˌgræntəd
ðə ˌraɪt əv ˈsʌfrɪdʒ‖ ðɪ aɪˌdɪə hwɪtʃ wəz rɪˈspansəbəl fɚ ðə
ˈfaundɪŋ əv ðə ˌlig əv ˌwɪmən ˈvotɚz‖ ˈwʌz ðət ɪn əˈkwaɪrɪŋ
ə vot‖ ˈwɪmɪn hæd ˌtekən ɪntə ðɚ ˌhændz‖ ə trɪˈmɛndəsɪr ˈpauɚ-
fəl ænd ɪmˌpɔrtn̩t ˌtuwəl‖ fɔr ˌbɛtɚ ɔr fɔr ˌwɝs‖ ænd ðət ðe
wɪʃt tə lɝn tə juz ɪt ˈwaɪzlɪ‖ ɪn ɔrdɚ tə prəmot ðə ˈdʒenərəl
ˈwelˌfɛr‖ ˈðæt wəz ə naˈɪvlɪ ˈnju aɪˈdɪə ɪn ðə pəˌlɪtɪkəl
ˌfild‖ ˈno grup əv pipl̩‖ ˈebl̩ tu əˈten ðə ˈprɪvəlɪdʒez əv
ˌself ˈgʌvəmənt‖ hæd ˌɛvɚ bɪˈfɔr ˈdautɪd ðɛr ˈon əˈbrɪlɪtɪ tu
dɪsˈtʃardʒ ðɛr rɪˈspansəˌbrɪlɪtɪ‖ æz ˌnjulɪ ˌflɛdʒd ˈrulɚz
ʌv ðɛr ˈon ˈlænd....]

Eddie Cantor
American Actor (d. 1964)

[a ju ˈsɪtɪ̩ŋ ˈkʌmftəblɪ ɪn jɚ ˌon hom əz jə ˌhɪɚ maɪ ˈvɔɪs?‖
a ju ˌðɛə wɪð ju ˈfæməlɪ‖ ən dɪˈsaɪdəd tə tɝn an ðə ˈredɪo tu
ˌlɪsən tu wʌˌtɛvə ˈkʌmz?‖ aɪ kænət ˈpraməs tə prɪˌzɝv ðɪs mud
əv ˈkwaɪɛt ən wel ˈbiɪŋ‖ aɪ ˌwɑnt ͡tə mek ju ˈæŋgrɪ ‖ aɪ ˌwɑnt
tə mek jʊə ˈblʌd ˈbɔɪl‖ ən jʊə ˌhaːt ˈek‖ aɪ wɑnt· tu tɛl ju
əbaut ˈʌðɚ ˌhomz hwe ˈdɛθ ɪz ə ˈkanstən(t) ˈgɛst‖ æn dɪˈspɛr ən
ˌsepəˈreʃən a ðə ˌdɛlɪ ˈpɔeʃən ə(v) ˌfaɪn ˈwɪmən laɪk jʊə ˈwaɪf
æn swit ˌtʃɪldrən laɪk jʊron ˈsʌnz‖ æn ˈdɔtɛz‖ ju ˈar ən əˈmɛr-
ɪ͡kən‖ æn ˈæz ən əˈmɛrɪ͡kən ju ˌo ðə ˌʌndɚˈstændɪŋ jʊə ˈkaɪndd-
nəs‖ ænd jʊr əˈsɪstəns‖ ju ˌo ət·tə ðɛm fə ˈmɛnɪ ˈrɪzənz‖ bət
ˈtʃiflɪ ͡ bɪˌkɔz ju ˈar æn əˈmɛrɪkən huz ˈlaɪf ən gʌvəmənt a
ˈmotəvetəd ˌnat ˌonlɪ baɪ ˌwɝdz laɪk̩ dəˈmakrəsi æn ˈfridəm‖
bʌˀt baɪ ˌwat ðɪz ˌwɝdz ˈmin‖ ju ˈowʌt ͡tə ðɛm fɔr jʊr ˌom
pəˀtekʃən əz ˈwɛl‖ fɔr ɪf ɪn ˌɛni ˈstaɪflɪŋ ˈgɛtow‖ ðɛr ɪgˌzɪst
ˈmɛn ˈwɪmən ən ˈtʃɪldrən hu ˌno ðət ðɪ ˈæks‖ æn ðə naɪf‖ æn
ðə ˈhæŋmənz ˈrop a ðɪ ˌonlɪ ˈsɝtəntɪz ɪn ðə ˌbɪtɚ ˈlaɪf‖ ˈju‖
æn əˈmɛrəkən‖ ˈkænət rest ˌɪzɪjən ju ˈbed‖ ju ˈkænət ˌdu ˈðæt
bɪˌkɔz‖ ɪ̇n ə ˌwɝl(d) wɪtʃ pəˌmɪts ˌsʌtʃ‖ ˈharəz‖ ðə rɪˈzʌˤlts
wɪl ˈsip ˈθru tu jʊrˌon ˈtʃɪldrən‖ juˌron ˌwaɪf‖ jʊrˌon ˈgræn-
tʃɪldrən‖ ˈnau‖ ɔe ˈletɚˌan....]

Joseph Davies
American Diplomat (d. 1958)

[...wʌn wik frəm nɛkst ˈmʌndɪ| ðə prezedən(t) ənd ðə ˈvaɪs
prezdənt wɪl| æz wi se bæk hom| bi sworn ɪn|| ɔlˈredɪ| ɪn æn-
ˌtɪsəˈpeʃən əv ðiː vɛnt| ˌgrænd ˌstændz ə bɪɪŋ əˈrɛktəd ɪn frʌnt
əv ðə ˈhwaɪt ˌhaus| æt ˈvæntɪdʒ pɔɪnts əlɔŋ hɪsˈtɔrɪk pənsəl-
ˈvenjə ˈævənu| æn ɪn ðə plazə ɪn frʌnt əv ðə neʃənz kæpət||
hwɛr ðə prezdənt wɪl tek ðɪ oθ əv ɔfɪs| æn dɪˈlɪvə hɪz ɪˈnɔg-
jərəl ədres|| æz ðə det əˈprotʃəl| ðə dʒɔɪnt kənˈgreʃnəl ɪˈnɔg-
(jə)rəl kəˈmɪtɪ əv ðɪ juˈnaɪtəd stets senet| ŋ ðə haus əv repre-
zentətɪvz| æn ðə prezdənts ɪnˈɔgjərəl kəˈmɪtɪ| wɪð ɪts ˈmenɪ
ˈsʌbˌkəmɪtɪz| ar prɪˈperɪŋ ðɪ fainəl (ə)rendʒmənts| fɔr ðɪs
ˈmemrəbəl əkeʒən| æn prɪˈperɪŋ ɪts welkəm| tu ðə θauzənz əv
ar ˈfɛlo sɪtəzənz hu plæn tu parˈtɪsəpet ɪn ðiz ˈseɹəmoɪz
hɪr|| ði æktʃuəl ɪnˈdʌkʃən əv ðə prezdənt ən ðɪ vais prezdənt
ɪntu ɔfɪs| ɪz ˈverɪ sɪmpəl....]

Frank Gannett
American Publisher (d. 1957)

[aur fɝst ˈdutɪ tə ˌsɪvəlaɪˈzeʃən| ɪn ðɪs jɪr əv wɜld ˈkraɪ-
sɪs| ɪz raɪt hɪr ɪn ðɪ juˈnaɪtəd ˈstets|| bətwin nau æn noˈvɛm-
bɚ fɪfθ| ænd ðɛr ə ˈonlɪ ˈhʌndrəd en ˈnaɪntɪ ˈfaɪv dez biˈfɔr
ɪˈlɛkʃən| wi mʌs dɪˈsaɪd ðə fjutʃɚ əv əˈmerɪkʌ|| hweðɚ wi ʃæl
bi e fri pipəl| ɔr slevz ʌv ðə stet|| hweðɚ wi ʃæl ˈmenˈten aur
sɪstem əv ˌkanstəˈtuʃənəl ˈgʌvəmənt æn fri ˈentəpraɪz| ʌndɚ
hwɪtʃ ðɪs neʃən æz gron ˈgret æn ˈstrɔŋ ɔr hweðɚ wi ʃæl go
fɚðɚ| ˈɪntu næʃənəl ˈsoʃəlɪzəm| nu ˈdiəlɪzm| ˈfæʃɪzəm| ˈnætzɪ-
ˌɪzəm| ɔr ˈkamjənɪzəm|| tɔrd wʌn mæn rul| e ˈdɪktetəʃɪp|| ˈri-
səntlɪ ðɪ pɔrts əv ˈnɔrwe wɚ opənd tu ðɪ ˌenəmɪ| baɪ tretɚz.
ˈɪnˌsaɪd ðə ˈkʌntrɪ|| wi ɚ rɪˈmaɪndəd əv ðə ˈstɔrɪ əv ðə wudn̩
ˈhɔrs| æn ðə fol əv trɔɪ|| hwen ðə ˈtrodʒənz ædˈmɪted ðə wudn̩
hɔrs| kənˈsilɪŋ soldʒɚz ʌv dɪˈstrʌkʃən| ðə wɚˈʌnəˌweɪr əv
hwʌt ðə wɚ ˈduwɪŋ|| ðə wɜst ˈenəmɪ əv ˈselfˌgʌvəmənt| ɪz ˌʌnə-
ˈwernəs|| hɪtlɚ hwaɪl ˈraɪzɪŋ tu pauwɚ æn ˈfæsənɪŋ ʃækəlz əv
ˈtɪrənɪ an ðə dʒɝmən pip|| ˈædolf ˈhɪtlɚ| sed|| ɪt gɪvz ʌs
ˈnætzɪz speʃəl plɛʒɚ| tə sɪ hau ðə ˈpipl̩ əbaut ʌs ar ˈʌnəwer
əv hwʌt ɪz ˈrɪəlɪ ˈhæpənɪŋ ˈtu ˌðəm|| ɪzn̩t ðæt ðə sɪtʃəˈweʃən
ɪn əˈmerəkə....]

H. Styles Bridges
U.S. Senator from New Hampshire (1937–1961)

[æz wʌn əv jɔ ˌsenətəz ɪn ˈwɔʃɪŋtən| aɪ wʌnta ˈkʌm ɪntə jɔ

'hom te|naɪt| ən dɪskʌs wɪð ju ə|gɛn ðæt grev 'prabləm| wɪð
hwɪtʃ wi ar |ɔl kən'sɜnd|| |nu 'trælətɪ | n ðə 'pis əv aʊə |kʌn-
trɪ|| wɪ|ðɪn ðə wik ɑɪ wəz |gɪvən ðə| prɪvlɪdʒ əv 'spikɪŋ tə
|ju ɑn ðɪs |sem |sʌbdʒɪkt|| ət ðæt tɑɪm a(ɪ) med |sevrəl 'stet-
mənts| hwɪtʃ ɑɪ |wəd lɑɪk tə rə|pit ə'gɛn fɚ 'ɛmfəsɪs|| ɑɪ səd
|ðən |ən ɑɪ rə|pit ə|gɛn| ðət ðə |gretɪst dɪ'zaɪɚ əv |aʊr pipl|
ɪz tə rɪ|men æt pis|| wɪð ðæt |stetmənt wi ar |ol ɪn kəm'plit
əg'rimənt|| ɜɪɪ ðɪs wik ɑɪ |olso |stetɪd| ðæt ɪt wəz |klɪɪlɪ
'evədənt| ðət ðə gret |bʌlk əv 'aʊr 'pipəl| sɪmpə'θaɪzd wɪð
wʌn saɪd| n ðə prɛzənt |jʊrə'pien kanflɪkt....]

SECTION 2 PROFESSIONAL ACTORS AND READERS

"Beauty," by Lord Byron as read by Tyrone Power:
[ʃi 'wɔks ɪn 'bjutɪ|| lɑɪk ðə 'naɪt əv 'klaʊdləs 'klaɪmz
ænd 'starɪ skaɪz|| ænd ɔl ðəts best əv 'dark ænd 'braɪt mit ɪn
hɚ 'æspɛkt| ænd hɚ |aɪz|| ðʌs 'melod tə ðæt tɛndɚ laɪt| hwɪtʃ
'hevən tu 'godɪ de di'naɪz|| wʌn ʃed ðə mor| wʌn re ðə ləs|
ðæt hæf ɪm'perd ðə 'nemləs gres wɪtʃ 'wevz ɪn 'ɛvrɪ revən
tres|| ɔr 'sɔftlɪ laɪtənz ɔr hɚ fes|| hwer θɔts sə'rinlɪ swit|
ɛk'spres haʊ pjur haʊ dɪr ðer 'dwɛlɪŋ ples|| æn an ðæt tʃik|
ænd or ðæt braʊ soʊ sɔft| sо kam jet |ɛloʷ'kweɪnt|| ðə smaɪlz
ðət wɪn| ðə tɪnts ðət gloʊ|| bət tɛl əv dez ɪn gʊdnəs spent||
ə maɪnd æt pis wɪθ ɔl bi'lo|| ə hart huz lʌv ɪz'ɪnoseⁿnt....]

From "The Book of Job," as read by Herbert Marshall:
[lɛt ðə de 'perɪʃ hwerɪn ɑɪ wəz bɔ:n|| ænd ðə naɪt hwɪtʃ
səd| ə mæn tʃaɪld ɪz kənsivd|| lɛt ðæt de bi da:knəs|| me gad
əbʌv not sik ɪt| nɔə laɪt ʃaɪn əpɒn ɪt|| lɛt glum æn dip
'da:knɪs klem ɪt|| lɛt klaʊdz dwel əpan ɪt|| lɛt ðə 'blæknɪs
əv ðə de 'terɪ|faɪ ɪt|| ðæt naɪt| ðæt sɪk da:knəs siz ɪt|
lɛt ɪt not ri'dʒɔɪs əmʌŋ ðə dez əv ðə jɪə| lɛt ɪt not kʌm
əntʊ ðə nʌmbər əv ðə mʌnθs|| je| lɛt ðæt naɪt bi bærən| lɛt
no dʒɔɪfəl kraɪ bi hɜd ɪn ɪt|| lɛt ðoz kɜs ɪt hu kɜs ðə de|
hu a skɪld tu raʊz ʌp lɪ'vaɪəθən|| lɛt ðə sta:z əv ɪts dɔɪn
bi da:k|| lɛt ɪt hop fɚ laɪt bʌt hæv nʌn| no si ɪt 'aɪ|dɪz
əv ðə mɔ:nɪŋ|| bɪ'kɔz ɪt dɪd not ʃʌt ðə dɔ:z əv maɪ mʌðəz wum|
no haɪd trʌbl frəm maɪ aɪz|| hwaɪ dɪd ɑɪ not daɪ æt bɜθ|
kʌm fɔθ frəm ðə wum ænd ɪk'spaɪə|| hwaɪ du ðə niz rɪ'siv mi|
ɔ hwaɪ ðə brɛsts ðət ɑɪ ʃud sʌk|| fɔ ðɛn ɑɪ ʃud əv len daʊn
ən bin kwaɪət| aɪ ʃud hæv slept|| ðɛn ɑɪ ʃud hæv bɪn æt rɛst...]

From "Death," by John Donne as read by Frank Silvera:

[dɛθ| bi nɒt praud|| ðo sʌm hæv kɔld ði 'maɪtɪ ænd 'dredful||
fɔ ðau ɑ nɒt so|| fɔ ðoz hum ðau θɪŋkst ðau dʌst ˌovə'θro| daɪ
nɒt| puə dɛθ|| nɔ jet kænst ðau kɪl mi|| frəm rest ænd slip
hwɪtʃ bʌt ðaɪ pɪktʃəz bi| mʌtʃ plɛʒʌ|| ðen frəm ði mʌtʃ mɔə
mʌst flo| ænd sʌnset ɑə best men wɪð ði du go|| rest əv ðə
bonz| æn solz dɪ'lɪverɪ|| ðau ɑːt slev tu fet| tʃans| kɪŋ æn
desperət men| ænd dʌst wɪθ pɔɪzən wɔr ən 'sɪknɪs dwel|| æn
'pɒpɪ ɔ tʃɑːmz| kæn mek ʌs slip əz wel| ænd betə ðen ðaɪ strok||
hwaɪ swelts ðau ðen|| wʌn sɔːt slip past| wi wek i'tɜnəlɪ|| æn
dɛθ ʃæl bi no mɔə|| dɛθ ðau ʃælt daɪ]

From "Sonnet XXX," by William Shakespeare as read by
Hurd Hatfield:

[hwen tuᵊ ðə seʃənz əv swit saɪlənt θɔt| aɪ sʌmən ap rɪ-
'membrəns əv θɪŋz paˣst| aɪ saɪ| ðə læk| əv 'menɪ ə θɪŋ aɪ
sɔt|| ænd wɪð old woz| nju wel| maɪ dɪə taɪmz| west|| ðen kæn
aɪ draun æn aɪ| ʌn'dʒust tu flo| fɔ presəs frendz| hɪd| ɪn
dɛθs 'detləs naɪt|| ænd wip əfreʃ| lʌvz lɒŋ sɪn(t)s kænsəld
wo| ænd mon ðɪ ɪk'spen(t)s əv 'menɪ ə 'vænɪʃt saɪt|| ðen kæn
aɪ griv æt grivənsəz fɔ'gon| ænd 'hevɪlɪ| frʌm wo tu wo| tel
ɔə ðə sæd əkaunt əv fɔbɪ'monəd mon|| hwɪtʃ aɪ nju pe| æz ɪf
nɒt ped bəfɔ|| bʌt ɪf ðə hwaɪl| aɪ θɪŋk ɑn ði| dɪə frend| ɔl
lɔsɪz ɑ rɪ'stɔːd| ænd 'saroz| end]

From Annabel Lee," by Edgar Allan Poe as read by Basil
Rathbone:

[ɪt wəz 'menɪ æn 'menɪ ə jɪr əgo|| ɪn ə kɪŋdəm baɪ ðə siː||
ðət ə medən ðə lɪvd hum ju me no baɪ ðə nem| əv ænəbel li||
ænd ðɪs medən ʃi lɪvd wɪð nò ʌðə θɔt| ðæn tu lʌv| æn bi lʌvd
baɪ mi|| aɪ wəz ə tʃaɪld ænd ʃi wəz ə tʃaɪld ɪn ðɪs kɪŋdəm baɪ
ðə si| bet wi lʌvd wɪθ ə lʌv ðæt wəz mɔə ðæn lʌv| aɪ æ æᵊn maɪ
ænəbel li|| wɪð ə lʌv ðæt ðə wɪŋəd serəfs əv hevn kʌvətəd hɜːr
ən mi|| ən ðɪs wəz ðə rizn ðæt lɒŋ əgo ɪn ðɪs kɪŋdəm baɪ ðə
si| ə wɪnd blu aut ə ðə klaud| 'tʃɪlɪŋ maɪ 'bjutɪfəl ænəbel
li| so ðət ə haɪ bɔːn kɪnzmən kem aut ən bɔ hər əwe frʌm mi|| tu
ʃʌt hər ʌp ɪn ə 'sepəlkɜ | ɪn ðɪs kɪŋdəm baɪ ðə si|| ðɪ endʒəlz|
nɒt hæf so hæpɪ ɪn hevn| went 'envɪɪŋ hɜːr ən mi|| jes| ðæt wəz
ðə rizn| əz ɔl men no ɪn ðɪs kɪŋdəm baɪ ðə si|| ðæt ðə wɪnd kem
aut əv ðə klaud baɪ naɪt| 'tʃɪlɪŋ ən 'kɪlɪŋ maɪ ænəbel li|| ðə
lʌv əv ðoz hu wɜ old ðæn wi| əv 'menɪ fɑ waɪzə ðæn wi| ən
niðə ðɪ endʒəlz ɪn hevn əbʌv| nɔə ðə dimənz daun ʌndə ðə si
kən ɛvə dɪ'sevə maɪ sol| frəm ðə sol| əv ðə 'bjutɪfəl ænəbel li||

fɔə ðə mun nɛvə bimz wɪˈðaut ˈbrɪŋɪŋ mɪ drimz əv ðə ˈbjutɪfəl
ˈænəbɛl li|| ænd ðə staːz nɛvə raɪz bət aɪ fil ðə braɪt aɪz əv
ðə ˈbjutɪfəl ˈænəbɛl li|| ənd so ɔɪ ðə naɪt taɪd| aɪ laɪ daun
bə ðə saɪd əv maɪ dalɪŋ maɪ dalɪŋ maɪ laɪf ən maɪ braɪd||
ɪń ðə ˈsɛpəlkɜ ðə baɪ ðə si| ɪn hɜ tum baɪ ðə ˈsaundɪŋ si]

From "Father William," by Lewis Carroll as read by
Cyril Ritchard:

[ju a old faðə wɪljəm ðɪ jʌŋ mæn sed| æn jɔ he hæz bɪˈkʌm
ˈvɛrɪ waɪt| ænd jeᶻt ju ɪnˈseᶻsəntlɪ ˈstænd ɔn ju hed| dju
θɪŋk ət jɔ edʒ ɪt ɪz raɪt?|| ɪn maɪ juθ| faðə wɪljəm rɪˈplaɪd tu
ɪz sʌn| aɪ fɪəd ɪt maɪt ɪndʒə ðə bren|| bət nau ðət aɪm pɜfɪktlɪ
ʃuɹ aɪ hæv nʌn|| waɪ aɪ du ət əgen æn əgen|| ju a old sed ðə
juθ æz aɪ menʃənd bɪˈfɔ| ænd hæv gron most ʌnˈkamənlɪ fæt| jet
ju tɜnd ə bæk ˈsʌməsɔlt ɪn æt ðə doə| pre hwʌt ɪz ðə rizən əv
ðæt?|| ɪn maɪ juθ sed ðə sedʒ| æz i ʃuk ɪz gre lɒks|| aɪ kept
ɔl mɪ lɪmz vɛrɪ sʌpəl baɪ ðɪ jus əv ðɪs ɔɪntmənt| wʌn ˈʃɪlɪŋ
ðə bɒks| əlau mi tə sɛl ju ə kʌpəl|| ju a old sed ðə juθ æn
jɔə dʒɔz ó tu wik fə ˈɛnɪθɪŋ tʌfə ðən ˈsjuət| jet ju ˈfɪnɪʃt
ðə gus wɪθ ðə. bonz ænd ðə bik| pre hau dɪd ju ˈmænɪdʒ tə du
ɪt?|| ɪn maɪ juθ| sed ɪz faðə| aɪ tʊk tu ðə lɔ° | ænd agjud
ɪtʃ kes wɪθ mɪ waɪf|| æn ðə ˈmʌskjulə strɛŋθ hwɪtʃ ɪt gev tə
mi dʒɔə| həz lastəd ðə ɹɛst əv mi laɪf|| ju a old sed ðɪə
juθ| wʌn wəd haːdlɪ səpoz ðət jɔ aɪ wəz əz ˈstɛdɪ əz evə|
jet ju bælənst ən il ɔn ðə endəv jɔ noz| hwʌt med ju so ɔ°flɪ
klevʌ|| aɪv ænsəd θri kwestʃənz æn ðæt ɪz ɪˈnʌf| sed ɪz faðə|
dont gɪv jɔsɛlf ɛəz|| dju θɪŋk aɪ kən lɪsən ɔɪ de tuə sʌtʃ
stʌf|| bi ɔf| ɔr aɪl kɪk jə daun stɛəz]

From "The Mad Gardener's Song," by Lewis Carroll as read
by Cyril Ritchard:

[hi ˈθɔt i sɔ æn ˈɛlɪfənt| ðət ˈprækˌtɪst ɔn ə faɪf|| hi
lʊkt əgen| ænd faund ɪt wəz ə ˈlɛtə frəm ɪz ˌwaɪf|| ət ˌlɛŋθ
aɪ ˈrɪəlaɪz| hi sed| ðə ˈbɪtənəs əv laɪf|| hi θɔt hi| sɔ ə
ˈbʌfəlow əpɒn ðə ˈtʃɪmnɪᶦ ˌpis|| hi lʊkt əgen ən faun ət wəz
hɪz ˈsɪstəz ˈhʌzbəndz ˈnis|| ʌnˌlɛs ju liv ðɪs ˈhaus| hi sed|
ˌaɪl ˌsen fə ðə pəˈlis|| hi ˌθɔt hi ˌsɔ ə ˈrætlˈsnek| ðət
kwestʃnd hɪm ɪn grik| hi lʊkt əˈgen ənd ˌfaund ət wəz ðə ˈmɪdl̩
əv ˌnɛkst wik|| ðə ˌwʌn θɪŋ aɪ rɪˈgrɛt| hi ˌsed ɪz ˌðæt ɪt
ˈkænɒt ˈspik|| hi ˌθɔt hi sɔ ə ˈbæŋkəz ˈklak dɪˌsɛndɪŋ frəm ðə
ˌbʌs|| hi ˌlʊkt əˈgen æn ˌfaund ɪt ˌwaz ə ˌhɪpəˈpatəˌmʌs|| ɪf
ˌðɪs ʃʊd ˌste tu ˈdaɪn| hi ˌsed|| ðɛ ˈwont bi ˈmʌtʃ fər ˈʌs||
hi ˌθɔt hi ˌsɔ ə ˌkæŋgəˈru ðət ˌwɜkt ə ˈkafɪᶦ ˌmɪl||| hi ˌlʊkt

əˈgen| æn ˌfaʊnd ɪt wəz ə ˈvedʒətəbəl ˌpɪl|| wɚ aɪ tə ˌswɑlə
ˈðɪs| hi ˌsed| aɪ ʃʊd bi ˈverɪˈ ˌɪl|| hi ˌθɔt hi ˌsɔ ə ˌkotʃ
ən ˈfɔə ðət ˌstʊd biˌsaɪd hɪz ˈbed| hi ˌlʊkt əˈgen æn ˌfaʊn
ɪt wʌz ə ˈbeə wɪˌθaʊt ə ˈhed|| ˌpʊə ˌθɪŋ| hi ˌsed| ˈpʊə ˌsɪlɪ
ˌθɪŋ| ɪts ˌwetɪŋ tʊ bi ˈfed|| hi ˈθɔt hi sɔ ən ˈælbətrɒs ðət
ˌflʌted raʊnd ðə ˈlæmp| hi ˌlʊkt əˈgen| æn faʊnd ɪt wəz ə
ˌpenɪ ˈpɒstɪdʒ ˌstæmp|| ʃʊd ˌbest bi ˌgetɪŋ ˈhom| hi sed| ðə
ˌnaɪts ɑ ˈverɪ ˌdæmp|| hi ˌθɔt hi sɔ æn ˈɑːgjument| ðæt
ˌpruvd hi wəz ðə ˈpop|| hi lʊkt ˌegən| ən ˌfaʊnd ɪt wəz ə
ˈbɑr əv ˌmatld ˈsop|| ə ˈfækt ˌso ˈdred| hi fentlɪ ˌsed|
ɛkˈstɪŋwɪʃɪz ˈɔːl ˌhop]

Narrow Transcriptions

Following are some examples of transcription which is narrower than has previously been presented. Illustrations are given of the use of more detailed modifying symbols and of pitch notation. The speech samples are "generalized" as they might be spoken.

SECTION 1   NARROWER TRANSCRIPTIONS

A few lines from the Declaration of Independence in a very substandard style:

[wi hoɬ iz truz də biˑ sʌɬf ɛvə(d)n̩|| ət ɔmeˣn ə krɛɪːd
ikwə(l)|| ət ɛ̈rəndad bəðɛr kretəˈ| wɪ sɜn ɪnɛlnəbə raɪs|| ət
əmʌŋ nizɚ laɪf| lɪbdɪˈ| ənə pəsut ə hæpənəs|| æt ə skjɚ ɪz̠
raɪs gʌməns rɪnsˑtud mʌŋ mɛ̈n| draɪvin ɛ̈r pɑrz frʌm ə kənsɛn
ə ðə gʌvən(d)|| æt wənvɚ ɛ̃ɪ fɔrm ə gʌmən bɪkʌmːstrʌktɪv ə
d̠ðiz ɛ̈nẕ ɪzə raɪðə pipɬ taɪdɚ tə baɬïʃt]

A portion of "the seven ages of man" from "As You Like It," by William Shakespeare: (colloquial GA pronunciation)

[ˈʔɔ| ðə ˌwɜˑl(d)z ə ˈstejdʒ| ən ˌɒlə ˌmenː n̥ ˈwĩmən ˌmɪrlɪ
ˈpˤlerrz̩|| ˌðej hæˑɣ ð̥ə ˈɛksəts| ʔən ðɚ ˈɛ̃n̬ˤr̃ənsz|| æ̃n ˈwʌˑn
ˈmæ̃nː hɪ̈z tˤʌrm| plɛɪz ˌmɛ̃nɪ ˈpɑrts|| hɪ̈z ˌæks bɹɪŋ ˌsɛ̈vn-
ˈerdʒɪz̥|| ʌtˉfɚs t̪θˌrː nfɛ̃n̯ˤ| ˈmjulɹˑŋ ən ˈpjukˤɹˑŋ ɪn(d)ðə
ˌnɜsz ˈɑrmz|| æn ˌd̥ð̥ᵉn d̥ð̥ʊ ˈ(h)wʌɪnɪŋ ˈskuwəl ˌbɚɪ wɪ̈ðəz
ˌsæˑʃəl| n̩ ˌʃʌɪnɪn ˌmɚrnɪŋ ˈfejs| ˈkˤrijpɪˑŋ lʌɪk ˈsnejəl
ʌn̩wɪlɪ̈ŋlɪ tə ˌskuᵛl|| ʔæ̃n ˌd̥ð̥ʊ̃n d̥ð̥ʊ ˈlʌˑvə| ˈsajɪŋ lʌɪk
ˈfɚnᵉs| wɪ̈ðə ˌwowf| ˌbæːləd ˉ| mejd tɔwɪz̥ ˌmɪstrɚˑs: ˈɜ̃r-
ˌbrʌw|| ðenə ˈsoʊldʒɚ| fʊl əɣ ˌstrejndʒ ˈowð̥z| æn ˌbɪrdəd
lʌɪk ə ˈpˤɔrd| ˈdʒʌləs ə ˌn̥ɑ̃n̥ə ˈsʌdn̥n̥ ˌkwɔː rəl| ˌsijkˤɹˑŋ
ðə ˌbʌb| rɪ⸱pjeˈtˤeʃən| ivə nɪn ð̥ð̥ʊ ˈkænᵉnz ˈmaʊθ]

From the writings of James Boswell:
[ĩn ˈbɑrbərəsˉsəsˌaɪ⸱etɪ| səˌpɪrɪ⸱jɔ⸱rɪtɪˈ əv ˈpɑrts ɪz
əv ˈrijəl ˈkã̃nsᵉɪ⸱kwẽn(t)s|| ˌgreɪt strɛ̃n(k)θ ˉɚr ˌgreɪt
ˈwɪ̃sdəm| ɪz ə mã̃tʃ væˤljə t̪ˤuw ən ˈĩndᵉɪvɪdʒəwəl|| bədĩn
ˌmɒˤr ˈpaljˤstˉt̪ˤɑ̃ɪmz̥ ˈ ðer aː(r) ˌpɪjpl tə duw ˈɛvrɪθɪ̃ŋ fɚ
ˌmʌnɪ⸱|| ən d̥ð̥ẽn ðer ˌar ə ˈnʌmbə rʌv ˈʌð̥ɚ səˌpɪrɪ jɚˤrətɪzs:|
sʌtʃ əz ˌð̥oz ə(v) ˈbɚθ ən ˈfɔˤrtʃən| ən ˈrã̃ŋk| ð̥ə ˈdɪsəˌpeɪʔ
mẽn̥z ə'tˤẽ̃n(t)ʃən| æ̃n ˌɪrjv̊ ˌn̥ɒɣ ˌɛkstrəˈɔrdn̥ẽ̃rɪ ˈʃer əv
rɪ̈sˈpekt fɚ pɚsn̥| æn(d) ˌɪntʃlˈɛkʃẽwəl səˌpɪrəˈjɔˤrətɪˤ||
ð̥ɪsz waɪzlɪˈ ˈɔˤrdəd̥bɚ ˈprɒvədᵉn̥(t)s| tə prɪˌzɜv̥ ˈsʌm
ɪkˤ'walətˤrɪˈ əˌmã̃n ˌmæ̃n'kã̃ɪnd]

SECTION 2 PITCH MARKS
From the writings of Daniel Defoe:
[²ðer ⁴aːr ³sʌm ²pip| ˈɪn ðə ²wɜld↗ || ³hu⸱→| ³naɣ ⁴ð̥ʃɪ ɚ
ˈʌn²pɚtˤst↗| ˈen rɪ²dustːu ˈen ɪ²kwɔlətɪ wɪð ³ʌð̥ɚ ˈpip|²↗|
²ænd ʌndɚ ³strɔːŋ ˈen ³ve²rɪ dʒʌːst æpˈrɪ³hen̥ʃənz əv ²bɪɪŋ
³fɚ²ð̥ɚ trited əz ð̥ej dɪ³zɜːv̥↗|| ˈbɪgɪ³↗|²wɪð ³i⸱saⁱps kaːk→|
ˈtə ³priⁱtʃ ʌpːis ²en ³jun'jən↗| ³æn ðə ³krɪstʃən ²duˤtɪ əv
³maⁱdə²rɛɪˈʃən↘|| ˈfɔr⁴ge⸱ˈtɪŋ ðət hwen ⁴ð̥ej ³hæd ²ð̥ə ˈpaʊ²ɚ
ɪn³ð̥er ˈhændz↗| ³ð̥ɒ̥z greɪˤsez ˈwɚ ³stren²dʒɚ̥z ɪn ð̥er gets↘]

From the writings of Percy Bysshe Shelley:
[²aɪ met ə ³træv²lɚ ˈfrəm ən ³æntik ²lænd→| hu sed→||
³tu: ²væst'n ²trã̃ŋkləs legzə ˈston↗| ²stænd ĩn ðə ³dɛ̃zɚt↘||
³nɪɪ ˈðem↗| ²ɒn ˈðə ²sã̃nd↗| ³hæf ²sʌŋk↗|| ˈə ⁴sæt²əd
³vɪ³ɪdʒ lɑɪz↘| hùz fraʊn ˈən²rɪŋk̩d lɪp↗| ²ænd ⁴snɪɚ ˈəv
⁴kɔːld ˈkəm²ænd↗| tel ðət ɪtsːkʌlptɚ³wel ²ð̥oz pæʃənz red→|

ʹhwɪtʃ ²jɛt sɜvaɪv→| ³stæmpt ²an ðiz ³laɪfləs ʹ²θɪ̃ŋ•z↘||
ʹðə³ hænd ʹðɛt³ maˑkt ²ðɛm↘| ʹænd ðə³ hɑrt ʹ ðɛt³ fɛd↘||² ænd
³an ʹðə³pɛdʹɛstəl↗|³ ðiːz²wɜˑdz əprɪr̩ʹ↘||³maɪ nɛm² ɪz
²ɑˑzə³mæn²diəs↘|²kɪŋ ʹav³kɪŋz↘||²luk əpan maɪ wɜks ʹ ji
maɪ²tɪ↗|ʹən³dɪspɛr²↘||²nʌθɪŋ bɪsaɪd rɪmenz ʹ↘]

Keys to the Exercises

KEYS TO THE EXERCISES OF CHAPTER 1

Exercise 2 Slurvian translations

1 Rock-a-bye baby in the treetop.
2 Pat-a-cake, pat-a-cake, baker's man.
3 Turnabout's fair play.
4 A rolling stone gathers no moss.
5 Sing a song of sixpence.
6 London Bridge is falling down.
7 Time and tide waits for no man.
8 Put two and two together.
9 Mighty oaks from little acorns grow.
10 Old Mother Hubbard went to the cupboard.
11 I pledge allegiance to the flag.
12 If at first you don't succeed, try again.
13 When it rains it pours
14 When in Rome do as the Romans do.
15 The early bird catches the worm.

Exercise 5   Pronunciation preferences. The D key indicates whether the first (1) or second (2) pronunciation tended to be favored by the dictionaries. The P key indicates which pronunciation was favored by a group of about 100 students.

Word	D key	P key	Word	D key	P key
1	2	2	17	2	1
2	1	1	18	2	1
3	1	1	19	1	2
4	1	2	20	1	1
5	1	2	21	2	1
6	1	2	22	tie	2
7	2	2	23	2	1
8	1	2	24	2	tie
9	2	2	25	1	2
10	2	1	26	1	1
11	1	2	27	2	1
12	1	2	28	tie	1
13	2	2	29	1	2
14	1	2	30	2	1
15	2	2	31	2	1
16	2	1	32	2	1

KEYS TO THE EXERCISES OF CHAPTER 2

Exercise 3   Counting syllables and segments

Line of Type	Syllables	Sounds
1	23–25	53–58
2	17–19	46–54
3	21–22	49–52
4	6	16–19

Exercise 4   Illustrative word structures

Single-Syllable Words

V	"ah"	CCVC	"stop"
CV	"lah"	VCCC	"arks"
VC	"ought"	CCCV	"straw"
CVC	"taught"	CCVCC	"spots"
VCC	"ox"	CVCCC	"parks"
		CCVCCC	"sparks"
		CCCVCC	"strips"
CCV	"slaw"	CCCVC	"scram"
CVCC	"shops"		

Two-Syllable Words

VCV	"Ernie"	CCVCVC	"sticking"
CVCV	"topper"	CVCCVC	"resting"

VCVC	"open"	CCVCCVC	"spanking"
CVCVC	"topic"	VCCCVC	"arctic"
CCVCV	"story"	CVCVCC	"topics"
CCVCCV	"stamper"	VCCCCVC	"explode"

KEYS TO THE EXERCISES OF CHAPTER 3

Exercise 10 Sentences containing the fragments

1 The stove industry
2 Sound and fury
3 Football player
4 Amazing to think
5 Keep 'm open
6 Busy drawing
7 Push Alfred
8 Coded and filed
9 Perhaps he did
10 Last night
11 Hum a tone
12 Picture town
13 Inkwell spilled
14 Sing often
15 This chop
16 Roy visited
17 Future policy
18 Shoe shine
19 Tuesday notices
20 Before a lunch

Exercise 11 Reduced forms of words

baut	klɛkt	dɪnt	ɑr	rɛglɚ
bʌv	klɪʒen	spɛʃli	potri	ʃunt
kɛpæsti	kʌmpni	faɪrɪŋ	prɛzdṇt	sɪmlɚ
kæfətɪrjə	kwɑpret	flɑurɪŋ	prɑbli	tɔrd
tʃɑklət	dɛfnət	nætʃɚli	rilaɪz	wunt

KEYS TO THE EXERCISES OF CHAPTER 6

Exercise 5 Open junctures in transcription

[spik⁺ðə spitʃ⁺aɪ pre ju trɪpɪŋli⁺ɔn ðə tʌŋ]
[aɪ θɪŋk⁺aɪ bɛtɚ go tə klæs⁺sun]
[ʃud⁺wi go tə lʌntʃ⁺æftɚ/⁺ə hwaɪl]
[hi wəz⁺stæbd⁺durɪŋ⁺ə faɪt⁺læst⁺naɪt]
[kəm⁺ɑn⁺ovɚ⁺ən⁺hæv⁺lʌntʃ⁺wɪθ⁺mi]

Exercise 7 Short Slurvian translations

You think so
Keep on
Six years
Castor oil
Pie plate table
Ice cream
Battle axe
He thought
What'll become of her
Cried out

I quit taking   By-law
No news   No time

KEYS TO THE EXERCISES OF CHAPTER 7

Exercise 5   Reading rate norms averaged for six speech science students

Passage	Rate	Time, sec	Words/ sec	Syllables/ sec	Sounds/ sec
	Fast	13	2.15	6.77	16.4
Multisyllabic	Normal	17	1.65	5.18	12.5
	Slow	23	1.22	3.83	9.3
Monosyllabic	Fast	12	4.83	4.83	14.9
	Normal	16	3.63	3.63	11.2
	Slow	23	2.52	2.52	7.8

Exercise 15   Weak forms of words

[ə]	[bət]	[səm][sm̩]
[ən][n̩]	[fər][fɚ]	[əf]
[ðɪ][ðə]	[ət]	[sə]
[ə][əv]	[tə][tʊ]	[ər][ɚ][ɝ]

Exercise 16   Stressing on phrases

[ˌhaʊ du aɪ ˈdu haʊ dəˈju du]
[ɪts ɪmˈpɑsəbl̩ fɚ mi tə go]
[ɪts ɪmˌpɑsəbl̩ fɔr ˈmi tə go]
[ɪts ɪmˌpɑsəbl̩ fɚ mi tə ˈgo]

Index of Selections Transcribed by Authors

Index of Speakers Transcribed

Name Index

Subject Index